Experiences in Language

Fourth Edition

Experiences in Language

Tools and Techniques for Language Arts Methods

Walter T. Petty

Dorothy C. Petty

Marjorie F. Becking

ALLYN AND BACON, INC.
BOSTON LONDON SYDNEY TORONTO

Production Coordinator: Helyn Pultz

Library of Congress Cataloging in Publication Data

Petty, Walter Thomas,
    Experiences in language.

    Includes bibliographies and index.
    1. Language arts (Elementary) I. Petty, Dorothy C.
II. Becking, Marjorie F. III. Title.
LB1575.8.P47 1985   372.6'044   84-14522
ISBN 0-205-08192-4

Printed in the United States of America

10 9 8 7 6 5 4 3 2 1   89 88 87 86 85 84

Photos on pages 95 and 134 are by Christopher Morrow/Stock, Boston, Inc.
Photos on pages 1, 12, 23, 49, 69, 181, 189, 332, 366, 378, 421, 427, and 455 are
    by Talbot D. Lovering, Allyn and Bacon staff photographer.
Photos on page 74 (top right and bottom) are also by Talbot Lovering.
Photos on pages 155, 249, 281, 309, and 351 courtesy of Lifland et al.,
    Bookmakers.
Photos not otherwise credited are by Peter Walders, Ellicott Road Elementary
    School, and Walter T. Petty.

To our children and grandchildren

Blane, Bruce, Claire, Michelle, Roy,
Tom, Toni, and Shelley

Contents

Chapter 12   **Teaching Children to Read**   309

Chapter 13   **Reading and Study Skills**   351

Chapter 14   **Children and the Library**   387

Preface

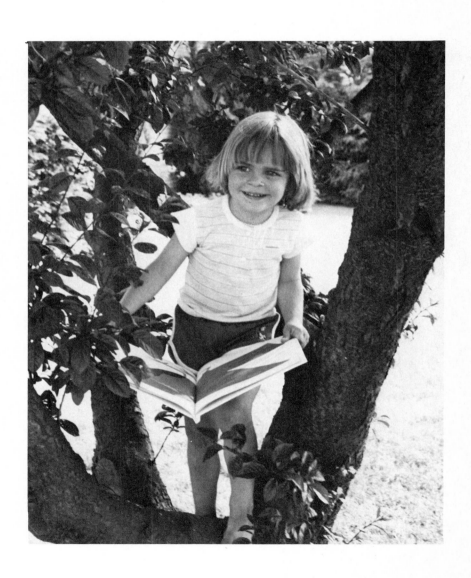

In this edition we again affirm our belief that the language arts are the core of the elementary school program, and that effective teaching of both the expressive and the receptive language arts provides the foundation for learning in all curriculum areas and therefore is vital to the entire program of the school. One does not acquire learning, to any great extent, without reading and listening, nor is that learning communicated without speaking and writing. Thus the language arts not only are intertwined but are basic to learning itself.

We have reorganized and rewritten much of this edition to show readers—more effectively, we believe—the possibilities open to the teacher for interrelating the teaching of the language arts and for integrating this teaching with the teaching of other areas of the curriculum. However, we continue to include chapters about the teaching of writing, listening, spelling, etc., not only because we believe that direct teaching of certain aspects of each language arts area is generally needed, but because this organization allows us to show the specific skills and understandings needed for each area, to suggest a sequence for teaching them, and to indicate the types of activities that may help to establish and reinforce these skills and learnings.

We have added to this edition a chapter on preprimary language development, both because of a recognition of the importance of early experiences to language development and because of the increasing number of children who attend some kind of preschool. Further, we have placed additional emphasis on the teaching of writing—an area that we believe has received inadequate or even improper attention in many classrooms.

For their contributions to our thinking in developing this book we again express our appreciation to teachers we have known and to graduate and undergraduate students who have attended our classes. We also appreciate the help of editors and reviewers of this and earlier editions.

W.T.P.
D.C.P.
M.F.B.

Language, Language Learning, and the Language Arts

1

Language is such an integral part of our lives that we tend to take it for granted—to use it in our everyday activities without giving thought to the miracle that it really is or even to its importance in our lives. Yet today the exchange of ideas and knowledge is increasingly crucial to each person's social, economic, political, and psychological well-being. At the same time, the vocational and personal environments of all of us are becoming more and more specialized, with the result that specialized vocabularies and ways of using language are developing within these environments. These factors surely limit the exchange and may lead to or increase class and status barriers that result in a loss of the give-and-take essential to democracy. Thus developing in each child his or her full capabilities for using language maximizes the possibilities for eliminating the barriers we already have and for avoiding the establishing of others. Beyond this, such development should foster a respect for the rights, privileges, and responsibilities of every human being.

LANGUAGE

Webster's Third New International Dictionary defines language in a number of ways. Some appear to limit language to speech and to human beings. Others are broader, including, for example, any method of communicating ideas, such as "signs, sounds, gestures, or marks"; "the transmission of meaning, feeling, or intent by act or manner"; and even "the means by which animals communicate or are thought to communicate." Such definitions would not seem to exclude music or other art forms, a lifted eyebrow or a friendly smile, the chatter of a frightened squirrel or the tail-wagging of a friendly dog.

While teachers are certainly aware of the effectiveness of "body language," as well as the many other means of communication suggested by these broader definitions, in the classroom they ordinarily think of language as the verbal symbols, either vocal or graphic, that are associated with ideas and objects and that are produced in systematic patterns to convey meaning from one person to one or more others. Our primary concern in this book is with teaching and learning the use of language thought of in this way.

2

Characteristics of Language

The Alaskan natives of the North Slope are said to know more than eighty different kinds of snow—and to have words for all of them.

New Words

backlash
bionic
centrism
guru
macho
pixel
troika

The systematic arrangement of symbols is a key characteristic of language. The systematic nature of any language is shown by intertwined and inter-related principles that cause the language to operate in regular ways. Each language has its own system—a system peculiar in at least some respects to no other language—but every language is systematic and every language has arbitrarily attached vocal (and generally graphic) symbols to the ideas and objects that are a part of the culture it serves.

Thus, arbitrariness is a part of language related to its systematic nature. The people of every culture have simply designated a sound or set of sounds to represent something they need to talk about. The French say *le chien*, the English say *dog;* both are arbitrarily designated symbols (both in sound and graphic forms) that represent the same object, and they do so regularly and systematically. Those who use a language also make it as com-plete as necessary for their culture. We have the term *nuclear physics;* an American Indian language of the year 1600 had no need for such a term. This difference makes neither language any less "advanced," complete, or systematic than the other. Each is a social instrument facilitating commu-nication between people about the things they want to communicate about.

Still another characteristic of language is that it changes. Evidence of the change in English is apparent, for example, if one compares pages from the King James version of the Bible, a Shakespeare play, a Hemingway novel, and an issue of *Time*. These changes in language occur in many ways. We readily think of new meanings being attached to words and of new words or combinations of words being used for new or changed objects or ideas. Perhaps we can think of pronunciation changes or spelling changes, though the latter tend to take longer to occur, and we may not be aware of them unless we read something written a hundred or so years ago. And if we look back far enough we can even find changes in word order.

The Systematic Nature of Language

As stated above, language—any language—is systematic. The system may be described in terms of sounds, groups of sounds arranged as words or word parts and their classification as to function, and the ways words can be arranged or ordered in sentences or parts of sentences. These terms are defined and briefly discussed in the remaining paragraphs in this section.

The basic sounds of a language are called *phonemes*. Phonemes are de-fined as the smallest units of sound by which different meanings may be distinguished. A phoneme is actually not a single significant sound, but a class of sounds heard by the typical native speaker as the same sound. For example, the sounds represented by *p* in *pin, spin,* and *lip* are actually artic-ulated slightly differently, but for all practical purposes they are the same. On the other hand, the differences between the sounds represented by *b* and *p* in *bit* and *pit* are also slight, but they are differences that we all rec-ognize and they distinguish meaning.

Phonemes are represented in written form by using virgules, in order to distinguish between letters and the sounds they represent. For example, to show the sounds in mat, *the linguist writes* /m/ /a/ /t/.

Phonemes, of course, are not letters of the alphabet. The same phoneme may be represented by different letters of the alphabet or even combinations of letters. The /s/ phoneme is represented by *s* in *send, c* in *cent,* and *sc* in *scent.* Conversely, a letter of the alphabet may represent different phonemes. For instance, the *g* is the graphic form of the initial sound in *gun* and *gene* and the medial phoneme in *regime.*

Linguists differ as to the number of phonemes that are called segmental—that is, through simple voicing and articulation, the continuous stream of sound is divided into segments that are recognizable as meaningful units. The differences are relatively minor—the numbers ranging slightly greater and slightly less than forty—and are due to differences in classification systems used.

In addition to the segmental phonemes, there are suprasegmental features which also describe the language we use. These include four degrees of *stress* in the flow of language, three levels of *pitch* in the voice, and four *junctures* or interruptions in the stream of speech. The degrees of stress are similar to the familiar accent, but they go beyond this—each syllable is identified as having a relative degree of emphasis in comparison to others. Pitch, of course, is the relative voice height in speech.

The smallest units in language that cannot be divided without eliminating meaning or changing it drastically are called *morphemes.* Morphemes may be thought of as the building blocks of the language. They relate sound and structure aspects of language to meaning. Morphemes may be *free* or *bound.* A morpheme is often a word, as in such lexical items as *cat, walk,* and *laugh.* These are free or lexical morphemes. A bound or grammatical morpheme is one that must be combined with another morpheme; examples are *-s, -ed, anti-.* Thus, *cat* is one morpheme (three phonemes) and *cats* is two morphemes (four phonemes).

Words may be classified into four large *form* classes or parts of speech (nouns, verbs, adjectives, and adverbs). Placement in these classes in most present-day descriptions of language is determined by four basic considerations, none of which give particular emphasis to meaning or function in the traditional sense (for example, that a noun is the name of a person, place, or thing). The considerations used include affixes, word order, particular structures or function, and the sound stress given. Thus, a noun is a word that will take the inflectional endings *-s* or *-es, -'s,* and *-s'*; it will take derivational suffixes such as *-er, -or, -ment, -ness, -ism,* etc.; it may be signaled or marked by such words as *the, a, each, some, many, my;* or it receives major stress on the beginning syllable (for example, *sus'pect* is a noun while *suspect'* is a verb). Of course, a word can be classified as a noun by applying only one of these criteria; there are few instances in which all can be applied. The other form classes—verbs, adjectives, and adverbs—also use word order, signal words, and affixes to determine classification.

Function or Signal Words

Noun markers—*my, some, two, the, an*
Verb markers—*am, is, were, had, will*
Phrase markers—*into, above, down, up, out*
Clause markers—*because, that, if, why, how*
Question markers—*who, when, what, where, why*

In addition to the four form classes, our language has *structure* or *function* words. These include the signal words, qualifiers (*very, rather, quite,* etc.), prepositions (*on, in, after,* etc.), and conjunctions (*but, and,* etc.). The structure words relate words of the form classes to each other and provide an essential structure so that our language has fluidity and cohesion.

The meaningful arrangement or order of words in sentences or parts of sentences is the fundamental aspect of system in language. This is known as *syntax,* which may also be defined as the grammar or description of a language. There are several approaches to describing word ordering in English sentences (see Chapter 3). The arrangement or order of words is particularly important in English, since it is a major way of expressing grammatical ideas and is essential in making meaningful sentences. For example, the words "selected book the quickly girl the" express grammatical meanings by structure signals and endings, but the meaning is not clear until they are arranged into "the girl quickly selected the book."

The Uses of Language

M. A. K. Halliday in *Explorations in the Functions of Language* describes the language learner's perception of its uses.

Language has no value independent of its uses. It serves people, and because it is systematic—a fact recognized usually unconsciously by most people—those uses are made possible. The first of its services is that of *communication.* Communication involves at least two persons, one to present the idea or thought and another to receive it. The effectiveness of the communication depends entirely upon the degree to which both persons know the language and have relatively corresponding abilities in using it. *Knowing* the language in this sense means having acquired a level of development of those elements of the system discussed above which makes possible language use, understanding the meanings of the words used, and being aware (though perhaps not at a conscious level) of any social or cultural forces that may bear upon the communication.

Language may also serve as a means of *releasing tensions or reacting to a specific personal incident.* This use is very personal and may range from the ludicrous to the sublime. Thus, one may mutter imprecations after a poor golf shot or while working on an income tax form, exclaim aloud at the sight of Niagara Falls, or shout "Bravo!" after hearing an outstanding musical composition.

Language is also the principal means for the *transmission of culture.* Literature, as considered in its broadest sense, records the ideas, opinions, and actions of individuals and of society. This record, vital to education and to future development, exists principally because of language.

Possibly the most important use of language is its role in *thinking.* While not all of the symbols needed in the mental manipulation necessary for thinking are language symbols, the majority are. A primitive people could likely exist by thinking in terms of mental images alone as they sought food and shelter. However, as rules, laws, customs, and social mores developed, symbols were needed to represent them. Thus, language was needed, and now language symbols representing the many abstractions of our culture are crucial to our thinking.

Variety in Language

Any language is an entity only in a limited sense. The language each person uses is largely a reflection of that person's early environment and education

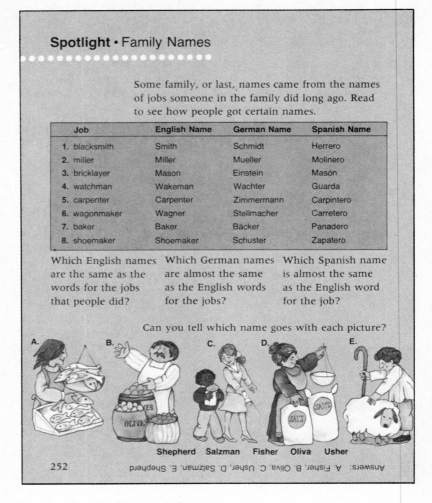

Spotlight • Family Names

Some family, or last, names came from the names of jobs someone in the family did long ago. Read to see how people got certain names.

Job	English Name	German Name	Spanish Name
1. blacksmith	Smith	Schmidt	Herrero
2. miller	Miller	Mueller	Molinero
3. bricklayer	Mason	Einstein	Masón
4. watchman	Wakeman	Wachter	Guarda
5. carpenter	Carpenter	Zimmermann	Carpintero
6. wagonmaker	Wagner	Stellmacher	Carretero
7. baker	Baker	Bäcker	Panadero
8. shoemaker	Shoemaker	Schuster	Zapatero

Which English names are the same as the words for the jobs that people did?

Which German names are almost the same as the English words for the jobs?

Which Spanish name is almost the same as the English word for the job?

Can you tell which name goes with each picture?

A.   B.   C.   D.   E.

Shepherd   Salzman   Fisher   Oliva   Usher

252   Answers: A. Fisher, B. Oliva, C. Usher, D. Salzman, E. Shepherd

Learning about family names is fun.

From LANGUAGE: SKILLS AND USE BOOK 3. By Ronald L. Cramer et al. Copyright © 1980 by Scott, Foresman and Company. Reprinted by permission.

How do you say these words?

creek
greasy
roof
wash
stomach
hog

and the social situation in which he or she is speaking. The variation in language that is most obvious is in dialect. Dialects, like the language of which they are a part, are systematic, adequate for communication among their users, and to a large extent predictable in structure and use. In general, dialects differ in matters of pronunciation and vocabulary to a greater extent than they do in grammatical features. Some dialects are also identifiable by the rate of speech and variations in pitch. The slow drawl associ-

To get water, do you turn on the:

faucet
hydrant
spigot
or tap?

More about dialects is found in Chapters 3 and 16.

See Chapter 4 in Johanna DeStefano's *Language, the Learner and the School.*

What others can you think of?

Early settlers created:

underbrush
bluff
gap
warpath

ated with the South and Southwest and the nasality in the southern hills are familiar examples. Most of us know that *Mary, marry,* and *merry* are pronounced identically by most natives of the northern midwestern United States, whereas in New England the natives pronounce these words differently. We also know that groceries are placed in a *bag* in some sections of the country but in a *sack,* or perhaps a *poke,* in others. There are many other examples of differences in pronunciation and vocabulary and some paralanguage differences. Sentence structure, on the other hand, remains essentially the same in most English-speaking communities.

Even though everyone (not just people in the South or Brooklyn or Boston) speaks a dialect, each person's language within a dialect is, to some extent at least, unique. This is an individual's *idiolect.* Also, each of us varies his or her language from one expressional situation to another, particularly after becoming an adult. Such variation is known as *register switching* or, more commonly in written expression, changing styles. Each of us uses a colloquial or homely language in speaking with close friends and family. This language is certainly less formal than that used in giving a speech or writing an article. A person may also use particular words and expressions—localisms—in his or her own town or neighborhood that would probably be avoided in another geographical location. Thus, although we may say that a person speaks *a* dialect, that dialect has variations, just as there are variations among dialects.

Any dialect is an adequate means of communication for its users, but if it deviates too much from what the community considers to be "standard" or "acceptable" English (discussed in Chapter 3), a problem is created for the speaker, one that the school must recognize and attempt to solve.

Language Change

English is a particularly adaptable and flexible language, partly because it is a polyglot one, rich in words contributed by other languages. For example:

- Scandinavian: *saga, ski, rug, geyser*
- French: *rouge, vignette, surveillance, coup*
- Spanish: *sombrero, guitar, corral, adobe*
- Italian: *violin, replica, ghetto, broccoli*
- Dutch: *buoy, skate, yacht, pickle*
- Hebrew: *amen, cherub, sabbath, camel*
- Persian: *caravan, bazaar, shawl*

Besides adopting words from other languages, we coin words to describe new commercial products, processes, and discoveries, or new or different ways of thinking about things: *jetliner, stereo, amplifier, missile, sneakers, Freon, Teflon.* Others occur from abbreviating or compounding, or as acronyms: *OPEC, TV, pro, hype, motel, houseplant, scuba, offbeat, paperback.* Still others move into the language from slang, although much slang simply gives new meanings to words already in the language. Also, very little slang

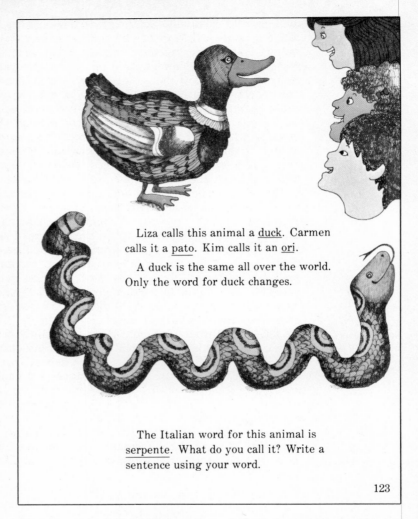

Liza calls this animal a <u>duck</u>. Carmen calls it a <u>pato</u>. Kim calls it an <u>ori</u>.

A duck is the same all over the world. Only the word for duck changes.

The Italian word for this animal is <u>serpente</u>. What do you call it? Write a sentence using your word.

123

Language textbooks for children are increasingly giving attention to wider aspects of language study.

has much permanence (have you heard *neat, square,* or *cool* lately?), although such words as *crank, fad, pluck,* and *slump* were once considered slang.

LANGUAGE LEARNING

Children generally learn to talk without much difficulty. This learning begins at birth, with the first sounds a child hears seeming to trigger a propensity to communicate. The fact that language is systematic facilitates this learning, as does the desire of persons around the child to communicate with him or her. The child's experimenting, trying to communicate, leads rather quickly to a discovery of how the language works, what the system is. Of course, not everything about the system is discovered at once. In fact, some aspects of it are still being learned well into the elementary school years, but the essentials for talking are learned by most children by about age two.

Controversy as to how this learning occurs has led to the advancement of several theories. The differences among these center largely on the extent to which language learning depends on innate ability as opposed to imitation. There is agreement that there must be some exposure to language, but that is the extent of agreement among the theories.

Language Acquisition Theories

The several theories about how children acquire language are controversial and complex. They are modified from time to time by their advocates and by different researchers, and they tend to be intertwined to some extent by some of their interpreters. Because of such complexities, and since the basics of a child's language are acquired in infancy rather than in school settings, only brief descriptions of the theories are attempted here.

See Chapter 6 in Inquiries into Child Language *by Diane Nelson Bryen, © 1982.*

One theory, usually called *behavioristic,* holds that each newly born human has an innate learning potential but does not have any specific learning abilities, such as a special innate capacity for acquiring language. The language learning that occurs, like other kinds of learning, is a result of the environment: Japanese children learn Japanese, and American children learn English. More specifically, though, the first learning, at least, is of the particular dialect—that is, the way the language is spoken in the immediate environment. In this theory, all learning, including that of language, is shaped by positive reinforcement of desirable behavior and negative reinforcement of undesirable behavior. Thus, an infant in the babbling stage is rewarded for uttering an appropriate sound (part of a word in the language of the attending person) by being fed, by a smile or a pat, or simply by a soothing tone. Later, the baby begins to self-reinforce by hearing and recognizing the familiarity of his or her own utterances.

Sometime before the end of the first year of life, the infant will probably say *da-da* or *ma-ma* when one or the other is nearby. The word will be repeated by the adult, who perhaps will point to himself or herself and reinforce the infant's utterance by a cuddle or a smile and another repetition of the word. Other words may be learned in the same manner. This reinforcement, then, is essentially how the meanings of the first spoken words are learned.

Young children differ greatly in their tendency to imitate as well as their ability to do so.

This theory, unlike the theories discussed below, treats language learning like any other learning. Human infants have the physical makeup to produce sounds and to pattern them in imitation of those they have heard and been encouraged to repeat. In learning the language of their environment, infants are not always able to repeat what they hear, but according to this theory the stimuli and reinforcement of the environment encourage them to make the effort, to experiment, until they master the system to the extent necessary for life in this environment.

A second theory, variously called the *innatist, rationalist,* or *nativist* (and having some variation in interpretation of its bases by its advocates), primarily differs from the behaviorist theory in the belief that humans are endowed with a specific process (some would say a skeletal framework) for learning language (any language). According to this theory, because of this innate ability or mechanism (which only humans have), the learner has a start on "knowing" the system of a language in its basic design. This innate basis (called the language acquisition device, or LAD) only needs to be triggered by the language environment of the infant for the surface expression of language to occur quite rapidly. Advocates of this theory hold that the imitation and the stimulus-response conditions of the behaviorists cannot account for the rapidity with which a child in any culture learns the essentials of the structure of the language.

The nativist also points out that a young child speaks sentences or parts of sentences that are not imitations of adult speech; thus, exposure to an adult model is needed only to give the child examples from which he or she induces the underlying rules as to how the language system works. While the LAD is still basic to this theory, great emphasis is currently given to the *interaction* between the child and adults. The nature of this interaction (not all verbal) requires the adult to use language differently from the way he or she would use it with another adult, since the adult does everything possible to help the learner figure out how the sounds relate to meanings and what the underlying organization is.

See the article by Fleming.

In further support of their theory, nativists cite studies of language acquisition in different cultures, which show that children of differing intellectual abilities, or even ones with physical or environmental handicaps, will ultimately acquire whatever language they have access to, and the acquisition sequence will always be substantially the same. On the other hand, experiments with teaching language to chimpanzees have challenged the position that language acquisition is restricted to humans. While chimps do not have the physical equipment to produce speech, researchers have shown that they can be taught to manipulate language symbols other than verbal ones (including those of the American Sign Language). The nativists counter this by pointing to a difference between acquiring language and being taught it and to the fact that (so far) the most intense efforts to teach chimps a humanlike language have resulted only in a level of development similar to that of two- or three-year-old children.

See *Language Arts,* November/December 1974, March 1975, for readable articles on language acquisition and development.

A third theory relates language acquisition to cognitive processes. While holding to the uniqueness of humans in learning language, this theory emphasizes the development of basic cognitive (thinking) structures prior to the development of corresponding linguistic structures, implying that thought is at least initially independent of language. The LAD is not discounted in this theory but is considered to be related more to meaning relationships than to syntactic ones; thus, semantic concepts are the generating force in the learning process. Basic to this theory, as well, is the interaction between the learner and the language users in his or her environment, as discussed above.

While theories about how language is acquired are interesting, and are important to many language researchers, acceptance of one theory by teachers is not necessary. What is significant to teachers is the rapidity of children's learning, the naturalness of this learning, the importance of experience with language in the early learning, and the fact that children largely understand how language works when they enter school.

Language Development

More about language development is found in Chapters 3 and 5.

Children begin at birth to experiment with their vocal organs, to make sounds. This experimenting progresses through cries and cooing, sounds which are detected as expressing pain, fear, anger, or joy. These early vocalizations show little system or little relationship to the language spoken by those caring for them. At about four months of age the infant shows signs of responding to human sounds—turning the head and eyes to look for the speaker. Shortly thereafter the cooing will change to babbling, which with increasing practice shows considerable mastery of the basic elements of the vocal mechanism. The child does more "practicing," gaining a great deal of control of volume, pitch, and articulation as shown by the ability to repeat sounds that are heard. By the time the normal child has reached the first birthday, he or she is producing sounds to which adult listeners can genuinely attach meaning. Usually these first "words" are consonant-vowel in form—*ma-ma, da-da, bye-bye*—with the child possibly not attaching the same meaning to them as the adoring father and mother do, although the experimenting will soon enable the child to relate the sounds to the adult meanings. The majority of first words are usually nouns—*ball, man, bird*, etc.—but such action words as *want, give,* and *more* also appear before the child begins to put two or more words together.

Children's first words often seem to be attempts to express complex ideas, suggesting a words-as-sentences hypothesis. The term *holophrastic speech* is often used to convey this idea. Of course, there is no way for us to know if a child has the idea of the content of a sentence in mind. The child who says "milk" is likely to get more milk, but the adult who hears the word doesn't know whether the child had "I want more milk" in mind but was limited by memory, attention, or linguistic skill or simply recognized that the one word was sufficient to accomplish communication.

Most children acquire at least fifty words before beginning to put two or more of them together.

Children normally, however, at around eighteen to twenty months of age begin to put words together. The experimenting in doing this is similar to that done with words. The first combinations of words tend to follow the pattern of a few words in a particular utterance position joined with a variety of other words ("bye-bye, daddy," "bye-bye, mommy," "bye-bye, doggie"). The experimenting continues, with more of these singled-out words being tried out with other words and combinations of words. Gradually, then, the child perceives the notion of word order—that some words belong first and some words second. Sometimes this early perception is faulty in respect to the language system. More often, though, word order is satisfactory, but frequently some words are omitted. The child says "I see car" for "I can see the car." This is *telegraphic speech* (as in telegrams) and is simply further experimenting. All such experimenting is a normal stage in development, a stage in learning how the language works.

By the time most children are two years of age they will have a fund of words that represent objects and actions and will be able to use them in ways that are understood. They test hypotheses about noun and verb endings, frequently overgeneralizing about the rules by saying *foots*, *goed*, and *mines*. This "sorting out" continues for some time (in some aspects of syntax to about age nine and perhaps beyond), but by the time the average child reaches kindergarten age he or she speaks in sentences, the complexity of which depends on mental maturity, language aptitude, and experiences.

From the very beginning the child's use of language is purposeful, not perfunctory. The child who has learned to talk enough to use language for satisfying immediate physical needs soon becomes absorbed in making the acquaintance of a great variety of things. Children ask "What's that?" over and over. Asking questions is the characteristic type of language activity at this stage of preschool language development. Two- to five-year-olds struggle to identify the many objects in the environment; they seek to bring order into a wide world of sight, sound, smell, and feeling. The responses to this exploring are very important to language development. Thus, narrow experiences and limited responses result in language development that is less advanced than that of the child who has had broad experiences and has secured responses to expressions of curiosity.

The family environment is the most important factor other than the

Language learning results from experiences and from talking about them.

A Note to Parents

Work daily to help your child acquire language.

In your speech use expansions of the language the child uses.

Ask questions which require more than one word in answer.

Help the child give labels to everything in the environment—from apples to sun, car, geese, and taxi.

Remember that your language is the model.

Talk to the child, and listen.

Encourage, but do not push!

Read to your child daily.

child's maturity pattern in determining the language facility that develops and the speed with which it is developed. For instance, an only child may have closer association with adults than one who has brothers and sisters. This closeness may result in the development of a larger vocabulary and more maturity in expression. Similarly, the child who is talked with a great deal develops language facility earlier than one who grows up being ignored or told to be quiet. In addition to providing the child with language experiences, the family provides the language model—the kind of language to imitate.

Children's mental development and progress in using language move along together, both thoroughly interwoven through the experiences of life. Every experience bears upon a child's development, especially intellectual and language development. Each new experience or enrichment of an earlier one results in greater knowledge and understanding. A child soon learns that language is important to the gaining of knowledge and understanding and makes use of it in exploring the environment.

The things children encounter in this exploration determine the language they use, the words they learn, and the meanings they attach to those words. A preschool child living in a city apartment house certainly has different experiences from those of the farm child. One will certainly know the words *woods, pasture, hedge,* and *pig,* and the other will as certainly know *taxi, curb, lobby,* and *elevator.* Of course, each may know some words in both lists, or they may attach different meanings to the same word (e.g., an *elevator* is used to store grain, and in street parlance a police officer may be called a *pig*), since words, lexical units, have meaning only as they are used in context.

THE LANGUAGE ARTS

The language arts are the *receptive* language activities of reading and listening and the *expressive* activities of speaking and writing. Involved in both reception and expression is *thinking,* which is sometimes called the fifth language art.

Although "language arts" is the most widely used term, there are other names given to the portion of the school program devoted to teaching language communication skills. "English," of course, is the historical term, but "the communicative arts," "the English language arts," and simply "language" are also used. It is also true that many teachers think of reading, spelling, composition, and the like rather than thinking more broadly of the language arts; hence they use no inclusive term.

The "language arts" seems to be the designation that best describes the activities of speaking, writing, listening, and reading and recognizes their interrelatedness. It focuses on language, as opposed to the more narrow and traditional elements of writing, grammar, and literature associated with English or to the broad aspects of communication involving sound, sight, feel, and smell without the use of language.

The Language Arts

RECEPTIVE		EXPRESSIVE
↔	T	↔
	H	
	I	
listening	N	speaking
	K	
	I	
reading	N	writing
	G	

Elements of the Language Arts

The use of the term "language arts" aids in focusing on the interrelatedness of the four aspects of language communication. If we are to use an all-inclusive term, however, we must define the various elements and know how they are related to one another.

Writing encompasses the skills of spelling, handwriting, punctuation, capitalization, and, most importantly, composition—putting together ideas and information in a coherent and appealing manner, recognizing the value of proofreading and editing what one has written, and using conventional forms where needed. The major element in speaking is also composition, but here the skills of articulation, pronunciation, and voice projection, as well as those related to physical posture and manner, are also included.

Reading and listening have common characteristics. Both are concerned with perception of either graphic or oral symbols, with the identification of unknown words and terms, and with the use of these, along with one's experience, to gain meaning.

Thinking is very much a part of each of the language arts. Children think as they compose, spell, form letters and words, listen to a speaker, read a selection, and so on. Our thinking is largely a language manipulation activity; thus any shortcomings in understanding how language works and how it may be used will adversely influence thinking. Conversely, limitations in thinking ability will limit the uses of language.

Cutting across the receptive and expressive aspects of the language arts in a like manner to thinking (and related to it) are elements of grammar, vocabulary, dialect, and usage. Equally important are the study skills involved in using a dictionary, locating information, and utilizing the library.

Furthermore, the language arts include attitudes toward language usage, communication activities, and the aesthetic components of these activities. For example, reading is more than merely gaining meaning, for literature is a part of this aspect of the language arts. In a like sense, listening is done both for useful purposes and for pleasure, and writing may be both "practical" and "creative."

Interrelationships among the Elements

At the elementary school level the language arts program may sometimes be separated into particular facets—spelling, handwriting, reading, etc.—for instructional purposes. Yet it is not possible to keep the various segments from merging, since even the most superficial examination of language arts instruction will lead to the conclusion that rarely does any language skill function independently.

The interrelationships among the language arts are many and varied, as will become even clearer in the chapters that follow. At the heart of the interrelationships is the presence of language in each element of expression or reception and the fact that an experience affecting one facet will usually affect others. For example, if you seek to teach children to read without recognizing their desire to write and the importance of listening and speaking skills to readiness for reading instruction, you will meet with frustration. Similarly, listening and speaking skills require knowledge of vocabulary, writing requires spelling and penmanship, both oral and written expression require language organizational skills, and so on. A teacher who is sensitive to interrelationships will not wait until confronted by a problem to note the commonness of elements, but will keep the carry-over effects in mind when teaching any of the facets.

The sequence of development of the language skills is listening, speaking, and later—in our culture, usually at school—reading and writing. Although the infant's cries, gurgles, and related sounds are language in its broadest sense, an infant's first contact with language as most of us think of it is through hearing it. Thus, even though hearing is the only language ability infants possess for much of the first year of life, the interrelated nature of the language arts soon becomes evident. At an early age children learn to relate their vocalizing to sounds they hear, and soon they develop skill in saying the sounds they have heard and practiced. The fact that deaf children do not learn to speak during this early period provides evidence of the close relationship between speech and listening.

Both listening and reading entail receiving messages. Thus, there is considerable similarity in the skills needed for determining what these messages are. Ability in reading correlates significantly with development of vocabulary as well as with both interest and proficiency in speaking and writing. Children early want to write and to read what they and others have written. What they read or listen to is often the substance or the motivation for their writing. Writing and speaking are of course interrelated in a manner similar to the way listening and reading are.

All children come to school with patterns of speech based on what they have heard, speech they have used in whatever environments they come from. The speech that a child uses is of basic importance in any effort to instruct him or her in learning to use language as effectively as possible. Every child also comes to school with habits of listening, and many even have some ability in writing and reading. Virtually all children have observed and "practiced" writing and reading and have developed attitudes toward the language skills and their importance. All of these abilities, habits, and knowledge must be considered in instruction, and there must be recognition that growth in one language arts area often reinforces the others and that all language activities need to be rich and varied in order to assure optimum growth in each facet of the language arts.

A FINAL WORD

Because language is the major means by which ideas are shared, it is basic to all living and learning. For this reason, the language arts are the foundation of the school curriculum, and the teaching of the language arts is perhaps the teacher's most important task. To accomplish this task requires a knowledge of language—the way it works, the way it grows and changes, how children learn it, and the way it affects the lives of all of us. It also requires that a teacher know what to teach, when to teach it, and the best procedures for teaching. The intent of the chapters that follow is to help you accomplish this task.

References

Bryen, Diane Nelson. *Inquiries into Child Language.* Allyn and Bacon, 1982.

Cazden, Courtney B. *Child Language and Education.* Rev. ed. Holt, Rinehart and Winston, 1981.

Dale, Philip S. *Language Development.* 3rd ed. Holt, Rinehart and Winston, 1981.

DeStefano, Johanna S. *Language, the Learner and the School.* John Wiley & Sons, 1978.

deVilliers, Peter A., and deVilliers, Jill G. *Early Language.* Harvard University Press, 1979.

Fleming, Joyce Dudney. "Field Report: The State of the Apes." *Psychology Today* 7, no. 8 (January 1974), 31ff.

Halliday, M. A. K. *Explorations in the Functions of Language.* Elsevier, 1977.

Pflaum, Susanna W. *The Development of Language and Reading.* 2nd ed. Charles E. Merrill, 1978.

Saville-Troike, Muriel. "Language Development." *Encyclopedia of Educational Research,* Harold E. Mitzel, ed., pp. 1023–1040. The Free Press, 1982.

Teaching Resources

FILMS

Development of the Child: Language Development. Harper and Row (20 min.).

Discovering Language Series. Coronet (5 color films; for grades 4–9).

Regional Variations. Stuart Finley (28 min.; for teachers).

Social Variations. Stuart Finley (27 min.; for teachers).

RECORDINGS

Americans Speaking. National Council of Teachers of English (cassette).

The Changing English Language. Folkway Records (middle grades).

Culture, Class, and Language Variety. National Council of Teachers of English (cassette to accompany book with the same title).

Our Changing Language. National Council of Teachers of English (record).

Activities for Preservice Teachers

1. Collect a list of slang expressions (you'll probably need help from upper elementary or high school students). Interview people from various age groups and occupations as to the meanings of the expressions you have collected. Report your findings to the class.

2. Find examples in modern-day English for which changes can be traced from Old English (A.D. 600–1100) through Middle English (A.D. 1100–1500). What sorts of things might account for these changes?

3. Begin a file of ideas and sources for an activity with children about how animals communicate. What animals could be watched, and where could the children go to see them? What books might help? (Bil Gilbert's *How Animals Communicate,* Pantheon Books, 1966, is a start.) What films could be used?

4. Recall your language arts experiences as a student in elementary school. What did the teachers seek to teach you? What was your opinion of this? What do

you recall about their teaching procedures related to this content? Did you react favorably? Why or why not?

5. Visit a classroom for approximately half a day and observe one child specifically. What can you say about his or her language? Can you make any judgments about the child's early language experiences?

6. Look up the pronunciations of *aunt, brooch, dais, orange, garage, root, route, suite,* and *stoop* in several dictionaries. Report to the class what you found.

7. Examine the treatment of the following in a number of other textbooks on language arts methods:
a. Elements of the language arts.
b. Interrelationships among the language arts.

c. Language acquisition theories.
d. Language development of children.

8. Tell with which regions of the country (and why) you associate each of the words or phrases in these pairs: string beans, snap beans; pail, bucket; sweet corn, roasting ears; porch, stoop; cherry pit, cherry seed; pavement, sidewalk.

9. Visit a classroom and talk with children who did not begin their schooling in the school they are now attending. Find out the reasons for their having moved. As the children talk, listen for variety in language patterns and usage. What might any or all of this mean to you as a language arts teacher?

Activities for Inservice Teachers

1. Ask the children in your classroom (or another to which you have access) to write the meanings of these trite expressions. Suggest that they ask their parents for help and that they add to the list any others they are told about.

neat as a pin	my better half
picture of health	ripe old age
green with envy	the bitter end
work like a horse	like rats in a trap

2. With a group of children (any age level) discuss what is appropriate talk for various situations and settings: dinner table at home, living room when parents have guests, when mother and child are in the kitchen, etc. Make notes as to any guidelines the children suggest, what problems they have in deciding, factors affecting talk in the various situations, and the like, so that you can report these to your class.

3. Survey the professional materials available to you in your school. What in them is related to the content of this chapter? Report to the class.

4. What evidence do you have that the differences in language abilities among children in your class are reflections of their family environments? List your observational evidence for four of your children.

5. Which of the four areas of the language arts receives the least attention in your classroom? Write a paragraph telling why this is so.

6. Think about what things concerning our language and how it is learned might interest children. Categorize these by age and grade levels and then for one level outline what you might teach and how.

7. Investigate nonverbal language (often called *body language* or *silent language*). See such sources as Edward Hall, *Silent Language* (Doubleday, 1959), and Julius Fast, *Body Language* (Evans, 1970). Also observe the uses of this type of communication by the children in your classroom.

2

Planning for Teaching and Learning

Do you remember when you were an elementary school student? What do you remember about the writing and speaking you did? What were lessons in these areas like? Did you fill in many blanks? Do drills? What did you write about? Do you remember the language books? Did your teachers tell stories? Read to you? How often? Did what you were learning about language seem important to you? Were the things you were being taught useful to you? Did they deal with "real life"?

Your reflections about what you remember, particularly as to what was good or bad, what was useful and relevant and what was not, can be very important to your teaching. Using your common sense in regard to these reflections can tell you a great deal about what to teach and how to teach it. Think about these things as you read this chapter—and, in fact, as you read all of the book.

The purpose of this chapter is to give you an overview of effective language arts teaching and the planning and organizing that are so important in maximizing children's learning. The content of this chapter has application in each of the chapters that follow—and you may find yourself referring back to it as you study them.

PRINCIPLES OF PLANNING

Planning is not something that can be done once and then dropped. Planning needs to be done for the long term, for intermediate periods of time, and for daily lessons. While long-term planning (what should be accomplished this year, this term, this month) is crucial, plans need to be made, changed, dropped, and remade as circumstances change and as children learn. Thus, the principles suggested here are just as applicable to daily planning as they are to long-term planning. Of course, the amount of time given to daily planning will be less than that given to more extensive planning. One reason for this is that daily plans are simply portions of those for longer amounts of time.

The basic element in all planning is the children—the children who are actually in your class. You need to know what knowledge, skills and abilities, and attitudes they have and what their needs are. Determining all of this is a big task and one that has to be worked on all year long (see the

Who are the children?
How are they alike?
How are they different?
What are their needs?
How will you find answers
to these questions?

20

section Planning for Pupil Differences later in this chapter). To start, though, before meeting the children and having personal contact with them, review their school records so that you have some idea of their abilities and needs. Remember, though, that a child's school record sometimes presents a biased picture of achievements, possible problems, and potential. Test scores, teachers' comments, and "confidential" information may give an accurate picture, but they may also reflect personality conflicts, cultural differences, and judgments made hastily. Use records carefully and recognize that no person can be put on paper.

In addition to knowing the children, you also need to know the curriculum content generally identified for their age and ability level, including the range of this content required to care for the differing needs and abilities of a typical group of such children. Furthermore, it is helpful to have your own philosophy fairly well defined, as well as to know what the administrative and supervisory personnel in your school believe about children, what should be taught, and how it should be taught.

Determination of Content

What should be taught is important to organizing a language arts program, but how content is selected—on what premises and by what principles—is of utmost concern if teaching effort is to accomplish anything worthwhile. The findings of research, the contents of curriculum guides and textbooks, and the policies and standards of the school provide guides, but the responsibility for determining what is taught is primarily the teacher's. Sometimes teachers say this is not true—that the principal tells them what to teach or that the textbooks and other materials structure the program for them—but this contention is too often an easy way to avoid planning and exercising personal initiative. The teacher presents whatever is presented in his or her classroom for the children to learn; the teacher is the major controlling force.

Guiding principles for exercising this responsibility include the following:

Examine textbooks for your class very carefully. Are these principles observed? Remember that a textbook is a resource, not a recipe.

1. The content of the program should be selected after consideration of statements of objectives formulated by the school or district. If objectives have not been stated, are too general or not clear, or are simply thought to be understood, then the formulation of objectives is a necessary first step. For this formulation, basic reliance should be on research evidence rather than on custom, the opinion of some school authority, or the resources available.

2. The emphasis in teaching should be on using the skills of communication rather than on learning subject matter. In other words, it is more important for a child to have the skills necessary for effective expression and reception of ideas and information than to know rules about language structure, punctuation, etc.

3. The selection of content should take into account the communication needs of the children in the classroom—their experiences and development, the types of communication they can and cannot handle, the things they will need to have mastered before progressing further in school, and the ongoing activities that develop from day to day in the classroom.

To help you decide what skills, abilities, attitudes, and knowledge the children in your class need now and as they progress through their school years, you should ask yourself the questions below. Answering them may not be easy, but you should rely on your own honest, sensible judgment in seeking the answers rather than first turning to the teacher next door or to textbooks and their manuals. Both of these resources—and others—may help you to find answers, but essentially those answers must be yours.

1. *How frequently is this needed and used in the life activities of children and adults?* For example, writers use colons much less frequently than they use commas, people do more storytelling than choral speaking, and seldom does one need to identify the adverbs in a sentence.

2. *How important is this when the need for it arises? Will the need arise?* For instance, many people do not write business letters frequently, but when the need arises, it is usually important that the letter be well written.

3. *How universally is this skill or ability encountered in the various life activities?* For example, giving a book report is a school activity for most people, but conversing is something everyone does.

4. *What evidence is there that this will meet a permanent need?* For example, some of the first words a child should learn to spell are the same words adults use frequently in their writing.

5. *Which children, if any, in my classroom are ready to learn this?* In other words, attention must be given to the needs of the children, the experiences they have had, and what they have already learned. Dictionary instruction will have little value for the child who has not learned alphabetical order.

Making Instruction Systematic

Systematic instruction is planned instruction.

How the content selected is to be taught is also important. This "how" includes the techniques for the specific teaching of the content, but the key element in the "how" is the overall instructional plan to be followed. This plan should be a systematic one to be most effective, not one that deals with the content incidentally or perhaps accidentally. Systematic instruction is really not complicated; it simply means that all teaching effort is directed at the content decided on by the criteria stated above.

Events occur in every classroom that cannot be foreseen and planned for, but without systematic attention to the content that has been selected after considerate and careful thought, too much is left to chance. Such incidental teaching may result in no attention to some experiences that develop language ability, the overlooking of skills that should be taught for their later importance, and a waste of time through needless repetition and interference with instructional objectives in other curriculum areas or at other instructional levels.

Systematic instruction, on the other hand, does not preclude taking advantage of a "teachable moment" or working into plans those unforeseen events that will further the objectives. Actually, a truly well-planned program provides for using the ongoing activities of a classroom—including many of those that cannot be foreseen—for the meaningful teaching of the knowledge, skills, and attitudes that have been selected.

*Planning together is
important to children.*

Inform parents of your instructional goals and plans. *Be specific.*

Neither does systematic instruction imply a nonintegrated program. If the principles and guiding questions suggested above are adhered to, *genuine integration of language arts with other areas of the curriculum will be fostered when such integration furthers children's learning.*

Cooperative Planning

The most important kind of planning involves the children, since they will learn more effectively from the participation. This planning should be done on various levels and throughout the year—overall planning for the year, planning a unit of work, and planning for a particular activity that may take place in a single day or a short segment of a day.

The ability to plan is not equally developed in all teachers, and it certainly varies from child to child. Nor is the ability to plan in conjunction with others equally developed in all of us. We have to *learn* to respect the rights and ideas of others—it does not just happen. However, cooperative planning can be learned by doing. Below are some suggestions for involving children; you will discover others for yourself as you continue to plan with them.

First, do not abdicate your responsibility. The amount of responsibility that pupils should assume or can assume varies according to their maturity and their experiences with planning. Second, make sure that some genuine choices are open to the children. If the pupils are really to feel that they have participated in the planning, there must be some real options. If you intend to have things done your way, planning by the class is a waste of time and may do far more harm than good. Third, when plans are made, try to stick with them. If the plans are bad, learning this fact may result in better planning the next time. Of course, plans sometimes have to be changed, so be realistic. Finally, make certain that the planning is not being done by only a few members of the class. Children can be as unmotivated by the authoritarianism of their classmates as by that of the teacher.

Recognizing Principles of Learning

All planning needs to recognize that learning is a complex act, and descriptions of the process are sometimes superficial or misleading. However, observations of the results of learning provide evidence as to how learning may be expedited. This evidence can be stated in several principles—principles that every teacher needs to heed.

LEARNING IS INDIVIDUAL. Children differ from one another in many ways, including the ability to learn. This difference is shown in learning capacities and rates and in the effectiveness of various modes. Further, in addition to differences in inherited and intellectual and physical endowments, children differ from one another in terms of emotions, previous experiences, and motivation and may differ in age, sex, maturation, and physical condition. Thus, children's participation in a classroom activity will reflect these factors. A teacher can do something about some of the factors but not about others, yet all have to receive consideration in teaching.

LEARNING IS AN ACTIVE PROCESS. While much of what we know seems to have been learned subtly—possibly because the human mind is much like a constantly running computer ready to take in data—learning is a seeking process. An individual's environment almost constantly presents the need for that individual to transact with it, to try to overcome any disequilibrium felt. The school environment needs to take into account children's backgrounds and needs in such a way as to facilitate many of their transactions even while presenting tasks that establish disequilibrium. That is, if the learning tasks are challenging rather than frustrating, the seeking process will be encouraged.

LEARNING IS DEVELOPMENTAL. Anything learned is built on and added to previous learning. Learning will not occur without readiness; therefore, it is important to determine what children know, their maturation levels, and their learning rates and capacities, as well as to plan for the proper sequencing of their experiences.

LEARNING IS MOTIVATED. The disequilibrium that an individual's environment may cause him or her to feel is a motivation for reacting, for learning. As suggested, this may be a very subtle process. However, for much learning—particularly in the classroom—there is more than a simple reaction. There will be a conscious drive established if the challenge, the motivation, is strong enough.

LEARNING REQUIRES REINFORCEMENT. Anything learned but not used moves rather quickly out of the conscious mind. It may be forgotten. If it is used, on the other hand, it becomes established. Thus, those things we want children to learn in school need to be practiced. This practice, of course, needs to be meaningful and satisfying to the children. Reinforcement does not occur if what is learned is separated from its use.

LEARNING MAY TRANSFER. Ordinarily, transfer of learning takes place from one situation to another to the extent that identical elements are shared by both. Learning will transfer if proper attention is given to what is taught, when it is taught, and whether children are helped to see the similarity of the situations.

PLANNING IN ACTION

Daily, unit, quarterly, and yearly plans must mesh if goals are to be achieved.

Using the principles for the selection of content, and with the involvement of the children as appropriate, a decision needs first to be made regarding the objective or objectives of a teaching-learning effort—a day's lesson, a unit of work, or an activity requiring an even larger time segment. Sometimes this simply means the clarification of an idea for the activity or unit of work—one that may come from you, from the children, from previous

Recognize and value children's planning.

events, or from a textbook or curriculum guide—but this clarification is important and means stating the goal in terms that are understandable to all.

The next step is to decide on the scope of the objective in terms of specific problems to be solved. This should be done rather broadly at first so that refinement in scope will naturally follow later. For example, suppose the class is about to begin a unit on colonial America. After a discussion with the children of what they might expect to learn from this unit, these questions are decided on and written on the board:

What famous people lived during that period? Why are they famous?
What events occurred during the period that are important to us today?
How did the people of that time live?

Finding answers to these questions becomes the broad objective of the unit.

Plan for purposeful *use* of language.

After the objectives have been clearly defined, decide on a number of ways the objectives might be accomplished. From this decision, further decisions can be made as other factors are considered and a definite plan of action evolves. Suppose you have decided to concentrate first on the third question above and have chosen several avenues for discovering the manner of living in colonial times:

- Using the textbook and other references that have been assembled in the room.
- Visiting the library to find other helpful books.
- Visiting a museum, an old fort, or some other historical site.
- Inviting a local collector to show antique items and tell about them.
- Viewing films about colonial times.

At this point you and the children should think together about materials that may be needed in order to utilize the suggested means for accomplishing the objectives. These should be listed and consideration given to any

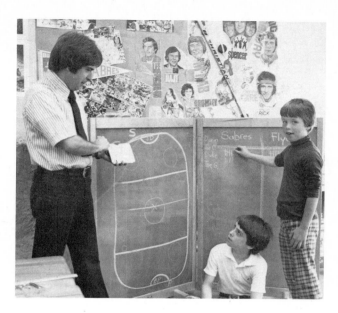

Planning to write about favorite hockey players.

problems related to getting or using them. Obtaining library books, for example, might entail learning about or reviewing library procedures and how to find information in books. Materials brought by the antique collector would require making arrangements for displaying them and perhaps discussing how a person should be introduced and interviewed.

The next step is to identify some of the problems that may be encountered in achieving the objective and to discuss how these problems may be overcome or avoided. In the sample unit, one problem might be arranging transportation for the museum trip.

One important consideration is the needs of the class members and what each can contribute to attaining the objective. This calls for assessment of individual abilities, interests, and possible assignments. Might a shy child be ready to introduce a speaker or perhaps help display materials? Might a child who is reticent about speaking build a model and show it to the class?

When all possibilities have been considered, the scope can be refined, specific means and materials selected, and assignments decided on. Perhaps the class might be divided into groups, each choosing a particular aspect of colonial life to study and report on (clothing, transportation, food, etc.). You could work with each group to decide on the best way of reporting to the class—demonstration, oral reports, dramatization, etc. It is important that the children participate actively in the planning, but as coordinator you can guide them in providing variety in the presentations.

Once these specifics have been decided on, a tentative time schedule should be set up for the activity and for segments of it as it progresses, with time allowed each day, or at regular intervals, for children to work on their projects.

The final step is to decide how the activity will be evaluated. This should include plans for determining whether or not the objectives have been achieved and what to do if an objective has not been accomplished. It is important that the children be included in this step as well as in the others. Let them help to set standards for conducting the work planned, for guiding individual performance, and for evaluation.

Although the steps here focus on an example from social studies, the same kind of planning is needed if the focus is science, health, language change, or whatever. The significant point is that effective communication is a second center of attention. This is integration of subject areas, and it is through such integration that language skills are most effectively taught. For a particular unit of study to achieve its objectives, children may need to use library skills, take notes, and organize material; they may need to introduce speakers, listen courteously, and discuss what has been heard; they may write and present reports, produce dramatizations, and perhaps even do some creative writing. Some of the skills needed may already have been mastered; others will have to be introduced or reviewed.

A BASIC INSTRUCTIONAL APPROACH

The diagram opposite illustrates a basic plan for teaching the skills needed in such expressional activities as those suggested in the preceding section. The plan calls for two types of lessons: one in which the emphasis is on the communication and one in which the emphasis is on improving the specific skills used in that communication. The plan has several parts and operates in a cyclical fashion; that is, an expressional activity is followed by an instructional lesson which is followed by another expressional activity, another instructional lesson, and so on. The effectiveness of the communication should improve with each subsequent expressional activity.

Basically, this plan seeks to integrate the teaching of the subject matter in such areas as social studies, science, and health with the reading, listening, writing, and speaking that children do as they learn about colonial America, how magnets work, why exercise is important, and so on. As illustrated in the diagram, one type of expressional activity is dealt with at a time—giving reports, participating in a discussion, writing stories, etc.— although any activity will involve a multiplicity of skills and abilities. The expressional activity, however, need not always be directly related to a subject matter area of the curriculum. There are many *ongoing activities* in all classrooms, which a teacher can use as teaching/learning situations. For example, children may describe a TV program or movie, discuss playground behavior, tell stories they have heard, report on items from newspapers, introduce parents to you and the other children, and write imaginative stories. These—and many more—are natural activities that require expression and may be utilized.

The expressional activity should focus on the communication itself and the purpose for it as well as the role of the audience in the process and the use of models, standards, or guidelines as aids in making the expression effective. The standards or guidelines should be flexible; that is, they should get progressively (from activity to activity throughout the year) more stringent and precise. They should be formulated by the class, but the textbook may provide suggestions that will be helpful.

The final aspect of the expressional activity should be evaluation by you alone, by you in conjunction with the class members, and by each pupil individually. As is suggested later, most evaluation should be informal and directed at learning rather than at giving grades or comparing children with one another. It should result in identifying for you and for each child the

Language Arts Instructional Plan

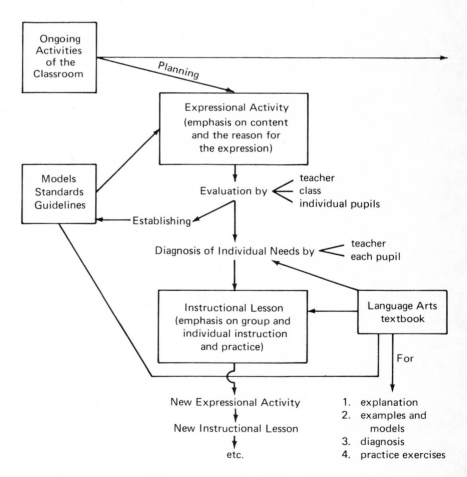

level of development he or she has achieved in skills and abilities needed for a particular language activity. A further element of the evaluation is the identification of a limited number of items for emphasis in instructional lessons. For example, evaluation of an activity in which the children wrote reports might result in the determination that organizational skills need instructional attention. Later, a similar activity might show a need for attention to handwriting improvement.

The instructional lesson should focus on both group and individual needs, but, as suggested above, it should not be so extensive that you dissipate your instructional effort by trying to teach too many things. The objective is to make the next expressional activity more effective, and the key to the plan really lies in the immediacy of the instruction that is given and the fact that it is based on genuine needs. The expressional situation provides motivation; this is lost when instruction is directed at errors made last month or those which may be made next month.

The instructional lesson should conclude with practice activities or exercises designed to establish the learning and reduce or eliminate the same faults or errors in the next expressional activity.

The textbook may be used at several stages in this instructional plan, as the diagram shows and as is suggested later in this chapter. The textbook is only one instructional resource, however. Others include the library, reference books, audiovisual materials, people, and community institutions.

While this approach is identified as a plan for teaching the expressional language arts, its essentials may be used in teaching the receptional ones. For example, there are many activities that require listening; standards for listening may be established, the effectiveness of the listening may be evaluated, and instructional lessons may focus on what the evaluation and diagnosis show is needed. Reading, too, is done for specific purposes, the success of which can and should be evaluated and instruction provided for deficiencies found.

PLANNING FOR PUPIL DIFFERENCES

We know that each person is unique. Yet aside from observing obvious physical differences, a teacher may not really recognize the range of differences that exist among the children in his or her class. In terms of pupil achievement, only about one-third of a typical class achieve at or near the norm for that grade level on a standardized achievement test. The other two-thirds are usually about equally divided above and below the norm, with the range (distances from the norm) increasing as the grade level advances. For example, a classroom of sixth graders may show 40 percent at grade level, 20 percent at seventh grade level, 10 percent at eighth grade level or above, 20 percent at fifth grade level, and 10 percent at fourth grade level or below. And since the achievement test does not measure many of the language skills, we can assume that the range among all pupils for all skills, abilities, and attitudes important to language communication is even more startling.

Refer to Chapter 16 regarding "special" or "exceptional" children and *mainstreaming*.

Teacher Identification of Differences

To determine the specific differences among pupils and hence determine their instructional needs, it is necessary to carry on a continuing program of evaluation. Relying on possibly casual observations and your memory about each child's strengths, weaknesses, and needs is likely to result in instruction that is less effective than it could be. More is needed, and below are specific evaluative devices and procedures you may use.

Make note of both strengths and weaknesses.

1. Observe and record on a note or checklist the speech performance of each child, including his or her speaking skills, mannerisms, and behavior as a member of an audience.
2. Make observational notes on individual pupils at regular intervals with respect to usage problems, difficulties in organizing expression, and lack of ease in speaking.
3. Use checklists or inventory forms to note achievements and deficiencies in specific language activities such as conversations, discussions, letter writing, or story writing. (Examples of these evaluative techniques are given in later chapters.)
4. Construct tests to determine each pupil's knowledge and abilities in choosing correct expressions, punctuating and capitalizing properly, and constructing sentences.
5. Tabulate the writing errors each pupil makes.
6. Use standardized tests in a planned program to measure growth and achievement in language arts.
7. Make recordings of speech and oral reading activities, and analyze them for particular problems.
8. Keep anecdotal records of information for special teachers, parents, etc.
9. Keep samples of children's written expression for comparison at intervals throughout the school year.
10. Discuss with children their problems in expression.

We are all well aware that record-keeping is a chore, but the procedures suggested above are relatively easy to implement. The task can be simplified by varying procedures throughout the year, by using checklists wherever possible, and particularly by keeping records up to date. A few minutes at the end of each day will save hours at the end of the month—as well as enabling you to attack problems as they arise rather than at some later date.

Pupil Self-Appraisal

Not all pupils need to use the same self-appraisal techniques.

Stimulating a pupil to identify his or her own language needs—the knowledge, skills, abilities, and attitudes needed for effective communication—is a basic motivational procedure that will pay rich dividends if you can do it successfully. Some methods teachers have used advantageously to help pupils identify their own needs are listed below. With patience on your part every child can learn to do some of the following:

Vary the self-appraisal procedures throughout the year.

1. Use checklists, preferably ones that the child has helped to devise or that are based on standards he or she has helped to develop.

2. Proofread and edit his or her own work. A proofreading checklist is usually helpful (see Chapter 10).

3. Check his or her own work as much as possible; for example, children can check their own spelling tests. (Having pupils exchange papers for checking does not help the child to discover his or her own problems.)

4. Write in a notebook things that need to be worked on—spelling words, new vocabulary, usage errors.

5. Keep charts of errors, such as those made in handwriting.

6. Compare his or her work with models (business letter form, for example) and scale examples (handwriting).

7. Look at the materials in a folder that contains samples of the child's work and records of his or her achievement.

8. Work as one of a pair or as a member of a small group in identifying areas in which improvement is needed.

9. Plot or record his or her own standardized test scores and compare them with the results of previous testing.

10. Participate in class discussions of needs, efforts to attain class-established standards, and plans for learning activities.

11. Meet with you to discuss problems and needs.

ORGANIZING FOR TEACHING AND LEARNING

There are many ways of organizing the programs of an entire school or of a classroom. The intent of each plan is to facilitate teaching and learning—the interaction of teachers and learners. Apparently, however, no one plan of organization of a school or of a class of youngsters is the ideal, one that research or practice has shown to be the most effective. Each plan is affected by many factors, including the number of children involved, the characteristics of the children as a group, the community and its traditions, legal regulations, fiscal and space requirements and limitations, curriculum decisions that have been made, and the philosophies of school board members, administrators, and teachers.

It is not our intent to review all possible organizational plans or to discuss any in great depth. There are published resources that do both. However, we do believe that every language arts teacher needs to know something about school organizational plans and how he or she may best organize a classroom of children for the maximum learning of each individual to occur.

Classroom Grouping

For much instruction in a classroom—and generally too much—the children are taught as a single group. Storytelling, reading aloud, dramatic ac-

Group when doing so will facilitate learning. *Don't* group for your convenience.

Grouping and individualizing instruction are discussed in many other chapters.

Keep parents informed about your classroom organization and management.

tivities, choral speaking, discussion, and written expression are examples of aspects of the language arts for which total-class instruction may be appropriate. On the other hand, all of these activities may be equally appropriate for smaller groups. When the need for specific instruction in regard to particular skills or knowledge does not apply to the entire class, or when some pupils are not ready for it, then small group or individual instruction may be mandatory.

Most teachers do at least some teaching of groups within the classroom. The children may be grouped according to abilities, skills, interests, needs, and so on. In fact, children will often get together in groups of their own accord if given the opportunity—and they certainly should be given such an opportunity. Grouping does not have to be limited to the traditional three reading groups; abilities and interests vary in all things children do. Neither does grouping need to be so lacking in flexibility that a child is always in the (so-called) "dumb group."

Grouping is not easily done by many teachers, as observation of a number of classrooms soon forces one to conclude. However, a teacher who has confidence in the children and feels that he or she can rely on them seems to have much greater success with grouping than does that teacher's counterpart who is more authoritarian or less inclined to involve children in the planning and conducting of activities. In addition, recognition of the limitations of evaluative instruments in pinpointing needs should not result in failure to use the instruments and to devise others to supplement them. Furthermore, grouping for instruction is easier when objectives are clearly defined.

In addition to the need for your objectives to be clear, you should think about the children's needs and interests and their personalities, the materials available to work with, how the groups will operate, and how you will handle time and space needs. Keep in mind that no grouping should be set in concrete. Sometimes plans just don't work out. Sometimes you learn more about individual children and their needs. Sometimes they take spurts in learning.

Individualizing Learning

Be wary when using commercial and other types of individualized learning packages. They may provide a rigidity that you want to eliminate.

There are many ways for providing instruction to meet individual needs. The organizational plans and related activities suggested below are only a few. As you read other chapters and think further about the importance of individualizing learning opportunities, you will add to the ideas presented in this section.

There has been considerable interest expressed in recent years for the "open" or "informal" classroom. While descriptions about how such a classroom is organized and operates vary considerably, the basic idea is to focus on individual needs, with children themselves identifying these needs in relation to their interests. Independent learning in good open classrooms occurs as children largely work by themselves on individual tasks and at their individual rates in learning centers. These centers may be simply tables, areas of a room partly screened off, or whatever; the idea is to provide opportunity for independent work. Frequently, there are centers for writing, listening, reading, science experimenting, research in books, mathematics projects, etc. In the following paragraphs we suggest ways in which assignments and special interests may be worked on individually or in small groups. Many suggestions for making this concept a reality are given in the chapters that follow, and at the end of each chapter are specific examples of independent learning activities. Like all other activities suggested in this book, these are only samples. If activities are to meet specific needs of individual children, they *must* be designed with those needs and those children in mind.

Regardless of the school or classroom organizational plan or plans, it is possible to provide individualized practice on specific skills for children who need such work. For example, some children can profit from exercise materials that require them to make decisions about which words should be capitalized. On the other hand, it is obvious that many language skills cannot be practiced with paper-and-pencil exercises. In fact, one of the big errors made by many teachers (and encouraged by some textbooks) is the use of written practice exercises as a means of changing the way children speak. However, discriminating use of practice materials, in ways such as those suggested below, may be helpful. For example:

- Practice exercises can be secured from workbooks, old textbooks, and clippings from teachers' magazines. These materials should be cut up so that the exercises that apply to a particular skill can be filed together.
- Often it is profitable to have two copies of workbooks that you intend to use in this manner so that the material on both sides of a page can be used. These exercises can be placed in clear plastic envelopes in order to keep them clean and to permit children to write on them with crayon that can be washed off. Answers to the exercises should be provided (perhaps on the back of the exercise page) so that pupils can check their own papers.
- Since many commercial materials (e.g., the pages of a workbook or textbook or a card in a kit) may either provide unrealistic and useless practice or try to give practice on more than one skill, exercises that you make yourself may be the most helpful.

Integration of the language arts with other areas of the curriculum provides many opportunities for individualization of instruction not only in the subject matter areas but also in the language arts. Integration with social studies (as in the example in the Planning in Action section) is relatively easy since both the receptive and expressive language arts are essential to most social studies activities. The same is true for several other curriculum areas, and even in science instruction—which tends to be highly structured by textbooks and other commercial materials—integration which may foster individualized instruction is possible. For example, if a class of third graders is studying the use of water by plants, there would be a need for children to be given library research to do—and to report orally to the class. Individual children could be assigned to list and assemble materials needed for the several experiments (plants watered and not watered, tracing absorption of water by a plant, how water gets out of plants, etc.) the activity would call for, while other children could keep records (of water levels, times needed for absorption, etc.). Children could write descriptions of the experiments, with the difficulty of these adjusted for individual pupil abil-

Note the similarity to the Basic Instructional Approach on page 29.

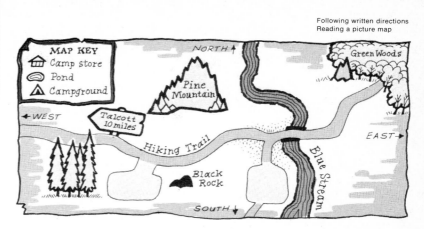

Following written directions
Reading a picture map

Dear Nancy,

    Hi! I'm sending you a map so you will have the latest scoop on my vacation. Yesterday we arrived at the trailer park, which is on the west shore of Blue Stream.

    Early the next morning, Blip my dog wanted to go out. I figured he'd return for breakfast, so I let him out.

    By midmorning when Blip hadn't returned, I decided to hunt for him. Between some tall pines and Black Rock was the campground. There an angry woman informed me that Blip had run off with a package of hot dogs.

    I headed for the camp store, which is located on Hiking Trail near the Talcott road sign. A man at the store said Blip had taken a box of chocolate cookies.

    When I reached the pond on the south side of Pine Mountain, someone fishing told me Blip was last seen heading toward Green Woods.

    Arriving at the woods, I heard loud barking. I discovered Blip sitting at the base of a huge pointed rock. Perched on the rock was an excited squirrel. Blip sure had a busy morning!

Love,

Jason

    Using the MAP KEY, follow the directions to complete the map.

DIRECTIONS

Put an **X** near the place where trailers are parked.

Draw the picture for the campground where it belongs on the map.

Draw the picture for the camp store where it belongs on the map.

Draw the picture for the pond where it belongs on the map.

Put a check at the place where Blip was found.

Comprehending maps, graphs, and charts is reading.

1

From *Skills Book*, Level 12, of *The Laidlaw Reading Program*, Second Edition, Copyright © by Laidlaw Brothers. Used by permission of the publisher.

ity. Vocabulary words would need to be looked up in a dictionary and possibly written on a chart. All of the children would be involved in conversations and discussions about the activity.

    Related to the above procedure is one in which children enter into "contracts" to do specific tasks. These contracts usually develop from pupil-

*Children may need help in
organizing for contract work.*

teacher conferences in which previous work is evaluated in terms of objectives agreed on earlier. Since children vary in their capacities to plan and in their abilities to assess their own capabilities and interests, it is appropriate for the teacher to provide alternatives that may be contracted for. Suggestions may also be made regarding pacing, although it is important for each child to discover his or her own working speed. Decisions will also need to be made regarding the way the product of a contract will be evaluated.

Other suggestions for individualizing include the following:

- Children who finish assignments or activities before their classmates do may be encouraged to make copies for the bulletin board of something they feel they have written well.
- A child who does good work in a particular area may help others who are having difficulty.
- Each child may keep a notebook for unassigned writing of a personal nature, and should have the option of showing it to the teacher only if he or she wishes.
- Children who finish assignments early may be permitted to browse in the library, work on special reports, listen to recordings, etc.

MAXIMIZING CONDITIONS FOR LEARNING

From the moment children at any age level enter a classroom door, there are opportunities for developing their language abilities. Children are ready to learn, and your program should capitalize on their abilities, backgrounds, and interests. Specific and careful planning is needed, but this planning, this organizing, must take into account conditions not discussed earlier, including ones you need to create.

Experience and Learning

An effective language arts program recognizes in three ways the importance of experience in the development of children's ability to use language. First, the program is based on an awareness that every child entering school, whether he or she comes from a white middle-class neighborhood or from a highly diversified socioeconomic and ethnic one, has a background of many experiences. While these experiences—including the language ones—may not have been used as learning tools and built upon to the extent that is desirable, they are important. Second, an effective program provides experiences that build vocabulary and concepts, develop multiple meanings of words, and familiarize children with the kinds of sentence patterns and ways of expressing themselves that they will encounter in school. Third, an effective program provides these experiences in settings that focus on genuine, lifelike communication activities that have meaning for the children involved and provide motivation for learning.

Awareness that every child has a language background developed prior to entering school—one which continues to be developed outside of the classroom—means more than overcoming any bias about a "disadvantaged" or "deprived" child having had little language experience or being "non-verbal." Children's language backgrounds are simply different, and to assume a background of experience on the basis of family economic conditions, race, ethnicity, or anything else is a fallacy. It is important, though, to try to determine just what the experiential background of each child is and to find out which experiences important to the school curriculum are lacking. To take for granted a background of experience and an understanding of concepts is dangerous. For example, teachers frequently report that inner-city children do not have a concept associated with the word *pet*, yet reading readiness books and first primers usually have pets in their stories. One teacher recently told one of the authors that children (and these were not "deprived" children) in her class had difficulty choosing a picture of a writing pen as representing a word which rhymes with *hen*. They apparently knew *pen* as the name of an enclosure for the chickens, but they did not know another meaning for the word. Probably their parents write either with a pencil or with something called a "ball point." Another teacher found an entire class of sixth graders who could not verbalize a definition of *physician*. It is possible, of course, that they would have known *doctor* or *pediatrician*—we must remember that language is constantly growing and changing.

There is a need in language arts programs to build on children's experiences, and for the focus of this building to be on developing language ability; experiences of children both inside and outside of the classroom are opportunities for this to happen. An experience is simply any occurrence, but more importantly it needs to be thought of as the reactions and feelings of the participants about the occurrence. Thus, the activities in a classroom provide differing experiences to different children, and some may provide little to any of them. The key is the quality of the activity—the experience—how it is planned, how it relates to the learning objectives, its realism, children's interest in it, and the guidance given by the teacher toward achieving the objectives.

Providing Input

Because of the differences discussed, there should be provision for diversity in children's school experiences. At the same time, a teacher should attempt to provide a common core of experiences because of the similarity of many children's needs. Children will be limited in their use of language by the experiences they have had. A child will not be able to express feelings about "early morning on the farm" if he or she has never been on a farm and arisen early. In the same way, a child will not react with feeling about the dazzling wonders of the snowflake if he or she has not seen snow—or even if snow has only been something to contend with rather than to appreciate (though the opportunity may be present to help such a child discover the wonder and beauty that accompany the hardships of snow).

Children must have an abundance of opportunities to gain new ideas, new impressions, and new feelings, and to relate these to the experiences they have had. The number of ways to give children these experiences is

Prepare children for experiences. For example, before a field trip, encourage the children to help plan it, generate questions, and discuss vocabulary and possible follow-up activities.

Talking about things that are real and important.

almost infinite: reading aloud from a variety of materials; talking with them about news events and other things of interest; providing for interesting visitors to the classroom; making available television and radio programs, recordings, films, and still pictures; providing books in profusion and the opportunity to read them; and giving special attention to expressive words and apt phrases and how they may be used. Particularly important are excursions or field trips. These may be merely excursions into the schoolyard or another part of the building, they may be visits to various points of interest in the neighborhood, or they may entail more extended trips.

Helping children be more aware of their senses is particularly needed and will result in input that builds language growth. Children, like most adults, are seldom good observers, although too often time for observing is simply not provided for in a crowded school day—and this is sometimes the case on a field trip or some other experience-building activity. While various observation games are available or can be created—such as displaying a number of objects, removing one, and asking what is missing—the observation of natural phenomena is more helpful. Taking time to observe cloud formations, how the wind has drifted the snow, a flock of geese overhead, or the spread of the roots of a sprouting bean seed will interest children, cause them to use language, and facilitate the learning of new ideas and words.

Children themselves can provide much input. With very little encouragement they will bring butterflies, leaves, worms, rocks, and innumerable other objects to the classroom.

A Few Awareness Books

Find Out by Touching by Paul Showers (Thomas Y. Crowell)

I See the Winds by Kazue Mizumura (Thomas Y. Crowell)

Rain Drop Splash by Alvin Tresselt (Lothrop, Lee and Shepard)

What Is Your Favorite Smell, My Dear? by Myra Gibson (Grosset and Dunlap)

Activities such as the following are all useful in adding to children's knowledge, and are things they will communicate about.

Take time to observe:

the swooping of a swallow
the chugging and blinking
 of a helicopter
a bird's nest in a tree fork
the swaying of a tall pine
the ripple on the water
 caused by a fallen leaf
waves creeping up a sandy
 beach
the bouncing run of a
 rabbit

- Keeping an aquarium or terrarium.
- Noting temperature differences in sunshine and shade.
- Watching flying formations of birds.
- Collecting leaves of different kinds or colors.
- Collecting kinds and shapes of rocks.
- Tasting particular substances, such as pickles, berries, fruits, spices, or nuts.
- Feeling various materials, such as velvet, fur, aluminum foil, sand, wool, and silk.
- Caring for a classroom pet.
- Observing the growth of different kinds of seeds.
- Keeping a weather chart.
- Bringing in pictures of things of interest, such as a new baby at the zoo.
- Feeding birds or squirrels in winter.
- Observing soil erosion.
- Listening to stories and recordings.
- Participating in singing games.

A Learning Climate

Children's growth in language depends on many things, not the least of which is the atmosphere or climate in a classroom. The climate desired is

A good classroom climate encourages the exchange of ideas and experiences.

one that fosters goodwill, respect, and friendliness on the part of all concerned. It is one in which an effort is made to ensure that each child will feel relaxed, at ease, and accepted as an important member of the group. Such a climate respects each child's personality, heritage, and the social and emotional effects of his or her out-of-school environment. Creating the climate for developing each child's potential is largely your responsibility, and it will evolve chiefly from the children's feelings of acceptance, freedom, and shared responsibility.

While there are differences among teachers (and who would want it otherwise?), every teacher ought to be a vital, interesting person, one who is sensitive and encouraging. These qualities are reflections of attitude, and your attitude can be shown in many ways. These include the following:

1. Show each child that he or she is an accepted and important member of the classroom group.
2. Encourage an attitude of friendliness and mutual respect among the children—including respect for differences as well as likenesses.
3. Talk with and listen to children individually and in groups, and encourage them to exchange ideas and experiences.
4. Be receptive to ideas and interests expressed by the children.
5. Show appreciation of each child's efforts at expression.
6. Be enthusiastic—and allow the children to be—about the activities of the classroom.
7. Show sensitivity to and awareness of the world about you—encourage children to notice the way things look, sound, smell, and feel.
8. Let children see your own enjoyment of the stories you read, the way words sound, and the images they create.

Classroom climate is also affected by the general learning environment or climate of the school. The principal, office workers, lunchroom helpers, custodians, bus drivers, and teacher aides are all involved in setting the learning conditions in classrooms. The principal is a key person in this. He or she must understand children, know the curriculum and materials, and see the importance of a busy and interesting classroom, one in which the children are active participants. If a teacher has an aide, this person certainly should share the teacher's feelings about children and seek to develop the same attitudes that the teacher has or is developing. A custodian needs to be interested in what a class is doing and be willing to accept possible personal inconveniences such as a disarranged classroom. Other school personnel should also appreciate children's curiosity and enthusiasm. You cannot control the actions and reactions of these people, but you can do much to influence their attitudes by talking with them about what the children are doing and why they are doing it. Try inviting each of them to be a special guest of the class for a particular activity or program. Also, try involving them in a class activity—making something, telling about something, giving their opinion on something, etc.

Physical materials in the classroom are also important. Little stimulation of language growth or creativity will come from drabness. Wall and bulletin-board decorations, displays, pictures, and objects to handle and talk about are all important. And, of course, there must be language: signs, titles, and name plates to show the use of words; records, tapes, and tables and shelves of books to show the delight and knowledge they can bring. Further, a classroom where language growth is taking place is one that shows evidence that the children themselves have taken part in planning, preparing, and arranging the decorations and displays and that many activities are in progress there. This does not necessarily mean neatness, though children must learn that materials left strewn around the room are not easily found when needed or may not be in condition to be used again. Nor does it mean that absolute peace and quiet must reign; children learn as they share their experiences, discuss their activities, and help one another with problems.

TEACHING RESOURCES

Anything in the children's world—in the classroom and outside of it—may be a teaching resource. However, in a more narrow sense, the principal resources are the textbook and materials intended to supplement it, or those materials—films, cassettes, cards, and so on—intended to be used as a replacement for the textbook.

Textbooks

Recognize weaknesses in textbooks as well as strengths.

Virtually every classroom has textbooks. They are the most readily accessible instructional aids a teacher has, but they are *aids*, not directors or regulators. To begin the instruction for the year on the first page of a textbook and to continue throughout the year in a page-by-page manner fails to take into account the language abilities and needs of a particular class, to say nothing of the varying needs and abilities of individual children in that class.

The language arts textbook can be an important aid to teaching, but it is not a teacher, nor can it do everything. It can serve several functions if properly used, as suggested earlier in the Basic Instructional Approach section. However, not every textbook will provide for those aspects of the approach identified for it. In general, though, language textbooks present a point of view about the teaching of skills, attitudes, and information that should be useful to you in objectifying your own philosophy. They also identify skills and content the authors believe to be suitable for a particular grade level, thus serving as a reminder and a base against which the instructional program may be evaluated. In addition, textbooks suggest methods for teaching many language skills, provide practice materials and suggest activities for establishing the learning of the skills and abilities taught, provide evaluation materials, and suggest other materials and techniques.

The limitations of most language textbooks are many, particularly if the textbooks are relied on too heavily. In the first place, the presentation of the program is likely to be too formal. In addition, the emphasis in many textbooks is on aspects of language study that children either already know or have no valid reason for learning. The suggested activities are for a hypothetical class and may not be suitable for a particular group of children. The practice exercises and activities suggested are usually inadequate in number and type because of being directed at a hypothetical class, and because of limitations in the size of the textbook. Also, many language activities need to be oral ones, and textbooks simply cannot adequately take care of that need. Further, the teaching suggestions in the textbook and sometimes in the teacher's manual may be too brief because of space limitations, or they may be too detailed and fail to recognize knowledge that many teachers (or pupils) already possess. Finally, the evaluation aids are also limited by space and by the inability to focus on evaluating a particular class.

The important thing to remember is that innumerable occasions for genuine language teaching occur as a teacher and children work, play, and study together. The textbook may help you to take advantage of these occasions in several ways. First, suggested settings for language activities, such as an imaginary conversation pupils might have or a hypothetical occasion for reporting orally, may be altered so that they apply to current work in a classroom or they may be used as a guide for taking advantage of similar settings. In addition, the textbook provides information regarding communication activities (for example, what should be included in giving directions, procedures to follow in conducting an interview or doing research for a report) that is useful in taking full advantage of natural situations. The textbook also may provide models of letters, outlines, and reports, which may be used in discussing the content, organization, and mechanics needed for effective writing in each situation; and it may provide examples supporting the explanation and suggestions you give regarding punctuation and capitalization items, choices of words, construction of sentences, and so on.

Other Resources

An effective language arts program regards virtually everything and anything as a teaching resource. Children are interested in the world and want to communicate about it. They learn outside the classroom as well as inside—in many ways they learn more outside. Thus, we lose touch with much of the child's world if we limit our teaching resources to just that which is within the walls.

Parents should be told and shown how the textbooks and other resources will be used.

There are, however, many resources other than the textbook that can be made a part of the resources inside the walls, and bringing these into teaching often puts the textbook in proper perspective. These resources include trade and reference books, newspapers, displays, art work, globes, maps, puppets, bulletin boards, computers, television and radio, film, recordings, cassettes, filmstrips, transparencies, and visual slides. Because of their importance in attaining an effective language arts program, we have listed at the end of each chapter examples of some of these resources so that you can bring them into your planning and instruction.

Reviews of educational
software for
microcomputers are
available from:

Association for Educational
  Data Systems
1201 Sixteenth St., NW
Washington, DC 20036

Classroom Computer News
Box 266
Cambridge, MA 02138

Computers, Reading and
  Language Arts
Box 13247
Oakland, CA 94661

The Computing Teacher
Dept. of Computer Science
University of Oregon
Eugene, OR 97403

Courseware Report Card
150 West Carob St.
Compton, CA 90220

MicroSIFT Reviews
Northwest Regional Educa-
  tional Laboratory
300 S. W. Sixth Ave.
Portland, OR 97204

Popular Computing
70 Main St.
Peterborough, NH 03458

School Microware Reviews
Dresden Associates
Box 246
Dresden, ME 04342

These resources are often referred to as audiovisual aids, but they are more than aids. When used in a well-planned program, they will heighten motivation for learning, provide for better retention of what is learned because of their concreteness and multisensory aspects, give the program freshness and variety, provide reinforcement for other learning, encourage active participation of pupils, widen the range of experience in a manner that has special attraction, and appeal to varied abilities and interests.

Much of the above applies particularly to television. Too often television in the classroom is used only as an aid in teaching some aspect of a subject matter area. Little writing or speaking (other than questions and answers) seems to follow a viewing session. Even less is likely to precede it. Also, there is the television viewing that children do at home. While there is disagreement about the positive and negative effects of television, surveys show that in any case most children watch about as many hours of television programs daily as they spend in school. Therefore, why not write about what has been viewed—changing an ending, adding other characters, describing a character or place, researching an idea presented, etc.?

The eighties have already become the *computer decade*. Libraries are replacing card catalogs with computers. Children are composing on word processors. They are reacting emotionally and intellectually to the diagrams, charts, and pictures that computers display on their screens. Educational software is available in such confusing quantities that teachers will be obliged to become skilled in evaluating this software for quality. The authors of this text cannot envision all of the ways the computer can be a resource for a language arts program, but we do know that nothing other than tradition and teacher lethargy can limit it.

EVALUATION AND GRADING

Too often evaluation is equated with giving a grade, but it is much more than this. Evaluation is a process, an essential component of the larger process of instruction. It is directly related to instructional goals and to the attainment of these goals. Evaluation determines what has not been effectively taught—what else needs to be taught. Grading, on the other hand, is done for the purpose of reporting to pupils, to parents, and to school authorities. Grading should be based on evaluation; therefore, evaluation is necessary for grading. However, the converse is not true—grading is not required for evaluation.

The Role of Evaluation

*Finding out what a child
knows or can do is the first
step in teaching.*

Evaluation is a process that includes all the procedures used by the teacher, the children, the principal, and other school personnel to appraise the outcomes of instruction. As a process it includes formulating goals in terms of behavior that can be measured or appraised, securing evidence from representative situations regarding the extent of the achievement of the objectives, summarizing and recording the evidence, interpreting or analyzing the evidence in terms of the objectives and the instructional procedures, and using the interpretation to extend and improve instruction.

In relating these steps to a particular aspect of an instructional program (perhaps a writing activity, the giving of an oral report, or learning to use the dictionary), begin by giving an inventory test or by using some other appropriate means for appraising what the learner already knows or can do that is specifically related to what you plan to teach. Then teach the skills, knowledge, or attitudes needed by the learner as shown by this appraisal. Provide motivation for learning the things taught by designing situations in which they are actually needed and used; this will establish learnings firmly. Next, give a test or make an appraisal similar in content and form to that used during the inventory stage, using the results of this appraisal to determine the extent of learning and discover specific deficiencies. And finally, reteach for these deficiencies, giving practice as needed; if necessary, continue the process by retesting, reteaching, and so forth.

Techniques and Instruments

As suggested earlier, instruments and procedures for evaluation vary widely in type, structure, and function. The procedures include the administration of tests, questionnaires, inventories, checklists, and observation forms, as well as conferences, examination of biographies and folders of pupils' work, and oral or written questioning. Tests vary, too—they may be oral or written, standardized or teacher-made, essay or short-answer. In addition, there are models, statements of standards, progress charts, logs and diaries, and scales.

Many of the instruments and procedures are discussed in later chapters where specific reference is made to their use. At this point the emphasis is on the importance of evaluation and the fact that there are many instruments and procedures available. It is also important to recognize the imprecision in commercial materials for evaluating oral and written language abilities—a fact reflected in the paucity of tests available for evaluating many important objectives. Thus, it is necessary to do much informal evaluation—to make use of checklists, records, charts, and inventories; to collect pupils' work in folders; to keep logs and diaries; to have conferences; and to help pupils develop models, scales, and statements of standards.

Reporting Progress

A teacher must observe the reporting policies of the school and district, of course, and in many cases this means putting letter or numerical grades on a report card. You can go further than this, though, by sending home samples of children's work, evaluative statements and explanations, and the results from using various instruments and procedures. While some teachers think doing these things is too time-consuming and others simply don't

Try to have conferences with parents early in the year, before problems develop.

know what to say in evaluative statements (often because of having done too little evaluating), the value of more adequate reporting cannot be denied. In addition to better and more detailed written reports, you should arrange to confer with parents about their children's progress and needs more often than once a year.

Children should also be reported to, but again this does not mean that every paper or activity has to be marked with a grade. Pupils will appreciate talking with you about their progress, seeing your marks on checklists and observation forms, and participating in interpreting data obtained through testing, using scales, etc. This kind of active participation, along with helping to establish criteria before activities are begun, will help children to learn habits of self-evaluation and to understand what is expected of them.

Telephone or send a short note to parents about their child's accomplishments.

All reports—to parents, to pupils, and to school authorities—should be based on evidence that can be shown and understood; they should be made in consideration of the child and the effect of the report on the child and his or her learning; and they should be as accurate an assessment of achievement or progress as is possible and without subjective bias of any sort—or as nearly so as possible.

A FINAL WORD

This chapter gives only a brief overview of the organizing and planning needed to teach language arts effectively; suggestions will be expanded on in the chapters that follow. Principles for selecting content and guidelines for planning become operational only when you consider the particular children in a classroom, how well they speak and write, and what problems they seem to have. In the same manner, the instructional plan suggested and the means for implementing it can become truly meaningful only when considered in connection with specific content and procedures for teaching speaking, listening, reading, and writing.

References

Blake, Howard E. *Creating a Learning-Centered Classroom.* Hart Publishing Co., 1977.

Carkhuff, Robert R., *et al. The Skills of Teaching: Interpersonal Skills.* Human Resources Development Press, 1976.

Hoover, Kenneth H., and Hollingsworth, Paul M. *A Handbook for Elementary School Teachers.* 3rd ed. Allyn and Bacon, 1982.

King-Stoops, Joyce. *The Child Wants to Learn.* Little, Brown, 1977.

Klugman, Edgar. *Teaching in the Elementary School: A Guide to Planning.* Fearon Publishers, 1970.

Petty, Walter T., ed. *Curriculum for the Modern Elementary School.* Rand McNally College Publishing Co., 1976.

Shiman, David A.; Culver, Carmen M.; and Lieberman, Ann. *Teachers on Individualization: The Way We Do It.* McGraw-Hill, 1974.

Magazines for Elementary School Teachers

Childhood Education. The Association for Childhood Education International, 3615 Wisconsin Ave., NW, Washington, DC 20016.

Early Years. Allen Raymond, Inc., P.O. Box 1266, Darien, CT 06820.

The Horn Book. Park Square Bldg., 31 St. James Ave., Boston, MA 02116.

Instructor. The Instructor Publications, Inc., 757 Third Avenue, New York, NY 10017.

Language Arts. National Council of Teachers of English, 111 Kenyon Road, Urbana, IL 61801.

Learning. Pitman Learning, Inc., 530 University Ave., Palo Alto, CA 94301.

The Reading Teacher. International Reading Association, 800 Barksdale Road, P.O. Box 8139, Newark, DE 19711.

Teacher. Macmillan Professional Magazines, Inc., 77 Bedford Street, Stamford, CT 06901.

Activities for Preservice Teachers

1. Interview an elementary school teacher, asking about the range of intellectual abilities and academic aptitudes of the children in his or her classroom. Also ask about the principal means used to give instructional attention to the differences.

2. Obtain copies of your state or district syllabi for language arts. Study these to determine what children are expected to learn at each grade level.

3. List the advantages and disadvantages of subject-matter departmentalization in the elementary school. Indicate the sources you used for determining these.

4. Prepare a learning activity for social studies, science, or some other area, giving particular attention to relating one or more areas of the language arts with the subject matter you intend to teach.

5. Use syllabi, texts for the grade level of your choice, and/or methods textbooks to prepare a learning activity for social studies, science, or some other area, giving particular emphasis to interrelating the language arts with your planned lessons.

6. Make an appointment with the individual in your local school system who is most involved with the testing program and ask to see and discuss the tests used for language arts evaluation. Report your findings.

7. Visit an elementary school and ask the teachers how they group for instruction in different subjects. See how many different grouping designs you can find and what teachers believe to be the strengths and weaknesses of each.

8. Make an appointment with an elementary school principal or assistant principal and ask to be shown the different types of records that are found in a child's cumulative folder.

9. Read articles from professional journals about varying organizational plans and/or designs for grouping. List advantages and disadvantages of each and decide which you would like to try.

10. Go through a year's issues of such journals as *Instructor*, *Learning*, and *Teacher* for ideas about special weeks and days. These journals indicate where kits for observance of these special events can be obtained (for example: The American Bar Association, 1155 East 60th St., Chicago 60637, has material on Law Day U.S.A., and Lutheran Brotherhood, 701 Second Avenue South, Minneapolis, MN 55402, has a kit for fire prevention week).

Activities for Inservice Teachers

1. Plan an informal meeting with other teachers in your school or district who teach at your grade level and make an outline of the major subjects that should be covered. You might want to include such topics as materials (including media), sharing of materials, interrelating all of the language arts, teacher-pupil planning, and evaluation.

2. Develop a plan (including techniques and/or devices) for evaluating your pupils in the language arts areas, one that will provide you with information helpful for your instruction and for reporting to parents. Keep in mind both simplicity of use and adequate coverage.

3. Plan an *interesting* program for parents designed to explain the language arts: teaching goals, importance, evaluation, and how parents might help at home or as volunteer aides in your room. Discuss the program with your administrator before presenting it.

4. Evaluate a commercial kit purported to provide basic or supplemental instruction in a language arts area (i.e., spelling, composition, listening). Base your evaluation on the curriculum-planning principles in this chapter.

5. Make several individual, self-correcting practice exercises for reinforcing a specific language arts skill. Report to the class how you would use them.

6. Prepare a card file of the audiovisual material available in your district that you have previewed and believe to be useful to you in your language arts program. Each card should tell how the material can be obtained, its major use, the time it requires, a synopsis of its content, and a brief evaluation of its value to your program.

3 | *Grammar and Language Usage*

The teaching of grammar has long been a tradition in elementary schools, and traditions tend to persist—unfortunately, in this case. The tradition of teaching grammar is reinforced by the content of most language textbooks for children—and in many cases the grammar content of these has even been increased as a result of the recent concern for teaching the "basic skills."

Teachers are obliged to use these textbooks as well as to deal with parents and others who view acquiring the "basic skills" as learning terminology and rules and doing exercises. Further, and despite their own judgment and observations, they are faced with articles in professional journals that are flavored to a large extent with teaching suggestions which ignore the research evidence accumulated over eighty years.

In addition, there is confusion about the difference between grammar and usage and between both of these and mechanics or conventions. Also, *standard English* and *dialects* are terms whose meanings may be unclear and which are brought into the content and practices labeled in common parlance as "grammar teaching."

It is because of the misunderstandings that appear to exist, as well as the existence of grammatical terminology and exercises in textbooks, that we have placed this chapter early in this book.

GRAMMAR LEARNING AND TEACHING

Chapter 2 in Lindfors' *Children's Language and Learning* gives a good discussion of "knowing grammar."

In everyday language, and often in school as well, the word *grammar* connotes "the rules" for speaking and writing correctly, including those concerning the mechanics of expression (more properly called *conventions*). The layperson may (and usually does) include spelling and handwriting as grammar when complaining about the schools' "not teaching grammar anymore." Little concern is shown for the term *usage*, which refers to the form of expression—the choice of words one makes in structuring speaking and writing—although "good grammar" may convey the same idea. The important point is that saying "It is me" or "We was going" instead of "It is I" or "We were going" is a usage choice. *Grammar*, on the other hand, refers to the system of word structures and word arrangements in expression. All of the examples above are grammatical; expressions such as "Were going we" and "All the boy and girls are going" are ungrammatical.

50

Development of Grammar

Native speakers of English have the ability to judge whether or not a string of words is arranged in an acceptable manner—that is, "acceptable" in the sense of conveying meaning, without regard to whether the words are polite or rude. Native speakers know the grammar of the language. We have what may be labeled as an *intuitive* knowledge of the organizational possibilities of English units. We acquired this intuitive knowledge unconsciously as infants and children as we sought to communicate our thoughts, to learn meanings, and to bring order to our lives.

As we stated in Chapter 1, at about eighteen to twenty months of age children begin to put words together—the first observable evidence that the grammar of the language is being learned. Most of their early word combinations tend to follow a pattern: singling out a few words for use in a particular utterance position with a variety of other words. This type of experimentation lasts only a short time, but it is an important step. The child who says "chair mama" at twenty months (and who also says "chair dada" and "see chair") is trying out word order. The child perceives that some types of words come first and others second. As compared to those of an adult, the perceptions are sometimes faulty, but they do show the development of a system or grammar representative of the child's level of maturity.

Thus, children learn the classes of words early (but, of course, not the grammatical terminology) as they demonstrate by using many of their first words in different contexts. The repeated words are likely to be nouns and verbs and, less often, adjectives. At this stage, the meanings expressed are largely dependent on the context. The young child who says "Mommy sock" may mean "Mommy, put on the sock" or perhaps "It is Mommy's sock." The child continues to talk predominantly about the here and now but will begin to use longer utterances: "Me push truck" and "Me push truck there." Various sentence types appear, such as "He no hit you" and "Where daddy go?" Pronouns begin to be used: "I go bed" and "That my ball."

The examples of utterances are from Chapter 4 of Bryen's *Inquiries into Child Language.*

This early development shows that children attach meanings to the words they use, that they know that the functions of these words may differ, and that conveying meaning depends on the order in which the words are spoken. Again, the young children's utterances provide evidence that they have developed an understanding of the language system. These utterances reflect the development of a grammar—not yet the grammar of a more mature speaker of the language, but a definite stage toward it. They have not yet learned how such things as auxiliary verbs, prepositions, and inflectional endings work, but their experimenting continues, and they do learn to use them. In fact, they begin very early to try out noun and verb endings with such constructions as *foots, goed, mines,* and so on. Using these overgeneralizations, they gradually learn from the responses of other persons that some ways of saying things are wrong. Children usually add many irregular verb forms to their vocabularies before many regular ones and construct generalizations as they discover new rules. As they mature, they learn how to apply the rules, but some of this learning takes a while.

The important fact to recognize is that children have reached quite a complex level of development by the time they enter school. They do not need to be taught the grammatical relationships of classes of words and their functions, which textbooks seek to teach. Of course, not all children are at the same level of development when they enter school (or at any time during their stay), and some grammatical development does continue during the early school years (using the passive voice, for instance).

Children entering a nursery school or even kindergarten or first grade are not yet literate as we think of literacy, but they understand sentences when they hear them, and they know if a part of a sentence has been omitted or is in the wrong place. They speak in sentences and phrases that reflect their knowledge of language patterns. They know many words, and they know the language system well enough to realize that structural changes can be made in some words to achieve particular purposes and meanings (e.g., adding endings such as *-s, -es, -ed, -er, -ing*). Certainly, some children will occasionally mix up word order, add the wrong ending or fail to add an ending at all, or have a problem in holding to tense or person. But the basic understanding of the system is present and developing—if it were not, the children would not have been able to communicate during their preschool years.

Values Attributed to Grammar Teaching

There are several reasons proponents of grammar teaching give for including it in the curriculum. Traditionally, many thought that only through an understanding of the grammar of the language could anyone learn to write and speak effectively. It is true, of course, that an understanding of language contributes to effective communication, but this understanding is gained from experience in communicating rather than from the ability to verbalize facts about the language system. However, even though repeated studies have shown that studying grammar (including any of the "new" ones) does not result in improved speech and writing, many people have been slow in accepting this overwhelming evidence.

See *Research in Teaching English* 10 (1976), pp. 5–21, and *English Journal* 66 (December 1977), pp. 86–89, for reports of grammar studies.

Closely akin to the argument that teaching grammar improves skill in communication is the belief that a knowledge of grammar is necessary for success in later education. For years elementary teachers have been prodded into teaching grammar by the complaints, both real and imagined, of secondary school teachers that pupils come to them unable to identify the parts of speech or to tell a subject from a predicate. Secondary school foreign language teachers frequently express the same concerns. However, there is no evidence that grammar teaching in the secondary school has any more bearing on writing and speech than it does in the elementary school. Furthermore, there has been evidence for about forty years that the teaching of English grammar—of whatever type—has no bearing on the learning of a foreign language.

You may want to read Weaver's small book about grammar teaching.

Perhaps the most valid reason given for teaching grammar is that advanced by many linguists, who believe that an understanding of the way language works is valuable in and of itself. They argue that language is the thing that sets humanity apart from the animals, that it is a uniquely human thing, and that children therefore ought to know about their own language. It is important to remember, however, that few linguists advocate the teaching of grammatical systems in the elementary school or the teaching of grammar in a formal or prescriptive manner. They generally believe that grammar teaching should be done in an eclectic and empirical way; the teacher should select only those items that are appropriate to the children and help them to discover *about* language through much experience, observation, and practice.

Although linguists vary in their opinions about how much—and when—grammar should be taught, most believe that any intensive study of grammar should be postponed until the secondary school, and some believe that even then it should be done on an elective basis. Another important distinction lies in the fact that, in general, they speak of helping children to discover "about *language*," not "about grammar." The former is certainly a more inclusive term and may include many things that are not strictly grammar: word histories and derivations, the use of the dictionary, how style and structure can contribute to meaning, and more. In light of this interpretation, every good elementary language arts program includes much study "about language."

Grammars Old and New

Grammars—defined as descriptions of the structure of a language—have developed in different forms and at different times, a process that continues as language scholars seek better explanations for the workings of the complex phenomenon that is language.

TRADITIONAL GRAMMAR. *Traditional grammar* is a description of the English language that is based on the system of the Latin language. Historically, it has simply been called *grammar* and only recently has the adjective been added. The description arose some 400 years ago in an effort to explain why certain words were used or certain sentences constructed rather than others. The fallacy in this description was the assumption that all languages have the same system (although all do have some system) and the failure to recognize that language grows and changes.

Another problem with traditional grammar is that it has generally been taught formally. Rules, definitions, and diagrams for showing relationships have been emphasized, with little or no attempt to relate these to students' actual speaking and writing. Most classroom time has been spent conjugating the forms of verbs, naming the parts of speech in sentences, and memorizing rules. The focus in traditional grammar teaching has been on teaching the system as the basis for prescribing what is "correct" in expression.

STRUCTURAL GRAMMAR. *Structural grammar* is the product of linguists' scientific study of the way we speak. Structural grammar does not prescribe what is "correct" but simply reports the language as it exists, including its growth and changes. In structural grammar, the ways words are put together into utterances have been categorized, and from this categorization certain principles and patterns of the language system have emerged. One difficulty with this grammar is determining how people actually do speak, a matter that is basic to the categorization that produces the patterns. Not everyone speaks the same way; that is, there are social and regional differences in usage and pronunciation. Then there is the problem of completeness. How large a sample of language must be examined to determine whether or not all possible patterns and principles of the system have been discovered? Of course, both of these weaknesses are of no greater importance to structural grammar than to any other, except that since the basis of this grammar is its scientific determination, they introduce some limitations to generalizing about the completeness of its patterns as a description of the language system.

Structural grammar identifies basic sentence patterns in English and describes the form and function of words in those patterns. In traditional grammar a word is described in terms of meaning: "A verb is a word that expresses action" or "A noun is the name of a person, place, or thing." In structural grammar a word is a noun because it has a particular function or is signaled in a particular way. In addition, the levels given to the parts of speech in structural grammar are somewhat different from those of traditional grammar. For example, words such as *a, an, the,* and *some* are called determiners or noun markers; they signal that a noun is to follow: "*My* mother went to *the* store." There are also verb markers (*can, could, might*— also called auxiliaries), clause markers (*because, if, how*), and phrase markers (*in, down, toward*), as well as intensifiers or qualifiers (*very, just, less*) and connectors or conjunctions (*and, but, for*); but the four major classes are the well-known noun, verb, adjective, and adverb.

TRANSFORMATIONAL GRAMMAR. *Transformational grammar* came into being after the development of structural grammar, as a result of the recognition by some grammarians of the impossibility of securing factual information on all possible sentences the speakers of the language may use. This grammar has a theoretical base rather than the empirical (observable or factual) base of structural grammar. To overcome the problem of examining actual utterances, transformational grammar assumes a *deep structure* system that leads to a *surface structure* (the sentences actually said and written). There are two basic types of sentences: kernel and transformed. Kernel sentences, of which there are a relatively small number, are the core of the system. They are sentences that cannot be derived by analysis from other sentences (e.g., "The children ride bicycles"). All other sentences are transformed sentences. They can be constructed by transforming kernel sentences ("Bicycles are ridden by the children" "Do the children ride bicycles?" "Don't the children ride bicycles?", etc.). Sentences can also be constructed by expansion of the noun phrase of a kernel sentence ("The children *in the fifth grade* ride bicycles") or the verb phrase ("The children ride bicycles *all day long*"), by the coordination of kernel sentences ("The children *and their parents* ride bicycles"), or by subordination of one or more sentences to another ("Since parents have other activities, they do not ride bicycles all day as their children do").

This grammar makes use of terminology similar to that used in structural grammar. Like structural grammar, it is not prescriptive, except in the sense of indicating whether or not an utterance is grammatical. There is no prescription as to correctness of the words used. However, transformational grammar (sometimes called *generative* or *transformational-generative*) can be taught as formally as was traditional grammar, and this often is the case. Teaching it can have much of the same emphasis on rules, relationships of words and phrases to one another (usually by a new kind of diagramming), isolation of the study from the expression of children, and activities that have little interest for or little meaning to children. Of course, the same can be said for structural or any other grammar.

A Functional Approach

What can teachers do to break away from the traditional emphasis on grammar teaching, even though they are supposed to use textbooks that have this emphasis? The answer is that they must know the research evidence, understand and be able to explain the difference between grammar and usage, and know the kinds of things that can be done to improve youngsters' speaking and writing. They must also know a good deal about the kind of language study that will appeal to children.

Children are not likely to generate much enthusiasm if the program is centered around a textbook that insists that it is wrong to say "Don't go *in* the house" and that it is normal and proper to say "The team is *we*, the athletes." Nor will they have much interest in exercises calling for identifying the nouns, verbs, adjectives, etc., in sentences; for underlining the "complete" predicates; for categorizing common and proper nouns; and so on. Children like to talk and they like to write; they want to tell what they have discovered and what they think about something. Thus, the program should focus on *using* language—speaking, writing, reading, and listening. A textbook may suggest ideas for using language. It also may be a source of examples and explanations (as suggested in Chapter 2). The grammatical terminology need not be taught or the exercises used.

However, we did suggest that any of the grammars described might be taught in a formal manner or dealt with in a functional way. In functional teaching of grammar the focus is on expression and its purpose rather than on grammar. However, to the extent that grammar enters into it, there is the implication that the grammar taught is of value—is functional—in making expression more effective. While there is little evidence in favor of bringing grammar into teaching with this focus, if grammar is taught (for any of the reasons suggested), it seems to make sense that an effort should be made to relate it to expression rather than to teach it as something entirely separate from the natural expression that occurs as children communicate.

Chapter 9 has many suggestions about sentence construction and sentence combining.

It is natural for children to learn the names of parts of sentences as they construct and reconstruct their own sentences and as they learn how to make their sentences more effective. Attention should be given to the terminology of the language system only as it relates to the children's expression and to the improvement of that expression in terms of its purpose.

If children construct sentences well and thus convey the message they intended, there is no need to teach grammatical items. On the other hand, if a child says "The boys is going," the opportunity *may* be present to teach about agreement of subject and verb. Certainly the child may be taught that *is* is a verb, not just something referred to as "this word." In a similar way, if a child describes the black bear in a film the class has viewed as simply a "black bear," there is a functional situation for teaching about using other adjectives—*big, lumbering, awkward,* etc.—to give a better word picture of what the child has seen.

Teaching about language functionally means that teaching about nouns cannot be allocated to the fourth grade, nor can it be done in a series of isolated lessons. Functional teaching requires that understanding be developed from the very first contacts teachers have with children. The kindergarten or first grade teacher who says "Who can give me another sentence telling about one thing we saw at the bakery?" is teaching grammar. So is the fifth grade teacher who says "Let's see how we can make this sentence more exact. Have we used the best adjectives to describe the carts the natives use for hauling grain?"

There is no need to avoid using grammatical terminology when it is natural to use it. A verb is more properly called by that term than an "action word," and *verb* is no more difficult to learn than many other words that children readily use. We don't call a television a "box that shows pictures" or a wheel "something that goes around," and children have no trouble with these words or the basic concepts which they represent.

Functional language teaching should be done informally and always in relation to actual expression. The Basic Instructional Plan suggested in Chapter 2 can be the framework for such teaching. This plan does not leave the teaching of language skills to unplanned or incidental occasions; with careful planning, opportunities arise that require the use of particular language skills and hence provide situations for functional teaching.

Activities

In thinking about ways in which the normal activities of a class may be structured so that interest in language, its variety, and its structure are furthered, consider again the "black bear" illustration used in the preceding section. In addition to merely thinking of adjectives to describe the bear, the children might learn to make sentence structures more complex and varied by experimenting with turning the adjectives into phrases, clauses, verbs, or adverbs. For example, "the awkward, lumbering black bear" might become "the awkward black bear with the lumbering gait," "the black bear who lumbered toward us with an awkward gait," or "the black bear lumbered awkwardly toward us." This kind of activity can also lead to a discussion of how words change form and position when they are used differently and, if it is done often, should lead to much greater variety in children's sentences.

An understanding of word order and form is also encouraged by the use of sentences made up of nonsense words, and children will have a great deal of fun while they are learning. A sentence such as "Ra slishy glugged ra rigit" immediately initiates the discovery that *ra* must be a noun marker—an article or determiner—and therefore *slishy* and *rigit* have to be nouns. Similarly, *glugged* is probably a verb in past tense because of its position and the *-ed* ending. Ask the children what would happen to *slishy* and *glugged* if their positions were exchanged, and see what kind of discussion ensues.

For word order, present simple sentences in jumbled order: "had many about airplanes Joe read books." Children will have little trouble putting this sentence in order, but try adding phrases and clauses ("in his younger years," "while he was growing up," "which were used in World War II"), and they will soon discover that word order is important to sentence sense. This kind of exercise should be helpful also for children who tend to misplace modifiers or use danglers. Using some of the children's own sentences will also help them to see how the way a sentence is put together can contribute to meaning and effectiveness.

A similar activity that encourages an understanding of sentence parts and sentence completeness involves using strips of tagboard on which are printed noun phrases and verb phrases. Distribute these to the children; then ask each child to see how many mates he or she can find that will make meaningful, complete sentences. As the children advance in sentence mastery, add coordinating conjunctions—*and, but*, etc.—and subordinating or adverbial conjunctions—*if, because, when*, etc. In this case, one child might be chosen to begin a sentence, with others volunteering to continue and complete it. The class would judge whether the resulting sentence was a good one and possibly experiment with revisions. This activity could also be done with teams, points being given for finishing first, having the greatest number of parts to a sentence, and, of course, having a well-constructed sentence.

Another excellent way to help children discover the importance of word order and structure is to use the overhead projector to show a paragraph in which all sentences are simple ones and the words are in natural order (i.e., subject, verb, object). To demonstrate the need for variety, have them try altering each sentence in the same way. Depending on the maturity of the children, they might invert order and make every active verb passive, add an adjective before each noun in the subject position, begin each sentence with a prepositional phrase, make all sentences compound by connecting each pair with the word *and*, etc. After doing this in several ways, have the children select one sentence from each rewrite to make a new paragraph, perhaps experimenting with several different combinations. Then evaluate the results by determining which paragraph is most interesting. (Reading the paragraphs aloud is a good way to demonstrate monotony in structure.)

In the upper grades the need for variety in structure can be illustrated by revising a famous speech such as Lincoln's Gettysburg Address or Patrick Henry's "Give me liberty, or give me death," keeping vocabulary the same, insofar as is possible, but structuring all sentences in the same way.

In the middle and upper grades, children often have difficulty with tense sequence, agreement, and staying in the same person as they write. Activities such as those suggested above can be structured to develop a better understanding of the way language works in these areas as well. For example, if you are using the tagboard strips, include various tenses of the same verb, both singular and plural forms of nouns, or a selection of pronouns (definite and indefinite, singular and plural, all persons). Or play a game in which no one is allowed to use plurals, past tense, or a particular pronoun for a certain period of time. This could be done in several ways; one is similar to "Ghost," with a child becoming one-third of a ghost the first time he or she uses the forbidden construction, two-thirds the second time, and so on. Obviously, some badly constructed sentences will result, but the children will become more aware of the grammatical need for different kinds of constructions.

These are only a few suggestions; obviously, the activities selected for a particular class must be chosen according to the needs and maturity of the children. The important point to remember in planning activities is that they should be directed at helping children see how the structure of language works in a positive way to make expression more effective and more meaningful.

USAGE AND DIALECTS

We have emphasized in this and earlier chapters that the language any of us use is largely a matter of our early environment—although by the time a person is an adult he or she has learned a great deal about choosing language appropriate to the communication situation. Such choosing does not mean that we invariably change the pronunciation of words or that we modify the expressions we learned in childhood, but we do pick up the jargon of our profession and social group, and in some situations we avoid language that might be labeled "nonstandard."

The above suggests that there are levels of language, and a few years ago differences in usage were seen as being on different levels. These levels were often termed *formal, informal,* and *colloquial,* and sometimes—in an attempt at finer distinctions—*illiterate, homely, informal standard, formal standard, literary,* and *technical.* There was also the idea that an individual used the language of one of these levels—apparently all or most of the time. We now know that each person's language usage varies. However, usage is still largely termed as standard and nonstandard, even though these terms are difficult to define.

Acceptable Usage

Deciding what the school should do about usage teaching is a major problem. In the first place, determining what items of usage are unacceptable is difficult at best. A textbook is only a partially satisfactory guide, as it is directed at a hypothetical classroom rather than an actual one. Also, too often the authors are unrealistic about which language usages are acceptable and which ones are not. Language scholars for some years have recommended that only a very few usage items should receive instruction or attention in the elementary school. In support of this attitude, one authority says,

See the report by Pooley.

(1) the constant repetition of a relatively small number of deviations constitutes over 90 percent of the nonstandard usage problems in the elementary grades [and] (2) a large number of "errors" listed in textbooks and language workbooks are not errors at all but standard colloquial English appropriate to the speech and writing of children and adults alike.

The reluctance of many teachers to accept certain usages is the major reason why the number of usage items identified here and in most textbooks is not more limited. A study done more than thirty years ago showed that teachers were only about half as accepting of "Can I have another helping of dessert, please?" "Everyone put on *their* coats and went home," "Go slow," and "It is me" as were a group of editors and writers. Observations by the authors of this book suggest that the extent of nonacceptance by many teachers has not changed much. Supporting our observations, a study by Johnson (see References) showed that five items of usage identified as acceptable by linguists were regarded as incorrect (particularly in writing, but also in most cases in speech) by teachers. This study dealt with the following examples of "incorrect" usage:

1. Everyone put *their* name in the upper left corner of the paper.
2. I *will* go to the store tomorrow.
3. The *reason* the page is missing *is because* Johnny tore it out.
4. They invited my friends and *myself*.
5. *Who* did you see?

Even more startling, this research also showed that 99 out of the 100 teachers in the study actually used at least one of the "incorrect" usages in either their own writing or speech, or both!

The list below is intended as a guide to the kinds of usages that should receive attention in the elementary school. It is not likely that the children in any one class will use all of them—and of course they should not be attacked unless the need is present. In no case, however, should all of them receive direct teaching effort in a single year. If a large number of them are used by the children, it is best to select those which occur most frequently and concentrate on them so that teaching effort is not dissipated.

ain't or *hain't*	my brother, *he*
yourn, hern, ourn	*her* and *me* went
hisen, theys	there *is* four
youse	there *was* four
onct	they *knowed*
hisself, theirselves	I, they *growed*
hair *are*	haven't *no*, isn't *no*
a orange	*leave* (for let)
have *ate*	haven't *nothing*
they *eats*	that's *mines*
was *broke*	where *it* at?

he *brung*	where is she *at?*
he *come*	he *run*
clumb	have *saw*
had, have *did*	I *says*
she, he *don't*	he *seen*
it *don't*	*them* books
didn't ought	*this here*
hadn't ought	*that there*
he *give,* he *walk*	*us* boys went
me and Mary went	we, you, they *was*
she *taken*	with *we* girls
I *likes* him	have *went*
I *drunk, drunks*	have *wrote*
can't hardly	the *mens*
does we have	*learn* me a song

Since language does change and since the studies cited earlier suggest that teachers and textbooks are often slow to recognize this change, aid may be needed in deciding what to teach. One way to obtain this aid is to listen to the speech of educated people and to read current newspapers and magazines; doing this with particular usages in mind can be very revealing. Another way is to check the appropriateness of words and expressions in reference books about usage, although sometimes these are not really current, and they may largely reflect the point of view of their authors.

Dialect Differences

A Various Language: Perspectives on American Dialects, edited by Juanita V. Williamson and Virginia M. Burke (Holt, Rinehart and Winston, 1971), is a readable compilation of articles dealing with various dialects.

It is certainly true that the pronunciations, vocabulary, and language structures of some children are such wide departures from the standard language or prestige dialect of the community that they cannot be ignored in classrooms. On the other hand, the dialects of other children may differ from the prestige dialect, yet they do not depart widely from the language that one hears and reads in the community. Thus, the attention given to these usages may be minimal, since many of the differences will cause no real communication difficulties and will add color and individualism to expression.

However, dealing with dialect differences becomes very important if other children laugh at the way a child speaks or say "He talks funny," if the dialect is of such low prestige and differs so markedly from "school" language that a genuine problem exists, or if understanding the child is difficult. If a youngster pronounces words such as *pin* and *pen* or *cheer* and *chair* the same way, there is a possibility that he or she will have difficulty with phonic analysis in reading—that is, a lack of sensitivity to a child's language may create a reading problem. Similar kinds of problems may appear in spelling instruction, but in neither of these language arts areas, or in any others, should it be assumed that the youngster's pronunciation must be changed or that the child should be told he or she is speaking incorrectly. All that is needed is to know the child's dialect and be able to reinforce learning when necessary. This is the only way to avoid mistakes like that of the teacher who asked a child what "canal" meant, was told what sounded like "a dish of water," and then proceeded to give an elaborate explanation of the concept of "canal."

See McDavid's chapter in *Linguistics in School Programs* for a discussion of differences.

Grammatical differences from the standard or prestige dialect of a community are often indices of the dialects of the disadvantaged. The following are the principal types of grammatical differences that may be found:

1. Absence of inflectional endings [*s, es, 's, s', en, ed, ing*] for noun plurals, noun genitives, third-singular present indicative, past tense, present participles, and past participles.
2. Analogical forms such as *hisself* or *theirselves* and the absolute genitives *ourn, yourn, hisn, hern,* and *theirn.*
3. Double comparatives and superlatives, such as *more prettier* and *most lovingest.*
4. Omission of the copula *be* [usually *is*, e.g., "He a cop"] with predicate nouns, predicate adjectives, and present and past participles.
5. *Be* as a finite verb ["He *be* fast" for "He runs fast"].
6. Differences in the principal parts of verbs, such as *growed, drawed, taken* as past tense, *rid* as the past participle of *ride*, and *clum* or *clim* as the past tense or past participle of *climb.*

These differences in grammatical features result in such expressions as the following:

He be absent yesterday.
She come to school every day.
He ax me can I go.
She had three sister.
Daisy is more taller than Eileen.
I drawed the picture.

It is important to recognize that a child using such expressions is not being careless. Careful listening will reveal that there is a system to the sentence construction as well as to the pronunciation and the vocabulary used. The child is using language that is familiar and that has worked well in meeting his or her communication needs.

In addition, no teacher should overlook the fact that his or her speech may not be fully understood by a child. Not only may the teacher use words unfamiliar to the child, but the pronunciations or the names given to objects or actions may be new as well.

Standard English

Parents and others in our society expect schools to teach "good English," meaning that they want children to learn the English that "important" people in the community use. This is the *standard English* referred to earlier that is so difficult to define. In fact, it simply cannot be defined in terms of specific words or pronunciations. However, it can be thought of as expression that is appropriate to the purpose of the speech or writing, that is consistent with the system of the language, and that is comfortable to both the expressor and the audience. It is language that is natural and uncramped by rule, reflecting custom that is widely accepted by society because it serves the needs of society. It is never static but changes with the communication needs and other changes in society.

This definition is based on criteria that the National Council of Teachers of English has long urged teachers to observe: acceptable usage (1) is determined by the living language of today; (2) recognizes dialect, geographical, and vocational variations; (3) is judged by its appropriateness for the purpose intended; (4) recognizes that there are situational levels of speech; and (5) takes into account the historical development of the language.

LEARNING ACTIVITIES

A. Answer these questions on your paper.

1. Where do you get water from?
   tap/faucet/spigot
2. What do you scramble eggs in?
   spider skillet/creeper/fry pan/frying pan
3. What do you eat for breakfast?
   flapjacks/griddle cakes/hotcakes/pancakes
4. What do you eat at a ball game?
   hot dog/frank/weiner/red hot
Do you know anyone who uses one of the other words?
What part of the country does he or she come from?

B. In each of the following sentences, the underlined word or expression comes from a particular regional dialect. Copy each sentence and rewrite it the way *you* would say it.

1. We ate the roast beef and mashed 'taters for dinner.
2. Carol caught angleworms before she went fishing.
3. She ordered a regular coffee.
4. The home team is going to larrup the Colts next week.
5. My pa stayed home from work today.
6. We ate sandwiches at nooning.
7. Tom and Jerry are in a heap of trouble.
8. We told that old dog to mosey along.

● 5

Children are interested in dialect differences.

TEACHING USAGE

Judgments about people are frequently made on the basis of the language they use. Fair or not, this is a fact. Thus, even though the way a child uses language at home and in his or her neighborhood may be useful for immediate communication needs, it may not serve lifetime needs, and the child may later feel cheated if the school has not attempted to teach a more widely acceptable dialect. It is important, then, to help each child to see the advantage of learning and using standard English, but it is equally important to do this without condemning his or her original dialect.

Procedures for teaching language usage are not as well defined by either research or established practice as we would like. However, the following sections suggest instructional principles and practices that appear to have the best foundation in research evidence and learning theory and to have received the greatest acceptance by teachers. These should help teachers who are frustrated by the failure of efforts they have made to bring about changes in the language children use. Many teachers do not modify their procedures in spite of being aware that what they have been doing is often fruitless—possibly because they do not know how these procedures might be changed. It is also possible that they do not really appreciate the fact that language habits are really that—habits—and habits are not easily changed.

To expect children to change their language habits because a teacher or a textbook says they should be changed is unrealistic. What is realistic is to recognize that the daily program in every classroom abounds with opportunities for children to use a more generally acceptable language for genuine communication purposes. What is also realistic is to realize that pupils learn to do what they do. If pupils are to speak and write a standard dialect, they must have practice in speaking and writing it. Rules and exercises are too far removed from genuine communication to have much value.

Analysis of Usage Problems

It is not possible to indicate the specific items of usage that you may need to teach, since the language backgrounds of children vary widely. The usage items suggested earlier in this chapter are a guide (as are those in language textbooks), but specific needs of children in a specific class must be determined by a survey of the oral and written usage of the children in that class. The example on page 64 shows how a survey form may be used to record usage items that need instructional attention. Listening to the children in the classroom and on the playground and observing their writing will provide the usage items. Note language patterns (grammatical structures) as well as individual words.

Another form that may be useful is the one shown on page 65, which focuses on items previously selected and provides a simple means for noting particular improvements by pupils.

	Usage survey for _____			
	verb forms	pronouns	redundancy	illiteracies
Michael	he growed			yourn
Amanda			John he	
Scott			this here	
Toni	be tall			yourn
Debra	axt			
Brian				
Jeffrey		it's		
Julie	has took			

Basic Instructional Procedures

The most vital factor in teaching acceptable usage is motivation. Therefore, every possible device must be utilized to relate the activities of the classroom to the basic goals of each pupil. Children must be made to feel that standard English is actually in widespread use (thus, as suggested earlier, the items taught must be realistic ones) and that learning it will benefit them personally. They must be shown that their communication is, at least in many situations, more effective when they use standard English.

Acceptance of children and the language they use is most important in teaching usage. Finding fault doesn't work; this is a fact that all adults recognize in their own experiences. And acceptance means more than simply recognizing that children can and should use their own dialect when it is appropriate—on the playground, for example. It means also accepting each child's cultural heritage—family, neighborhood, style of living, and so on. It means encouraging children to talk and write about their experiences and the things that are important to them.

Begin by surveying your class early in the year and at intervals throughout the following months. From these surveys choose only a few usage items for concentrated teaching effort. A few items will probably apply to

	Chris	Kelly	Jill	Todd	Kurt	Miguel	Danielle	Rosalita	Linda	Barbara
I goes	✔		✔	✔				✔		
brung	✔	✔		✔						✔
he don't				✔		✔	✔			
hisself	✔	✔								
me and _____			✔		✔		✔			
drawed	✔	✔				✔				
he be late	✔		✔	✔						
he a tall boy	✔									
rid for rode		✔								

the entire class, and these may receive total class instruction. Items needed by only a few may be worked on individually or in small groups. Only the most frequently used and grossest departures from acceptable usage should be selected for teaching—perhaps by comparing the children's speech with lists of divergent dialect features or misused words such as those presented earlier in this chapter. After these have been selected, identify them for the children, along with the reasons for their selection, without making any child feel inadequate because he or she employs a particular usage.

These items may be attacked in two ways. First, and most important, opportunities must be provided for the children to use the particular items being emphasized in natural communication. The focus should always be on the communication rather than on the usage, but teaching directed toward the particular items need not be minimized by this focus. Simply see to it that the children use the accepted forms of the items selected, and do so without fault-finding or placing undue stress upon them. Second, continue to work toward building interest in words and expressions—and in language generally. This is done principally through providing many experiences with language of many kinds. Read to children often from prose and poetry, imaginative and factual materials; call attention often to the pictures created by words, as well as to the emotional reactions they call forth. Particular attention should be given to variations in language used for different purposes—for example, a science lesson and a story containing conversation.

This kind of activity can be combined with discussions about dialect, colloquialisms, and differences in situational usages. Children might collect sentences heard on the playground and revise them into language appropriate for an assembly announcement and for a social studies report. Activities such as those suggested earlier in this chapter for teaching grammatical concepts can also be adapted for usage practice. For example, tagboard strips containing noun and verb phrases can be combined, with children saying sentences aloud as they are formed. Both seeing and hearing the accepted forms will help to provide reinforcement.

As much as possible, the children themselves should assume the responsibility for making changes. Encourage them to work independently, both individually and in groups, keeping their own lists of individual problems and charting progress they make in learning new forms. This will help to focus their attention on their own particular problems and provide motivation by concentrating on improvement.

In short, then, providing for much use of language (both oral and written) in meaningful situations, presenting many opportunities for children to see and hear language that is well used (through books, records, films and filmstrips, and your own language), and including frequent, *brief* drill on a limited number of items that have been selected for your particular pupils should result in some measure of success in teaching children to use language effectively.

References

Bryen, Diane Nelson. *Inquiries into Child Language.* Allyn and Bacon, 1982.

Cazden, Courtney B., ed. *Language in Early Childhood Education.* National Association for the Education of Young Children, 1972.

Johnson, Robert S. "A Comparison of English Teachers' Own Usage with Their Attitudes Toward Usage." Doctoral dissertation. Teachers College, Columbia University, 1968.

Lee, Doris M., and Rubin, Joseph B. *Children and Language.* Wadsworth Publishing Company, 1979.

Lindfors, Judith Wells. *Children's Language and Learning.* Prentice-Hall, 1980.

McDavid, Raven I., Jr. "The Sociology of Language," in *Linguistics in School Programs,* Albert H. Marckwardt, ed., pp. 96–97. The Sixty-Ninth Yearbook of the National Society for the Study of Education, Part II. University of Chicago Press, 1970.

Pooley, Robert C. *The Teaching of English Usage.* National Council of Teachers of English, 1974.

Reed, Carroll E. *Dialects of American English.* Rev. ed. University of Massachusetts Press, 1977.

Weaver, Constance. *Grammar for Teachers: Perspectives and Definitions.* National Council of Teachers of English, 1979.

Teaching Resources

FILMSTRIPS

Fundamentals of English. McGraw-Hill, 1964 (6 color strips).

Learning about Our Language Series. McGraw-Hill (4 sets of 6 each; primary).

Using Language Correctly. Eye Gate House (color; intermediate).

Words We Need. Filmstrip House (grades 2–4; 4 filmstrips, 4 LP records, 4 scripts).

RECORDINGS

Instructional Record for Changing Regional Speech Patterns. National Council of Teachers of English (by Ruth I. Golden; Folkways record).

Activities for Preservice Teachers

1. Research the literature concerning grammar teaching. What conclusions do you reach?

2. Lindfors (see References) suggests presenting this sentence to children of various ages: "The grok muffed the rupple bleet with his malfoon." She then suggests that such questions as these be asked: "What did the grok do? What did the grok muff? What kind of bleet was it?" The purpose is to see what relationships the children understand through word order and suffix signals. Try it, and report the answers you get.

3. Read "Sense and Nonsense about American Dialects" by Raven I. McDavid (*PMLA* LXXXI, no. 2, March 1966, pp. 7–17) and be prepared to report to the class on it.

4. Observe a particular class and make a record of usages that need to be worked on by most or all of the class, by small groups, and by individual children. Use resources suggested in this chapter to determine which usages should be attacked.

5. Plan a lesson that will bring about practice in one of the forms selected in question 4.

6. Compose a paragraph using only simple sentences (as suggested on p. 57) and plan the kinds of revisions a particular class might be asked to make.

7. Examine several elementary school language textbooks for their grammar content. Does the content seek to teach *about language* or *about grammar*? Is there enough content about *using language*? Which, if any, of the textbooks would you want to use?

8. Note and report differences in usage that you hear on TV and radio and among your associates. Which would you call examples of dialect differences and which nonstandard?

Activities for Inservice Teachers

1. Ask teachers in your school to define *standard English*. Compare these definitions with those you find in textbooks similar to this one.

2. Find out from secondary school English teachers in your district their views as to how much grammar should be taught by elementary school teachers. Evaluate these views in terms of the content of this chapter.

3. Listen to and watch television programs that demonstrate dialect differences. List these programs and assign pupils to watch and listen; then plan class discussion around the language differences noted.

4. Prepare a checklist similar to the one in this chapter. Evaluate your class, then contract with them to eliminate usage errors, one or two at a time.

5. Review the language teaching activities in this chapter and select several to use with your class. Keep a record of the use, including the planning.

6. Evaluate your own ability to identify parts of speech. Assess this knowledge in terms of the degree to which you use this knowledge in writing and speaking. React to this assessment and to the exercises and practice material commonly given to children.

Independent Activities for Children

1. Let a child make her own checklist of expressions she needs to work on in her writing. For example, she might list these in two columns:

Words I Use with Friends   *Words I Use in Writing*

I ain't gonna do it.   I am not going to do it.

Only a few expressions should be worked on at a time. When these have been mastered, the child can add others.

2. Prepare exercise materials that ask the child to change a given expression to standard English. Expressions that might be used in such an exercise include these:

    have ate
    he give
    have went
    he brang
    was broke
    them books

3. Write on cards sentences in which the child is to substitute phrases that he thinks of. For example, a sentence such as "He wanted to go to the store" might be used with directions to the child to substitute other phrases after the first *to* (e.g., "ride around the block," "play ball," "go to the circus").

4. Prepare a set of cards with a two-word sentence on each ("Boy walked." "Dog barked." "Snow fell."). Adding one or a few words at a time, the child is to expand each into a series of sentences. For example:

    Snow fell.
    Snow fell steadily.
    Snow fell steadily all day.
    Snow fell steadily all day long.

5. To help individual children with word order, make cards with simple instructions, such as the following:

Write a simple sentence. Then add an adverb to make your sentence more specific. Tell how, when, or where. For example:

    The horse jumped.
    The horse jumped *suddenly*.

Rewrite the sentence with the adverb in another position. Keep your adverb list for your free writing time.

6. Prepare cards or ditto sheets from which the child can select sentence exercises such as the following:

Put in missing words.

The _____ man _____ scolded the _____ boy.
There was a _____ storm _____ night.

Directions may include listing as many words that would "make sense" as possible for each blank.

7. Give the child tagboard strips containing noun and verb phrases. Have her see how many she can match so that they make meaningful sentences. An extension would be to provide coordinating conjunctions—*and, but,* etc.—and subordinating conjunctions—*if, because, when,* etc.—on other strips for forming compound and complex sentences.

8. Using a compartmented tray or box, place in separate compartments cards containing determiners, nouns, verbs and verb phrases, adjectives, adverbs, prepositional phrases, and conjunctions or clause markers. Use ink or marking pencil of a different color for each category. The child may experiment with word order and structure by making sentences from these. At the upper levels, gerunds and participles may be added.

4 | *Attention to Vocabulary Development*

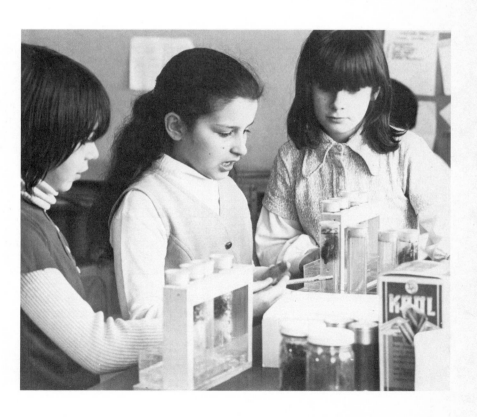

Do you know that an adult
dictionary may list a dozen
or more meanings for the
word *trace?*

There was no trace of their
  having been here.
There was a trace of sugar
  in the jar.
Can you trace the diagram?
Look closely as I trace our
  route on the map.
The bear left a trace in the
  dust.
The police will try to trace
  the missing child.

Ours is a world of words. Individuals who possess vocabularies of substantial breadth and depth can communicate their ideas, desires, and needs, and are aided in gaining understanding and appreciation of the language used by others. The knowledge each of us has of words and how to use them comes largely from simply living in this world of words—from all the activities that involve language, are described by language, or provide a reason for speaking, listening, reading, and writing. This is the basic means for developing vocabulary.

While experience and individual learning efforts are the means by which we as adults strengthen our vocabularies, direct teaching of vocabulary—plus the providing of many experiences—is needed if children are to develop their vocabularies to the point where they will be fully equipped to meet their life needs, both in school and out. Words important to a subject area, a unit of study, or any class activity need to be understood if children are truly going to learn the concepts, attitudes, and skills which are a part of that study or activity. And they must learn the skills and attitudes needed for gaining the meanings of new words or new meanings for known words that they meet in independent reading and listening.

BASIC CONSIDERATIONS

Most children entering the first grade understand several thousand words. Of course, they do not use all of these in their speaking, nor can they explain the meanings of many. But they have encountered such a large number of words so frequently in their preschool years that they "know" them with varying degrees of understanding. Certainly "knowing" a word does not necessarily mean that one is confident in using it (or even willing to try), nor does it mean understanding all of the multiple meanings possible for most words. Regardless of these limitations, however, children do understand and use a large number of words, and this means that an amazing foundation is present for further vocabulary development.

70

Kinds of Vocabulary

Every person has several vocabularies; we tend to use one group of words for speaking, another for writing, another for reading, and still another for listening. There is usually considerable overlap among these vocabularies, but all evidence indicates that they are not the same.

Our listening vocabularies are usually larger than those we have for reading, speaking, and writing. This is especially true for young children, since they have not learned to read or write, or are just learning to do so. Children's speaking vocabularies are generally their second largest, but this is often not true for adults because adults are able to read, to write, and to spell the words they need in their writing.

In the early stages of learning to read, gaining an adequate vocabulary for reading tasks is difficult for some children. This is not because most children do not know many of the words in the reading materials; it is because they have the task of determining what they are in graphic or printed form. As reading abilities approach or reach considerable maturity, reading vocabularies become very large, and the average person understands many words he or she is unlikely to use in either speaking or writing.

Speaking vocabularies are somewhat more informal than those needed for reading or writing. However, every person has several speaking vocabularies: one for home and among friends, one for working hours (including, perhaps, professional or other specialized terms of one kind or another), and one used in formal social situations—among strangers, at meetings, and so on. People who are effective communicators have learned to use the vocabulary appropriate for the various occasions. These vocabulary differences and the importance of using appropriate vocabulary should be recognized by everyone (especially teachers), since the traditional tendency has been to teach formal language and to attempt to insist on its use. This point was discussed in earlier chapters and will be reemphasized in those that follow because of its major importance.

Preschool Vocabulary Development

As we have stated, children's levels of language development are determined both by their experiences and by their innate intellectual abilities. The words children have learned prior to coming to school are those that they have needed in the environments in which they have lived. How they pronounce these words and how they put them together in utterances reflect these environments. By the time you meet these children they will have learned a great deal of language; their vocabularies will be of considerable size. Naturally the sizes of the vocabularies will vary from child to child, and this fact must be recognized and planned for. It is also important that as much as possible is known about each child's knowledge of words as you plan your vocabulary teaching.

The meanings preschool children give to words that they "know" are particularly significant to teachers. Anyone who has associated with chil-

See the study by Dale and O'Rourke of when children know some meanings.

dren of age five or under knows that these children do not use some words to mean the same things that adults do. This does not mean, of course, that the words even very young children use are without meaning to them. In fact, the meanings they have for words are not only consistent but also systematically related to their adult meanings. A teacher does have the responsibility, though, for helping children learn the adult meanings.

In addition to attaching somewhat "skewed" meanings to some words, young children often do not know that most words have more than one meaning. Even in grades four and above some common meanings of frequently used words are not known by large numbers of children. Yet many words that children meet early in their school days (e.g., *bed*, *fire*, *hard*, *table*, etc.) may be used in ways unfamiliar to the children, especially as they are used in figures of speech.

From Dale's *Language Development*, p. 192.

While teaching young children new words and new meanings—or clarifying and extending the understandings that they have—must be a concern of teachers, Dale points out that "it is easy to be impressed by the magnitude of the differences in semantic sophistication between child and adult" and not properly respect the semantic abilities of young children. The key is to build upon the knowledge and abilities that the children have.

Of particular concern to teachers and to all of society is the education of children from underprivileged environments. Children who have not had the educational, social, and economic experiences of the middle class—to which school curriculums are so frequently tied—naturally will not have vocabularies comparable to those of children who have. Of course, there are many exceptions, but, for whatever reason, different environments usually result in somewhat different needs, including language needs. A child from an educational, social, and economic background that is different from the norm will have a vocabulary that is different from that norm. He or she will not necessarily be "poorly" languaged, nor will that language be either superior or inferior to any other; it will simply be different.

On the other hand, there are often conditions attached to poverty and restricted social and economic opportunities that affect a child's vocabulary development in ways other than those related simply to a different experiential background. These include such factors as self-image, expressional freedom, and the persons who most affect children's development. Numerous writers who have studied children whom society tends to label as disadvantaged have stated that these children often suffer from a negative self-image and limited opportunities for language exchange with adults due to the pressure on the adults they are associated with simply to accomplish the tasks required to provide basic life needs. There is an emphasis on the immediate: getting the meal, getting to sleep in order to be rested for the next day's work, caring for the food, shelter, and clothing problems of a family under crowded physical conditions, and so on. All these concerns tend to restrict a child's use of language. The child learns to do what he or she is told to do and to avoid situations that might interfere with the pressing tasks. The words learned are those that are needed, but there is a good deal of sameness to the tasks and hence a sameness to the words.

The child of poverty also has a restricted environment in the physical sense. There is no money for travel; the traveling that is done is usually connected with the adult's job and with getting groceries and other necessities. There may be no easy means of transportation to the country, the park, or even other neighborhoods within the city. Poor children's travel is often limited to going to school, to church, to neighborhood stores, and to the homes of friends. It is not unusual to find children in ghetto areas of cities who have never been more than a few blocks from their homes (and rural children who may never have been on a highway or to a city).

Children from economically deficient backgrounds are not nonverbal; they are nonverbal about things they don't know about. This is natural. All of us keep quiet in strange surroundings. The surroundings may be strange because we are in a foreign country, at a meeting of nuclear scientists, or observing a construction crew at work on a building. Certainly the advent of television has increased the knowledge of deprived children—and of other children as well. Doubtless it has also added to their store of words. But television alone cannot provide the exchange of ideas and the experience in using language that are needed to prepare the child for the school environment.

It is not only poor children, however, who suffer from a lack of verbal exchange with adults. Increasingly, schools are finding that children from comfortable homes in attractive neighborhoods lack vocabulary and concepts that many of us consider commonplace. One first grade teacher found that some children could not give any name to cocoa, or hot chocolate, although every child had tasted it. This phenomenon may be an outgrowth of today's social and economic milieu, in which parents may be divorced or separated or both parents may hold jobs and have many other interests outside the home. The "poor little rich girl" of yesteryear may be found at any social level in today's world. It becomes even more important, then, for the teacher to help each child to acquire the kinds of experiences, and to learn the concepts and words to describe them, that will make the evolving school environment—including its language—a familiar one, one in which the child can function successfully.

EXPERIENCES AND VOCABULARY GROWTH

See Chapter 13 for alphabet and concept books.

While the experiences children have had prior to their coming to school—experiences significantly responsible for the learning they have gained and the habits, attitudes, emotions, and interests that make up their personalities—the building of further background is important to all children. This background should be built as much as possible by experiences that place the children in direct contact with concrete objects and real-life situations and those that permit words to be associated specifically and meaningfully with objects and concepts. Opportunities for direct, firsthand experiences may be provided in many ways and in all areas of the school program.

Experiential Opportunities

A creative instructional program provides endless opportunities for vocabulary development. Each day is filled with experiences, and every experi-

Many types of experiences develop the vocabularies of young children.

ence holds the possibility of teaching at least one child a new word or a new meaning. There is no end to the activities that may be carried on in a classroom: cooking Indian food, constructing an aquarium, making adobe bricks, building a simple generator, etc. Each activity will lead to new words. For example, building a terrarium might lead to the Latin base word *terra;* to *charcoal, peat moss,* and *drainage;* and to the names of the plants placed in it. The real issue is in making these experiences worthwhile for as many children as possible and in as many ways as possible, including that of further developing the children's vocabularies.

**Vocabulary development
may occur from:**

1. Making a mural.
2. Planning and giving a
   puppet show.
3. Looking at and discussing pictures.
4. Drawing pictures of objects, people, and
   places.
5. Writing stories.
6. Planning for and mak-
   ing an exhibit.
7. Viewing films and television programs.
8. Talking with classroom
   visitors.

Put new words on charts,
and display charts
prominently.

Help children replace
"tired" words in their
vocabularies.

Manipulative activities that involve handling various materials, tools, and equipment bring children into direct contact with objects and ideas and provide opportunities to learn new words and concepts, to understand directions, to gain ideas of how things work, and to relate the objects to things read and talked about. Included in such activities are those which use blocks, art materials, science instruments and models, construction tools, and audiovisual equipment.

Social experiences within the classroom, such as the show and tell period, the daily news or current events period, small-group committee work, free conversation periods, and class discussions, provide opportunities for new words to arise, for their meanings to be learned, and for the words to be put to immediate use. Emphasize vocabulary in these experiences. For instance, if a boy tells about his dog barking in the night and awakening the household, you might promote a discussion about what the bark sounded like (was it a yip, a yelp, a growl, or what?), how he felt when he was aroused from sleep (drowsy, alert, curious, frightened?), or what others in the household did.

Direct observations of people, things, and processes through trips away from the classroom are particularly conducive to vocabulary development. These may be extended field trips to a museum, a farm, a factory, city hall, etc., or they may be excursions to places close by such as to see the nests in the shrubs at the back of the school ground or to the principal's office to learn what records are kept. Each trip requires planning, observation, and follow-up discussion. Many trips will require practice in observing, writing letters and making charts, and giving some preliminary attention to the vocabulary that will be encountered on the trip.

Any oral or written expression that occurs spontaneously in a classroom, as well as all expression that may be considered of an "assignment" nature, provides opportunity for vocabulary development. Encourage children to make a conscious effort to select words that express thoughts exactly. Children tend to overuse a small stock of verbs, adverbs, and adjectives, but they can be successfully led away from repeated use of such omnibus words. One teacher led children to discuss words that might be used instead of *said*. Her fourth grade class discovered 104 words that could be used. You can generate a great deal of interest in finding better choices in particular contexts for such words as *nice, real, pretty,* etc. Even a word like *ran* may not be as accurate as *scurried* or *dashed*. As is suggested later in this chapter, the emphasis should be on the image to be gained by the listener or reader. Help children to see that the choice of words affects the picture or image received, and thus communication hinges upon the vocabulary that is used.

Simply observing things brought into the classroom or seen from the window produces ideas and words. You and the children can bring in rock samples, tree leaves, insects, growing plants, seeds, etc. The classroom may have its rabbit, gerbil, hamster, duck, or whatever. Observing the growth of a plant from a seed may lead to learning the words *chlorophyll, carbon dioxide, stem, dissolve, blossom, respire,* and *ecology*. If attention is not directed to learning new words, however, a seed can be planted, the soil faithfully watered, and growth observed and measured, without any vocabulary development taking place.

Visualizing and Listening

Since there are always some limitations in the degree to which actual experiences can be depended on to develop children's vocabularies as much as is desirable, the use of visual and auditory materials and reading are the practical substitutes. Reading as a means for providing experiences in which new vocabulary is learned generally has been a part of school programs, as has the development of vocabulary as a way to improve reading abilities. However, in spite of the abundance of audiovisual equipment and the often first-rate materials (software) available to use with it, not enough recognition is given in school programs to the value of other-than-print media for giving breadth and depth to children's experiences and the consequential development of their vocabularies. Even the general awareness of the public that the television experiences of preschool children foster vocabulary development has not had the use impact on the school curriculum that might have been expected.

With older children, don't overlook words associated with their interests in sports, music, movies, television, and the news.

Through television, children have seen Mt. St. Helens erupt, the spaceship *Columbia* take off and land, Olympic events, animals in their natural habitats, and the devastation caused by hurricanes and floods. They have explored ocean floors, climbed mountains, seen native peoples in several corners of the world, and laughed at Fat Albert. But they have also seen human slaughtering almost at first hand, become absorbed by the unrealistic activities of "private eyes," and watched untold numbers of movies, many of which have much violence and "gutter" language. The TV watching that children do in their homes cannot be controlled by teachers, but teachers can be knowledgeable about the programs children watch, discuss these with them, help them to evaluate story lines and to make fantasy-reality distinctions, and suggest programs that would be good for them to watch. And, certainly, teachers can pursue and clarify understandings of concepts and meanings of words with the children. They can encourage children to use new words and new meanings in their writing, to look for them in their reading, and to listen for them at home and at school.

For a free schedule of quality programs, write to Television Information Office, 745 5th Avenue, New York, NY 10022.

Television can be used directly in the classroom, but this viewing needs to be planned for, including planning for vocabulary growth. But television is not the only means for the visual and auditory building of experiences. Films, filmstrips, phonograph and cassette recordings, photographs, and drawings and paintings can all substitute to some extent for field trips, interviewing resource people, and handling objects; and many of these materials provide experiences that go far beyond the direct experiences possible for a school to provide.

The Role of Reading

Reading has been and is the principal means that most of us have used in developing whatever breadth and depth of vocabulary we have. However, reading as a means for developing children's vocabularies is sometimes limited by their reading skills, by the interest they show in a particular reading activity, and by the availability of reading materials that provide the depth

Making analogies

Here is a word game you can play. Read each of the following cards and circle the number next to the answer.

Horse is to **cart** as
engine is to ___.

1. track 2. train 3. stop

Tame is to **wild** as
wrinkled is to ___.

4. old 5. smooth 6. rough

Color is to **purple** as
toy is to ___.

7. child 8. play 9. ball

Dainty is to **delicate** as
stout is to ___.

10. cherish 11. thin 12. fat

Annoyed is to **furious** as
interested is to ___.

1. fascinated 2. bored 3. sympathetic

Truckdriver is to **truck** as
pilot is to ___.

4. jet 5. racing 6. slow

Crayon is to **coloring** as
bicycle is to ___.

7. game 8. toy 9. riding

Painter is to **brush** as
writer is to ___.

10. type 11. pen 12. story

Warm is to **hot** as
happy is to ___.

1. angry 2. thrilled 3. sad

Big is to **little** as
tall is to ___.

4. short 5. huge 6. pretty

Plane is to **fly** as
ship is to ___.

7. craft 8. house 9. sail

Gravy is to **potato** as
butter is to ___.

10. slice 11. margarine 12. toast

Now add the numbers you circled in column 1. Did you get **32**? Good. You are a winner. Add the numbers you circled in column 2. Did you get **48**? Good. You win again.

65

A vocabulary-building experience.

From *Skills Book*, Level 12, of *The Laidlaw Reading Program*, Second Edition, Copyright © 1980 by Laidlaw Brothers. Used by permission of the publisher.

and breadth of vocabulary development desired. Also, much reading material is written with an expectation of vocabulary development—particularly with respect to knowledge of several meanings for words—that requires vocabulary teaching before the selection can be read. Therefore, a teacher

New Words

Do you know their
meanings?

Afro
cassette
fallout
flipside
hovercraft
minibus
paramedic
update

A Bulletin Board Idea

WHAT IS THE
DIFFERENCE
BETWEEN:

a cheetah, a bobcat,
and a lynx?
odor, fragrance, and
stench?
tall, high, and lofty?

must discuss these new words as well as use direct experiences, films, film-strips, models, dramatizations, and so on to supplement the discussion.

Even after aids have introduced new words, meanings, and concepts, reading needs guidance—no less for its vocabulary development aspects than for the learning of word recognition skills. It is particularly important to remember that the context in which a word appears often does not provide a satisfactory clue to its meaning. For example, in the sentence "The ship set sail for the tropics," there is no clue to the meaning of *tropics* if this word is unknown. Even if *sail* is known, there is nothing to show whether it was actually a sailing vessel that departed or some other kind of ship. And, of course, a child might have absolutely no difficulty "reading" this sentence. This sentence and the many similar ones a child encounters illustrate that what the context of any reading material reveals to a particular reader depends on that reader's previous experience and on the clarity of the relationship between an unknown word and the other words near it.

Teach the children to note and make use of clues to meaning that are provided by the context. Such clues include an example in the context that explains an unknown word, a restatement of an unknown word in a form that is in effect a definition, or the presence of a modifying phrase or clause that reveals meaning. The best way to teach children to use these clues is through selecting paragraphs and sentences that contain one or more of these types of context clues and using them for illustration and practice.

> *Example:* He was truly *vicious;* for instance, he never had a kind word for his children and he beat his dog cruelly for no reason at all.
>
> *Restatement:* She recited her story *monotonously;* her voice droned on and on without change in tone or rate of speaking.
>
> *Modifying:* People looked at him as if he were a *leper* whom everyone was afraid to approach for fear of catching the dreaded disease.

Provide practice in making inferences, that is, in reading between the lines. This practice is possible with much material used in reading lessons, including that in basal readers, if the questions asked require making inferences rather than simply giving factual answers. For example, this quotation might be useful for such practice:

> The house had a lonely look. Its paint was peeling, the front gate hung by one hinge, and a forlorn rosebush struggled for existence among the weeds.

Questions might include:

> What kind of people do you suppose lived in this house?
> Were they neat, orderly people?
> Did they like flowers?
> If the yard was not cared for and the rosebush was being choked out by weeds, what do you think *forlorn* might mean?

Teaching punctuation items that are particularly relevant to understanding the meanings of words can also be helpful. One example of such an item is the use of commas to set off words used in apposition:

> The *pachyderm,* a huge bull elephant, was an awesome sight.

Words set off by parentheses or dashes also frequently give clues to word meanings:

His *unkempt* appearance (he surely hadn't shaved for at least a week) startled us. He was protesting *vociferously*—I'm sure everyone in the building could hear him.

Basic to word study is the ability to use the dictionary effectively (see Chapter 13). Children should be encouraged to use the dictionary to verify their inferences about words, to find meanings of words for which no context clues are given, or to discover variant meanings.

Use of the thesaurus, too, should be introduced and encouraged as soon as children have the reading ability and facility in dictionary skills to use it effectively. It may be introduced when children are writing—possibly a group composition—or searching for synonyms or a "better word." Middle and upper grade children should turn to the thesaurus as readily as to the dictionary.

Giving special attention to particular categories of words can broaden the children's understandings and add to their skills in both the receptive and expressive language arts. For example:

- Words often used figuratively, such as *face, leg, arm, table* (e.g., *face of the cliff, tableland*).
- Relationship words, such as *over, under, among, between, across, first, second*.
- Judgment words, such as *great, heavy, long*.
- Indefinite words, such as *some, several, most, few*.
- Common idioms, such as *clear up, hold out, bring down, close out*.

In order to be ready for reading and other first grade activities, a child must understand relationship words, such as those listed above. The concepts associated with these words are important for every child to learn through direct experience. Children can find things that are *over* other things, *under* the table, *across* the street, and so on. They can discuss whether one jump rope is as long as another and whether one child is as heavy as another. They can also consider what is meant by the *arm* of the chair and the *face* of the clock. Children in the middle grades can have fun competing to see who can compose the greatest number of sentences using "body words" figuratively (*heart, throat, body, foot*, etc.). They can also make charts of words that belong in particular categories. These can be used in the children's writing and can be searched for in reading materials. The most successful procedure, however, is to teach the meanings of these words as they are encountered in reading and other activities in the classroom.

OTHER TEACHING/LEARNING ACTIVITIES

New words and their meanings can be brought to the attention of children through many activities which have appeal for them and which are inherently interesting or can be made so. Much can be done somewhat indirectly (as has been suggested) if you are alert to the possibilities. More teaching

---

In Other Words, A Beginning Thesaurus (grades 3 and 4) and
In Other Words, A Junior Thesaurus (grades 5 and up) are available from Scott, Foresman and Co.

How many meanings can you think of for these words?

ball	pass
bank	turn
iron	string
head	sweep

A Bulletin Board Idea

SOUND WORDS

buzz	hum
bang	ping
crunch	zing
chirp	tick
clatter	smack

should be done directly, however. Some activities that can be used in a direct way and the kinds of experiences related to them are given in the following pages. These are only suggestions; they should be modified and added to according to the needs of a particular class.

Word Activities

A major kind of vocabulary-building activity involves giving special attention to words. This activity is not a vocabulary exercise in the ordinary sense that we all remember, nor does it call for procedures related to teaching the meanings of words directly. The idea is to make the activities focus upon the appeal of words and the many interesting facts that can be learned about them. One such activity is to list on the board or on charts new words found in daily classroom activities. These may be words from social studies, science, or other subject areas; words used by the children in the classroom or on the playground; or words they heard on TV, saw on a sign on the way to school, or heard used by a visitor to the classroom. Little learning will result, of course, unless these lists appeal to children. For example, lists might include places that have retained Indian names, science terms derived from people's names, slang expressions and their origins, or foreign words that have been assimilated into our language.

Charts may be made of words in particular categories, such as "quiet" words, "sad" words, or Christmas words; these can be related to many activities. Charts may also be made of words to use instead of commonly overworked ones (*real, nice, pretty*, etc.) and of words for special occasions or special interests, such as football, camping trips, or art class. Charts of synonyms and antonyms can also help in building vocabulary. One class found thirty words that were better in various contexts than *mad* to describe the incidence of *anger*. Finding synonyms and antonyms for such words is also an activity that could be on a task card in the language arts center of your classroom. Chart making can be an activity for the entire class, for individual pupils, or for small groups, and the charts can be made in final form or planned so that they may be added to.

Children are interested in figures of speech, and good writers and speakers use these to get their ideas across. Figures of speech include personification, simile, metaphor, hyperbole, and euphemism. Children may be interested in collecting and categorizing these, keeping charts of good ones to use, finding their meanings, or deciding which are clichés to be avoided.

Personification is the giving of human or personal qualities to anything that is not human: in terms familiar to most children, the speaking in "Bugs Bunny" TV cartoons or "Little Toot." A simile makes a direct comparison: "as slow as molasses in winter" or "He fought like a tiger." A metaphor also compares, but it is not introduced by *like* or *as:* "He became purple with rage" or "She has a finger in every pie." Hyperbole is an exaggeration for effect, a figure of speech in which the truth is stretched: "I was scared to death" and "He can throw the ball a mile."

The above figures of speech are based on similarity; euphemism is based on contrast. We use euphemism to express an unpleasant fact indirectly.

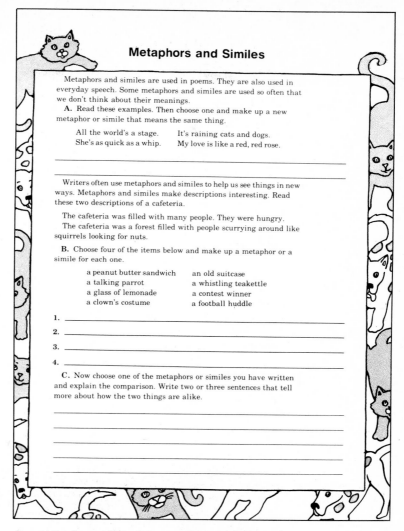

Metaphors and Similes

Metaphors and similes are used in poems. They are also used in everyday speech. Some metaphors and similes are used so often that we don't think about their meanings.

A. Read these examples. Then choose one and make up a new metaphor or simile that means the same thing.

All the world's a stage.   It's raining cats and dogs.
She's as quick as a whip.   My love is like a red, red rose.

_____

Writers often use metaphors and similes to help us see things in new ways. Metaphors and similes make descriptions interesting. Read these two descriptions of a cafeteria.

The cafeteria was filled with many people. They were hungry.

The cafeteria was a forest filled with people scurrying around like squirrels looking for nuts.

B. Choose four of the items below and make up a metaphor or a simile for each one.

a peanut butter sandwich   an old suitcase
a talking parrot   a whistling teakettle
a glass of lemonade   a contest winner
a clown's costume   a football huddle

1. _____

2. _____

3. _____

4. _____

C. Now choose one of the metaphors or similes you have written and explain the comparison. Write two or three sentences that tell more about how the two things are alike.

_____
_____
_____
_____
_____
_____

An activity for teaching about metaphors and similes.

For instance, in referring to someone who has died we say "passed away" or perhaps "gone to the happy hunting ground." We also *perspire* instead of *sweat, withdraw* instead of *retreat,* or have a tooth *extracted* instead of *pulled.*

Children can be encouraged to keep individual lists of words they have learned and want to use. For this to succeed, the children must really be interested in the words; an assignment of so many words a day becomes drudgery. This means that each child keeps his or her own list and that you help each one find words which appeal, that you show interest in their words and make learning new words an important part of classroom activities. Some provision should be made for having a child tell about these words—perhaps in spare moments throughout the day different children can tell about words they have added to their lists.

Campaigning for the adoption of new words is fun, but it should con-

---

Lesson 4   **Where Words Come From**

Just as English and other languages have histories, each individual English word has its own history, too.

Thinking It Through

Most English words come down to us from the distant past. Many were borrowed from other languages. Often the pronunciation and spelling have changed over the years, and sometimes so has the meaning. Usually, if you see the old and new forms together, you can see similarities.

Tracking down the histories of words is called **etymology.** This term also means the history of a particular word.

Look at the dictionary etymology for *umbrella*.

etymology ——— **um brel la** (um brel´ə), a light, folding frame covered with cloth or plastic, used as a protection against rain or sun. *n.*, *pl.* **um brel las.** [*Umbrella* comes from Italian *ombrella*, and can be traced back to Latin *umbra*, meaning "shade, shadow."]—**um brel´la like**´, *adj.*

● From what language was the word *umbrella* borrowed?
● What was its form in Italian?
● What did the original Latin word mean?

Although most English words either come from Old English or are borrowed from other languages, there are other sources for words. Some words, such as *pasteurize* and *china*, come from the names of people and places. Other words, such as *zoom*, *whiz*, and *chug*, imitate the sounds of things and actions.

Working It Through

A. Use each imitative word below in a descriptive sentence about a thing or action that the sound of the word imitates.

1. boom	**4.** crunch	**7.** gurgle	**10.** slurp
2. buzz	**5.** flip	**8.** hiccup	**11.** squeak
3. cluck	**6.** gulp	**9.** jump	**12.** strum

216

Word sources add interest to vocabulary study.

tinue for only a few weeks or interest will lag. Such a campaign may take the form of introducing one or more new words daily by showing pictures and drawings that give the meanings; by putting questions on the bulletin board asking "How is it pronounced?" "Can you find it in the dictionary?" "Have you heard anyone use it?" or "Can you use it in two sentences?"; and by providing situations in which the new word can be used. Or possibly each day a different pupil might select a word and present it to the class. Some teachers like to supervise this selection; others prefer to let children exercise their ingenuity in finding words, even though some turn out to be less than useful.

There is also value in teaching words and word elements directly, including the meanings of important root words, prefixes, and suffixes. The teaching may develop the meaning of a root (for example, *port*) with as many prefixes and suffixes added as possible (*report, import, deport, portage, portable, porter, reporter, export,* etc). Learning the meanings of commonly used suffixes and prefixes—along with the various forms some of them can take (*in-*, for example)—can help children to unlock the meanings of many new words they meet. Give them active practice in looking for familiar elements in words, such as prefixes, suffixes, Latin or Greek roots, and English base words. For instance, the child who knows the word *limit*, the suffix *-able*, and the *il-* variation of *in-* should have no difficulty in arriving at a reasonable definition of *illimitable*. Other direct teaching might include listing words and phrases that prompt images (e.g., "shimmering snow," "rolling waves," "shattering blast," etc.), discussing the meanings, and suggesting other phrases that create images. Children may also be encouraged to notice and discuss alliteration and rhyme in slogans. Similarly, many opportunities can be capitalized upon for noting words whose meanings have shifted or for which new meanings have been added. Consider the "space" words: *junk, clean, stage, capsule, pad, bird.* Other categories for word study include manufactured words (*rayon, dacron*), words with multiple meanings (*pitch, fall, lean*), and "loaded" and emotional words (*time-tested machine, loved ones*).

Learning and reinforcing the learning of new words through expressional activities that do not use language has great appeal. Children can make cartoons or drawings to illustrate word meanings and accurate word choices; they can dramatize meanings of words in specific contexts; and they can even play charades, using new words they have learned.

Vocabulary Exercises

Although the major emphasis in vocabulary building should be upon teaching new words in natural and meaningful situations, exercises that focus upon specific words can also be valuable. These exercises use paper and pencil and require filling in blanks, writing a numeral or letter to indicate the answer, or circling or underlining a word or a number. Such exercises smack heavily of "busywork" and are too often used in such a way that little genuine learning occurs. However, the shortcomings of such exercises can be overcome if they are selected with care and not overused.

Many vocabulary books, workbooks that accompany reading textbooks,

Roots and Words

color	circle
colorful	circus
discolor	circular
colorless	circumference
Colorado	encircle
move	telephone
remove	microphone
movable	saxophone
movement	phonics
moving	symphony

What do they mean?

shoulder the burden
put your back into it
cog in the wheel
get things rolling
none of your lip
elbow grease
put the finger on him

and dictionary and spelling workbooks offer vocabulary exercises. The following exercises, typical of those found in such sources, may be used to reinforce learning of particular words. Exercises modeled on the ones below can also be constructed by the teacher to suit the needs of a particular group.

1. Write the word for the young of each animal family.

bear	cub _____	horse	_____
dog	_____	lion	_____
duck	_____	sheep	_____
cow	_____	goat	_____

2. Circle the definition of *huff*.

hurry   fit of anger
excitement   anxiety
moment's time

3. See how many different meanings you can find for each word. Write a sentence to show each meaning.

pool   running
rock   picking
blank   cutting
strike   feeling

Here are some examples:

Blane's favorite game is *pool*.
The swimming *pool* is my favorite spot in summer.
Connie drives in a car *pool*.

Children can make their own thesaurus. Have them find words that describe a particular smell, taste, kind of weather, noise, texture, emotion, etc., and then list synonyms for each of their words.

4. Write each word in column 1 next to its antonym in column 2.

1	*2*	
present	broad	_____
victory	civilized	_____
smooth	retreat	_____
dull	absent	_____
advance	tight	_____
barbaric	bright	_____
narrow	defeat	_____
loose	rough	_____

5. Write a synonym for each of these words.

swift	_____	journey	_____
error	_____	wane	_____
mend	_____	depart	_____
rich	_____	huge	_____
visitor	_____	dress	_____

6. For each word choose the prefix that will make its meaning become the opposite of what it is without the prefix. Write the words you make, and use each in a sentence.

   im-   dis-   il-   un-   in-

clean	_____	legal	_____
like	_____	definite	_____
cover	_____	honest	_____
mature	_____	possible	_____

7. Choose the suffix that will make each sentence read correctly. Be sure to make necessary spelling changes.

   -ness   -ment   -less   -ed

   Happy___ is spending holidays together.

   We are waiting for the announce___ to tell us when the plane will leave.

   It seems hope___ that our team will go to the Super Bowl.

   We are please___ to see you ski so well.

   You must be kind or you will be friend___ .

For fun with words, see:

If You Talked to a Boar by Michael Sage (Lippincott)
Nailheads and Potato Eyes by Janet McCaffery (Morrow)
Pick-A-Riddle by Ennis Rees (Scholastic)
Word Twins by Mary White (Abingdon)

8. See how many palindromes (words or sentences spelled the same way backward as forward) you can find. Here's a start: *madam, repaper, level.*

9. What do the prefixes mean in these words?

Word	*Prefix meaning*
antifreeze	_____
reaction	_____
prepay	_____
subtotal	_____
disagree	_____

10. Add words to the ones below to make compound words.

    snow_____   base_____   sun_____
    class_____   arm_____   mail_____

11. Find the correct words for these sentences.

    A desk has a _____ but cannot spin it.   (top)

    A chair has an _____ but cannot raise it.   (arm)

    A rug has a _____ but gets no rest.   (nap)

    A clock has a _____ but cannot smile.   (face)

12. How many words can you write to rhyme with the words below?

    | meat | flame | book | slow |
    | _____ | _____ | _____ | _____ |
    | _____ | _____ | _____ | _____ |
    | _____ | _____ | _____ | _____ |

Pick out words from what children are studying in social studies, science, etc., and what they talk and write about when you make exercises like these.

13. Write homonyms for these words.

haul _____   role _____

our _____   wait _____

tale _____   sent _____

road _____   hole _____

14. Underline the word that does not belong in each group.

good	slow	real
decent	idle	false
corrupt	lazy	proven
honest	active	true

Make sure the exercises are challenging for the children.

15. Write the meaning of each expression.

The idea overwhelms me.
She was the understudy to the actress.
The disease is incurable.

16. Draw a line from each word in column 1 to the word in column 2 that makes you think of the word in column 1.

1	2
narrow	thin
marrow	bone
tired	attempted
tried	weary
angle	corner
angel	wings
trial	path
trail	test

Games

Word games can be fun, and they can be used to provide variety in vocabulary-building activities. They can involve all the children, small groups, or, in many cases, individuals. Games are not an adequate substitute for direct attention to broadening vocabularies or providing the depth of understanding needed to use words comfortably, but they can be a useful part of the total program. Below are some to try; many will give you ideas for variations.

Also see *The Arrow Book of Word Games* by Murray Rockowitz (Scholastic).

GUESS THE RHYMING WORDS. Make up sentences and have children supply the missing words to complete the rhymes. For example, "My brother *Bill* sits on the window _____" and "We looked into the *hall* when we heard a loud _____." Discuss the meanings of words the children give, particularly those with more than one more meaning, and help them to find as many words as possible that rhyme and also make sense.

WHAT'S THE ANSWER? Ask children riddles, such as "What has four legs, one head, and one foot?" (bed) or "What has a heel but only one toe?"

(shoe). This game can be extended into an interesting investigation of the use of figurative language, with the children finding examples of words used figuratively.

HINKY-PINKY. The object of Hinky-Pinky is to find a pair of rhyming words where the first describes the second: *motion–ocean, tasty–pastry, cook–book, fleeting–greeting.*

ADD-A-LETTER. Have one child start with a letter. Each has to add one letter, in each case making a word. For example:

a	i
an	in
ran	tin
bran	thin
brand	think
brandy	

LITTLE WORDS. Put a long word on the board—often it can be a word associated with a special event, such as Christmas, Halloween, vacation, or graduation. Challenge the children to find as many "little" words in it as they can. Vary the rules from time to time; for example, the rules can specify whether the letters of words must be in the order found in the long word or whether they must simply be included in it.

WORD JUMP. Start with a word and have a pupil think of a new word that begins with the last letter of the first word—for example, *book, kite, elephant, table, egg, gym, money, yardstick,* etc. Continue until you get to a stickler. Generally it is best to make all words nouns, but this can vary. Rules regarding use of the dictionary can vary but should be established before the game starts.

JUST THE OPPOSITE. Have one child use a word in a sentence. For example:

young: He is a young man.

A second child should reply with something like

He certainly isn't very *old.*

The second child then chooses another word and uses it in a sentence, a third child responds with an antonym, and so on. Children must drop out of the game if they fail to give a sentence or choose a correct antonym. Dictionaries should be available for checking the antonyms. (This game can also be played with teams.)

PAIRS. Divide the class into teams, and assign each team a pair of letters. The objective is to make a list of words that contain these letters as a pair. For example, one team might be assigned the diphthong *oy* and the other *oi*. One team might list *employ, alloy, coy, decoy, envoy,* etc., and the other team might list *soil, boil, coin, poison, voice,* etc. Pupils may use their dic-

A **pun** is the amusing use of a word that can have different meanings. Read what each person below is saying and underline the word that is used in an amusing way.

81

Puns are fun.

From *Skills Book*, Level 12, of *The Laidlaw Reading Program*, Second Edition, Copyright © 1980 by Laidlaw Brothers. Used by permission of the publisher.

tionaries, and the team with the longest list wins. Discuss the meanings of words listed.

GIVE A SYNONYM. The class is again divided into teams. A member of one team gives a word and a member of the other team must give a synonym. For example, *ran–dashed*. Have the teams take turns giving the first word.

A FINAL WORD

Like any other portion of the curriculum, vocabulary can be dull and stereotyped when it is presented for a certain number of minutes each day in isolation from any other part of the curriculum. It is doubtful whether much learning takes place in such a setting; certainly little excitement about words will be generated. Many of the activities suggested in the preceding pages might be used in such a program, as might any activity that seeks to build a skill or present a concept. The secret lies in planning and organization.

It is important to reiterate here what we have said or will say about every area of the language arts curriculum. *Effective instruction must have objectives and it must have a plan for accomplishing these objectives.* If these objectives and these plans are meshed, motivation for learning needed skills will probably result. For example, if learning prefixes is one of the vocabulary skills your class needs, plan to coordinate this with a reading lesson in which a number of new words contain prefixes, a spelling lesson that includes words with prefixes, or a social studies unit in which this learning is meaningful.

In short, this is what we mean when we speak of an *integrated* curriculum: needed skills are combined with the acquisition of concepts or knowledge to create a meaningful experience.

References

Dale, Edgar. *The Word Game: Improving Communications.* The Phi Delta Kappa Educational Foundation, 1975.

―――――, and O'Rourke, Joseph. *Techniques of Teaching Vocabulary.* Field Educational Publishers, 1971.

Dale, Philip S. *Language Development, Structure and Function.* 2nd ed. Holt, Rinehart and Winston, 1976.

Deighton, Lee C. *Vocabulary Development in the Classroom.* Teachers College Press, 1959.

Hennings, Dorothy Grant. *Words, Sounds, & Thoughts.* Citation Press/Scholastic, 1977.

Norton, Donna E. *Language Arts Activities for Children.* Charles E. Merrill, 1980.

Tiedt, Sidney W., and Tiedt, Iris M. *Language Arts Activities for the Classroom.* Allyn and Bacon, 1978.

Teaching Resources

SOME CHILDREN'S BOOKS FOR BUILDING VOCABULARY

Adelson, Leone. *Dandelions Don't Bite: The Story of Words.* Pantheon Books, 1972.

Asimov, Isaac. *Words from the Myths.* Houghton Mifflin, 1961.

Churchill, E. Richard, compiler. *The Six-Million-Dollar Cucumber.* Watts, 1976.

Cohen, Peter Z. *Authorized Autumn Charts of the Upper Red Canoe Country.* Atheneum, 1972.

de Angeli, Marguerite. *The Door in the Wall.* Scholastic, 1972.

Dickson, Paul. *Words: A Connoisseur's Collection of Old and New, Weird and Wonderful, Useful and Outlandish Words.* Delacorte Press, 1982.

Espy, Willard R. *The Game of Words.* Grosset and Dunlap, 1972.

Gwynne, Fred. *The King Who Rained.* Dutton, 1970.

Hall, Donald. *Ox-Cart Man.* Viking, 1979.

Hefter, Richard. *Yes and No: A Book of Opposites.* Larousse, 1975.

Lindgren, Astrid. *Pippi in the South Seas.* Scholastic, 1959.

Mayer, Mercer. *Bubble Bubble.* Parents Magazine Press, 1973.

Nevins, Ann, and Nevins, Dan. *From the Horse's Mouth.* Prentice-Hall, 1977.

Nurnberg, Maxwell W. *Fun with Words.* Prentice-Hall, 1970.

Parish, Peggy. *Amelia Bedelia.* Scholastic, 1963.

Provensen, Alice, and Provensen, Martin. *A Peaceable Kingdom: A Shaker Abecedarious.* Viking, 1976.

Schwartz, Alvin. *Tomfoolery—Trickery and Foolery with Words.* Lippincott, 1973.

Tremain, Ruthven. *Fooling Around with Words.* Greenwillow, 1976.

FILMS

Fun with Words. Coronet Films (3 films; 11 min. each; primary).

Magic Words. BFA Educational Media (9 min., color and sound; primary).

COMPUTER SOFTWARE

Word Games. Lakeshore Curriculum Materials (for Apple II; grades 4 and 5).

FILMSTRIPS

Language—The Mirror of Man's Growth. Centron Educational Films (5 filmstrips with cassettes or records, teacher's guide; grades 5–8).

Word Study Series. McGraw-Hill Films (set of 6 strips; intermediate).

RECORDINGS

Building Word Power. Coronet (9 cassettes, response books, teacher's manual; intermediate and upper).

Imagination and Me. Good Apple (record and teacher's guide).

Vocabulary Building. 3M Co. (10 cassettes, workbooks; intermediate).

KITS

Everyday Vocabulary. EBSCO Curriculum Materials (12 cassettes, masters, lessons; grades 4–6).

Vocabulary Builder. Eye Gate Media (filmstrips, cassettes, masters; intermediate).

Vocabulary Builder Series. Curriculum Associates (cards, masters, guides; grades 3–9).

Vocabulary Games. Barnell Loft (20 game packs; grades 1–6).

Word Play. Random House (6 cassettes, worksheets, guide; intermediate).

Words Plus. Listening Library, Inc. (4 cassettes, filmstrips, guide, duplication masters; grades 4–6).

Wordworld. The Economy Co. (19 cassettes, booklets, posters, manual; intermediate).

WORKBOOKS

Basic Skills Vocabulary. ESP, Inc. (books for grades 1–6).

Words Are Important. Hammond, Inc. (grades 4–8).

Wordly Wise. Educators Publishing Service (series of 9 workbooks; grades 4–12).

Activities for Preservice Teachers

1. Develop lists of words that will interest children of the ages you plan to teach. For example, you might include words borrowed from the American Indians (*moose, squash, pecan*) or the French (*boulevard, chalet, envoy*); words that have become generalized (*kleenex, ghetto, coke*) or specialized (*maid, corn, city*); and words derived from mythology (*Achilles heel, cupid, Pandora's box*).

2. Investigate books about words and language written for children. Develop a file indicating where these can be obtained and how you would use each.

3. Investigate the use of computers in the elementary schools of your area. In particular, find out if computers are used for vocabulary building.

4. Plan a field trip for a grade level of your choice. List the new vocabulary the children should have the opportunity to learn.

5. Prepare a bulletin board designed to help build vocabulary. Have in mind a specific grade level and a particular lesson or unit of study with which this bulletin board would be used.

6. Make a list of words with multiple meanings and collect pictures to illustrate the various meanings—e.g., *park* the car; play in the *park*.

7. Obtain as many different texts as you can for the grade level you prefer (language, social studies, spelling, science, etc.). Prepare ten different vocabulary development worksheets for this level based on material from these texts and the suggestions in this chapter.

8. Read a chapter in an intermediate grade social studies or science book. Establish objectives for teaching the vocabulary in the chapter, and plan how you would go about accomplishing your objectives.

9. If you are able to, talk with several preschool children and show them various objects. What are some words they "know" whose meanings are somewhat at variance with the ones you might have for them?

Activities for Inservice Teachers

1. Using the media resources in your school, preview materials that might be appropriate for building vocabulary in connection with content areas. Add these to your media file, along with notations concerning vocabulary to be developed and methods for developing it. Be sure to include call numbers or other markings (color codes, etc.) to assist you in locating materials.

2. Use your content texts to plan specific vocabulary development lessons before the children read assignments. Introduce new words and concepts as you do in reading—using new words in a context that will assist readers in gaining meaning.

3. Have the children in your class report new words, figures of speech, localisms, and their meanings. Make lists of these on charts, discussing and adding to the lists periodically.

4. Prepare charts for vocabulary development similar to those illustrated in this chapter. As you plan and perhaps illustrate these charts, remember that they must be interesting, stimulating, and fun and that they must be a part of your total curriculum (not apart from it).

5. Work with the children in your class in developing charts of interesting words on different subjects. For example, a list of words dealing with the American Revolution, the human body, the history of mathematics, or regional dialects should make good charts.

6. Visit the instructional resources center in your school district. Look through catalogs for vocabulary development materials that are not presently available in your school but would be desirable and appropriate for the age and ability levels of the children you work with. Meet with your principal or immediate supervisor and explain why money should be allotted for these in the next budget.

7. From the Independent Activities for Children section in this chapter, select activities that would be suitable for enrichment or remediation for the children in your class. Adapt and expand these to fit individual needs.

8. Map reading calls for a specialized vocabulary. In connection with an appropriate social studies or science lesson, develop a plan for teaching the vocabulary needed to understand and use the various kinds of maps found in an atlas.

Independent Activities for Children

1. Make a vocabulary bulletin board featuring a large tree with many branches. (This could be a mobile, if space is limited.) Have children cut leaves, flowers, fruit, birds, nests, or even monkeys or other animals that could be found in a tree from colored construction paper; place these in an envelope or box nearby. When a child meets a new word in any curriculum area, he writes it on one of the cutouts and hangs it on the tree. During free time, children practice reading the words on the tree and using them in sentences.

As children master words, they can be replaced by others. Or, periodically, old words can be removed and each one awarded to the child who is first to use it correctly in a sentence.

2. Let each child keep a word file or dictionary of interesting new words that she meets. Have the child look up the correct pronunciation and meanings of each word she decides to "keep," and fix it in her memory by using it as many times as possible, both in speech and in writing.

3. Word exercises for children to do in their free time can be prepared on cards (3 × 5 cards, for example). The cards might contain one of the following:
a. A large word (*hippopotamus*) in which small words can be found (*hip, pop, pot*) or letters rearranged to make words (*must, top, pit, ship, post, shop*).
b. A word category (for example, sports) for which the pupil writes all the words he can think of (*goalie, quarterback, basket, glove, football, bat, net, foul, puck, dribble*).

4. Prepare lists of words for which a child can find homonyms. For example:

1	*2*	*3*
know	too	new
feat	sale	weight
our	peace	roll
hole	led	knight
grate	fair	do

5. Using a list of homonyms which have been identified, a child writes one sentence using each word, placing these on separate 3 × 5 cards. When enough cards have been accumulated, children can use them to play games similar to Old Maid or Rummy.

6. Children can also develop lists of homographs—words that are spelled alike but pronounced differently (*bow, live, read*). They can then write sentences demonstrating how the context determines the pronunciation:

Chip has a bow tie.
Please bow when you meet the king.

These can also be used in matching games.

7. For practice with synonyms, put sentences on cards, each containing an underlined word for which a child may find synonyms. Here are some sentences:

The thunder breaks the silence.
Rain pelted the window glass.
The snow fell steadily.

He ran across the road.
The engine started when he stepped on the starter.

8. Prepare a file of cards containing lists of words with multiple meanings. For example, on one card might be such words as *bank, store, shop, park,* and *box,* along with directions to the child to write sentences showing different meanings for each word.

9. Individual children can prepare lists of "food" words by categories. The categories might be cereals, meats, dairy products, vegetables, and fruits. Encourage children to be observant at home and in stores so that lists will be long.

10. Have a child make a list of words that have taken on new meanings in recent years. Start her with *capsule, pad, stage,* and *rock.*

11. Provide lists of "special" words whose origins a child can trace. For example:

From proper names—*braille, cologne, ampere*
From other languages—*veto, exit, vacuum, nest*
Recently coined—*helicopter, amplifier, laser, missile*
Names of states—*Connecticut, Wisconsin, Oregon*

12. Have a child make a list of words heard on TV during a particular week that he would like to add to his vocabulary. He can enlist the aid of parents in writing them down, or he can jot down the context in which the word was used and spell it phonetically, checking the dictionary later for correct spelling and meaning.

13. A child can use crayon, fabric, clay, or any other available material to make an object, then make a list of all the words she can think of to describe it. For example: *mud—squishy, dirty, oozing, fun.*

14. Have a child look in a full-length mirror and try to think of an adjective to describe each feature or part of his body. This can be followed by writing a self-description or drawing a self-portrait.

15. Put pictures on a bulletin board and have individual children look in magazines for words, phrases, and sentences to describe them. These can be cut out and placed around the pictures to make a word bulletin board.

16. Two children can play a game using antonyms. One child reads words (adjectives and adverbs) from a list she has made, or simply says words she thinks of. The other child must furnish an antonym for each. After the second child misses, he reads words, and the first child supplies antonyms.

17. Individual children can make lists of incomplete sentences to share with the class at a later time. Other children then try to think of words and/or phrases that fill the blanks and make interesting sentences.

I looked out the window and saw _____ .

Sitting on the front doorstep was _____ .

He _____ the cake _____ .

18. Have a child prepare a chart for the bulletin board of words that can be used instead of such "tired" words as *awful, pretty, big, nice, fun,* etc.

19. Place small pictures from magazines or ones that you draw on 3 × 5 cards. Print the name of what is pictured on each card. With enough of these cards children can make up their own games—for example: matching pairs of homonyms, homophones, antonyms, or synonyms. After you get them started, children can make or find pictures for cards to add to the set.

20. Have children talk about their hobbies or favorite sports using, and perhaps illustrating or explaining, the specialized vocabulary of the hobby or sport.

21. Decorating words to look like their meanings can help individual children think more creatively about language. For example:

22. At holiday time, a child might list all the words she can think of to describe the holiday and customs associated with it. These might be verbs, nouns, adjectives, and adverbs—or they could be limited to one of these categories.

23. When children in the upper grades study and discuss careers, they might make charts of words used by people in particular occupations. For example, a person selling automobile insurance might use such terms as *no-fault, assigned risk,* and *mass marketing.* The help of parents and other adults might be enlisted for this activity.

5

Beginning Language Arts Programs

As discussed in earlier chapters, the language development of children begins and progresses quite rapidly in the years before they enter first grade or kindergarten. Research of the past twenty years has shown us a great deal about this development: how it occurs and what its stages are, conditions that foster or retard it, and its relation to a child's cognitive growth and social maturation. This research has also shown or implied the importance of giving greater attention to this development than had been the case in organized preschool programs, kindergartens, and the primary years of elementary schools.

This chapter discusses preschool programs and the relationship between them and what is generally thought of as elementary school language arts, focusing on the role of early programs as a foundation for the attainment of the goals of effective language arts programs. We suggest activities and teaching/learning situations for early programs which will help to build competence in using language. It should be recognized, however, that the suggestions vary in their application to the several levels of preprimary programs, as they do for kindergarten or even the first grade or beyond, since differences in the development of children *must* be recognized and appropriately dealt with by teachers in all programs. The latter sections of the chapter discuss young children's writing and reading, their development in these areas, and issues concerning early development and teaching attention.

PREPRIMARY SCHOOLING

The education of young children has increasingly become an issue of national importance. While the research concerning the crucial role of a child's early years in the development of his or her potential in the school years or beyond has been a major factor in raising this issue, there have been other forces bringing it to prominence: the changing roles of women, economic conditions causing the need for two incomes in a family, the increase in one-parent family units, and curricular changes in school programs.

Why Preprimary Language Arts Programs?

The answer to this question is a twofold one. First, language ability is crucial in learning. Second, an astounding number of children are in preschool programs, and virtually all five-year-olds are in kindergartens. The 1978 census estimated that 1,824,000 children were in nursery school and 2,989,000 in kindergarten. Added to these numbers, again by this census estimate, there were more than one and a half million children in licensed day care or family day care services. Then there are those children who are in unlicensed centers or cared for by relatives or "block mothers." These numbers certainly reflect societal changes—working mothers—but they also indicate that there is a growing awareness of the need for young children to interact with peers and adults other than those in present-day family units.

Growth in language is fostered by experiences which require talking and listening—a responding, active verbal interaction. Growth is not fostered by passively watching a TV screen, by being told to go play alone, or by any situation that limits exploration and exchange. Furthermore, children's social development is affected by language development; hence it too hinges on the emotional and experiential setting. Finally, each child's mental development and conceptual framework are complexly interwoven with his or her language development.

A Book for Parents

Your Home Is Your Child's First School by Norma Rogers (International Reading Association)

Of course, the desired climate and experiences do not require a school setting. Many mothers (as well as fathers) do talk with—not just talk to—their young children and do provide a wide variety of experiences that children can respond to; but, as indicated above, in many instances it is increasingly difficult for them to do this. While working parents may provide a quality environment for young children *when they are with them,* this time may be quite limited. Also, the fact that families are smaller lessens the opportunities for interaction with siblings and other adults that existed in the extended families of an earlier time.

Language Development

The language development of a child is an active process, a process of exploring and experimenting concerning language structure and how language is used. The child of two has ordinarily made rapid growth in vocabulary and has begun to put two or three words together in statements, questions, and responses. By age two and a half he or she has mastered vowel and many consonant sounds, although often with some articulation difficulties (e.g., *birfday*), by three is using sentences of four or five words (e.g., *The dog is barking*), and by four or five has all of the basic, common sentence structures of English. This latter achievement may be illustrated as follows:

noun–verb	*Doggie run.*
noun–verb–noun	*Timmy ate breakfast.*
noun–verb–pronoun	*Billy gave me a cookie.*
noun–linking verb–noun	*Miss Smith is my teacher.*
noun–linking verb–adjective	*The doggie is big.*

Fortunately for the child, regardless of the richness or impoverishment of the language environment, language development does meet his or her communication needs in that environment at any preschool age level. It may not, however, be sufficient for the school setting at age five or six or be indicative of the child's language or cognitive potential. In addition, language development, in both structure and vocabulary, does not end at age five, but at that age is dependent upon what has developed before.

Characteristics of Good Programs

Good preprimary programs are essentially no different from effective programs in elementary schools, except for being less structured and task-oriented. All programs should view children as dynamic, whole individuals, with no aspect of their development receiving overwhelming attention or being excluded from the others. Preprimary programs, though, especially need to provide for activities involving trial and error, self-selection, verbal interaction, and manipulation. Particular attention needs to be given to getting children to talk; thus, programs should recognize that children talk about things important to them, things they care about (don't we all!).

Adults working with young children need to listen carefully and watch closely. They should avoid command, directive monologues (e.g., "Put the paint brush in the can" or "Now, let's all sit still"), remarks that call for no response (e.g., "I like what you're doing"), or an "interviewing" approach (e.g., "What is your name?" or "How many brothers and sisters do you have?"). Open-ended questions ("I wonder why that happened?") and informative comments work better since they evoke responses.

Teachers at any level of schooling ought to be language models—in fact, they always are—using language that is more precise and often more complex than that which the children are using.

BEGINNING PREPRIMARY AND PRIMARY ACTIVITIES

Activity is a key aspect of preprimary and primary language arts programs. Teachers in these programs need to ask and answer a number of questions about the activities they propose to provide. For example: Why should we have this activity? Is it appropriate for the children engaging in it? Why should it take place at the time planned? Why and how will it benefit the children? What materials are needed for it? Particularly important in the answers should be the extent to which language responses and thinking will occur because of the activity.

Materials and Expression

A tub of water makes a good beginning. There's no question that it is a sloppy thing to have in a classroom, but playing in water is fun and the children become so involved that they forget about themselves and their shyness and begin to chatter like chipmunks. There are any number of activities that can result from water play, all of which encourage language development. Discussing what will float, what won't, and why is one; others are washing toy dishes and doll clothes, talking about animals that live in water and those that don't, and "painting" the school sidewalk. (The children will talk about what they are doing and what happens to the water.) Adding bubbles and letting the children just play and talk about the bubbles can also be successful.

Sandboxes are also guaranteed to be messy, but they do help to promote the freedom of expression and thought so necessary for school success. Pretending to be a truck driver hauling sand or building roads and lakes creates an opportunity for a child to talk with others and leads to other conversations. Sand can even be colored with tempera paint to add interest to children's constructions.

Manipulation of objects helps children to know and understand them. For example, objects as simple as balls and building blocks of different sizes can lead to discussions of likenesses and differences, concepts such as small, large, round, square, etc., as well as vocabulary associated with these concepts. Blocks are also good for fostering creativity, as children pretend to be driving cars or trucks, cooking, or doing things they have seen or heard about their fathers and mothers doing.

A display of materials that children may handle will bring about new understanding of words, as well as awareness of everyday things in our world. Remember to encourage discussion of how things look, feel, and smell, as well as of likenesses, differences, and uses of materials. The display might consist of burlap, cotton, suede, velvet, wool, and nylon. The amounts needed are small and can be obtained easily and inexpensively from a fabric shop.

Things that can be smelled provide a way to bring about a good deal of talking. Children can be encouraged to describe the various smells and to talk about smells they have encountered, which smells they like or dislike and why. This may lead to a discussion of what smells tells us and the recognition that not all liquids that look like water are indeed water. In fact, using water, rubbing alcohol, and white vinegar is a good way to begin a discussion of the difference between looks and smells. Such a discussion can lead to further vocabulary development, of course, as well as inducing discussion and concept building.

Another simple way to start discussion is to ask every child in the room to bring in the top from a jar or bottle. Each child may show his or her top to the other children, who handle it and ask questions. For example, a discussion may begin with "Is this from a catsup bottle?" "What do you use catsup for?" "If I put mustard on my hamburger, why isn't the top of the catsup like the top of the mustard? They are used for the same purpose." "Could we put a catsup cap on mustard?" Such a discussion might lead to the discovery that differences may be very slight or not immediately obvious. For example, though the consistency of both *appears* much the same, catsup will pour, whereas mustard will not.

To expand this discussion you might bring in catsup, mustard, and a variety of relishes and onions. The children may taste these and discuss the differences in the way they taste, the ones they like, those they don't like, and why. This lesson is more enjoyable if hamburgers or hot dogs can be served, but that is not always easy to arrange.

Other activities might include planting a terrarium, blowing soap bubbles, preparing fruit for eating, making and wearing paper masks, looking at objects through a magnifying glass or a microscope, and examining by feel and then describing objects in a sack.

Concentrating on an idea.

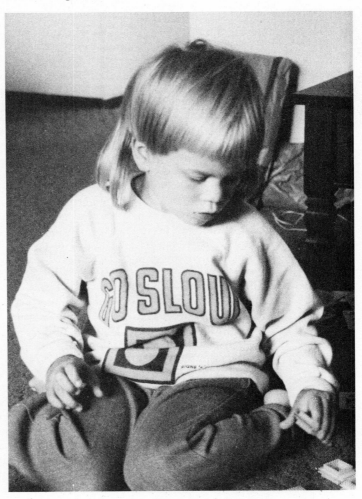

One of the most important factors to remember when developing language through sense awareness is to start with items that are fairly certain to be in the children's environment. Build on their knowledge and encourage them to talk about what they know. Encourage expansion of creative expression and thought through discussion of other ways to use the objects and materials.

Physical and Rhythmic Activities

Communication is not, of course, exclusively tied to language. Often a message—a thought, an idea, a feeling—comes from someone's eyes, a bodily stance, the way a head is held, or the extension of a chin. The bodily movements of young children are often expressive and are forerunners of the gestures and facial expressions of older children and adults that frequently accompany conversations, discussions, reports, and dramatics.

The physical activity of children often seems to be expressed in perpetual motion. A child sways, bends, skips, runs, prances, and jumps. He screws up his mouth; she wrinkles her nose and sticks out her tongue. These are natural movements, and they express feelings and reactions. These natural and expressive movements and gestures are communicative; many occur as children are talking. The fact that they are natural to children can and should be capitalized on in beginning language arts programs. Particularly important are rhythmic activities. Each child possesses an individual rhythm in speech, walk, and other movements, and these movements are expressive of a personality, background of experiences, and physical and mental maturation. But a little observation will show very real differences among the children in their coordination and their abilities to make fundamental movements. Make allowance for these differences instead of expecting the children to perform like a ballet group. In addition, take note of those children who appear to have particular difficulty with bodily control and coordination and plan additional ways to help them. Bodily control and coordination can be helped by play on balance beams, slides, and gym sets. Obstacle courses are good, too, because of the various movements and the coordination required to do them.

A fundamental way to get children to express themselves through body movement is to have them listen to music and react to it. Children enjoy improvising to music or to rhythm instruments by running, walking, galloping, trotting, hopping, jumping, bending, stretching, swaying, crawling, creeping, and so on. Much spontaneous music occurs with physical activity. Walking about the classroom, children often will sing softly to themselves or chant rhythmically. Running or skipping, jumping rope, and riding a seesaw are also activities that bring forth rhythmic chants by the children as they engage in them. While music may stimulate movement, children often feel the desire to move first, later asking for the music or accepting it and possibly adjusting the tempo of their movement to it. Early emphasis, then, should be upon spontaneity and individuality, with interpretation of music coming later.

Fundamental rhythmic activities include the following:

- Walking to a rhythm tapped by you.
- Clapping in unison.
- Walking and clapping to a beat.
- Walking to music.
- Walking and running to changing rhythmic tempos.
- Moving from walking to running with an increase in the beat of the rhythm.
- Skipping rope.
- Hopping to a musical rhythm.
- Combining a leap with other movements.
- Galloping, tiptoeing, swaying, etc., to rhythm.
- Creating a repetitive pattern of movement (e.g., walking, running, hopping—walking, running, hopping).

Finger Plays and Other Action Verses

Finger plays and other action verses call for bodily movements, coordination, and rhythm. They teach children new words and unison speaking, and they are fun to do. The fun is in the action and the repetition of familiar favorite verses. Demonstrate to the children using the entire verse; then, doing a line at a time, have one or two children join in.

The verses and the directions below are only suggestions. The children will have many of their own—perhaps nursery rhymes they know or verses they make up. They should be allowed to express their creativity in the verses they make up and in the variations they give to the words and actions.

LITTLE LEAVES

Little leaves fall gently down,	*(Raise hands and lower them,*
Red and yellow, orange and brown;	*fluttering fingers like*
Whirling, whirling round and round,	*falling leaves)*
Quietly without a sound;	*(Repeat above motions)*
Down—and down—and down—and down!	*(Lower bodies gradually to the floor)*

STRETCH, STRETCH

Stretch, stretch, way up high;	*(Reach arms upward)*
On your tiptoes, reach the sky.	*(Stand on tiptoe and reach)*
See the bluebirds flying high.	*(Wave hands)*
Now bend down and touch your toes;	*(Bend to touch toes)*
Now sway as the North Wind blows;	*(Move body back and forth)*
Waddle as the gander goes!	*(Walk in waddling motion back to seats)*

TEN LITTLE FINGER MEN

Ten little finger men,   *(Hold up ten fingers)*
Who will clap for me today?
"I will, I will," all my fingers say.   *(Clap hands on "I will")*
Ten little finger men,   *(Hold up ten fingers)*
Who will write for me today?
"I will, I will," all my fingers say.   *(Draw circles in the air)*

FIVE LITTLE RABBITS

Five little rabbits under a log;   *(Hold up fingers of one hand)*
This one said, "Sh! I hear a dog!"   *(Point to little finger)*
This one said, "I see a man!"   *(Point to ring finger)*
This one said, "Run while you can!"   *(Point to middle finger)*
This one said, "I'm not afraid!"   *(Point to index finger)*
This one said, "Let's hide in the   *(Point to thumb)*
   shade!"
A man and his dog went hurrying by,
And you should have seen these
   rabbits fly!

THIS LITTLE BOY

This little boy is just going to bed.
Down on the pillow he lays his head,   *(Palms together at side of face)*
Wraps himself up in his blankets   *(Hands folded across chest)*
   tight,
And this is the way he sleeps all
   night.
Morning comes. He opens his eyes.   *(Sit up tall)*
Back with a toss the cover flies.   *(Spread arms apart quickly)*
Soon he is up and dresses for play,
Ready for school and a bright new
   day.

HOUSES

Here is a nest for the robin;   *(Cup both hands)*
Here is a hive for the bee;   *(Fists together)*
Here is a hole for the   *(Finger and thumb make a
   bunny;   circle)*
And here is a house for   *(Fingertips together to make
   ME!   a roof)*

THREE LITTLE WITCHES

One little, two little, three little   *(Hold up fingers one by one)*
   witches
Ride through the sky on a   *(Clasp hands together in front as
   broom;   though grasping broomstick)*
One little, two little, three little   *(Repeat action in first line)*
   witches
Wink their eyes at the moon.   *(Wink one eye while making a
                                              circle with arms)*

THIS LITTLE CLOWN

This little clown is fat and gay;	*(Hold up thumb)*
This little clown does tricks all day;	*(Hold up index finger)*
This little clown is tall and strong;	*(Hold up middle finger)*
This little clown sings a funny song;	*(Hold up ring finger and wiggle it)*
This little clown is wee and small,	*(Hold up little finger)*
But he can do anything at all!	

RIDING THE MERRY-GO-ROUND

Ride with me on the merry-go-round,	
Around and around and around.	*(Move hand in circles)*
Up go the horses, up!	*(Raise arms in the air)*
Down go the horses, down!	*(Lower arms)*
You ride a horse that is white;	*(Point to neighbor)*
I ride a horse that is brown;	*(Point to self)*
Up and down on the merry-go-round,	*(Raise and lower arms; then move one hand in circles)*
Our horses go round and round.	

THE ANGEL ON MY CHRISTMAS TREE

Two small hands that touch in prayer,	*(Touch hands in prayer)*
A golden halo in her hair,	*(Make a circle above head with one hand)*
On her back, two silver wings;	*(One hand on each shoulder)*
Once each year my angel brings	
The Christmas story back to me,	
While she rests upon my Christmas tree.	*(Touch hands again in prayer)*

FIVE LITTLE GOBLINS

Five little goblins on Halloween night	
Made a very spooky sight.	
The first one danced on his tippy-tiptoes;	*(Hold up first finger)*
The second tumbled and bumped his nose;	*(Hold up second finger)*
The third one jumped high up in the air;	*(Hold up third finger)*
The fourth one walked like a fuzzy bear;	*(Hold up fourth finger)*
The fifth one sang a Halloween song.	*(Hold up thumb)*
Five goblins played the whole night long!	

THE WIND

The wind came out to play one day.	
He swept the clouds out of his way;	*(Make sweeping motion with arms)*

He blew the leaves and away they flew.	*(Make fluttering motion with fingers)*
The trees bent low and their branches did, too.	*(Lift arms and then lower them)*
The wind blew the great big ships at sea;	*(Make sweeping motions)*
The wind blew my kite away from me.	

MR. DUCK AND MR. TURKEY

Mr. Duck went out to walk	*(Hold up thumb)*
One day in pleasant weather.	
He met Mr. Turkey on the way,	*(Hold up other thumb)*
And there they walked together.	*(Move thumbs together)*
"Gobble, gobble, gobble,"	*(Move one thumb back and forth)*
"Quack, quack, quack."	*(Move other thumb back and forth)*
"Good-by, good-by."	*(Nod both thumbs)*
And they both walked back.	*(Move thumbs apart)*

COUNTING ACTION RHYME

One, two; sit up. Please do.	*(Children sit tall)*
Three, four; feet flat on the floor.	*(Feet on floor)*
Five, six; stir and mix.	*(Motion of stirring)*
Seven, eight; close the gate.	*(Clap)*
Nine, ten; make a pen for a hen.	*(Interlace fingers)*

READY TO LISTEN

Let your hands go clap, clap, clap.	*(Clap hands three times)*
Let your fingers snap, snap, snap.	*(Snap fingers three times)*
Let your lips go very round,	*(Make lips round)*
But do not make a single sound.	
Fold your hands and close each eye;	*(Follow action indicated)*
Take a breath . . . and softly sigh.	
Ah_____!!	*(Follow action indicated)*

STAND UP TALL

Stand up tall,	*(Stand)*
Hands in the air.	*(Raise hands)*
Now sit down	
In your chair.	*(Sit)*
Clap your hands.	*(Clap three times as words are said)*
Make a frown.	*(Knit brows)*
Smile and smile,	*(Smile)*
And flop like a clown!	*(Relax with arms dangling)*

A READINESS GAME

Make one eye go wink, wink, wink;
Make two eyes go blink, blink, blink.   *(Suit actions to words)*
Make two fingers stand just so;
Then ten fingers in a row.
Front and back your head will rock;
Then your fists will knock, knock,
   knock.
Stretch and make a yawn so wide;
Drop your arms down to your sides.
Close your eyes and help me say
Our very quiet sound today.

Talking about Things

Many preprimary and primary teachers start the day's activities with "Talking Time" or "Sharing," though perhaps they have not labeled the time. The point is that children often come to the classroom bursting to tell something. This is a particular time for a teacher to *listen*, encourage, and respond. It is also a time (as appropriate to the level of the children's maturity) for guiding them in amenities in conversation and discussion: taking turns, listening to others, telling events in sequence, articulating and pronouncing clearly, and using good sentences.

Talking in a class-sized group may be frightening to young children, even some in first grade. It often is best to talk with only three or four children and later provide for groups of four or five to talk together. Much "sharing" may occur in such groups, particularly by children who are shy or less verbal.

In the primary grades, the morning "Talking Time" sometimes takes the form of a newspaper for which the children report items, with the teacher writing them on the board or on a chart. Some decisions usually need to be made about what are suitable items for the newspaper or even for the more informal "Talking Time." Things that everyone knows need not be reported, nor should items that have limited interest. The children can help decide these matters.

Teachers sometimes put the newspaper on a sheet of newsprint twenty-four by thirty-six inches in size. The upper half may be left for a picture, and children can take turns illustrating the "news." Special events such as birthdays may mean a departure from "turns," with the one who has the birthday drawing a picture of his cake or a present she received.

At this level, the newspaper provides an opportunity to teach the names of days and months, their abbreviations, punctuation of dates, and capitalization skills. However, the emphasis should be on the content and on making the experience bring forth oral expression from the children.

The familiar "Show and Tell" is also an activity that children soon learn to like and that promotes talking. "Show and Tell" has an advantage over "Sharing" because showing an object—a new sweater, colorful leaves, a

Children can "Show and Tell" about:

a colorful rock
seashells
a bird's nest
a photograph
a self-drawn picture
foreign stamps
toys
books

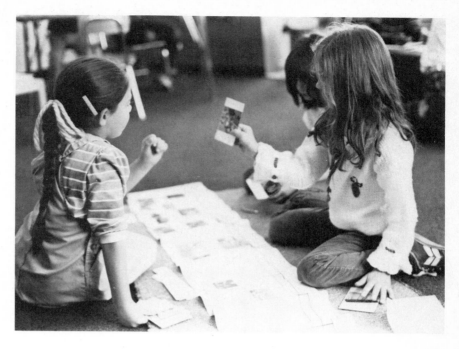

Language growth requires interaction.

new toy—causes the speaker to focus attention on the object and thus not to think about himself or herself or any nervousness felt about talking. "Show and Tell" tends to be more organized since there is less likelihood of rambling on when something is being shown and talked about.

"Show and Tell," like other talking situations, does not have to be a total class activity. Small groups, again, often work better and are less formal. In "Show and Tell" and other activities, the following suggestions are helpful:

1. Urge children to talk to the group rather than to you.
2. Encourage questions and comments.
3. Insist upon attention and good listening.
4. Practice good listening yourself.
5. Limit the number of children who show or share on a single day, thus eliminating boredom and providing adequate time for each child.
6. Do not formalize "taking turns" too much.
7. Remember that informal seating will promote expression.
8. Do not force any child to share or show.
9. Take special care to praise the efforts of shy children.

10. Include the children in the planning and management of the sharing period.
11. Take advantage of the opportunity provided by the sharing period to note children's interests, possible speech defects or articulation difficulties, and nonstandard usages that may need teaching attention.
12. Encourage variety in the types of objects children show and talk about.

Creative Play

From the time children first walk around the house in their parents' slippers, role playing and other forms of dramatic play are an exciting part of their lives. Young children love to live in a land of make-believe. Early in life they begin to play "house," "school," and other games based on aspects of life about them. Much of children's emotional and social growth, cognitive development, and knowledge about their environment—and, of course, language development—occur through this form of creative experimentation and expression. Creative play, in essence, forms a bridge between the developing minds of children and the external world; therefore, schools should foster opportunities for this naturally occurring activity to continue.

Opportunities for creative play occur throughout the school day. Children may experiment with adult words as they play in the housekeeping corner, build roads and houses in the sandbox, shop for bargains in the classroom grocery store, or carry on imaginary telephone conversations. In a more structured type of situation, children may act out what they will do when the principal comes to visit them or play at introducing themselves or each other to a class guest.

Other opportunities for informal dramatization may be suggested by conversations or situations that occur on the playground or in the classroom. Suppose children playing a game get into an argument about the rules. Later, the situation could be dramatized, and the children themselves could work out a solution to the problem. Naturally, the focus should be on discovering a better way to resolve the disagreement, *not* on placing any child or children in an awkward or embarrassing position. This will not happen, of course, if the classroom is one in which every child feels that he or she is an accepted and important individual.

Dramatizing Stories and Rhymes

An activity liked by young children that is also helpful in developing abilities in all of the language arts is that of hearing and saying rhymes. Many colorful and attractively illustrated nursery rhyme books are available in book stores and libraries, and every classroom should have several. Choose one or two rhymes that the children in your group will particularly enjoy. Then establish listening purposes by telling the children to listen to the rhyme as you read it so that they can tell you what happened. You may need to read the rhyme several times, asking them to listen for the answer to a specific question each time. Next, one child may relate the sequence of events in correct order. (The child need not march to the front of the room to do this.) Once the children know what happened, they may act out the rhyme as you read. It is sometimes helpful to select the most extroverted children to participate first, as they will generate enough enthusiasm to encourage others to try.

The next step is to encourage the children to act out the rhyme using the words they want to say. Particular attention should be given to whether or not children use the rhyme when they are speaking. If no child mentions that the words sound alike at the end, this may be pointed out after the dramatization. Read the rhyme once again, asking them to listen for the rhyming words. Or, if you wish, do this the first time you read the rhyme.

Children know much about rhyming and may pick up the wording of the rhyme, but memorization should not be required. Keep in mind that spontaneity of expression and ease with language are the goals. Some children, particularly those who are extremely self-conscious, may not readily respond to these activities, and to do some of them may take months, even with six-year-olds. Gently encouraging these children will help. Patience and knowledge of the particular children involved are the keys in planning such activities.

Some suggested Mother Goose rhymes to dramatize are these:

This Is the Way the Ladies Ride	Three Little Kittens
Rock-a-Bye-Baby	Baa, Baa, Black Sheep
Jack Be Nimble	Simple Simon
One, Two, Buckle My Shoe	Old King Cole
Jack and Jill	Polly, Put the Kettle On
Georgie Porgie	Old Mother Hubbard
Humpty Dumpty	Wee Willie Winkie
Little Miss Muffet	

Many others are as suitable as those listed. Always be on the lookout for poems well suited to dramatization or to pure enjoyment.

Once the children have had experience with dramatizing simple rhymes, move on to the dramatization of stories that have more plot and a greater variety of actions—but do continue to use rhymes. Simple, brief stories of a repetitive nature but with much action are good to begin with in teaching young children. Try these:

The Three Billy Goats Gruff	*Millions of Cats* (Wanda Gag)
The Three Little Pigs	*The Little Brown Hen* (Martin)
The Three Bears	*Cinderella*
The Elves and the Shoemaker	*Chicken Little*
Peter Rabbit (Beatrix Potter)	*The Snowy Day* (Keats)

Simple props related to occupations and tasks are helpful.

Formal dramatization at this level is seldom desirable. If you wish to plan a program for parents or another group of children, the informal dramatization discussed will suffice. It may be rehearsed, but only to a limited extent; and since spontaneity is a goal, the "final" production may vary from an earlier one. And by all means use only the simplest of props—half a yardstick can become an old man's cane or a soldier's sword, and an apron transforms a little girl into a mother, becomes a shawl for an old woman, or creates headgear for a princess. Let the children's imaginations, not costumes and props, create the desired effect.

Reading and Telling Stories

Magazines for Young Children

Humpty Dumpty's, P.O. Box 567B, Indianapolis, IN 46206 (K)
Playmate, P.O. Box 567B, Indianapolis, IN 46206 (first grade)
Sesame Street Magazine, P.O. Box 2892, Boulder, CO 80321
Turtle, P.O. Box 567B, Indianapolis, IN 46206 (preschool)
WOW Magazine, Box 1925, Marion, OH 43302

Teachers should read stories *daily*, not just to children who have not yet learned to read but at every elementary school grade level. Of almost equal importance—and perhaps greater at preprimary levels—is storytelling. The two should really be thought of together since doing either effectively requires planning its introduction; using the voice skillfully to communicate plot, mood, setting, etc.; gaining the attention and eye contact of the audience; and anticipating interruptions and questions. Each method of presentation has its particular advantages. Some stories should be read—because they are told in rhyme, or because illustrations or vocabulary add greatly to enjoyment. On the other hand, telling a story allows greater freedom in using gestures, permits better eye contact, and frees the hands for using aids such as flannel-board figures. When telling a story, however, be sure you know it well (but do *not* memorize), and avoid simplifying your language "because the children are young."

Of course, the primary purpose for reading or telling stories should always be to provide pleasure through language; but these activities also provide opportunities for language growth through acquiring new vocabulary, developing more varied language patterns, sharing ideas and feelings, and learning story schema or developing a "sense of story," important both to writing and to reading.

Encourage parents to keep reading to their children.

Children should be comfortable when stories are told or read to them. For young children this means sitting in a close group—and not a large one usually—with the adult also sitting on the floor or on a low stool. Some children may not want to listen to a story—they may be actively doing

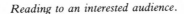
Reading to an interested audience.

something else—so it is often a good idea to have a means for announcing "Story Time." A puppet is usually a good "announcer."

See Maxim, *The Very Young*, for storytelling suggestions.

Selecting stories to read or tell is usually not a problem since young children will quickly tell what they want to hear—frequently stories they have had read or told to them. You will need to do some selection, though, in order to introduce new ones. For this selection, consider first the ages of the children. Three- and four-year-olds like short stories, with some action and with characters like themselves (even with their names), but they don't like stories with a strong element of fear. For five- and six-year-olds, more content is required, and characters, locales, and story lines are needed. Plots should be uncomplicated, evolving around a great deal of direct conversation among characters who are themselves interesting and easily identifiable to the children. And any story told or read to children should be one that appeals to you.

When a story is suitable, children may be involved in role playing: "Let's stretch as tall as the tree" or "Let's all hop like the rabbit." After they have listened to a wide variety of stories, they will want to dramatize many, and they will also begin to tell stories they know and some they "make up."

Experience Stories

More on experience stories is found in Chapter 12.

An experience story is a story dictated by a pupil or pupils to the teacher. The teacher records on the chalkboard or on a large sheet of chart paper what a child or group of children say. The story is usually based on some experience—most often something the entire group has experienced. Recording directly on chart paper is usually more practical than recording on the board. It saves time and avoids the possibility that the story will be erased inadvertently.

First experience stories are not written for children to read. The dictation simply serves to help the children understand that written symbols stand for spoken words. It also gives children a new reason for expressing their ideas and helps them to develop feelings of self-confidence and status. As children begin to recognize some words, experience stories can and should be an important part of the readiness and reading programs.

The sharing period, dramatic play activities, materials and objects in the classroom, and the class events the children participate in can all become subjects for experience stories. The arrival of a gerbil in class, which necessitates a discussion of what it eats and what kind of cage it should have, may serve as the basis for a three- to five-line story, depending on the maturity level of the children. A schoolyard walk, the planting of seeds, or an educational film can also serve as the basis for a story. With the exercise of a little imagination and effort, the possibilities are endless.

Unless the children have developed a good deal of spontaneity, you will need to use guiding questions to help them formulate ideas for an experience story and to aid them in organizing these ideas. Such questions should lead children to recall the experience in sequence, to avoid leaving out important details, and to state what they really mean to say.

CHILDREN'S EARLY WRITING

Adults generally have thought that children learn to write at school, after they learn to read. They have thought of learning to write largely as a matter of learning the mechanics of handwriting, even though they have been aware that children write simple stories in the first grade after they have learned to "print." Mothers and nursery and kindergarten teachers, though, just as generally have known that children begin "writing" much earlier—even though adults may have thought of it as scribbling and drawing—and have even been surprised that some of it has "made sense" to them. Of course, all of it makes sense to the children.

Recent research (described in some detail in Chapter 8) which involved observing young children and more closely analyzing their "writing" has made us aware that children can make significant strides toward learning to write in a way similar to that of learning to speak: through observation, practice, and informal corrective feedback. Thus, children's early efforts are a significant aspect of developing competence in writing. And the research concerning young children's writing growth tells us a good deal about what elementary school (and beyond) writing programs should be like.

Beginning Writing

See Marie Clay, *What Did I Write?* and Temple et al., *The Beginnings of Writing.*

Young children (particularly those younger than three years) often think that the story being read to them is contained in the pictures in the book. This gradually changes because of parents and others pointing to words in books or on packaging and saying things like "This says *milk*. See, *m, i, l, k.*" Children also will see that words are made of letters as their names and other words are printed for them. Thus, children as young as three may understand that a picture is not writing, that writing is a series of marks or figures placed horizontally across a page, and that this writing has marks of different shapes. They usually don't know that writing moves from left to right, and unless they are highly gifted, they don't know what the marks mean or how to make them.

Children with opportunities to write will soon *pretend* that the marks they make stand for something. The pretending, though, may be an adult perception; to the child a particular mark or group of marks does stand for something, and the child knows what the something is. Some of the early marks or figures will resemble conventional letters, although they may sometimes be upside down or backward, and some will be created by the child. The marks or figures made at this stage are meant to represent words and not sounds. However, children will soon begin to combine this *word* representing with letters or letterlike figures that represent *sounds*, particularly as they recognize that their names have several sounds and as they see them printed above clothes hooks, on chairs, and on paintings and drawings they have done. Gradually, they will progress to representing words with one or more of the letters in these words. There will still be problems with orientation of the letters (i.e., which way they face, placing them on their sides, etc.) as well as spacing between "words" and left-to-right movement, but linearity in their writing will be generally observed. If a word is represented by a single letter, the letter is often a consonant, probably because so many words begin with consonants or sound as if they do (e.g., *elbow, engine, arm*). It is not unusual, though, for some words in a child's sentence to be represented by more than one letter (e.g., representing initial and final sounds, a letter for each sound, or even a conventional spelling), while others may still have a single-letter representation.

Thus, children try to represent the words in the messages they write. They experiment with these representations, "inventing" spellings (discussed in Chapter 10). The attempts of many children gradually get closer to conventional spellings (sometimes succeeding quite early), and their compositions become more mature as they are read to, begin to read themselves, see in written form more and more words that they use in speaking, are guided and encouraged by teachers, and have opportunities for doing the writing they want to do. Writing materials such as pencils, crayons, felt-tipped pens, paper of various sizes, slates, and chalk should be easily accessible. Books, alphabet sets, and the like should also be available.

Young Children and the Writing Process

The discussion above focused on motor skills development and thought processes relative to the fundamental mechanics or conventions of writing: forming letters, spelling words, spacing, and writing movement. But the most significant element in anyone's writing—child's or adult's—is the content, the message. Children's scribbles are done for the joy of movement and the satisfaction felt from making marks. With knowledge that the marks signal meaning comes the desire to convey meaning. In these attempts children aren't particularly writing for an audience; more likely they write something they would say aloud, although they do often want to read or show what they've written. Their writing is usually accompanied by a drawing, ordinarily one done prior to the writing—although the drawing may be changed during the writing or afterward. Early writing does show that it is a three-stage process (more fully discussed in Chapter 8) of *rehearsing*, *drafting*, and *revising*, although close observation is often necessary to note these stages. A child's drawing is evidence of rehearsing, as is the talking aloud the child does and verbal interactions with others before the writing begins. Marking out, erasing, inserting additional "letters," and more talking aloud show that drafting is occurring; and looking at the writing, possibly changing or adding to it, and showing it is the third stage for the child.

See articles in Pinnell, *Discovering Language with Children*.

In addition to providing children with writing materials, places to write, and time in which to do it, teachers need to encourage children and to respect their writing efforts. As the children develop—in the kindergarten and first grade particularly—teachers can give more direct guidance. Conferring with children about their products (at all stages) is important. They will need to be taught to write their own names in manuscript and to be given help in writing captions and short sentences. They can copy words and letters below teacher models, or they may trace over them. Some children will soon want to move beyond tracing and copying and have the ability to do so, while others will continue to need considerable encouragement in learning to make letters, to space between words, to move from left to right, etc. Even more encouragement will be needed for some children to attempt writing their "stories" if they feel too inadequate about those abilities.

PRE–FIRST GRADE READING

Books for Parents

Getting Ready to Read by Susan Mandel Glazer (Prentice-Hall)
Helping Children Learn about Reading (National Association for the Education of Young Children)
The Reading Triangle by Linda Clinard (Focus Pub. Co.)

Although most children are given instruction in reading in the first grade, grounding for this instruction begins long before this in the experiences the children have had, what has been read to them, and the interactions they have had that bear on their cognitive and language development. While this grounding is generally recognized, there are differences of opinion about whether it is part of "reading instruction." Is it "reading instruction" to help children recognize their names in print, learn the names on cereal boxes, or know what *Stop* on a sign or *Men* or *Women* on a rest room door means? Or is "reading instruction" learning which letters represent what sounds or the meanings of root words and suffixes? Even those who lean toward affirmative answers to the latter question differ as to when this instruction should begin.

It is not our intention to discuss the teaching of reading here (see Chapter 12). Rather, since reading programs of varying degrees of formality have entered many kindergartens, the issue of whether such programs are appropriate is related to the preceding sections of this chapter.

Early Readers

Dolores Durkin refers to this as a "language arts approach."

It is generally known that some children learn to read at age five or younger. This fact has influenced changes in kindergarten programs, as have pressures on elementary schools to move much curriculum content to earlier age levels. Also, some people feel that children are maturing earlier because of TV watching and attendance in preschools. What has often been overlooked is that the research on early readers showed that they had great interest in written language (asking questions such as "What does that say?" "Where does it say that?" and "How do you make a *k*?"), and that they lived in homes where much reading was done, trips were taken, books and writing materials were available, and language interaction with adults occurred. Also overlooked has been the fact that typical reading "readiness" and beginning reading instructional programs tend to be highly structured and formalized, with too little concern for the many differences among children; thus, these programs differ greatly from the individualized, supporting, learning (not teaching) settings experienced by the early readers as reported in the research literature.

Concern about Kindergarten Reading Programs

Because some kindergarten reading programs were begun without proper consideration of the research about early readers, because relatively little was actually known about the effectiveness of the pre–first grade reading instruction being given, and because of observations various educational leaders had made of the current practices in such instruction, a committee sponsored by seven national educational organizations issued a report (in 1977) expressing concerns about early programs and stating some recommendations for teachers and school administrators having or considering starting pre–first grade reading programs. These concerns and recommendations are given below:

Concerns

See the committee statement in *Language Arts* (April 1977).

1. A growing number of children are enrolled in prekindergarten and kindergarten classes in which highly structured prereading and reading programs are being used.

2. Decisions related to schooling, including the teaching of reading, are increasingly being made on economic and political bases instead of on our knowledge of young children and how they best learn.

3. In a time of diminishing financial resources, schools often try to make "a good showing" on measures of achievement that may or may not be appropriate for the children involved. Such measures all too often dictate the content and goals of the programs.

4. In attempting to respond to pressures for high scores on widely used measures of achievement, teachers of young children sometimes feel compelled to use materials, methods, and activities designed for older children. In so doing, they may impede the development of intellectual functions such as curiosity, critical thinking, and creative expression, and, at the same time, promote negative attitudes toward reading.

5. A need exists to provide alternative ways to teach and evaluate progress in prereading and reading skills.

6. Teachers of pre–first graders who are carrying out highly individualized programs without depending on commercial readers and workbooks need help in articulating for themselves and the public *what* they are doing and *why*.

Recommendations

1. Provide reading experiences as an integrated part of the broader communication process that includes listening, speaking, and writing. A language experience approach is an example of such integration.

2. Provide for a range of activities that is broad both in scope and in content. Include direct experiences that offer opportunities to communicate in different settings with different persons.

3. Foster children's affective and cognitive development by providing materials, experiences, and opportunities to communicate what they know and how they feel.

4. Continually appraise how various aspects of each child's total development affect his or her reading development.

5. Use evaluative procedures that are developmentally appropriate for the children being assessed and that reflect the goals and objectives of the instructional program.

6. Ensure feelings of success for all children in order to help them see themselves as persons who can enjoy exploring language and learning to read.

7. Plan flexibly in order to accommodate a variety of learning styles and ways of thinking.

8. Respect the language the child brings to school, and use it as a base for language activities.

9. Plan activities that will cause children to become active participants in the learning process rather than passive recipients of knowledge.

10. Provide opportunities for children to experiment with language and simply to have fun with it.

11. Require that preservice and inservice teachers of young children be prepared in the teaching of reading in a way that emphasizes reading as an integral part of the language arts as well as the total curriculum.

12. Encourage developmentally appropriate language-learning opportunities in the home.

While the statement of concerns and recommendations was directed at pre–first grade reading programs, it applies in many instances to reading programs in the first grade and beyond. It is also supportive of much that we have advocated in this chapter and earlier ones as well as much that will receive attention in the chapters that follow.

References

Allen, Roach Van, and Allen, Claryce. *Language Experience Activities.* 2nd ed. Houghton Mifflin, 1982.

Cataldo, Christine Z. *Infant and Toddler Programs: A Guide for Very Early Childhood Education.* Addison-Wesley, 1983.

Clay, Marie M. *What Did I Write?* Heinemann Educational Books, 1975.

Cohen, Monroe D., ed. *Primary School Potpourri.* Association for Childhood Education International, 1976.

Durkin, Dolores. *Getting Reading Started.* Allyn and Bacon, 1982.

————. "A Six Year Study of Children Who Learned to Read in School at the Age of Four." *Reading Research Quarterly,* 10 (1974–1975), pp. 9–61.

Evans, Ellis D. *Contemporary Influences in Early Childhood Education.* Holt, Rinehart and Winston, 1975.

Hess, Robert D., and Croft, Doreen J. *Teachers of Young Children.* 3rd ed. Houghton Mifflin, 1981.

Hildebrand, Verna. *Introduction to Early Childhood Education.* 3rd ed. Macmillan, 1981.

Maxim, George W. *The Very Young: Guiding Children from Infancy Through the Early Years.* Wadsworth, 1980.

Ollila, Lloyd O., ed. *The Kindergarten Child and Reading.* International Reading Association, 1977.

Pinnell, Gay Su, ed. *Discovering Language with Children.* National Council of Teachers of English, 1980.

Robinson, Helen F. *Exploring Teaching in Early Childhood Education.* 2nd ed. Allyn and Bacon, 1983.

Sealey, Leonard; Sealey, Nancy; and Millmore, Marcia. *Children's Writing, An Approach for the Primary Grades.* International Reading Association, 1979.

Temple, Charles A.; Nathan, Ruth G.; and Burris, Nancy A. *The Beginnings of Writing.* Allyn and Bacon, 1982.

Teaching Resources

FILMS

Magic Moments. Encyclopaedia Britannica (5 units of 4 films each, 2–8 min. each; primary).
Ready. Learning Corporation of America (set of 12 color film loops, 3–4 min. each).

FILMSTRIPS

Early Childhood Series. Bowmar (records and sound filmstrips; N–3).
Let's Look For. Bowmar (5 strips and cassettes).

RECORDINGS

Sound, Rhythm, Rhyme and Mime for Children. Folkway Records (record; primary).
Talkstarters. Scott, Foresman and Co. (books and records; primary).

KITS

Language Big Box. Developmental Learning Materials (picture cards, puppet, books, sequence cards).
Peabody Early Experiences Kit. American Guidance Service (puppets, objects, cards, pictures).
Peabody Language Development Kits. American Guidance Service (kits for several developmental levels).
Primary Thinking Box. Benefic (filmstrips, cassettes, posters, guide, etc.).
The Reading/Language Kit. Slosson Educational Publications (activity cards, guide).
Spacetalk. Bowmar/Noble (20 cassettes, handbook, response folders; primary).

OTHER AIDS

Ready for Reading: Classroom Games for Reading Readiness. Technomic Publishing Co.
What Comes Next? Sequencing Kit. Lakeshore Curriculum Materials (manipulative letters and numerals).

Activities for Preservice Teachers

1. Read one of the references listed for this chapter. Be ready to report on it to the class.

2. Investigate commercial materials intended for pre-primary and/or primary use. The listing for this chapter represents only a small sample of materials available. What did you find that you believe to be useful? What criticisms of these materials do you have?

3. Visit a preschool or kindergarten class. Make a note of differences among the children in size, physical coordination, willingness and ability to express themselves orally, and extent of vocabulary.

4. Watch several TV programs for young children, such as "Romper Room," "Sesame Street," "Mister Rogers," or "Calliope," and evaluate them in terms of how effective they are in developing language abilities, building vocabularies and experience backgrounds, and teaching social skills.

5. From friends who teach preprimary classes or parents of children aged three to five, collect samples of children's "writing." Can you read it? Are some letters conventional in shape? Is there evidence of linear motion in putting them on paper? Are some figures (possibly letters) repeated frequently?

6. Observe children on the playground or during a physical education period. Select several children and compare their coordination with that of the other children. If you notice a child who seems to be particularly lacking in coordination, ask the teacher how he compares with the others in articulation, handwriting, spelling, and reading.

7. Use chart paper or shelf paper to write an imaginary experience story on a topic such as "Our Fish," "Dirt," or "Flowers." On a separate sheet, outline the steps you would use in helping children to write such a story. Be sure to include a description of the motivating experiences.

8. Prepare a bibliography of good stories to read to primary children. See recent publications of the American Library Association, International Reading Association, National Council of Teachers of English, and the Association for Childhood Education International for assistance.

9. Find other finger plays to add to those in this chapter. Paul Anderson's *A Second Book of Stories to Tell* (Denison, 1962) is one source. Primary teachers often have their own collections, too, and will share with you.

Activities for Inservice Teachers

1. Make a surprise box filled with objects that are interesting to touch. Include such items as a smooth pebble, a piece of sandpaper, satin cloth, tree bark, and a feather. Use this with your class to develop concepts and/or vocabulary.

2. Make a box similar to the one described above, but use objects to be smelled (children can wear blindfolds). Items might include a piece of orange peel, a cinnamon stick, a coffee bean, an evergreen twig, and a piece of leather.

3. You might also have a "tasting party." Serve bite-sized portions of raw fruits and vegetables (e.g., green pepper, cauliflower, tomato, pineapple, etc.). Use this as a basis for extending children's experiences and encouraging oral expression.

4. Tape-record (or video-tape) a "Sharing" or "Show and Tell" session. This makes a good record of children's abilities and needs. Children will enjoy your playing it, and some self-evaluation may possibly occur (depending on the maturity levels).

5. Prepare a listening, speaking, and motor-skills coordination checklist for use with young children. As the children participate in activities suggested in this chapter, evaluate them in terms of the criteria you have established for their age level. Then, based on your observation, prepare a card for each child listing his or her strengths and weaknesses. Include a brief statement about how you plan to adjust the curriculum to meet these needs.

6. Describe steps that might be taken to help a shy child participate more in classroom activities.

7. Write on the board or ask the children the following questions: "Do you like to pretend? What would you like to pretend you are? Can you draw a picture about your pretending?" After pictures have been drawn, ask for volunteers to tell about their pictures. This activity may be either for the whole class or for small groups.

8. Regardless of the grade level you are teaching, try a group story (i.e., experience story) with yourself as the scribe. What evidence do you find of the children's story sequencing/organizing abilities? What else can you report to the class about the experience?

9. Find out what is occurring in your school or a neighboring one about writing and reading in the kindergarten.

Independent Activities for Children

1. For preprimary children provide alphabet blocks and puzzles for sequencing letters, letter practice cards, story sequence cards, etc.

2. Discuss "news items" with the children and then provide newsprint for them to individually illustrate these "items."

3. Prepare paper bags, each containing a single object. The objects should be of varying shapes, sizes, and textures. Have a child reach into the bag and feel the object and describe it to a second child. The objective is for the first child to describe the object well enough for the second one to guess what it is.

4. Provide a variety of puppets and a puppet stage for children to use informally for their puppet shows.

5. Provide a box of old clothing, shoes, hats, etc., for children to use in creative dramatics.

6. A child can choose materials from an "odds and ends" box to make "pretend" animals. These may be shown to the class, stimulating a discussion which the child who made the animal would lead.

7. Collect sets of pictures from magazines for individual children to place in sequence for a story. The pictures may be mounted on cardboard with flannel patches on the back so that the child can place them on a flannel board.

8. Provide a writing "center" supplied with writing materials and encourage the children to use it whenever they have time (i.e., when they are not working directly with you) and want to write. Provide for each child to have his or her own pocket for storing words. Move into the center frequently to assist children wanting help.

6 | Developing Speaking Skills

Earlier chapters have discussed children's acquiring the ability to speak and the growth of this ability. The preceding chapter stressed the importance of building upon this ability in preschool and beginning school experiences. This chapter discusses the importance of extending each child's ability, suggests activities which foster children's inclination to talk with others, and focuses on the speaking skills and knowledge of speaking situations that are necessary for meeting children's school needs and that are important to adults.

THE IMPORTANCE OF SPEECH

Many teachers provide opportunities for children to talk, for they recognize that this is the way language power develops and that children have practical needs for speaking in various types of situations, both in and outside of the classroom. However, evidence of the cliché "the good classroom is a quiet classroom" still exists, and there are also classrooms in which children talk a good deal but where there is little evidence of guidance toward learning the skills and behaviors important to the speaking situations commonly met.

There are also many teachers, but not nearly enough, who recognize the importance of speech to children's success in attaining competence in listening, reading, and writing and consequently to their learning in many areas. Of course, levels of language maturity are not *always* reflected in a child's (or adult's) speech, but the preponderance of research evidence indicates that they usually are. For example, Loban, in reporting his thirteen-year study, stated that children "superior in oral language in kindergarten and grade one before they learned to read and write are the very ones who excel in reading and writing by the time they are in grade six."

See Loban in References.

The relationship between a child's proficiency in oral expression and his or her personal and social development is significant, bearing upon the child's potential for learning and affecting the self-concept. Teachers have often noted that personality differences among children seem to be related to their speaking. An aggressive child frequently assumes a great deal of classroom leadership, possibly monopolizing speaking activities. Perhaps the child's assurance in speaking fosters this behavior, or possibly the aggressive personality provides speech confidence. On the other hand, a shy, retiring personality could be due to language immaturity, or it may be that the child's shyness has undermined confidence in speaking. Cause-and-effect relationships are not clear, but the fact that there apparently *is* a relationship adds to the reasons for emphasizing oral language in language arts programs. Surveys have shown that many adults fear speaking before a group; surely it is reasonable to assume that giving little—or haphazard and sporadic—attention to speaking situations during children's school years may well result in their becoming such adults.

THE SPEECH SKILLS

Skill in oral expression results from practice in the various situations in which an individual needs to speak. The instructional program, then, must provide many speaking situations, and it must utilize these situations to direct attention to speech skills, to behavioral attitudes and habits, and to content.

Naturally *what* is said, the content, is of primary importance in any speaking situation. Effectiveness in communicating this content is affected by its organization and development, by the vocabulary used, and by the skills discussed below: (1) control and use of the vocal mechanism, (2) use of facial and bodily expression, and (3) development of audience-speaker rapport.

Vocal Control

Effective speech is pleasing to the ear. It is produced with ease and confidence. It is rhythmic and free from hesitations, repetitions, and interruptions. The tempo and volume are suitable to the content and the audience, and all sounds are clearly articulated and distinctly enunciated. To aid children in developing this kind of fluency the teacher must do three things: help each child to feel confident and secure in speaking situations, help each child discover his or her own weaknesses and have the desire to improve them, and help each child learn to speak as clearly and distinctly as is physically possible.

A person's emotional state is often indicated by voice quality, tone, pitch, and tempo. This is especially true of children. A child who is upset, tense, or worried shows it in his or her voice. A self-reliant, alert child shows confidence by a pleasing voice. An eager, happy child is usually friendly and talkative. A diffident child who is emotionally and socially insecure is unable to achieve fluent, articulate speech. A child who is overly aggressive, perhaps also reflecting emotional insecurity, is apt to speak in a strident voice and insist on monopolizing speaking situations.

You cannot, of course, be expected to solve all of your children's personal and social problems, but you can create a classroom atmosphere in which children feel secure and free to speak. You can provide many activities and experiences which encourage talk and, by your personal and verbal interactions with each child, build his or her self-concept.

Choral speaking, which is discussed more fully in a later section of this chapter, is an excellent activity for building the confidence of the shy child or for tempering the speech of the overly aggressive one. Choral speaking also has value in helping children develop an understanding of the importance of rate, pitch, rhythm, stress, uses of pauses, etc. Experimenting with different ways of reading lines helps them to see how these factors contribute to effective speech.

Few of us really listen to our own voices except through artificial means. Therefore, one of the best ways to help children discover their individual needs with respect to pitch, volume, and rate of speaking is to record their voices and have them listen to the recordings. This may be done individually, in small groups, or with the entire class participating. The clearly established purpose of the listening, of course, should be to seek ways to improve, not to find fault. Listening to recorded speech may also be helpful in formulating standards; these should not be unrealistic, but they are not likely to be if the children participate in setting them. They can be posted and referred to in evaluating each new effort—and refined as the children progress in speaking abilities.

Articulation

Children in the early school grades sometimes do not articulate sounds clearly. This may be due to the retention of early speech habits, missing teeth, or eagerness in talking. Generally, such articulation difficulties are eliminated by the time children reach the middle grades, especially if teachers have been good speech models and the children have engaged in many speaking activities. There may be, though, some children who have real problems in making certain sounds correctly. The problems of these children may have been noted in a speech screening program and the children may be receiving help from a speech therapist. However, if such is not the case, you may do the following:

1. Show the child how the sound is made as he or she listens and observes the movement of your lips and tongue.
2. Have the child imitate you and examine his or her attempts by watching in a mirror.
3. Have the child repeat the sound several times.
4. Have the child say syllables and words that include the sound.

In teaching the production of speech sounds, time should not be wasted in drilling on those that present only minor difficulties, since to be motivated to improve, a child must feel that proper production of the sound is important to communication and not just something to be done during a practice period. The child, of course, will readily recognize that minor speech faults do not interfere with communication.

Individual attention is usually more effective than teaching a given sound to the entire class. The instruction should be as close as possible to the time when the difficulty with the utterance occurs. Finally, throughout the instruction make your own speech an example of good articulation, distinct enunciation, and correct pronunciation.

One fourth grade set these standards:
1. Don't talk too fast.
2. Speak clearly and loudly enough so everyone can hear.
3. Be sure you know how to pronounce all the words.
4. Don't use too many *and's.*
5. Look at the audience.
6. Use facial expressions and gestures.
7. Be interested in what you are saying.
8. Try to look relaxed; don't fidget.

See Chapter 16 for suggestions for children with speech handicaps.

Gestures and Bodily Expression

Children need to be aware that oral communication often includes more than speech. It is virtually impossible for a person to express things orally without using some body movements, and these movements should be natural and in harmony with the speech activity and the content of the communication. The rhythmic activities, finger plays, and action verse suggested in the preceding chapter are both fun for children and a means for developing harmony between speech and physical movements. Children may, though, develop annoying mannerisms such as fidgeting, head jerking, hand twisting, exaggerated facial expressions, and other undue physical movements. The avoidance of their development is usually accomplished by the elimination of self-consciousness; this can be accomplished through careful planning and participation in speaking situations that have real meaning.

Showing aids telling.

In the primary grades, the activity of showing an object while telling about it may relieve a child's nervousness by taking his or her attention away from self. Similarly, the middle or upper grade child might use a map, chart, or other aid in giving a report; this will also encourage natural gestures and more purposeful body movements. Group and individual pantomimes, discussed below, as well as creative dramatics can also teach the value and proper use of gestures and body movement. And, of course, you are a constant example; just as you try to set a model in speaking, so you should also be aware of your own use of facial expressions, gestures, and body movements throughout the school day.

Pantomime

Pantomime follows rather naturally and easily the physical movements, rhythmic activities, creative play, and beginning dramatization described in Chapter 5. Besides the fact that pantomiming is fun, its relation to the oral expression that will occur both before and after it is done makes it an important part of language arts programs.

Beginning Pantomimes

a boy who has ripped his
    pants
a tree being pruned
someone walking an unruly
    dog
a shopper with an armload
    of packages
building a snowman
getting dressed in the
    morning
a girl washing her hair
a football fan watching a
    game on TV

Pantomime is expression. It tells something. It is imitation. The familiar is easy for children to show by pantomime. Therefore, start with simple ideas. Encourage children to work their pantomime from the inside out, to use their own thoughts and feelings, and to pantomime both in groups and individually. Children may imitate a parent driving a car, caring for a baby, shopping for groceries, or playing golf, or they may imitate the look on someone's face when that person is happy, surprised, angry, or sad. Other actions they may want to mimic are swimming, watching television, vacuuming a rug, playing with a dog or cat, or building a snowman.

The entire body is brought into pantomime when children pretend to be one of the following (add your own suggestions or have children add theirs): a rag doll, a tin soldier, a runaway horse, an angry dog, a dish of Jell-O, a monster, a tree on a windy day. Or perhaps a fat person trying to tie a shoe, someone who just sat on a tack, a firefighter climbing a ladder, or even a coffee pot perking.

Individual Pantomimes

practicing the violin
being a school crossing
    guard
roller skating
getting gum from a
    machine
opening birthday presents

Pantomime activities can also be used to develop sense awareness. For example, a child might pretend to put a foot in a tub of ice water, or may

Group Pantomimes

playing catch
doubles ping pong
a mouse is loose in the
    room
building a campfire
raising the flag
putting up a tent

look at an apple, think how good it will taste, bite into it, chew it—and find half a worm. Another might act out putting a finger into a hot pie, eating a hamburger, smelling something burning on the stove, hearing noises in the night, etc. While one child does the imitation or pantomime, other children will enjoy guessing what role or activity is being portrayed. These pantomime activities, which appear to children to be a game, provide many opportunities for language development. Encourage questions and responses that go beyond one word. That is, when a child asks "Why?" it may be appropriate to ask "Why, what?" in order to get a good question. In the same manner, one-word answers may be changed to sentences.

A full-length mirror in the classroom will give children the opportunity to practice their pantomimes and try out variations before an audience of only one. It can prove to be an invaluable aid in many other oral activities as well, in addition to providing an opportunity to talk about good grooming and discuss why we should look clean and neat.

Audience-Speaker Rapport

Am I a good listener?

1. Do I pay careful attention and not distract the speaker by doing something else?
2. Do I use facial expressions to show that I do not understand or that I am interested in what is said?
3. Do I show appreciation without calling attention to myself by commenting or laughing too loudly?
4. Do I jot down questions or notes for discussion after the speaker has finished?

Aside from the explorative type of talking done by a young child—and the talking-to-ourselves that we adults often do—an individual speaks because he or she has something to say: an opinion to express, facts or information to present, a question to ask. The need is to say something to someone, to an *audience*. The audience may be one person or many, but the audience is very much a part of any oral expression.

It is important for a speaker to establish and maintain a relationship with this audience in which there is interplay, in which there is genuine communication. The people in the audience will show that this communication is taking place by their posture, their eyes, their facial expressions, their courtesy in listening, the incisiveness of their questions, and their voiced reactions. The skilled speaker shows a sensitivity to the audience in his or her response to their reactions. For the child this is often difficult; it is only learned through experience and careful planning.

OPPORTUNITIES FOR ORAL EXPRESSION

Natural situations—the class discussing a problem, a small group working on a project, two or three children conversing—should be the basis for much of the instruction in oral expression. In addition, the teacher must plan other opportunities in connection with the ongoing activities and studies of the class—reports, dramatizations, etc. Genuine and meaningful activities that are truly concerned with communication provide the best opportunities for giving attention to specific speech skills, to behavior related to speech activities, to the content of the speech, and to listening abilities.

Each school day abounds with such natural situations, since teaching and learning in every subject area require at least some oral expression. In virtually every chapter in this book some reference is made to using language orally, with suggestions or implications for its teaching. This section is de-

Provide places and time for conversations.

voted to the kinds of oral language situations and activities that are not adequately discussed elsewhere and for which particular skills, attitudes, and behaviors need to be taught.

Conversation

A wise teacher shows interest in his or her students by being available to talk with the children when they first come to school in the morning. This "chatting time" before school should not be considered a waste, since many children have no one in the home who will listen to or talk with them. To develop favorable self-concepts, children need to know that others are interested in them and their interests.

The desire to communicate thoughts and ideas to others continues throughout the school day. Whether it is a discussion of the room arrangement, a future assembly program, a social studies or science project, or current news events, certain habits and courtesies must be agreed on and practiced by those involved.

For effective conversation, the listener must be attentive in order to react to what the speaker is saying; the topic must be of mutual interest; and both participants must be polite (even when angry) and tactful (especially when being truthful). A good conversationalist will be friendly and will remember that a conversation is not a battle of wits in which one attempts to disarm another. A good conversationalist will also be enthusiastic about what he or she has to say and about what others say. Being enthusiastic requires being informed and knowing about many things that become the

Decide on some conversation topics and then divide the class into groups of two or three to talk about the ones they choose.

subjects of conversations—books, movies, television, political and social events, and the like.

Many behaviors in conversational situations are suitable for dramatization by pupils or for discussion in large and small groups. The first week of school is a good time to discuss conversational abilities and courtesies, with a review whenever it seems appropriate.

It is important to remember that conversing is an activity of some intimacy and that the necessary intimacy is difficult to achieve in a formal physical setting with a classroom of children. A shy child who will not talk from his or her seat may find it easier to talk in a conversational group of four or five children where it is possible to talk in a low voice and to feel secure in the physical nearness of others. However, even in a small-group setting, it may be necessary to have one or more self-confident children included in order to keep the conversation rolling and to foster the participation of the other children.

Telephoning

Some teachers say that so many children begin using the telephone prior to their coming to school that instruction and guidance in telephoning skills and courtesies are not necessary. To some extent this may be true; however, we think some teaching and reviewing are worthwhile. Certainly telephoning is an activity that provides its own motivation and opens the door for numerous language arts activities. If possible, actual situations involving the use of the telephone that arise either at school or at home should be used. Such situations might include telephoning the mother of a child who is ill to give information about assignments or class activities, phoning to make arrangements for an interview, using the telephone to ask someone to come and speak to the class, or calling to inquire about suitable dates for a trip to a museum or another place of interest.

Having a unit on using the telephone is sometimes a good idea since it will stimulate interest and provide the opportunity for direct attention to telephoning skills and courtesies. Telephone companies often have kits that may be borrowed for this teaching. Such kits may include materials about using telephones as well as telephone hookups for the classroom. Due to the increasing ability to buy telephones relatively inexpensively, as well as the science interests of a good many children in the upper grades, it is even possible that a school may have its own equipment for such a unit.

Discussion

Many of the problems that arise in the daily activities of the classroom lead to discussions among the pupils. With guidance, these discussions can lead to the development of skill in critical thinking, reasoning, problem solving, and expressing ideas orally in a rational and organized manner. Through discussion children gain information, learn to stick to the point of the topic being discussed, and develop the ability to express themselves effectively.

Discussion differs from conversation in that it ordinarily has a topic that was at least somewhat agreed upon and a more purposeful goal, but it is

Tips on Telephoning

1. Formulate messages, orders, and other detailed information as concisely as possible before starting to call.
2. Identify yourself to the person being talked to clearly and courteously when making or receiving a call.
3. Explain clearly and courteously the purpose of a call.
4. Speak as courteously as in a face-to-face conversation.
5. Allow the person who made the call to close the conversation.
6. Ask permission to use another person's telephone.
7. Place calls at times convenient to the persons called.
8. Avoid monopolizing a party line or the telephone in your home.

How We Discuss a Topic

1. Everyone thinks before speaking.
2. Only one person talks at a time.
3. Everyone listens carefully.
4. Everyone is given a chance to talk.
5. We keep to the subject.
6. We are polite.

similar to conversation in the need to take turns, to be courteous, to avoid repetition, and to speak so that all can hear. Discussion is not the same as arguing, although some arguments may occur as a discussion progresses. Arguments, however, arise from an attempt to defend a point of view, whereas a discussion seeks to arrive at an answer or a solution to a problem.

Discussions need not involve the entire class. Round-table and panel discussions are good activities and call for a limited number of participants especially to prepare and to agree about rules for the discussion (e.g., order of speaking, amount of time each one has to speak, etc.). A tape recorder is useful to participants in round-table and panel discussions since it gives them the opportunity to judge their speaking skills and the content of what they have said as a basis for planning future similar activities. In addition to the more or less formalized panel discussions, having a small group of children discuss a topic is often very useful and can be tied to having one or more of the group report to the entire class on the discussion and the conclusions reached.

In teaching skills for any discussion format, attention should be given to helping the children discover what needs discussing and to defining the subject accurately so that irrelevant talking can be avoided. However, the children also need to learn the importance of and reasons for various viewpoints. And they need to learn how to agree on rules or limitations to the discussion (such as the number of times an individual may speak and how a conclusion will be reached).

Reports

The giving of oral reports is an extension of the "Show and Tell" activity of the primary grades and should have many of the same characteristics. That is, the content of the reports should be organized and be limited in scope rather than being rambling accounts, but many should be given because the children want to give them. Children beyond the primary grades will volunteer to show something or to tell about personal interests and events. This volunteering, if encouraged, can lead to effective reporting on social studies and other content area topics, even if these report topics are assigned.

Good reports don't just happen—they need to be motivated and planned. A good report must communicate something to an audience that is important to them. Thus, children will need to develop the ability to select material appropriate to the topic and to the audience, the ability to collect and organize material (this will require skill in reading critically, taking notes, summarizing, and outlining), and the ability to face the group and give the oral report with accuracy, interest, and avoidance of "ah—hmm—well a— you know" and the like. They also need to recognize that a report can often be made more meaningful to the audience if they use a map, diagram, chart, or flannel board with words or pictures relevant to the content of their report.

If topics are assigned to children, there should be some choice so that each child can select one that interests him or her. Children should not have to give reports, however, if they need to develop more security in speaking

Oral reporting can be fun.

through some other situation first. Instruction is generally needed in location of information, preparation of notes, and the avoidance of plagiarism. Children will also need help in judging the amount of time available for the report, developing good beginnings and endings, and selecting visual aids.

A bulletin board with steps for children to follow in preparing reports may be useful. Here is one example:

STEPS IN PREPARING A REPORT

6. Develop good opening and closing sentences.

5. Think: Is this report too long? Should it be cut?

4. Choose interesting vocabulary and illustrations.

3. Review your notes and outline the report.

2. Check the encyclopedia and other references—take notes to answer your questions.

1. What questions might be asked about this topic? List them.

Decide what opportunities there are for genuine and useful reporting. Here are some suggestions:

1. Topics related to social studies or science are suitable. See the end of each chapter in textbooks or in teacher's editions.

2. Reports may be an extension of reading. Perhaps the class has read a story about a Scottish family and the children want to know more about Scotland. The more able readers could be asked to give reports on Scotland to the class after they have consulted additional resources.

3. New plans or rules of the school can be determined and reported upon.

4. Extensions of current events topics may be the subjects of reports. For example, events as they are discussed in different newspapers would furnish excellent topics for reports during a study of propaganda techniques—detecting bias in a writer's viewpoint, the use of "loaded" words, etc.

5. Other opportunities for group or individual reports include interviews, trips to places of interest, and reviews of movies, books, or television programs.

When the children give their reports, you should be a model listener in the audience. But you should mentally note, and perhaps jot down, individual weaknesses in usage, organization of the material, eye contact with the group, voice control, and the like. The weaknesses you note, as well as strengths, can later be recorded on a checklist or put into a file of notes you are keeping on individual children or on various types of speaking situations. A tape recorder may be useful to you and to the children. However, until children become accustomed to being recorded, you will want to use this sparingly. On the other hand, children are sometimes "given a boost" if listening to the recording causes them to believe they gave a better report than they had thought.

Children should be encouraged to set up criteria and to evaluate their individual reports. There is some danger that children will tend to set their standards too high, so you will want to participate too. Group evaluation of a talk should be carefully guided; children are sometimes cruel to one another. However, if your criticism is helpful and constructive, the children are likely to follow suit.

Giving a Report

Was my topic interesting?
Did I have a good beginning?
Did I have the attention of my audience?
Did I speak clearly?
Was my report well organized?
Did I have a good ending?

Announcements and Directions

Giving announcements has become a part of school life, and many schools have regular opening announcements that come over a speaker system. A few schools allow children to make some of these announcements, as well as some of their own. In addition, there are many opportunities in classrooms for children to make announcements. Outside school, children may make announcements at Scout meetings, club meetings, and parties.

Announcements should be given in a clear, brief, and friendly manner. The announcement usually has "who, what, when, where, and how" qualities. Standards for announcements should be developed by the class in consideration of these qualities and manner of presentation. The standards can then be used as the basis for instruction and as a guide for the preparation and delivery of announcements that members of the class make.

Children also have many opportunities to give and follow directions during a school day. They may give directions for playing a game, participating in a scavenger hunt, performing a science experiment, or getting to their homes. Standards for giving directions should also be established by the class as a group; they should stress accuracy and sequence, as well as delivery.

The skills and abilities necessary for making announcements and for giving directions are similar to those needed in most oral language situations. The language used must be organized and presented in terms that will be understood by the audience. Acceptable language should be used, but greatest attention should be upon the conciseness and clarity of the message and its appropriateness for the particular audience.

Interviews

For teaching outlining and note taking along with interviewing, see Chapter 13.

An interview is a good method of securing information and provides the interviewer with the opportunity to use speaking skills, organize his or her thinking, and develop listening ability.

Many situations occur that give children the opportunity to conduct interviews. Intermediate grade children studying a foreign country may wish to talk with someone who has lived in or visited that country. The children themselves may know of such a person, possibly a parent, a friend, or even a child in another class. If not and if you are new to the community, you may have difficulty in locating interviewees. Try one or all of the following:

1. Talk with other teachers or the principal, who may know someone who has spent time in that country.
2. Contact the local Chamber of Commerce office or a senior citizens' group to obtain a speakers' bureau list.
3. Send letters to parents with a list of countries the class will be studying during the year and invite any of them who have knowledge of a country to talk with the group.

For interviewing favorite authors, contact Dial-an-Author, School and College Department, Bantam Books.

Interviewing parents and other adults about their occupations or hobbies will also enrich the curriculum. In planning for these interviews, emphasize their importance to the community, their uniqueness, or their relation to subjects being studied. It is amazing how unaware both children and adults are of services that are provided in communities. For instance, when children drop money into a juke box or soft-drink machine, do they think about how the machine got there or who keeps it running? Have they ever thought that someone earns a living this way?

What is necessary for an interview experience? First, preplan by listing questions that the class or individual would like answered. Develop enough knowledge of the topic that sensible questions can be asked. This often means that the children may need to do some library research. Above all, it is important that an interview have some purpose other than simply giving the child experience in interviewing.

Some people will be able to come to school for an interview, but others will not, and plans will need to include arrangements for these interviews.

Information from Interviews

Books, newspapers, and magazines are not the only sources of information that you can use for a report. People are also sources. Perhaps you know someone who has a good knowledge of the subject on which you wish to report. If so, you may wish to interview this person.

There are three steps to holding an interview: making an appointment, preparing questions in advance, and taking notes.

Making an Appointment

Kathie had long been interested in becoming a doctor. She decided to write a report on "A Career in Medicine." She knew that the woman who lived next door, Dr. Robinson, would be a good person to interview.

Kathie asked Dr. Robinson for an appointment on Saturday morning. She told her why she was asking for an interview and what the topic of the interview would be. She mentioned one or two questions she would ask and said she would like to stay about fifteen minutes.

Preparing Questions in Advance

Before the interview, Kathie wrote in a notebook all the questions she wanted to ask, with space left for the answers. Here is her list of questions:

1. Are there any special subjects that help prepare you for medical school?
2. How many years must you attend medical school?
3. What is an "intern"?
4. What is a "resident"?
5. Can a medical doctor have a career in medicine besides private practice? If so, what are some examples?

Now Kathie was ready for Saturday's interview.

127

Proper planning and preparation are necessary if language activities are to be meaningful.

From LANGUAGE FOR DAILY USE, Explorer Edition, Level Purple, by Mildred A. Dawson et al., © 1978 by Harcourt Brace Jovanovich, Inc. Reprinted by permission of the publisher.

In addition, plans should include ways the information gained may best be utilized. Children may want to use a cassette recorder for an interview if one is available. They should know, however, that if an interview is to be recorded, permission should be obtained from the person being interviewed. Nonprofessional speakers are sometimes frightened by the thought of having their words recorded.

Standards that could be developed for interviewing include the following:

1. Introduce yourself and state the purpose of the interview.
2. Avoid sentences like "The teacher says we have to ask you about _____."

3. Remember that the interviewer should open and close the interview.

4. Have the questions to be asked firmly in mind or on paper so that you stick to the topic.

5. If it seems advisable, give the person to be interviewed a list of the questions to be asked. This can be done when the appointment is made, thus giving the person time to consider his or her answers.

6. Discover appropriate times for an interview appointment.

7. Give the person being interviewed some idea of the amount of time the interview is to last.

8. Take notes during the interview (see Chapter 16).

9. Find a way to end the interview other than "Well, our time is up so we have to quit."

10. Always be courteous, listen carefully, and express appreciation for the information.

Debate

Debating is ordinarily considered a secondary school or college speech activity. However, some children in the upper grades of the elementary school can be attracted to the idea of a "formalized" argument. If there are children in a class who are so attracted, and if they are mature enough, the research that goes into preparing the arguments is good practice for using reference skills and doing logical thinking.

Debating calls for two children to present one side of the debate topic and two children to present the other. Each speaker makes a presentation and a rebuttal, with a time limit set for each turn at speaking.

An entire class can become involved in a debate through the listening they must do in order to judge which team won. How to judge a debate usually should be a discussion topic for the class, with the discussion leading to standards for judging.

Meetings

Intermediate grade children are of the "let's form a club" age. When this interest is expressed, it is time to teach parliamentary procedure. The name and type of club as well as the desire for it should come from the children. It is possible, for example, to have science, book, and class clubs all at the same time with different members and officers. A fair amount of guidance will be needed, since children sometimes become quite cliquish within clubs and may hurt others' feelings.

Interest in forming a club does not automatically mean interest in parliamentary procedure. Prior to starting one, you may need to initiate a discussion of the importance of learning how to operate a club effectively. The children need to be taught the purpose of rules for conducting a meeting as

**Basic Elements of
Parliamentary Procedure**

1. The chair calls the meeting to order.
2. The chair asks for minutes of the last meeting to be read; the secretary does so.
3. The chair asks for additions or corrections to the minutes.
4. The minutes are approved. Strictly speaking, this is done by vote, but in most cases the chair simply says, "If there are no objections, the minutes stand approved as read" (or corrected). Any objection, of course, requires a vote.
5. The treasurer's report is asked for, given, and acted upon as above, except that the chair usually asks if there are questions concerning the report.
6. Committee reports are asked for, presented, and discussed as needed. No motions are made at this point.
7. The chair asks for old business. If there is any, proper motions are made, discussed, and voted on.
8. The chair asks for new business. New business is discussed; motions are made, discussed, and voted on; any necessary committees are appointed.
9. The chair asks if there is further business to come before the group.
10. If there is none, the chair asks for a motion to adjourn. This is voted on, and the meeting is adjourned.

well as the rules to be followed. Although rules should not be too detailed or formalized for beginning groups, a chart of the rules agreed on could be posted and referred to during meetings.

As the children become more experienced with clubs and their meetings, they will need to develop some understanding of parliamentary procedure and its vocabulary. What is a *motion*? How do you make a motion? What does it mean to *amend* a motion? What do we mean when we say that only one person may *have the floor* at a time? What are the possible omissions, additions, or corrections that are asked about following a secretary's or treasurer's report?

The following is a guide to making motions and voting upon them that may be useful.

1. The individual who wishes to make a motion stands and says, "Mister (or Madam) Chair."
2. The chair replies, "The Chair recognizes Tommy Blank."
3. Tommy then says, "I move that we be permitted to have a morning and afternoon snack in our room." (Note that correct wording is "I move," *not* "I make a motion that . . .")
4. Another child says, "I second that motion." (Remember that a motion must be seconded before it can be voted upon.)
5. The chair then says, "It has been moved and seconded that we be permitted to have morning and afternoon snacks in our room. Is there any discussion?"
6. After discussion the chair may need to repeat the motion. The chair then calls for a vote by saying, "All in favor say 'Aye.' Those opposed say 'No.'" (If there is doubt about the outcome of a voice vote, a member may say, "I call for a show of hands.")
7. The chair announces, "The motion has been carried" (or defeated). Once a motion has been voted upon, there need be no further discussion of it in the meeting.
8. Members of the club need to keep in mind that only one motion may be on the floor at a time and that a motion must be voted upon before a second motion may be made.

The above is a simplified list, but is should be quite adequate for the needs of most groups of either children or adults. If several children—or the entire class—become particularly interested in studying the fine points of parliamentary procedure, obtain a copy of *Robert's Rules of Order*.

Parliamentary procedure should *only* be taught when children have the desire and need for this procedure. If the children are not interested in clubs, or only in quite informal ones, it is not necessary to teach these procedures. However, some form of organization is important in even an informal group activity.

In addition to learning how to conduct and participate in club meetings, the children should also learn that meetings will be more orderly and fewer arguments will arise if a simple set of bylaws or standing rules is agreed upon. These might include such items as the number of officers, the length of their terms of office, whether they can succeed themselves, the time and place of meetings, the amount of dues (if any), etc.

Storytelling

Storytelling, particularly by teachers, was discussed briefly in the preceding chapter and receives further attention in Chapter 15, but as was suggested in the earlier chapter, children can and should begin telling stories when they are in the primary grades. It is an activity they enjoy, both as tellers and as listeners, so it should be engaged in not only then but as they continue in school.

Children's storytelling usually begins with their recounting of personal experiences, since storytelling is essentially an act of sharing. These first stories may be laced with both reality and fantasy, reflecting their actual experience as well as things they have heard about or seen on TV. But they do show a recognition that stories have a framework—although a teller's eagerness sometimes disguises this. Sketchy as such a framework may be, however, it does show that the element of organization has begun to enter into children's thinking—an element vital to all communication, both oral and written.

Storytelling is natural for children if informality is maintained.

These first experiences in sharing may be followed by encouraging the children to tell stories they've heard and liked and, later, ones they've read. In the telling of these, story beginnings and endings are used, characters and settings appear, and story lines are followed—again, aspects of composition. However, as important as this foundational element is, the major reason for encouraging children to tell stories should be the joy they will gain from both listening to a good story and being able to tell one—a joy that may be experienced throughout life.

Storytelling is more informal than most other forms of expression, but the speech skills needed are those required for all speaking activities. Listening to and watching an adult who is a good storyteller will help children to see the advantages of utilizing voice tone, gestures, and facial expressions. But experience is still the best teacher—children must practice the skills for oral interpretation and the techniques for holding an audience.

Jokes and Riddles

When children are about eight, they develop a real interest in telling jokes and riddles that may last for years. This interest can be utilized to develop oral language skills. Begin by having joke and riddle books on the library table and occasionally reading a joke or a riddle to the class.

Using jokes and riddles is often good for a time when you and the children are experiencing a letdown. One way to overcome such doldrums is to cover a bulletin board with black paper, cut out white stars, and use a red marking pen to write a riddle on each star. Use another star for the back, since the marking usually goes through the paper. This second star, which has the answer printed on it, should be fastened to the one with the question. The bulletin board title could be "The Answer Is in the Stars" or "The Stars Know—Do You?"

After the bulletin board has been made and used, the children have listened as you read jokes and riddles, and they have looked at the joke and riddle books on the library table, they should be sufficiently motivated to want to tell jokes themselves.

A class discussion is in order to establish rules for telling jokes and the types of jokes to tell. The discussion may be used to bring out the point that jokes should never hurt another person's feelings or make fun of someone in any way. Children may want to tell jokes about nationalities, races, or religions because they have heard their parents or friends tell them and know that people have laughed. A child may say, "My dad tells jokes about _____ all the time." There is no good answer to this; certainly jokes about nationality, race, and religion are reappearing—and perhaps this is a sign that prejudices are beginning to disappear! Perhaps you might say that adults sometimes see things differently (children should certainly agree with that), and suggest that you might laugh at a joke about teachers when told by another teacher, but be very hurt if it was told by one of the children in the class. In short, avoid even implied criticism of a child's family or friends, but reemphasize that a joke should not hurt another's feelings. If interest is present and the class sufficiently mature, you might even go into

Books Children Will Enjoy

Jest in Pun by Bil Keane (Scholastic, 1969)
Nailheads and Potato Eyes by Cynthia Basil (Morrow, 1976)
Noah Riddle? by Ann Bishop (Whitman, 1970)
What If . . . ? by Joseph Low (McElderry Book, Atheneum, 1976)

the changes that have taken place in comedy: the disappearance of the blackface comedian, the shiftless Negro servant, the Irish cop, etc.

From the class discussion, lead the children to set up rules for telling jokes. The following are good:

1. Tell the joke to the teacher first to be certain that it is good joke for the class.
2. Look at the audience when telling a joke.
3. Know the order in which events happen in the joke so you don't have to say, "No, wait a minute; I forget; let's see—ah—then he went . . ."
4. Don't laugh at your own joke until it is over.
5. Remember the punch line. Use your voice to lead up to the punch line, and then deliver it quickly.

A good way to begin is to let the children take turns telling jokes or asking riddles as a part of the daily opening exercises. Later, extend the class time for telling jokes and riddles to an assembly program. For such a program each child in the room might dress as a clown or wear another costume of his or her choice. The entire program could consist of jokes, riddles, funny songs, and funny dances. Many or all of the children in the class should know all of the jokes so that if one child is ill there is not a crisis—his or her spot can be filled.

Watching a comedian on television can help children learn about such things as expression, timing, and mannerisms when telling a joke. Children can *report* to the class what they have learned about telling jokes from watching a particular individual. Work on listening skills at the same time by asking each child to remember one joke a comedian told and to tell it to the class.

The telling of jokes and riddles is a good way to develop many oral language skills. It is especially useful with a class that has negative ideas toward school and learning, since it will develop interest and may cause them to decide that school can be fun. Reading is also taught, as children turn to books for jokes and riddles. For a child to remember a joke it is essential that he or she comprehend and remember what was read and understand the sequence of events. Even children with negative attitudes toward reading will generally read a book of riddles or jokes.

The telling of jokes and riddles can also be related to daily handwriting lessons through having the children work on their handwriting problems by copying riddles from the board or writing their own. These handwriting papers can be collected and later made into a riddle book. Saving answers to the riddles until the end of the day will promote class conversation as children try to guess answers.

More Joke Books

A Frog Sandwich: Riddles and Jokes by Marci Ridlon (Follett, 1973)

Monster Jokes and Riddles by Norman Birdwell (Scholastic, 1972)

Witcrackers—Jokes and Jests from American Folklore by Alvin Schwartz (Lippincott, 1972)

Choral Speaking

Choral speaking is a most enjoyable way to interpret literature orally. Experience with choral reading helps children learn to sense mood development, to understand the role of rhythm in speaking, and to realize the importance of volume, tone, and quality of voice. Fluency, clarity of enunciation, and speaking with expression are improved through choral speaking.

Choral speaking requires interpretation as well as knowing very well the selection to be spoken. Sometimes a poem or verse may be memorized; other times it may be read. In either case, the children will need to read the selection several times and discuss the meanings of phrases as well as the entire piece. Speaking will need to be tried, varying the pace, rhythm, emphasis, and tone in order to decide how the piece may be most effectively spoken, but this should not be overdone or children will tire of it. Trying out can be fun, though, and even disagreements about meanings and aspects of the reading can add zest to the activity.

Choral speaking also has value in helping children speak in other situations. Children who are too shy to speak tend to lose their shyness when they are just members of the group in choral speaking. Children who never seem to close their mouths learn to discipline themselves when they become a part of the group. Children who hate to read may develop more positive attitudes toward reading while engaged in this activity. As with everything else in the classroom, your enthusiasm will be the factor determining whether or not children enjoy choral speaking and profit from it.

Several types of choral speaking are described below. You will likely need to try different types with the children you are teaching before deciding what works best and what they like. You may also want to experiment and perhaps modify the suggestions given.

REFRAIN. A selection such as "Poor Old Woman" appeals to children, for this is a form of choral speaking in which a soloist reads the narrative and the others join the refrain. When introducing this poem to the class, you can make it more appealing by showing pictures of each bug or animal as it is mentioned. These pictures can make a delightful bulletin board and certainly sharpen imagery and highlight meanings.

Give each class member a copy of the selection. Ask the class to follow with their eyes while listening to your reading of the selection, paying particular attention to the expression. Read it again with the children joining in on the refrain.

POOR OLD WOMAN

Sometimes holding up a "prop" (picture of cow, fly, etc.) helps shy children.

SOLO:	There was an old woman who swallowed a fly.
ALL (*dramatically*):	Oh, my! Swallowed a fly!
(*slowly*)	Poor old woman, I think she'll die.
SOLO:	There was an old woman who swallowed a spider.
(*slowly*)	Right down inside her, she swallowed a spider. She swallowed the spider to kill the fly.
ALL (*dramatically*):	Oh, my! Swallowed a fly!
(*slowly*)	Poor old woman, I think she'll die.
SOLO:	There was an old woman who swallowed a bird.
(*said in an aside*)	How absurd to swallow a bird!

(more quickly)	She swallowed the bird to kill the spider, She swallowed the spider to kill the fly.
ALL *(dramatically):* *(slowly)*	Oh, my! Swallowed a fly! Poor old woman, I think she'll die.
SOLO: *(slowly and deliberately)*	There was an old woman who swallowed a cat. Fancy that! Swallowed a cat!
ALL:	She swallowed the cat to kill the bird, She swallowed the bird to kill the spider, She swallowed the spider to kill the fly. Oh, my! Swallowed a fly! Poor old woman, I think she'll die.
SOLO: *(as if telling a secret)*	There was an old woman who swallowed a dog. She went the whole hog! She swallowed a dog!
ALL:	She swallowed the dog to kill the cat, She swallowed the cat to kill the bird, She swallowed the bird to kill the spider, She swallowed the spider to kill the fly. Oh, my! Swallowed a fly! Poor old woman, I think she'll die.
SOLO: *(slowly and carefully)*	There was an old woman who swallowed a cow. I don't know how, but she swallowed a cow.
ALL: *(with increasing momentum)* *(slowly and deliberately)*	She swallowed the cow to kill the dog, She swallowed the dog to kill the cat, She swallowed the cat to kill the bird, She swallowed the bird to kill the spider, She swallowed the spider to kill the fly. Oh, my! Swallowed a fly! Poor old woman, I think she'll die.
SOLO:	There was an old woman who swallowed a horse.
ALL:	She died, of course.

ANTIPHONAL. Antiphonal choral speaking contrasts light voices with heavier ones. For example, boys may read questions and girls answers, or poems containing dialogue may be used. Poems of contrast are also excellent, with heavier voices taking parts that contain long vowels. Middle and upper grade children do well with this type of choral reading.

Use the tape recorder so children may hear themselves.

Give the children copies of the selection and have them follow as you read aloud to give the pattern for the children to imitate. Have several children try parts of the selection until class agreement is reached on voice quality, inflection, and timing. One good selection is Christina Rossetti's "Who Has Seen the Wind?":

HEAVY VOICES: Who has seen the wind?

LIGHT VOICES: Neither I nor you:

HEAVY VOICES:	But when the leaves hang trembling The wind is passing thro'.
LIGHT VOICES:	Who has seen the wind?
HEAVY VOICES:	Neither you nor I:
LIGHT VOICES:	But when the trees bow down their heads The wind is passing by.

Of course, this poem could also be done with one group asking the question in each stanza and the other responding, but the above division is a bit more unusual and gives each group an opportunity for creativity in reading the lines.

Other poems that can be used in this way include "Baa, Baa, Black Sheep" (Mother Goose), "Little Boy Blue" (Mother Goose), "Night" (Sara Teasdale), "It Is Raining" (Lucy Sprague Mitchell), "The Little Elf" (John Kendrick Bangs), "Father William" (Lewis Carroll), and "What Is Pink?" (Christina Rossetti).

LINE-A-CHILD. In the line-a-child choric form a single child or small groups of two to four children speak a line or couplet. The selection is continued by another child or group, then another, and so on until the end. It is necessary that the selection have lines or couplets that are naturally separated from one another—possibly marked off by semicolons or periods.

A bulletin board display or individual pictures may serve as an introduction to the selection. Each child should have a copy of the poem, and you should point out where each line or couplet ends. (*Note:* combine this oral language activity with a written language lesson on thought units and punctuation.) Read the selection with the children listening to get the feeling of the poem and to determine which words or expressions need emphasis. Discuss these and then place the individuals or groups according to the order in which they speak so that they can remember their turns. Speaking on cue is essential for the continuity of the poem.

Good poems to try include "Jump or Jiggle" (Evelyn Beyer), "The Little Turtle" (Vachel Lindsay), "The Barnyard" (Maude Burham), "My Zipper Suit" (Mary Louise Allen), "The End" (A. A. Milne), "Only One Mother" (George Cooper), "Merry-Go-Round" (Dorothy W. Baruch), "Mice" (Rose Fyleman), "Someone" (Walter de la Mare), "The Wind" (Robert Louis Stevenson), "Spring Rain" (Marchette Chute), "Very Lovely" (Rose Fyleman).

UNISON. Teachers are often surprised to discover that unison speaking is the most difficult of all choral work. Lower elementary children have great difficulty in coordinating their voices, and this precision is essential for quality unison speaking. This form also requires the greatest skill by the director. If you wish to see whether young children can do unison speaking, try Mother Goose rhymes, as they are easily interpreted and can serve as a beginning for pantomime and dramatics.

Try these:

"There Was a Crooked
  Man" (Mother Goose)
"Galoshes" (Rhoda W.
  Bacmeister)
"Silver" (Walter de la
  Mare)
"Snow" (Dorothy Aldis)
"The Sun" (John
  Drinkwater)
"Someone" (Walter de la
  Mare)
"The Monkeys and the
  Crocodile" (Laura E.
  Richards)
"Witch Ways" (Ethel
  Jacobson)

A wealth of poems are suitable for unison speaking in the intermediate and upper grades. One example is "The Purple Cow" by Gelett Burgess:

> I never saw a purple cow,
> I never hope to see one;
> But I can tell you anyhow,
> I'd rather see than be one!

Choral reading or speaking has advantages as an assembly presentation. First, all the children in the class become involved and are on stage. Second, all children will learn the selection; then if the child selected as soloist comes down with measles on the day of the production, others know the part. Those who have been involved with the trauma of having a sick child on the day of a program will appreciate this advantage of choral speaking.

Creative Dramatics

Creative dramatics in the elementary school as discussed here is essentially a continuation of the activities and suggestions made in Chapter 5 about creative play and dramatization of stories and rhymes. The emphasis should still be upon informality and creativity, with no more attention to scenery, props, costumes, or memorization of lines than is natural for the children to be concerned about. Certainly dramatics in the elementary school should seldom, if ever, reach the production level of high school presentations. Formal "play production" is time-consuming, may be traumatizing to children, and hinders rather than fosters creativity.

The essence of creative dramatics is improvisation; children are inspired to use imagination in choosing words and actions that will convey the desired impression. They can experiment with tone, rate of speaking, use of gestures, and even bodily stance as they try to create a believable mood or character. All of these require creative thinking.

Dramatize moods, such as happiness, sorrow, pain, excitement, etc.

In addition, the use of creative dramatics promotes both personal and social growth. Children release energy and express emotions as they respond to music or some other stimulus and as they create characters and scenes. A shy child can gain confidence through pretending to be someone else, as well as through working in a group. The aggressive child learns to work as a part of a group, and all children learn how important cooperation and planning are to achieving a desired outcome. And, finally, children gain a better understanding of themselves and others as they "become" other people and discover the commonality of human emotions.

Children may also react to personal problems they are experiencing or have heard or read about, or plan how they will behave in particular situations (e.g., conducting an interview, going on a field trip) through *role playing*, a form of creative dramatics. This has the value of possibly clarifying issues, solving problems, and indirectly teaching skills and behavior.

If the children have not had a background of experience in dramatic play and other oral activities, it would probably be best to start at the beginning of the year with activities similar to those used in the primary grades:

rhythmic response to music, pantomime, and re-creation of incidents from literature. Dramatizing an incident such as Charlie's visit to the chocolate factory or Tom Sawyer conning his friends into whitewashing the fence is not difficult, yet it presents an opportunity for creativity. From there you might graduate to using a different ending to a story or to creating another incident involving the same characters (e.g., "What do you think might have happened if Tom's friends had decided to turn the tables on him?").

Creative dramatics can add understanding and depth to almost any area of the curriculum. A child who has helped to create a rhythmic dance based on a mathematical concept (e.g., a square, subtraction, etc.) will not find arithmetic dull. Similarly, dramatizing a day spent traveling across Kansas in a covered wagon will give students a deeper understanding of the hardships of the westward expansion.

All the skills required for any oral activity can be developed through creative dramatics. Like any other activity, it should not be overdone, but it should be an integral part of your language arts program.

Suggestions in Chapter 9 for stimulating writing are adaptable to creative dramatics.

Puppetry

Puppets and marionettes can be useful tools for teaching oral expression. Besides, they are fun! Puppets are more helpful than marionettes, unless a teacher is experienced with marionettes. A marionette is usually operated from above by strings, which often isn't easy for children to do, whereas a puppet is operated by hand from below. Interest in puppets may first be

Making puppets helps children learn to follow directions.

Puppets, creativity, and talk!

developed when a child brings a hand puppet for "Show and Tell." Children may wish to use this puppet to recite a favorite Mother Goose rhyme. Talking for a puppet instead of one's self tends to bring out a shy child rather easily. Once interest has been generated, you will want to encourage each child to make his or her own puppet. Making puppets and putting on a play is an excellent way to teach children to follow directions and to strengthen language skills. And the children will have a delightful time while they are learning.

Puppet Books

Creative Puppetry in the Classroom by Mary Fredericks and Joyce Segal (New Plays Books)

Easy-to-Make Puppets by Frieda Gated (Harvey House)

Easy-to-Make Puppets by Joyce Luckin (Plays, Inc.)

Wooden Spoon Puppets by Audrey Dean (Plays, Inc.)

When making puppets, start with simple ones such as cutout stick puppets, empty-bag puppets, or vegetable and fruit puppets.

CUTOUT STICK PUPPETS. To make stick puppets, figures or faces may be drawn, colored, and cut from cardboard, or paper dolls may be used. Coloring books often have outlines of figures or faces that can be pasted on cardboard. Tongue depressors or ice cream sticks can be glued to the bottoms for the children to hold. If a puppet needs support up the back, a longer stick will be needed—one long enough so that the hand holding it will not show if the puppet is used in a puppet stage. Stick puppets can be clothed with either cloth or paper. Old wallpaper, leftover gift wrap from Christmas, or even colorful shelf paper can be useful for making attractive paper clothes, and remnants or scraps from mothers' sewing bags can provide materials for cloth garments.

EMPTY-BAG PUPPETS. Children can make and use empty-bag puppets if the bags are not too large for them to handle. Place the bag flat, with the folded bottom part up. Draw or paint the upper part of a face on the bottom of the bag, and the lower part of the face on the side. If you want the puppet to have a moving mouth, the upper part of the mouth should be on the bag bottom, and the lower lip on the side. If the eyes are to move, the lashes

Styroform Stick Puppet

Paper Bag Puppet

should be on the bottom, with the lower part of the eyes on the side. The puppet is operated by placing fingers in the bag so that the folded-down bottom can be moved up and down to show a mouth moving (or eyes, eyelashes, or eyebrows). Yarn, crepe paper, or cotton can be glued on for hair.

VEGETABLE AND FRUIT PUPPETS. Potatoes, carrots, beets, radishes, apples, and oranges are a few of the vegetables and fruits that can be mounted on sticks and used as other stick puppets are used. Faces can be made in a variety of ways: they can be cut out with a vegetable peeler, drawn on with paint or a felt-tip pen, or made from paper or felt and pasted on. Or thumb tacks or paper stars may be used for eyes, with other features added in one of the above ways.

MORE ADVANCED PUPPETS. At a little more advanced level are *sock puppets*. These are simply socks with buttons sewed on for eyes and with crayons or paint used to make other features. The *stuffed-bag puppet* is an extension of the empty-bag puppet. The bag is filled about halfway with crumpled paper. (This simply fills out the bag, which is used in about the same way as described above.) If the bag is large, it can be partly drawn together with a string to represent a neck and shoulders below the face. Usually stuffed-bag puppets are decorated or dressed more than the simpler puppets.

THE STAGE. You will need some kind of stage to use puppets for dramatization. Of course, hand puppets are good for storytelling, getting children's attention, and just talking, but to get full value from the puppets children make, dramatization is needed.

The stage should be inexpensive and easy to make. Tip a card table on its side; the children can sit behind it and raise puppets above the table edge. A large box or carton—the kind refrigerators or stoves are shipped in—also works well. Part of a side is cut out and the part visible to the audience is painted. The children sit inside and raise their hand puppets to the "stage floor" level.

THE STORY. Almost any situation can be dramatized with puppets. Here are some ideas:

1. Accepting responsibility for tasks at home and at school, such as cleanliness of a room or completion of a task. Let the children plan their own dialogue for this.
2. Good sportsmanship on or off the playground.
3. Correct behavior in social situations.
4. Stories from literature. Try these:

   Amiable Giant (Louis Slobodkin)
   The Three Bears
   Andy and the Lion (James Daugherty)
   Hansel and Gretel
   Snipp, Snapp, Snurr (Maj Lindman)
   Pet Show (Ezra Jack Keats)

SPECIAL CONSIDERATIONS IN TEACHING

The sections that follow emphasize special concerns in teaching oral communication. These are important to oral situations and should receive attention in many teaching activities.

Social Amenities

Social amenities are best taught when the situation demands their practice. Many teachers undoubtedly would like to think that these are taught in the home, but most of us know that often they are not.

The atmosphere in your classroom and your attitude toward teaching and toward each child are of prime importance in teaching social behavior. Since nearly every classroom has at least one child who is disliked by the other children, or perhaps several children who come to school so dirty that you may hesitate to touch their papers (to say nothing of their bodies), the need for teaching social amenities is readily apparent. The basis for such teaching is acceptance and mutual respect among all concerned—you and each child.

If you are having difficulty getting children to accept a particular child, talk with the librarian about a bibliotherapeutic book that may help bridge the gap. These books are designed to improve children's attitudes toward themselves or toward adjusting to a difficult situation. Reading a book about such a situation to the class may help the children to develop understanding and acceptance. Hopefully, the children will follow your lead and become pleasant and accepting of each other. Social amenities that children particularly need to learn are making introductions and extending and responding to greetings. Children need to learn the conventions followed in these amenities, and this is best done through the many genuine occasions that arise in every classroom. For example, visitors who come into the room may be greeted by a room host or hostess, who introduces them to the teacher and the other children. Good practice can also occur during an open house, parents' night, or similar occasion. In addition, there are many situations in which these amenities can be taught through dramatization.

In making introductions children should learn to say, "Mrs. Smith, this is Sue," or "Mary, I'd like you to meet Jimmy." The first name mentioned should be the person honored—an older person, a woman, or a special guest.

Children should also learn how to respond: "I'm very glad to meet you, Sue" or "How do you do." Encourage them to shake hands firmly (but not too firmly) and to look at the person they are being introduced to.

Rules that are helpful include these:

1. Speak each person's name clearly (if a name is not understood, ask that it be repeated).
2. Use an introduction to start a conversation, with the person making the introduction beginning the conversation.
3. When introducing yourself to another, be certain to give your name clearly and add some identifying remark.

Situations That May Be Dramatized

introducing a mother or father to a school friend
introducing one friend to another
a parent introducing his or her child to a friend or guest
introducing oneself to a stranger
introducing a visitor to the class

4. Speak the name of a person you are introduced to and use it when speaking to him or her to help remember it.

Discuss with children the awkwardness of a situation in which two people are talking and are joined by a third person, known to one of the first

---

Making Introductions

Have you ever had to introduce two strangers to each other? If so, did you have any trouble deciding how to do it?

Read what Manuel says.

1. "Dad, this is Alan Johnson. Alan plays on my team. Alan, this is my dad, Mr. Ruiz."
2. "Jill, this is my neighbor Tim Thomas. Tim, this is my friend, Jill Levine. She just came home from a camping trip."
3. "Ms. McCarthy, my name is Manuel Ruiz. My sister Amy won't be able to come to tumbling practice today. She has the flu."

To Discuss

1. When Manuel introduced a younger person to an older person, which name did he say first?
2. Why did he tell Tim that Jill had gone camping? What would you say to Jill if you were Tim?
3. Could Manuel have given Ms. McCarthy the message without telling her his name? Why do you think he introduced himself?

Practice

1. Select two classmates. Decide on a situation like one of those above. Practice introducing them the correct way. Check the rules before you begin.
2. Act out your introduction.

9

Children should learn social amenities as part of the program.

From LANGUAGE FOR DAILY USE, Explorer Edition, Level Orange, by Mildred A. Dawson et al., © 1978 by Harcourt Brace Jovanovich, Inc. Reprinted by permission of the publisher.

two but not to the other. The person who knows the one who has joined them does not introduce her because of having forgotten her name. This should be no excuse; the person should simply apologize, ask her name, and then introduce her. Children will be eased by knowing that many people feel shy and embarrassed in this situation—that this is natural but needs to be overcome.

Other situations to discuss with children might include the following:

1. What can be said to make a new child feel welcome?
2. What words should be used in such situations as thanking an aunt who has given a boy a shirt that he thinks is ugly? What can he say about the shirt without lying or hurting the aunt's feelings?
3. What might be said and done if a group of children are playing ball and notice some strange children watching? What do you do?
4. Suppose you are having dinner at a friend's house. What do you do and say after dinner?
5. What do you say if you want a person to sit in a particular place?
6. A friend invites you to a movie. What do you say?
7. What are some situations in which you should offer assistance? For example, in removing a coat, what do you say?
8. Suppose the teacher asks, "Who discovered America?" and a child replies, "George Washington." Is it polite to laugh?
9. How do you respond to courtesies shown you?
10. Someone knocks at the door. How do you greet this person?

Classroom Courtesy

Manners and courtesy are essential if people are to get along in a pleasant atmosphere. It might help to begin the year with a discussion of "what we need to do to make our room a pleasant place in which to live and work."

This may also be the time to discuss the ways in which courtesy and safety work together. The discussion of classroom behavior might well lead to a unit on courtesy and the necessity for obeying the rules on school buses, in the lunchroom, or on the playground.

You can get help with such units from several sources. For example, most police departments will send someone who will talk with children about safety. Some bus drivers and cafeteria workers might be pleased to help. Inquiry should also be made to state education departments, AAA offices, and organizations such as Boy Scouts and 4H. Materials related to safety and courtesy may often be obtained from insurance agents, since many insurance companies provide a wealth of materials on these subjects. For example, write to Public Relations, Kemper Insurance Company, 4750 Sheriden Road, Chicago, Ill 60640, for free material on several aspects of school safety.

The library is important in teaching courtesy; there are numerous books, films, and filmstrips available on this topic. You might want to read to your

Also by the same author are *What Do You Do, Dear?* and *Dear Dragon* (Harcourt Brace Jovanovich).

class *What Do You Say, Dear?* by Sesyle Joslin. Magazine pictures may also be used to promote discussions of good manners; use these on a bulletin board or show them to a group using an opaque projector.

After discussing courtesy in the room and the importance of courtesy and safety when coming to or going from school as well as on the playground, discuss courtesy and safety in the school building—the corridor, cafeteria, auditorium, and office. Perhaps the principal will be able to come to the room to discuss the importance of courtesy and how the children can help by being polite and following school rules (or a child may interview the principal). Teachers are often hesitant about asking school administrators to talk with their classes, but many are flattered to be invited. Other people who work in the school building may be willing to discuss their jobs with the children and tell how good manners make their work easier. Or a safety patrol member or crossing guard may discuss why good manners and following directions are essential for safety.

Children may also discuss correct behavior and courtesy in public places such as stores, museums, libraries, zoos, parks, restaurants, pools, movies, or ball games. Courtesy and behavior on escalators, elevators, streets, and public buses should also be discussed. It is essential that children learn appropriate physical and verbal behavior, since there really is no excuse for rudeness by people of any age.

Through dramatization—actually playing roles—children can learn many social amenities that will be useful to them. In fact, teaching the amenities provides an opportunity to use a variety of oral language experiences. Discussion, role playing, telephoning, interviewing, committee work, puppet plays, making announcements, and giving directions can all be used to further children's understanding of behavior that shows concern for others.

The Role of Parents

It is the sharing of experiences that broadens children's knowledge of the world about them, increases their vocabularies, and develops their ability to express themselves. Most teachers agree that it is from a child's experiences and his or her discussion of them that concepts necessary for future learning are developed. Yet schools are not able to provide all the experiences that a child needs—much is the job of the parents. Consider planning a program for parents with the purpose of informing them of the role of experience in learning. Include in such a program an explanation of the importance of talking with and to children at every age level. If a program is not possible, perhaps the school might place an article in the local paper or you might send a list of suggestions home to parents. Caution is needed in wording such a message, as most parents do not want to be *told* how to raise their children. Yet parents do want their children to do well in school. The following types of suggestions for encouraging a child's oral language development might work:

1. Is it possible for most or all of your family to eat meals together? Mealtime conversation can help children to know that you are interested in them and to talk more freely.

2. Answer children's questions when you can. If you don't know the answer, perhaps you can help them to find it.

3. Instead of trying not to use words that children do not understand, explain the meanings of new words to them.

4. Encourage children to talk in sentences, but do not be so demanding about this that they stop talking at all.

5. Remember that children will model their speech after that of adults who live around them.

6. Discourage baby talk; help children learn to talk so that they can be understood by strangers as well as by the family.

7. Stories, poems, nursery rhymes, and records should be a part of every child's life. Read to your child as much as you can, and talk about the stories and the people in them.

8. A child's experiences contribute to his or her school work. The more people, places, and things a child sees, the better prepared he or she will be for speaking, reading, and writing. Take the child with you whenever you can, even to the grocery store. Talk about the people and things you see.

9. Plan special trips with children. Take them on walks, go with them to the zoo or museum, visit places of interest in the area, and talk with them about these experiences.

10. When your family goes on a trip, short or long, talk about the things you see along the road or highway, the names of rivers, mountains, etc. Try to stop occasionally at historical markers along the road or at places of particular interest.

Such statements may seem too direct; you might wish instead to write a short letter to parents, embodying these or similar ideas. The point to stress is that encouraging language development is something that can be done by talking with children and providing them with experiences and that the important ingredients are time and attention rather than financial outlay. It is possible that many parents who are willing to spend the time have simply not realized this.

EVALUATING ORAL EXPRESSION

There are tests of articulation ability, auditory discrimination, and verbal development. They do not measure abilities in social speaking situations.

There are no standardized tests for measuring children's abilities in the types of oral communication activities described in this chapter. However, this does not mean that the skills and abilities of children in speaking situations should not be evaluated. Evaluation can and should be a part of virtually every speaking situation. This does not mean formal evaluation or the testing that first may come to mind, but it does mean appraisal, determining what children can and cannot do adequately for their maturity levels. Such evaluation is a basic element in teaching if children's speaking skills and abilities are to improve from one speech activity to another.

The evaluation/appraisal done should be based upon the objectives of your total program and the objectives for specific speaking activities: conversation, discussion, interviewing, etc. To some extent these objectives

How to Be Good Conversationalists

1. Always be polite.
2. Only one person should talk at a time.
3. Speak clearly and listen carefully.
4. Use good language.
5. Do not intrude on the conversations of others.

Rules for Giving a Report

1. Pick an interesting topic and stick to it.
2. Have a good opening and closing.
3. Look at the audience.
4. Make your voice loud enough to be heard.
5. Organize your report carefully.
6. Use good sentences and interesting words.

may be set by curriculum guides developed for your school and/or formulated by yourself. However, even in consideration of these, the objectives determined by pupils must not be overlooked.

Standards

Guidelines, rules, or standards for performance in oral expression can be developed for all oral language situations. These standards should be developed by you and the pupils. They should reflect the children's way of looking at things, but if they are too restrictive or are beyond the performance levels possible, some modification may be necessary. Standards should always be thought of as evolving.

Evaluation should always be made in terms of the standards developed by you and the children and, most importantly, in terms of each individual child and the amount of progress he or she has made toward achieving these goals. In addition, you should evaluate the extent of each child's capabilities in the speech skills discussed earlier in this chapter, as well as his or her efforts to make any needed improvement. The evaluation of oral expression is bound to be somewhat subjective, but it will be less so if goals are clearly understood, if progress in achieving these goals is discussed regularly by you *and* the children, and if each child is evaluated according to individual abilities, needs, and achievements.

Checklists

Checklists are similar to lists of standards in that they also suggest appropriate behaviors. The items on a checklist are usually questions that can be answered with "Yes," "No," or a check mark. Checklists may be used by individual pupils for self-evaluation or by the teacher.

A checklist may be extended to include questions about specific usage items of concern, physical mannerisms exhibited by pupils, and more details regarding the content and organization of the material.

Checklists should be used at regular intervals, and comparisons made of the responses from one time to another. And checklists, like standards, may need to be revised as children's abilities progress.

CHECKING UP ON MY SPEECH

	Yes	No
1. Is my voice pleasant to hear?	____	____
2. Do I speak so everyone can understand me?	____	____
3. Do I adjust the volume of my voice for different situations?	____	____
4. Am I prepared for speaking activities?	____	____
5. Do I think before speaking?	____	____
6. Do I use good words and sentences?	____	____

Other Records

While checklists are relatively easy to use, they may not be constructed so that enough details about individual children's strengths and weaknesses can be recorded. Some teachers prefer to keep notebooks with pages for individual students. Still others like to keep individual files, putting notes in them from time to time. Whatever the record system used, there should be provision for determining growth. The system also needs to deal with specifics so that such needs can be focused on in instruction.

References

Bamman, Henry, *et al. Oral Interpretation of Children's Literature*. William C. Brown Co., 1971.

Bauer, Caroline Feller. *Handbook for Storytellers*. American Library Association, 1977.

Carlson, Ruth Kearney. *Speaking Aids through the Grades*. Teachers College Press, 1976.

Currell, David. *Learning with Puppets*. Plays, Inc., 1980.

Eisenson, Jon, and Ogilvie, Mardel. *Communication Disorders in Children*. 5th ed. Macmillan, 1983.

Heining, Ruth. *Creative Dramatics for the Classroom Teacher*. 2nd ed. Prentice-Hall, 1981.

Loban, Walter. *Language Development: Kindergarten through Grade Twelve*. National Council of Teachers of English, 1976.

Lynn, Elizabeth M. *Improving Classroom Communication: Speech Communication Instruction for Teachers*. Speech Communication Association, 1976.

McIntyre, Barbara M. *Creative Drama in the Elementary School*. F. E. Peacock Publishers, 1974.

Meers, Milda J. *Helping Our Children Talk*. Longman, 1976.

Philpott, Violet, and McNeil, Mary Jean. *The Know How Book of Puppets*. Sterling Publishing, 1975.

Renfro, Nancy. *Puppetry and the Art of Story Creation*. Nancy Renfro Studios, 1979.

Sloyer, Shirlee. *Story Dramatization in the Classroom*. National Council of Teachers of English, 1982.

Stewig, John W. *Spontaneous Drama: A Language Art*. Charles E. Merrill, 1974.

Willbrand, M. L., and Rieke, R. D. *Teaching Oral Communication in Elementary Schools*. Macmillan, 1983.

Teaching Resources

FILMS

How to Make a Puppet. Bailey Film Associates (10 min., color; primary and intermediate).

Let's Try Choral Reading. McGraw-Hill Films (12 min., color; grades 2–6).

Storytelling: Can You Tell It in Order? Random House/Coronet (11 min., color or b/w; primary).

Storytelling Is Fun. Random House/Coronet (11 min., color or b/w; intermediate).

RECORDINGS

Animal Puppets and Tape. Developmental Learning Materials (5 puppets, tape, scripts).

FILMSTRIPS

Good Manners at Play. Eye Gate House.

Talking Time Series. McGraw-Hill (2 sets of 8 strips each; grades 2–6).

KITS

Communicative Competence. Opportunities for Learning (manual, filmstrips, cards, etc.).

Oral Language Development. Developmental Learning Materials (booklets, manual, duplicating sheets).

The Storytelling Process. Random House (filmstrips/cassette; for children and teachers).

Activities for Preservice Teachers

1. Learn several stories well enough to tell to children. Try your storytelling skill with neighborhood children or those at a nearby school. You may want to practice with peers first.

2. Think about the various speaking activities and situations described in this chapter and make a list of ways to use a tape recorder in aiding children's learning.

3. Interview the speech correctionist in a school district to find out what kinds of speech problems he or she encounters and what kinds of remedial procedures are used.

4. During your observations of various classrooms, see if you can discover a child whose difficulty in speaking appears to stem from feelings of insecurity. Ask the teacher's permission to help work with this child. Over a period of several weeks, see if you can detect any signs of increased confidence due to the additional attention.

5. Observe a class during some oral activity and use a checklist to evaluate both individuals and the group. From this evaluation, decide which skills, attitudes, or abilities should have teaching priority for the entire class and which children need individual help.

6. Compile a booklet of poems that would be appropriate for choral speaking. Determine which type of choral activity each is best suited for.

7. Plan a lesson utilizing creative dramatics for a grade level of your choice. Be sure to include motivation, kinds of activities that might develop, and follow-up activities.

8. Develop a file of ideas that children might like to dramatize. These ideas can be written on 3×5 cards and should include little more than the nucleus of the idea. Identify each as to the number of children to be involved. Some ideas might be "Children in the Cafeteria Lunch Line," "The Family Loads the Car for a Vacation," "Sitting on the Bench at a Big Game," and "The School Office."

Activities for Inservice Teachers

1. Have the children find examples (from observing parents, neighbors, friends, TV) of gestures, expressions, and body language that convey messages.

2. Assist the children in your class in forming a club based on their interests. Use the information in this chapter and perhaps that in a language textbook to teach the children the parliamentary procedures needed by their club.

3. Prepare a card file of information on books of jokes, riddles, and speech games that children may use.

4. Arrange for children in your class to interview various persons around the school—custodians, clerks, bus drivers, etc. Make certain that suggestions in this chapter for preparing for interviewing are followed.

5. Develop a Drama Book Shelf. This should include books with good stories to dramatize. Criteria for selection of stories should include: simple sequences, clear-cut climax, significance of content, and possibilities of characterizations.

6. Plan a choral speaking activity with your class that could be presented to another class, a school assembly, or a parents' night.

7. List the steps you would use when making puppets with a group of children. What problems might you encounter? How would you resolve them? Now that you've planned, try puppet making with your class. Evaluate the experience in terms of children's interest, participation, and opportunities to use language.

8. Collect and file in a small box selections for choral speaking that can be used in the small periods of time that become available daily. Use these for the minute spent waiting for the bell, for settling-down time after a physical activity, for those in the class who have finished their cleaning up, etc.

9. Develop a lesson that will use creative dramatics in a curriculum area other than language arts. Evaluate the success of the lesson and report results to the class.

10. Prepare a page that could be sent home to parents suggesting ways they might foster the development of their children's speech in various situations.

Independent Activities for Children

1. Two children may work together to plan a play to demonstrate good manners. For example, one might be a guest visiting the classroom and the other could greet and introduce her, or they might illustrate ways to disagree in a conversation without being discourteous.

2. Have a child plan a skit for a special day (Citizenship Day, the anniversary of the Boston Tea Party, United Nations Day, Washington's Birthday, Flag Day, etc.). The planning may include writing a script, getting props, researching, selecting participants, etc.

3. A child can relate to a small group an incident in a story he has read, telling it as though he had been one of the characters. (He may wish to rehearse this before a mirror or record it on tape before presenting it to the group.)

4. Allow children to select a "visitors' committee" who will greet guests to the classroom, explain activities of the class to them, and otherwise act as hosts. Ask school personnel and parents to visit regularly to provide practice for the hosts. New members should be appointed at regular intervals.

5. Children can make puppets independently if they are provided with a place and materials—paper bags, paint, scissors, socks, sticks, stapler, etc. Have a few puppet models, but encourage individual departures from copying these.

6. Stories can be made up to tell using puppets. Children may make up these stories independently and practice them in front of the mirror before telling them to the class or to a small group.

7. A child can make and use finger puppets to dramatize nursery rhymes for a friend who has been out of school for several days.

8. Paper dolls and their clothing can be cut out and used for dramatic play. One or two children may create a play with paper dolls.

9. Keep a card file of topics or situations calling for oral activities. These might be filed under types (conversation, discussion, interviews, storytelling, explanations and directions, etc.) or they might be labeled simply *individual* or *group*. When children have free time during the day, they draw a card at random and develop the activity suggested. Group activities can be enjoyed and/or evaluated by those participating; individual activities can be recorded on tape or presented to the class at odd moments—before lunch, for example. Topics should not be too specific or directive. A conversation card, for example, might read "A new neighbor has moved into the house next door. Decide just how you might meet and carry on conversation. Be yourself, not some imaginary person."

The children themselves should be encouraged to add topics; they may also help to rotate cards so topics do not become stale.

10. Give a child a list of words that are sometimes not pronounced correctly or that are not clearly enunciated so that they are confused with other words. Have her record these and listen to herself. You may also check her recording or have her do this with another child so that they check one another. Some words to use are *quote, quota; compile, compel; partial, parcel;* etc.

11. A child can prepare a talk to give to the class on a topic such as:

> How to make a kite
> How to build a snowman
> How to build and care for an aquarium
> How to make a stamp collection

12. Give a child a collection of pictures from magazines and have him record on tape a story based upon these pictures.

13. Children may also record original stories on tape. At a special time, such as once each week, tapes may be played to the class for practice in listening and discussion.

14. Let children keep a file of pantomime ideas. Provide a mirror in a corner of the room where individual children can experiment with pantomimes and prepare to present them to the class or to small groups.

15. Individual children may prepare and present announcements at school assemblies or over the school public address system.

7 | Fostering Effective Listening

At a party, were you ever caught in the middle of two or three conversations taking place at once? How was your listening? Does the rock music coming over the radio in your home affect your listening? What about traffic noise that almost literally shakes the windows?

Most of us are concerned with screening our listening—with noise "pollution." Yet we are also concerned about receiving the newscaster's words accurately and about gaining "the message" from members of our family—including the children. And we want the listening skills of our children at home and at school to be effective.

Listening is more than just hearing: Hearing frequently cannot be avoided because sounds cannot be screened out. However, we can do something about deciding what we listen to and how this listening can be done most effectively. Likewise, we can help children attain listening skills.

LISTENING CONCERNS AND ISSUES

By the time children come to school for the first time they have had five or six years' experience in listening. From listening they learned the language of their homes, of their neighborhoods, and possibly of much of the world (through travel and television). No one has taught them to listen, although they have likely been told many times to "pay attention." They have probably acquired some listening habits and skills, but they have probably not developed the concern and many of the practices for learning by listening that teachers desire.

Although we sometimes say we "half listen" and although we often listen intermittently or in a somewhat passive manner to music or to someone talking, real listening requires participation. Like the reader, the listener must actively engage in the perception and recognition of words and phrases, in the comprehension of ideas and facts, and in conscious or emotional reaction to these in relation to his or her background of experience. Listening is not an activity that should be separated from expression. Listening to speech requires a speaker. Listening to music requires a performer. Someone or something is always producing the sounds heard; thus the active nature of listening is further emphasized.

156

Hearing and Listening

Listening is affected by the acuity with which a person receives sound waves of various frequencies (tones) at various intensities (levels of loudness). An inability to respond to normal frequencies and intensities represents a hearing loss, which may range from minor to serious. Although a hearing loss affects an individual's ability to perceive sounds and discriminate among them, it is possible for a person to have normal hearing and yet have difficulty with sound perception and discrimination. This is particularly the case with people who have speech problems and with those unfamiliar with a language or a particular dialect. There should be, at most, only minimal problems with children who speak the language or dialect and who do not have speech or hearing problems. Many children who seem to have difficulty with perception and discrimination are probably reflecting a lack of understanding of what they are asked to do, unfamiliarity with aspects of the language (e.g., the words used), little motivation to retain (remember) what they heard, or inattention.

Hearing is also affected by fatigue and masking. Masking is simply a failure to hear because of the superimposition of sounds that interfere—the many voices at a cocktail party. Related to this, but with a physical base, is inadequate binaural hearing. Binaural hearing may be thought of as similar to depth perception in vision; that is, without adequate binaural hearing the individual cannot locate a particular speaker among several talking at once.

There are a number of factors related to hearing and listening that may interfere with reception:

- a speech that is too rapid for reception (usually because the content is unfamiliar)
- slow speech, which leads to "mind wandering"
- lack of interest in the topic or speaker
- waiting for the opportunity to take issue with the speaker
- inadequate knowledge of the topic
- distractions caused by sounds, movement, or the physical surroundings
- an "overacceptance" of the speaker and/or the topic
- inadequate development of the skills needed for listening
- poor organization of the material to be listened to
- preoccupation with personal interests and problems
- a hearing loss

Listening and Reading

Since listening and reading are receptive acts, there are many similarities between them. Both require as a first step readiness for reception. This means that interest in what is to be heard or read must have been aroused; there must be appeal or curiosity—a motivating force. Both reading and listening also require accurate perception of sounds. If *build* sounds to the listener like *filled*, it may not be possible to get the message. In the same manner, the child who sees *black* instead of *blank* will have trouble understanding the sentence "Fill in the blank spaces." Reading and listening also both require that the words or other lexical units (e.g., *rocking chair, push broom, town house*) heard or read are ones whose meanings are either known or can be determined from the context or other clues.

Comprehension in both reading and listening results from understanding phrases, sentences, and statements of greater length—the paragraph, for example—rather than a single word. Therefore, both require relating what is received to past experiences, so that the content of what is heard or read can be thought about and examined creatively and critically. Furthermore, both processes require active attention to signals—punctuation marks, pauses, intonations, key words (e.g., *next, for instance, perhaps, on the other hand*).

Reading and listening can take place in many situations and can be done for many purposes. The closeness of their tie has been shown over and over again by the similarity of activities and exercises designed to teach their skills. In fact, since listening has begun to receive instructional attention, many reading series provide listening activities and suggest that teaching listening skills is one way to improve reading skills.

Ability to listen and ability to read do not necessarily go hand in hand, but a planned program that builds on the relationships between them should improve children's skills in both areas. For example, children may follow a story with their eyes and listen to it being read (using earphones and with the listening part of the activity on a tape cassette). Other examples include giving oral directions (they may be taped) for reading assignments, presenting material in social studies and other curriculum areas through both listening and reading, and motivating reading by having pupils listen to stories with related themes or subjects.

Some Purposes for Listening

1. To get the main idea.
2. To select details.
3. To establish a mood.
4. To answer questions.
5. To summarize information.
6. To separate fact from opinion.
7. To gain a visual image.
8. To appreciate and enjoy.
9. To recognize propaganda, bias, or prejudice.
10. To determine the speaker's purpose.
11. To adapt information presented to a particular need.
12. To evaluate in terms of some criteria.
13. To perceive relationships.
14. To interpret unusual or especially appealing language.
15. To show courtesy.

Types of Listening

We all listen in different ways at different times and in different situations, and this fact needs to be taken into account in an instructional program. While listening is an active, interacting process, the level of activity on the part of the listener varies. Interest in what is being heard affects this level, as do emotional and intellectual factors. Sometimes we only listen marginally, as when a radio is on, but we are basically thinking about whatever we are working on. We often listen to music to appreciate it, perhaps being involved to some extent emotionally but to a lesser extent cognitively. At other times, we listen for particular information but are not otherwise actively involved. At still other times, we are very attentive, listening totally for understanding and perhaps critically analyzing what we are hearing. There is response to any listening, of course, or it is not listening, but the response is rather passive in marginal listening situations. However, in situations in which the listener seeks information or understanding, desires satisfaction of an emotion, or wishes to make a judgment, the listening act is an active one.

Types or levels of listening are not as discrete as perhaps is suggested above. Certainly, listening instruction should not have the objective of "moving" children from a "lower" (marginal or passive) level to a "higher" one. Rather, the objective is to teach children how they may more effectively listen in the situations and settings for which they have the need to listen.

THE LISTENING SKILLS

Listening skills have been listed by many researchers, but with the increase in the number of these lists there has arisen more and more skepticism about their validity. Obviously, though, there are factors that make the reception of sounds meaningful. Possibly listening is something of a state of mind. The young child who has received no instruction in listening can listen well when he or she wishes to do so. No child who is hungry has to be called twice for lunch. Every child has shown considerable effectiveness in listening in order to have learned the language he or she speaks and the ideas and concepts that can be expressed.

Yet young children have generally not had occasion to listen for the kinds of purposes that exist in classrooms. Even older children often lack many of the skills that would aid their listening, or perhaps they do not know what they should be listening for in various situations.

Listening to language, like the related receptive language arts reading, is an information-processing act. In both reading and listening, it is not a single sound or letter—or even a word—that is the unit of comprehension required, although we may use the clues any of them provide in the processing. Essentially, the process first requires perception of something that is meaningful to the receiver—language structure that is known and used, a "chunk" of language whose content is related to something the listener already knows, or perhaps only a word, a tone, or a gesture that gives a clue to the meaning. A listener (unlike a reader) cannot stop listening in order to analyze a sequence of sounds, and usually it is not possible to "go back" and relisten. Yet a listener can learn to gain meaning from (1) the context of what is heard, (2) the clues in a speaker's facial expressions or gestures, (3) the organization of the content, (4) the redundancies that occur in most speech, (5) the voice inflections—tone, rhythm, and volume—a speaker uses, and (6) the clues provided by such signals as *on the other hand, first, however,* etc.

The perception of all or some of the language heard, by the listener's knowledge of elements of it or by any of the ways suggested above for gaining the necessary understanding, is only part of the listening process. Responding to the information perceived completes the process. For such responding to occur, the listener must be skilled in such cognitive abilities as (1) determining the main idea of what was heard; (2) accurately noting relevant details; (3) following directions; (4) understanding denotative and connotative meanings; (5) following the sequence of a plot, explanation, or

See Lundsteen, *Listening: Its Impact on Reading and the Other Language Arts.*

argument; (6) recognizing relationships of cause and effect, time, space, and place; (7) understanding figurative and idiomatic language; and (8) distinguishing among fact, fiction, and fantasy.

These skills are closely related to the purposes for listening—purposes that arise throughout each day for almost everyone. For example, in the classroom children and teacher must listen to one another as they discuss topics of interest, plan activities, and stimulate each other's thinking and study. Each child needs to listen so that he or she can answer questions about social studies events, a story the class has read, or an arithmetic problem. The child must listen in order to separate fact from opinion (in a newscast, a political speech, a TV advertisement, or a talk given to the class); he or she must listen in order to summarize material (such as that given in a science report), follow directions for a game or a project, or get the main idea from a story, a TV program, or a class report. Children also listen to gain appreciation of music, a story, or a poem. They listen to establish a mood for thinking and reacting. They listen for particular words or phrases (e.g., *the reason for this is, my first point, in conclusion,* etc.), to nonspeech sounds other than music (e.g., to start ideas flowing for a creative writing activity), or for words that relate to particular gestures, voice tones, or mannerisms.

Guidelines

Listening can be improved by:

1. Setting specific purposes for listening.
2. Giving directions only once.
3. Listening courteously to children.
4. Setting an example by clear enunciation and accurate pronunciation.
5. Organizing material presented orally to children so that it is systematic, explicit, and brief.

A number of guidelines or principles are helpful in planning a program to improve children's listening. To begin with, a classroom climate that is conducive to listening avoids distracting physical and emotional conditions. This climate includes a relaxed, unhurried, nonthreatening teacher's voice, along with facial expressions that are expressive and varied but that are directed at promoting accurate listening.

Second, purposes *for* listening should be suggested or developed with the children; one should not simply demand that children listen *to* something. Listening should be done *for* information that can be gained, *for* appreciation of the language in a poem, *for* propaganda words, *for* directions, etc. Establishing standards, providing for class reactions, and discussing listening behavior will all help children discover the need for and the importance of listening.

The discovery will be further enhanced if listening activities are related to the ongoing activities of the class—this is our third guideline. These activities should be within the interest and comprehension levels of the pupils so that they become personally involved, thus avoiding "tuning out." Interest is also more likely to be maintained if the listening periods are not too long and if a change of activity is provided—questions, discussion, drawing or writing something as a result of the listening.

The teaching of listening provides opportunities for planned integration.

As much variety as possible should be provided in listening experiences used for teaching the skills. For example, films, debates, individual and group reports, dramatic activities, demonstrations, music, descriptions, explanations, discussions, and conversations may all be used. Some variations in the seating arrangement will also help. That is, if you are reading a story and showing illustrations from a book, the children might be grouped closely about you, while for a film they might sit in rows (with care taken to see that children at the perimeters can see well).

An effective listening program also provides for individual differences. This will include seating those children who have hearing losses as advantageously as possible, as well as providing activities of varying levels of difficulty and with varying purposes for different individuals and groups.

Of course, and most importantly, provision must be made for activities and lessons for learning and practicing the listening skills or abilities identified earlier. Directions for these activities should be well organized, and they should be presented once, with children being encouraged to think before asking to have them repeated. Attention should also be given to helping children practice ignoring distractions.

Teachers' Listening

In planning instruction for children, teachers should first give attention to their own listening. They should genuinely "pay attention," "be courteous to speakers," and observe all the other behaviors that they urge upon children. Doing so will avoid such catastrophes as that of the teacher who responded to a child, "Isn't that nice, dear. Now go play and have fun" after the child announced that his grandfather had died last night!

You may find yourself at a loss for words when given some valuable piece of information by a pupil. If a child says, "We got new gravel in our driveway," you may find yourself wondering, "Who cares?" But the child does care; this is something to talk about. Perhaps you might begin a discussion of stone size, the difficulty one encounters in riding a bicycle on new gravel, etc. Give the child a sense of pride by truly listening and giving a positive response.

Teachers also need to remind themselves of factors that foster their own listening effectiveness, especially of those that block their listening. Doing so should cause them to recognize that the same factors bear upon children's listening. Even the most positive conditions for listening will not ensure that a child who is hungry, sleepy, or emotionally upset will listen effectively. None of us listen very well if we are upset, thinking of other things, or simply not interested in what is being said.

LISTENING ACTIVITIES

The opportunities for teaching listening are unlimited. This is a speaking and listening world, and every classroom is a part of it. But children must be taught to listen effectively in the many communication situations of the classroom, and this teaching can be done with varying degrees of formality. That is, you can plan lessons that focus on teaching particular skills, engage in activities that require listening for specific purposes, and use other activities of a more general nature that call for listening as a part of them.

Readiness

Make the teaching of listening a part of all your classroom activities.

Since both reading and listening are receptive communication acts, activities children engage in as a foundation for reading instruction are helpful for listening. The term *readiness* is somewhat overused, and too often is identified only with activities in the kindergarten and first grade. There needs to be, of course, readiness for any new learning—at any age or grade level. However, the activities in this section are ones that are normally for young children: listening for rhyming sounds, discriminating among speech sounds and relating them to letters, and identifying nonspeech sounds. They also include listening to music and rhythms, listening to stimulate imaginative thinking, and listening for basic communication purposes. Most listening readiness activities are enjoyable to children and set the stage for teaching skills related to specific purposes. However, developing in a child the ability to listen to a speaker and get the message—including, for example, the ability to sift out the facts the speaker gives from his or her opinions—comes from direct teaching of the specific skills rather than from the development of a generalized listening ability.

While activities which give attention to sounds—identifying and discriminating among them as suggested below—are important, as much focus as possible should be placed, even at this early stage of a listening program, on gaining meaning. Children can listen to stories, responding with their ideas and feelings about characters, how a story ended, or what it reminded them of. And, as suggested in earlier chapters, attention to meaning can be given as children listen to one another at sharing times, as directions are given, and as they engage in creative dramatics.

Rhyming activities help children identify speech sounds, discriminate among them, and gain practice in auditory memory. Readiness activities include having the children listen to and repeat rhyming words (*cold–told, Jill–hill, quick–stick, fast–last, cat–rat,* etc.), listen for words that rhyme in stories, and listen to supply missing words in simple rhymes. (For example: "We traveled far/in our new____. We saw a cat/who was very____. Go into the hall/to play with the____.") Children may say nursery rhymes together (try "Jack Be Nimble," "Little Boy Blue," "Hickory Dickory Dock," "Little Bo-Peep") or play rhyming games ("I rhyme with sled. You sleep in me. What am I?"). It is also fun to divide the class into teams, with one team giving a word and another supplying a word that rhymes with the first one.

Related to rhyming activities are those that call for discriminating among sounds and words. For example, you might say pairs of words (*three–free, ship–chip, chair–share*) and have the children tell if they are the same words or different ones. Or have some of the pairs begin with the same sound (*mother–man, boy–ball*) and others begin with different sounds (*little–ball, dog–log*) and let the children tell which pairs begin with the same sound. Still another variation is to say groups of words and ask the children to pick the word that begins with a different sound from that of the others in the group (*mice, fish, money, mouse / fire, fact, dog, fence / top, tent, tool, cat*). The children will also enjoy games such as having those children stand whose names start with the same sound as the word you say. The same game can be played with the names of the streets they live on, the cars their parents drive, or their brothers' and sisters' names.

Simply listening for sounds is an activity often used to stimulate thoughts in a creative writing lesson, but it is also a good listening readiness activity. Have the children close their eyes for a number of seconds and then tell what sounds they heard. Or have them go on a sound hunt in the room to find the objects that make sounds—record player, water faucet, bells, clock, window closing, etc. Many of these sounds can be imitated, as well as other sounds that the children are likely to know, such as animal calls, screeching tires, etc.

Listening for Sounds around Us

Street sounds—horns tooting, gears grinding, dogs barking, people talking
Sounds on a trip—getting on the bus, the bus going over a bridge, entering a pet store
Classroom sounds—footsteps, blocks falling, singing, whispering

Listening Centers

Wire tape and cassette players for stations permitting individual and/or small group listening.

Early Grades

Many of the activities of the general "readiness" nature can be continued or extended into the primary grades and beyond. For example, you might give the children a sentence with a word missing, but supply the first letter (letter name, not sound) of the missing word. A sentence such as "The man leaped on his h____ and dashed off" is an example of this. You might even try listen-and-rhyme games. They are silly, but they do require listening and surely help to develop sentence sense.

TEACHER: I baked a cake.

PUPIL 1:   You baked a snake?

PUPIL 2:   No, she backed into a lake.

PUPIL 3:   She baked a snake and stepped on a rake.

PUPIL 4:   My goodness sake!

Give the children the last letters of a word, and have a child supply a consonant or blend that will make a word (*end–send, ead–bread*) and then go to the board and write and pronounce the word. Other children may say words that begin with a different consonant or consonant blend but end with the same syllable. Once the list is complete children may dictate silly rhymes to you.

> I had a hen
> Who talked with men
> As she sat in the den
> And wrote with a pen.

Collect these and put them on ditto sheets which the children can make into books to illustrate and take home to read.

A completion activity that helps develop attentiveness involves simply giving the beginnings of sentences that they are to complete: "Our class is going to . . ." or "John is . . . ." At first one completion is sufficient; later, depending on the age and maturity level of the children, they may be asked to repeat what has been said and supply a new item: "John is a boy," "John is a tall boy," "John is a tall boy in a red sweater," etc.

Children, especially at this age, love to be helpful to the teacher. You can capitalize on this to help them form habits of listening, so they won't miss the opportunity to do a chore. Let them carry oral messages and run errands: "Bruce, please tell the custodian that our sink is leaking again" or "Jennifer, will you please go to the storeroom and ask the clerk for a box of chalk?" Even kindergarten children can perform such errands if they have been made familiar with the building and its personnel. As they mature, the requests can become more complicated: "Jerry, will you collect all the pictures from the children in your row and put them on my desk? Then give each person a sheet of this paper." To avoid confusion and attract the attention of the child addressed, always say the child's name before giving directions. To involve more than one child, sometimes give directions such as this: "Has everyone finished? Will the third person in each row collect the pictures for his or her row?"

Since giving instructions is so much an integral part of the school day, there is little need to construct opportunities. It is helpful, however, to be guided by three principles:

1. Use some signal to gain attention (this might be a name, a question, possibly even a note struck on the piano).

2. Speak clearly so that those involved can hear accurately.

3. Form the habit of giving directions only once.

Plan for:

children to listen to each other
your listening to children
a balanced and not over-powering amount of listening
readiness for a listening activity

Primary grade children are not too young to begin to select what is relevant to a particular listening purpose. The kinds of discrimination exercises suggested for listening readiness are a beginning. Try also giving a list of objects—for example, *cookie, muffin, fork, cake, bowl*—and asking them to name those that belong in the same category.

Activities for helping children learn to listen more effectively should of course be genuinely interesting and appealing. Carefully selected stories, read or told, have this appeal and are an essential part of the language arts program. For example, in the story *Harry the Dirty Dog*, which has great appeal, the children may be asked to listen to find out why Harry ran away (main idea) or what happened after Harry ran away (sequence). Listening to a story for the purpose of retelling it is also excellent for learning sequence—as well as for providing valuable oral activity.

A Listening Tip

Before reading to the children, write on the board words which may be unfamiliar to them. Have the children pay particular attention to gaining meanings of these words.

You may need to help children ferret out the main idea, determine what the sequence really is, or identify important details. Sometimes ideas that seem obvious to us are missed by children. Try asking what is important about a story or report that could be told in one sentence (main idea). Listing details on the board will help children learn to discover those that are important and to determine sequence or organization. Telling part of a story can aid in developing many skills. Children will need to listen for the main idea, for the sequence of events, and for particular information to adapt. In addition, such an activity will help them learn to draw inferences from what they hear, since the end of the story must fit the characters, the scene, and the events that have gone before. With young children, begin by using a single sentence and having the children add another: "As I was walking through the woods one dark and stormy night, I suddenly saw a flash of light. . . ." If this is too difficult at first, perhaps several suggestions may be made and written on the chalkboard; the children can then decide which ones fit best with the original sentence.

Middle and Upper Grades

As children grow a bit older, the opportunities and need for their giving oral reports and engaging in various forms of discussion increase, thus increasing the possibilities for a more direct focus on the development of listening abilities. Again, greater success is possible if the talks and reports are on subjects of concern to the pupils. Perhaps the building of a new school might occasion special attention to some things especially desired by the children, such as basketball backboards or a listening room in the library. Some ideas included in a talk are likely to be pertinent; others are not. Listeners should have paper on which they can separate points according to whether they are fact or opinion, record details, note new words, etc. After a talk the group should discuss its content and the manner of presentation.

A Listening Tip

Let the child who is giving a talk observe the group and comment on the listening behavior of the audience after he or she has finished.

A natural follow-up to talks is to have the children listen to newscasts and to comments made by political figures. This listening is particularly good for practice in determining what is fact and what is opinion.

Children can tell stories or give descriptions, with their listeners responding by making drawings about the story. For example, at Halloween the ugliest monster imaginable might be described. This will surely result in drawings appropriate for the season of the year.

Activities derived from listening to your reading are also very good. Read a descriptive scene to the class; have the children draw pictures depicting what they heard. Read descriptions of well-known people—perhaps persons studied in connection with social studies—and have pupils guess who they are. Read a story or folktale to the children—perhaps one from a country the class is studying. Stop before the story is finished, and let the children guess the ending.

Children at all age levels enjoy poetry. They could listen to a poem to determine mood and feeling. A poem like Vachel Lindsay's "The Congo" is especially good for this type of listening. In addition to mood and feeling, children could also listen for pitch, stress, pauses, rhythm, and tone. In fact, both poetry and stories that are unknown to the children may be read for many purposes. Two such purposes might be to determine a title and to give practice in the development of effective use of context clues to determine word meaning.

Sentences may also be read, with one or more words in each omitted and the children supplying the missing words. Some sentences should be of the type that requires "listening on" (similar to "reading on") to determine the missing words. For example, "Last year the _____ nearly killed a man, even though the Park Rangers affectionately called him 'Old Grizzle.' "

Many television shows can be used for listening activities, including programs watched at home. For example, children who watch the cartoons can listen for and record usage "errors." These can be discussed in class. They might also record the television that they watch for a week in preparation for a class discussion on listening habits.

The use of audiovisual aids can add much to listening activities. For instance, before giving an oral report, the child can list on the board, or use an overhead projector to show, questions pertaining to the report. Afterward, these questions can serve as a guide for a discussion of the main ideas, details, and sequence of what was said. At first, the children will need help in selecting and wording the questions.

Repeat-and-add games keep children interested and help to develop interesting sentences as well as to foster good listening habits.

PUPIL 1:   Thunder.

PUPIL 2:   The thunder roared.

PUPIL 3:   The thunder roared and the lightning flashed.

Another activity that is fun is for the children to listen to classmates reading orally and try to determine the punctuation. They may also evaluate the reader in terms of his or her ability to read with feeling, to "capture" the audience, and to convey the author's message. Encourage ques-

For information on obtaining audiotapes of educational radio programs, write to National Public Radio, 2025 M St., N.W., Washington, DC 20036.

tions related to specific listening skills. For example: "What did Jim talk about?" (main idea) or "What did he say first, next, and last?" (details and sequence). Giving tests orally also provides useful practice in listening. That is, instead of writing questions, read them to the class (this works best for questions requiring short answers). Also try assigning various children the task of listening to and recording assignments so that they can be telephoned to a child who is absent.

An activity that is valuable in helping children understand usage problems, appreciate differences in speech, and understand various speakers is listening to different dialects. The New Englander's speech is not the same as that of the Southerner or the Midwesterner. Likewise, the male adult's speech and the female adult's speech often present different listening tasks. Try recording the speech of friends and acquaintances who speak different dialects, have high or low voices, speak rapidly or slowly, and so on. Keep in mind, too, that music, such as the songs of Stephen Foster or modern country-western songs, offers excellent opportunities for listening to dialects.

For other listening activities, see books such as *Language Arts Activities for Elementary Schools* by Burns and Bassett.

LISTENING LESSONS

The following are examples of the types of listening exercises that may be constructed. Content for these may come from textbooks for the subject areas or it may even be adapted from reading exercises in teachers' manuals and workbooks, since the purposes for reading and listening are so closely related.

Selecting Details

Ask the children to listen for details about Virginia City and how it became a ghost town as you read the following:

> The miners living in Virginia City in 1860 lived in frame shanties and tents made of canvas, potato sacks, old shirts, and blankets. Two years later, however, the shacks and tents had been replaced by hotels, rooming houses, and homes—all of substantial construction. Three years after that the silver mines were closed because the silver ore began to give out. It seemed that Virginia City would become a ghost town, but new veins of silver were discovered and the life of the city revived. In 1875 a fire devoured the city, and that event, combined with a decline in mining, brought on the ghost town appearance of Virginia City as it is today.

Follow the reading by asking questions such as these:

> What were the tents of the early miners made of?
> When was the fire in Virginia City?
> What was mined in Virginia City?
> Why did Virginia City become a ghost town?

Finding the Main Idea

Write these sentences on the board and cover them:

> The burro is a very gentle animal.
> Children ride on their burros.
> The burro is a favorite pet in Mexico.
> The children give names to their burros.

Ask the children to listen carefully to what they are about to hear and to think of the one idea it tells about. Read the following:

> Many children in Mexico have burros for pets. The burro is so gentle that a small child can take care of him. The children enjoy riding on their burros. Sometimes the children ride them in parades. They call their pet burros by name, and talk to them just as they talk to one another. Often a boy will carry sugar in his pocket. His burro will follow him, sniffing in his pocket to get the sugar.

Uncover the sentences and read them aloud. Ask the children to write the sentence that is the main idea of the paragraph.

Following Directions

Distribute one sheet of lined paper to each pupil and say something like "Today we are going to make a terrarium. But first we need to go over the directions. I'll read them to you, step by step. Listen carefully, and write down just a few words to remind you of each step. When we know exactly what we must do to build the terrarium, we will begin." The directions might be as follows:

1. Lay out the pieces of glass (except the piece for the top) on the table. Put the largest piece in the center and the smaller pieces around it, matching the smaller pieces with the sides of the large piece.
2. Fasten the largest piece of glass (the bottom) to each of the side pieces using wide adhesive tape.
3. Make sure that all exposed edges of the glass are taped.
4. Use tape to hinge the glass for the top to the rear of the terrarium.
5. Remember that the top is taped to the rest of the terrarium only on the rear side.
6. Tape the edges of the hinged top so that no glass edges are exposed.
7. Place the terrarium on a solid surface, and cover the bottom with about an inch of fine, clean sand.
8. Place the plants in the sand, leaving them in the pots.
9. Add pieces of driftwood, rocks, and other objects to make the terrarium attractive.

Getting Word Meanings

Write the words *exalt* and *ravine* on the board. Ask the pupils if they know the meanings of them. Write the meanings they give on the board and then ask them to listen to this paragraph to find out if they were right.

> A little way off, to the left, stood a small house; and to the right was another, before which stood the wagons belonging to his father. Directly in front was a wide expanse of rolling prairie, cut by a deep ravine. To the north, beyond the small farm, which was fenced, a still wider region rolled away into unexplored and marvelous distance. Altogether it was a land to exalt a boy who had lived all his life in thickly settled Wisconsin.

Following the reading the meanings of the words should again be discussed and looked for in a dictionary if necessary.

Distinguishing between the Relevant and the Irrelevant

Ask the pupils to listen to the following selection and to be ready to tell which sentences are needed to gain the meaning and which do not really relate to the remainder of the selection.

> There were six boys beside the campfire. The dry sticks blazed and the heavy logs glowed with the heat. It was almost time to put the fish in the frying pan. The boys had poked the potatoes in their foil wrappings and already they were softening. Jim's older brother had stayed at home. He was going to college this fall. All the boys were hungry and were anxious to eat. Bill put on more wood and Bob got the frying pan.

Ask the pupils to tell why the sentences that do not relate to the remainder of the paragraph are not needed to gain the meaning.

Drawing Inferences

Tell the pupils to listen to the following paragraph in order to answer some questions that can only be answered by listening "between the lines."

> The air was crisp and clear, but a wet snow had pelted the windows last night. I breathed deeply, glanced toward the snow-covered cars parked along the curb, and thought, "What a beautiful day." Suddenly I came down with a bump on the sidewalk.

Ask these questions and discuss the meaning of making inferences:

Why did the speaker fall?
Does the speaker live in town or in the country?
Had it stopped snowing?

TEACHING RESOURCES

There are many resources available to aid teachers in the development of more effective listening. As suggested in the preceding section, the content of listening lessons may come from textbooks in various subject areas of the curriculum. These should not be the only sources for lessons, however, since so many other materials are now available for providing variety and interest in the listening program.

Tape and Cassette Recorders

The increasing prevalence of inexpensive tape recorders, particularly of the cassette type, provides teachers with many opportunities to extend their teaching. Directions, tests, questions, stories, and various types of information can be recorded, leaving the teacher free to observe the children as they work, give individual help, and discover individual problems. Directions for seatwork can be placed on tape: "In row 1 put an x on the picture that begins with the sound you hear at the beginning of boy, ball, and book." Or you might tape questions to be used following silent reading of a lesson in social studies or some other subject area (these should be short-answer questions). Sometimes allow space on the tape for recording children's answers so that it can be kept and used by individual children or groups in studying for a test. Test questions, too, can be taped. Many teachers tape their spelling tests, for example. Then children can take their

Listening games can be fun.

own pretests, check their spelling (correct spellings are included at the end of the tape), and, when they have studied the words misspelled, take their final tests.

Directions for games can also be taped; one like "Simon Says" is particularly suitable for listening. Another, for which the children can prepare themselves, is called "I Am a Fellow American" or "Guess the Mystery Guest." For these, the children choose characters from their social studies lessons, find additional information about them in encyclopedias or other supplementary books, and tape short sketches of the persons chosen. The other children then guess who each person is. A variation of this game is to have children tape several statements about a particular person; the other children then discuss these and decide which are fact and which opinion. This can also be done with the children making statements about themselves.

Children can also be encouraged to use the tape recorder to evaluate their own performances and discover their own errors. The child who has enunciation or pronunciation problems may enjoy "playing teacher"—recording his or her own reading of a story and then listening to the tape to discover and correct errors. You will need to work with most children to help them learn this technique, but if you think children cannot hear their own mistakes, try listening to your own recorded voice and see how many speech mannerisms and habits you discover that you were unaware of. Taping is also very effective when children are preparing for a play, a choral reading presentation, an oral report, or any other activity to be presented before an audience—even if that audience is only the class itself.

You will find recording helpful for activities suggested in other chapters as well. For example, in connection with a study of interviewing, the children would enjoy taping and then listening to an opinion survey program on a topic such as the following: "Should the frog replace the bird as a decorative symbol?" There could be a discussion of frog wallpaper, frog placemats, frog lampposts, frog's nest soup, frog watchers, and who knows what else to stimulate listening and stir creative thinking.

Taping chapters or portions of chapters may help children who do not read well with difficult reading in the content areas. To establish listening purposes, preface the reading with taped questions, perhaps selected from those given at the end of the chapter. As reinforcement, provide written copies of the questions to be answered, or begin the tape with an instruction something like this: "Before you listen to the tape, turn to page 46 in your textbook and read questions 1, 2, and 3. Read carefully; then reread to be sure you remember what to listen for. Keep your book open as you listen so you can check yourself. Now turn off the tape recorder until you have read the questions and are ready to begin listening."

Records

Combining the teaching of listening with music activities is helpful and enjoyable. For example, children can be given pictures of musical instruments along with information about the sounds produced by each instrument.

Then, as they listen to *Peter and the Wolf*, for example, the children hold up the picture of each instrument as it is played. This may be varied by giving each child only one or two pictures; the children will need to listen carefully so that they will not miss their instruments.

A good motion activity is to play music and have the children move in time to the rhythm. They love to march to something like Sousa's "Semper Fidelis." (Older students might be stimulated to learn more about Sousa and his life as bandmaster of the United States Marine Corps band.) More creative interpretations of rhythm and mood may result from "The Dancing Doll" (Edward Poldini) or "Claire de Lune" (Claude Debussy).

Such pieces as "Claire de Lune," "Parade of the Wooden Soldiers," or "Danse Macabre" are good for drawing out what the music makes a child think of. (The children should not be told the titles.) Sometimes their interpretations might be in the form of pictures which could be displayed and discussed. The composer's purpose can also be discussed, with this discussion leading to a comparison of the composer's inspiration with their reactions.

This procedure may be reversed, of course, by telling the children the story behind a particular composition, such as *The Sorcerer's Apprentice* (Paul Dukas), and then having them listen to see how the music and the instruments reflect the theme and mood of the story.

Music is a natural corollary to social studies. Martial music of different wars, folk songs of many types and lands, spirituals—these and many other types of music will help children to truly understand the people who lived in other times and in other lands. Ask your school music director for help in selecting music of these types.

Books

There are many books that build interest in listening, suggesting things to listen to and for. Many others have stories that are appealing to listen to and are helpful in making children aware of listening and in teaching listening skills. Here are some:

Alexenber, Marvin. *Sound Science*. Prentice-Hall, 1968.
Baylor, Byrd. *Plink Plink Plink*. Houghton Mifflin, 1971.
Borten, Helen. *Do You Hear What I Hear?* Abelard-Schuman, 1960.
Branley, Franklyn M. *High Sounds, Low Sounds*. Thomas Y. Crowell Co., 1967.
Brown, Margaret. *Steamroller*. Walker, 1974.
Brown, Margaret Wise. *The City Noisy Book*. Harper and Row, 1939. (Also *The Country Noisy Book*, *The Seashore Noisy Book*, and *The Winter Noisy Book*.)
Elkin, Benjamin. *The Loudest Noise in the World*. Viking, 1954.
Emberley, Ed. *Klippity Klop*. Little, Brown, 1974.
Guilfoile, Elizabeth. *Nobody Listens to Andrew*. Scholastic Book Services, 1973.
Hanson, Joan. *Sound Words: Words That Imitate the Sounds Around*. Lerner, 1976. (Also *More Homonyms: Steak and Stake and Other Words That Sound the Same but Look as Different as Chilli and Chilly; Homographic Homophones: Words That Look and Sound the Same*.)

Johnston, Tony. *Night Noises and Other Mole and Troll Stories.* Putnam, 1977.
Mayer, Mercer. *What Do You Do with a Kangaroo?* Four Winds Press, 1973.
O'Neill, Mary L. *What Is That Sound?* Atheneum, 1966.
Showers, Paul. *The Listening Walk.* Thomas Y. Crowell, 1961.
Tresselt, Alvin. *Wake Up, City!* Lothrop, Lee and Shepard, 1957. (Also *Wake Up, Farm!*)

EVALUATION OF LISTENING

Without some form of measurement or testing, a teacher does not know whether listening lessons and activities are achieving the desired objectives. Equally important is the fact that each child needs feedback to guide his or her learning. Of course, well-designed lessons provide considerable evidence to both the teacher and the children of how effective the listening was for the particular lessons. Some evidence beyond that attained by this procedure, however, is needed to determine growth.

Standards

Developing standards or guidelines for specific types of listening activities or lessons—e.g., oral reports or panel discussions, watching a film, listening to a story—is very useful. Not only do such standards provide a measure of guidance to speakers, but they give individual children a means for making judgments about their listening. They also provide guidance for a class or group evaluation.

The following is an example of a set of second grade standards:

> A GOOD LISTENER
>
> Looks at the person talking.
> Doesn't talk.
> Thinks about what is said.
> Remembers what he or she is listening for.

Standards should become more specific than this example as the children mature and as they focus on different types of listening situations and purposes. Standards should always, however, be developed with the children rather than being imposed upon them. Intermediate grade children can develop standards based on such questions as these:

Do I keep in mind the main idea of what I'm listening to?
Am I courteous in my listening?
Do I reserve judgment until the end of a presentation?
Am I aware of transitional phrases and what they mean?
Do I recognize bias on the part of the speaker?
Do I remember what I am listening for?

Listening Skills

Everyday you receive a great deal of information by listening. You may even start your day by listening to the radio. Listening to directions and reports are part of your daily school work.

● Think why you should listen carefully in each of the following situations.

Someone is telling you how to walk to his or her house.
The coach is telling you how to play soccer.
Your teacher is telling you what you should do in case of fire.

You may be surprised to learn that listening skills are very much like reading skills. When you listen to a talk or speech you listen for the main idea. You also listen for important details that tell about or explain the main idea. You must practice to become a good listener just as you practice to become a good reader.

Here are some rules to help you become a good listener.

1. Look directly at the speaker.
2. Do not talk to others while you are listening.
3. Try to think only about what the speaker is saying.
4. Listen for the main idea. The speaker usually states the subject at the beginning of the speech.
5. Try to remember at least two important details that the speaker gives.
6. When the speaker is finished, take notes by writing the main idea and details immediately.
7. Ask questions about what you can't remember or don't understand.

Language textbooks can often help you teach listening; they suggest activities and identify the skills that need to be developed.

Series E: Macmillan English, Book 5, by Tina Thoburn et al. Copyright © 1982 Macmillan Publishing Co., Inc. Used by permission of the publisher.

Checklists

Statements of standards can be translated into checklists, such as the one below, and these can be used by pupils to keep a written record of their listening skills.

MY LISTENING CHECKLIST

	Yes	No
1. Could I hear and see the speaker?	____	____
2. Was I ready to think about what the speaker said?	____	____
3. Was I ready to learn?	____	____
4. Was I able to discover the direction the speaker was taking?	____	____
5. Did I determine the main idea?	____	____
6. Did I use clues the speaker provided?	____	____
7. Was I able to pick out information supporting the main idea?	____	____
8. Was I able to summarize what the speaker said?	____	____

There are a few standardized tests which purport to measure listening ability or skills. The *California Achievement Test* (kindergarten battery only) contains a "Listening for Information" section in which children respond to the teacher's reading. Graded listening tests are a part of the *Cooperative Primary Tests* (grades 1–2 and 2–3). In these tests, the teacher reads words, stories, poems, and so on. Children indicate their comprehension by marking illustrations.

Another standardized test is the *Durrell Listening-Reading Series,* which is designed to provide a comparison of children's reading and listening abilities. The several levels of the test (grades 1–3.5, 3.5–6, 7–9) seek to measure both vocabulary knowledge and comprehension ability. Essentially, this test measures auditory perception and discrimination rather than listening comprehension. Tests such as the *Illinois Test of Psycholinguistic Abilities* (ITPA) and the *Wepman Auditory Discrimination Test* (WADT) allow assessment of auditory perception, discrimination, and sequencing. However, these tests are generally administered by speech therapists or learning disability teachers to individual children rather than to a class, and they do not measure children's abilities in comprehending speech.

The various standardized and other published tests can serve as models for a teacher's own tests. Teacher-made tests can be directed at measuring achievement in specific skills. For example, to test pupils' abilities to listen for details, present material orally or by tape that contains details to listen for. In the same manner, direct test content and questions at evaluating skill in separating fact from opinion, in answering specific questions, in getting the main idea, in recognizing propaganda, or in using contextual clues to get word meanings. The listening lessons suggested earlier in this chapter provide examples of the way such tests can be constructed.

A FINAL WORD

Listening occupies a baseline position in relation to speaking, reading, and writing. In a quantitative sense, it is most important, since about half the average adult's or child's day is spent in listening. In a qualitative sense, listening is equally important: the "knowledge explosion" requires that information be processed as rapidly as possible—in school and out. Listening is a major means by which this may be accomplished; thus, teaching listening must be a concern of every teacher.

Providing direct and regular instruction in the listening skills results in more effective listening and improved attitudes. Such teaching, however, must be based upon clear-cut purposes understood by both teacher and pupils and must be followed by evaluation of pupil learning.

References

Barker, Larry L. *Listening Behavior*. Prentice-Hall, 1971.

Burns, Paul C., and Bassett, Randall. *Language Arts Activities for Elementary Schools*. Houghton Mifflin, 1982.

Durrell, Donald D., *et al. Durrell Listening-Reading Series*. Harcourt Brace Jovanovich, n.d.

Friedman, P. G. *Listening Processes: Attention, Understanding, Evaluation*. National Education Association, 1978.

Kirk, Samuel A., *et al. Illinois Test of Psycholinguistic Abilities*. University of Illinois Press, 1968.

Lundsteen, Sara W. *Listening: Its Impact on Reading and the Other Language Arts*. National Council of Teachers of English, 1971.

Smith, Charlene. *The Listening Activity Book: Teaching Literal, Evaluative and Critical Listening in the Elementary School*. Fearon Publishers, 1975.

Tutolo, Daniel J. "A Cognitive Approach to Teaching Listening." *Language Arts* 54 (March 1977), pp. 262–265.

Weaver, Carl H. *Human Listening: Process and Behavior*. Bobbs-Merrill, 1972.

Wepman, Joseph M. *The Auditory Discrimination Test*. Language Research Associates, 1973.

Teaching Resources

FILMS

Most films made for children can provide worthwhile listening experiences. Companies such as Weston Woods, Learning Corporation of America, Encyclopaedia Britannica, Random House, and many others have marketed appealing films.

Films and filmstrips available from National Geographic Educational Services on such subjects as pollution, energy, cities, explorers, and government provide good opportunities for using listening skills.

FILMSTRIPS

Adventures in Listening. Random House/Coronet (6 filmstrips, records or cassettes; primary).

Learning to Listen. ESP, Inc. (grades 2–5).

RECORDINGS

Listen and Learn. Educational Progress (8 tapes, book, guide).

Listening Skills Program. Opportunities for Learning (cassettes, guide, activity sheets).

KITS

Listening Comprehension. Educators Publishing Service (inventories, games, masters, manual).

Listening Comprehension Skills Kits. Opportunities for Learning (cards, manual; several levels).

Listening Skills Program. Benefic Press (cassettes, activity book, guides, charts; two levels: grades 1–3, 4–6).

Listening to the World. American Guidance Services (gameboards, picture cards, sound book, cassettes, guide).

Scholastic Listening Skills. Scholastic Book Services (scripts and masters, two units; primary).

SRA Listening Language Laboratory Series. Science Research Associates (cassettes, masters, teacher's handbook; primary and intermediate).

Think, Listen and Learn. Listening Library (12 cassettes, masters, guide).

Activities for Preservice Teachers

1. Talk with several teachers about what they do to teach listening. Do they relate teaching of listening skills to their teaching of the content areas of the curriculum? Do they use records and/or cassettes? A commercial program? Record games and activities themselves? Or only as listening teaching occurs in the reading program? Report to the class about what you found.

2. Using as a base the various books and other commercial resources identified in this chapter, write for catalogs from companies offering materials that may be useful for teaching listening.

3. Ask some teachers you know about the children in their classrooms who are good listeners. Particularly ask if the teachers find these children to be good readers.

4. Plan an activity for which you would need to give specific directions. Include in your plan the sentences you would use.

5. Examine publishers' catalogs for materials useful in teaching listening. Give particular attention to materials that relate listening to other aspects of the curriculum.

6. Collect pictures of objects that children can name and categorize according to beginning sounds, etc.

7. Describe the arrangement of a classroom which would maximize attention to teaching the listening skills.

8. Add to the list of "listening books" given in this chapter.

9. Examine one of the major language textbook series for the attention it gives to the teaching of listening. Report to the class.

Activities for Inservice Teachers

1. Identify the types of listening that children do in your classroom. Relate each type you identify to specific activities or situations. Are these the types of listening the children should be doing in these activities or situations?

2. Develop plans for a "listening center" in your classroom. What materials will you need? How much space? What sorts of listening activities would you have in the center?

3. Use a tape recorder in your class. How many different ways can you find to use it? Keep a record of the uses of the tape recorder.

4. Visit the instructional media center of your school or district to determine what materials are available for teaching listening skills in your classroom. Make notes (perhaps a card file) so that you can readily request the materials you want.

5. Experiment with the physical conditions in your classroom and their effects upon listening. Keep a record of different conditions you create and how you measure the effects on listening.

6. Look in the curriculum guides in the school or district professional library. Record on cards the listening activities suggested in these guides.

7. Find out from other teachers in your school how they teach listening. Keep a record of what you are told.

8. Prepare sets of listening lessons of the types given in this chapter for use with your children. Try these lessons and report the results and your observations to the class.

9. Prepare your own tape recordings of selections you can play for your class to help them to listen for main ideas, details, etc. Incorporate outlining and note taking into this activity.

10. Start a file of listening activities you could use with your class. Begin with activities suggested in this chapter.

11. Tape directions for games. While the children are listening and following the directions you can observe and evaluate their ability.

Independent Activities for Children

1. Tape sounds of common objects such as a doorbell, electric mixer, telephone, lawnmower, water faucet, garage door, etc. Find and mount pictures of these and other objects. A child may play the recording and select the correct pictures, placing them in sequence. Be sure to space sounds just enough to allow time for selecting the pictures. Items may be named at the end of the tape so the child can check the accuracy of her listening.

2. A child may listen to a series of recorded sounds and write a word associated with each. For example:

faucet—gurgle, drip
rain—patter, pelt

3. Tape recordings of stories can be useful in many ways. For example, one child could listen to the story and select the "best" title from a list of possibilities provided on a card. Another could listen for the main idea or the sequence of events. A third could listen to discover the feeling or mood or to find words that bring to mind particular pictures—tall house, round face, worn shoe, etc.

4. Have a child perform an experiment or construct an object after listening to directions only once. Directions may be taped or they may be read by another child. Taped directions should be spaced to allow time to perform each step; the tasks might be simple ones such as folding paper to make a hat. Oral directions for three to five simple tasks could be given all at once, for example, "Go to the window and raise the shade about two inches. Then come back, sit down in your chair, and fold your arms." Children will enjoy thinking up unusual directions and attempting to perform tasks accurately.

5. Record tests such as those in *My Weekly Reader* for children to take individually.

6. Have a child listen to a recorded story or description and then draw a picture of the scene described or an episode in the story.

7. A child can prepare cutouts for the telling of a flannel board story from listening to a tape recording. Listening individually permits the child to relisten to parts of the story in order to develop the sequence and to decide what illustrations he needs.

8. Have a child make a list of all the sounds she hears in a particular place—in the lunch line, on the playground, at a certain street corner on the way to school, etc. As an added bonus, she might use the list to write a "sound picture" of the spot, or she might try to find the best words to describe each sound.

9. As a variation of the above, a child can sit quietly in a corner of the room listening for sounds such as a clock ticking, a car going by, a whistle, a buzzer, a dog barking, or walking in the hall. He should write down a word or two for each sound heard. Or two children can listen for the same period of time and compare the number of sounds they have heard.

10. A child can listen to records such as those "Sesame Street" produces for a variety of purposes:

Rub Your Tummy—following directions
A Face—vocabulary development
One of These—aural discrimination

11. A child can listen to the weather report on radio or TV and be prepared to present a forecast to the class, including expected temperature range, probability of precipitation, etc.

12. Newscasts can be listened to for the major topic reported, the name of the newscaster, the name of a public figure mentioned in the newscast, etc.

13. Have a child take notes on an assembly program or a program presented to the class for the purpose of preparing a written summary for the class diary.

14. Oral presentations may be improved if a child tapes a poem or story she is going to read to the class and then listens to it several times to discover ways to improve the reading.

15. Children can work in pairs, with one child reading a sentence and the other naming words that sound alike. Sentences such as the following might be used:

Jane knew her mother would bring a new dress.
The whole class saw the hole in the fence.

16. Working in pairs, children can use simple walkie-talkie sets to give directions to one another.

17. Keeping a log or diary of listening activities for several days will help a child recognize the importance of learning to listen effectively.

8 Children's Writing: Program and Practices

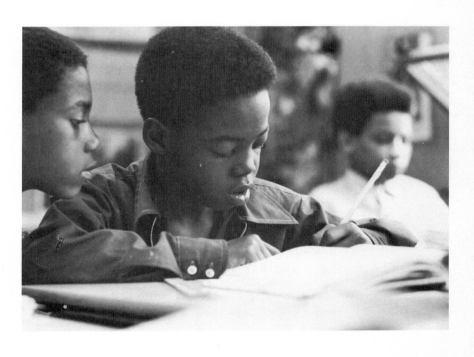

You don't need to be told that there is public concern about the teaching of writing in elementary and secondary schools. The media periodically cite examples of students' garbled sentences, misplaced modifiers, and horrendous spellings. There has been considerable reaction to such examples and to the public concern by teachers and school administrators, college professors, publishers of educational materials, and professional organizations—reaction which has led to an increase in both desirable and undesirable teaching practices. Unfortunately, it seems to us that the increase in undesirable practices may be winning out in too many classrooms.

The teaching of writing has long been an important element in the elementary school curriculum, although the emphasis given to it has varied from time to time. Regardless of the emphasis, however, the teaching of writing has too often been conducted in a framework of lessons isolated both from genuine communication purposes and from the interests of children. Many teachers have sought to improve writing quality through grammar exercises, while others have urged that children do much imaginative writing. In either case there has been little attention given to either the content or the form of this writing. In general, it is probably fair to say that too few teachers show evidence of knowing how to teach writing, and the differences in emphasis and techniques used reflect their struggles in determining "what to do."

In this chapter—the first of two concerned with teaching writing—we briefly discuss recent research findings and related opinions about what writers do and what programs should and should not be like. We then state factors and principles important in fostering and teaching writing, detail a virtually limitless number of opportunities for children to do many types of writing, and, finally, make further suggestions for maintaining children's interest in and opportunities for writing. Chapter 9 focuses on techniques for making writing more effective, form and conventions that are a part of writing, and the evaluation of children's writing efforts and of the program and practices in classrooms.

WRITING: RESEARCH AND THEORY

Writing is a complex process involving language, thought, feeling, personal experience, and expressive ability. It is a purposeful, individual activity. It is a "putting together," a composing effort in which the writer in reality discovers what he or she wants to say and how to say it. It is a thinking endeavor that requires selecting, combining, arranging, and developing information and ideas into sentences, paragraphs, and larger units of discourse. It is a process that we all engage in at various times, although as adults we write for varying purposes and in differing amounts and forms.

Chapter 3 stated that historically a major reason for teaching grammar was the belief that its teaching would lead to improvement in writing. That belief, which has by no means been discarded by many people, influenced not only the content of language textbooks and classroom instruction but also much research about teaching writing. An effort by the National Council of Teachers of English to determine what was known from research about teaching writing, reported in the 1963 publication *Research in Written Composition* (see Braddock *et al.*), resulted in a single substantiated finding: that grammar teaching *did not* improve students' writing. The authors of the report did make another significant statement: "Some questions which seem fundamental in the teaching and learning of written composition apparently have gone almost untouched by careful research."

The observation made in the report began to affect researchers in the early 1970s, causing them to focus efforts on observing writers—skilled and unskilled—of various ages to find out what they do in writing. This research led to findings that supported the insights and practices of those too few teachers who were effectively teaching writing, and it is changing the practices of many others who have been frustrated by the lack of success from their efforts.

Some Research Findings

The researchers soon observed that, for an individual to write, time is needed, and several stages are passed through in developing a written product. Thus they concluded that writing is a process rather than a single act. So it is not surprising that giving children a writing topic and saying, "Now you have your topic, so get busy and write," really doesn't work. The researchers discovered that writers of any age, particularly the better ones, *explore* and *plan*, both before putting words on paper and as the writing is being done. This exploring and planning—identified usually as the "prewriting" stage of the process—consists of a wide variety of activities, such as sketching and drawing, listing, talking to oneself and others, looking up information, and so on, all directed consciously or unconsciously at getting the writing started, clarifying thinking about what to write, and to some extent "rehearsing" for the actual writing. The next stage is writing—better thought of as *drafting*. In this stage exploring and planning often continue. The young child changes his or her drawing, thinks aloud or talks to classmates, pauses and rereads, and perhaps checks on information. The older writer may do much the same—marking out, drawing lines to change the organization of the content, and reflecting about what is being written. The final stage is *revising*, followed by proofreading and editing, contemplating the product, and doing something with it.

The research has generally shown that the better writers do more exploring and planning, spend more time drafting, and show more sensitivity to a reader than poorer writers do. The poorer or less skilled writers tend to write in a way that imitates speech and are more preoccupied with matters of spelling and punctuation than are the better writers, particularly at the drafting stage.

The research with young children has shown that they are eager to write, as was discussed in Chapter 5, and that they themselves will decide what to write about if given the opportunity. There is also evidence that they will write more under this condition than they will if writing is assigned. Of particular importance to teaching practices is the finding that teacher participation is needed in all stages of writing—encouraging, guiding, listening, and responding. Assigning a writing topic and returning to the desk to count milk money or to put red marks on papers is simply a bad practice.

See articles by Burrows, Calkins, Glatthorn, and Graves.

Beginning Writers

Again, as stated in Chapter 5, children come to school convinced that they *know* how to write. To them drawings and lines on a paper are not pretend writing; they are very real. Kindergarten children's first writing is drawing and naming objects with one-word labels. Children can tell a teacher these words so that he or she can write them on their papers. The drawings soon become more complex so that a one-word label is not satisfactory, and gradually a child will want to copy what the teacher has written. This and other

A proud beginning writer.

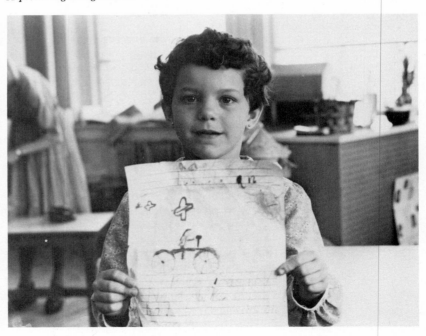

observations the child has made lead to the forming of some letters. As soon as this happens, writing becomes even more real. Great independence in writing occurs as soon as a child learns to form a few letters (i.e., about half a dozen of the most commonly written consonants). Of course, this limited ability will not permit the child to spell words correctly, but it is enough for the child to write a sentence that he or she can read: RCRBKD ("Our car broke down"—from Temple *et al.*, p. 57). With encouragement, more letters are learned, spaces are left between "words," vowels are put in, and the writing becomes real even to adults.

The big "hang-up" for most young children (and some not so young) in writing about things they know about is spelling. Accepting children's spelling attempts (i.e., "inventions"—discussed in Chapter 10) is an important element in fostering the earliest writing of young children, but of course it does not mean that attention will not be given to spelling later.

See accounts *by teachers* in the book by Newkirk and Atwell.

Of special significance is the discovery by teachers of first, second, and third grade children participating in the recent research that children show interest in revising their own writing. Under the encouraging classroom conditions in these studies, children want the information in their stories and accounts to be accurate; they want their writing to tell what they really want to tell. And revising done with the guidance and encouragement of teachers, revising that the children want to do, has been shown to result in better sentences, more accurate spelling, and neater papers.

What Writers Do

There has been considerably less research done in recent years in the intermediate and upper grades, even of the case study–observation type, than has been done in the primary grades and with preprimary children. However, older children and adults—even professional writers—appear to do many of the same things a beginning writer does. Of course, they will likely have considerably less difficulty with spelling, punctuation, and sentence construction, but to some degree at least they explore, plan, draft, and revise. Murray, a teacher and professional writer, has identified "steps followed by most effective writers—businessmen and poets, scientists and journalists." He summarizes the content of these steps as seven skills that writers need: (1) discovering a subject, (2) sensing an audience, (3) searching for specifics, (4) creating a design, (5) writing, (6) developing a critical eye, and (7) rewriting. It is not too difficult to recognize in this listing of skills the prewriting planning, searching, rehearsing; the thinking and rethinking during drafting or writing; and the contemplating and revising that the observational research has found. Thus, there is considerable agreement about what writers do, and this is a basic consideration in deciding upon writing programs and teaching practices.

See *A Writer Teaches Writing* by Donald M. Murray.

Writing and the "Basic Skills"

We mentioned at the beginning of Chapter 3 that concern for teaching "basic skills" was being interpreted by much of the public, as well as some teachers, as a need to teach grammar. Apparently researchers and educators

See the article by Charles Chew.

at all levels have to keep fighting this belief. Chew, basing his conclusions on a study of sources available to teachers for use in teaching written composition, has pointed out that "In textbooks used to prepare teachers, curriculum guides, student textbooks, evaluative materials, and publications from the National Council of Teachers of English, the major emphasis is placed on grammar and mechanics." In fact, he says, the emphasis is "overwhelming."

In the preceding sections, we have summarized much of what research and observation have shown to be *basic*. Clearly there is considerable difference between these findings and what is emphasized certainly in most textbooks, guides, and other resources. In the remainder of this chapter and the following one, as well as in other sections of this book, we present and discuss teaching suggestions and activities for children to aid them in attaining the skills, abilities, attitudes, and knowledge that we believe to be basic.

FOSTERING WRITING

The teaching of writing will not be successful unless the total classroom program is meaningful and challenging. If ideas abound in the classroom and communication is genuine, and if children are respected, a foundation is present for teaching writing. Motivating children to write will be little needed or will be very simple if there are apparent, meaningful purposes for the writing. Children will write because there is a genuine need to do so—to communicate information or to express ideas or feelings. They will write because they have something to say and feel that someone will appreciate or learn from what they have written.

Keep in mind the importance of an audience.

The Classroom Environment

A "Writers' Corner," possibly partially screened and furnished with writing materials, will stimulate much writing.

A good writing environment is actually no different from the environment that should be created for any learning. Every environment consists of people, things, processes, purposes, feelings, and relationships all blended together. But a good learning environment is one in which all of these elements are brought into harmonious play with one another. Creating this harmony in a classroom is an ongoing, dynamic process—one that requires effort by both teacher and children. But it is a process that cannot be left to chance; therefore, the major responsibility is the teacher's.

The keys to meeting this responsibility are purpose and respect—purpose in what children do and respect for their learning efforts. Both can be achieved, though, by a well-planned, challenging curriculum in which communication is a genuinely integrated part and by understanding each child's aspirations, abilities, and potential. A child will write a report readily enough, for instance, if she feels that the information included in it is needed in the social studies class—and if that class is interesting. Another child will gladly keep a record—and do so to the best of his ability—if he is convinced that this record will actually be referred to and used later. A third will write a summary of a science experiment if she enjoyed working on it and knows that the summary will be sent to her parents. Others will write the dialogue for the skit on good health habits because the skit will be presented to the second graders.

Input and Experience

As adults we know that we cannot write very effectively, if at all, about something that is largely beyond our realm of knowledge. We do not write about a chemical experiment unless we have sufficient background in chemistry to do so; we do not write about politics unless we have studied and experienced political activity. The knowledge that we have about ourselves and what we could or could not write is a most important clue to the teaching of written expression.

Children will write about subjects they know about, things they have experienced, things that have meaning to them. Equally, they will write in forms that they have had experience with. They will write letters if they know how letters are written (and there is reason to write them). By the same token, they will write reviews of books if they know the form and organization of reviews, tall tales if the purpose and form of these is understood, poetry in cinquain form if this is known and appreciated, and so on.

We have earlier pointed out that children have had many experiences before coming to school, that they continue to have many experiences outside of the classroom, and that these experiences must be respected and capitalized on in our teaching. We have also emphasized that children must have abundant and continuous opportunities for gaining new ideas and information, associating these with previous experiences, and learning vocabulary related to them. Not all experiences need to be firsthand, but as many as possible should be. Looking at pictures, listening to music and speech, talking with and watching other people all provide experiences.

Particularly important also is reading; much poor language expression—oral or written—is an almost direct consequence of a background of little reading. Reading to children and encouraging them to read are tremendously important to a writing program. Through the reading of good literature, genuinely expressive language insinuates itself into the mind, generates thinking, awakens ideas, and gives impetus to creativeness. Reading challenges children's thinking, enriches their other experiences, and leads directly to many writing activities.

As important as direct experiences and those gained from reading and other vicarious means are, fostering writing that is genuinely effective and individually as creative as possible requires a good deal of direct teaching. Most children must be guided in being observant enough to see how the spider web seen during the walk was intricately woven—or even to see the web. They must be taught to give thought to the hardships of the southern sharecropper seen in a film or to appreciate the artistry of a wood carving from Africa. We must recognize that children may do as we often do—see, hear, read, feel, or taste at a level that leaves only vague impressions and ideas and seldom provides the base for expression that should be possible.

Things to Listen for

the first raindrops tapping hesitantly at the window
a lonely puppy wailing in the night
the howling wind demanding to be let in
the crunch of your boots on new snow
the conversation "levels" at different tables in the cafeteria

In addition to providing a broad range of experiences and to giving a good deal of direct guidance in helping children gain as much as possible from them, specific attention will need to be given to teaching children about a variety of forms or types of writing. Without knowledge about a particular form, a child will not be able to write effectively, if at all, in that form. Thus, children need the input of hearing and seeing the various forms of writing that you want them to use in their expression. This, of course, cannot all be given at once. As children engage in writing, it can be given through models, demonstrations, and group compositions, and as with all input, it should be a continuing and recurring process.

Other Ways to Give Input

listening to music
attending plays
observing dancers
making lists of words (synonyms, words related to objects or ideas, etc.)

Program Principles

There is no one way to teach writing, no single key to unlocking children's potential, no pattern for every teacher to follow. But writing can be taught. Children can learn with guidance, encouragement, and the teaching of some skills. Not all teachers will do the same things in teaching and guidance, and not all children will show like interest in writing or will develop the same abilities. Many useful principles for developing writing programs and teaching have been suggested or implied in the preceding sections. These are amplified and extended below.

1. Provide for much and varied oral expression: sharing, discussing, "brainstorming," role playing, and the other activities discussed in early chapters—and more. Encourage talking about interests and thoughts. Listen to the children, encouraging the clarification—and extension—of ideas.
2. Guide children in being observers of things about them, from the spelling of some words in advertisements to how geese fly in formation or how an author "paints a picture" of a character in a story.
3. Provide input by reading and telling lots of stories, reading poetry, taking field trips; bringing in people to talk with the children; examining objects and processes (i.e., integrating with science); looking at pictures, graphs, and charts; and looking at and listening to TV and films.

Read all types of literature:

fables
tall tales
autobiographies
fairy tales
historical fiction
folk tales

4. Encourage children to explore on their own, to seek ideas and information, and to plan. Direct instruction will usually be needed to supplement the encouragement in the planning, as well as in using media of all types in the library and the classroom.
5. Have a comprehensive program, one that has the children writing in all of the forms and situations discussed later in this chapter. A comprehensive program also includes using these writing forms in all curriculum areas, thus providing for meaningful integration and recognizing that writing is a way to learn.
6. Encourage and provide time for much "free writing," and possibly provide space and materials. At any grade level, providing or arranging for journals to write in is a good idea. Respect children's privacy in regard to this writing. Remember that as adults we don't want to show everything that we write.

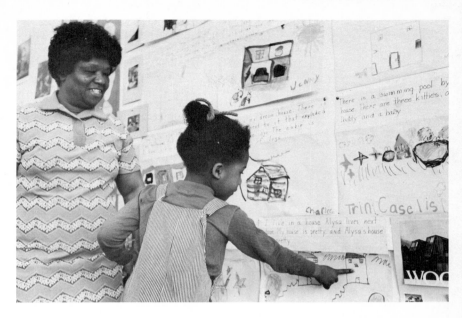

Children like their writing products to be displayed. This is satisfying to them, and it also leads to self-evaluation of their work.

Publishers of Children's Writing

Children's Express, 20 Charles St., New York, NY 10014

Ebony, Jr!, 820 S. Michigan Ave., Chicago, IL 60605

Highlights for Children, 803 Church St., Honesdale, PA 18431

Jack and Jill, 1100 Waterway Blvd., P.O. Box 567B, Indianapolis, IN 46202

The McGuffey Writer, McGuffey Lab School, Miami University, Oxford, OH 45056

Stone Soup, Box 83, Santa Cruz, CA 95063

7. Some assigned writing will be necessary—particularly beyond the primary grades. Make every effort, though, to provide for self-selection as to topic or task by the children in recognition of both their interests and their abilities.

8. Encourage children to write for real audiences, which means that writing should be done for genuine purposes. While many children will determine the purpose of their writing if the environment fosters this, others will need teacher guidance.

9. Value ideas, originality, precision, and vividness of language above competence in spelling, sentence construction, and the use of conventions.

10. Provide for positive feedback to children concerning their writing. This can be done in individual conferences and/or when children ask questions or show their writing.

11. Encourage children to do their own revising of content and editing of spelling, conventions, and syntax. Such encouragement may occur in conferences and other feedback activities, as well as less specifically through aspects of the classroom climate.

12. Provide for both indirect and direct instruction in rhetorical skills as well as matters of form and convention. Much indirect instruction may occur as children are encouraged in their revising. To the extent that this is not accomplishing satisfactory gains, lessons and activities may be needed.

13. Provide for a purposeful disposition of writing: displaying, class or school publishing, publishing in a magazine or newspaper, sending home, making available for classmates to read, etc.

14. Recognize that growth in writing occurs in spurts. These spurts will vary from child to child, and usually will be difficult if not impossible to trace to anything in the program. After all, adults have "off days," and it is certainly probable that some of our own earlier writing is better than some that has been done recently.

15. Recognize that the textbook doesn't teach writing. While some language textbooks may have some writing activities that appeal to children, by and large they are loaded with such exercises as filling in blanks, underlining parts of speech, or arranging sentences in a prescribed sequence. Textbooks can be a resource; they are not satisfactory program guides.

16. Evaluate your teaching. Are you flexible, recognizing differences in children's abilities, backgrounds, and interests? Are you a "trusted reader" of children's writing, a reader who respects private views and a child's wish not to display a piece or to be judged on it? Do you write—and do the children know this—in order (if for no other reason) to be more conscious of a writer's struggles and joys?

A recent study by Brogan of several textbook series reports an emphasis on filling in blanks, writing one-word responses, copying textbook sentences to supply missing punctuation, and expanding textbook sentences by including specified parts of speech.

WRITING ACTIVITIES

Many opportunities for children to write for purposes that are meaningful to them occur in classrooms every day. An opportunity may stem from a science lesson, a field trip in social studies, the information brought by a resource person to health class, the development of a story, or any of numerous other activities that are integral parts of the curriculum. This section identifies many possible writing situations and suggests the kinds of activities that can and should be planned for in a classroom where children are encouraged and helped to communicate their ideas and feelings.

Experiential Writing

While many young children may do much writing on their own, and most are anxious to, teachers can help foster this by putting on paper for them the ideas and information the children have. The youngest of children are eager to talk about their pets, presents they have received, places they have been, and things they have done. They are equally eager to have these accounts recorded in writing. The same is true about their school experiences if these have been appealing and challenging.

Dictation to the teacher can begin when children are in preschool or kindergarten and at first will probably consist of just one or two sentences, or possibly only a title for a picture. Individual and group dictation of stories and other forms of composition should continue in the primary grades as children are learning to make letter forms and are doing independent writing. With the teacher doing the writing, children are freed from handwriting problems, and the focus can be on the ideas being expressed and choosing the best ways to express them. Yet attention can also be given to spelling, punctuation, capitalization, margins, etc., in a meaningful and nonthreatening way. Experiential writing—with the teacher remaining as

Our Weather

It snowed last night. The wind is blowing the snow. It is cold.

An Experience Chart

OUR HALLOWEEN PARTY

We had a Halloween party. Our mothers sent cookies. Mr. Fall gave us milk. We played and had fun.

scribe—is a valuable activity at any grade level because it allows children to focus on the organization and content of what is written—and this is where the emphasis in teaching written expression should be.

Stories can be written on the chalkboard, on chart paper, or, if composed by an individual pupil, on ordinary-size paper. In each case questions can direct attention toward composition and organization: How shall we start the story? Can someone think of another way? Which way do you like? What should we say next? Is this the way the story should end? Have we told the story in the proper order? Let's go back over this and decide which sentences we need to keep in the story and how they should be arranged.

Even in the very first productions, attention should be paid to the mechanical skills. At first, simply pointing out capital letters and periods will help children to become accustomed to their use. Later you could say, "How do I begin this sentence?" The same procedure can be used with other punctuation, margins, placing the title, and possibly spelling some words. However, it is not wise to introduce or to dwell on a great number of these skills at one time, particularly when writing a chart for young children.

Children in higher grades can be scribes for younger children.

To encourage young children's sense of participation in writing experience stories, copies may occasionally be made and given to children so that they can put their names on them and take them to their parents. As children begin to be experienced with stories dictated by the group, they may dictate individual endings. Again, these may be taken home, or they may be posted so that children can find out how others completed the story. Stories individually dictated to the teacher might be placed in a class book of stories. Other forms of writing that children dictate should also be used—for instance, records and titles posted, letters mailed, and so on.

Story Writing

Story writing really begins with the first oral sharing and experience writing activities of children, even though some of these may be more similar to the reports they will write later. In the early stage of story writing, however, this distinction need not be made. To children a story is something they want to tell, and they will do this both orally and in writing when they are encouraged to do so and have the necessary skills.

Bind stories and give to younger children.

Children's first stories are usually about something that happened to them or that has been read or told to them. But given their inborn imaginative and creative abilities, their stories soon become ones that they "make up" or at least embellish considerably. Teachers generally encourage children to use their imagination, "to be creative," and of course the encouragement of children's creativity—in all of their endeavors—is desirable. But creativity is more than imagination; it draws upon imagination, but it also draws on an individual's emotional resources and propensity to be curious and to think independently. It requires divergent thinking, but the expression of this thinking—the product—results only if there is some degree, at least, of convergent thinking.

We are not suggesting any diminishing of teachers' efforts to foster children's creativity. In fact, we think teachers should generally exert more effort. This effort, however, must be more than simply telling children to "write something creative." Too often this direction results in wildly imaginative pieces that have few characteristics of stories and/or creative expression—even though such a piece may contain ideas or ways of phrasing them that are indeed genuinely creative. Too often, too, there is no encouragement or guidance in revising this writing. Stamping a smiling face or writing "good" on the paper does nothing to teach writing. It isn't even satisfying to the child.

Children can be awakened early in their experiences to features of stories. Dictating to the teacher—with questions by him or her that help children think about catching a reader's interest with the story's beginning, the order in which they want to tell the story, and so on—will help. The same sort of thing can be done in time spent with children as they consider writing they have done themselves. As a teacher reads or tells stories or relates personal experiences, children will begin to learn the importance of sequence in relating events and details. And, of course, pointing out these characteristics of stories is an integral part of teaching reading and listening comprehension. Yet when children begin to write, many of their "stories" may have an appealing beginning, but then the sequence of events becomes confused, a climax is absent, and finally the "story" just stops (often with the child writing "THE END").

Story ideas and forms may come from literature.

Trying too hard to be imaginative is one cause for a story's being poorly developed, but attempting too broad a scope is possibly even more often a cause. Limiting a topic—for a story or for other forms of writing—is a problem for all writers, children or adults. Help children to discover that if the scope is limited to a particular event or time span, the story can be developed more interestingly. For example, the title "Sam Got Out of the House Last Night" lends itself more readily to sequencing events and using specific details than does "My Pet Cat." Or "The First Indian I Ever Saw" is more easily handled than "Crossing the Prairie in a Wagon Train."

Deciding how to limit the topic is part of the exploration, the prewriting phase of writing. With careful questioning and responding by the teacher, children will learn to do this kind of thinking. It won't amount to total planning, but it will set the stage, helping as the children write and their stories develop. By the time children reach the middle grades, it might prove helpful to formulate standards that can be posted and called to their attention each time they write. These might include such points as the following:

THINGS TO THINK ABOUT BEFORE I WRITE

1. What is the story about?
2. Where did it happen?
3. Who are the characters and what are they like?
4. Who is telling the story?
5. How will it begin?
6. What is the high point, or climax, of the story?
7. What events or actions lead up to this climax?
8. How will I end the story?

This may seem like a good deal for a child to think about, but children often can do more than we think—especially when they have some idea of what to do. And if the standards are posted, children can refer to them as they plan and as they write.

Children should learn, of course, that this preplanning is not iron-clad. Sometimes plans need to be modified—possibly even abandoned. But they do help in getting started and in organizing content. The child who has some idea of where he or she is going is more likely to produce an interesting story than one who simply begins.

Even with planning and modifying of the plan during the writing, stories usually need revising as the writer contemplates them or as they are read to peers or the teacher. Thus, reference will need to be made to standards or "story guides" and to what listeners or readers say.

If attention is given to all that is said and implied above, dashing off a "story" in a Friday afternoon "creative" writing period is not possible. Time is needed to produce stories satisfactory to their authors and readers. This is true for authors of any age—as teachers who have tried to write stories themselves have found out.

Letter Writing

Letter writing is one of the most frequently used writing forms and therefore should receive instructional emphasis in the elementary school. Like other writing forms, it is best taught in situations where the need is genuine rather than manufactured, and such situations abound in the average classroom. Some examples are listed on page 194.

Probably you can think of other occasions or of other people for children to write letters to. You might try asking parents to send in names and ad-

Learning about the parts of a letter.

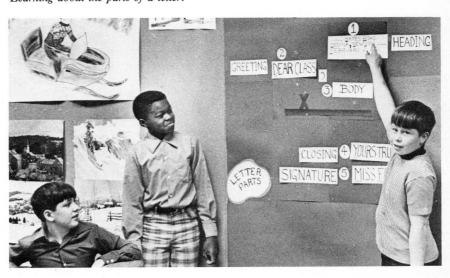

Write to the National Council of Teachers of English for a pamphlet for parents, *How to Help Your Child Become a Better Writer* (available in both English and Spanish).

Use charts and models to show letter form. Label the parts: heading, greeting (salutation), message, closing, and signature.

OCCASIONS CALLING FOR LETTER WRITING

Invitations	To friends to visit the classroom.
	To parents to come to an activity.
	To another class or school to come to a program.
	To the principal or supervisor to observe an activity.
	To a guest to show slides.
	To the custodian or nurse to tell about his or her work.
Replies	Of acceptance of an invitation from another class.
	Of regret at not being able to come to a program.
Sympathy	To a sick classmate, teacher, or relative.
	To a teacher or family of a classmate after a death or accident.
Greetings	To others at school on a holiday.
	To parents at Christmas, on Mothers' Day, and on other special occasions.
	To the principal and other teachers on birthdays.
	To various friends on special occasions.
Friendly letters and postcards	To another classroom or school.
	To a former classmate.
	To last year's teacher.
	To a student in a foreign land.
	To authors of favorite books.
	To grandparents.
	To a sports star.
Thank-you notes	To someone for talking to the class.
	To friends and relatives for presents at Christmas.
	To another class for the use of books or other materials.
	To a parent for the loan of materials.
	To the principal for some special favor.
Requests	To a company or individual for information.
	To a shopkeeper for materials.
	To someone for permission to visit his or her business or home.
	To the principal for permission to take a trip.
	To organizations for free materials.
Orders	To a business for class supplies.
	To a publisher for a magazine subscription.
Applications	For a position on the school paper.
	For a job in the school office.
	For summer work.
	For after-school jobs.
Complaints	About an article in the newspaper.
	About a practice on the playground.
	About a product to a consumer agency.

Names of pen pals are available from (some charge fees):

English Speaking Union
Pen Friends
16 East 69th St.
New York, NY 10021

The International
Friendship League
40 Mt. Vernon St.
Boston, MA 02108

League of Friendship, Inc.
P.O. Box 509
Mt. Vernon, OH 43050

Student Letter Exchange
910 4th St.
Austin, MN 55912

World Pen Pals
1690 Como Ave.
St. Paul, MN 55108

Two books about letter writing, *P.S. Write Soon!* (elementary) and *All About Letters* (upper elementary and high school), produced by the United States Postal Service and the National Council of Teachers of English are available from the latter for $1.50 each. Both have many ideas about places and people to write to, as well as addresses.

Middle grade children will enjoy *Dear Dragon* by Sesyle Joslin.

More Ideas for Teaching Letter Writing

1. Post model letters, including those written by children.
2. Show letter makeup by outlining the form with a felt pen.
3. Use dittoed work sheets, lined in such a way that the child is forced to write in correct form.
4. Keep collections of letters showing various forms.
5. Use construction-paper cutouts to show form and shape.
6. Have pupils exchange letters for correction of matters of form.

dresses of grandparents and other relatives children could write to. In fact, arranging for children to start their own address books is a good idea. The point is that letter writing can be done for genuine purposes. Practice will be real. Children will learn when it is appropriate to write notes of sympathy or congratulations, that one should write a thank-you note to someone who has sent a gift or done a favor, that it is courteous to express respect when writing to someone older than they are, how to acknowledge invitations, and to give reasons when regrets are necessary. They should also develop the ability to select appropriate writing materials (paper, pen, typewriter) and the realization that letters should be answered and mailed promptly. Like any other piece of writing, a letter should be read before it is mailed, and attention should be given to spelling and neatness. And, finally, a letter is personal; one should not read a letter addressed to someone else unless asked to. This courtesy may be emphasized by asking children's permission before posting letters or having them exchanged for correction—and respecting a child's wish *not* to have his or her letter read by others.

While younger children will sometimes have occasion to write business letters, principal instruction should begin in the middle grades, with emphasis on the need for more formal language, appropriate salutations and closings, and the kinds of information that should be included in the body of the letter (whether money is enclosed, how to write out dollars and cents, the importance of stating exactly where merchandise or information is to be sent, etc.). Whenever children first write to an individual (rather than a firm) and request a reply, they should learn that a stamped, self-addressed envelope should be enclosed. And they should know that any letter written to a stranger—even if it is a letter of complaint—should always be courteous; rude or angry letters seldom get the desired results.

In the upper grades, introduce or reinforce any of the above items that children do not seem to be familiar with, and also bring in, discuss, and post business letters with various formats, such as block and indented styles. At this level, some pupils may also be learning to type, so they should know that it is good form to write *and* type the signature on a business letter.

Most of us do not write business letters often, but when we do it is sometimes important that they convey a particularly good impression (letters of application, for instance). Impress children with the importance of neatness, the placement of the letter on the page, and the inclusion of needed information in the body of the letter. Again, no letter should be sealed and mailed until it has been proofread. One or two inked corrections are better than mistakes left uncorrected; if there are many errors, the letter should be rewritten.

There are many matters of form that are particularly important in letter writing—the placement of the parts of a letter, capitalization of particular items, abbreviations of titles such as Mr. or Dr., wording of the salutation or complimentary closing, etc. Children will master these only through actual letter writing experiences. Certainly letters should not be emphasized to the exclusion of other forms of writing, but letters are often crucial, and therefore the writing of letters should not be neglected in the school program.

Reporting

There are always many opportunities for children to write reports. In fact, the classroom activities that pursue children's interests and recognize that the teaching of writing should not be separated from the teaching of other subjects—social studies, science, health, and so on—demand the writing of reports. Among the kinds of reports are the following: summaries of books, speeches, articles, movies, and television and radio programs; summaries of student council, class, or club meetings or of assembly programs; research accounts based on interviews, reading on specific topics, or science experiments; accounts of personal and class experiences.

Sending reports home informs parents about their children's learning.

Reporting begins in the primary grades—both in many "stories" written by children themselves and in those dictated to teachers—when the emphasis is on conveying information. This early reporting is a good foundation for later reporting on many topics and for many occasions. The following should suggest the unlimited possibilities:

1. Writing one-paragraph reports on famous people.
2. Visiting a museum and reporting on an object observed.
3. Writing a report on a hobby or special interest.
4. Keeping records of baseball and football games and reporting on them.
5. Explaining the organization and work of a club.
6. Describing an incident from a particular point of view.
7. Reporting on controversial issues in committee meetings.
8. Writing an account of a holiday celebration.
9. Reporting briefly on the history and derivation of a word.
10. Giving personal reactions to characters and situations in books.
11. Reporting on the steps through which a character in a story changes.
12. Reporting on the history of a custom, superstition, or place name.
13. Reporting on an interview with the principal.
14. Summarizing newspaper articles on a topic of current interest.
15. Reporting on background information relative to a current news story.

Don't overlook the possibility of putting cover pages on reports so they can become part of the classroom library.

Chapters 13 and 14 discuss teaching children to locate information, take notes, outline, and correlate information—skills needed for making reports as effective as possible. Since reporting, either orally or in writing, is important to many classroom activities, it is a good idea to initiate a class discussion aimed at formulating a set of procedures. By the time children reach the upper grades, these should probably include the following steps:

1. Decide what facts or information should be included.
2. Determine the most likely sources for this information—observation, interviews, reading.
3. Use these sources to find the information needed.
4. Recheck 1 to see whether all needed information has been found and whether new items should be included.
5. Decide on the order in which facts should be presented and the best way to present each one—illustrations, details, or reasons.

Reviews

Making and writing new book jackets appeals to children.

A specialized type of report is the review. Reviews may be written about books, television programs, movies, and cultural events. A review should be a teaser, a reaction by the writer, and not a dull account of "what happened." Before children write reviews, particularly of books they have read, they should be made familiar with reviews such as those found in *Language Arts* and *The Horn Book*. Most newspapers have reviews (of varying quality) of television, movies, and local events. Various reviews should be discussed with children so that they learn how a review differs from other kinds of reports.

Essays

Ideas for Personal Essays

I Wish I Were____
If I Were President
Thoughts on a Rainy
    Afternoon
The Meanest Man in the
    World
If I Had a Hundred
    Dollars
The Day I Forgot
I Like____
How It Feels to Be Me
On Being Ten Years Old
Walking Barefoot in the
    Mud
Skiing the Bumps
My Hockey Team

See Chapter 15 for writing suggestions related to literature.

The word *essay* has fallen into disuse, except in literature classes, yet it is an apt term for a type of writing that offers endless opportunities for creative expression. In simple terms, an essay is the expression of one's own beliefs or feelings about a person, an event, or an idea. Thus much of the writing and speaking that we do, both as children and as adults, has some of the qualities of an essay—even a personal letter is a loosely organized essay, since it reflects the writer's own personality. Likewise, many of the experience stories that children write or dictate to the teacher are essays.

The essay has several advantages as a vehicle for creative expression. First, it is a form with which children have had experience; thus they can focus major attention on choosing the best way to express their ideas and feelings. Second, by its very nature the essay is creative, since it is a personal expression. Third, children want to express their own likes and dislikes, their fears and desires, so this form should appeal to them. It may even help to improve the self-image of a child who believes that his or her feelings are unimportant to others. And finally, the essay is somewhat similar in form to the kinds of writing most commonly used by children and adults—more so, at least, than are stories and poems. Thus children can learn organization and methods of developing ideas while they are also developing their creative talents.

News Articles

News writing can begin in the primary grades with group-dictated news written by the teacher on the chalkboard.

A classroom newspaper can be extremely challenging for motivating writing. Children will become intrigued with discovering and reporting events around the school, in the neighborhood, and in their homes. The newspaper can be typed—parents often will help, as will upper grade or high school students—or written by children, preferably in manuscript form. It may have the organizational features of a regular newspaper—that is, staff, editorials, and various types of sections. It can be published weekly, monthly, or only occasionally for special holidays and events. Frequency should be determined principally, of course, by the amount of learning and enjoyment the children gain from this activity, but other factors must be considered too. Will this frequency of publication fit into the schedule without replacing other activities that may be even more valuable? Can the paper be planned to call forth the kinds of writing practice and skills needed by the children? Is time available for typing and duplicating, or can parents and/or students be depended on for at least a part of this work?

The writing in a newspaper may be of many types, since newspapers ordinarily include many things—news stories, special features, letters to the

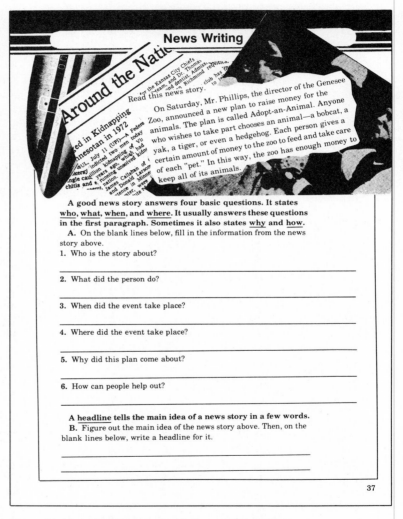

From this kind of activity move to using real news articles.

editor, jokes, advertisements, poems, and comics. Organizational skills are also called into play in making decisions about what things should be placed together.

Many upper grade reading programs include material on how to read a newspaper. This may provide a starting point for a class or school newspaper. Children might read newspapers in class and analyze them, cutting out clippings of various sorts to illustrate what they have learned. Various sections of a paper (sports, world news, society news, etc.) should be noted, and special attention should be given to sources of material for these sections—syndicated columns, wire services, publicity handouts, and local reporting. Journalism has its own vocabulary, and children can learn the special meanings of words such as *copy, deadline, proofreading, layout,* and *editor.* The school newspaper should receive high priority in a program of written expression because it is a live (not book) activity, it builds class and school spirit, and it appeals to all children, regardless of creative abilities. Every child in the classroom may participate in some way, because there is such a wide variety of forms of writing. And almost every area of the curriculum may be utilized in the newspaper—social studies, science, art, health, etc.

Records

Graphs and charts can supplement written records.

Children's interest in nature and in everything going on about them provides opportunities for writing records of things that happen. Since most record keeping requires straightforward, factual writing, and not a taxing amount, many children who have difficulty with other forms of writing can keep records. Here are some kinds of records that can be kept:

1. The time the sun sets, recorded at weekly intervals.
2. Weather calendars.
3. Growth of plants in the classroom windows.
4. Steps followed in making pudding.
5. Spelling words missed by the class.
6. Classroom duties assigned to pupils.
7. Class diary of daily events.
8. Books read by each child. (Avoid making this too competitive.)
9. Daily temperatures, wind direction, etc.
10. Dates of appearance of first robin, ducks flying, etc.
11. Height and weight records.
12. Foods eaten for breakfast, hours slept, etc.
13. The changing appearance of the polliwogs, cocoon, etc.
14. Visitors to the classroom.

Other Records

stories read
topics written about
sports schedules and scores

15. New words learned in various subjects.
16. Science experiments.
17. Points to remember about a film.

18. Daily attendance and daily schedule.

19. Standards or rules for class activities.

20. Events to be reported on in the yearbook.

Forms

Offers on cereal boxes interest children and can provide practice in filling out forms.

Everyone has occasion to fill out forms. Neither children nor adults can avoid doing so; therefore children need to learn and to practice this kind of writing. There are many day-to-day activities in which children must fill out forms. These situations should be utilized to teach careful reading, the importance of legible writing (or printing), and the need for accuracy. Some school situations for filling out forms are these:

1. Enrollment cards.

2. Questionnaires regarding personal history.

3. Questionnaires concerning health facts.

4. Library loan cards.

5. Call slips for books at the library.

6. Information called for on a standardized test.

7. A money order for materials for the class.

8. An application card for an account in the school savings bank.

9. A deposit slip for a school savings account.

10. A withdrawal slip.

11. A subscription blank for a magazine.

12. Coupons for samples advertised in magazines.

13. An order to a publisher for a reference book.

14. An application blank for membership in a magazine club.

15. A book plate for use in a textbook.

Announcements, Labels, and Notices

Many school activities call for written notices, labels, titles, and announcements. This type of writing requires specificity and brevity. Moreover, such writing may not be read unless it is interesting and clear. Teaching emphasis should be upon these factors. Activities such as the following may be helpful:

1. Making oral announcements that hold to standards of brevity, accuracy, etc.

2. Giving oral directions for a game or other activity.

3. Examining the weaknesses of notices and announcements in newspapers.

4. Reporting on notices, signs, and labels seen around the school.

5. Scoring announcements and notices as to appeal, clarity, neatness, etc.

The factors to be considered can be listed on a score sheet and points assigned to each as an announcement or notice is examined.

Poetry and Rhymes

Send *extra special* poems by children to Dr. Leland Jacobs, c/o *Early Years*.

Every child should have some experience with poetry—hearing it, reading it, speaking it individually or as part of a group, and writing it. Certainly no one class will produce many—if any—poets of great stature, but the number of children who can create a truly charming, humorous, or actually poetic bit of verse is often surprising.

Children should not be expected to write poetry unless they have heard much of it. Poetry in its various forms needs to have been read to them, and they should have experienced saying it in choral speaking activities. Opening activities in a classroom provide a natural time every day for reading poetry to children, but many activities also provide natural times if you have appropriate poetry ready to read (see Chapter 15). There are equally many natural and fun times for children to experience speaking poetry. Important, too, as background for children's writing of poetry are experiences that have extended their language powers: finding and talking about words and phrases that create visual and sound images, words with a musical lift, new ways of saying things, and words related to their emotions.

A class poem is a good beginning. Decide on a type of poem with which the children are familiar and which they have enjoyed, read aloud several examples, and then suggest that they might compose a poem like this. With the background suggested, children should be able to think of topics, words and phrases, rhyming words (if needed), and even entire lines. Possibly you may need to encourage such suggestions by stimulating one or more of their senses. Even a weed picked on your way to school may prompt thoughts about its structure, color, or smell and bring forth words and phrases about how ugly or beautiful it is, its uniqueness, and so on. The children can then discuss which words and phrases sound best or fit the subject or rhythm best. In this way they will learn how to go about the process of creating a poem.

It is not important to teach poetic techniques as such, but call attention to them when it is appropriate. For example, kindergarten children cannot be expected either to pronounce or to remember *onomatopoeia*, but they can readily grasp that *buzz* is something like the sound that a bee makes. Upper grade pupils, on the other hand, might be extremely proud of the fact that they have used a technique called *alliteration* in creating a phrase like "the sad, silken syllables of the breeze." Emphasis should always be on the product rather than the technique, however.

After several class poems, it may be appropriate to encourage group poems (three or four children) in order to give children more confidence, since the responsibility for success or failure does not then rest on a single child and the exchange of ideas often leads to better language choices. With little encouragement some children will want to write poetry themselves, if they have heard a good many poems and if they are not forced into attempting a form that doesn't appeal. Others will do little poetry or verse writing by themselves regardless of the amount of poetry they hear or read and the encouragement they receive. They should not be pressured to write, but the door should be kept open for them to try when and if they want to. Sometimes a simple observation or sensory experience will elicit feelings—words and phrases—from even the most reticent and may lead to an almost spontaneous writing of verse.

Writing poems based on a specified pattern or formula will assist some children. Again, such pattern writing can be overdone. There are several short and rather structured forms, however, that children particularly enjoy using because the form itself creates a challenge and furnishes rather definite guidelines, thus helping them to achieve greater success with their first efforts.

COUPLETS AND TRIPLETS. Reading readiness activities calling for the use of rhyming words may produce the children's first attempts at composing poems. At this point there is no need to be concerned with rhythm, although children love rhythm and they may well try to produce it. Simply encouraging them to make the second rhyming sentence relate to the first is sufficient, however.

Helping them to find words or phrases that sound better or improve the rhythm will help them to develop aural discrimination and to learn about sentences, capitalization, and end punctuation while they are taking their first steps toward creativity and having a great deal of fun as well.

CINQUAIN. Cinquain is not difficult to write, and it is excellent for helping children to become aware of the special quality of poetry—its appeal to the emotions and the senses. It has a very specific formula:

First line: one word, giving title
Second line: two words, describing title
Third line: three words, expressing an action
Fourth line: four words, expressing a feeling
Fifth line: one word, a synonym for the title

This is too restrictive a form to stay with for very long, but it does allow some freedom in the choice of words and phrases, and almost any child can achieve some degree of success with cinquain. To show how the formula works, here are two examples:

SAM

Warm, friendly,
Licks my face
To show his love.
Puppy.

DARKNESS

Thick, eerie;
I whistle loudly;
I fear the night;
Black.

Books for Children to Read

City Talk by Lee Bennett Hopkins (Alfred A. Knopf, 1970)
For Me to Say by David McCord (Little, Brown, 1970)
It Doesn't Always Have to Rhyme by Eve Merriam (Atheneum, 1966)
Miracles by Richard Lewis (Simon and Schuster, 1966)

FREE VERSE. Free verse places no restrictions on total length and number of syllables or words to a line and prescribes no rhythmic pattern. The writer decides where to break lines or begin new stanzas, and when the poem is complete. In a sense, free verse may be thought of as *free thought*. The length of the thought might be one sentence by a third grader or several stanzas by a creative sixth grader.

If children experience activities in which they talk about and use words and phrases that express their feelings, that create images, about commonplace but important things to them—family, friends, fear, happiness, pain, etc.—then writing these feelings will follow.

LIMERICKS. Middle grade children can have a great deal of fun with limericks, and certainly children should know that poetry can be humorous as well as serious. That, in fact, is the essence of poetry—it expresses all our emotions at one time or another. Limericks have a set form with which most of us are familiar: the first, second, and fifth lines rhyme; the third and fourth lines rhyme and are shorter. Show children that the "trick" is to find a number of words that rhyme and then see if several of them suggest an idea; they will need at least three rhyming words for lines one, two, and five. Then show them how they can experiment with word order or find synonyms in order to make the meter work out correctly. The beginning couplet should be established first; then the same kind of experimentation can produce lines three and four. The final line should come rather easily after this much has been done.

> There was an old woman named Snow
> Who couldn't get flowers to grow.
> She planted some seeds
> But grew only weeds.
> What happened I really don't know!

OTHER FORMS. Obviously there are many more verse forms than have been discussed here, and children may be encouraged to try any that they are interested in. *Haiku* is a lovely Japanese verse form that many teachers have children try. Haiku has a total of seventeen syllables in three lines: the first line has five syllables, the second seven, and the third five. There is no rhyme or meter. The central image is usually from nature, with the final line making an observation about life. The teaching of this poetry form in the elementary school has declined, however, because of the emphasis typically given to counting syllables without enough regard for the feelings the words express. The beauty of haiku lies in the right choice of words to create the image and express the idea of the poem. Some authorities, at least, believe that elementary school children have neither the vocabulary storehouse nor the life experiences to create haiku. The same might be said about other Japanese poetry forms—*tanka*, which adds two lines of seven syllables each to haiku; or *senryu*, which has three lines but may add two or three syllables.

Some teachers, together with their students, have invented their own forms, such as triante and diamente. These can be structured according to the age and abilities of the children. We especially like triante, because it calls for "sense" words, as follows:

First line: one word, giving the title
Second line: two words, telling how it smells
Third line: three words, telling how it feels
Fourth line: four words, telling how it looks
Fifth line: five words, telling how it sounds

Poems can also be made in shapes; that is, a poem about a cloud might be shaped like a drifting cloud, one about Halloween might be in the shape of a pumpkin, etc. The important fact to remember is that poetry is yet another way in which ideas and feelings may be expressed. In the kind of world we live in today, it is important for children to learn to express their emotions verbally and to exercise care in selecting the words they choose to express those emotions. In addition, reading and hearing poetry can add dimension to their lives, and creating poetry will undoubtedly extend this dimension.

Other Writing Activities

Many other activities can serve to stimulate children's writing. Much of what children read will particularly serve this function, with the writing also providing useful reinforcement and supplement to reading lessons as well as to reading in other curriculum areas. The following are other forms of writing that may be based on these experiences.

CHARACTER SKETCHES. Sketches based on the characters in a story may be written by children. They should think about the character selected, search for details about that character and the things he or she does, and speculate about his or her behavior. A character sketch can take any of several forms; it can be thought of as a "verbal snapshot" or an impression gained by a "first glance," a description that tells what kind of human being a person is, a combination of these, or a sketch that concentrates on an example or examples of one trait.

BIOGRAPHIES. Children can research and write biographies of people in the news or people they have learned about in social studies. They can also write "made up" biographies or autobiographies of characters in stories. These provide not only fun but also good motivation for reading. Forms of writing such as personification can be used if a story lends itself to such treatment. An old car, a horse, or a towering tree can write its early life through the imagination of the child.

DESCRIPTIONS. Literary selections often demonstrate how a professional writer uses composition skills. For example, at the beginning of "Rip Van Winkle," Washington Irving describes the Catskill Mountains as "swelling

24 Notes and Summaries

Have you ever come home from school and found a message like this on the kitchen table?

My dear child,
    I have to work late at the biology laboratory this evening. I must finish some experiments that have to be done today. I expect to arrive home at about 9:00 P.M. If you get hungry before then, don't hesitate to prepare yourself something.

> Very affectionately yours,
> Mother

You've probably never received a message quite like this one. Your mother does not need to be so formal with you. If she were going to be late, she might write this way:

Dear,
    Must work late tonight. See you about 9. Fix a snack if you want.

> Mom

This kind of writing is called a note. Its purpose is to give information simply and clearly.
    Writing notes is an important skill with many uses. For example, you can take brief notes to help you remember things you read about or hear in class.

Help children recognize that communication requires different language styles.

Using Our Language, 1977 edition, Level 5; copyright © by Bowmar/Noble Publishers, a Division of The Economy Company. Used by permission of the publisher.

up to a noble height, and lording it over the surrounding country . . . when the weather is fair and settled, they are clothed in blue and purple, and print their bold outlines on the clear evening sky; but sometimes, when the rest of the landscape is cloudless, they will gather a hood of grey vapors about their summits, which, in the last rays of the setting sun, will glow and light up like a crown of glory.''

In discussion, help the children to discover how the use of devices such as personification and simile adds vigor to a description, how the use of verbs as well as adjectives and adverbs gives strength, and how a few well-chosen details, instead of a wealth of them, can set scene and mood. This can be followed by thinking about a familiar setting and giving details about it. These details can then be woven into a description.

MORE LETTERS. Corresponding with an author is a way for a child to share with others some of his or her reading experiences. The possibilities for such correspondence may be limited, but trying it might bring surprising results.

Children can also write letters to the librarian, to another teacher, or to children in another grade about the books they have read. These are effective whether the writer is recommending or criticizing the book.

In the middle grades, book characters may exchange letters. Have pupils write to one another as the characters might have done. For example, Henry Reed might ask Homer Price all about the doughnut machine, and Amos might be very interested in discussing French customs with Anatole.

COMMENTARIES. Another variation of the book report involves encouraging children to relate the most humorous incident, the most exciting happening, the part they liked best, or the saddest part of a book. This will help children learn to seek certain types of materials from books and stories.

RIDDLES. Children can prepare a series of clues concerning a character, a setting, an event, or an object in a story. The reader must guess who or what is being described. Sometimes it is possible to create interest by deliberately choosing ambiguous terms.

CAPTIONS AND HEADLINES. For children who have difficulty expressing ideas in writing, short forms of composition should be sought. Writing labels for pictures related to stories is one example. These labels should be more than simply one or a few words. Instead of writing "The Snowstorm," a child might be encouraged to write a sentence about it, such as "When I awoke everything was white and clean."

In addition to writing labels for pictures, the less able children may be encouraged to write headlines—to give in short sentences the "big idea" of a story they have read.

DIARIES. For units where stories revolve around colonial times or other periods in history, students may pretend to be living during the period and keep diaries. They can also write letters to friends telling about some of the experiences or first-person stories in which they describe events as though they had participated in the action. It is particularly important to limit the scope in this kind of writing. For example, a diary entry might cover only one day, or even a part of a day; a first-person account could be limited to a single aspect of an important historical event—for instance, what the foot soldier felt like at Valley Forge.

MORE ON MOTIVATION AND WRITING

If early school experiences have been ideal, children in, say, the fourth or fifth grade may independently write a good deal, as well as readily engage in writing that is assigned. However, not all school conditions are ideal—input and oral expression may have been neglected and exercises emphasized rather than purposeful writing—so even if a teacher makes writing an integral part of a meaningful and appealing curriculum, something more is often needed. Sometimes, too, children simply need an extra push; their experiences and desire to write about something do not quite trigger the writing process. This is particularly true for writing that does not have the specific communication purpose of a letter, report, or announcement. For some children to write stories, essays, or poetry, this push or immediate form of motivation may be especially needed. Some may need only a glimmer of an idea—a topic, a picture, or an object—to start their thinking and writing; others may require more to set the stage.

SPECIFIC TOPICS. If a teacher simply writes a topic or topics on the board and asks children to begin writing—even if he or she provides time for them to think before actual writing begins—the writing expected may not result. In fact, some children may write little or nothing.

There are several ways to avoid this. First, it is probably better to provide a choice of topics; a single topic is not likely to suit the interests and abilities of the entire group. If the general topic is one that has grown from a particular study unit, suggest different ways of treating the topic or different aspects that might be dealt with. Second, it is wise to take a few min-

Having the use of a typewriter often motivates a nonwriter.

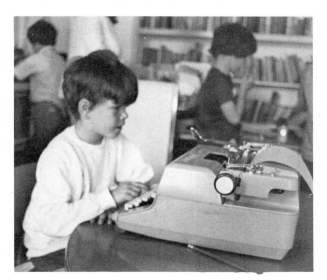

utes to discuss the topics, suggesting—or having children suggest—ways in which they might be treated; this may spur pupils to think of others themselves. Another possibility is to select a particular topic and list on the board, again with the children's help, some words that might be suitable to use in connection with this topic. The list need not include every word that can be dredged up—only enough to get the children's thinking started. It should, however, include nouns, verbs, and adverbs, as well as adjectives; children should discover early that adjectives are not the only words that describe. Topics should be chosen with an eye toward children's interests and experience—either actual or vicarious. No one can be expected to write well about something that is uninteresting and unfamiliar.

To avoid forcing children to write about a topic that has no appeal for them, or about which they know little, you might have the children make a chart of questions they might ask themselves and thus decide on their own topics:

What do I know a lot about?
What do I want to learn something about?
What would my friends like most to read or hear about?
Do I know how to do something that I could tell about?

Some children may not think they have answers to such questions, but perhaps if they are interviewed by other children they will have. Topics determined by children themselves are almost always more appropriate than those a teacher suggests.

PICTURES. Using pictures as bases for ideas is another technique for getting children to write. Collect pictures of various sizes and on various subjects, mount them on heavy paper if necessary, and file them for ready reference. The filing is usually by topic (e.g., dogs, winter, children, farm animals, colors, etc.). Mounting pictures adds to the amount of filing space needed, but it also keeps them from becoming dog-eared; probably temporary mountings are best, since they may need to be changed for different purposes. (To make a temporary mount, simply fold several pieces of Scotch tape, sticky side out; attach one side to the mount and the other to the back of the picture.)

Pictures can be used in several ways: a large picture can be displayed to the entire class, smaller pictures can be distributed to individual pupils, or individual pupils or small groups can choose from a display in the chalk tray, pictures in story books, or those in readers or other textbooks. Showing a large picture to the entire class is usually good for beginning writing activities because the ensuing discussion often stimulates many ideas.

The following suggest the kinds of "thinking about" and "talking about" questions that are helpful:

1. What is happening in the picture? (Encourage various possibilities.)

2. What kind of people are these? Do they belong to the same family, are they friends, or what? Do you think you would like them?

3. What might have happened just before the time of the picture? What might happen next?

4. Think of words and phrases that describe the action in the picture. What words might describe the people or the way they feel?

5. What are some words that describe the scenery in the picture?

6. If you were going to tell a story about this picture, how and where would you begin?

It is important that such questions be exploratory, not directive; creative writing does not result in every child's turning out the same story. On the other hand, children should discuss whether or not suggestions fit the picture: a wrinkled, ragged crone might find a long-lost child, but she is not likely to marry Prince Charming or find a lucrative job unless she is in disguise or a fairy godmother has been at work!

A STORY FRAMEWORK. If a topic or a picture does not give the child enough of a setting to start his or her thinking and writing, an elaboration or extension of the topic may be helpful. This extension usually provides a framework around which a story can be created. Sometimes, too, the framework stimulates thinking that leads to a story that is not directly attributable to the framework. A file of such "frames" can be useful; listed below are some that have proved successful.

1. You are a young boy who plays the drum for an army company that is part of Washington's Revolutionary Army. Tell what happens one day while you are waiting in camp for the general to arrive.

2. You are traveling on a wagon train from St. Louis to California. Many of the wagons are lost crossing the Red River. What happens the next morning?

3. Pretend you are an inanimate object such as a parking meter, a "No Parking" sign, or an object on display in the drugstore window. Describe your feelings about one of the people you "see" daily.

4. You are a famous explorer who has just returned from a trip. Tell about one of your discoveries and why it is important.

5. You wake up suddenly in the middle of the night. Everything is quiet and it is pitch dark. Suddenly you hear a clanking sound that reminds you of a TV program. Tell what happens next.

6. The chair is rocking, but no one is in it. As you watch, the rocking increases in speed and a faint glow of light travels across the room. What happens next?

7. You are lying on the bank of a lake watching your fishing line. Suddenly you hear a rustle in the bushes behind you, followed by some loud sniffing. Tell how you feel and what happens when you discover what caused the noise.

8. Describe some common happening on earth as if you were an invisible observer from another planet visiting the earth for the first time.

9. Pretend you are a statue in the park. Tell about some of the things you have seen and the changes that have occurred over the years.

10. Halloween is a time for fun. Think of some of the things you have done on Halloween, some of the ways you have dressed, some of the things you have seen and heard. Think, too, of smells and tastes and how they were related to what you did. Can you make up a story about an ideal Halloween?

Brainstorming can be used by groups as a way of generating story beginnings.

A STORY BEGINNING. Sometimes a child cannot think of a beginning for a story but can finish one or even add more than simply the ending if the beginning is appealing. Furthermore, most children enjoy writing a story from a given beginning. One way to start stories is for the class as a group to make up an opening; then each child finishes the story individually. Magazines for teachers and for children often have story beginnings that can be used as they are or with modifications for local circumstances. Many kinds of beginnings may be used. Some actually indicate how the story should end, and only minor variations are possible. Others simply start the "wheels" turning, so that the various stories the children write reflect their creativity and individuality.

It is a good idea to have some story beginnings on hand, just as you have files of topics, pictures, and story structure statements. Here are some that teachers have used:

1. There was a strange silence along the main street of the town, even though it was only 9 P.M.
2. On the table was a stack of books; the top one was open.
3. Bulldozers began climbing the hill as the sun appeared.
4. The rain beat against the window pane as the sky darkened and lightning flashed.
5. There was a fluttering of wings, and the quail rose from the bushes.
6. She looked over the edge of the building and gasped at what she saw many floors below.
7. The door banged. Then it opened quickly and a tall, grizzled cowboy came through.
8. All the way home I kept looking at my clothes and thinking about what I might say to my mother.
9. The old house looked interesting. The rocking chair on the porch had a red cushion in it and the screen door was hanging by one hinge.
10. As I passed the house I caught a whiff of . . .
11. Bill stood on the dock, his legs stiff and refusing to move. Then he felt dizzy.
12. He really was mean. He did mean things. Why, one time I remember . . .

Story beginnings that go beyond a sentence or two are also helpful. Again, it is a matter of what is needed to start children thinking of things they can write. The following are examples of types that you might try.

1. John and his younger brother were playing on the beach when they found the strange footprints. They seemed to come from the water and to go along the shore toward the trees in the distance. John started to follow his brother, who was racing after the footprints.
2. The last weak rays of the sun streaked coldly across the graying sky. Linda shivered and touched her heels gently to the horse's flanks, remembering that the field would soon be swallowed by the fog and clammy darkness. Then she heard the scream—a piercing, wailing cry.

3. George manages the family, but not always very well. He forgets that he is a dog and that there are some things a dog can't do. I remember when he tried to . . .

4. I could see the fire in the distance. The blaze danced above the tree tops and the smoke billowed away in a darkening cloud. Just then three deer burst through the undergrowth and dashed past me. What should I do? Was there a chance?

5. It's fun to watch ants. They are so busy and seem to know what they are doing. Sometimes I have fun pretending I am an ant.

6. The roar of the waterfall could be heard above the patter of the rain on the trees. I listened carefully for another sound. No, I could not hear it. I wondered why. I surely was close enough. Maybe I was on the wrong side of the river.

7. The strange sound got louder and louder until it was almost deafening. We had stopped walking when it started, and now we stared at one another. Fright began to show on John's face, and Bill's eyes were blinking. Then the sound stopped and an eerie silence ensued. We wondered what might happen next, but we still didn't talk.

8. I pounded and pounded, but the door wouldn't open. Looking around for something to use as a hammer, I spotted a large rock lying in the driveway. I ran to get it and was hit by . . .

9. The light got brighter and brighter as the ship settled toward the earth. Then there was a slight flutter and it came to rest. I held my breath, wondering what would happen next. Suddenly a hole opened up in the bottom of the ship and a ladder came swiftly down. The figure that followed was round, spindle-legged, and silver colored—just as an "outer space" creature was supposed to look. What should I do? Should I speak? Should I run? I decided . . .

10. It was a very good movie, especially the music. It reminded me of the time we visited Yellowstone National Park and saw the geysers, although we didn't have the trouble with bears that the girl in the movie had. But wait, let me tell you about it.

Words about Weather

sunny	blustery
bright	hot
foggy	stifling
sultry	warm
snowy	humid
stormy	changeable
cloudy	windy
dry	smoggy
wet	drizzling
cold	tepid
clear	misty

WORDS AND PHRASES. Seeing and discussing words and phrases that remind them of experiences or stir their imaginations may stimulate children to write. Often these words and/or phrases can be collected by the class, and perhaps because of this they will work particularly well. Sometimes, however, pupils may need help in getting thinking started. Phrases such as these may help them to think of others:

pelting rain on the window
a prancing horse
silver-gray smoke rising
a seagull floating noiselessly above
sunlight dancing upon the blue water
the swaying, bending trees
a dewy spider web in the bush
snow blowing in waves across the field

Nothing creative is likely to result from such phrases, however, unless children have come to enjoy words and the way they are used. As you read aloud to children, comment on an unusual word or show your appreciation of an apt phrase. Talk about words; help children to enjoy the way they sound and the way they conjure up pictures. Encourage them to discover new words and learn new meanings for words they already know. Only a true appreciation of language will bring about expression that shows sparkle and imagination.

References

Blake, Robert W. "Setting Up an Effective Writing Program in the Schools." *Impact on Instructional Improvement* 15 (Winter 1980), pp. 11–20.

Braddock, Richard; Lloyd-Jones, Richard; and Schoer, Lloyd. *Research in Written Composition.* National Council of Teachers of English, 1963.

Brogan, V. Shirley. "Instructional Writing Suggestions in Elementary School Language Arts Textbooks: An Analysis Based upon Opinions of Writing Authorities." Unpublished doctoral dissertation, State University of New York at Buffalo, 1983.

Burrows, Alvena T. "Research into Practice," in *Help for the Teacher of Written Composition*, Sara W. Lundsteen, ed. Clearinghouse on Reading and Communication Skills, 1976.

Calkins, Lucy McCormick. "The Craft of Writing." *Teacher* (October 1980), pp. 41–44.

Chew, Charles R. "Basic Skills in Written Composition—Our Task." *The English Record* (Winter 1976), pp. 15–16.

Clapp, Ouida H., ed. *Write On, and On, and On!* Buffalo, New York Public Schools, 1981.

Glatthorn, Allan A. "Demystifying the Teaching of Writing." *Language Arts* 59 (October 1982), pp. 722–725.

Graves, Donald H. "Children's Writing: Research Directions and Hypotheses Based upon an Examination of the Writing Processes of Seven-Year-Olds." Unpublished doctoral dissertation, State University of New York at Buffalo, 1973.

———. "An Examination of the Writing Processes of Seven Year Old Children," *Research in Teaching English* 9 (Winter 1975), pp. 231–242.

———. *Writing: Teachers and Children at Work.* Heinemann Educational Books, 1982.

Haley-James, Shirley, ed. *Perspectives on Writing in Grades 1–8.* National Council of Teachers of English, 1981.

Jackson, Jacqueline. *Turn Not Pale, Beloved Snail: A Book about Writing among Other Things.* Little, Brown, 1974.

Murray, Donald M. *A Writer Teaches Writing: A Practical Method of Teaching Composition.* Houghton Mifflin, 1968.

Newkirk, Thomas, and Atwell, Nancie, eds. *Understanding Writing: Ways of Observing, Learning, and Teaching.* Northeast Regional Exchange, 1982.

Petty, Walter T. "The Writing of Young Children," in *Research on Composing*, Charles R. Cooper and Lee Odell, eds. National Council of Teachers of English, 1978.

———, and Finn, Patrick, eds. *The Writing Process of Students.* Department of Learning and Instruction, State University of New York at Buffalo, 1975.

Sealey, Leonard; Sealey, Nancy; and Millmore, Marcia. *Children's Writing.* International Reading Association, 1979.

Wille, Fred. *The ABC's of Creativity and Language Arts.* Good Apple, 1978.

Teaching Resources

FILMS

Let's Write a Story. Churchill Films (11 minutes; color, b/w; primary and intermediate).

Writing Different Kinds of Letters. Random House/ Coronet (11 minutes; color, b/w; intermediate).

FILMSTRIPS

Beginning Writing Skills. Society for Visual Education (filmstrips with cassettes, skill sheets, guide; primary).

The Writing of Poetry. Harcourt Brace Jovanovich (4 boxed filmstrips, guides; upper elementary).

KITS

Classroom Authors' Kit. Curriculum Associates (game with desk plates, masters, etc.; upper grades).

First Experiences in Creative Writing. Prentice-Hall (filmstrips, cassettes, guide; grades 1–4).

Letter Writing Basics. Eye Gate Media (4 filmstrips, 2 cassettes; intermediate).

Report Writing Skills. Random House (8 cassettes, masters, guide; intermediate and upper).

SRA Composition. Science Research Associates (cassettes, model cards, handbook; grades 4–6).

Activities for Preservice Teachers

1. Write something yourself—a report, essay, description—and make notes as to what you do and in what order during all three phases of your writing. What did you learn about what children may do when they write?

2. Demonstrate to the class exactly how you would go about helping a class of first graders write a group composition. Be sure to include a description of motivational activities.

3. Find a letter written by some well-known person that might be used in connection with letter writing activities. Prepare a demonstration showing how you would use it.

4. Select a unit of study for a particular grade level and plan the writing activities that might grow out of it. Include a list of skills or writing forms that might need to be introduced or reviewed at this grade level.

5. Plan a lesson for children at a grade level of your choice to write imaginatively something other than a story or poem (e.g., cartoon dialogue, essay, advertisement).

6. Begin a file of pictures that would be useful in motivating creative writing. Be sure to include some that show actions, some of single individuals, some that convey mood, etc.

7. For each of the pictures you have collected (for no. 6), jot down a list of questions that would be appropriate for starting discussion before writing begins. Or make a list of possible writing topics based on the pictures.

8. Select one of the references listed in this chapter to read and report on to the class. Make sure that your report conveys the substance of the article or book.

9. Observe in a kindergarten or first grade when children are writing. Try to plan your observation so that you observe both "assigned" and "free" writing.

10. Report to the class about what the public media and the professional literature are reporting as "basics" needed to enable children to write better.

Activities for Inservice Teachers

1. Use a checklist to note individual children's interests based on your observation of their drawing, writing content, and conversations. Provide a "Writing Box" with miniature models of objects related to their interests. Children can choose an object as a base for their writing.

2. If you are not in the practice of conferring with children about their writing, try it for a few weeks. Keep a record of changes in the children's writing that could be attributed to the conferences.

3. Investigate the free materials that can be secured by writing letters. Give special attention to those that could be written for by the children. Then get the children started writing.

4. Select one child in your class to observe for a week. Record the types of writing he or she does, including all kinds of writing: titles, announcements, labels, stories, reports, letters, etc.

5. Parents often state that they have no idea what their children do in school. Plan a biweekly newsletter for reporting class activities to parents. Precede this activity by a study of newspapers and a visit to a local paper.

6. Survey your classroom as objectively as possible to determine the degree of creativity fostered by the environment. Do children's ideas abound or have they been suppressed? Is the classroom yours or does it "belong" to the entire group?

7. Try writing something yourself while the children are writing. Try to think of yourself as another student in the class, obliged to do what you have assigned or what the children have chosen to do. Afterward try to recall the problems you had, the pauses you made, the revising you did, etc.

Independent Activities for Children

1. Provide bulletin board space for an "Announcement Center." This space can contain information or directions about daily activities that children can sign up for (if the classroom is operated as an informal or open one), special events, children's own announcements, pertinent news clippings, and school happenings. Most of the materials should be written by the children; in fact, this can be a provision for using the space.

2. Contact a local nursing or convalescent home for names of people who might enjoy receiving letters from children. A child can "adopt" one of them as a grandparent and write letters to him or her, telling about class activities, personal interests, etc., and possibly including an occasional story or poem the child has written.

3. Encourage children to write daily in journals (e.g., a spiral notebook). They should be allowed to write anything they wish, and to choose whether or not to show it to you or their peers. Provide time for this writing.

4. Have a child collect business letters received by parents and friends and make a display of different forms, using colored pencil to point out variations in placement and to underline kinds of language appropriate for salutations, closings, and the body of the letter.

5. For the child who can't think of a story to write or who doesn't believe his or her experiences are worth relating (or doesn't know how to relate them), record keeping or making and observing a window garden may be the answer. Have the child bring the soil and container (paper cup, egg carton, etc.), and you furnish the seed (tomato, bean, etc.).

6. Prepare collections of materials to spark children's writing. The collections (usually a box is needed for each) might include the following:

comic cartoons from newspapers
photographs of interesting places and events
cloth and other objects of different textures
newspaper stories
pictures from magazines

7. Place pictures on a bulletin board and have a child write sentences and short paragraphs describing them.

8. Cut up workbooks containing pictures that tell a story in sequence. Fasten each group together with a paperclip or rubber band, and keep them in a shoe box covered with gift wrap or contact paper. A child selects a group, places the pictures in sequence, and then writes a sentence about each, thus making a paragraph.

9. Have a child adapt a story for dramatization, writing a script with dialogue and stage directions.

10. Suggest that children exchange stories or other writing with children in other schools. These may be children whose names were obtained from one of the Pen Pal sources, or they may be children in a nearby school. Each child should write to the other child, inviting him or her to exchange writing and to react to the writing that is exchanged.

11. Diaries can be kept by children for a pet, a story character, or a toy. An individual child can regularly write in the diary of one "character."

12. Individual children can write reports on topics of their choice after trips, such as a nature walk or a visit to the fire station or a construction site. Suggest possible topics:

birds or animals seen
the tall fireman
building machinery
what I saw that nobody else did

13. Given children's interest in television, motivating the writing of letters to TV stars is little needed. Addresses for writing are as follows:

(Name of star)
ABC-TV, c/o Manager,
   Audience Information
1330 Avenue of the Americas
New York, NY 10019

(Name of star)
NBC-TV, c/o Vice President,
   Information Services
30 Rockefeller Plaza
New York, NY 10020

(Name of star)
CBS-TV, c/o Vice President
   of Press Information
51 W. 52nd St.
New York, NY 10019

9 | *Extending Writing Abilities*

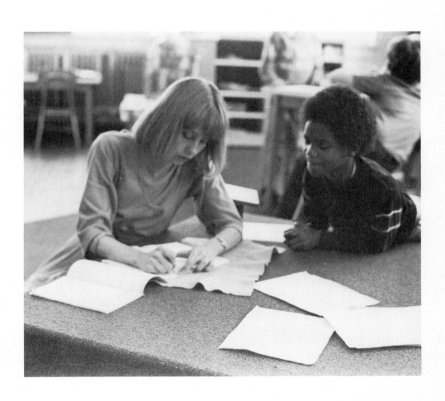

Children have a natural interest in writing, a kind of fascination with putting on paper something that they and others can read; but for children to learn to write effectively requires time, encouragement, and teaching. The preceding chapter discussed the writing process and teaching principles that emphasize the process nature of writing as well as the many writing activities that occur naturally or may develop in a challenging and well-planned language arts program.

This chapter discusses ways to help children organize their writing better, construct more effective and varied sentences, and make the best word choices. Included also are matters of form and convention in writing; revising, proofreading, and editing; and evaluating writing programs and products.

IMPROVING WRITING EFFECTIVENESS

All language expression, both oral and written, is largely effective to the degree that its content is organized so that it clearly conveys the thought of the speaker or writer, its sentences are well constructed and have appeal and clarity, and the word choices reflect both preciseness and variety. Children's writing will be improved to a considerable extent in these aspects if they have done a great deal of writing, have been guided and encouraged in doing it, and have thoughtfully revised what they have written. However, direct teaching attention is also needed.

Teaching Organizational Skill

Children need to learn that the best way to present a thought effectively is to organize the expression so that it sticks to the point and presents the information in an interesting and suitable sequence. Organization is reflected in the construction of sentences, paragraphs, and the discourse as a whole. No expression—be it one sentence or more—is effective unless it is well organized and thoughtfully composed.

When a child begins to recognize relationships, he or she is beginning to organize. Activities such as the following call for organizing skills and are first steps in learning to organize thoughts in written form.

- Putting pictures related to a story into proper sequence.
- Putting a puzzle together.
- Classifying objects by size, color, shape, etc.
- Telling in sequence the things seen on a trip.
- Deciding what classroom tasks need doing.
- Telling how to play a game.
- Giving words that are associated with special days or events.

Guidance in helping children organize their expression should begin as they tell about experiences and continue as they dictate more than a single phrase or sentence and write independently. Organization is a thinking skill that develops through guided practice; therefore early guidance in oral expression is particularly important to organized writing. This guidance should be subtle, so that free expression is not stifled, but it does need to be offered. Dictation to the teacher provides especially good opportunities for such guidance, and this is the major reason that dictating to teachers by individuals and groups should not stop just because children have learned the basic writing skills.

As children engage in the writing process—from initial planning through revising—much of the focus should be on organization of content. This focus is reflected in suggestions in the preceding chapter regarding stories, reports, and other forms of writing. In addition, activities such as the following may be helpful:

1. Write a short paragraph on the chalkboard or duplicate it. Have the children tell the main idea of the paragraph in one sentence. The paragraph might be taken from a social studies or science book.

2. Have children look at and discuss the content of a picture and then state in one sentence the main idea of the picture. A variation of this activity is to choose a title (without regard to whether it is a sentence).

3. Write several sentences on the chalkboard, and have the children select the ones that could be put together into a paragraph.

4. Provide the children with paragraphs that contain one or two sentences unrelated to the idea of the paragraph. Have the children cross out the unrelated sentences.

5. Provide the children with a paragraph in which the sentences have been scrambled, and have them rearrange the sentences in the most effective order.

6. Give children paragraphs in which the beginning or ending sentences are missing. Have them compose appropriate sentences to make the paragraphs complete.

7. Provide opportunities for pupils to discuss and list ideas and information before they begin writing. This should be done regularly at all grade levels; it is one of the most valuable ways in which you can help children learn to organize their thinking.

8. Encourage the children to watch for ways in which professional writers move skillfully from topic to topic and use paragraphs in their writing.

Outlining (discussed in Chapter 13) is useful in organizing expression as well as in studying. Unfortunately, observations of writers tell us that few do much outlining, possibly because of the formality with which outlining has been taught. But outlines helpful to organizing writing need not be formal; in fact, it is probably best if they are not, for attention should rest on the ideas and information to be presented, not on the form of the outline. Neither should a writer be held to an outline made before writing has begun; we do think as we write. But thinking about what to write and the order of this content should begin before the drafting stage, and outlining will help in this thinking.

Developing Sentence Sense

Much expression is not as effective as it might be because of faulty sentences. While there are no shortcuts to skill in constructing effective sentences, there are some things teachers can do which will help, as well as some that are often done which probably do not help. In the latter category are teaching a grammatical definition of a sentence, identifying parts of speech in sentences, and having children do sentence construction, punctuation, and capitalization exercises totally unrelated to their interests and their own writing. Basically children need to learn that a sentence is a means of expressing an idea. The focus is on the idea and on expressing it in a way that is clear and exact, a way that makes *sense*. The expression of the idea must be lucid and complete; it must avoid trying to tell so much that the meaning becomes confused or lost.

As frequently mentioned earlier, children should have many opportunities to express themselves orally, and this is a good time to encourage them to express ideas clearly. This does not mean that every response need be a "complete" sentence in the sense that most of us have had drilled *at* us in grammar study. However, questions may be asked or issues and problems advanced that require more than a "Yes" or "No" answer.

In the primary grades, provide activities in which each child tells one thing—and only one—about some personal experience, such as a trip, a project, or a picture. Or ask questions and have children answer in sentences that tell only one thing. Such statements or answers help convey the idea of a sentence. As you act as scribe for children's writing and as they begin their own writing (often telling only one thing), attention should be given to sentence markers—capitalization, periods, and question marks. As you write for children you can say, "I'll capitalize the first letter of this word since it begins your sentence" or "Let's put a period here since your sentence is ended." Major emphasis, however, should be on guidance in formulating ideas and developing continuity of thought. For instance, after a trip to the zoo, questions can be designed to lead to an organized composition about the experience:

> **TEACHER:** Tell me one animal you saw at the zoo.
>
> **CHILDREN:** We saw monkeys at the zoo.

Gradually expand the group stories and accounts of which you are the scribe. This provides opportunities for utilizing various types of sentences and forms of punctuation.

TEACHER:	Now tell me one thing the monkeys were doing.
CHILDREN:	They were hanging by their tails.
TEACHER:	How did they look?
CHILDREN:	They looked funny hanging upside down.

Of course children will have more than one answer to such questions. Perhaps several answers to each question might be recorded, and the class could choose the ones to be used—or possibly combine them into several compositions.

This kind of activity, if used often, can guide children in developing concepts about capitalization and punctuation, sentence construction, and organization of ideas. Such guidance should continue, of course, when children begin to write their own sentences and paragraphs. Care should be exercised, however, to avoid stifling originality by calling for only one possible answer or statement.

Sentence sense also develops from exposing children to hearing good sentences. This generally means that you will need to read to children in a voice that portrays "sentence feeling." Sometimes it is helpful to have children listen to recordings of their own speech, noting how the voice tends to drop at the end of a group of words—that is, at the end of a sentence. Another way to illustrate good sentence structure is to write two stories told by children in contrasting forms—one in which good sentence sense is evident and one in which the sentences are poorly or improperly constructed. Then have the stories compared and evaluated and the poorly written one reconstructed.

Don't overlook opportunities presented by conferences and other feedback situations for encouraging children to focus on creating sentences that *make sense.*

Activities such as those suggested in the preceding paragraph can be used at all grade levels by simply varying the length and difficulty of the material used, as can punctuation and capitalization dictation exercises (particularly helpful after a new item has been introduced), exercises in which children match subjects in one column with predicates in another, or those requiring pupils to organize sentence elements into their proper relationships to make good sentences. At every grade level, expose children to good sentences that are read well. This means reading well-written materials frequently in a voice that clearly portrays sentence feeling.

You may also want to try activities such as those suggested below. They are listed in ascending order of difficulty, but many can be varied to suit different ability levels.

1. Display a large picture to the class and ask, "Who has a sentence about this picture?" A picture of a cowboy might elicit responses such as the following:

   The cowboy has a big hat.
   He sure is tall.
   I saw a cowboy on TV last night.

   Write the sentences the children give you on the board. Do not write a child's response unless it is a sentence. Don't be adamant about this. Rather, suggest rephrasing.

2. Write declarative sentences on the board. Have them read orally by pupils. Then have these sentences changed to interrogative or negative forms. For example:

Billy is at his desk.
Is Billy at his desk?
Billy is not at his desk.

3. Write sentences on the board from a story the children are reading or have read, scrambling the order of words in them. Have individual children or small groups rearrange these so that sentences are formed.

4. Give each child an envelope containing words printed on small pieces of durable paper. These may be words taken from their reading and other class activities. Each envelope should contain nouns, verbs, adjectives, adverbs, connectives, determiners, pronouns, etc., so that sentences can be made. Have the children see how many sentences they can compose, making sure that each sentence makes *sense*.

5. Write a sentence on the chalkboard. Ask the children to add phrases to make the idea clearer. A variation is to add adverbs and adjectives rather than phrases.

6. Write on the board several phrases that elicit mental pictures. For example: a pile of clothes on the floor, wet leaves on the window pane, the smell of bananas. Have pupils combine and/or add to the phrases to make sentences.

7. Have the children revise "time" sentences found in their reading. For example:

When Edith's mother came to the door of the kitchen, all of the children were exclaiming about the dessert.

This might be revised in one of these ways:

The children were exclaiming about the dessert as Edith's mother came to the door of the kitchen.
Edith's mother came to the door of the kitchen just in time to hear the children exclaiming about the dessert.

8. Write a sentence such as "He will play" on the chalkboard. Have the children add details that provide more information by answering such questions as "Who?" "What?" "How?" "When?" and "What kind?"

He will play with Bill.
He will play baseball with Bill.
He will play baseball with Bill on the school diamond.

Changing "the Picture" by Changing the Sentence

The bear came down the road.
The bear ambled down the path.
A brown bear shuffled along under the trees.
A small brown bear loped down the path.

Remedying Sentence Faults

Children's thinking sometimes runs ahead of both their speaking and their writing, resulting in the omission of some sentence elements. Children also tend to run sentences together by overuse of *and* or, in writing, by simply running them together without a conjunction or punctuation and capitalization. Other common faults include using launchers (you know, well, okay) which do not function as transition words or contribute to meaning and making unnecessary repetitive and/or irrelevant statements.

Activities such as those suggested for developing sentence sense will help to remedy these faults. The idea of "making sense" causes children to realize that these faults interfere with making sense, that they make communication less effective or even impossible. Again, the kind of attention you give as children write and revise, proofread, and edit (see sections later in this chapter) can do much to eliminate or minimize these faults. Practice exercises that provide for distinguishing between fragments and sentences, correcting run-on sentences, adding or deleting words to make sentence meaning clear, or making sentences out of nonsentence groups of words are also needed. Here are some examples of exercises that you might make:

1. Write on the chalkboard a story composed of a series of run-on sentences. Have several children take turns reading the story, stressing the idea that they are to attempt to read it paying attention only to the punctuation they see. Following such attempts have the story read again, this time emphasizing how natural reading shows where sentences begin and end. Then have the children rewrite the story, breaking it into sentences and omitting "and" when they think it preferable.

2. Write sentence fragments (perhaps from children's own work), such as:

   Because she did not go
   After the story ended
   While the class finished the game

   Have the children decide whether these are sentences and then how each might be made into a sentence.

3. Write sentences on the board, such as:

   Linda said that it was a good story.

   The children can then try various changes to make the sentence more interesting. For example:

   Linda declared that the story was very appealing.
   "What a good story!" said Linda.

4. Have children write sentences in different ways, experimenting with the placement of parts.

   During recess she will play with her friends in the gym.
   She will play with her friends in the gym during recess.
   She will play in the gym during recess with her friends.

5. Write sentences on the board for the children to rewrite and clarify.

   He saw four live ducks on the way to the market.
   There was much action in the movie that I didn't understand.

Sentence Combining Activities

One difference between the writing of young children and that of adults is that adults (and older students) write sentences containing more and longer clauses. Research directed at teaching students to write these more syntactically complex sentences by having them do sentence combining exercises (largely done at the junior high or middle school level or above) has shown that the students doing the exercises write more of these sentences than do students not doing them. This research has led to interest in using sentence combining in the elementary school and to the inclusion of such exercises in a number of elementary school language textbook series.

The exercises in commercial materials usually have models—i.e., two (or sometimes more) sentences written separately and then combined—showing in the combining either compounding, subordinating, or substituting. Each model is then followed by a number of groups of sentences to be combined as those in the model were. While some practice like this has value, it often has the disadvantage common to many drill materials—that of being unrelated to children's own work. It usually is better to take sentences children have written or to write ones related to things they are studying and then to let them experiment with combining to achieve greater clarity, emphasis, focus on the image the writer desires the reader to have, ease of reading, or variation in style.

You might simply write two sentences on the board and ask the children *if* they can be combined into one sentence. For example:

> The fifth grade classes are having a Christmas party.
> The party will be in our room.

The children will easily find several ways to combine these sentences, so you may readily move into asking them to combine several sentences into one. Emphasize that the ideas from the sentences can be combined in different ways. For example, one might take the following sentences:

> The children got off the bus.
> John got off the bus first.
> As soon as the bus emptied the driver closed the door.

These might be combined as follows:

> John was first as the children got off the bus, just ahead of the closing door.
> John got off the bus first, and after the other children followed him, the driver closed the door.

You may want to emphasize combining in particular ways to show how style may be changed. For example,

1. by using a connector:

> The girl played hard.
> The girl won the game.
> The girl played hard, and she won the game.

2. by not using a connector:

> The girl won the game by playing hard.
> By playing hard, the girl won the game.

Still another activity is to write words such as *when, after, until, there, where, if, because, then,* and *since* on the chalkboard. Then write pairs of sentences such as these:

> Everyone sat down to dinner.
> The children came in from playing.

These are example sentences. Use ones related to your children and their activities.

We will go to the airport early.
My grandmother is coming from Syracuse.

Have pupils combine the sentences in each pair using one of the words from the board. For example:

After the children came in from playing, everyone sat down to dinner.

There are many variations in these sentence combining activities that may be used for showing children ways that sentences may be constructed. Children usually are intrigued by the possibilities in manipulating language, and these activities have appeal if they are not used to the extent that they become boring or interfere with writing for the many purposes suggested in Chapter 8.

Improving Word Choices

A Bulletin Board Idea

THINGS WE AVOID IN OUR WRITING

1. Overworked words.
2. Inactive verbs.
3. Vague references.
4. Misplaced modifiers.
5. Stale, wornout phrases.
6. Inaccurate expression.
7. Sweeping generalizations.

The quality of the words selected in a piece of writing is as important as the quality of the sentence structures. Care in choosing words can add brightness, vitality, and appeal to the writing, as well as make the statement of the message more effective. Thus children need to be guided in making the best choices possible to convey the information, ideas, and feelings they seek to express.

In the preceding chapter *precision* and *vividness* of language were mentioned as aspects of writing products to be especially valued. Precision means exactness, so children should be encouraged to replace such words as *thing, something, a man,* etc., with the names of the objects or persons. Replacing such expressions as *made a face* with *scowled* or *frowned, slowly walked* with *sauntered,* or *got away* with *escaped* will add to exactness as well as be more appealing to a reader. Thus vocabulary building is vital, since choosing better words is possible only if the writer has a storehouse of words to choose from. Choosing can be aided, though, by the use of a thesaurus or sometimes a dictionary.

Children usually know many more words than they use in their writing, however. This may be because they can't spell some of them, but it is more likely because they have not been encouraged to substitute better words for those they have been accustomed to writing. As suggested in Chapter 4, with only slight encouragement children will list from their own knowledge substitutes for "overworked" words. And they will be intrigued enough to search for others to add to the list. Making lists may not mean that the words will be used by the children in their writing, but calling attention to such words will remind the children that they can and should be used, and consequently at least some of them probably will be.

Since a word is a symbol that stands for or refers to an object, action, idea, or possibly even a relationship, one might assume that its referents will be known if the word is known. This isn't true, though. Many words have multiple meanings, and others mean different things to different people. Writers need to be aware that if they use words for which they and their readers may have different referents, the intent of their writing may be lost. To avoid this, children should use words whose referents are as specific as possible. For example, *T-shirt* is more specific than *shirt*, *pizza* is more specific than *food*, *oak* than *tree*, and *spaniel* than *dog*. Such attention to word choices may appear to be too advanced for elementary school children, but it need not be. Questions probing what a writer really means to say, and whether meaning could be misunderstood or lost because of some words, if used frequently and in a supportive manner, will accomplish a great deal.

Writing is improved also by choosing vivid verbs that carry the weight of several adverbs with them: for example, *amble, trudge, march, slink*, or *pace* rather than *walk*. Similarly, adjectives should be carefully chosen: such words as *bulky, enormous, huge, vast*, and *burly* convey meaning much more accurately than *big*. As we stated above, children will know many better, more vivid verbs and particularly descriptive adjectives, and they will be interested in learning even more and using them more often as they realize that the words add clarity and appeal to their writing.

Figures of speech—personification, simile, and metaphor, and certainly onomatopoeia—should be included in children's writing. Personification—the granting of human characteristics to nonhuman objects—is no stranger to children who have heard about the Gingerbread Man, Br'er Rabbit, and the Cheshire Cat or have seen Mickey Mouse and Huckleberry Hound. They have heard a cake described as being "light as a feather"; and they know the expression, "quick as a flash." And from their earliest years they've been delighted by such words as *tinkle, boom, pop, purr*, and *zoom*. These forms ought not be taught formally, with definitions and distinctions, but children should be encouraged to try them.

On the other hand, too much emphasis on figures of speech, highly descriptive adjectives, and others of the suggestions can lead to distraction from the meaning to be conveyed. Often children will overuse similes or become preoccupied with adjectives, particularly as they first experiment. Helping them focus on exactness of meaning but with enough variety to add appeal will soon remedy this.

Some Noise Words

thump
thud
sigh
slurp
murmur

FORM AND CONVENTION IN WRITING

Most teachers seem to agree that the vital element in written expression is the content. Unfortunately, though, some appear to believe that conventions of writing—the mechanics, the matters of form and appearance, the agreed-on customs of putting language symbols on paper—are of little importance. Such teachers are likely doing their pupils a distinct disservice.

Certainly the conventions must be seen in proper perspective. They are aids to communication, not ends in themselves. Children need to learn that communication will be lost if attention is not given to them. Teachers should remember that habits, good or bad, tend to "stick," and thus recognize that good habits in respect to the conventions will stand children in good stead for the rest of their lives.

Form and Appearance

A neat and attractive-looking paper, whether it is a letter, a report, an announcement, or a story, is a courtesy to the reader and helps make the expression more effective. Although there are few set rules about many matters of form, there are some generally accepted ideas about such matters as leaving margins at the top, bottom, and sides of the paper, indenting the first line of a paragraph, placing a title, avoiding crowded writing at the end of a line, and eliminating untidy erasures and messy blots. Children should learn about these.

FORM AND APPEARANCE IN WRITING

Kindergarten	Usually little child writing, but the teacher should call attention to titles of stories and their placement, to attractive arrangements of work on paper, and to general neatness.
Grade 1	Margins at left, right, top, and bottom of page. Even spacing between letters and between words so that writing is not crowded. First word of a paragraph indented. All writing should be neat.
Grade 2	All taught in grade 1. Title centered at top, with space between it and story. No crowding of writing at ends of lines; recognition that right margin will be uneven. Name and date on all papers.
Grade 3	All taught in earlier grades. Attention to neatness.
Grade 4 and above	All taught in earlier grades. Words at ends of lines divided correctly. Use of appropriate paper for particular writing occasions. Using only one side of paper.

A Bulletin Board Idea

THIS IS THE WAY WE HEAD OUR PAPERS

name

school

grade

date

title

Keep the focus on content. Teach form and appearance in the context of the children's writing.

Developing a handbook of forms and conventions for a classroom (for the whole school is even better) will help both children and teachers.

This chart is *only a guide* and should be used the way any list of skills or learnings is used—with the recognition that not all children will progress at the same rate and that no child should be expected to master skills listed for any grade level until he or she has achieved those given for earlier grades.

Children should know what is expected of them. It is a good idea to work with them early in the year to establish standards of form and appearance for written work. These standards should be simple and should include only items needed for identification, neatness, and correctness. Items might include position of name and date on papers to be handed in, the extent of margins, regulations about writing on one or both sides of the paper, types of paper to be used for written work, etc. By all means let the children themselves participate in setting these standards. Discuss the reasons for having such standards, and then post them until habits become established, making sure that they are adhered to consistently in order to avoid confusing the children.

Form in writing can be introduced in first grade—and perhaps incidentally in the kindergarten program. At first the teacher will do much of the writing—of letters, experience stories, and charts—and should call attention to how these look, particularly with respect to margins.

When independent writing begins in grades 1 and 2, attention should again be directed to margins, neatness in writing, and the mechanical skills that have been introduced. Indenting the first word of a paragraph may be taught, as may the indentation of the closing and signature in a friendly letter, since children should be learning to write letters to friends.

Punctuation

Punctuation can be overemphasized, but it does have an important place in writing: it helps to transmit meaning. Simply stated, punctuation is a method for showing, by the use of a number of agreed-upon marks, meaning that cannot be shown—or is only partially shown—by words and the arrangements given to them. In speech these meanings would usually be transmitted by the rising and falling tones of the voice, by emphasis or stress on certain sounds, and by pauses in or the breaking off of the stream of speech.

There are, of course, punctuation items that are unique to written discourse—marks used in writing that are not meant to symbolize speech features. These include such things as a period after an abbreviation, a hyphen to show the division of a word, the underlining (or italicizing) of a book title, and quotation marks around the title of a story.

There are also features of stress, pitch, and juncture in speech that are not reflected by punctuation in written expression. Stress is usually shown by meaning. For example:

She signed the *contract* without hesitating.
As the pavement began to *contract*, a crack appeared.

Pitch can sometimes be shown by punctuation, as in the sentences "He will go with us" and "He will go with us?" Although end punctuation is the most common clue to an intonation pattern, other punctuation marks sometimes indicate the need for a change in pitch. For example, "The boys without coats were very cold" will not be read orally the same way as "The boys, without coats, were very cold."

The breaks in the stream of speech, the junctures, can sometimes be signaled by punctuation marks—for example, the more pronounced juncture at the end of a sentence. However, since any sentence (The man/next to me/ was laughing) has breaks in the flow of its utterance (as indicated by the /), it is a fallacy to assume that every pause requires a punctuation mark. This is particularly true with the current deemphasis on close punctuation. We see "My friend Jim Smith will go with us" just as often as we do "My friend, Jim Smith, will go with us," and no one fails to get the meaning. Also, when one wants to indicate a pronounced interruption (a double bar juncture //, for example), there is no particular punctuation form that must be used. The sentence "My brother (actually my half-brother) will meet me in Boston" can be written "My brother—actually my half-brother—will meet me in Boston." Nothing about the way the two sentences are said indicates the difference in punctuation.

Punctuation teaching may be aided by relating the items taught to intonation patterns in speech when this is appropriate. When children read orally, opportunities for calling attention to punctuation marks and what they signal often arise. Major attention, however, should be given to functional and direct teaching. That is, punctuation should be taught as it is needed by pupils in their writing, and attention given only to those items that are important to that writing.

Teaching Punctuation

Observe conventions in chart stories.

Punctuation teaching should begin in the primary grades. The first sentences that are put on the board, met in a reader, or written on a chart or under a child's drawing provide opportunities for beginning punctuation teaching. Although this teaching should be informal and secondary to the expression, it can be specific and direct.

Children can learn most easily to use punctuation properly (and other matters of mechanics and convention) by doing a great deal of writing, if teachers give encouragement and appropriate guidance. In the New Hampshire observational studies, Calkins (see References) reported on the effect of such a writing program: the children in a third grade classroom whose teacher emphasized individual writing could define and explain approximately three times as many kinds of punctuation as could the children in a classroom in which punctuation drills and exercises had been emphasized. This shows the importance of the teacher both in deciding what to teach and in the attention he or she gives to children's questions, interests, and thoughts.

The following sections give other suggestions for teaching the most common punctuation items.

THE PERIOD. The first writing children experience calls for a period *at the end of a sentence*. For example:

We went to the park.

Call attention to the period. Point out that the little dot is a traffic signal called a period. It means that a stopping point has been reached and there must be a pause before going on to the next set of words. Later a more formal explanation may be given, such as, "A period tells us this is the end of a statement."

As children begin their own writing, remind them of the need to signal the end of a statement they write. To help them, provide charts with properly punctuated sentences as models.

Early in children's experience they will also encounter three other uses of the period. They will see it in *abbreviations of titles of persons and of place names*. For example:

Mill St.
Dr. Hill

They will also find it after *initials in proper names*. For example:

H. O. Downs

Finally, they will encounter it after *numerals in lists*:

1.

2.

Each of the above four uses of the period should be introduced to pupils in kindergarten and first grade and directly taught in the first, second, or third grade as pupils begin their writing and encounter situations that require the use of the period.

THE QUESTION MARK. First grade children should be introduced to the question mark. Since children come to school asking questions, it is natural for you to place a question mark *at the end of a direct question* in a story they dictate. It is also natural for them to write questions in their first stories, and they will readily place the correct mark if it has been introduced. In fact, children probably have less trouble with question marks than with any other type of punctuation.

A second use of the question mark is *after a direct question in the context of a larger sentence*, as " 'Are you going to the store?' Billy asked." This is more difficult for children to understand and should not be introduced until the late third or early fourth grade.

THE COMMA. There are many common rules, but children should be taught only those they actually need in their writing. In the primary grades, as you write experience stories and notes to be copied by the children to take home, some uses of the comma can be introduced. These include the comma between the date and the year, between city and state, after the salutation in a friendly letter, and after the complimentary close of a letter. Children can also begin to become aware of the comma used to separate words in a series, although this use should not be directly taught until the third grade.

Punctuation practices vary. For example, a comma may or may not precede and *in sentences containing words in a series.*

QUOTATION MARKS. Children in the primary grades will encounter quotation marks in their readers and storybooks and will naturally have questions about them. This is the right time, then, to introduce their use. A good way to do this is to have children take the parts of characters in stories in which the speech is set off by quotation marks. They will learn that these marks signal speech. The use of quotation marks may also be shown in group stories you write on the board as the children dictate. Use these group stories often, even after the children begin to write compositions of more than two or three sentences by themselves, for they are useful in many ways—for example, for developing vocabulary and organizational

A PUNCTUATION GUIDE

Item	Use	K	1	2	3	4	5	6	7	8
Period	At the end of a statement	★	★	†	'	'	'	'	'	'
	After initials	★	★	†	'	'	'	'	'	'
	After abbreviations	★	★	★	†	'	'	'	'	'
	After numerals in a list	★	★	†	'	'	'	'	'	'
	After letters or numerals in an outline				★	★	†	'	'	'
	In footnotes and bibliographies						★	★	†	'
Question mark	After an interrogative sentence		★	†	'	'	'	'	'	'
	After a question within a larger sentence				★	†	'	'	'	'
Comma	Between the day of month and the year	★	★	†	'	'	'	'	'	'
	Between city and state	★	★	†	'	'	'	'	'	'
	After a salutation in a friendly letter		★	†	'	'	'	'	'	'
	After a complimentary close		★	†	'	'	'	'	'	'
	To separate parts of a series			★	†	'	'	'	'	'
	To set off words of direct address				★	★	†	'	'	'
	To separate a direct quotation					★	†	'	'	'
	Before and after appositives					★	★	†	'	'
	After introductory clauses					★	★	†	'	'
	After introductory words: yes, no, interjections					★	†	'	'	'
	Before the conjunction in a compound sentence						★	†	'	'
	Before and after a nonrestrictive clause						★	★	†	'
	Before and after parenthetical expressions						★	★	†	'
	In footnotes and bibliographies							★	†	'
Apostrophe	In contractions		★	★	†	'	'	'	'	'
	To show possession		★	★	★	★	†	'	'	'
	To show plurals of figures and letters				★	★	★	†	'	'
Quotation marks	Before and after a direct quotation		★	★	†	'	'	'	'	'
	Before and after titles (other than titles of books)			★	★	★	†	'	'	'
Exclamation mark	At the end of an exclamatory word or sentence		★	★	★	†	'	'	'	'
Colon	After the salutation of a business letter				★	★	†	'	'	'
	To separate the hour from minutes			★	★	★	†	'	'	'
	Before a long series or list					★	★	★	†	'
	To denote examples						★	★	★	†
Hyphen	At the end of a line to show a divided word		★	★	★	†	'	'	'	'

*Introduction   †Suggested teaching   'Maintenance

skills. As you write, point out punctuation and paragraphing, making special mention of the placement of commas and question marks in relation to quotation marks. Put some of the stories on charts, so the children can use them as models. And, above all, work with the children as they write; if good habits are established from the beginning, many future problems may be avoided.

The punctuation chart suggests grade levels for the introduction, direct teaching, and maintenance teaching of the punctuation items usually taught in the elementary school. Keep in mind, however, that these are approximations only; each class progresses at its own rate, as does each child in it. Punctuation marks—and their various uses—should be taught as they are needed in the children's writing.

In an active language arts program children will have encountered these marks in their reading, and their uses as aids to understanding meaning, as well as to reading orally, will have been pointed out. They will have participated in group writing of many kinds, and individually they will have written sentences, lists, experience stories, friendly letters, etc., by the time they reach the middle grades. If this has not been true, you may need to start virtually at the beginning, but in any case see that there is a genuine need to write letters, directions, notes, reports, reviews, announcements, news articles, and so on, and provide both the time for writing and guidance during the writing. The teaching of needed punctuation items will be a natural adjunct of such a program.

Research has shown that as children advance through elementary school they tend to make many errors in punctuation and they show little improvement in punctuation skills. This surely means that one or more of the following are true: (1) children regard punctuation as of little importance; (2) teaching has been inadequate; (3) insufficient opportunity has been given for the use of punctuation items in genuine writing situations; and (4) evaluation has not resulted in review and further use of items needing attention. If punctuation is taught in connection with situations where there is a need to communicate and if children are shown that it contributes to this communication, there should be fewer problems.

Capitalization

Capitalization is another mechanical element of written expression about which a great deal is known in relation to children's needs. The capitalization needs of the children in a particular class can be determined by examining their spontaneous and assigned writing. Textbooks and course guides often list recommended grade levels for introducing and teaching capitalization uses (as shown in the capitalization chart), but, as always, such lists are merely guides, not firm requirements. The best guide is the writing the children actually do.

There are a number of ways to teach capitalization skills. When children first begin to learn about letters, they discover that each letter has two forms. When they write their own names, they learn to use capitals. Later, when they see words and sentences written on charts and on the chalkboard

CAPITALIZATION CHART

Words to Capitalize	K	1	2	3	4	5	6	7	8
First word of a sentence	★	★	†	'	'	'	'	'	'
First and last names of a person	★	†	'	'	'	'	'	'	'
Name of street or road	★	★	†	'	'	'	'	'	'
The word I		★	†	'	'	'	'	'	'
Name of a city or town		★	†	'	'	'	'	'	'
Name of a school or special place	★	★	†	'	'	'	'	'	'
Names of months and days	★	★	†	'	'	'	'	'	'
First and important words in titles	★	★	★	†	'	'	'	'	'
Abbreviations: Mr., Mrs., St., Ave.	★	★	†	'	'	'	'	'	'
Each line of a poem[a]			★	†	'	'	'	'	'
First word of a salutation of a letter		★	†	'	'	'	'	'	'
First word of a complimentary close		★	†	'	'	'	'	'	'
Initials		★	★	†	'	'	'	'	'
Titles used with names of persons			★	★	†	'	'	'	'
First word in an outline topic				★	★	†	'	'	'
First word of a quoted sentence			★	†	'	'	'	'	'
Names of organizations			★	★	†	'	'	'	'
Sacred names			★	★	★	†	'	'	'
Proper names generally: countries, oceans, etc.			★	★	★	†	'	'	'
Proper adjectives					★	★	†	'	'
Titles of respect and rank and their abbreviations			★	★	†	'	'	'	'

★Introduction   †Suggested teaching   'Maintenance

[a]Be sure to point out that there are exceptions to this, particularly in modern poetry.

or printed in their readers and storybooks, they encounter many of the kinds of words that are customarily capitalized. The next step is experience stories, and capital letters can be pointed out as these are written on the chalkboard: "Notice that I am beginning the sentence with a capital letter" or "Bruce begins with a capital letter because that is his name."

Direct teaching begins the moment children first start to copy words from charts or the chalkboard; letters to be capitalized should be pointed out (and reasons given) so that children begin with an awareness of the need for both capital and small letters.

When children begin to write independently, it is important to observe their written work, noting errors (without red-marking the papers) and planning lessons to correct the errors and to introduce new uses as they become appropriate. At this point children are fascinated with writing anything, so group and individual dictation drills can be especially helpful in emphasizing capitalization situations to which particular attention is being given or which pupils find difficult. Pupils can also compare their capitalization with that shown in models and make their own corrections. Group correction of papers, with special attention to capitalization, is possible through the use of an overhead or an opaque projector. Good habits formed at the very beginning are far more effective than any amount of corrective work.

If good habits are formed, unnecessary capitalization will probably not be a problem, but it may be necessary with some children to reteach certain usages or provide practice activities to eliminate unnecessary capitals. In particular, children who capitalize words for purposes of emphasis should be helped to overcome this habit.

Above all, however, teaching children to proofread their writing and then insisting that they practice this proofreading will accomplish more than most teaching activities.

Good habits in the conventions of writing are like good driving habits—they become established through regular use.

Punctuation and Capitalization Activities

In the lower and middle grades, the teaching of punctuation may be enlivened by making cardboard stick puppets representing various punctuation marks. These can be given names such as Rollo Period, "Slim" Exclamation Mark, Paula Apostrophe, etc.—or let the children choose names they like. Each character can tell what he or she does and from time to time can come out and remind pupils of what they have forgotten.

Children can also play matching games, matching punctuation symbols with their uses. Make tagboard cards, printing a symbol or a use on each one. For example, make a period on a card; then on four additional cards print the words "at the end of a sentence," "after an abbreviation," "after initials," and "after a numeral in a list." A symbol card will be needed for each use. If desired, an additional set of cards can show illustrations of these uses.

Another game that can add interest is a version of "What's My Line?" The children can plan this by choosing "guests" to represent punctuation marks; the guests are then questioned by the panel about their functions and appearance. A guest might be introduced with "He is rather shy and seldom appears more than once in a sentence" (period), "Our first guest always appears in pairs" (quotation marks), or "This guest is very lively" (exclamation mark). This could make a good assembly program, with the "panel" selected from the audience. Both panel and guests should be cautioned that questions may only be answered by "Yes" or "No."

The importance of punctuation and capitalization can be shown in many ways. One is to have pupils find examples of specific punctuation and capitalization items in books, newspapers, and magazines. For instance, they might look for sentences in which commas set off words in a series, a period is used after an abbreviation, a word is divided by a hyphen, or parentheses are used to enclose material that is not part of the main thought. These examples can be used to make wall charts or a bulletin board.

Another way to emphasize the value of punctuation and capitalization is to present the children with a paragraph that has none. Choose this paragraph carefully, selecting one in which meaning is actually obscured by the lack of signals. Or let the children try reading some of Don Marquis's *Archy and Mehitabel*—this will quickly convince them.

It is fun occasionally to present "trick" sentences for pupils to punctuate. Sentences such as these can be used:

Sixty, three, and eleven are the numbers.
Sixty-three and eleven are the numbers.

No water is coming through the pipe.
No, water is coming through the pipe.

Bill, said Joe, is very noisy.
Bill said Joe is very noisy.

An important aspect of teaching any skill is helping children to become aware of their own errors. A good way not only to help them become aware of their errors but also to lead them to assume responsibility for overcoming them is to have pupils keep individual folders for papers that have punctuation and capitalization errors marked. From these they can compile lists of items that need to be studied and select drill materials to help them overcome their problems. Papers should be dated so that children can examine them regularly (perhaps once a month) to determine their own progress.

Avoid workbook types of practice activities in which there are several or even many different items on a single page. Individual children or groups may be helped by using practice activities, but the practice should be upon a specific need. For example:

1. Write each sentence, using capital letters wherever they are needed:

   it was uncle jim who took me.
   we went to the zoo in glenwood park.
   will mrs. jones be at the picnic?
   last christmas we visited sarasota, florida.

2. Write the following sentences, using commas where they are needed:

   Where did you get the bike Jim?
   I think Mom that I may be late.
   John come over after school and play.
   Alice aren't you going to school today?

A good variation of the above is to use the children's sentences. These can be gathered by listening and making notes as they talk or jotting down appropriate sentences from their writing. Exercises can also be made by dittoing material from reading, science, or other textbooks without capital letters or without punctuation (or the particular marks being studied). The children can supply the needed items and then compare the results with the text. (Allowance should be made, of course, for legitimate variations.)

Dictation exercises can furnish variety, and they can be used in several ways. Children can dictate to each other, or dictation can be recorded and used by individuals who need practice on particular items. Spelling words that need review can even be included in dictation drills. Dictation can also be done by the teacher when a large group or the entire class needs practice on a specific skill or as a general review. When dictating, read the selection three times: once so pupils will know the length and get the gist of what is said; a second time, very slowly, so they can write it; a third time, more rapidly, so the writing can be checked.

A duplicated paragraph is good for a general review of punctuation and capitalization, again with specific directions as to the number of items to be supplied.

> *Directions:* Rewrite the following paragraph, using eight capital letters, three periods, and four commas.
>
> no one was allowed to leave boston and this could have been disastrous for paul revere had he not known the city so well in the darkness he was able to reach the charles river where he had hidden a rowboat a few days before and two friends were waiting to row him across it would be a very dangerous mission for their boat would have to pass near the enemy

It is a good idea to have a generous supply of practice materials of all types for individual children or small groups to use when they need drill and to keep these materials filed in such a way that the particular type can be found quickly. These can vary in difficulty according to the grade level and the needs of the particular children in the class. Answer sheets should be included in each folder so children can check their own work.

REVISING, PROOFREADING, AND EDITING

Revising begins with reflecting. The writer tries to view what he or she has written somewhat from the perspective of a reader—but not entirely, for first viewing is also from the perspective of the writer: Have I stated what I want to state? Where am I not clear? Have I left out some details? Are the transitions between ideas or paragraphs effective? Do they help hold ideas together? All writers, even the youngest, do some reflecting, but without guidance and encouragement by a teacher the reflecting will likely be superficial, leading to few changes in the writing product. If a teacher is to provide guidance to the writer, the teacher must have reflected about the product, assuming the writer's perspective as much as possible and considering the maturity of the child's writing.

Recall the Basic Instructional Approach suggested in Chapter 2.

Revising means changing openings and endings, adding details, varying sentence types, changing words to get the most precise ones, examining and possibly changing transitional devices, possibly changing the order of paragraphs and sentences, eliminating excess words or phrases, adding or deleting modifiers, etc. The focus in revising is on the content. The objective is to make that content convey the writer's message in the best way possible.

Writers often revise a good deal as they write, and this should be encouraged, but with the caution that too much revision may result in ideas being lost. Major teaching effort should be expended in individual conferences with children, beginning with first drafts of what they've written and

An informal writing conference.

*Reading a writing product
aloud often emphasizes faults
that need revising.*

continuing with successive drafts. Some group instruction is helpful—for example, revising the draft of a group story or account. Too, the various teaching suggestions made earlier in the chapter regarding organization, sentences, and word choices give attention to specific problems or needs.

It may be helpful to show the children one of your first drafts of a paper, a letter, or any other piece of writing that you considered important enough to edit and rewrite. Or find a biography of a famous author that shows reproductions of first versions of well-known works and compare these with the finished versions. Accompany this evidence that even experienced writers need to edit with exercises in actual rewriting. For example, a particularly wordy paragraph can be written on the board or placed on a transparency for use with the overhead projector, and the children can work together deleting, condensing, and revising where necessary. The same thing can be done with some of the children's own first drafts—or even with presumably finished products when the need is shown. To be truly helpful, this type of editing must be done in a spirit of discovery. Questions must encourage constructive, rather than adverse, criticism: How many other ways can you think of to say this? Which one gives the best picture? Can you think of other details (reasons, etc.) that could be added? Is there any other way the same idea could be developed? Working cooperatively in this way will help pupils to discover that sometimes it is even a good idea to start over again entirely or try a different method of development.

Proofreading is related to revising, since the reading and reflecting suggested are certainly a part of proofreading; however, proofreading more often connotes looking for errors. Simply telling children to proofread is not enough. They need to learn to proofread by degrees; that is, first they need to proofread for only one or two elements—possibly checking to see if each statement is a sentence, as shown both by its "sense" and by its capitalization and punctuation. After children learn to check on one or two things, others can be added. In the various stages of developing skill in proofreading, the children should decide as much as possible for themselves

---

Lesson 6   **Improving Your First Draft**

You can improve the first draft of your story by adding details about your characters and by adding conversation.

Thinking It Through

Read part of Jim's story with some of the improvements he made in it.

Proofreader's Marks

≡ Make a capital letter.

⊙ Add a period.

℮ Take out.

∧ Put in one or more words.

ꟼ Begin a new paragraph.

∧ Put in a comma.

> Bobbie could hardly wait for the steer judging to begin⊙ She had spent four long years on her project∧ raising ^Reggie^ a steer from a calf to a ^1200-pound^ reserve grand champion. ꟼ Bobbie's entry was to be judged last. As she waited for the judges to reach her stall, she ^paced up and down and^ fiddled with her ^the^ scarf∧ ^around her ponytail^ Then she shined the ^scuffed^ tops of her boots on the back of her ^stiff, new^ jeans. Her ^sweaty^ hands showed she was nervous. Her knees felt funny, too.
>
> Finally, the judges came to her. One judge introduced herself⊙ ℮ then she asked Bobbie her name and her steer's name. Another judge asked what she had been feeding him ∧and ^whether^ if℮ the steer had ever been sick or injured.

- Which details did Jim add to improve the descriptions of his characters' looks? thoughts and feelings? actions?
- What marks of punctuation did Jim add?
- Where did Jim decide to start a new paragraph? Why?

292

Children may be motivated to rewrite by learning basic proofreading and editing skills.

From LANGUAGE: SKILLS AND USE BOOK 6. By Ronald L. Cramer et al. Copyright © 1980 by Scott, Foresman and Company. Reprinted by permission.

what to look for. As they progress through the grades, they should be encouraged to develop their own standards for guiding their proofreading.

In the middle and upper grades, the use of proofreading marks to note errors can interest children and help to avoid confusion. They will also feel less embarrassed if they know the marks used are actually those used by editors and that errors are made even by professional writers and printers—hence proofreading. These might be placed on a chart where children can see them.

A PROOFREADING CHART		
"Why can't I go outside," I asked.	✓ ?/	insert apostrophe insert question mark
"there isn't any- thing to do in in the house and I've finished my work.	cap ⌒ ⌃ ⩍	capitalize omit insert comma insert quotation mark

Since the purpose of proofreading is to find errors or faults in writing, it follows that the errors—misspellings, absence of punctuation, etc.—should be corrected and the faults—in sentence structure, organization, etc.—remedied. In some instances this means a child will need to copy what he or she has written with the changes made. Other times, especially if more than looking for mechanical errors is included in proofreading, rewriting is needed.

It is possible to interest children in revising, in proofreading, and in rewriting, but if suggestions made in this chapter and the preceding one are ignored or seldom observed, children will resist rewriting and any forced "copying over" (which, in effect, is what it would be) will likely not result in an improved piece of writing.

The objective in teaching revising and proofreading is for the writers to be editors, or polishers, of their own works. And no one learns to be a good editor quickly.

EVALUATING WRITTEN EXPRESSION

Evaluation is one of the major elements in the total teaching-learning activity. From evaluation both you and your pupils should discover what has been learned and what has not. From evaluation you should plan your future teaching. But because evaluation is often difficult and because there is a reluctance to criticize a child's creative efforts, some teachers do little evaluation of children's writing or of their own teaching of writing.

However, evaluation need not be as difficult as it is often thought to be if its focus is realistic and instruction-centered rather than directed at giving grades, making red marks, and finding fault.

Evaluating Your Teaching

What other questions
should you ask yourself?

The first concern in evaluation should be the program itself—its objectives and the teaching procedures and materials used. Such questions as these should be considered:

1. What is the atmosphere in the classroom? Is it one in which each child feels free to express ideas and make contributions to projects and discussions? Is there anything that might tend to repress individual expression?

2. Does the physical appearance of the classroom reflect creativity (on the part of both teacher and children), or is it dull and unattractive?

3. Is there sufficient input of many kinds throughout the year and in all areas of the curriculum?

4. Do children have many opportunities to read and hear well-written stories, poems, etc.? Is there a real interest in words and the way they are put together?

5. Do children have enough skill in the mechanics of writing to be able to express their ideas? Is the emphasis on mechanics so great that they are afraid to try new ways of expressing themselves?

6. Are motivation and preparation for writing adequate, or are children expected to write without really having a purpose or knowing what is expected of them?

7. Is writing a genuine part of the total curriculum? Is advantage taken of the many opportunities that occur for children to do purposeful writing?

8. Do the children write in many forms and for a variety of purposes and audiences? Do they have adequate knowledge of the many forms of and purposes for writing?

9. Does each child receive constructive responses—from you and others—at various stages in the writing process? Does each child feel free to ask questions, try out ideas, and seek help?

These are questions to be asked and answered by you the teacher. In part, though, your answers must come from a consideration of the children's writing. Is the writing generally vapid, superficial, and trite? Does it neither interest nor communicate? Surely children are not like this. They are eager and sad, exhilarated and frustrated, interested and bored, possessing and giving. If their writing fails to express these feelings, if it is unimaginative and nonindividualistic, then something has happened. Something has come between the children and the papers they turn in.

Possible causes for children's failure to achieve the results desired (both by them and by the teacher) include the following:

- Lack of direction and guidance.
- Fear of teacher disapproval.
- Stifled oral expression.
- A meager vocabulary.
- Ignorance of the forms of writing.
- A deficiency of input.
- Failure to recognize the importance of the audience.

- No working knowledge of composition skills.
- Putting paper before the children too soon.
- Overemphasis on teaching mechanical skills.

Evaluating Specific Products

Evaluation of any piece of writing is largely an appraisal of its quality in terms of its purpose. From the beginning writing efforts of children, the practice of having them evaluate their own work should be fostered. They should learn to examine carefully what they have written in terms of selection of thought or idea; organization, clarity, and appeal of the product; and courtesy shown to their readers by legibility, correct spelling, acceptable word usage, and meaningful punctuation. This does not mean that everything a child writes needs to be given this kind of scrutiny. But when a child writes to communicate and to express, as all children will unless their desire for expression is shut off or no opportunities exist, he or she should appraise what was written. Children's self-evaluation can be aided by providing them with models, when possible and appropriate (letter writing form, for example), for guidance and comparison. Proofreading and editing checklists or lists of standards to be observed will also help. A checklist such as the one shown may be useful to you, but it also may be

Checklist for Written Reports	Linda	Ian	Kim	Carlos	Marie
Information					
Organization					
Vocabulary					
Sentence structure					
Appearance					
Usage					
Punctuation					
Capitalization					
Spelling					

modified and duplicated for children's use. That is, the spaces for the children's names could be used for a child to write in information identifying specific pieces of writing. Thus, the child could determine which areas he or she needs to work on most, where improvement is occurring, and so on, particularly if points (say from 1 to 5) are assigned to each item rather than a "yes" or "no."

The checklist can be expanded, but only if there is time available and knowledge present for using an expanded version. For example, organization can include introduction, body, conclusion, etc.; appearance can be divided into title, margins, and handwriting. Items included, of course, should vary according to grade level and standards previously established.

The better scales for evaluating writing are those developed by school districts. The Grosse Pointe, Michigan school district has been a leader in doing this.

Individual pieces of writing may also be evaluated for content, organization, mechanics, style, etc., by a scale which provides for the assigning of points for each of the aspects of writing in the scale. Scales either will have short examples of different levels of quality for the characteristics being assessed or will have statements upon which to base judgments, as in this example of a portion of a scale.

SEQUENCE

High   The order of events is clear even if the writer at times tells about the past or the future.

Middle   A few times it is not clear which event happened first.

Low   It is impossible to determine which event comes first or follows any other event.

Any teacher can make a scale to aid in judging a piece of writing. With guidance, children can do this too. A scale has particular value in guiding consistency in judgments about pieces of writing from the same individual and in aiding an evaluator to form judgments about examples of writing of a class.

Writing products are increasingly being evaluated by a *holistic* method. That is, rather than evaluating aspects of composition and assigning points which are then totaled for a score for the piece, the evaluator makes a judgment as to the quality of the piece as a whole. Holistic scoring is usually done on a schoolwide (or even wider) basis to get an assessment which can be compared with earlier ones or ones in other settings. Judgments of the quality of each piece of writing (preferably more than one piece per writer) are made by two or more teachers who have come to some agreement about the bases for their judgments. Holistic scoring has some advantages but does not have the diagnostic features that scales and checklists have for determining what aspects of writing need teaching attention.

Informal Records

Making valid judgments about the quality of an individual's writing as a whole or about aspects of it is not easy. Certainly, if we recall that writing

Parents are interested in such records, which are a good means for giving them evidence of their child's ability and growth.

ability grows in spurts and that every writer has "off days," judgments should not be based on evaluating one or even several pieces of writing. In order to determine a child's strong points and weaknesses, various techniques should be used. One is using a checklist or scale at intervals during the year. Others include keeping folders of children's writing; anecdotal records for each child—derived primarily from individual conferences; observational records of prewriting, writing, and postwriting behaviors; and tests of knowledge and application of punctuation and capitalization skills, paragraphing, and showing variety in sentence structure.

Group Evaluation

Another valuable technique is group evaluation, which may be done in several ways. One is to have the child read his or her paper to the class and let the class evaluate it for content and organization. Another is to have children work in small groups, reading papers and making suggestions for improvement. (This is particularly helpful following the first draft of a paper; children can then use the comments in revising and formulating final drafts.) A third method is to have several children write at the board (this calls for carefully lined chalkboards) so that all the children can see several "compositions." A fourth method is to use the opaque or overhead projector to show papers and have the children make corrections and suggestions. This can be a valuable teaching technique if papers are preread so that those selected illustrate weaknesses common to many children in the class or, conversely, if they demonstrate especially good vocabulary, organization, or method of development.

Many teachers prefer to tell children before writing begins if there is to be class or group evaluation, to read papers themselves instead of having children read them, or—when the projector is to be used—to have each child put his or her name on the back of the paper rather than on the front, so that no child will be embarrassed. Much embarrassment can be avoided, however, if evaluation is approached in a constructive manner and if belittling others is discouraged at all times. It is probably wise, however, either to forewarn children when writing is to be evaluated by anyone other than the teacher or to give each child the right to specify that he or she does not wish to have the paper read by others—freedom of expression must not be inhibited by fear of having intimate revelations exposed.

Standardized Tests

There are standardized tests that purport to measure ability in written expression or some aspect of it. However, these measures do not actually do what is often claimed for them. For example, a test may determine a pupil's knowledge of grammatical terminology or rules, but this kind of knowledge has nothing to do with writing ability. Identifying good and poor sentences (or fragments), choosing acceptable words and expressions (standard usage), arranging sentences in order, identifying misspelled words, and indicating where punctuation items should be placed are other activities that appear on standardized tests (although not all of these appear in all tests that purport to measure writing ability). These items, of course, are all related to writing, but they simply sample the test-taker's ability to distinguish between standard and nonstandard forms and to proofread for some types of errors rather than performance in the individual's own expression.

Assigning Grades

Assigning a letter or number grade to a child's paper should be avoided unless there is a school policy requiring it. If there is such a policy, the grade assigned should be supplemented by noting commendable aspects of the writing, such as a good choice of words, an apt expression, a neat margin, or good organization of thought. Every written product from every child has something about it that can be commended. Perhaps it may only be a better formed letter, fewer erasures, or greater promptness in turning it in, but, whatever it is (or, one hopes, they are), this should be made the focus rather than the grade.

Grading in some form is necessary, since grading is reporting—reporting first to the child and later to the school system and the parents. However, whenever possible such reporting should be done by a statement or series of statements rather than by the traditional letter grade.

A FINAL WORD

Teaching children to express themselves effectively by writing is one of the most complex tasks of the elementary school teacher. Ideas, organization, knowledge of forms, sentence structure, vocabulary, usage, and spelling—all these and more are inextricably bound up with written expression. When we speak, gestures, facial expressions, personal appearance, and intonation can supplement the actual words; further explanation or argument can even be added if the thought is not understood or accepted. On the other hand, written expression must often stand alone. This does not mean that the teaching of oral expression should be minimized in language arts programs, but a letter of application, a friendly note, the minutes of a meeting are often matters on which one is judged. It is important, then, that children know how to write in these and other special forms and have the skills to do so effectively. The ability to write effectively is also an aid in thinking and a means for self-expression, both important in all of our lives.

References

Calkins, Lucy McCormick. "Andrea Learns to Make Writing Hard." *Language Arts* 57 (1980), pp. 569–576.

———. "When Children Want to Punctuate: Basic Skills Belong in Context," in "Research Update," Donald H. Graves, ed. *Language Arts* 57 (1980), pp. 567–573.

Elbow, Peter. *Writing with Power*. Oxford University Press, 1981.

Graves, Donald H. "What Children Show Us about Revision." *Language Arts* 56 (1979), pp. 312–319.

Hennings, Dorothy Grant, and Grant, Barbara Moll. *Written Expression in the Language Arts: Ideas and Skills*. Teachers College Press, 1981.

Kirby, Dan, and Liner, Tom. *Inside Out: Developmental Strategies for Teaching Writing*. Boynton/Cook, 1981.

Larson, Richard L., ed. *Children and Writing in the Elementary School: Theories and Techniques*. Oxford University Press, 1975.

Petty, Walter T., and Hall, Mary Bowen. *Slithery Snakes and Other Aids to Children's Writing*. Prentice-Hall, 1967.

Teaching Resources

FILMS

Punctuation. Bailey-Film Associates (6 min.; color; intermediate).

Punctuation for Beginners. Coronet Films (11 min.; color, b/w; primary).

FILMSTRIPS

The Comma. McGraw-Hill (color; 2 strips).

Steps to Better Writing. Thomas S. Klise (5 filmstrips with records or cassettes, guides).

Using Punctuation and Capital Letters. Prentice-Hall Media (series of 6 strips).

KITS

I Can Punctuate Anything. Anything? Anything! Sunburst Communications (3 filmstrips, 3 cassettes, worksheets, guide; grades 4–8).

Punctuation Power. Coronet (6 cassettes, response books, manual; intermediate and upper).

Think and Write. Developmental Learning Materials (cards, masters, manual).

WORKBOOKS

Organization Skills. Curriculum Associates (30 lessons; grades 5–8).

Activities for Preservice Teachers

1. Make a checklist to use in assessing children's writing. Include such factors as vividness of language (intensity, freshness, vigor), picturesqueness of speech, involvement of feelings, element of surprise, etc. Decide on the range of points you will assign each item. Check out your list and the points awarded for each item with someone who is now teaching.

2. Prepare a set of transparencies to be used for group practice in proofreading at a particular grade level.

3. Plan a bulletin board using "fun" sentences in which meaning is changed by changing the punctuation.

4. Make puppets representing the various punctuation marks and plan a play in which the various characters explain themselves. This may be as imaginative as you wish.

5. Prepare several paragraphs to use in teaching organization, incorporating the suggestions in this chapter or devising ideas of your own.

6. Report to the class on what one commercial language textbook series does about teaching sentence sense, organizational skills, and making word choices to improve children's writing. Several students could each take a textbook series for this analysis.

7. Discuss with several kindergarten and first grade teachers what they do about teaching the skills covered in this chapter. This may take some probing because they may feel that they do little or nothing. And while this may be true, it also may not be.

Activities for Inservice Teachers

1. Select a child in your class who does little writing. Observe this child closely for a week or two. Note his or her activities, interests, and abilities. What does the child do when he or she could be writing? Analyze your observations and plan what you might do to create more interest in writing and to develop confidence in doing it.

2. With the children in your class, prepare a bulletin board on editing. The editing signs (sp = spelling error, lc = small or lowercase letter, etc.) will interest children.

3. Keeping in mind the abilities of your class as shown in the written work they have done, prepare a list of their needs in order of importance for a bulletin board. Hold a class discussion on proofreading; encourage the children to establish realistic criteria. Contract with each child for improvement of a weakness. Carry on this project for a month, then evaluate the results.

4. Prepare a punctuation checklist for your class. Use it as a focal point for a bulletin board. Plan a series of activities based on practical, interesting uses of punctuation, and add the products of the activities to the bulletin board.

5. Prepare similar activities for capitalization. Combine these (as well as the punctuation activities) with practice in proofreading written work.

6. Analyze the writing done by your class by collecting all written work for a week and tabulating both the number and frequency of punctuation items used and the capitalization and punctuation errors made.

7. Collect samples of children's writing at several grade levels. Analyze these in terms of growth in ability to capitalize and punctuate.

8. Tape individual children reading orally. Have them listen to themselves while following along in the book, noting how their reading was influenced by punctuation. Discuss the importance of punctuation to oral reading. Let the children practice for a week, then record and evaluate again.

Independent Activities for Children

1. Prepare cards with sentences that can be rewritten without changing the meaning. Children can use these to gain practice in varying structure. For example:

When the book fell from the table, the boy jumped.
The boy jumped when the book fell from the table.

2. Give the child sentences to finish using simile or personification.

I am as strong as _____
The car sounded _____
The tree in the front yard is as tall as _____

3. Keep an idea box where any child can place an idea for a story and any other child can use it. This could be kept in the "writers' corner," a special spot in the room furnished with a table, several chairs, paper, pencils and pens, a dictionary, and a thesaurus. Children could be allowed to go to this corner and write, just as they go to the library corner when they want to read. It may be necessary for you to begin or add to the idea box; if so, try to find ideas that may stimulate a new way of thinking. For example:

Tell about your walk home when you were blindfolded.
Describe the biggest dog in your neighborhood.
Suppose you were a bear in the zoo and didn't like marshmallows.

4. Have the children make a chart showing commonly used abbreviations. The chart can be illustrated with pictures of a street, a man, a doctor, etc.

5. Record short selections on tape that a child can listen to and copy. The copying will require punctuation, capitalization, and attention to neatness and form. Dictate slowly and select material that will interest a child. Various interesting facts that can be gleaned from almanacs, facts books, etc., can be put into appealing dictation paragraphs.

6. Individual children can design posters or bulletin boards on punctuation and/or capitalization for the classroom. The objective should be to make these informative, interesting, and colorful.

7. Prepare groups of sentences for a child to arrange into paragraphs. Some of the groups should include sentences that would be extraneous if included in the paragraph.

8. Prepare on ditto sheets paragraphs containing errors in spelling, capitalization, and punctuation. The child is to proofread these, making corrections as he or she finds the need. Other paragraphs may be poorly organized; instructions should then call for putting the ideas into logical order.

9. Prepare cards or dittoes containing simple sentences with verbs or verb phrases underlined. Individual children may select from these and find more colorful words to substitute for the underlined portion. For example:

Sentences	Substitutes
He *bit into* the apple.	crunched
	munched
	devoured

10. When children need to learn about the use of hyphens to divide words at the ends of lines, turn to the newspaper. Because newspaper columns are short, they contain many hyphenated words. Have the children look for these, cut out the columns, and circle the hyphens with a red crayon. Put the articles on a chart or bulletin board. Using the display, help the children formulate generalizations about the use of hyphens to divide words.

11. A child or several children working together might do any of the following:

Make lists of colorful phrases.
List adjectives describing objects in the classroom.
Find good beginning sentences for stories.
Collect objects that provide sensory feelings.

12. Have children collect particularly good similes, metaphors, and images. They might then work in groups to compile booklets of those they like best.

13. Two children can play a game with cards bearing various types of punctuation—periods, quotation marks, exclamation marks, etc. One child draws a card; he or she must compose a sentence that uses the mark on the card, giving the proper inflection. The other child guesses which mark was on the card. Individual children can play this game by drawing cards and then writing sentences using the marks correctly.

14. Two children can work together: one writes a question, using the correct capitals, spelling, and punctuation, and the other writes a statement in reply to the question. The children can check each other. (This is also excellent practice in spelling, changing person and forms of verbs, etc.)

15. One child prepares sets of sentences with different punctuation marks at the end. He or she reads them to a friend, giving the correct inflection. The second child guesses what the punctuation mark is.

That's your dog.
That's your dog?
That's your dog!
You don't know the answer.
You don't know the answer?

10 *Children Learn to Spell*

The basis of effective spelling instruction is a school program that appeals to children and provides for genuine communication activities. If writing activities are meaningful to children—if the writing that is done is recognized by children as important—then correct spelling is important. If children's interest in writing is not fostered—if there is little or no genuine reason for writing—then spelling instruction will not be effective.

PROGRAM OBJECTIVES

The basic goal in spelling instruction is to teach children to spell the words they use in their writing. This means the writing they do in school *and* the writing they will do after their school years. Of course it is impossible to determine all of the words any person may need to spell in a lifetime, but everyone should learn to spell the words that are most frequently written. It is also important to encourage children's increasing awareness of the structure of their language and how aspects of this structure relate to spelling specific words. Finally, a positive attitude toward spelling correctly and habits which support this attitude need to be developed.

Since spelling requires putting into written form words that are familiar from speaking, reading, and listening, two important abilities are needed. One of these is the ability to recall how words look—the words that the child has studied and those that have frequently appeared in his or her reading. The other basic ability is that of associating letters and patterns of letters with specific sounds. These two abilities become closely allied in the spelling efforts of most children, and both are influenced by the children's understanding of syntactic and morphemic aspects of the language.

A good speller naturally must know the letters of the alphabet and how to write them in both lowercase and uppercase forms. He or she should know how to alphabetize words and how to use this knowledge to find the spellings of words in dictionaries and glossaries. He or she should be able to pronounce words clearly and accurately and to use a dictionary, including its diacritical markings and key words, as well as phonetic and structural aids to help with pronunciations.

A person who spells well shows a concern for doing so by proofreading his or her own writing, by looking up the spellings of unknown words, and

See Chapter 13 for a discussion of dictionary skills and activities.

250

by establishing a specific study procedure for learning to spell new words. Thus the objectives of teaching the child habits of proofreading, studying, and using the dictionary properly are very important.

These basic objectives should be kept in mind as you read the remainder of this chapter, as you plan your program, and as you select and use materials in the program.

SPELLING READINESS

The time and effort spent on readiness activities in preschools, kindergartens, and first grades is generally directed toward the reading program, but a similar level of readiness should be fostered toward writing—and spelling. Of course, the ability to recognize some words—a major step in learning to read—is an ability also important to spelling. A child who looks at *ball* and *tall* and does not see that *b* and *t* are different letters is going to have difficulty in both reading and spelling. The one who cannot hear the difference in the way these words are spoken may likewise have difficulty.

Readiness for spelling, like readiness for reading or any other school subject, differs with individuals. Children at any age level are at various stages of development in their ability to express themselves orally and graphically. They also differ in receptive language ability. All of these differences are especially noticeable among children in preschool, kindergarten, or first grade—although, in actuality, the differences are likely to become greater later. In all cases, however, to foster the development of each child, recognition must be given to differences and plans for learning made accordingly.

As was pointed out earlier, children learn to talk by active involvement in a speech environment. This involvement is one of both imitating and experimenting—a problem-solving process—until knowledge functional in the speech environment is obtained. While children are usually encouraged to talk, like encouragement often is not given for learning to write—or to read, for that matter—since writing (or reading) is thought of as something to be learned at school. But with environmental conditions which foster and encourage writing, a similar problem-solving process will occur.

Early Writing and Spelling

See the article by Henderson and Beers.

We stressed in earlier chapters that young children want to write. They want to "put down" on paper their ideas and feelings—mainly for themselves; they want to create rather than to communicate with someone. To do this, at first they draw pictures or simply make marks that no adult can interpret. Later, they learn about letters, what their shapes are (or approximately), and that letters represent sounds. Mother writes SUSAN, and Susan copies it as best she can. Susan will see other letters—on TV, in books, or when brothers or sisters write their names for her. Gradually, then, in her "writing" she will go beyond marks and drawings to writing letters to represent words associated with what she wants to "put down." *S* may be her "spelling" of *sun*, or she might "spell" it *N*. She might not even come that close to adult logic; the letter or letters she writes may not be found in the spelling of her "word," but she will show that she knows that words are made up of letters and that a word represents sounds.

Considerable attention is being given by researchers to such attempts of young children to spell the words they want to write. These attempts have been labeled "invented" spellings, and the researchers have focused much of their attention on how these "inventions" change as children ask questions about the spelling of words and as they see more and more words. Observations by the researchers of children and their spelling inventions have led them to conclude that children move through a series of spelling strategies over an extended period of time. This movement, of course, is not the same for all children, and the "inventions" often differ even when the children are at comparable developmental stages. The movement of a child from one stage to another in approaching ability to spell the words he or she writes is likely based on both the child's experimenting and a good deal of informal instruction—often not thought of as such or perhaps not observable by researchers—applied primarily by an adult. This results in the enhancement of children's ability to associate sounds and letters and to remember how letters and words look. That is, they increasingly are able to secure useful impressions and to recall them—the fundamental abilities needed in learning to spell the words one wants to write.

While the use of the term "invented" is new, the fact that young children experiment with spelling and that they "spell" words to suit themselves has long been known. What is important about the research in regard to spelling, though, is that greater recognition is being given to the value of affording young children many opportunities to write and fostering their attempts to achieve conventional spellings. Encouraging early writing is a definite factor in developing the readiness needed for success in the spelling program.

Readiness Activities

Many activities develop readiness for beginning spelling instruction. As suggested above, encouraging young children in their creative efforts to "write" certainly is important. But emphasis on writing should be part of a rich program involving all of the language arts: reading and telling stories to children, encouraging their talking with adults and other children, and providing many opportunities for them to see words (on labels, signs, charts, etc.—and in books). Besides such involvement in language, and even before children make much of a beginning in their "writing," activities that involve auditory perception and discrimination, such as the following, are helpful:

- Show pictures of objects and have the children tell which have names that begin with the same sound. For example, you might have pictures of a bear, a baby, a lion, a cat, a ball, a cup, a lamp, and a box.
- Do the same for ending sounds. For example: *sled, bread, bed, cap,* and *lamp.*

- Write the names of the objects under their pictures and underline the beginning letters of the names that are the same. For example, <u>b</u>ear, <u>b</u>aby, <u>b</u>all, and <u>b</u>ox. Ask the children if they know the names of these letters. Ask if they see other letters that are the same. Underline them: be<u>a</u>r, b<u>a</u>by, c<u>a</u>t, etc.
- Say a key word, followed by several others, and have the children hold up their hands for each one that begins with the same sound (or ends with the same sound or has the same middle sound). For example: *soft*, followed by *dot, sit, sing, bought, sand, song.*
- Activities similar to the ones above can be developed for consonant or vowel clusters (*st, gr, oy*, etc.), as well as for single phonemes. Further, associating similarities or identifying differences in words rather than simply in sounds calls for much the same type of exercises.
- Say pairs of words and have the children hold up their hands when the two begin with the same sound (or end the same way or rhyme with each other). For example: *big—boy; fill—ball; live—give.*
- Ask a child to name objects, and have the other children supply words that begin with the same sound (or end, etc.).
- Have the children think of words beginning with the same letter (*boy, bat, bear*), say these words, and then compare the beginning sounds and letters.

In addition, attention should be given to visual perception and discrimination. Begin by having children match objects of the same size, shape, or color. Later, have them find like and different letters and word forms. This sort of activity can also be combined with auditory activities.

- Have the children match pictures of objects whose names begin with the same sound (or letter) as their own names.
- Write letters on the board and have the children select pictures of objects whose names begin with the same letter (or end with the same letter or have the same medial letter). This activity should be used with caution, since the children may match sounds that are represented differently. For example, a picture of a bear might be readily and correctly matched with the letter *b* for the beginning letter or with *r* for the ending letter, but there might be difficulty with the medial sound representation.

THE INSTRUCTIONAL PROGRAM

We believe that teachers should follow specific spelling instructional programs. When this instruction should begin *should* vary from child to child, but, given the constrictions of school programs, it usually does not. For most children, however, a formal program should not come before grade 2. And at that grade level, as well as later ones, it should be based on the best research evidence available. Some researchers and reporters of research on "invented" spellings seem to believe that it is not necessary to give instructional attention to learning to spell specific words. However, this belief has not been substantiated by long-term research, nor does it take into account economy in the use of teachers' and children's time.

There certainly is nothing wrong about a school program in which chil-

Correct spelling is a concern of parents. Make sure that they understand your program.

dren have much interaction with written language through daily reading and writing. In fact, such a program is strongly advocated throughout this book. But whether such interaction needs to be supplemented by direct instruction or not is the issue, an issue of concern to teachers obligated to teach spelling (or reading, writing, listening, or speaking).

In any case, as has been pointed out, the ability to spell is largely contingent on the effectiveness of two processes—reception and recall. Reception comes from *recognizing* letters, noting their sequence, and associating with them sounds and knowledge of word structures, individually or in patterns. Recall requires *remembering* the sequence of letters and/or remembering associations that aid in achieving the correct sequence. Essentially, then, these processes are what children engage in as they "invent" and seek to improve their "inventions." A specific spelling program gives them practice, and the practice concentrates on words that research has shown are written with great frequency.

Fostering Positive Attitudes

Are you a good speller?

Here's how to tell:

1. Do you think spelling all words correctly is important?
2. Do you try to spell correctly every word you write?
3. Do you know how to learn to spell new words?
4. Do you know how to look up the spelling of unknown words?
5. Do you proofread for spelling errors?

A truly good speller is one who endeavors to spell all words correctly. A good speller possesses an attitude of concern and knows how to learn to spell a new word, how to get help in spelling unknown words, and how to make the best use of the knowledge of words that he or she has. Good attitudes toward spelling may be encouraged through continuous attention to correct spelling in your own writing. Show the children that correct spelling really matters by proofreading your own writing and by using a dictionary when necessary.

Showing the children that the words they are required to learn to spell are ones they consistently use in their writing and have need to spell is also useful. A simple tabulation of the words they write or of the words written by their parents and friends will show this—and will produce a list very similar to the one on pages 256 and 257.

Requiring the children to learn only those words that spelling tests and actual writing situations have shown they are unable to spell makes sense to the children and avoids the development of the negative attitudes that often result from studying words that are already known. It is also important to make certain each child knows and uses a specific and efficient method of learning to spell new words.

Encouraging in the class a spirit of mutual pride and cooperation in spelling achievement builds good attitudes. Children enjoy helping one another study, giving proofreading help, and providing encouragement to one another. Also emphasize individual and class progress in spelling, making each pupil aware of the progress he or she has made. Records of progress should be kept by the pupils themselves, although you may want to keep supplemental ones.

Encouraging high standards of neatness and accuracy in all writing is very helpful. Standards can be developed for the class to apply, and these should be referred to as often as necessary to see that they are maintained. It also helps to conduct an efficient spelling period—avoid dragging tests out too long or permitting procedures to develop which encourage dawdling and other poor habits. Negative attitudes toward spelling should be attacked immediately, although fault-finding should be avoided in favor of determining the causes of spelling failures and encouraging and stimulating the efforts children make.

Developing Desirable Habits

Although a favorable attitude toward spelling correctly is basic to a successful program, merely desiring to achieve will accomplish little unless certain basic habits are developed. The following are particularly important habits that can be developed:

- *Being concerned about the spelling of words used in written expression.* This means teaching children that anytime they are in doubt they should think, "Is this word spelled correctly?" and "Am I sure?" This habit is established by the development and maintenance of standards in written work and by the concern you show about correct spelling.
- *Proofreading all written work carefully.* Proofreading must be taught so that a child will not simply stare at the paper and think he or she is proofreading. In proofreading for spelling errors, each word must be looked at letter by letter.
- *Checking the spelling of all words about which the child is in doubt.* This does not mean that every doubtful word must always be checked in a dictionary— though knowing how to use the dictionary is essential—since sometimes a spelling can be checked in a reading text's glossary, by asking a classmate, or by asking you.
- *Using a specific procedure for learning the spelling of new words.* Although the procedure may vary slightly from child to child (as is discussed later), there are specific steps that are important and should be thoroughly learned and practiced.
- *Working efficiently during the spelling period.* Following a specific study procedure is an important part of working efficiently during the spelling period, but listening attentively to the pronunciation of words during testing, completing the spelling exercises promptly, and simply not wasting time are also important habits to be encouraged.

Teaching Specific Words

A great deal of evidence has been accumulated about the words people write most often. Many commercial spelling materials provide for the teaching of these words, although some materials tend to emphasize the teaching of words that illustrate "spelling patterns" (for example: *cap, cat, catch, pack, cab, cad, badge, bag, jam, pan*) even though some of these words are not likely to be written—at least not frequently—after the completion of the lesson.

The commercial spelling books that seek to teach a core of important words usually present 3,000 to 4,000 (grades 1 through 8) for children to learn. Materials emphasizing spelling patterns may include a greater number of words (including many of the "most commonly written" ones) in order to illustrate the patterns and to show exceptions to them.

The following words are of particular importance. Elementary school children should be able to spell these words without hesitation by the time they reach the fifth grade (or sooner).

A 1972 study by Thomas showed that 1,000 words account for 83% of all words used in children's writing; 2,000 words account for 89%.

Another study found these words account for over 36% of all words written:

the	of	on
I	is	they
and	was	that
to	have	had
a	my	she
you	are	very
we	he	will
in	for	when
it		

a	children	game	land	only
about	close	gave	large	open
after	coat	get	last	or
again	cold	getting	let	order
ago	come	girl	letter	other
all	coming	girls	like	our
along	could	give	line	out
also	country	glad	little	over
always	cut	go	live	
am		going	long	part
an	daddy	good	look	people
and	day	got	looked	place
another	days	grade	lost	play
any	dear	great	lot	played
are	did	grow	lots	please
around	didn't		love	pretty
as	do	had		put
asked	does	hand	made	
at	dog	happy	make	rain
away	doing	hard	man	ran
	doll	has	many	read
baby	don't	hat	may	red
back	door	have	me	rest
bad	down	he	men	ride
ball		hear	milk	right
be	each	heard	more	room
because	eat	help	morning	run
bed	end	her	most	
been	even	here	mother	said
before	every	him	much	same
best		his	must	sat
better	fall	hold	my	saw
big	far	home		say
black	fast	hope	name	school
book	fat	hot	never	see
boy	father	house	new	seen
boys	feet	how	next	send
bring	few		nice	she
brother	find	I	night	should
but	fire	if	no	show
buy	first	I'm	not	side
by	five	in	now	sister
	for	into		sleep
call	found	is	of	snow
called	four	it	off	so
came	friend	its	old	some
can	from		on	something
car	fun	just	once	soon
cat		know	one	started

stay	there	top	we	would
stop	these	town	week	write
such	they	tree	well	
summer	thing	two	went	year
sun	things		were	years
sure	think	until	what	yes
	this	up	when	yet
take	thought	use	where	you
teacher	three		which	your
tell	through	very	while	yours
than	time	walk	white	
that	to	want	who	
the	today	wanted	will	
their	told	was	wish	
them	too	water	with	
then	took	way	work	

A Spelling Program Plan

The spelling program in a classroom is often determined by the textbook or other materials available. Most commercial spelling textbooks make use of one of two basic plans. These plans are usually called the *test-study* and *study-test* plans. We believe that evidence clearly favors the test-study plan as the most efficient and satisfactory approach because it focuses on individual differences among pupils and because it fosters positive attitudes by requiring pupils to study only those words they do not know how to spell. The test-study plan consists of these features:

Children learn to spell many words from their reading; therefore, they may know how to spell many of the lesson words.

1. A test is given at the beginning of the term or month to determine the general level of spelling achievement of the class and of individuals in the class. It can be constructed by randomly selecting words from the lessons to be covered during the term or month. Select as many words as the pupils can attempt without becoming overtired or losing interest (usually twenty to twenty-five words are enough).

2. Pupils may be grouped for instruction on the basis of the preliminary test, or individualized teaching may be planned. For example, high achievers may be released from spelling instruction for other activities and low achievers may be assigned other materials, given fewer words, or provided with planned, individualized study help.

3. The weekly assignment begins with a test. This permits you and each child to determine the specific words that require study. You may want to precede this test (perhaps only occasionally) by pronouncing the words and having the pupils pronounce them. If you think there are words whose meanings are not known, these may be discussed. However, this is usually not necessary if the words have been selected properly.

4. The words that each pupil misspells on the pretest are identified by the child (see the following section on the weekly spelling lesson) and become his or her study list for the lesson.

5. In studying each word, the children use the steps that have been worked out by the class, or by you and individual children if modifications in the class steps seem to be necessary.

6. A final weekly or lesson test is used to determine the degree of mastery each child has achieved (a midweek test is also usually advisable, since attempting to spell—trying to recall—for a test is a good learning procedure).

7. Each child keeps a personal record of spelling achievement on a chart or similar device.

8. To prepare for reviewing, each child records in a notebook all words misspelled on the final test. Review words are studied using the steps followed in studying new words.

9. Each child is tested on the words in his or her review list at regular intervals until these words have truly been mastered.

10. A final term or monthly test is given to measure the progress made since the administration of the first test. This test may be a sampling of the words or it may include all of the words taught during the period of time (perhaps in more than one sitting).

A good instructional plan in spelling also provides for allowing children to correct their own tests and for giving most tests in list form. Having pupils correct their own tests makes the testing a learning experience, for pupils see exactly what mistakes they have made. Having the test corrected by another pupil or by you practically eliminates the possibility of any learning occurring from the procedure.

Some variation in testing is useful. For example, you may dictate sentences, each containing a spelling word, or perhaps a paragraph containing several or all of the words in a lesson. However, the difficulty with this form of testing is that other words used may not be known by the children. Thus, the list test should be used most often because it is economical of time and focuses on the objective of learning to spell the words in the lesson.

The Weekly Lesson

The spelling of a word important in most writing should be taught whenever the opportunity to do so occurs. However, it is also wise to have regular spelling lessons. Following are the principal features of a five-day lesson plan. The weekly lesson might be done in three days by including the second day's activities with those given for the first day and the fourth day's activities with those of the third day. Too, some children may not need all of the visual and auditory impression activities; and, as suggested in the preceding section, especially good spellers may need little or none of the weekly program.

Research shows that no more than 75 minutes per week should be devoted to direct spelling instruction.

FIRST DAY. Administration of a pretest of the words in the lesson (pronouncing the word, using it in a sentence, and pronouncing again); checking the test (each pupil checking his or her own); making individual study lists of words misspelled; discussing the words as necessary—their meanings and use, any unusual spellings, the application of any rules, or etymological matters that are appropriate and of interest.

SECOND DAY. Visual and auditory study of structural and phonemic elements in the words; direct study of the words on individual spelling lists.

THIRD DAY. Administration of a test (usually including all words in the lesson as a means of ensuring that guessing did not account for some correct spelling on the pretest); checking the test; again with each pupil checking his or her own; studying the words misspelled.

FOURTH DAY. Continued practice in visual-aural analysis of the words; learning new meanings for the words; extending word knowledge through practice in using linguistic principles; studying words misspelled on the third-day test.

FIFTH DAY. Administration of the final test; checking the tests, still with each pupil checking his or her own; writing words in a review list; marking achievement on a progress chart.

In addition, time may be given as it is available to practice in using the dictionary, to use of vocabulary building exercises, and to participation in games and enrichment activities. Some study of language, particularly of word origins, is also appropriate for inclusion in the lesson as time permits.

Grouping for Instruction

The above lesson outline indicates that much of the learning and teaching effort is individualized; for example, each pupil makes his or her own study list, each pupil studies the words he or she misspells individually, each pupil writes his or her own review words, and each pupil marks his or her own progress chart. However, the plan does not indicate how to go about grouping for instruction.

Actually, grouping is not difficult. It may be done in a manner similar to that used for reading or mathematics instruction. The first step should be administering a quarterly, semester, or yearly pretest of twenty-five to seventy-five words (depending on the ability of the pupils to handle the mechanics of writing). The words on this test should be randomly selected from the words for the particular quarter, semester, or year. Children who misspell none or very few of these may be considered the high achievers; those who misspell 10 to 50 percent should be considered the average group; and those who misspell more than half of the words should be considered the slow group. Some teachers make the average group larger than suggested and limit the slow group to only a few pupils.

The high and average groups should be given all of the words in a lesson, though some enrichment words may be added to the list for the high group if such words are carefully selected because of their need in writing.

Pupils' Study Procedures

There is general agreement among spelling authorities that the spelling of a word is learned by a series of steps involving impression and recall. The impression or image steps generally include visual, auditory, and kinesthetic impression. The recall steps usually suggest "seeing" the word in the mind and then writing from memory. Children who are very good in spelling can often learn a new word after seeing it only once; hence the other steps may not be necessary. The poorer spellers need help and encouragement in learning the steps and putting them into practice. They may also need to have the steps individualized by the addition of extra ones to help them say the words properly or to gain better visual, auditory, or kinesthetic impressions.

The following method of study is suggested as suitable for most children. You may wish to modify it in some manner for your class, but keep in mind that alternating impression and recall procedures are needed.

Learning to spell is a series of:

impression
↓
recall
↓
impression
↓
recall

1. Look at the word carefully and pronounce it correctly. Say it slowly, naturally, and clearly, looking at it as you say it.
2. Cover the word with your hand or close your eyes. Say the word and think how it looks. Try to visualize exactly the way the word is written as you say each letter in sequence to yourself.
3. Look at the word again to be sure that you said it and spelled it correctly. If you did not, start again at 1.
4. Cover the word and then write it, thinking carefully about how it looks.
5. Check your spelling. If you misspelled the word, begin again at 1. If you spelled the word correctly, go on to the next word.

Practices to Avoid

A number of the practices sometimes used by teachers should be avoided. Often these are used because the teacher is frustrated or simply does not know they are of no value or may even be harmful. For example, calling attention to possible "hard spots" in words may implant a spelling difficulty that could be avoided through a positive approach to learning. The practice of "writing" words in the air is also sometimes used in an effort to give children a kinesthetic-tactile impression of words. This is not a valid procedure, since to give a true kinesthetic-tactile impression of a word, the shape of letters should be felt (in sand or on chalkboard) and the muscle movement should be approximately that used when the word is actually written.

Sometimes teachers have a child write a word ten or some other number of times without intervening attempts at recall. Simpy copying a word is not likely to create a permanent impression. This practice is related to the less frequently used one of assigning the studying or writing of spelling words as a form of punishment. Neither practice does much to promote positive attitudes toward spelling, nor does reprimanding children for asking how to spell a word.

OTHER INSTRUCTIONAL CONSIDERATIONS

Other matters related to spelling instruction are discussed in this section. There are differences of opinion concerning some of these, and these differences are frequently reflected in the content of commercial spelling materials. Even with the less controversial matters there is disagreement regarding the amount of instructional attention each should receive.

Language Structure and Spelling

There is a long history of attempts to relate in some way the twenty-six letters of the English alphabet and the approximately forty (depending on the dialect) sounds, or phonemes, the letters must represent, so that learning to spell can be simplified. Various rules for representing or spelling some sounds have been promulgated in commercial spelling books for many years. Most research regarding this effort has focused on discovering how the various phonemes are represented. For example, Ernest Horn reported about thirty years ago that an examination of 10,000 words showed that "the *k* sound is spelled with *c* 64.36 percent and the *s* sound with *s* 71.19 percent of the time." A few years later researchers at Stanford University reported on a study of 17,000 words in which they took into account phoneme position in syllables and the stress given a syllable, as well as letter representations of the phonemes. Some of their findings regarding representations were similar to Horn's, and others were different, but these researchers used the word "regular" to identify the most common letter representation of each phoneme and suggested the teaching of generalizations concerning them. This study influenced the content of many commercial spelling materials and school programs despite the fact that these researchers had also shown that programming a computer with an algorithm of several hundred complex rules resulted in only 50 percent of the words being spelled correctly.

Other researchers have extended the Stanford study by pointing out that the representation of a sound may be influenced by the sounds adjacent to it, concluding that the percentage of "regularity" would be higher if this were done. For example, one points out "that the final 'j' sound of *fudge* is spelled *dge* because it follows a short vowel sound but is spelled *ge* in words such as *huge* and *large* because they contain other kinds of vowel sounds" (from Hodges, p. 6).

The importance of this information to a spelling program, valid as it is, seems debatable. Will a child seeking to spell *pajamas* be helped by knowing this? The 'j' sound does follow a short vowel, as it does in *pageant* and *digit*. And the child may still need to spell *gem, jug, general, joy, agent, tragedy, urge, major, reject, hinge,* etc.

We do believe that children need to learn likely representations of sounds in order to avoid completely irrational spelling attempts. And it is true that some sounds are represented by a single letter or a cluster of letters with considerable frequency (the 'b' sound, for example), but others, particularly vowels, are variously represented in many commonly used words. Further, if we take into account the dialect variations in speech, the "regularity" of representations decreases. So it seems that efforts to teach generalization about "regular" sound representations are likely to be unprofitable, if for no other reason than that, as stated in the report of one study (see Johnson *et al.*), "A comparison of words that children have difficulty spelling with words that can be constructed from common spelling patterns will show very little overlap. Words that confuse children include *said, friend, their, too, beautiful, people, holiday, finally, scared, experience,* and *silver*. These words cannot be constructed from common spelling patterns and yet they are words that children commonly use in writing and which they frequently misspell." Certainly time used in attempting to teach generalizations about sound-symbol correspondences and word patterns could be better spent.

Currently researchers are giving less attention to phoneme-grapheme correspondences and more attention to verification of theories concerning the nature of English orthography. They are discovering that the nature of

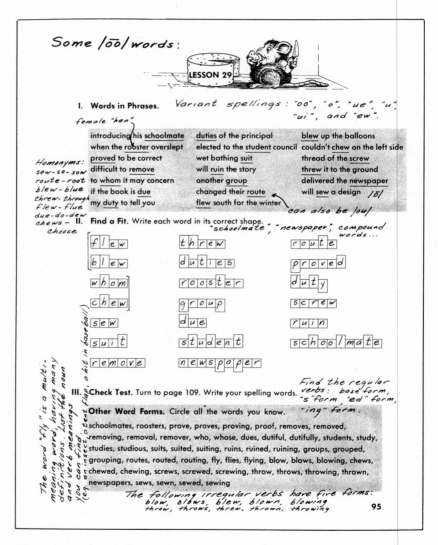

Illustrating variant spellings of sounds.

From *Working Words in Spelling*, Level E, Teacher's Edition. Copyright © 1977 by Curriculum Associates, Inc. Used by permission of the publisher.

this orthography closely parallels what mature, efficient spellers know about the language system and its graphic representation. The thrust of their advice regarding spelling programs is that children be provided with many opportunities to explore the ways in which their knowledge of spoken language relates to spelling. Many of them also admit that learning to spell is complex enough to warrant regular spelling programs.

Many teachers and researchers have long recognized that the issue, variously identified over the years as "phonics and spelling," "linguistics and spelling," or "pattern spelling," is really one of *teaching versus learning*. The average mature speller has *learned* the most likely representations of individual sounds and patterns of sounds and exceptions to them. The mature speller has also learned that in deciding how to spell a word consideration must be given to the placement of its sounds in syllables and to their sequence, to the stress given to these syllables, and to the relationship of the word to other words in terms of meaning and structure. How this learning has occurred, though, is less well known. Many recognize that mature, efficient spellers have done much writing and reading. However, the role in this learning of what some writers like to label "traditional" spelling programs cannot be discounted.

Spelling Rules and Generalizations

Use rules cautiously. Will rules help you spell these?

birch	curse	beard
church	hearse	weird
perch	terse	feared
search	worse	leered

Despite the concern evinced in the preceding section, the program should give attention to generalizations that are helpful to spelling. A helpful generalization should not be taught in such a way that children simply learn to verbalize it but then show no ability to apply it in spelling as they write. Rather, generalizations should be presented during lessons on words to which they apply or at times when children encounter a spelling problem that a generalization will help to eliminate. No more than one generalization should be dealt with at a time, exceptions to it should be noted, and opportunities for reviewing it and other generalizations should be provided. Any instruction should also take into account dialect differences; the fact that pronunciations given to some words vary with the context of speech, the situation, and their grammatical use; and the fact that generalizations which may be useful in reading may not be useful in spelling. An example of the latter is a commonly used reading generalization: "When there are two vowels, one of which is final *e*, the first vowel is usually long and the *e* is silent" (*bake, tone, fine*). This is helpful to a reader seeking to pronounce the word and thus determine what it is, but the reader is *looking* at the word. The speller gains no clue from this generalization about how to spell the word.

Particularly important generalizations that have few exceptions are the following:

1. Words ending in a silent *e* usually drop this *e* before a suffix beginning with a vowel (*make-making*) but keep the *e* before a suffix beginning with a consonant (*time-timely*).

2. For words ending in a consonant and *y*, change the *y* to *i* before adding a suffix, unless the suffix begins with *i* (*candy—candies; baby—babying*).

3. For words ending in a vowel and *y*, do not change the *y* to *i* when adding a suffix (*play—played; enjoy—enjoying*).

4. For those words of one syllable or accented on the last syllable that end in a single consonant preceded by a single vowel, double the final consonant when adding a suffix beginning with a vowel (*run—running; begin—beginning; need—needed*).

5. The letter *q* is always followed by *u* in common English words (*quite, quart*).

6. English words do not end with *v* (*believe; give*).

7. Proper nouns and most adjectives formed with proper nouns begin with capital letters (*France; French*).

Note such slang words as rev, luv, shiv.

Rules concerning the use of the apostrophe are also useful, since improper use of the apostrophe is the cause of many spelling errors. The following are helpful rules:

1. The possessive of a singular noun (including those ending in *s*, *z*, *ss*, or *x*) is formed by adding an apostrophe and *s*.

It is also correct to simply add an apostrophe to singular nouns ending in s *(e.g., Ms. Jones' house). However, it is simpler for children to learn one rule than two.*

John's idea	Congress's action
father's hat	box's top
Ms. Jones's house	Buzz's pitch

2. The possessive of a plural noun ending in *s* is formed by adding an apostrophe.

girls' coats	Matthewses' relatives
Smiths' house	states' rights

3. The possessive of a plural noun not ending in *s* is formed by adding an apostrophe and *s*.

women's hats	data's use
teeth's whiteness	children's books

4. Personal pronouns do not take the apostrophe to show possession.

his	theirs
hers	whose
its	

5. Pronouns that are not ordinarily possessive show possession by adding an apostrophe and *s*.

someone's coat	each other's dog
everyone's house	another's name

6. An apostrophe is used to indicate missing letters in contractions, letters omitted to show speech, and the missing part of a date.

'ere's to you	your 'ome
don't (do not)	we'll (we will)
it's (it is)	you're (you are)
the winter of '92	the class of '72

There are rules regarding the formation of plural forms that are also useful:

1. Plurals of most nouns are formed by adding *s* to the singular.

boy—boys   book—books

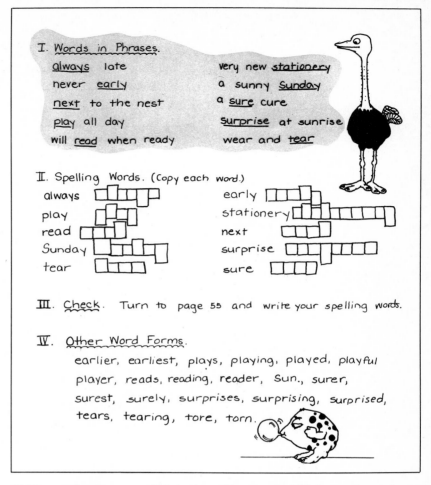

I. <u>Words in Phrases.</u>

<u>always</u> late	very new <u>stationery</u>
never <u>early</u>	a sunny <u>Sunday</u>
<u>next</u> to the nest	a <u>sure</u> cure
<u>play</u> all day	<u>Surprise</u> at sunrise
will <u>read</u> when ready	wear and <u>tear</u>

II. Spelling Words. (Copy each word.)

always	early
play	stationery
read	next
Sunday	surprise
tear	sure

III. <u>Check.</u> Turn to page 55 and write your spelling words.

IV. <u>Other Word Forms.</u>

earlier, earliest, plays, playing, played, playful player, reads, reading, reader, Sun., surer, surest, surely, surprises, surprising, surprised, tears, tearing, tore, torn.

Children need to learn to spell derivatives of base words. This lesson also emphasizes visual impressions.

A part of Lesson 22 in *Spelling Words in Use* by G. Willard Woodruff and George N. Moore. Curriculum Associates, 1977, p. 46. Used with permission.

2. When a noun ends in *s, x, sh,* or *ch,* the plural is generally formed by adding *es.*

   buses   foxes   bushes   churches

3. A noun ending in *y* preceded by a consonant forms its plural by changing the *y* to *i* and adding *es.* Words ending in *y* preceded by a vowel do not change *y* to *i.*

   body—bodies   boy—boys

4. Plurals of a few nouns are made by changing their forms.

   woman—women   mouse—mice   scarf—scarves

Integrating Spelling and Writing

Although a major objective is to teach children to spell correctly all words that they write, it is even more important to teach them to be *concerned* with spelling correctly. When children write imaginatively they want to get their ideas on paper before they are lost, and in their enthusiasm for writing they frequently use—or want to use—words they do not know how to spell. This

---

Spelling Sound-Alikes

Some possessive pronouns sound exactly like other words. Although they sound alike, they are different in other ways.

- Read the following sentences.

> Jane and Eddie wrote <u>their</u> report.
> Now <u>they're</u> finished with the typing.
> The children put the report over <u>there</u>.

How are the underlined words different? *Their, they're* and *their* are different in two ways. They have different spellings and different meanings.

> <u>Their</u> shows what two people have. It is a possessive pronoun.
> <u>They're</u> is a short way of writing <u>they are</u>.
> <u>There</u> means <u>in that place</u>.
> Words like <u>their</u>, <u>they're</u>, and <u>there</u> are homonyms.

Homonyms are words that sound alike but have different spellings and different meanings.

- Read the following sentences.

> Is this <u>your</u> magazine?
> <u>You're</u> welcome to read it.

Do the sentences give you a clue to their meanings? *Your* shows what you have. It is a possessive pronoun. *You're* is a short way of writing *you are*.

- Now read these sentences.

> This television has <u>its</u> own antenna.
> But <u>it's</u> broken.

In the first sentence above, *its* means *belonging* to it. In the second sentence *it's* is a short way of writing *it is*.

126 SPELLING: *Homonyms*

Learning the meanings and spellings of homonyms is often a problem for children.

From *Series E: Macmillan English*, Book 5, by Tina Thoburn et al. Copyright © 1982 Macmillan Publishing Co., Inc. Used by permission of the publisher.

is a problem that every child and every teacher faces. Certainly it is more important to get the child's expression on paper than it is to have the child spell every word correctly. Too, since many of us skip over spelling problems in our first drafts, it makes sense to permit a child to do so as well. For example, permit children to write only the first letters of the words they cannot spell or simply draw a line to show where a word was left out. In addition, you can help forestall spelling problems by listing on the board words that the children may want to use, by permitting children to ask one another for help—if they can do so without interfering with the other child's writing—and by encouraging them to use a dictionary, pictionary, file of words, or textbook to find the word they want to use. Help children yourself with words they cannot spell if their other efforts fail or if their thinking seems to be stymied by a spelling problem.

Encouraging the children to experiment with problem spelling words by writing them on scratch paper to see if they recognize the correct spelling is also helpful. You should have the children proofread the final draft of their writing, but be careful of penalties, such as not putting a story on the board if it has misspelled words or requiring recopying. In some cases these things may work; in others the next attempt at writing will produce poorer results. The important concern in all writing is to get ideas on paper first, and then to give attention to sentence structure, vocabulary, mechanics, and spelling, so that the finished product will be as effective as possible.

Special Spelling Problems

Some words are frequently misspelled (these are the "demons" that most teachers know about) and will require persistent effort from you. There are reasons for the persistence of their difficulty, however, as discussed below.

Many words are misspelled because the children do not know or do not apply the rules that are workable, do not understand the use of the apostrophe, fail to capitalize properly, or do not have the linguistic knowledge they should have (for example, how compounds are formed). Here are some that are frequently misspelled:

coming	I'll	it's	studying	tried
didn't	I'm	getting	Sunday	truly
don't	its	sometimes	that's	writing

Homonyms also often cause difficulty. For pupils to learn these requires that meanings be thoroughly taught and that visual images be gained. Spelling authorities disagree about whether homonyms should be taught together. We believe that for the first instruction they usually should not. However, since much review of them is necessary, they should be presented together in the review to emphasize the differences:

there	hear	your	know	some
their	here	you're	no	sum
they're				

two	four	write	buy	piece
to	for	right	by	peace
too				

Attention to "correct" pronunciation must take into account dialect differences as
they are shown in pronunciations—e.g., some people give
the vowels in naughty and
knotty the same sound.

Improper pronunciation is a frequent cause of errors. Such words as *and, going, third, ask, today, Saturday, pretty, hundred, kept, been, library, children, desk,* etc., are pronunciation and spelling problems for some children.

Phoneme-grapheme irregularity which results in misspelling because of the misapplication of a generalization is also a problem. Commonly written words that fall into this category include:

ache	believe	enough	thirty
across	birthday	friend	though
afraid	build	guess	thought
again	color	heard	tonight
among	could	one	very
answer	cousin	sure	were
beautiful	decide	the	when
because	does	they	women

The following list of spelling "demons" has been developed from studies of misspellings of elementary school children. These words are important and should be learned by every pupil.

about	can	Friday	how
address	cannot	friend	how's
afraid	can't	friends	hundred
afternoon	children	from	
again	Christmas	front	I'll
all right	close	fun	I'm
along	clothes		in
already	come	getting	isn't
always	coming	goes	it
am	couldn't	going	it's
an	cousin	good	its
and		good-bye (good-by)	I've
answer	daddy	grade	
anything	day	guess	January
anyway	December	guest	just
April	didn't		
are	different	had	knew
arithmetic	dog	Halloween	know
aunt	doing	handkerchiefs	
awhile	don't	has	lessons
	down	have	letter
baby		haven't	like
balloon	Easter	having	likes
basketball	enough	he	little
because	every	hear	lots
been	everybody	hello	loving
before		her	
birthday	father	here	made
bought	February	his	make
boy	fine	home	maybe
boys	first	hope	me
brother	football	hospital	Miss
brought	for	house	morning
	fourth		mother
			Mr.

Mrs.	receive	teacher	vacation
much	received	teacher's	very
my	remember	Thanksgiving	
	right	that's	want
name		the	was
nice	said	their	weather
Nov.	Santa Claus	them	well
now	Saturday	then	went
nowadays	saw	there	we're
	school	there's	were
o'clock	send	they	when
October	sent	they're	whether
off	sincerely	think	white
on	snow	thought	will
once	snowman	through	with
one	some	time	won't
our	something	to	would
out	sometime	today	write
outside	sometimes	together	writing
	soon	tomorrow	
party	stationery	tonight	you
people	store	too	young
play	studying	toys	your
played	summer	train	yours
plays	Sunday	truly	
please	suppose	two	
pretty	sure		
	surely		
quit	swimming	until	
quite			

ENRICHMENT ACTIVITIES

Be certain that you use each word correctly.

Spelling programs can be enlivened through the use of games and other activities directed at learning the words in the spelling lessons and at building vocabularies. Activities and games are useful for motivating pupils, caring for individual differences, and providing variety in the program.

Vocabulary

The importance of vocabulary development was discussed in Chapter 4, where many activities for such development were suggested. For additional activities, look in commercial vocabulary and spelling materials. These can often be used at times appropriate to your program rather than at times indicated by the order in which they occur in a book.

Tired Words and Good Replacements

awful—horrible, dreadful
funny—humorous, strange
pretty—considerably, fairly
good—suitable, valuable
nice—pleasant, neat
real—genuine, actual
sure—certain, steady

Activities that build interest in words, help to teach spelling, and have appeal to children include finding substitutes for such overworked words as *awful, funny, scared, pretty, good, nice, real,* and *sure;* synonyms for such words as *small, cold, sad, big, work, see, happy, strong,* and *tired;* and homonyms for *blue, do, fair, great, hail, made, pain, rain, read, sew, sight, tail, whose, wait,* and *pause.* These can be found and put on charts by individual pupils or groups, or the project can involve the entire class.

In a like manner, antonyms may be collected (try finding them for *rise, new, bottom, full, empty, colder, front, never, short,* etc.); lists can be made of words that have the same root (*report, portable, import, portage, portly*); and words that have more than one acceptable spelling can be found (*judgment, judgement; gayly, gaily; driest, dryest*).

Exercises can be made which ask pupils to build compound words from other words. Words to start with might include *day, news, hall, base, stand, light, band, paper, ball,* and *way.* Or you might have the children form plurals for irregular words such as *wife, foot, mouse, leaf, woman, man,* and *calf.*

Children can become quite interested in words because of their origins, their forms, or changes that have occurred in them. For example, they might be asked to find the origins of such words as *braille, boycott, vandal, cologne, maverick,* and *nicotine.* They might also enjoy tracing the origins of words from other languages (*cipher, kimono, oasis, parka, pretzel*) or compound words (*warehouse, chairman, downtown, statehouse*).

Other interesting activities include seeing how many uses can be found for such common words as *run, head,* or *board;* finding words with different sounds represented by the same letter or letters, or vice versa (*enough, though; graph, rough; taught, taut*); discovering different ways in which the same meaning is expressed in various parts of the world where English is spoken (*lift* for *elevator, petrol* for *gasoline, lorry* for *truck,* and *sweets* for *dessert* in England; *tap* for *faucet* in Canada; etc.); and finding new words that have been added to the language and determining why they were created.

A Chart Idea

> **DO YOU KNOW THESE COMPOUND WORDS?**
>
> airbus
> audiotape
> fastback
> hovercraft
> skateboard
> trendsetter

Games

Games should not replace writing activities or the direct study of the spelling words in the program. However, games interest children, build class spirit, and provide a break in routine. If games are used, they should be ones that call for children to write words (reinforcement of learning) rather than spell them orally (which is an unlifelike activity). Often words chosen by the teacher for the games may be those that children have had difficulty spelling either in lessons or in their writing.

The games which follow are some that may be used. Too, many of the Activities for Children at the end of the chapter are gamelike and do not carry the negative element of competition between children.

STAND-UP. Divide the class into three or four teams. Assign each team one of these letters: *b, f, h, t, m.* Read the following list of words. A member of each team stands up whenever a word is read that begins with that team's letter. If a team member stands when the word does not begin with the team's letter, that member and another must sit down. The team that has all of its members standing first is the winner.

kite	*toad*	cook	clothes	us	*milk*
baby	*hear*	ate	*fairy*	*mouse*	got
old	*fat*	beach	cave	yet	*feet*
face	any	*fire*	*happy*	*moon*	bed
hand	*bad*	grass	*two*	write	bear
top	across	*her*	arm	*tiger*	candy
string	*feather*	did	*must*	*heel*	*fire*
get	wing	*teacher*	bag	wood	*hit*
my	*hard*	*mile*	*move*	won	*met*
back	very	*hen*	*airplane*	*fed*	garden
clay	*today*	*ten*	all	*ball*	*took*

SPELLING BALL. Spelling ball is an adaptation of baseball. Divide the class into two teams. Place a chair in each corner of the room to serve as home plate and first, second, and third bases. Select a pitcher for each team.

The team at bat lines up at home plate. The pitcher of the opposing team asks the first batter to come to the board and write one of the new words. A correct spelling is a hit, and moves the player to first base; an incorrect spelling is an out. A player on first base advances to second if a succeeding batter makes a hit, and so on until a run is scored. When a team makes three outs, the opposing team lines up to take its turn. The team with the highest number of runs at the end of the game wins. If the words become too easy for the children, have the pitcher use words from previous lessons.

TEAM SPELLING. Divide the class into two teams. Give each pupil a card bearing a letter used in one of the spelling words. When you say a new word, both teams spell the word by placing themselves in proper position. The team that spells the word first scores one point. Continue in this manner until all the new words have been used. The team with the most points wins. (*Note:* Be sure to provide two cards for each team for any letter that is used more than once in a word.)

GETTING AHEAD. Arrange a group of children in random order. Pronounce a spelling word to each one in turn. Continue in this manner without correcting misspellings. If a pupil in the group recognizes a misspelling and is able to correct it, he or she goes to the head of the group. The object is for each pupil to try to remain at the head of the group.

SPELLING ROW. Place the children in five or six equal rows. Pronounce a spelling word to the first row. The first child says the first letter, the second child says the second letter, and so on until the word has been spelled. The next group is asked another spelling word. The children in the second row respond in the same manner. This procedure is continued for each row. For each letter omitted or every word misspelled, a team is given one point. The team with the fewest points wins. It may be necessary to regroup occasionally in order for the children at the end of a row to have an opportunity to participate. (Or begin at one end for the first round, the opposite end for the second, and so on.)

SPELLING HUNT. Write the spelling words on slips of paper. Fold these and place them in a box. Ask one pupil at a time to take a slip. The child hands the paper to the teacher, who pronounces the word and asks the pupil to write it on the board. If the child misses the word, he or she takes the paper and studies it.

SPELLING SITDOWN. The spelling sitdown is played in the same manner as a spelling bee, except that the children who spell the words correctly take their seats. The team that has the fewest members standing wins. (The spelling may also be done by writing responses on the board. Children at their seats may write on paper the words you pronounce.)

RHYMING WORDS. Have one child stand in front of the room and say, "I am thinking of a spelling word that rhymes with tack." The other children try to spell the correct word. The one who spells it correctly has the next turn. The words should be written on the chalkboard.

PYRAMIDS. Starting with a vowel, have children take turns adding one letter at a time so that a word is spelled with each addition.

a	o	e
at	on	be
ate	one	bee
late	tone	been
later	stone	

Children can work singly or in groups. The objective is to see who can make the longest list of correctly spelled words within a given time.

SPELLING MATCH. Divide the class into six equal groups. Have members of each group number off (1, 2, 3, 4, etc.). Have the 1's go to the board and write as you pronounce several words. Correct their spelling and tally the number of misspelled words. Then the 2's go to the board and write an equal number of words. These words are checked and scored. When all the members have had a chance to write, scores are checked and the group with the fewest misspelled words wins.

THINK AND SPELL. Have one pupil stand in front of the class and say, "I am thinking of a spelling word that ends with an *e*." (Words from a single spelling lesson should be used for this.) The children who know the answer raise their hands. One child is called on to write the word on the chalkboard. If the child writes the word correctly, he or she becomes the leader.

Try having the better spellers make crossword puzzles using words from the spelling lesson or other words they might have occasion to write. Some commercial materials can provide puzzle models.

CROSSWORDS. One child on a team begins by writing a word he or she knows on the board. This child then asks another to spell a word that begins with the last letter of his or her word. Continue this, giving a point to the opposite team when a pupil cannot think of a word or misspells one.

SPELLING PLAY. Have a pupil dramatize the meaning of a spelling word. The player then chooses someone to write the word. The pupil who writes the word correctly takes the next turn and acts out another word.

GUESSING. Choose one child to write a new word on the chalkboard and cover it with one hand. The child then chooses a classmate to guess which word was written. The child who is chosen says, "Did you write *m-i-s-s miss?*" "No, I did not write *m-i-s-s miss.*" Another child is chosen and the same procedure followed until the correct word is guessed. The child who guesses correctly writes the next word on the board.

SPIN AND SPELL. Make a large clock face with a moveable hand. Number the face from 1 to 9 (a number for each spelling word). A pupil is called on to spin the hand and read the number to which the hand points. The child then must write the word that corresponds to the number. You should have a numbered list, so children do not have to memorize the order of the words.

WORD ENDINGS. Write on the board a number of words from which new words can be made by adding the endings -*ed*, -*er*, and -*ing*. See which children can make the longest lists of new words. Let the children compare their lists in order to prevent the learning of nonsense words. This may be made more challenging by including the possibility of adding prefixes as well as endings. Words that might be written include: *bring, clean, do, eat, end, grow, late, like, pen, play,* and *walk*.

ADD-A-LETTER. Divide the class into several equal teams. As you pronounce a word, the first member of each team goes to the board and writes the first letter of the word, then runs back and gives the chalk to the second member. This child then writes the second letter, and so on until the word is completed. The team that finishes first gets five points; second, four points; etc. One point is subtracted for each incorrect or unreadable letter. The team with the highest score wins.

NEW WORDS. One pupil starts the game by writing a base (root) word on the chalkboard (such as *write*) and then asks who can spell a word that has this word as a base (e.g., *writing, writer*). He or she calls on one pupil, who comes to the board and writes the new word. If the new word is written correctly, this pupil writes the next base word.

Other Activities

- Playing word games such as Scrabble and anagrams.
- Providing riddles that can be answered with words from a list.
- Providing crossword puzzles and having children make puzzles for classmates to work.
- Finding the histories of words such as *desperado, digit, festival,* and *vocation*.

Dictionary Challenges

How many can you find?
1. Synonyms for smart.
2. Meanings for dark.
3. Adjectives that describe food.

- Rewriting trite sentences using more interesting and specific words.
- Reporting on new words added to the language because of the space program, computer technology, environmental problems, etc.
- Making charts of synonyms, antonyms, contractions, abbreviations, or some other category.
- Having groups or individual children find words for various categories such as food words, TV words, words about our city, or holiday words.
- Using words in some form of creative writing. For example, children might write a story using *bronco, radar, calico, lizard,* and *desert.*
- Making individual graphs of spelling progress; making lists of words that are difficult; making lists of new words to learn to spell.
- Finding modifications of spelling in newspapers, TV advertisements, and signs.
- Making a word-picture dictionary.
- Searching for the origins of surnames (they are usually related to places or occupations).
- Writing descriptions of objects, using as many new descriptive words as possible and using them accurately.

EVALUATING SPELLING PROGRESS

Evaluation should begin with examining goals. As was pointed out earlier, the goals of a desirable spelling program are to create a number of attitudes, habits, abilities, and skills and to teach the spelling of a basic core of words. Each child's ability to spell the assigned words on the basic list can be evaluated by you during the year the child is in your classroom, but a true evaluation of many of the attitudes, habits, abilities, and skills cannot be made until after more than two or three years of spelling instruction. However, the difficulties involved in evaluating all the goals of your program completely should not deter you from making some attempt to evaluate each one. Of course, the child's ability to spell the words in the basic list in all of his or her writing is a good indication of the attainment of the other goals.

Tests

Children's ability to spell the words in a basic list can be measured in several ways.

Test for:

1. General spelling ability of class before teaching (a test using a few words from each lesson).
2. Study needs and achievement by giving a pretest and a final test in the weekly program.
3. Individual progress on review words.
4. Mastery of special words (from unit, other subjects, contractions, etc.).
5. Progress and achievement at end of month, semester, or year.

- The regular teaching program should include several weekly tests, perhaps monthly tests, and a test at the end of each term. Each of these tests should include only the words the children should have learned (or a sampling of them) during the particular time period. Provision should also be made to test words learned earlier (including previous grade levels). The form of these tests should be that suggested earlier for the weekly lesson.

- A standard spelling scale can be used to compare the spelling of your class with that of children of the same grade level as reported in the scale. The only usable spelling scale today is *The New Iowa Spelling Scale* (Bureau of Educational Research, University of Iowa, Iowa City, Iowa), which lists the percentage of children in grades 2–8 who spelled each of 5,500 words correctly.
- Testing through the spelling section of standardized achievement tests provides limited measures of spelling ability. The form of most tests is one of recognition rather than recall, and there are so few words tested that the results are useful only as guides.

Checklists

A checklist or similar device can help to systematize evaluation of children's attitudes, habits, and abilities. For example:

November Name	Proof- reads spelling pages	Proof- reads other work	Uses diction- ary	Uses study proce- dure	Uses gener- aliza- tions
Bill	*no*	*no*	*no*	*no*	*sometimes*
Roy	✓	?	✓	*no*	✓
Mary	✓	✓	✓	✓	*no*
Julie	✓	✓	*some- times*	✓	✓

Pupil Self-Evaluation

Children like to see the progress they are making.

Children should participate in evaluation whenever possible, including evaluation of the program and materials. They should especially learn to evaluate their own spelling, whether done in the spelling class or in their writing. Some ways in which they can engage in the evaluation process are the following:

- Keep individual progress charts of scores made on spelling tests.
- Keep progress charts on written activities that contain misspellings. For example, the number of words misspelled per 50 or 100 words written may be recorded periodically.
- Keep a record of the proofreading of their written work.
- Correct their own spelling tests and analyze the errors made.
- Keep individual spelling lists of words misspelled in their writing.
- Participate in class discussions of spelling achievement.

My Progress Chart

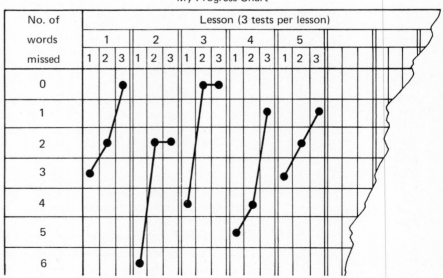

No. of words missed	Lesson							
	1	2	3	4	5	6		
0								
1								
2								
3								
4								
5								
6								

My Progress Chart

A FINAL WORD

The systematic teaching of spelling remains an important part of the elementary school language arts program. However, instructional attention must also be given throughout the school day. Developing an attitude of concern for spelling all words correctly should receive equal emphasis with the direct teaching of a basic core of important words. A carefully constructed program based on the suggestions offered here will result in effective learning in your classroom.

References

Allred, Ruel A. *Spelling, The Application of Research Findings.* National Education Association, The Curriculum Series, 1974.

Barbe, Walter B.; Francis, Azalia S.; and Braun, Lois A., eds. *Spelling: Basic Skills for Effective Communication.* Zaner-Bloser, 1982.

Fitzsimmons, Robert J., and Loomer, Bradley M. *Spelling Research and Practice.* Iowa State Department of Public Instruction and the University of Iowa, 1977.

Henderson, Edmund H., and Beers, James W., eds. *Developmental and Cognitive Aspects of Learning to Spell: A Reflection of Word Knowledge.* International Reading Association, 1980.

Hillerich, Robert L. *Spelling: An Element in Written Expression.* Charles E. Merrill, 1976.

Hodges, Richard E. *Learning to Spell.* Clearinghouse on Reading and Communication Skills and National Council of Teachers of English, 1981.

Horn, Ernest. "Phonetics and Spelling," *The Elementary School Journal* (May 1957), pp. 431–435.

Horn, Thomas D., ed. *Research on Handwriting and Spelling.* National Council of Teachers of English, 1966.

Johnson, Terry E.; Langford, Kenneth G.; and Quorn, Kerry C. "Characteristics of an Effective Spelling Program," *Language Arts* 58 (May 1981), pp. 581–588.

Middleton, Mildred L. *Improving Spelling Performance.* Kendall/Hunt Publishing Co., 1981.

Petty, Walter T. "The Teaching of Spelling," *Bulletin of the School of Education*, Indiana University, vol. 45, no. 6, November 1969.

Thomas, Ves. *Teaching Spelling, Canadian Word Lists and Instructional Techniques.* Gage Educational Publishing, 1974.

Wood, Margo. "Invented Spelling," *Language Arts* 59 (October 1982), pp. 707–717.

Teaching Resources

FILMS

Spelling for Beginners. Coronet Instructional Media (11 min.; color or b/w; primary).

Spelling Is Important. Macmillan Films (18 min.; middle grades).

FILMSTRIPS

Discovering Spelling Patterns. McGraw-Hill Films (set of 36 strips; intermediate).

New Spelling Goals. McGraw-Hill Films (set of 7 strips; primary).

Spelling. BFA Educational Media (2 strips; intermediate).

The Spelling Monsters. Scholastic (sound filmstrip; grades 2–3).

Words: Their Origin, Use, and Spelling. Society for Visual Education (set of 6 color strips; intermediate).

KITS

Independent Drill for Mastery. Developmental Learning Materials (cassettes, masters, manual, tests; grades 4–6).

Individualized Spelling Kit. Curriculum Associates (booklets, word cards, word finders, teacher's guide).

Spelling Spree. Prentice-Hall Media (3 sets of filmstrips, cassettes, masters, guide, etc.).

Word Growth II Spelling Kit. Curriculum Associates (grades 4–8; high achievers).

GAMES

Espy, Willard R. *An Almanac of Words at Play.* Clarkson N. Potter, 1975.

_____. *Another Almanac of Words at Play.* Clarkson N. Potter, 1980.

Grant, Niels, Jr. *Word Games.* Fearon Publishers, 1971.

Manchester, Richard B. *The Mammoth Book of Word Games.* Hart Publishing, 1976.

COMPUTER SOFTWARE

Magic Spells. The Learning Co. (elementary).

Spelltronics. Lakeshore Curriculum Materials (available for several different microcomputers; grades 2–6).

Whole Brain Spelling. SubLOGIC (preschool to adults).

Activities for Preservice Teachers

1. Test your own spelling ability by having someone test you on the list of spelling "demons" given in this chapter. List any you misspell and learn to spell them correctly. Continue to retake the test until you have mastered all the words.

2. Study teacher's manuals and advertising materials for several sets of spelling books to find answers to the following questions: How were the spelling words selected? What is the total number of words for each grade? Does the series use the test-study or study-test method? Are provisions made for good spellers and for poor ones? What activities are provided other than tests and direct study of words? Are study steps suggested?

3. Outline a spelling readiness program for a first grade. Include in your outline references to commercial or teacher-made materials you would use.

4. Select a spelling book for a grade of your choice and plan the spelling program for a week, basing it on one of the weekly lessons in the book. Show how you would provide for upper, average, and slow groups; in what ways you would use individualized instruction;

how you would use activities in the book; what enrichment activities you would add; and how the lesson might be integrated with other subject areas or other areas of the language arts. Be sure to stay within suggested time limits, except possibly when integrating spelling with other areas.

5. If you were a fifth grade teacher and had several requests from parents that their children be given spelling homework, what would be your response? Plan in some detail what you would do and report to the class.

6. There are many articles in professional journals concerning "invented spellings" in addition to the several referred to in this chapter. Examine four or five of these, comparing points of view and conclusions of the authors.

7. Discuss children's spelling with persons now teaching to determine (a) what they consider to be children's chief problems, (b) the range of abilities in their classes, and (c) if they are using practices advocated in this chapter.

Activities for Inservice Teachers

1. Work out a plan—and then put it into operation—for improving the attitudes of pupils in your class toward spelling correctly all the words they write. Base your plan on suggestions in this chapter.

2. Start a file of spelling games. The ones in this chapter can be the first ones in your file. Ask other teachers and look in other textbooks and in magazines for others.

3. Prepare a variety of materials for children who find spelling difficult. Letters cut out of wood, stiff paper, sandpaper, or felt are useful for a child to trace. A box of wet sand in which the child can write words also helps.

4. From a first grade teacher get examples of children's independent writing. Examine these for children's "invented" spellings. Report your findings to the class.

5. Prepare a card file of spelling puzzles, exercises, and games that children may do during free time.

6. Review the reading levels of children in your class. For example, list their names, reading scores (word attack, vocabulary, comprehension, total), and your observations on their reading so that the picture is before you. Then think of each child's spelling problems. Is there a relationship to reading ability? Do you need to modify or individualize the spelling tasks you have been giving some children?

Independent Activities for Children

1. Have the child prepare a chart for the bulletin board that lists the most commonly used contractions (*don't, aren't, can't, I'll*, etc.).

2. Prepare sentences with blanks that children can fill in with appropriate words from the spelling lesson—or several lessons.

3. Have each child tabulate over a period of several weeks the number of times each word appears in the reports, stories, etc., he or she writes. This will show children the importance of a relatively small number of words. It will likely also show them that several of these words are ones they frequently misspell.

4. Each child should keep his or her own list of spelling "demons"—words missed in writing activities or consistently misspelled in review lessons. He or she may study these during free time and practice using them in sentences.

5. Sheets can be prepared with questions, directions, and space for the child's responses. Such entries as the following might be on the exercise sheets:
a. Change the first two letters of *fright* and write the new words (*bright, slight, flight*).

b. Put prefixes before these words so that antonyms are formed:

_____ clear	_____ true
_____ spell	_____ correct
_____ patient	_____ sense

c. Write synonyms for these words:

throw   (hurl, cast, pitch, toss)
shut   (close, bar)

d. How many compound words can you make by adding words to these words?

fire   (fireman, fireplace, fireside)
ball   (baseball, football, basketball)
man   (fireman, chairman, mailman)

6. Put a series of compound words on cards—one word on each card. The child may add as many other compounds as possible that include one of the words in the given compound word. Some compound words to use are *cowboy, mailman, background, football*, etc.

7. Prepare cards, each with an interesting activity, from which children may select an assignment. Cards might have the following activities:

a. Write the plurals of these words:

wolf	woman	fish
leaf	sheep	church
shoe		

b. Rearrange the letters in each group and write the words:

lrig	pllse	drow	eerd

c. Combine these words into compound words:

ball	way	net
fish	door	foot

d. How many words can you write that begin with these letters?

cl	st	gr	tr	bl

8. A child can categorize words according to spelling patterns. Various patterns can be used. For example:
a. words with a certain sequence of vowels and consonants (vcv—*begin, major, music;* vccv—*summer, dollar, filled*)
b. words ending in *-ing* or *-ake* (*sing, bring, thing; cake, lake, take*); two-syllable words (*later, truly, pilot*)
c. words that begin with a two-symbol consonant cluster (*br—brother, bring, bright; sl—slip, sleep, sly*).

9. The slow learner may be helped by the use of crossword puzzles made up of words from the spelling list for the week or a list of words that have caused special difficulty. If desired, the puzzle may even be used in conjunction with a list of the words to be used, so that the child may learn the correct spelling as he or she copies the words from the list.

10. In a shoe or boot box, place letters cut from tagboard and backed with flannel, making sure to provide duplicates of vowels and the frequently used consonants (a Scrabble board makes a good guide to the number needed). Line the top of the box with flannel. Two or more children may take turns drawing letters; as soon as a child can form a word with his or her letters, the child places them on the flannel lid, each child keeping his or her words in a separate column. The first child to form a predetermined number of words is the winner.

11. Make a list of words commonly misspelled in children's writing, and have children make crossword puzzles from it. Children's puzzles then can be exchanged.

12. Have the children look in dictionaries (adult ones) for variant spellings of words. These can be put on a chart, which can then be used in a group discussion of why differences arise.

13. Children can find and list pairs of homophones. A variation of this would be to make a list of words which the children then match by sound with other words. For example: *plain, weigh, write, cent, feet, mist.*

14. Prepare cards, each with a word that has several fairly common meanings. The child is to find as many meanings as possible and to write sentences illustrating them. Words to use might be common ones such as *left, right, train, dress,* and *ship* or less well-known ones such as *bond, idle, type,* and *trim.*

11

Teaching and Maintaining Handwriting Skills

Some futurists say that the need for handwriting will disappear. This is unlikely, although the amount of handwriting adults do has undoubtedly decreased—and probably will decrease more. It does appear to be true, however, that teachers today do not give as much attention to handwriting instruction as did those of twenty years ago. How much this reduction in attention is due to a belief in the decline of the need for handwriting and how much is due to the expansion of the curriculum (which forces teachers to give only minimal attention to some subjects) is debatable. Concern about providing for individual needs and development has also led teachers to be much less prescriptive now than formerly about forms and sizes of letters and various other factors related to handwriting.

Instructional emphasis does vary considerably from teacher to teacher and from school to school, but observation in a number of classrooms—regardless of whether or not handwriting instruction is given—will reveal children sitting in all sorts of postures at their desks, with pencils and pens clutched in various ways, and with the papers on which they are writing in many positions. It is not uncommon to find papers with illegible or scarcely legible writing in the basket on the teacher's desk or posted on the bulletin board.

INSTRUCTIONAL OBJECTIVES

The major reason for teaching handwriting lies in its role in communication. Handwriting is a tool for written expression; for this reason it must be legible. Thus the principal objective of handwriting instruction is to help each child learn to write legibly. Since handwriting must be done with reasonable speed for it to be a useful skill, the development of satisfactory speed is the secondary objective.

Achieving handwriting skill is closely related to physical and mental development, and this must be kept in mind in planning the instructional program. Handwriting is a complex skill that involves both mind and muscles and the coordination of the two. Thus, evaluation of the way a child writes should be based on the degree of maturation of his or her motor skills abilities and what the child has been taught to do, not on something as artificial as grade level.

The developmental nature of the handwriting process does not mean that handwriting need not be taught. Rather, handwriting skill results from the direct teaching of forms and movements, along with adequate practice on what has been taught. Since legibility is the principal goal, recognition must be given in your program to factors that make for it, even though this may conflict with expressions of individuality. Particular attention must be given to the left-handed child.

Children's handwriting improves when they are motivated to diagnose their own handwriting needs, to evaluate their own progress, and to receive direct help with their problems. This motivation is largely based on their doing purposeful writing. Thus, handwriting should be taught throughout the day rather than being relegated only to instructional periods, although specific times should be reserved for working on problems or for teaching forms and movements.

Finally, your own handwriting, your understanding of the developmental nature of handwriting skill, the knowledge you have of effective teaching procedures, and your skill in using these procedures are important factors in creating a successful program.

Handwriting must be legible. Letters should be well formed and of the proper relative size, with adequate and uniform spacing between them. There should be uniformity of forward slant to the letters (or a lack of slant in the case of manuscript letters) and adequate and uniform spacing between words.

A written product with a pleasing appearance will result from good handwriting, which in turn results from work that is carefully and neatly arranged and writing of an even, smooth quality.

Good handwriting is done with ease. To write easily, the writer must have a comfortable posture (body, arms, hands), writing instruments and paper correctly positioned, free movement of the arm and hand, and a rhythm to the writing movements.

Readiness for Handwriting

See *What Did I Write?* by Marie M. Clay (Heinemann Educational Books, 1975).

As we have emphasized in several of the preceding chapters, young children are interested in scribbling and drawing, both "writing" to them. They often say that they are "writing my name," "writing a story," or "writing to daddy." Readiness for writing in terms of interest appears early; however, this interest does not mean that they are ready for any formalized instruction in forming letters and words. Children at the kindergarten level or younger typically have neither the neuromuscular control nor a long enough attention span for such instruction.

Draw arrows on the chalkboard and on children's papers to show directionality.

The suggestions made earlier, particularly in Chapter 5, regarding readiness for instruction in the various language arts bear upon readiness for handwriting instruction. Here we emphasize that kindergarten teachers, particularly, should strive to help each child achieve the ability to differentiate between the left and the right hand and the habit of left-to-right sweep in looking at charts, sets of pictures, and material on the board. At this stage, too, further development of eye-hand coordination is important, as is an awareness of likenesses and differences in sizes and shapes of objects and an understanding of space relationships—depth, height, width, distance, and comparative size. In the kindergarten it is also important for children to learn to concentrate on simple work tasks and to develop an awareness of handwriting and its purposes.

Prewriting and Early Writing Activities

As children participate in a wide variety of activities that require muscular coordination and perceptual skills, note which children would benefit from specific motor control activities and which need training in careful observation of size, shape, and spatial relationships. Some of the activities related to the prewriting objectives are the following:

See the article by Linda Leonard Lamme.

1. Learning to differentiate between the left and right hand.
   a. Saluting the flag with the right hand.
   b. Shaking hands with the right hand.
   c. Holding up the hand called for in games.
   d. Playing games such as "Looby Loo," "Hokey Poke," and "Simon Says."
2. Practicing left-to-right sweep.
   a. Noticing the left-to-right direction of a series of pictures, of writing on charts or on the board, or in counting a line of children.
   b. Watching the teacher's left hand sweep smoothly under titles of stories or under captions and signs as he or she *stands to the left* of written material on charts or on the board.
3. Becoming aware of sizes, shapes, and spatial relationships.
   a. Selecting puzzle parts and putting puzzles together.
   b. Choosing blocks of various shapes for building; putting blocks away according to size and shape.
   c. Modeling with clay or with a salt and flour mix.
   d. Arranging books on shelves according to size.
   e. Sorting shapes—triangles, squares, circles—into groups (correlate with mathematics).
   f. Sorting color chips and pictures into groups.
   g. Working with pegboards, tinker toys, etc.
   h. Recognizing the boundaries of work and play areas.
4. Becoming aware of handwriting and its purposes.
   a. Noticing and identifying one's name on name cards, art work, coat hooks, and personal possessions; on attendance, committee, and job lists. (Begin teaching with the child's name, even if the child does not speak English.)
   b. Participating in choosing captions for bulletin boards and titles for chart stories; noticing various captions, labels, and book titles.
   c. Noting signs around the school, on other buildings, and on streets.

Using Crayons or Markers

The skill a child attains in the use of crayons is an important index of the success he or she will have when handwriting instruction begins. These crayon pictures of fathers (reduced in size) made by kindergarten children

(a) Only a suggestion of form is evident; many details are missing; control of crayon is erratic (top left).

(b) Lack of perception of the relationship of the parts to the whole is apparent; details are missing; some details are over-elaborated (top right).

(c) Keener observation of form is noticeable; significant details are included, such as ears, arms, hands; hair placement is more accurate (center).

(d) An awareness of the relationship of the parts to the whole is shown; many details such as eyebrows, fingers, neck, and shoulders are included; broad strokes of the crayon are used consistently (bottom left).

(e) An understanding of body proportions is revealed; a variety of details makes a realistic picture; good crayon manipulation is evident (bottom right).

[*Adapted from* We Teach Handwriting, *Seattle Public Schools, 1963.*]

show progression in the development of readiness for handwriting instruction—the stages of mental development and motor skill achievement. Attainment of the levels shown in (d) and (e) indicates readiness for handwriting instruction. Remember that some children in the first or second grade may not have attained levels (d) and (e) and hence are not ready for handwriting instruction.

Other Readiness Activities

Readiness for handwriting instruction is also dependent on the child's ability to use language. Many children in the kindergarten and first grade need experiences that stimulate the desire for language expression and show the importance of writing. They need to listen to stories, look at pictures, dictate stories about their experiences, describe objects, play games that require speaking and listening, tell how objects are alike or different, retell stories, and play word and sound games.

There are other activities that give practice in basic movements needed for writing: making clocks, doughnuts, soap bubbles, Halloween faces, a Christmas tree with ornaments, a cat, stick figures, a square wagon with wheels, and so on.

Minimize these activities for children who want to do "real writing."

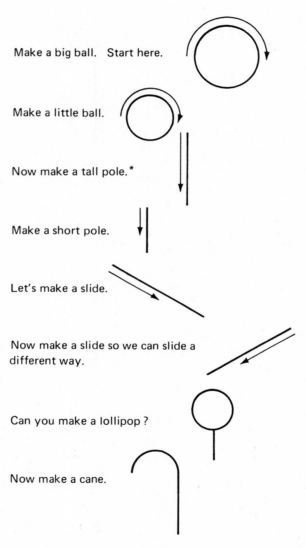

Make a big ball.   Start here.

Make a little ball.

Now make a tall pole.*

Make a short pole.

Let's make a slide.

Now make a slide so we can slide a different way.

Can you make a lollipop?

Now make a cane.

* Make certain that words such as pole, line, lollipop, slide, etc., are in the children's vocabularies.

BEGINNING HANDWRITING INSTRUCTION

Evaluating Handwriting Readiness

Affirmative answers to the following questions indicate the child's readiness for beginning handwriting instruction.

1. Does the child show a preference for one hand over the other?
2. Does the child show good dexterity in finger and wrist movement as shown in the use of scissors, for example?
3. Does the child follow a left-to-right direction easily when viewing a series of pictures or when following your writing?
4. Is the child increasingly aware of size, shape, and spatial relationships and does he or she demonstrate this awareness in art and building activities?
5. Does the child have in his or her vocabulary the terms that will be used in handwriting instruction, such as large, small, short, tall, straight, round, top, and middle?
6. Does the child listen accurately and with concentration for increasingly longer periods of time?
7. Can the child recognize his or her own name when it is written in the approved printscript form?
8. Does the child recognize reasons for writing, such as the need to say thank you or to send a message home?

The first few weeks of grade 1 are important in furthering readiness for handwriting instruction. Activities with shapes, as suggested previously, will help to provide clues to the children's readiness. Usually at least two to four weeks should be devoted to a continuation of readiness activities begun in the kindergarten, but these should not be regarded as fixed limits. No instruction should be given until a child possesses the necessary muscular coordination, the emotional and mental maturity required for learning the skills, and the desire to write.

Children are first taught printscript—probably more often called manuscript. The reasons for teaching manuscript rather than cursive form include the fact that it is considered easier to learn than cursive, since only simple curves and straight lines are required to form the letters, and that the formation of letters in manuscript is similar to that of letters encountered in reading. Manuscript is also typically more legible than cursive writing, and young pupils derive great satisfaction from their rapid progress in mastering it. The use of manuscript writing thus appears to contribute to achievement in reading and spelling, as well as help children produce more and better written language products.

Basic to handwriting instruction is the fostering of children's natural interest in writing. Encouraging their attempts by providing adequate time and materials and by displaying what they have written is important, as are writing their dictated stories on the board, on charts, and below pictures they have drawn; writing notes to be taken to the office (and reading those received); and writing reminders, schedules, and directions on the board (even if some or most of the children are unable to read them).

Writing on the Chalkboard

The chalkboard is a good place to begin handwriting instruction. A child has the space on the board to make use of the large muscles, which are better controlled than some small ones, so that corrections can be made easily. All writing should say something, so begin with a word (the children should have made the basic movements suggested earlier in this chapter as a part of the readiness program). Choose a word that is within the children's reading vocabulary and that has meaning for them. Demonstrate each letter of the word on the board. Call attention to how each letter is made. (You may want to call the vertical lines *bats* and the circles *balls*.) Write the word, say what it is, and then write it again, asking the children to tell you how each letter is made.

When you demonstrate letter forms at the chalkboard, make sure that all of the children are sitting facing the board.

Demonstrate how to hold the chalk. Have each child stand directly in front of where he or she is to write, holding a half-piece of chalk with the index finger (the child may call it a "pointer") near the tip, the middle fingertip next to it, and the thumb underneath. For straight lines, children should start at the top and pull down; letters with round movements should be done according to the directions for the handwriting system being used. The pupils should learn the movements for making each letter and be corrected if they do not do as directed.

Writing at the board can be done at first without lines, but after a short time children can be asked to evaluate their attempts in terms of whether their letters are "sitting" on a straight line (use a pointer or yardstick). Later draw lines on the board and have each child stand in front of one that is at eye level. Soon after this, attention can be given to spacing between letters, and, as more than one word is written, between words.

Writing on Unlined Paper

Basic Objectives of Beginning Instruction

1. To recognize and know the names of all the letters of the alphabet.
2. To follow instructions about how to make letters.
3. To sit, place the paper, and hold a pencil properly.
4. To write his or her first and last name from memory.
5. To write easily on lined paper a one- or two-sentence story.
6. To observe a two-finger margin at the sides of papers and a one-finger space between words.

Of course children will have written on paper of various sizes before actual handwriting instruction begins. When first instruction using paper begins, however, they should use unlined newsprint, 12×18 inches in size. Some teachers will supply the children with a thick-leaded pencil; others prefer a crayon or a felt-tipped pen. If a crayon or pen (may be messy!) is used, it should be held in the same manner as a pencil will be held later (see diagram on page 297). The first writing on paper may be done without attention to letter alignment. Later the folding sequence that is shown below can help pupils learn to keep their writing within spaces. The amount of time given to learning letter forms and to practicing each stage of the sequence will vary from class to class and from child to child.

Folding 12 x 8 Unlined Paper

No folds — dog

One fold — big

Two folds — the dog

Three folds — We go

Children should continue to use unlined paper in grade 1 until they are able to comply reasonably well with these standards:

1. Know the directions for strokes (down for straight lines and usually, depending on the system, from left to right and over the top for circles).
2. Observe size relationships of letters.
3. Make letters approximately fill the spaces between folds.
4. Hold the writing implement easily and move the hand freely.
5. Achieve some degree of body relaxation.

Writing on Lined Paper

It is generally agreed that after about ten weeks of instruction some children will be ready for lined paper, which also should be about 12×18 inches in size. The lines should be spaced about an inch apart. A little later, paper with narrower lines (to ½ inch apart) can be used. The use of a primary pencil (one that is small enough to be manipulated easily) with a thick black lead can begin at the same time the lined paper is introduced, or a short time before.

When writing on lined paper begins in a normal classroom, some children will still be writing at the board and some will be writing on unlined paper. Beginning handwriting instruction should proceed slowly, with careful supervision of all of the writing of each child. A slow and careful procedure will prevent the development of poor writing habits, fatigue, and loss of interest.

CONTINUING DEVELOPMENT

Handwriting Reminders

1. Join all letters properly.
2. Lift the pencil only at the end of a word.
3. Slant your paper to the left (to the right if you are left-handed).
4. Dot your i's and cross your t's when you have finished writing a word.
5. Leave even spaces between words.

The teaching of handwriting does not end with teaching children the manuscript forms, even though many teachers wish it did, considering the many things they are called on to do each day. Some school systems teach only manuscript, but in the majority the children continue using manuscript in grade 2 and then are taught cursive forms in grade 3. A few schools do not introduce cursive forms until grade 4, and an increasing number include a program for the maintenance of manuscript skills after cursive is introduced. Since many of the forms we are all called on to complete say "print," there is a need to maintain manuscript skill. Manuscript is also good for posters and other writing that is to be exhibited.

Grade 2

Practice develops habits; the habit of writing legibly and with adequate speed is needed by every child.

The program in grade 2 ordinarily consists of teaching manuscript to the few children who did not learn the forms in grade 1, providing practice in the use of manuscript to maintain and refine skills, and carefully evaluating all writing for the purpose of doing corrective teaching. The objectives include the following:

- Refining manuscript ability—keeping the letters well rounded; making firm, straight lines; spacing letters closely and evenly within words; leaving a space of one finger between words; and placing all letters properly on lines.
- Writing all the small and capital letter forms correctly by the end of the year.
- Maintaining a consistently acceptable hand position—holding the pencil about an inch from the point, keeping the hand and elbow below the base line of writing, and keeping an air space under the wrist.

Grade 3

The major event in the third grade handwriting program is the introduction of cursive (or, as many children say, "real") writing, usually near the beginning of the second semester. Actually there is a readiness for cursive writing just as there is for beginning writing, so ideally cursive form should be taught (regardless of grade level) when *a child* is ready. Evidence of this readiness includes the ability to write manuscript letters well from memory, the ability to read cursive writing that is written well, and the desire to learn the new form.

Until cursive writing is introduced, the objectives of the program are simply an extension of those for the second grade program. Letter forms should be made correctly, spacing should be improved (and done without finger measurements), and lines should be firm and made with even pressure.

Transition from Manuscript to Cursive

Zaner-Bloser Company has a number of pamphlets available to teachers, such as *The Left-Handed Child, Planning Kindergarten Instruction, Reversals in Writing,* etc.

While there is some difference of opinion about whether the learning of cursive form should occur as a transition or changing of manuscript to cursive or should result from the teaching of a system unrelated to manuscript, most authorities favor steps which show relationships. There is a shift in motor skills required, since cursive requires new movements, new proportions, and a slant to the writing. Some letters differ considerably from the manuscript styles, the pencil is not lifted from the paper between letters in a word, and the paper is placed differently.

Since commercial handwriting systems give instructions for teaching cursive forms, you should use the instructions provided with the materials you use. The following suggestions may be helpful in using the specific steps outlined for a particular system.

1. Show the relationships of cursive forms to manuscript forms by using illustrations such as the following:

2. Move from the simple to the complex. Introduce lowercase or small letters first, starting with the ones that are easiest to make: l, e, i, t (undercurve and slant strokes).

3. In introducing letters, use parallel guidelines on the board to show how each straight line slants the same way as the others. The parallel lines will also help

D'Nealian™ Manuscript Alphabet

D'Nealian™ Cursive Alphabet

D'Nealian™ Numbers

From *D'Nealian™ Handwriting* by Donald N. Thurber. Copyright © 1978 by Scott, Foresman and Company. Reprinted by permission.

in showing spacing between letters, the widths of humps in m's and n's, the width of the loop in an l, etc.

4. Introduce letters in words on the chalkboard, calling attention to the strokes, to the way the word begins, to the way the letters join, to the size of the letters, and to the ending stroke of the word.

5. Introduce new letters in several words, so that a new letter will appear in various positions—at the beginning, in the middle, and at the end of a word.

Intermediate and Upper Grades

After cursive form has been introduced, handwriting instruction is still very important for two reasons: (1) the skill in cursive writing acquired during and shortly after its introduction must be reinforced and maintained; and (2) the amount of handwriting done by the pupils in their school work increases at each grade level. To meet the increased demands, focus instruction on helping each pupil achieve the following specific objectives:

1. To write all letters legibly in both lowercase and uppercase cursive forms.
2. To understand how the terms *shape, size, space, line quality,* and *alignment* apply to evaluating his or her own handwriting.
3. To maintain attention to posture, hand position, and movement in writing.
4. To evaluate his or her own handwriting in terms of class standards and commercial models and diagnostic materials.
5. To maintain previously acquired manuscript skills and to use manuscript writing in appropriate situations (making posters, filling out forms, and labeling materials).

ALTERNATIVE WRITING SYSTEMS

See the article by Winifred Berry.

Criticism of the fact that children essentially learn two forms of handwriting (regardless of whether cursive is taught as a new form or by a transition approach) has been voiced because of the time that the learning of two forms requires and because the transition to or learning of the second form interferes with the development of children's ability in written composition. This criticism has led to advocacy for teaching only manuscript—an advocacy that runs counter to tradition and a substantial amount of public opinion.

The criticism has also led to the introduction in some schools of handwriting systems whose forms are in a sense both different from and similar to manuscript and cursive. One of these systems is known as D'Nealian. In beginning instruction this system calls for making letters that are oval rather than round and slanted rather than vertical. Most of the lowercase letters are made in one movement instead of two. Later children are taught to connect these letters, which, in effect, makes the writing similar to typical cursive.

A second system is a revived one, Italic. Italic letter forms are less slanted than D'Nealian ones and are unconnected in grade one. These letters are modified slightly during the second grade by joining the small letters with entrance and exit strokes. Capital letters are the same in both beginning and later instruction. Italic writing is attractive when done well, and probably most viewers of it would first regard it as connected manuscript. However, some of the letter forms are quite different from manuscript; early advocates of its use called it "true cursive" and stressed its similarity to present type faces.

It seems unlikely that the teaching of either of these forms will supplant the teaching of manuscript and cursive. The introduction of Italic writing in England more than twenty years ago caused little stir in the United States, possibly because it received some criticism. However, manuscript writing did not attain its present widespread use until more than thirty years after its introduction.

OTHER INSTRUCTIONAL CONSIDERATIONS

The preceding sections discussed how handwriting should be taught at the beginning stage, at the stage of transition to cursive writing, and in the intermediate grades, where the problem is the maintenance of skills. The issue of other systems or forms of writing was introduced. There are other instructional considerations that a teacher should give attention to. These are discussed in the following sections.

Emphasis on Practice

In addition to teaching handwriting directly and maintaining skills through the use of teacher's and pupils' guides and textbook materials, you should capitalize on opportunities to give attention to handwriting in all of the pupils' writing. Handwriting skill will diminish unless it is practiced, and this

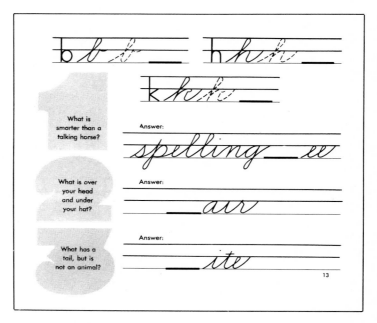

Motivate the transition to cursive form.

Walter B. Barbe et al., *Creative Growth with Handwriting*, Grade 3. Columbus, Ohio: Zaner-Bloser, Inc., 1975, p. 13. Reprinted by permission of the publisher.

practice must include corrective work on factors that cause the writing to be illegible or cause it to be done awkwardly or in a tiring fashion.

Keep a checklist for recording individual problems that need correction. Search for the causes of handwriting faults as well as for the faults or errors themselves—check for poor posture, improper paper position, poor lighting, a too tightly held pencil, or a writing instrument that is too large, too small, or too short. In addition to the checklist, it is a good idea to keep

---

OBJECTIVE: The student will:
write a paragraph when given sentences and a choice of phrases within each sentence.

Write this paragraph. Each time there is a choice,
pick the one you like best.

It was the | most beautiful / strangest / most horrible | thing I had ever seen. I could

hardly wait to | snap a picture of it. / tell my friends about it. / get as far away as I could. | The whole

thing was the color of | alphabet soup / rose petals / rusty water | and smelled like

springtime. / moldy cheese. / clouds. | Do you think other people will really | believe / like / fear

what I saw?   Pick – a – Story

Answers will vary.

_____

_____

_____

_____

_____

_____

_____

_____

_____

Directions: Have students complete the page independently, then elect a friend and read stories to each other.   **47**

Handwriting practice can be more than writing words and making letters.

Walter B. Barbe et al., *Creative Growth with Handwriting*, Grade 5. Columbus, Ohio: Zaner-Bloser, Inc., 1975, p. 47. Reprinted by permission of the publisher.

samples of the children's writing collected at intervals throughout the year. Supplement your analysis of the handwriting on these samples by asking the principal, or perhaps the next-door teacher, to rate them.

Children should also evaluate their own writing. They should make comparisons with levels of achievement shown on commercial scales as well as with their own previous writing efforts. Their efforts toward improvement may be encouraged by displaying samples on the bulletin board, holding a writing clinic with several of the best writers acting as "doctors" for specific problems, having children report on their handwriting (each child indicating his or her best letter, the most difficult letter to make, why his or her handwriting is improving, etc.), and giving emphasis to handwriting in all areas of the curriculum.

The opaque and overhead projectors are useful for looking at children's writing. In showing children's writing, emphasize improvement rather than finding fault. Do not stress details too much: dwelling on "the tail of the q is too long" or "the o is not round enough" will make handwriting improvement more difficult to achieve. Instead, have the children refer to handwriting charts that they can use to form their own judgments. Some discussion of handwriting will help focus on particular problems. For instance, one day talk about the effect of the slant of letters upon speed and legibility. On other days attention can be given to uniformity of size of letters, spacing, formation of letters, and so on.

Handwriting practice should grow out of the needs that arise as the children write stories, poetry, reports, summaries, diaries, minutes, letters, notes, announcements, signs, etc. Genuine communication will foster an appreciation of the importance of good handwriting to communication. It is usually helpful to set up one main objective for the class each week, with each pupil paying particular attention to any personal handwriting faults that relate to that objective. The objective might be maintaining parallel slant, gaining uniformity of letter size, closing letters properly, maintaining good margins, or using good posture.

Novelty can be added to practice through the use of such sentences as the following:

Zillions of zebras zipped by.
Well, Willie works willingly.
Buzzy, a busy bee, buzzed by.
A snappy turtle snapped at the stick.

To provide further variety in practice, tape a paragraph or two, speaking slowly but evenly and paying strict attention to the number of words per minute. If you have several tape recorders with listening stations, different children can practice writing different paragraphs (different content, different speeds, etc.).

Planning a handwriting project with another teacher of the same grade level can also provide motivation for practice. Pupils can write selections (without names on papers) to be exchanged between classes for other children's evaluation. A variation of this is to exchange letters with pupils in a more advanced grade or some other part of the country.

If a child's handwriting remains poor, consider the possibility that he or she may have an emotional problem. If so, it would probably be wise to

Don't overlook children who know or are learning how to type. Some commercial handwriting programs (such as *Writing Our Language*, Scott, Foresman and Co., 1973) devote some attention to typing. Typists do need to maintain handwriting skills, though.

forget about any intensive effort to help the child improve. Instead, try to give emotional support and look for ways to help with the problem. Persistently poor handwriting may also be caused by poor visual-motor control. Vision should be checked, of course, but sometimes readiness activities merely need to be continued.

Activities

Beginning pupils are always eager to learn to write. Later they are also motivated to learn cursive form. However, interest in practicing skills may lag. Special attention must be directed toward creating interest in handwriting and providing a freshness to instruction for a program to be successful. Try using some of the following activities to supplement the preceding suggestions and furnish motivation:

1. Combine spelling review with handwriting practice by having the children compose sentences using the spelling words.
2. Children can use bags or envelopes to make individual mailboxes. These mailboxes are then placed beside the pupils' desks, and the pupils may use them to send daily notes to one another. Legible notes may be read; illegible ones are sent to the dead-letter office where a committee of students studies them and reports on their weaknesses.
3. Pupils may do research on the history of handwriting, kinds of paper and how paper is made, the handwriting of famous people, kinds of handwriting tools, italic writing, graphology, or the handwriting of pupils in their school.
4. Children may report on writing they do at home—letters, thank-you notes, shopping lists, telephone messages. To help show the importance of writing, they may also report on writing their parents do.

Instruction Time

Research evidence indicates that ten to fifteen minutes of concentrated work each day should be sufficient for teaching and maintaining handwriting skills. Most primary grade teachers will find occasion and need for daily handwriting periods, whereas perhaps no more than a five-minute lesson on alternate days will be adequate at the middle and upper grade levels. The less frequent and shorter periods presuppose, of course, that attention is being given to individual diagnosis of need and practice.

In addition to having specific handwriting periods, devote attention during the day to handwriting skills in all areas of work in which writing is involved. Pupils must feel responsible for legibility in all their writing.

The way to eliminate poor handwriting is not to spend more time in handwriting periods but to better utilize the time that is devoted to its teaching and practice.

Position and Movement

A child's handwriting is affected by the fit of the desk and the child's position in relation to it. Handwriting is also affected by the position of the

Paper Position for Cursive

The relaxed angle of the forearm across the desk and the maximum convenience of the forearm and fingers to the paper decide the position of the paper. Usually the angle of the bottom of the paper with the edge of the writing surface should be 30 degrees. For the left-handed writer, the paper should be angled in the opposite direction.

paper, the way the writing instrument is held, and the movements of the handwriting strokes. If attention is given to each of these factors at the proper times, much time and energy on the part of both the child and the teacher will be saved.

A child should sit comfortably, with both feet touching the floor and both arms resting in a relaxed position on the writing surface. The writing instrument should be held lightly, and the index finger should be placed nearer to the point than the thumb, with both at least one inch above the writing point. The writing movement should involve smooth coordination of the whole arm, the wrist, and the fingers.

Speed of Writing

Attention to speed is not only useless but harmful if it begins before letter formation is spontaneously good. No end is served by making letters, words, and sentences rapidly and illegibly. Speed is important when letter formation has been properly established, since we all need to write rapidly at times. However, pupils usually make their own adjustments according to the nature of the work—pressure work, personal writing, or work that needs to be particularly neat and pleasing in appearance. Speed norms (see scale samples later in this chapter) are only rough averages and should not be used as arbitrary standards for all children or for every product of a child's writing.

Differences in Letter Forms

Paper Position for Manuscript Writing

For manuscript writing the paper is usually perpendicular to the edge of the desk. Some authorities suggest an angle of about 10 degrees.

A common instructional problem, particularly in the intermediate grades, is that different children in a class will write a number of different forms of the same symbol. These differences are particularly apparent in many capital letters, and they usually simply reflect the fact that the teachers the various pupils have been instructed by in earlier grades have used different commercial materials. Since there seems to be no conclusive evidence to demonstrate the superiority of a given letter form over other forms of the same letter, it is reasonable to permit pupils who have learned different forms to continue to use these so long as they are legible and can be made with sufficient ease and speed. However, it is a good idea for a school to adopt a single system, so that teachers will not confuse pupils further by advocating their individual ideas. Before adopting a system, a school may want to simplify some letter forms (removing loops and swings).

Handwriting Materials

Materials for handwriting include chalk, chalkboard, paper, crayons, pencils, pens, and usually commercial handwriting books. There is great variation in the use of these materials in different programs. Most programs call for the use of chalk and crayons in the primary grades, and many call for large beginner's pencils. As to the latter, there is less emphasis today on a larger than normal diameter for the pencil, but the lead should be thicker, since the essential requirement is that the beginning pupil is able to make a line that is easily seen.

There is also variation in the paper advocated for the various grade levels. You should insist that several types of paper be available to the children in your classroom—not all paper in grade 2 should have lines ½ inch apart, for example. In addition, there should be stationery available for letter writing. The following chart provides a guide to practice and instruction paper:

A GUIDE TO PRACTICE AND INSTRUCTION PAPER*

Grade 1	12 × 18 inch unlined newsprint (the use of this will depend upon the attention given to handwriting in the kindergarten)
	12 × 18 inch newsprint lined the long way
	12 × 18 inch (or shorter), with lines ½ inch apart alternating light and heavy
Grade 2	9 × 12 inch, with lines ½ inch apart alternating light and heavy
Grade 3	9 × 12, lined the long way with lines 1 inch apart
	9 × 12, with lines ½ inch apart alternating light and heavy
	9 × 12, with lines ½ inch apart
	8½ × 11 inch, with lines ⅝ inch apart
Grade 4	8½ × 11 inch, with lines ½ inch apart
	8½ × 11 inch, with lines ⅜ inch apart
Grade 5	8½ × 11 inch, with lines ⅜ inch apart

*Paper varies in size. Some beginning lined paper, for example, is 8½ × 11 inches (with the lines running the long way).

The Left-Handed Child

Five to ten percent of the pupils in a classroom are likely to be left-handed. These pupils are in a right-handed world and are probably taught by a right-handed teacher. If the pupil cannot imitate the teacher as the right-handed pupils do, he or she starts off with a problem. It is important, therefore, that you be aware of the left-handed pupils in your classroom, since their need for instruction is equal to that of right-handed pupils. First of all, it is necessary to recognize that left-handed children can be taught to write as well and as quickly as the right-handed ones. On the other hand, the time needed for development of particular skills is not necessarily the same for the left-handed pupils as for right-handed ones. In any case, it is important to avoid the implication that a child needs special attention because he or she is left-handed—simply pay attention to this child's individual needs as you do to those of other children.

Attention does need to be given to special instructional problems. For example, there should be much writing at the board in the early years, since when a child is writing at the board it is practically impossible to use the upside-down style some improperly taught left-handed writers use.

The best way to avoid upside-down writing is to make sure that the paper is angled in the opposite direction from that suggested for the right-handed child. In addition, encouraging the left-hander to hold the writing instrument slightly farther from the point helps, as does making sure that the top of the pen or pencil is pointed toward his or her left shoulder.

It is possible that some left-handed pupils will have developed the upside-down writing habit before they come into your classroom. Whether or not a teacher should attempt to change this habit after about the fourth grade depends on a number of factors. The pupil may not be psychologically or emotionally responsive to a change. In such cases, if the handwriting is reasonably legible and can be done with adequate speed, no attempt to change is advised.

Left-handed writers should not be expected to write with the same slant as the right-handed ones, although they may do so. However, if the paper is placed properly and the writing instrument held correctly, it is logical for the left-handed child's writing to slant in the direction of the writing movement—that is, to the right.

EVALUATING HANDWRITING

Handwriting can be evaluated either formally through the use of published scales or less formally by the teacher and the pupils. Since evaluation should lead to corrective practice and remedial teaching, the latter procedure is recommended. This evaluation should be pupil-focused and systematic and should be used as the basis for further teaching.

Diagnosis and Remediation

Most publishers of commercial handwriting material can supply instruments helpful in locating handwriting faults. Some extracts from one handwriting chart—*Handwriting Faults and How to Correct Them*—are given on pages 300 and 301.*

*Chart published by Zaner-Bloser Company in 1937 and periodically revised. Used by permission.

A Bulletin Board Idea

HOW IS YOUR HANDWRITING?

Put your paper in an envelope.

Good

Fair

Needs Improving

[This chart] is designed to reveal whether or not the pupil's handwriting violates one or more of the following essential qualities: (1) uniformity of slant, (2) uniformity of alignment, (3) quality of line, (4) letter formation, and (5) spacing. Three levels of quality—excellent, mediocre, and poor—are shown for each trait. In addition to illustrating these qualities, the chart contains excellent suggestions on ways to test a pupil's handwriting for each quality. The chart is particularly helpful because it enables both the teacher and the pupil to discover specific handwriting weaknesses that are in need of remedial treatment and makes helpful suggestions for correcting the defects.

How to test legibility: Make a letter finder by cutting a hole a little larger than the letter in a piece of cardboard. Place the hole of this finder over each letter in turn and mark the letters which are illegible. Have the pupils practice these letters separately, then write the word again and test as before.

How to test slant: Draw slanting lines through the letters and mark all letters which are off slant. If the slant is too great, the paper is tilted too much. If the writing is too vertical, the paper is too upright, and if the slant is backward, the paper is tilted the wrong direction.

How to test for spacing: Draw parallel lines between letters (see diagram). Place the paper in front of you and mark all letters and words which are unevenly spaced.

correct   incorrect

How to test alignment: Alignment and size are closely integrated and should be studied together. Use a ruler (a diagnostic ruler is best) and draw a base line touching as many of the letters as possible. Also draw a line along the tops of the small letters. Mark the letters above or below these lines.

correct   incorrect

How to test size of letters: Draw lines along the tops of the letters. Remember the minimum letters, i, u, v, etc., are ¼ space high; d, t, p are ½ space; capitals and l, h, k, b, d, are ¾ space high. All the lower loop letters extend ½ space below the line.

How to test for quality of line: Make a letter finder by cutting a hole a little larger than the letter in a piece of cardboard. Place the hole of this finder over each letter in turn and mark the letters which are illegible due to the quality of line.

Have pupils practice these letters from their writing books separately until the letters are perfectly legible. Then have them write the whole word again and test as before.

Handwriting Scales

Handwriting scales are often not used because of the feeling that children will attempt to copy the handwriting on the scale and thus lose their individuality in writing. However, scales do not have to be used for *grading* pupils' handwriting; they can simply be bases for the pupils to use in making their own judgments about the legibility of their handwriting.

One commercial instrument, *Guiding Growth in Handwriting Evaluation Scales*, provides five specimens of handwriting for each grade level and suggests that samples compared with these specimens be rated as good, medium, or poor.* There is also a numerical score for each of the five specimens. Two of these specimens are reproduced below.

SPECIMEN 3—MEDIUM FOR GRADE 5. Similar cursive handwriting may be marked 75. The standard speed for this grade is about 60 letters per minute.

> I live in America. It is good to live where you have freedom to work and play. As an American, I support my country and what it stands for.

SPECIMEN 5—POOR FOR GRADE 5. Similar cursive handwriting may be marked 65, and writing poorer than this may be evaluated accordingly.

> My name stands for me. I want to write it well.

Checklists

Procedures for evaluating handwriting were suggested in the section on handwriting practice, since practice should grow from diagnosis and evalu-

*Scales published by Zaner–Bloser Company in 1966. Used by permission.

ation. You can make a legibility checksheet such as the following, but be sure to list only the letters causing difficulty for your class. The checksheet can be added to as new problems are noted.

	NOT THIS	BUT THIS
Straight back stroke for e, l		
Avoidance of loop in a, i, n, t, u		
Points on r and s		
Well-rounded curves on m, n, u		
Carefully crossed t		
Open loops on b, f, h, k		
Avoidance of lazy ending on h, m, n		
Open loop on g, p, y, q		
Dot over i, j in line with letter		
Closing of f on the line		
Careful closing of a, d, g, q		

Individual pupil records such as the one on page 304 are useful for self-evaluation. You can modify the form for your own use by substituting pupils' names for the months; it can then be used in a periodic evaluation of the handwriting of your class.

A FINAL WORD

Handwriting instruction continues to have a place in the elementary school language arts program. There has been a shift of emphasis, however, to helping children develop a good bit of individuality in their writing if they can maintain legibility and reasonable speed. Instruction is needed in the way letters are formed and how the movements necessary can be made smoothly. Children must also recognize the importance of slant, spacing, and letter size to both legibility and speed.

MY HANDWRITING PROGRESS

KEY: S = Satisfactory   Name _____
          N = Needs improvement   Grade _____

	Oct.	Nov.	Dec.	Jan.	Feb.	Mar.	Apr.	May
Letter forms								
Letters to work on								
Size of letters								
Spacing within words								
Spacing between words								
Alignment of letters								
Slant								
Joining of letters								
Ending strokes of words								
Line quality								
Margins and arrangement								
Neatness								
Rate of writing								
Position and movement								

References

Anderson, Dan W. *What Research Says to the Teacher: Teaching Handwriting*. National Education Association, 1968.

Askov, Eunice N., and Peck, Michaeleen. "Handwriting," in *Encyclopedia of Educational Research*, 5th ed., Harold E. Mitzel, ed. The Free Press, 1982, pp. 764–769.

Barbe, W. B., and Lucas, V. H. "Instruction in Handwriting: A New Look," *Childhood Education* 50 (1974), pp. 207–209.

Berry, Winifred. "Italic Writing," *The Independent School Bulletin*, January 1961, p. 69.

Bissex, Glenda. *Gyns at Wrk: A Child Learns to Read and Write*. Harvard University Press, 1980.

Freeman, Frank N. *Guiding Growth in Handwriting*. Zaner-Bloser, 1965.

Lamme, Linda Leonard. "Handwriting in an Early Childhood Curriculum," *Young Children* 25 (November 1979), pp. 20–27.

Stewig, John Warren. *Exploring Language with Children*. Charles E. Merrill, 1974, Chapter 8.

Teaching Resources

FILMS

History of Writing. Encyclopaedia Britannica Films (25 min.; b/w; intermediate).

Improve Your Handwriting. McGraw-Hill (intermediate).

Written Word. National Educational Television Service, Indiana University (15 films, each 29 minutes; b/w). Titles include *Sign and Symbols, Between the Rivers, Keys to the Mysteries, Along the Nile, A B C's, Westward to Greece, Book Takes Form, Noble Roman Letter, Beautiful Book, Paper from China, Wood Blocks and Metal Type, Printing in Venice, The Perfect Book, New Worlds for the Book, Decline and Revival*.

FILMSTRIPS

Cursive Alphabet. Zaner-Bloser (4 strips; primary).

Manuscript Alphabet. Zaner-Bloser (2 strips; b/w or color).

KITS

Sounds and Symbols. Educators Publishing Service (30 cassettes and worksheets for teaching manuscript).

Activities for Preservice Teachers

1. The teacher's handwriting, both manuscript and cursive, will serve as a model for the children in the class. A teacher needs to be able to write neatly on unlined surfaces such as the chalkboard or chart paper. Using the guides suggested in this chapter or in a handwriting program, practice your handwriting for five minutes each day—manuscript and cursive. Keep a folder to note progress, and continue to practice until you feel that your writing will serve as a good model.

2. Evaluate the quality of your handwriting by several of the means suggested or explained in this chapter.

3. With a colleague plan a debate for the class on the pros and cons of not teaching children to write the cursive forms.

4. Observe handwriting lessons at several grade levels. Note differences in posture, hand and arm movement, quality of writing produced, handedness, etc. Note also what provisions are made for individual differences.

5. Examine samples of commercial handwriting materials for the grade level of your choice. Decide which you would like to use if you had a choice.

6. Obtain several samples of children's handwriting and try to evaluate them using a handwriting scale.

7. Plan a presentation to the class about what you would do to determine the level of readiness for one stage of handwriting instruction. This might be for initial instruction in manuscript, transition to cursive, practice after an initial learning stage, etc.

Activities for Inservice Teachers

1. Evaluate your own handwriting on the scale used in your school. Locate your weak letter formations and practice daily until your writing is close to the sample.

2. Make an informal survey of the handwriting in your school. Collect papers and analyze for specific handwriting faults. Note amount of writing done, posture, types of assignments, etc., and their relationship (if you can determine any) to handwriting ability.

3. React to the article by G. Halpin, "Special Paper for Beginning Handwriting: An Unjustified Practice?" (*Journal of Educational Research*, September 1976, pp. 668–669).

4. Have all the children in one classroom write the same paragraph; then arrange these so that you can identify three or four levels of quality. In other words, see if you can construct a handwriting scale.

5. Prepare activities for children in your class to do individually to improve their handwriting.

6. Have a "Handwriting Week" in your classroom. With the children plan special lessons and displays.

7. Start a file of examples of good and poor handwriting by adults. Try to get examples that are not signatures. Later, with children, examine the examples for specific illegibilities.

8. Purchase from a bookstore descriptive books on graphology. Use the study of graphology to stimulate interest in handwriting among upper grade children.

Independent Activities for Children

1. To develop small-muscle coordination, a child can snap clothespins on a clothesline or coffee can using only one hand, then remove them and try to do it faster the next time.

2. Fabric and torn paper can be pasted on paper to form designs or make houses, trees, etc. Pasting activities help develop eye-muscle coordination.

3. Children can also use the Montessori dressing forms to develop small-muscle coordination. The snapping, large button, zipper, bow-tying, and shoe-lacing frames are all helpful.

4. The child can keep his or her own handwriting improvement record by filing dated samples in order of quality, using a standard handwriting scale to help him or her make adjustments.

5. A child can enjoy and profit from making a personal handwriting scale, using samples of his or her own writing—from weak to improved—along with dates on which they were written.

6. Encourage individual children to use a diagnostic chart such as the ones suggested in this chapter to examine their handwriting and determine what they need to practice.

7. Have a child write his or her name—first, middle, and last—and compare individual letter formations with those found on a handwriting scale to determine which letters need improvement.

8. Provide a child with a device for determining the legibility of a single letter in a word. An easy device to make is a piece of tagboard about 1 inch wide and

3 inches long; near one end punch a hole with a hole punch. The child places the hole over individual letters and practices making those that are illegible.

9. For individual practice, prepare a holder with a pocket on one side and a sheet of acetate on the other (fasten it to the folder on one long side and on the bottom). In the pocket, place cards containing directions for the formation of letters and lists of words using those letters. A child selects a letter to work on and places it under the acetate. Using a marking pencil and with the card as a guide, the child first traces the letter, then writes it without tracing, and finally writes the words, comparing them with the model.

10. Some attention to speed is necessary in the middle grades, although legibility must remain paramount.

To practice speed, individual children can write short paragraphs and time themselves. Prepare paragraphs that should take about a minute to copy (about forty to sixty letters) at first. Paragraphs and sentences may be taken from handwriting scales, textbooks, or familiar books or stories.

11. As an incentive to improve, suggest that a child prepare a sample of his or her handwriting (enough so that most letters—upper- and lowercase—and numerals are included) and write a letter to a pupil in another part of the country to send with the sample suggesting an exchange several times during the year.

12. Have a child find examples of early picture writing and/or other alphabets—hieroglyphics, Indian picture writing, Greek alphabet—and prepare a demonstration for the class. As a part of the demonstration, several children might develop symbols depicting an activity the class is involved with and have the other children try to "read" what they have written.

12

Teaching Children to Read

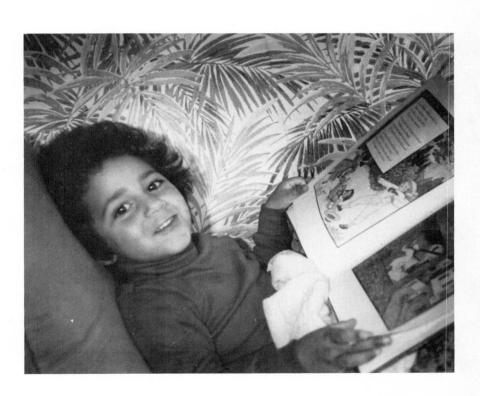

Reading is one of the language arts.

Children bring all of their experiences—those with language, those of thinking and emotion, and those with people and objects—to the challenging task of learning to read and to the development of skills needed by maturing readers after initial learning has occurred. Reading is not something that can be separated from these experiences, or from the other language arts or other parts of the school curriculum.

Practically all children come to school eager to learn to read. They usually have had experiences with books; they've been read to and have looked at and handled books—although too often they may not have had enough of these experiences. In spite of this general eagerness, however, many children become frustrated in their learning efforts, so that after only a year or so at school they have lost much of their curiosity and their desire to know; they may even ignore the appealing books that are available to them.

The causes of this change—which happens to far too many children—are many and varied. Differences in learning abilities, in experience backgrounds and readiness to learn what teachers seek to teach, and in adjustments to the school setting may not have been recognized and considered in instructional programs. Sometimes, too, the classroom instruction is contrived and forced; it does not focus on natural communication; it does not recognize that the reading act depends on the other language arts and is intertwined with them. Probably most of all, there are too many teachers who are not sensitive enough to each child as an individual and not enthusiastic enough themselves about the wonders of learning.

READING: AN OVERVIEW

A child does not learn to read suddenly or after only a short period of time, as one might learn to ride a bicycle. Of course a beginning reader may struggle with learning to remember what sounds certain letters represent or what word a series of letters stands for and then suddenly be able to remember these so that he or she can recognize a word or several words. But this is not reading.

Most adults are continuing to learn to read. The ability any person has as an adult is not the same ability he or she had in grade 2 or grade 3. Most adults have learned to skim, to draw inferences from content, to be expressive in oral reading, and to adjust their reading rate to the material being read and the purposes for reading it. Learning to read does not end with grade 3, with the elementary school, or with formal schooling at any level; as a developmental process it continues to develop as the individual's life changes.

What Is Reading?

Reading is a complex process that involves a series of equally complex sensory and mental processes. But this complexity does not mean that learning to read is difficult. Speaking is similar in complexity, yet children learn to speak, apparently without great difficulty.

Defining reading is not easy. Try to think of a one-sentence definition. What do you include? Is it attaching a sound to each squiggle that we call a letter so that putting the sounds together forms a word that the reader knows? Is it getting a clue to what several squiggles represent by any means possible—from pictures, from the shape of the pattern of squiggles, or by guess and inference? Is it saying each word either audibly or silently? Is it recognizing the meaning of a word, a phrase, or a sentence? Is it relating one's experiences to those of the writer? Is it a process of thinking that is stimulated by a special kind of object?

Over the years people identified as reading experts have defined, redefined, charted and modeled, and mulled over what it means to read. Definitions have ranged from "reading means getting meaning from certain combinations of letters," to "reading is a complex mental process that involves the doing of several things simultaneously," to "reading is a psycholinguistic guessing game," to "reading is proceeding from cognitive confusion to cognitive clarity." The educational literature abounds with such definitions and more, ranging from the glib to more thoughtful ones. You should formulate your own definition after further study, but for now consider the definition we like:

See *Teaching Elementary Reading* by Tinker and McCullough.

Reading involves the identification and recognition of printed or written symbols which serve as stimuli for the recall of meanings built up through past experience and further the construction of new meanings through the reader's manipulation of relevant concepts already in his or her possession. The resulting meanings are organized into thought processes according to the purposes that are operating in the reader.

No definition of reading, glib or extensive, tells one how to teach reading. On the other hand, almost any definition reflects an interpretation of the reading process that suggests, at least, a method for teaching. But no one really knows *a* best way to teach reading, and we know that some children learn to read regardless of the method and some do not.

Factors Affecting Reading

The extent to which any reading act is successful is affected both by the reader and by the material he or she is seeking to read. The reader must be ready for the specific reading effort. That is, he or she must have the men-

Readiness is necessary for any learning experience.

tal capacity, experience background, language maturity, and skill development required, as well as an interest in doing the reading. These factors are not unique to reading, however; none of us is successful in anything we attempt to do without readiness for doing it. If we do not have a background of some related experiences, an understanding of what is involved and what we need to do, and the physical and/or mental ability required, our effort will not be successful. And of course we would not even try any task if we weren't interested in doing it.

Reading readiness has traditionally been thought to embody activities that prepare a child for his or her first reading instruction—usually in the first grade. But it is important for every teacher to remember that readiness is an ongoing and ever-present concept. Every child must develop the readiness for each successive step in learning to read. Every person, regardless of age, must have the required readiness for any reading effort if reading is actually to occur.

Language development is a major aspect of readiness for reading at any developmental level, since it reflects the individual's mental abilities and experiences. Without sufficient language development, a reader will fail to adequately comprehend ideas formulated into sentences, determine word meanings from context, or use skills which aid understanding. Of course, the language structures of the material to be read may be so abstruse or awkward that even a reader with adequate language maturity may be unsuccessful in reading it. A reader may reject material also if its appearance

The beginning of a lasting interest in reading.

does not appeal—even if the content does. This is particularly true in the case of children. Style and size of print, spacing, length of lines, and number of illustrations are among the factors that may influence the interest of the reader and the ability to use the skills he or she possesses.

Of course, the content of the material and the vocabulary used affect reading, but these are more directly related to a reader's experience and ability. Because of this, though, they are especially important factors in reading instruction. Children can go a long way toward reading material whose content is generally familiar to them, especially if the content does not contain too many words and language structures that they have heard infrequently or do not use.

Other factors that bear upon reading include the ability to visually perceive adequately, the emotional state of the reader, and, particularly for the child just learning to read, the empathy and encouragement shown by the teacher.

Differences in Children That Affect Learning

1. Intellectual abilities.
2. Mental maturity levels.
3. Experiential backgrounds.
4. Verbal facility.
5. Emotional adjustment.
6. Attitude toward learning.
7. Exposure to print.
8. Physical coordination.
9. Visual and auditory abilities.

Objectives of Reading Instruction

The overall objective in teaching children to read is to develop in them the attitudes, abilities, and skills needed for securing information, fostering and reacting to ideas, developing interests and tastes, and deriving pleasure by reading. This fundamental objective may be met by a program which has or attains these objectives for each child:

1. The ability or skill to
    a. recognize many words at sight.
    b. gain meaning quickly upon meeting unknown words and expressions by using one or a combination of the following:
        analysis of structure,
        phonics,
        configuration of the graphic symbol,
        contextual analysis,
        the dictionary.
    c. comprehend and interpret the meanings of words, phrases, and sentences.
    d. read silently at speeds appropriate to the content of the material and the purpose of the reader.
    e. read orally with fluency, suitable speed, expression, correct pronunciation, and attention to enunciation.
    f. evaluate the content of what is read.
    g. use books efficiently—locate information, use the library, etc.
2. The provision of many opportunities for rich and varied experiences through reading.
3. The development of a lasting interest in reading.

Integrating Reading Instruction

Reading, like the other language arts, is an all-day, all-life activity; wise teachers are aware of this and use it to their advantage in reading instruction, in building children's understanding that reading and the other lan-

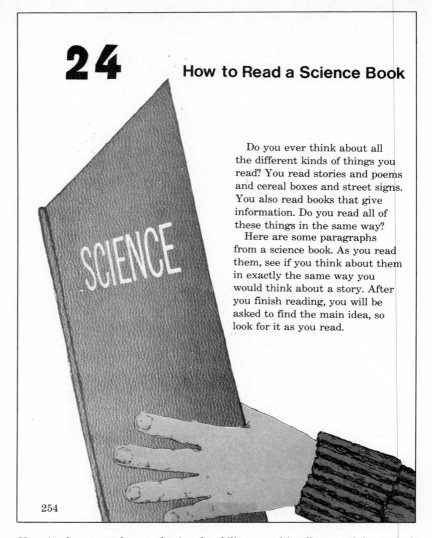

24 How to Read a Science Book

Do you ever think about all the different kinds of things you read? You read stories and poems and cereal boxes and street signs. You also read books that give information. Do you read all of these things in the same way?

Here are some paragraphs from a science book. As you read them, see if you think about them in exactly the same way you would think about a story. After you finish reading, you will be asked to find the main idea, so look for it as you read.

254

Knowing how to read means having the ability to read in all areas of the curriculum.

guage arts are our means for communicating, and in meaningfully integrating the curriculum.

The more the various areas of the language arts and other subjects are meaningfully related in instruction, the greater the possibility that learning will be enhanced and interest developed. The following chapters on study skills, library skills, and children's literature add to the instructional suggestions in this chapter. The interrelatedness of all of the language arts and

Children have not been taught to read until they can read their social studies, science, and mathematics books with an understanding of concepts, directions, and questions.

the need to use language skills and abilities in all areas of study make the teaching of reading easy to relate to vocabulary study, spelling, and handwriting, as well as to science, mathematics, and social studies. Because sharing personal experiences orally or through writing is highly motivational, the sharing can also be related to reading instruction. In many ways the interrelating of the various instructional areas is easy, but careful planning is required for the objectives to be achieved. Numerous aids to such planning have been suggested in earlier chapters, and others will be discussed in the chapters that follow. However, an alert teacher will find many more ways throughout each day to relate his or her instruction in reading and the other language arts to all the other areas of the curriculum. These natural occurrences usually top suggestions in any book, because they relate activities to real people in a genuine situation.

READINESS FOR BEGINNING READING

Many of the reading problems of concern to teachers (and, less directly, to the entire public) are a direct result of improper attention to children's readiness for the teaching effort directed at them. If readiness for the particular learning is absent, a cycle of frustration and failure is being thrust upon a child. Readiness for any learning can be encouraged and guided; it can never be rushed.

Determining Readiness

See Roger Farr and Nicholas Anastasia, Tests of Reading Readiness and Achievement (International Reading Assoc., 1969) for reviews of readiness tests.

Before instruction in reading begins, the teacher needs to look at many factors in a child's development to determine which areas must receive attention prior to the initial instruction in actual reading skills. Once this determination has been made, attention can be given to building readiness in those factors needing it. There may be some children, of course, who do have the readiness for initial reading instruction when they come to school, but most will range from "nearly ready" to needing both time and considerable attention to most of the factors. It is important to remember that at any stage of development every human being is ready to learn something, but readiness is not static, nor does it proceed in regular cadence for all individuals. Two children might both be ready for the first steps in initial reading instruction, but both may not be ready for the next steps. You must continually seek to elevate a child's readiness and know what the readiness level is for instruction to be most successful.

Factors that generally must be assessed to determine the readiness strengths and weaknesses of the child before reading instruction begins are indicated by the following questions:

A. Background experience: Has the child
   1. been on shopping trips to the market, department stores, etc.?
   2. visited a zoo, farm, office building, etc.?
   3. gone on trips to other parts of the country?

For Parents

Good Books Make Reading Fun for Your Child by Glenda Davis Sloan (International Reading Association)

How Can I Encourage My Primary Grade Child to Read? by Molly Kayes Ransbury (International Reading Association)

Raising Readers by Nancy Larrick (Walker and Co.)

Reading Begins at Home by Dorothy Butler and Marie Clay (Heinemann)

What Books and Records Should I Get for My Preschooler? by Norma Rogers (International Reading Association)

Why Read Aloud to Children? by Julie M. Chan (International Reading Association)

You Can Encourage Your Child to Read by Molly Kayes Ransbury (International Reading Association)

4. been to the library?
5. been read to at home?
6. looked at picture books at home?

B. Verbal facility: Does the child
1. have the ability to describe experiences to others so that they enjoy listening?
2. understand a variety of concepts and vocabulary—e.g., a peach is a fruit, a cow's baby is a calf?
3. know the meanings of most common prepositions—*over, under, between, above,* etc.?
4. use and understand the language of the school—*library corner, talking time, bring your chairs to the circle,* etc.?
5. have the ability to understand and repeat oral directions?

C. Intellectual and perceptual ability: Does the child
1. have the general intellectual ability and maturity of other children of the same chronological age?
2. have the ability to discriminate visually among shapes, words, and letters?
3. recognize and name the letters of the alphabet?
4. identify words that rhyme or begin alike?

D. Physical condition: Is the child
1. in general good health?
2. sufficiently rested and nourished each day?
3. able to hear and see adequately?
4. coordinated as well as others of the same age?
5. able to articulate sounds and pronounce words normally?
6. established as to eye, hand, and foot dominance?
7. able to use crayons, pencils, and scissors adequately?

E. Emotional-social stability: Does the child
1. modify behavior to adjust to changing situations?
2. work independently?
3. have the desire to learn and complete tasks?
4. work and play with other children?
5. listen to and react to others?
6. have a positive self-image?

These are not all of the questions that might be asked, nor is a negative answer to one or even several of these evidence of possible failure in the beginning stage of learning to read. But such questions do get to the heart of the abilities, attitudes, and skills that are important to first instruction, and therefore many "yes" answers are needed. "No" answers indicate the readiness program that should be planned for the child.

Invite parents to learn about your reading program. Be prepared to give them suggestions for helping their child become ready for your first instruction and for helping as the child is beginning to read.

The answers to such questions can be obtained by observing the children and talking with them, by interviewing their parents, and by administering commercial tests. Caution should be exercised in concluding readiness, however. Commercial tests are often not as diagnostic as is claimed, and there are differences among them as to what should be evaluated as evidence of readiness for initial reading instruction. Also, the things children and parents say may be misunderstood or may be inaccurate. The best procedure is to use a variety of means, formal and informal, but to remember that there is no absolute set of conditions that says a child is ready for the initial instruction.

Developing Readiness

Remember!

See that all readiness activities are planned and purposeful.

Make every lesson a diagnostic lesson.

Stop occasionally to think about how some of the things you do *routinely* can be made a part of the readiness program.

Don't overlook the fact that a readiness program must be individualized, since no two children need exactly the same program and very few children can move through a program at the same rate.

Utilize commercial readiness materials when they are suitable to your program and to the needs of individual children.

Finally, recognize that readiness never ends.

Chapter 5 suggested many activities for fostering children's social, intellectual, sensory, motor, and language growth. These activities build readiness for reading instruction as they do for learning in all curriculum areas. Too often, though, reading readiness is thought of in terms of commercial materials. These materials vary in quality, of course, and certainly some are helpful to teachers and to children, but for the most part they include many more worksheets and dittoing exercises than are needed or should be used.

The sections that follow suggest activities which build children's readiness for learning to read. Many are intentionally similar to activities suggested earlier, but concern about children's learning to read requires a particular focus on them here.

BUILDING EXPERIENTIAL BACKGROUNDS. Although children's experiential backgrounds vary greatly, all children need opportunities to have experiences that relate to school activities. These are some ways that may be used to build experiential backgrounds:

1. Read and tell stories to children in small groups and individually. Encourage the children to talk about what was read or told.

2. Encourage children to tell about things they have done, to make up stories, and to share information. Encourage them to bring objects to show and explain to the other children and to you.

3. Provide opportunities for dramatic play; for experimenting with clay, finger paint, and cold water paint; and for creative expression through music and rhythm.

4. Have places within the room for displaying interesting materials—leaves, flowers, rocks, etc. Show pictures—still, motion, filmstrip, slide—and encourage the children to talk about them. Conduct experiments with seeds, flowers, and plants. Observe animals, fish, etc. (have a classroom pet, an aquarium, or a terrarium).

5. Take many excursions—into the schoolyard and neighborhood, around the building, and to stores. Plan these with the children, write experience charts about them, and discuss both the trips and the organization, words, and sentences of the charts.

DEVELOPING SPEAKING ABILITIES. Children can best grow in their use of language through opportunities to talk to attentive listeners about things they are interested in. New words may be introduced as they are needed in these speaking activities. Explain the meanings of the words, using concrete objects or pictures when possible to give additional substance to the explanation.

In addition to naturally occurring speaking activities, try these:

- Have children create new endings for stories read.
- Provide for sharing experiences and showing objects—toys, pets, etc.
- Have art work interpreted orally.
- Encourage the dramatization of words like *walked, ran, crept, raced*.
- Use play activities, such as playing house, store, etc., to induce speaking.

DEVELOPING VOCABULARY. Many opportunities to develop children's vocabularies will present themselves during discussions, reading by the teacher, and sharing periods. These should be utilized whenever they occur. For example, in discussing something that Mary told in Show and Tell, have the children substitute words with the same meaning: Can you give us another word that tells how Mary felt? From Mary's description, can you tell what kind of day it was?

In other instances, dramatic activities can be used to develop word meanings. As children play at being firefighters, mechanics, parents, etc., they can be told new words (by other children as well as by you). Also simply talking about words with the children—discussing meanings, variations, the way words sound, etc.—is interesting and helps develop vocabulary.

UNDERSTANDING RELATIONSHIPS. Experiential backgrounds are also built through activities that focus on teaching new concepts and developing understanding of relationships among known concepts. For example, have the children tell what they would wear on a hot day, on a rainy day, etc. Have one describe how he or she would dress and the others guess the time of day. Fold a paper in half; then have children make and cut out pictures of objects that belong together and paste the pairs in the "boxes." Set up a play street of cardboard store fronts, with picture cutouts of items the children can pretend to buy in these stores. Many of the activities suggested in this section and in other chapters can be directed at showing relationships.

VISUAL SKILLS. Children need the ability to perceive and discriminate visually. Again, there are many activities for building these skills. For instance, give a child pieces of paper of different shapes to be sorted according to shape. Start with two shapes and increase the number (they may also be sorted according to color). After forms have been matched, the child can check his or her work by placing them side by side on the flannel board. You might also have form boards or puzzles to assemble, beads to string, pictures to color, and blocks to build with. Pictures can be classified for scrapbooks (dogs, cats, pets and not pets, types of food, etc.). Arrange objects on a table, cover them, and have the children recall the objects. Show a sample form (square, triangle, circle, etc.), remove it, and have the children draw what they saw. (This will also provide a check on eye-hand coordination.)

Discriminating visually among shapes of objects and drawings is not *the same as discriminating between words.*

Along with visual discrimination activities with objects and shapes, provide activities for matching like letters (in both upper and lower cases); matching like words (without teaching, except as children ask what the words are); noting sign words—*stop, go, slow, danger,* etc.; sorting "long" and "short" words on cards into piles; counting the number of letters in names; sorting words on cards into piles according to beginning letters; and so on. Ability to discriminate among letters and words will develop, too, as children see many words in chart stories, in titles under their drawings, and in the books they look at.

AUDITORY SKILLS. Since children have learned to speak, they obviously can perceive sounds reasonably accurately and can discriminate between similar ones. Beginning reading instruction may be aided, though, if children practice these skills. Activities for their development and practice include identifying and distinguishing among the sounds produced when different objects are struck; listening to music for high, low, soft, and loud sounds; identifying rhyming words (out in the snow/sat a black crow); finding the missing words in two-line rhymes (we went so far/in daddy's new _____); and making charts using pictures of objects whose names rhyme or begin with the same sound.

Children should also listen for and give words that rhyme or begin with the same sound. This can be done on a pupil-teacher or child-to-child basis. It can also be a team activity, but be sure that children who "drop out" early have a way to participate. In other words, do not make this an activity for those who already have good ability.

It is helpful, too, to vary regular classroom activities in which responses are asked for by rows or in some other ordinary way by using skill-building activities instead. For example, "All children whose names begin with the same sound as 'Mary' may collect the crayons and put them away."

Other activities include giving several words, some of which rhyme (or begin alike), and having the children tell which ones belong together and which do not; making different sounds in sequence and having the children tell which was first, middle, and last; having the children take turns imitating sounds of animals or machines while the others try to identify them (sometimes it may be desirable to determine *why* a particular response— right or wrong—was made); and using jingles or rhymes that repeat sounds or words (Jack Be Nimble, Hickory Dickory Dock, etc.).

Hearing and listening are not the same thing. Listening requires thought and often some action.

LISTENING. Children need to be encouraged to listen to and be courteous to other children as they tell about things. Children particularly need to listen to directions, so practice in doing this is needed. Directions should be clear and simple, and at first there should be only one thing to remember. It is also important to check to see that directions are understood, particularly in respect to any sequence involved, and then see that they are followed. Variation in teaching can be provided by follow-the-leader games or games in which the children give the directions.

Ask children questions about stories read or told to them to determine how well they have listened and understood. Begin with questions that will be easy for them to answer if they have been listening, such as the name of a character, but progress to ones concerning actions, whether the story is about real or imaginary events, and the relationship of the content of stories to their own lives.

SENSING SEQUENCE. Many activities are useful for helping children to learn the importance of sequence and to use sequence in stories they tell and later write. These include discussing the day's or week's program and other activities and experiences in terms of sequence; using dramatic play with dialogue or pantomime to tell a story; utilizing art work (a series of pictures, a class movie, etc.) to show the importance of order; and having the children retell a story heard or seen on a film or filmstrip or finish a partially told story.

Large plastic boats, wading pools, and tubs make good sandboxes.

EYE-HAND COORDINATION. Dramatic play activities, building with blocks, using tools, working with pegboards and puzzles, and playing on outdoor equipment are all useful for developing eye-hand coordination. A sandbox is also helpful; the children can write letters and names in the sand. Other activities include cutting and tearing, pasting, coloring, easel and finger painting, and working with clay.

LEFT-TO-RIGHT MOVEMENT. Since reading requires left-to-right movement, it is necessary to teach this to children. This can be done both directly and incidentally. For example, when reading to the children, hold up the book and run your finger under the words as you read. To teach more directly, you may have them arrange a series of pictures on the chalk tray to tell a story. Make sure that the pictures must be looked at from left to right to tell the story in proper sequence. Another activity is a directional game in which the children tell each other to go to certain places or perform certain actions, using the words *left* and *right*.

EXTENDING THE ATTENTION SPAN. Reading instruction is hampered and perhaps nullified if children do not pay attention to instructions. A young child has a short attention span, but it is possible to develop the ability to pay attention without unnecessary forcing. For one thing it is helpful to begin and end activities at systematic and logical times. Planning with the children will be useful, since they will better understand what they are to do if they contribute to the planning. Children can also be given jobs that require paying attention, such as housekeeping and other classroom chores. Observe children's actions at these times, and make sure not to give responsibilities only to those who are well-behaved or who do things well.

Above all, give purposes for doing things. Give the children something specific to watch for, listen to, or find out.

Chapter 3 of Teaching a Child to Read by Roger Farr and Nancy Roser (Harcourt Brace Jovanovich, 1979) suggests many readiness activities.

ADJUSTING TO THE SCHOOL SETTING. It is essential to help each child become acquainted with the school environment—the classroom, the building, the grounds, the people—since this environment is usually strange and perhaps even frightening.

Providing opportunities for expression and creative work, giving encouragement and praise, directing the child's attention to something outside the self, and helping each child achieve success are all useful in helping him or her make the adjustment to school. In all of these activities be friendly, calm, relaxed—and not overcritical of mistakes. Especially, be fair in all your dealings; give the child an extra smile or a pat on the back to show he or she is liked and wanted.

Practices more specifically related to reading are making a special point of introducing children to the books they will use, demonstrating how books and other reading material should be used, and giving practice in their use (see Chapter 13).

FURTHERING THE DESIRE TO READ. As suggested at the beginning of this chapter, most children are eager to learn to read and are curious about books. This interest should be encouraged through the following techniques:

- Make liberal use of labels on objects and pictures—name cards on desks; labels for articles made by children, paintings, drawings, science collections, and other materials and equipment.
- Make and use signs: "We are outside," "Gone for a walk," "Save."
- Maintain a library corner with many books available for children to examine. Time should be allotted for the use of the corner.
- Read stories, informational materials, and poems to the children. Be sure not to do all the selecting yourself; let the children choose what they would like to hear.
- Read other materials to and in front of the children. For example, when a notice comes to your room, make a point of the fact that you are reading it. Point out the importance of reading as a means of communication. When appropriate, print a notice on the board to serve as a reminder of what the note said.
- Write charts of the children's experiences. The children can "read" (tell) what these say.
- Send books home with children.

Provide private places to read:

in an old bathtub full of pillows
in a papier-mâché cave (with a light inside)
in a large box
under a long table on a rug
in a carrell

ORGANIZING FOR INSTRUCTION

For proper attention to be given to instructional procedures and techniques, use of materials available, and, most importantly, the differences in the abilities and achievement levels among the children, it is necessary to plan the organizational pattern of the teaching/learning program. Essentially, this planning must begin with decisions about the extent to which all of the children in a classroom will be taught as a group, in smaller groups, and individually. This planning must be of a continuing nature, since the factors influencing decisions will change.

Looking at Individuals

To make organizational plans it is necessary to learn a good deal about each child: various measures of his or her reading ability or readiness for instruction, intelligence, health or emotional problems, previous school achievement, home factors that may affect learning, experiences he or she has had, and any other factors that may influence achievement in reading.

Beginning as well as experienced teachers frequently have difficulty organizing the instructional program. One of the reasons is that often not all of the information suggested above as being important is available—or at least not readily. There is also the problem of systematically looking at the information that can be garnered and making decisions based upon it. We suggest that you record information about each child on a 5×8 card. Then, from the cumulative folders of the children, record standardized test scores (not simply cumulative scores, but those of the subtests: word recognition, comprehension, etc.), I.Q., last reading book or program completed (including test information on these), age, various teachers' comments, information about the child's background and interests, etc. With the information condensed in this fashion, basic needs may be identified and organizational ideas can be more readily explored.

Most teachers find rather quickly that planning to teach the entire class as a group of individuals with comparable abilities, potential, and interests simply will not provide effective teaching for many of the children. They also discover frequently that, although there are wide individual variations among the children, there are some common needs that suggest the use of groups for a good deal of instruction.

The card technique suggested above aids primarily in finding common or related abilities, backgrounds (including books read in earlier grades), and interests, but it is also useful in helping you understand the tremendous differences among the children in your class. We recently worked through a set of cards with a first-year fifth grade teacher and found a range in I.Q.'s from 75 to 145 and a range in reading levels (based on standardized test scores) from grade 2 to grade 11.

Although there is much to be said for individualized programs, particularly if the conditions suggested for them are met, experience tells us that, for best use of time, much instruction can and should be done in small groups.

Grouping Plans

The objective of most grouping plans is to narrow the range of differences so that a single set of materials and common objectives are appropriate for all the children in the group. Thus, in a classroom in which children are reading from first grade level to sixth grade level (which is not at all uncommon in third and fourth grade classrooms), four groups might be formed, each with its own materials and objectives. The children in one group might all be reading at about the third grade level; they could all use the same reading textbook and be given instruction in many of the same skills. Another group might be reading at a second grade level; they would use materials that they could read without frustration or boredom. A third group might be the few children who were still struggling with beginning reading skills; perhaps the reading materials for these children might be individualized as much as possible to meet their specific needs. The fourth group might be the more capable readers, who would generally read independently but would be taught needed skills as a group.

Other plans for instruction include grouping on the basis of interests rather than ability and grouping on the basis of social preferences. Interest grouping can be based on differences in the interests children show as they study social studies or science, play games, and read independently. Social preference grouping simply means that children are put in a group because they are "special" friends, live on the same street, have birthdays in the summer, have moved to the school from another town or city, etc. Both of these plans permit teaching fewer children at a time, just as ability grouping plans do, but they widen the range of reading abilities in the group considerably.

Examples of Seatwork Activities

1. Practicing handwriting.
2. Studying spelling.
3. Working in a reading workbook.
4. Writing a story.
5. Reading for fun.
6. Working on a science experiment.
7. Working on a social studies project.
8. Doing learning games and puzzles.
9. Practicing visual discrimination activities.
10. Classifying objects.
11. Listening to tapes and records.
12. Following suggestions on task cards.

Grouping can take still other forms. The entire class may be a reading group when they watch classmates dramatize a story or report on a project. Other variations include putting two ability groups together when they are working on a particular skill or when both are reading about something related to another area of the curriculum (e.g., both reading about peoples of the Far East).

Grouping may also involve the entire school. For example, at a given time of day all classrooms may have reading instruction, and each child moves to the classroom whose teacher is working with the children on his or her reading level. (This is known as the Joplin Plan.) This plan permits the narrowing of the range of differences to a greater extent than is possible in a single classroom but does present the potential problem of having some children taught by a teacher who does not know them as well as their regular teachers do.

A modification of this plan involves all teachers in a school who work with the same grade level. The teachers, acting as a team, discuss each child's strengths and weaknesses as discovered through observation and reading tests and agree on the group each will instruct, as well as on a common time for instruction. During the given period of time, each teacher works with about twenty-five children who are at approximately the same level. Teachers who have used this plan have found that they still need to do further grouping among those coming to their classrooms, although the range of abilities is certainly much narrower than in the ordinary self-contained classroom. The plan may be particularly difficult for the teacher who takes the slowest children, since even an excellent teacher will have difficulty in teaching reading to a class of twenty-five slow children in sixty to ninety minutes. These children have the greatest academic needs and are commonly the greatest behavior problems. Thus the teacher working with them should have fewer children—perhaps fifteen—along with an aide and a parent volunteer. A teacher with more able students can take a larger class, because these children are more likely to be independent workers.

Pupil-team grouping is being used in some schools. In this plan, superior readers give assistance and extra practice to groups of three to five children who need extra help. In fact, there are so many variations in how instruction can be organized for a particular class that usually the only limitation is the flexibility of the individuals involved.

Working with Groups

Although the effectiveness of an organizational plan depends to a great extent on the teacher's personality and the characteristics of a particular group of children, there are other factors that influence how well a plan meets instructional needs. The principal factor is the operation of the plan itself. That is, the operational scheme—the schedule—must be workable for the plan to be effective.

Any grouping plan will permit variation in the schedule or operational scheme. The following is an example of one way of scheduling three groups. A similar schedule could be made for four or any other number of groups. However, the management of more than four groups is difficult.

Amount of Time	Group		
	A	B	C
10 minutes	Teacher reading aloud, sharing newspaper reports, choral reading, etc.		
30 minutes	Teacher-directed activity	Reading library books	Independent work
30 minutes	Independent work	Teacher-directed activity	Reading library books
30 minutes	Reading library books	Independent work	Teacher-directed activity

More or less time than that indicated in this chart may be needed for some groups. Particularly slow-learning children may need more teacher direction, while a group of high-achieving children may work independently with only occasional teacher checking. All grouping, however, requires that children work independently at times while the teacher is teaching the others. For this to work, there must be meaningful independent or group activities that do not require much direct teacher attention. Listening to children read is not teaching, especially if the teacher is giving a substantial amount of attention to the other children in the room. Without planning, careful scheduling, and an adequate supply of materials for children to use, a teacher is "keeping school" rather than teaching.

Giving the same seatwork to all children is an injustice to them. Make sure that all seatwork has a purpose and is not just something to keep a child "busy"!

Planning for the Limited Reader

Some of the children at any grade level have very limited reading ability. These children and those who have learned to read very well are the major reasons for grouping and individualizing instruction. The child who can read the material assigned to his or her classroom—the social studies books, the science materials, and the reading textbook for the grade level—well or fairly well presents few problems. The child who has an instructional reading level considerably below the grade level to which he or she is assigned is a major problem for most teachers. And these children are found in most classrooms.

A teacher must accept the fact that these children do exist and that they are in most classrooms, and must ask, "What can I do?" The answer is not simple—it must vary with every teacher and every classroom. First, as suggested earlier, a teacher should take a look at the child's record. What do other teachers say about this child? What is his or her mental ability? A pattern should be looked for in tests—a weakness that can be pinpointed. For example, if enough information is available, it may be noticed that this child has low scores on the word recognition portions of reading tests and quite consistently has trouble with vowel digraphs (two vowels together that represent a single sound—*boat, meat, beet*) on spelling tests. Perhaps this is the pattern. If further investigation confirms the pattern, attention should be given to working on vowel digraphs.

Whatever the search for the cause or causes of a reading problem reveals, realistic action must be taken. This means finding something at which the child can succeed—something that will build ego and provide a sense of achievement. Begin with reading at a very easy level; perhaps a sixth grader may very easily read a book written at second or third grade level. Look, too, at the other books he or she has. Surely the sixth grader who reads at third grade level will have difficulty with the sixth grade spelling program; not only the words themselves but also the practice activities are likely to present a reading problem. Yet this child might find success in—and benefit from—a third grade spelling program. In other words, avoid the all-too-common mistake of placing a child at the correct instructional level for reading but at the same time expecting him or her to spell words or read social studies and science books at a reading level two or more grades above that level. After all, integrating curriculum areas means just that—providing each child with suitable materials in every area.

The Accelerated Reader

Children who are advanced in reading, who easily read above grade level, have the same basic needs as other children in terms of acceptance, encouragement, and recognition of achievement. Because they can read well in a literal sense, their instruction in study skills and interpretive and critical reading skills is sometimes neglected. They may learn these skills easily, of course, but they do need to be taught. Teacher direction and attention are needed also after such teaching as they work independently. The independent work these children are capable of requires that many books of all types be available—trade, information, reference, textbooks—along with opportunities for them to be used in meaningful projects. Projects may include responding to their reading by making dioramas, murals, bulletin boards, posters, and charts and by writing scripts, stories, reviews, and reports. Accelerated readers may also help librarians, read to younger children, and report to the class about authors.

TEACHING READING SKILLS

We have suggested factors—skills and abilities—important for children to have developed when the first instruction in reading is given. As this instruction begins, there is an immediate need for children to have other skills. The teaching of these does not take place all at once, even for the child who possesses a high level of development in all of the initial readiness factors. Rather, instruction in these skills is woven in over a period of time—usually two or three years—as children need them in order to read.

We want to stress that all of these skills or abilities are needed by a child if he or she is to be a successful reader. They are not ends in themselves; rather, they are means that permit the reader to get sense from what is written by associating what he or she knows with what the author has written. Beginning readers will make greater use of some of the word recognition or decoding skills or abilities than will mature readers—phonic and structural analyses, for instance—while the experienced, mature reader will have a large supply of sight words and will rely on context clues more heavily to gain meaning of unknown words.

In this section we suggest procedures and activities for teaching and developing these skills. However, you may want to seek further descriptions of procedures and more extensive suggestions of activities in reading methods books, in educational journals, and in reading materials published for use with children.

Word Recognition

The ability to recognize, recall, or otherwise identify or determine a word is basic to reading. There are several intertwined skills involved in word recognition. No one of these always works, nor do all children need an equal amount of instruction in all or any one of them. Some activities related to gaining these skills are discussed in the following sections.

SIGHT RECALL. Adults generally recognize at sight most of the words they encounter in their reading. We simply know the words and do not have to stop to figure out what they are. We have gained this ability by our experiences. We have heard many words, seen them often in written form, and possibly have written most of them ourselves. In other words, how they appear in graphic form has been memorized. Of course, we sometimes look up a word in a dictionary, ask someone what it is, or possibly stop long enough to see a clue in it that we relate to a word we do know.

Children who are ready for beginning reading instruction also recognize some words by simply seeing them. These words are ones they have seen frequently in stories that were read to them or in experience stories that they helped "write." Young children are great at pretending to read, and much of their pretending is recalling. Sometimes their identification of specific words is inaccurate, but they often actually do recognize some words and almost always have a genuine sense of the meaning of a group of words even if they don't know what all of them are. The first reading instruction builds on this knowledge and focuses on teaching a small number of words that a child will readily recognize by sight. These words are introduced slowly and with a heavy reliance on pictures, actual objects, or the experiences of the child so that meaning immediately becomes a part of the reading process. These words provide the foundation for future learning of other words and of ways to determine words that are known in speech but are unknown as graphic symbols. Not only do these words need to appear in context meaningful to the child, but they also need to appear frequently so that they can be learned.

A Book for Parents

The Reading Triangle by Linda M. Clinard (Focus Publishing Co.)

CONTEXT CLUES. The most important skill for determining the meanings of unknown words is that of using context clues. These clues are available to a reader because of some degree of shared experiences with the author of the materials and because of the reader's knowledge of how the language works. While most of the clues are verbal, pictures also provide clues to meaning, since they generally relate to the content. Thus, a reader using context clues to determine the meaning of a word that he or she does not recognize at sight draws information from the remainder of the sentence, other sentences in the context, pictures that appear to be related, and experiences that he or she has had with related ideas. In a sense this is a guess (as, actually, are all word recognition techniques other than using a dictionary), but it is an informed guess.

Children's skill in using context clues is closely related to the breadth and depth of their vocabularies (see Chapter 4). Knowledge of the multiple meanings of many words is necessary, as is knowing that many words have synonyms, figures of speech and idioms have special meanings, modifying phrases and clauses serve specific purposes, and particular words suggest the author's pattern of thinking (e.g., *first, also, on the other hand,* etc.). Activities such as the following can help develop this skill:

1. Write sentences in which one word has been omitted and have pupils supply as many words for the blank as possible. Vary this procedure by writing different first letters in the blank:

   John _____ to the store.
   John w _____ to the store.
   John r _____ to the store.

2. Write homographs (*bear, stick, fleet, flat, fair,* etc.) and illustrate their meanings with sentences:

   I cannot *bear* to see you suffer.
   The *bear* ran down the road.

3. Think of all the possible descriptive words that could be related to a particular object or action.

4. Write as many sentences as you can showing different meanings of common words. Try words such as *run, walk, back,* and *step.*

5. Write synonyms for words in a story. Will all synonyms for a word always fit the context?

6. Circle the clues to the meanings of the underlined words in these sentences:

   The <u>submarine</u> is a reliable underwater craft.

   After Bob bought the groceries for his mother, he <u>purchased</u> candy with the change.

STRUCTURAL ANALYSIS. Structural analysis involves looking for known parts within unknown words. Determining whether a part of a word is known by the reader—that is, that it has meaning that is understood—often leads to identifying the unknown word. Many words are compounds, and a reader may know the meaning of one of the words forming the compound. This may be enough of a clue (especially if other word recognition skills are used) for the reader to get the meaning of the compound. In the

Read the cartoons. Do what the direction sentence after each cartoon tells you to do.

Put a check beside two statements that are incorrect.

_____ Everyone can eat peanuts.

_____ Bob had money to spend.

_____ Bob wanted to buy everyone a treat.

_____ Juanita went home because she was angry.

Put a check beside two statements that are incorrect.

_____ The plants were in a windowbox.

_____ The pavement was wet.

_____ The rain watered the plants.

_____ The wet sidewalk meant that rain had fallen.

86

Total context affects comprehension.

From *Skills Book*, Level 11, of *The Laidlaw Reading Program*, Second Edition, Copyright © 1980 by Laidlaw Brothers. Used by permission of the publisher.

same way, clues may be provided by other word elements: inflectional endings—*s, ed, ing, ly*, etc.—prefixes, suffixes, and roots. Knowledge of how contractions work, plurals are formed, and words may be divided into syllables is also helpful in structural analysis.

Various teaching procedures or approaches are used for teaching structural analysis, in which varying emphasis is given to each of the elements. Often the ideal time to teach structural analysis is when unknown words which lend themselves to such analysis are encountered by a reader. However, timely as such teaching might be, a reader who is excitedly fulfilling his or her purpose for doing the reading should not be stopped. In such a situation the wise teacher will simply supply the unknown word, but will note it for later teaching. Activities useful in such teaching include these:

1. Write inflected and derived forms of words and have pupils underline the root word of each (e.g., *happier, making, shorter, carries, flies*, etc.).

2. Have pupils find the root common to all (or a certain number) of a group of words (e.g., *reporter, portable, portage*, etc.).

3. Make lists of words that have the same ending (suffix) and have the pupils see if they can determine the meaning of the suffix (e.g., *helpful, tearful, hopeful, fearful*).

4. Have pupils make lists of compound words or put words together to make compounds.

5. Provide lists of words to be divided into syllables.

6. Write prefixes on cards and place them in a box. Then have each pupil draw a card and give a word that has the prefix as a part of it.

7. Have children classify words in a list by common suffixes, prefixes, syllabication rule, or root.

8. Provide lists of contractions (*shouldn't, can't, I'll, won't*, etc.) for pupils to change to the contracted words.

PHONICS. Phonics is the relating of graphic symbols (one or more letters) to sounds (also one or more). The objective is to help a reader identify unknown words by putting together sounds associated with the graphic symbols, thus saying a word that is known. Various "systems" or approaches to teaching phonics have been advocated, each with varying numbers of generalizations or rules about the sound or sounds that are represented by a letter or group of letters and suggestions for blending of sounds so that a "sounding out" approximating the pronunciation of a word is produced.

Children should not be taught to depend exclusively—or even largely—on phonics for recognizing unknown words. There are simply too many exceptions to many of the rules or generalizations for them to be as helpful as some people state. Too, combining sounds does not always result in approximate pronunciations. Finally, the process may slow the reader down excessively. This slowing down causes a reader to lose the sense of the context and language structure and thus not use the clues these provide. On the other hand, phonics used in combination with structural analysis may be helpful in enabling a reader to gain enough sense of the context to make better use of the clues it and the language structure provide. The key is not

Sources of Further Activities Helpful to Teaching Reading

Learning Activities for Reading, 3rd ed., by Selma E. Herr (Wm. C. Brown, 1977)

100 Individualized Activities for Reading by Nicholas P. Criscuolo (Fearon, 1974)

Reading Activities for Child Involvement, 3rd ed., by Evelyn Spache (Allyn and Bacon, 1982)

Reading Activities for Today's Elementary Schools by Paul C. Burns and Betty D. Roe (Rand McNally, 1979)

Reading Aids Through the Grades, 2nd rev. ed., by Anne Marie Mueser (Teachers College Press, 1975)

What You Can Do with a Word: 300 Classroom Reading Activities by Dorothy Raymond (Academic Therapy, 1981)

to "overdose" children with phonics but to provide them with the phonics knowledge that may genuinely be useful at times.

There are many activities for developing phonics skills. Here are some ideas:

1. Change the beginnings and endings of words to make new words (*man—can; meat—meal; walk—talk*).
2. Underline the common elements in a series of words (the *cl* in *clouds, climb, clap, clang*).
3. Make charts of pictures illustrating words that begin with the same blend (or letter, prefix, etc.).
4. Have children come to the board and point to the letter (or blend or digraph) that begins the word you say.
5. Substitute vowels to form new words (*cap—cup—cop; big—bag—beg—bug*).
6. List "families" of words (*cake, take, lake, make, sake, rake, bake, snake, shake*).
7. Have pupils sort cards with words on them into groups with the same vowel sound (or same beginning sound, ending sound, beginning blend, etc.).
8. Match words with specific sounds at the beginning to words with the same sounds at the end.
9. Add letters to beginning blends to make words (*cr—crash, creek, crazy, creep*).
10. Make lists of new words that contain a part from a familiar word (*shoe—shop, ship, show, shine,* etc.).
11. Pronounce pairs of words (*pay—pat; head—said; cap—hat*) and have the pupils tell in which pairs they hear the same vowel sound.
12. Match cards to make words. Initial consonants may be matched with phonograms (*an, ink, eat,* etc.); suffixes may be matched with bases; or two words may make a compound.
13. Match pictures whose names rhyme (or begin with the same sound).
14. Write words with medial vowels omitted (*r__d, t__n, p__n*) and have children insert as many different letters as possible.
15. Have the children write the first letter or first two letters of the words you say.

THE DICTIONARY. Children should begin to have dictionary experiences as soon as they begin to make and know the names of letters. Not only will they learn many words as they investigate beginning dictionaries (Chapter 13), but they will learn that a dictionary is a reliable source of meanings of unknown words they encounter in reading. While words in the listening/speaking vocabularies of a reader can be recognized and thus meaning determined by the other means suggested, some words they meet cannot, and a dictionary is needed.

A Focus on Comprehension

The ability to read is more than identifying the words that the graphic symbols represent. The purpose of reading is to gain meaning, to comprehend; and comprehension is an active mental process. The printed page itself con-

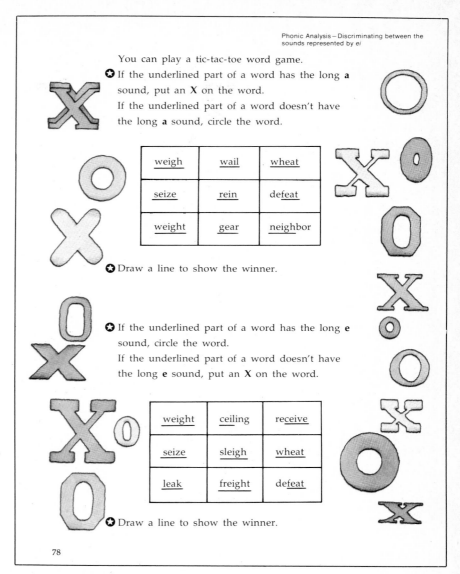

Phonic Analysis—Discriminating between the sounds represented by *ei*

You can play a tic-tac-toe word game.

✪ If the underlined part of a word has the long **a** sound, put an **X** on the word.

If the underlined part of a word doesn't have the long **a** sound, circle the word.

weigh	wail	wheat
seize	rein	defeat
weight	gear	neighbor

✪ Draw a line to show the winner.

✪ If the underlined part of a word has the long **e** sound, circle the word.

If the underlined part of a word doesn't have the long **e** sound, put an **X** on the word.

weight	ceiling	receive
seize	sleigh	wheat
leak	freight	defeat

✪ Draw a line to show the winner.

78

A phonics workbook activity.

tains no meaning. It is just ink on paper. Meaning comes from the mind of the reader. Comprehension requires the reader to relate his or her background of experience and knowledge of how language works to the words that have been recognized or decoded. Comprehension, then, occurs when the reader has a significant background of experience to relate to the content of the reading material and thinks about what he or she both knows and wants to know regarding this content. Thus, the problem in teaching comprehension is one of using and building upon children's experiences, developing vocabulary related to those experiences, selecting reading materials that relate to experiences the reader has had, and utilizing the skills that facilitate comparing the language on the printed page to this experience.

We have emphasized the building of children's experiences in many sections of this book. We have also focused on experiences in building vocabularies in Chapter 4 and elsewhere. This broadening and strengthening of children's experiential backgrounds must be a continuing process if children are to comprehend the contents of their textbooks, trade books, and reference sources. No stage in this process is ever complete, though, unless vocabularies are enlarged. New words—and new meanings of known words—need to be explored and discussed in relation to the new experience as well as to the children's earlier ones and their interests.

In addition to extending their experiences and to providing opportunities for them to gain in language ability, a teacher must equip children with a number of specific skills that will aid them in comprehension: they must know how to read for the main idea, for details, for the organization of the

Building children's experiential backgrounds is an important part of developing reading readiness.

content, and they need to be able to skim, to read critically, to outline, to use the dictionary, and to vary the reading rate (these skills are discussed in Chapter 13). Children must also be taught to go beyond the literal interpretation of what they read. They must learn to do cause-and-effect reasoning, to draw inferences, to arrive at conclusions, and to make generalizations.

Comprehension teaching should begin even before the first reading instruction. In fact, listening to stories and accounts requires many of the skills and abilities of comprehension possessed by the mature and highly effective reader. Comprehension is a thinking activity and should not be thought of as something to teach after word recognition skills have been learned and a storehouse of sight words accumulated. Children seek to comprehend from the beginning what they attempt to read. Thus, instructional attention should always be on reading purposefully, comprehending what is read and assimilating or reacting to it.

All classroom activities that aid the development of children's thinking powers help to improve their reading comprehension. To encourage thinking, of course, the activities must be purposeful, must relate to the children's experiences and interests, and must require some degree of reasoning or the testing of ideas. Here are a variety of activities to use or adapt to your class:

1. Encourage children to raise questions regarding a selection before they read it. Also encourage questioning during and after reading; the focus should be on meaning rather than on words or manner of reading.

2. Ask questions that require more than recalling facts and oral reading in response. Ask judgment and reasoning questions.

3. Question children about cause-and-effect relationships in things they talk about as well as read.

4. Aid children in constructing their own questions they want answered from their reading.

5. Have individual conferences with children to help determine how effectively they are comprehending what they have been reading and to aid comprehension by the exchange that will occur in the conferences.

6. Help children to recognize and interpret punctuation marks in material they read.

7. Ask children to paraphrase or tell in their own words what they have read.

8. Make specific efforts to teach sentence sense, variations in sentence and paragraph order, and organization of sentences, paragraphs, and larger units.

9. Encourage wide reading about topics of interest rather than intensive "digging" in only one source.

10. Have children illustrate favorite events in a story by drawing a picture or by dramatizing.

11. Encourage children to volunteer for oral reports on definite topics of special interest to them.

12. Have many projects going on around the classroom (science experiments, games, seatwork exercises, etc.).

13. Take time to point out and discuss figurative, idiomatic, and picturesque language. Encourage children to find other examples of these forms.

14. Have children describe a place or activity in one word and tell why the word is an appropriate description.

15. Use seatwork activities such as matching:
    • questions with answers in lists.
    • paragraphs with titles.
    • words with their synonyms (or antonyms).
    • pictures with sentences (or words or paragraphs).

16. Other seatwork activities include using selections in which the main idea is to be found, details related to the main idea listed, directions followed, an inference that is justified stated, or a conclusion written.

17. Have children prepare short oral or written summaries of science experiments or social studies units.

18. Have children fill in from words in a list missing words (usually every fifth word) in paragraphs whose content is not too unfamiliar to them.

Reading Rates

Give attention to reading rates in the middle grades.

Not all reading must be done as rapidly as possible. The type of thinking the content requires should determine the rate of reading. Thus, much of the problem in developing effective reading rates centers upon helping the child to recognize the type of reading required—appreciative, critical, or informative. Talking with the children about how different materials, such as newspaper articles, cartoons, science experiments, arithmetic problems, and social studies books, should be read will help. This kind of discussion gives focus to reading purposes.

In addition, direct attention should be given to increasing reading rates. Try timed reading activities. Pick selections with words the pupils are likely to know, and have them read for one or two minutes (gradually increasing the amount of time). Then have the pupils count the number of words read and divide by the number of minutes to get their reading rate per minute. Some testing of comprehension should accompany these exercises.

Oral Reading

Oral reading, in contrast to silent reading, is slow, requires the pronouncing of each word, and is inefficient for many purposes. Its indiscriminate use in a classroom can do much to develop bad reading and listening habits. It is most indefensible in reading activities of the "round robin" or "barber shop" type in which children in a group "follow along" while they await their turn to read aloud. Oral reading, nevertheless, is a form of communication and has a place in the classroom.

There are two types of oral reading: (1) sight reading, in which the reader has not prepared for the oral presentation; and (2) prepared oral reading for communication to and/or enjoyment of an audience. The first type can legitimately be used to determine a child's ability in (1) recognizing and pronouncing words and enunciating their sounds, and (2) phrasing and observing of punctuation marks in the content. This type of oral reading should be done individually, with only the teacher for an audience. It is for assessment and guidance of teaching needing to be done. The second type of oral reading calls for preparation so that what is read effectively relates a story, proves a point in a discussion, answers specific questions, announces something, or seeks to give enjoyment or create feelings, as in dramatic and choral situations. It is communicating to an audience.

Oral reading of the second type requires not only that the reader recognize the words and understand the content, but that he or she convey this understanding to the audience. Because of the need to convey understanding, silent reading (except as noted above) should always precede oral reading so that vocabulary and meaning problems are resolved before the reader faces the audience.

THE READING LESSON

The basis of effective reading instruction is the reading lesson. The lesson is the focal point on which a teacher brings his or her instructional knowledge and ability fully to bear. This requires careful planning for specific purposes and for individual children. We suggest that there are certain essential features involved in lessons—in planning for them, teaching them in a total class setting, modifying them for children with limited reading ability, and integrating them with the remainder of the curriculum. These features are discussed in the following sections.

Lesson Essentials

Naturally, a teacher must be flexible in the techniques used from day to day and from one particular teaching situation to another. Not every lesson should follow the same format; a teacher should show initiative in planning lessons. However, the focus should always be on reading to gain meaning and to interpret and use the ideas presented in print. (Most methods or approaches to teaching reading have this kind of emphasis, the principal exception being those that focus almost exclusively on decoding.) Hence the plan suggested here for daily instruction may be regarded as an outline. The essentials are the following:

I. Developing readiness for the reading activity
   A. Through a discussion of experiences that are related to the material to be read.
   B. Through the introduction of new words and new concepts and the relating of these to known words and concepts.
   C. Through relating children's interests to what is to be read and establishing purposes for the reading.

II. Guiding the first or survey reading of the selection
   A. By asking questions and by responding to children's questions so that the child is motivated to read for the purpose or purposes of the lesson.
   B. Through noting the organization of the selection.

III. Rereading for specific purposes, such as
  A. Answering specific questions.
  B. Doing interpretive oral reading.
  C. Finding specific words or explanations of particular concepts.
IV. Developing important habits and skills
  A. Through direct instruction and practice in using word recognition techniques, comprehension skills, and so forth.
  B. Through the use of workbook and teacher-prepared materials.
  C. Through evaluation of progress and the establishment of further instructional goals.
V. Providing for enrichment
  A. By following up on activities during rereading.
  B. By relating what has been read to interests and needs in other curriculum areas.
  C. By suggesting supplemental readings and other activities.

Planning a Lesson

Even an experienced teacher makes plans; these include writing out reminders of things to do during the lesson, planning the probable sequence of activities, and gathering together needed materials prior to the lesson. An inexperienced teacher should make rather detailed plans—even if the teacher's edition of the children's reader has extensive suggestions. The following indicates the general outline of a reading lesson plan, along with some suggestions regarding each point.

OBJECTIVES. Write out the objectives in terms of what you want the children to know or to be able to do as a result of the lesson. Think about how you will be able to observe what each child has learned. An objective is of value only to the extent that its achievement can be determined. For example, if an objective is to teach the children the meanings of certain words, whether or not they have learned these words can easily be determined.

MATERIALS. List everything you will need for the lesson: books, word cards, sentence strips, objects illustrating new words and concepts, pictures, etc.

TIME. How much time must be spent on this lesson? Is it a lesson that should extend over more than one day?

READINESS. What will you do to get the children ready to do the reading and to learn the new words and skills? If you are going to have a discussion of previous stories in the unit, what will you do to relate the discussion to this particular story? Readiness for the skills to be introduced or practiced must also be considered. Perhaps you will want to write sentences using the new words in a context more familiar to the children. You might need to list words that can help provide configuration (shape) clues, illustrate a phonic or structural principle, or teach a skill that can be used to determine meaning.

READING THE STORY. How much of the story do you plan to have read at a time before discussing it—a paragraph, a page, or some other unit? Or do you want the children to read the story in its entirety before it is discussed or otherwise reacted to? (Beginning readers should read no more than one page before discussing and responding to questions.) How are you going to use the pictures? Will you have the class discuss them to help build readiness? Reading should usually be done silently first, and then orally, but not every line needs to be read aloud. You will need to think about the purposes for specific reading acts. For example, you may list purposes such as the following: Read to find out why everyone in the picture is laughing. Now find out what happened next. See what the story tells about this picture.

SKILL DEVELOPMENT. The portion of your lesson devoted to skill development should include structural analysis and phonics activities, vocabulary building exercises and activities, and work on comprehension skills. Some of this can be done before the story itself is read. However, you may want to see if the children can independently identify or determine the meanings of words that are new to their reading experiences. If they cannot, this may mean that a phonics principle (for example) needs to be discussed, examples given, and the relation to known words and other principles shown after the actual reading is completed. Workbook activities are usually closely tied to this portion of the lesson and should be used. Examine the workbook activities as you plan the lesson, however, to determine their suitability to your purposes and their relationship to the teaching procedures you must plan for yourself.

EVALUATION. Don't wind up your lesson by asking, "Did you like the story?" Instead, discuss the mood or plot of the story, how the story relates to real life, etc. Plan evaluation in terms of the objectives. Are you going to give the children a worksheet in which they match words and definitions? Are you going to ask questions requiring answers that show understanding of the story read? What are these questions?

ENRICHMENT. There are usually enrichment suggestions in the teacher's editions of reading textbooks at the end of either a story or a unit. Typically these suggestions include books that are related to the story or unit, films or filmstrips that extend understanding and build further interest, and dramatic activities that relate to the reading. These enrichment suggestions should always be considered. While it may not be feasible to use all of them, those that can be utilized should be. Sometimes, too, the suggestions will cause you to think of other things to do.

MATERIALS AND INSTRUCTIONAL
APPROACHES

Reading instruction has been of educational concern for so long that a great quantity of reading materials has been developed, along with many procedures, methods, and approaches. Yet many teachers are faced with the task of caring for the needs of individual children without adequate materials. It is not unusual, either, for a school or district to purchase an excess of "packages" or "kits" of limited scope, rather than books, and then to have all children "put through" this material, which some or all of them don't need; thus many learn little or nothing from the experience. However, a teacher sometimes does have a choice of books and other materials (possibly from a district or school resources center) and always has a good bit of freedom regarding their use.

At the present time there are many approaches to teaching reading, each reflecting a philosophy and a definition of what reading is. Those most commonly used advocate similar fundamental procedures. Differences are often in the sequence of the teaching of specific skills, the stress placed upon the use of particular skills, the rate of introduction of new words, the amount and kinds of grouping for instruction, and the supplemental activities advocated. There are, however, rather large differences in the materials used in the approaches.

The following sections describe several approaches to teaching beginning reading (and beyond the beginning stage in a few cases) that are widely used. There are variations in all of these depending on the material or some author's or advocate's description of the approach.

The Basal Reader Program

The large majority of schools use one or more sets of books called a basal reader series. One source has identified 33 "major basal reading series," which indicates the quantity of materials published, the market for reading materials, and differences in points of view as to how best to teach reading (although, as suggested above, procedures are quite similar to one another). The principal premise underlying the use of a basal reading series is that systematic grading or sequencing of the reading skills is possible and necessary. That is, a basal series seeks to control the manner in which various skills are introduced, the sequence of their introduction, and the extent and timing of the reinforcement practice given for each skill. In addition, a basal series controls the vocabulary the child meets and the practice given on this vocabulary.

The first materials in a basal series are readiness workbooks, picture cards, and sentence and word strips that can be used to build the first stories and to teach the first sight words. Readiness materials are followed by preprimers, which use the words introduced in the readiness materials and which often contain stories with the same characters as those in the readiness materials. (Some of the more recently published basal books do not use the same characters and story line and introduce words and concepts not taught in the readiness materials.) A typical preprimer may have from

⊗ Read the sentences.

Carol Price was learning to sew. She practiced her stitches on anything and everything in sight. Here are some of the things she fixed.

⊗ Each sentence below tells what a person is thinking. Write the number of each sentence beside the matching picture.

1. Wearing these socks will be impossible.
2. Perhaps more stuffing will help the rag doll.
3. At least the rip in the jeans is mended.
4. None of the other members of the team will have a sweater like this.
5. Buttoning this shirt will not be easy.

118

Basal programs include workbook activities.

From *Skills Book*, Level 9, of *The Laidlaw Reading Program*, Second Edition, Copyright © 1980 by Laidlaw Brothers. Used by permission of the publisher.

twenty to fifty or sixty different words in it, which generally means that each word is repeated frequently, giving the child practice in recognizing it. Most basal series have three or four preprimers.

The preprimers are followed by a primer (usually the first hardcover book in the series), which continues to introduce new words and to give practice on those previously introduced. After the primer comes the graded series; usually one book is identified as level one (in schools with grade levels, the readiness materials, the preprimers, the primer, and the level-one book would ordinarily be completed by a child in grade 1), and there is a first-level and second-level book for each higher grade.

Since the competition among companies publishing basal reading programs is very keen, there has been a great increase in the amount and kinds of materials available to complement and supplement the core program found in the children's books and dealt with in teacher's manuals. Most companies have workbooks intended to aid in the development of specific skills and to provide practice in using them. These are frequently supplemented with duplicating masters of practice exercises, pretests, and posttests. Some series have filmstrips, records and cassettes, and supplemental books (sometime paperbacks) as part of their program. A few have computer software to supplement the teaching of some skills and to aid teachers in keeping records on children's progress.

Teacher's guides or manuals remain rather prescriptive in regard to use of the materials, but there is some recognition that teachers may need to modify the procedures suggested. A teacher should use his or her best judgment regarding the relevance of these procedures to the needs and capabilities of specific children.

Particularly noticeable in the newer basal programs is the emphasis given to eye appeal. The pictures are colorful and interesting. There is also a good deal of attention paid to picturing people of different races and ethnic groups and to variety in the reading content (including more than only middle-class families).

Although the instructional plans of various basal series are not alike, they do generally provide for preparational activities (introduction of new vocabulary, setting purposes for reading, establishing experiential backgrounds), silent reading to get the sense of the story, oral reading to check on the use of specific skills, the introduction to and practice of specific skills, and enrichment activities (supplemental reading, related arts, building additional experience backgrounds, etc.).

As has been stated, basal reading programs have been the subject of a great deal of criticism. Yet many teachers have used them quite successfully, and they are not likely to be replaced as the major resource for teaching reading. There is simply too much to be said for a systematic program that does not leave the teaching of skills and vocabulary to incidental encounters. We believe that the value of organized and planned teaching outweighs the criticism directed at basal series. Fortunately, though, the bases for much of the past criticism have been eliminated.

The best approach for most teachers, in our opinion, is that given in a basal program, but the basal program should be a balanced one. That is, it should not unduly stress phonics or any single word recognition skill, depend heavily on seatwork to develop the skills and abilities a reader needs, stress the learning of words over the comprehension of sentences and longer elements of discourse, or ignore either literature or informational content in its books for children. A high-quality basal program can be modified and supplemented in many ways to accommodate the *real* children in a classroom and the differences in abilities and personalities of teachers. It can and should be adapted to meet individual needs. It can be supplemented—and, again, should be—with many experience stories, trade books, and materials related to all areas of the school curriculum.

The Language-Experience Method

Experience charts can be written about:

daily classroom plans
the "news"
individual experiences of the children
group exercises
classroom helpers and tasks
school or playground rules
stories and poems that have been told or read
directions for doing something
sensory experiences—feeling, tasting, seeing, hearing
classroom pets
the weather

The language-experience method utilizes the experiential backgrounds of the pupils and their abilities to express themselves orally for the content and form of the reading materials. The basic premise of this method or procedure is that children need to see the relationship among speaking, writing, and reading. The procedure also stresses the idea that reading is for communication and that children want to tell about, write about, and read about their experiences. The feeling is strong among advocates of this approach that children will be successful in reading what they have actually written themselves and that the experience of failure will then be avoided.

There is no attempt to specify the content of stories by any means except the children's experiences. Thus, although a story in a basal reader might tell about an experience of a suburban family or an event in the life of a city youngster, an experience story can be about anything the children (or an individual child) want to tell about and then read. There are no vocabulary controls in the method, although a teacher may help to see that certain words are repeated in the content of the stories children dictate and some words will be repeated simply because they are used so frequently in everything that is said or written. There is no attempt to structure the sequence of skills taught from one reading experience to another.

Most teachers have routinely written stories that children dictated and have used these stories in their instruction. However, the uniqueness of the language-experience approach when it is the only approach or method used is that the reading skills are taught as they emerge from the story writing and reading. The responsibility for the program rests heavily on the teacher. Children's experiences are utilized in the stories, so many experiences must be provided to keep children's interest high.

The exclusive use of the language-experience approach is criticized because the children are reading content they already know about—they aren't reading to find out anything new. Critics also bring up the possibility that children will not learn all of the reading skills they will need to recognize unknown words and to react inferentially and critically to the content. However, whether in an exclusive program or not, using experience stories (and not just in teaching beginning reading) is a good way to teach composition, build vocabulary, maintain interest, and individualize instruction. The language-experience method is also particularly useful with children who need remedial treatment, who speak a nonstandard dialect, or who have had experiential backgrounds that are difficult to relate to the content of the reading series textbooks.

The Individualized Approach

Since children differ in ability, background, and interests, and since they learn at different rates and in different ways, there is reason to believe that each one should be allowed to progress at his or her own pace and to the extent of his or her own capacity. Many critics of basal reading programs maintain that it is difficult, if not impossible, for proper attention to be given to such differences if basal reading materials are used, particularly if they are used exclusively. Thus there is a strong feeling among some of these critics that individual children should select for themselves the books they want to read and be permitted to set their own pace and to follow their own interests. This is the essence of the individualized approach.

Reading authorities who advocate individualized reading suggest that at least 100 books be available to children at the primary level and as many as 500 to those in the intermediate grades.

This approach requires that many books be available for the children to choose from and that the selection be of a wide enough scope (in terms of the difficulty of the reading materials) that children can read extensively at whatever level of development they have achieved. The approach also requires that the teacher determine whether all the skills are being taught. In successful individualized programs, the teacher spends a great deal of time conferring with pupils individually—listening to them read orally, talking about what they have read, helping them attempt a book of greater difficulty, and teaching skills directly.

What appears to some critics of this approach to be an unstructured program is, in fact, a highly organized way to teach reading. A classroom teacher who uses the individualized approach should be a skilled diagnostician, able to determine quickly which skills the child needs additional help with and which ones have been mastered. The teacher must also be familiar with activities that develop skills and have available a wealth of prepared work materials to aid in the teaching.

Some teachers give their initial instruction in a language-experience format and then move into the individualized approach. Still others begin with the first books of a basal series. From the beginning, skills are developed on the basis of needs (the development might actually be done in small groups), with the teacher keeping records of each child's progress. Good record keeping is an integral part of effective individualized programs.

Two widely used individualized programs are published by Random House and Scholastic. Examine these—and others.

The individualized concept has been seized upon by many commercial concerns, resulting in many sets or packages of materials. This development is understandable, since the key to an individualized approach is that a large number of books be available for the children to choose from in their reading. Thus, companies have produced packages containing a wide variety of books (most often paperbacks) of varying levels of reading difficulty about many subjects of interest to children. In addition, the commercial materials provide forms for the record keeping an individualized program calls for, suggestions to teachers for using the program, and synopses of the stories.

In many ways the packaged individualized programs resemble the basal programs. The guide materials for teachers are not unlike basal readers' teacher's manuals, and there are cassettes, records, filmstrips, and tests with some programs. They are unlike basal programs, however, if the child is truly free to select what he or she reads.

The most effective individualized programs in our view are those in which there are many books available and the teacher is very competent. He or she must know the books thoroughly and must be a well-organized individual and a keen observer of children. Without such a teacher, packaged materials will not solve all of the instructional problems, although they are likely to produce results far better than those produced by a less effective teacher with an inadequate number of suitable books.

Programmed and Systems Approaches

Programmed instruction provides for the presentation of subject matter in small units, with each presentation calling for a response from the pupil. In true programmed instruction, each response is followed by an indication to the pupil of whether his or her response was correct or incorrect and what he or she should do next. The theoretical base for programmed reading materials is that the process of learning to read is a sequential one, the elements of the process are identifiable, and the order of their presentation is determinable. The objective of the programming is to permit each child to learn at his or her own rate—learning each skill before going on to a new one.

The programmed materials most recently put on the market are software for microcomputers. With the certain increase in the number of computers in schools, the number of these programs will undoubtedly increase. It is probable, however, that these materials will be largely of a supplemental nature to classroom teaching—that is, drill on word identification and comprehension skills. It is wise to select and use such programs very carefully, making certain not only that they seek to teach the skills and abilities needed by readers but that learning transfers as readers engage in reading books.

These newer programmed approaches are very much like the ones developed in the late 1960s in that they attempt to combine an individualized approach with a diagnostic-prescriptive system. Their mechanical nature (like that of the earlier, less sophisticated ones) holds fascination for children, and they will capture the attention of children for learning some skills—attention that a teacher often has been unable to get. The key point, though, is whether these children can and will then read material that is not on a screen.

Proponents of these programs stress the importance of following the program exactly and completely. They also emphasize the value of reinforcing learning, which the sequential steps provide for, and of giving pupils the opportunity to correct mistakes and remedy weaknesses immediately. Critics of programming are generally disturbed by its impersonal approach. They also question whether the skills necessary for effective reading can be taught by a machine, whether the programs are really used in an individualized manner, and the cost factor. There does seem to be evidence that some schools attempt to justify the cost of materials by putting all pupils through the program.

However, the advantages of programmed instruction should not be overlooked because of a reluctance to accept its mechanical type of teaching. Too often in traditional programs specific skills are neither well taught nor reinforced. Often, too, pupils do not have much feedback concerning what they are learning or how well they are learning it. And, of course, a great deal of teaching is unsystematic and without defined objectives. Programmed instruction at least attacks these faults.

Other Programs and Materials

See *Television and the Classroom Reading Program* (International Reading Association, 1973).

There are various other commercial programs available, some of which advocate approaches similar to those described. Often, though, these other less-than-well-known programs differ from basal programs in their materials. For example, so-called phonics programs emphasize the sequential and systematic teaching of phonic generalizations, and the materials in these programs reflect this emphasis. The modified alphabet programs seek to simplify the sound-symbol problem caused by English spelling, and their printed materials naturally use these alphabets. Some programs labeled "linguistic" emphasize the gradual introduction and extensive repetition of sound-symbol relationships, with the sentence structures in the books of these programs showing this emphasis. More recently this emphasis has shifted so that some programs labeled "linguistic" or "psycholinguistic" stress the pupil's use of his or her syntactic and semantic knowledge to gain meaning.

While not meant to teach reading skills, there are also many materials available that are identified as enrichment programs. These are essentially literature programs; they seek to develop interest in reading, to produce lifetime readers. In addition, there are many meant to supplement various types of programs. However, no commercial materials or any program under whatever name will teach children to read. The teaching must be done by a teacher who has definite goals, knows a variety of procedures, and reflects a genuine understanding of children's needs and abilities.

EVALUATION

Evaluation in reading is more than administering standardized reading and general achievement tests. Evaluation in reading involves making judgments about teaching procedures and pupil performance—judgments that are based both on children's performances on commercial and other types of tests and on observations made of children's reading behavior. Evaluation should *not* be a once- or twice-a-year activity; it should be a continuing process—a process that is very much a part of teaching.

Observations

Observations of children's reading should be made regularly. In fact, an observational evaluation should be a part of every reading lesson. There should, though, be system to evaluation by observation so that the result will be more certain to be recalled. This system can be very simple. A notebook with a page for each child permits notation regarding word identification stumbling, failure to observe punctuation marks (and which marks), phrasing difficulties in oral reading, and so on. The notations made should be as specific as possible since future instruction should be based on them. The alert teacher will observe children's reading at all times during the school day, noting such things as the use or nonuse of a dictionary or reference sources, library books chosen (and whether they are actually read), and problems a child appears to have in doing seatwork.

Individual reading lessons and interviews make possible detailed notations. Frequent interviews with children in which they talk about what they have been reading and problems they have had are especially useful both for noting something that has not been observed earlier and for providing clues about things to watch for in future observations.

Observation results may also be recorded on checklists and charts. Using these may simplify the noting of things observed. For example, children's names may be listed on a checklist which provides spaces for checking how each one is achieving in using various decoding skills or in reading for details, main ideas, etc. Teachers often have two or three types of checklists in order to note items related to all of the program objectives. Examples of types of checklists are given in other chapters.

Informal Reading Inventories

Another informal but systematic procedure for determining the levels of children's reading abilities and the problems they may have is the Informal Reading Inventory (IRI). Commercial reading programs often include such inventories for various reading performance levels, but teachers frequently decide to make their own because they know the abilities and interests of the children in their classes. Essentially an IRI consists of selections of several levels of difficulty chosen from basal readers other than those used in the instructional program. If the inventory focus is on word identification skills, the children read the selections aloud, beginning with the least difficult. The teacher marks on duplicate copies of the selections the errors made—substitutions, omissions, inversions of word order, miscallings, repetitions, etc. The selections may also be read silently and followed by questions directed at determining how well the children have comprehended the content. These questions, prepared in advance, should not be of the "yes" or "no" variety and should include ones which require critical thinking or judgment.

Standardized Tests

Most standardized tests are group tests that provide quantitative data as to how a child's work compares with either the achievement of a norming sample of children or a preestablished standard of performance. Standardized reading tests do not tell a teacher what he or she needs to do about improving the reading performances of individual pupils. They do provide

Helpful references on reading testing include the International Reading Association's *Tests of Reading Readiness and Achievement: A Review and Evaluation* (1969) and *Measuring Reading Performance* (1974).

a teacher with information as to the general level of achievement of his or her pupils in comparison with other pupils with whom logically they might be compared.

There are many standardized reading readiness and achievement tests on the market. Selecting a test appropriate for a particular group of children, the program objectives, and the procedures used is a substantial task. Attention should be given to the standardizing procedures the test-maker used, the population of children used for determining norms, the ease with which the test can be administered and scored, what the test purports to measure, and so on. Also, a teacher and others concerned about the testing (school administrators, for instance) should know what the test results really show and have clearly in mind how the results will be used.

A FINAL WORD

Sometimes, because of society's concern about children learning to read, teachers become too tense about the very important task of teaching reading, and they use materials and spend time and effort that may not actually help. Reading is a complex process, as we stated earlier, but it is one that every child of reasonably normal intelligence can and should learn. We strongly believe in the interrelatedness of the language arts and therefore have included suggestions in almost every chapter in this book that in reality bear upon the teaching of reading. However, you may want to examine several of the many textbooks devoted solely to the teaching of reading for additional suggestions.

References

Aukerman, Robert C., and Aukerman, Louise R. *How Do I Teach Reading?* John Wiley and Sons, 1981.

Burns, Paul C., and Roe, Betty D. *Reading Activities for Today's Elementary Schools.* Rand McNally, 1979.

Downing, John, and Leong, Che Kan. *Psychology of Reading.* Macmillan, 1982.

Durkin, Dolores. *Getting Reading Started.* Allyn and Bacon, 1982.

Farr, Roger, and Roser, Nancy. *Teaching a Child to Read.* Harcourt Brace Jovanovich, 1979.

Hall, Mary Anne. *Teaching Reading as a Language Experience.* 3rd ed. Charles E. Merrill, 1981.

Lapp, Diane, and Flood, James. *Teaching Reading to Every Child.* 2nd ed. Macmillan, 1983.

Mangieri, John N.; Bader, Lois A.; and Walker, James E. *Elementary Reading.* McGraw-Hill, 1982.

Mason, George E.; Blanchard, Jay S.; and Daniel, Danny B. *Computer Applications in Reading.* 2nd ed. International Reading Association, 1983.

Silvaroli, Nicholas J.; Kear, Dennis; and McKenna, Michael. *A Classroom Guide to Reading Assessment and Instruction.* Kendall/Hunt, 1982.

Smith, Frank. *Understanding Reading: A Psycholinguistic Analysis of Reading and Learning to Read.* 3rd ed. Holt, Rinehart and Winston, 1982.

Tinker, Miles A., and McCullough, Constance M. *Teaching Elementary Reading.* 4th ed. Prentice-Hall, 1975.

Teaching Resources

FILMSTRIPS

Bookmark Reading Filmstrips. Harcourt Brace Jovanovich (6 color sound strips and 6 cassettes for each grade 1–6).

Consonants: How They Look and Sound. Filmstrip House (16 strips and records; primary and intermediate).

Phonics Practice. Science Research Associates (2 strips).

Reading. Pacific Productions (sets of color strips on phonics, structural analysis, comprehension, etc.; total of 41 strips).

What's the Word? Houghton Mifflin Co. (12 strips on contextual aids, phonics, and structural analysis).

KITS

Auditory Discrimination in Depth. Teaching Resources (sound filmstrip, cassette, blocks, cards).

Comprehension Skills Series. Jamestown Publishers (booklets and cassettes).

Mix-and-Match Games. Teaching Resources (game boards and skills cards; grades 2–8).

The Primary Reading Series. Bowmar/Noble (booklets, worksheets, tests; grades K–3).

Reading for Every Day: Survival Skills. Sunburst Communications (activity cards, masters, guide; grades 4–7).

SCORE. Prentice-Hall Media (filmstrips, cassettes, stories and game book with tape, guides).

Silver Edition Skill Builders. Reader's Digest (supplemental readers; 4 at each level 1–6).

Specific Skills Series. Barnell Loft (booklets, teacher's manual, test package, etc.; several levels).

SRA Reading Laboratories. Science Research Associates (kits of graded reading selections and exercises for comprehension, speed, and listening for each grade level 1–6).

COMPUTER SOFTWARE

Prism. The Psychological Corp. (disks compatible with several microcomputers; grades 2–8).

Reading Comprehension: Our Weird World. Lakeshore Curriculum Materials (8 disks; available for several microcomputers; grades 4–6).

OTHER AIDS

Basic Word Sets. Barnell Loft, Inc. (36 titles; teacher's manual, tests, record sheets, and spirit masters).

Dolch Basic Sight Cards; Dolch Basic Phrase Cards; Consonant Lotto; Vowel Lotto; Group Sounding Game; Sight Syllable Solitaire, etc. Garrard Publishing Co.

High Interest/Low Readability Activity Program. Sunburst Communications (25 books, 25 activity cards, and teacher's guide).

Individualized Reading Instruction. Love Publishing Co. (games and activities).

Listening-Reading Program. D. C. Heath (records of completed and unfinished stories, response sheets, and teacher's manual; kits for grades 1–6).

Reader's Digest Reading Skills Media Centers. Reader's Digest Educational Division (skill-builder magazines and cassettes).

Reader's Digest Science Reader. Reader's Digest (6 books; grades 4–6).

Activities for Preservice Teachers

1. Examine, compare, and evaluate the diagnostic and evaluative suggestions in several basal reading series. Be ready to report to the class.

2. There are many more commercial materials available than those listed in this chapter. Check library and materials center sources for others that could be added.

3. Select two standardized reading tests and compare them as to content; quality of directions; ease of administration, scoring, and interpreting results; and standardization procedures used.

4. Outline a plan for teaching reading to a hypothetical class for one week. Show in the outline how you would include elements of individualized, basal, and language-experience approaches.

5. Examine two or three series of basal readers. Compare the vocabulary loads, linguistic emphases, story content, illustrations, and teacher's manuals.

6. Present arguments in favor of using an individualized approach to reading instruction rather than a basal program.

7. Locate and examine commercial reading materials identified as "linguistic" or "psycholinguistic." Report to the class your findings and impressions.

8. Observe a group of kindergarten or beginning first grade children for differences in verbal facility, social-emotional stability, and physical coordination. Consult the list of questions suggested in this chapter as you watch the children.

9. Design exercises for children (grade level of your choice) to practice finding the main idea, selecting details, and determining the organization.

Activities for Inservice Teachers

1. Identify situations occurring over a period of a week in your classroom in which purposeful oral reading by children could have been included but was not. Discuss this with your peers in the class.

2. How do you define reading? Is your definition now the same as it was when you began teaching? If not, to what do you attribute the change?

3. Write a critique of one reading lesson from a basal series and the corresponding teacher's manual suggestions. What would you add to or delete from the lesson and/or suggestions? Include your response to that question in your critique.

4. Investigate software for microcomputers related to reading instruction. The Mason reference should aid you in starting the investigation.

5. If you are grouping children for reading instruction, examine the advantages and disadvantages of your grouping system. Then work out a plan for making improvements. You may want to consult other teachers as well as educational literature for assistance.

6. Identify the reading levels and some of the interests of your class. Then, accompanied by two children acting as teacher's aides, go to the library and borrow for one month as many books (or more) as there are children in your class. With the children's help, set up a reading interest center and begin an individualized, free-time activity which stresses reading for relaxation and enjoyment.

7. Secure copies of reading tests, such as the California Reading Test, the Developmental Reading Tests, the Gates MacGinitie, and the Iowa Silent Reading, and consider the possibility of using them in your class. Before examining them, decide what you want to determine by testing.

8. Examine recent publications of the International Reading Association—including copies of the journals. Report to the class about your examination. How valuable are these publications?

Independent Activities for Children

1. Children like to work with a friend. Try "buddy reading." The pairs select books (with teacher guidance) and find a corner or other place in the classroom where they take turns reading to each other.

2. To give individual children reading practice, prepare cards that children can read and then respond to by:
a. Writing answers to questions about the selection.
b. Following directions.
c. Listing particular details given in the selection.

3. Have a small group (three or four) of children compare a science textbook for their grade level written in the 1960s with one written in the 1980s. They can compare tables of content, indexes, and the emphases given to topics. Their conclusions should be reported to the class.

4. The best "independent reading" activity for children is reading. A section of the room where a child can go to find a book or to read alone is very important. The fare from which he or she may choose must be varied and appealing, and time must be provided for "just" reading.

5. Type descriptions of items pictured in catalogs or magazines, making sure the language is appropriate for the abilities of the children. Cut out the pictures and have pupils match them with the descriptions.

6. Activities such as the following can be done by individual children or small groups for structural analysis practice:

a. Match cards with root words written on them with other cards containing prefixes or suffixes.

b. Write in the missing inflectional suffixes in sentences. For example:

We are go _____ to town.
This is the small _____ of the three balls.

Put the sentences on cards and place them in a file.

c. Prepare cards containing various words with common base forms. Have the child separate the cards into base-word categories. Words might be *green, greener, greenest; report, portal, portage, import;* etc.

d. Word cards can be sorted into those with particular endings (*-ed, -ing, -ness,* etc.), particular combinations of letters (*ake, ime,* etc.), or particular beginnings (*b, gr, str,* etc.).

7. Supply children with maps, graphs, and charts suited to their level and ask them to interpret the information provided.

8. Similar activities can be constructed for auditory discrimination and letter-sound association practice.

a. Prepare sets of unlabeled pictures. A child can then group them according to the initial or final sound of their names.

b. A child can sort words on cards according to the number of syllables in the words, words containing syllables that begin with a particular letter, those that rhyme, etc.

9. Prepare a bulletin board (one the children can reach) in which each section shows a letter or combination of letters. Under each section thumbtack a box. Children can find pictures of objects whose names begin with the letters and place them in the correct boxes. This activity can be varied. For example, instead of showing letters, the bulletin board sections can contain pictures. Another variation is to find pictures with names whose ending sounds match the letters on the board.

13 | *Reading and Study Skills*

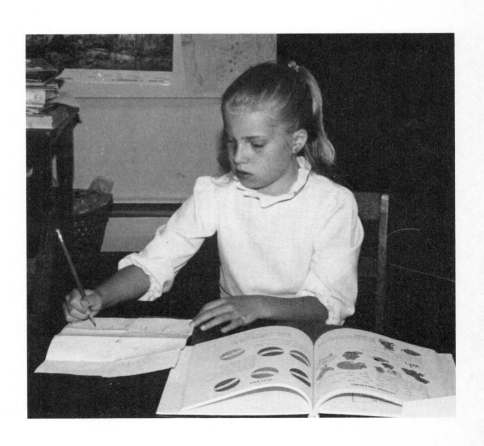

Study skills are not the exclusive domain of the language arts program. They are an integral part of teaching—and learning—in every curriculum area and at every grade level. When a kindergarten teacher asks, "When we go out to peek at the nest in the big mulberry bush, what are we going to look for? How will we have to behave?" he or she is laying the foundation for good study procedure by helping the children to set both purpose and method. In the fourth grade, a teacher may say, "Before you start to write your paragraph, make a list of the things you want to include. Then decide what should come first, second, and so on." This teacher is helping children to organize. Both are guiding children toward techniques that will aid them in learning effectively and independently. This guidance is one of a teacher's most important tasks.

LEARNING TO STUDY

Academic success or failure is often determined, or at least strongly influenced, by a student's knowledge of how to study—his or her ability to use the study skills. Time and again parents are told by a teacher, "Marie would do better if she worked harder." But "working harder" may not be very meaningful to Marie or her parents. They may well assume that it means she needs to spend *more time* studying—and possibly it does—but it may also mean that what she really needs is to learn *how to study*.

There is no reason to believe that children enjoy being failures any more than the rest of us do. It is the school's job to give them the tools with which they may achieve success. Important among these tools are the study skills, and these must be systematically and carefully taught, not left to incidental learning. This chapter will discuss particular skills needed and suggest ways in which they may be taught.

Assignments

Properly made assignments are an important part of teaching children how to study. Suppose, for example, that you write on the chalkboard a notation something like this:

Homework
Social Studies—read pages 140–145.

If this is the extent of the assignment, most children will probably read the pages because they are supposed to, but how much real learning will take place? What will the individual child remember from what has been read? On the other hand, such a notation may merely be a reminder to the children after you have thoroughly introduced the assignment. In fact, a visual reminder of page numbers, questions to be answered, etc., is good reinforcement. This may be written on the chalkboard (preferably with more than simply page numbers) or dittoed and given to the children as a study guide, or pupils may keep notebooks in which they jot down page numbers and other pertinent information about assignments. This is a good habit for them to form, particularly in the upper grades.

Well-made assignments are an integral part of planning for instruction.

To be truly meaningful, an assignment must guide study so that the desired learnings will occur. It should tell the child *what* he or she is supposed to do, *why* it is to be done, and *how* it is to be done. This requires more than simply assigning page numbers; it includes providing motivation, filling in necessary background, and giving specific purposes for the lesson. Suppose, for example, that pages 140–145 in the social studies text concern the colonial Southeast. The assignment might involve the following three steps:

I. *Motivation:* This could take the form of discussion centered around questions such as the following:

A. When we talked about the colonization of the New World, we discussed how the different colonies were founded. Do you remember how Virginia and the Carolinas began? What about Georgia and Florida?

B. Do you suppose life in the southern colonies was the same as that in New England or different? In what ways might it have been different?

C. What is the climate like in the South? Might this have anything to do with the crops they raised and the way they made their living?

D. We know that slavery developed in the South rather than in the North. Can you guess why?

II. *Background:* This might include briefly reviewing pertinent facts that the children may have forgotten, possibly listing the names of the southern colonies, and introducing new terms and vocabulary.

III. *Specific Purposes:* No assignment is complete until the children have specific things to look for as they read. You might duplicate or write on the board several questions to guide their reading, you might use some or all of the questions that are found at the end of a section or chapter in the text, or you might suggest the following procedure:

A. As you read, notice the headings in dark print. Turn each of these into a question and see if you can answer it in one or two sentences. For instance, on page 141 you see the heading "Important Money Crops in the Southeast." Turn this into a question: What were the important money crops in the Southeast? Read the paragraph and see if you can answer the question in one sentence.

B. As you read, try to discover one particular topic that you would like to find out more about and report on the rest of the class. A list of suggestions is on the board, but you may be able to think of another topic that would make a good report.

The example above not only illustrates one way of making an assignment meaningful but also shows how the language arts can be integrated with other curriculum areas. As previously stated, study skills should be taught in all areas; this particular assignment may lead to a need for library skills (see Chapter 14), skimming and locational skills, organizational skills, and speaking or writing skills. In addition, this assignment gives practice in the linguistic activity of turning headings into questions; the reading skills required to find details, discover the main idea, or answer specific questions; and even vocabulary, spelling, and handwriting skills. Needed review should be a part of reading, spelling, handwriting, and language periods, and certainly the preparation for oral or written reports should be the subject matter of the language arts class.

The three steps listed above—providing motivation, furnishing needed background, and outlining specific purposes—are vital to every type of assignment and every grade level. Even in the primary grades, where study is largely supervised, it is important to remember that children learn more readily when they know what they are doing and why they are doing it. For example, suppose a group of third graders are preparing to read "Miss Tibbett's Typewriter." Perhaps you might provide motivation by printing on the chalkboard " oday we are going o read a s ory called 'Miss ibbett's ypewri er,' " and asking the children "What is wrong with this sentence?" If they do not at first discover that only one letter is missing, print other sentences, or perhaps several children's names, each time with only one letter missing (not necessarily the same one in each).

This story can be found in *Secrets and Surprises* (Macmillan, 1980), pp. 210–223.

Most third graders will have seen many typewriters, but few will be familiar with the actual operation of one or with the way the keys are arranged, so you should have a typewriter on a table where children can group around it and examine it. Point out that both the capital and lowercase forms of a letter are on the same key, and call attention to punctuation marks and the arrangement of letters at each level. Children will probably want to know why the letters are not arranged alphabetically; show them how the most used letters are placed where they are easiest to reach, and demonstrate (if you can) the fingering used by trained typists.

Take advantage of opportunities to involve non-teaching personnel in classroom activities. The school secretary might be delighted to demonstrate the use of the typewriter for this story.

In this way, both motivation and background are provided, and children are ready to read the story with pleasure and understanding to find out what happened as a result of the missing letters and which letter was missing after each repair job. These questions, of course, furnish purpose.

These steps can be adapted to suit almost any kind of assignment or activity, whether it be solving an arithmetic problem, planning a field trip, or preparing for a science experiment. Obviously, variety may—and should—be introduced; nothing could be duller than to have every lesson, even for only one subject area, presented in exactly the same manner. Motivation, for example, might include reading a story or poem, bringing in a group of pictures, showing a film, or simply reminding the class that "We decided that we ought to write for some materials for our science experiment" (more opportunities for integration). Similarly, specific assignments must be varied; converting topic headings into questions is a valuable study technique for children to learn, but they would soon lose interest if they were asked to turn every topic heading in a textbook into a question.

Study Steps

Discourage reading only to find answers to specific questions through thought-provoking questions that call for more than factual information and discussions centering around *why, how, what was the result,* etc.

In addition to the guidance provided in assignments, a child in the middle grades needs help in learning certain study steps to use either in reading a textbook or in doing independent reading. A number of systems for reading and retaining written material have been advanced, and in keeping with current fashion, most are known by their acronyms—e.g., PQRST, POINT, EVOKER, PANORAMA. The number of steps in these may vary, but for most purposes good study procedure boils down to four basic points:

1. *Preview:* Read the introduction if there is one. Look at section headings, pictures, maps, graphs, etc. This will help you to get an idea of what the chapter (selection, unit, story) is about.
2. *Purpose:* Read the questions at the end of the chapter (and/or questions prepared by the teacher as a part of the assignment) *before* reading the chapter itself. This will help you to know what kind of information you are looking for—it establishes a purpose for reading.
3. *Read:* Read the chapter carefully, keeping in mind the questions to be answered.
4. *Review:* Read the questions again, and see if you can answer them. If not, review necessary sections. Or, look at section headings again, turn each into a question, and try to answer it in one or two sentences. For some assignments or for particularly difficult material, you may wish to use both of these methods.

Encourage children to jot down questions that come to mind as they study. These may be points requiring clarification or topics for discussion and further exploration.

When these steps are first introduced, children will think they are time consuming and therefore not worth using. But if you can persuade them to try this method, they will discover that they read faster because they know what information they are looking for, and that they are better prepared to take part in discussions or to report on their reading.

Children should also be shown that these steps can be adapted to many kinds of assignments and activities and can help them in many ways. The preview technique can be adapted for selecting a book for pleasure reading—a child might read the first few paragraphs, look at chapter headings and illustrations, and perhaps skim a page or two here and there to get a fairly reliable impression of whether he or she would enjoy reading the book. Or the child might use this technique to discover whether a particular article or book contains the information needed for a report. In this way, children may learn how to avoid wasting time reading something that is not suited to their particular purposes.

In a similar way, children may learn that establishing purposes for reading—that is, beginning with specific questions in mind—is also time-saving. The child who knows what he or she is looking for and who uses the preview method will be able to prepare a better report because the time spent will be devoted to fruitful efforts.

Further, the review step furnishes an excellent way to study for tests. Far too many students, even in high school and college, spend the night before an exam trying frantically to reread all the material covered; using the, suggested review method will not only refresh one's memory, but will reveal those sections that do need to be read more closely.

LOCATING INFORMATION

In addition to learning how to study, children need to learn certain skills that will help them to locate information quickly and easily. Library skills are discussed in the following chapter; those presented here are alphabetizing, using the dictionary, and note taking. Many of the activities suggested are directly related to reading, reading and spelling readiness, and handwriting; some involve using picture dictionaries, learning initial consonants for reading, and learning visual and auditory discrimination skills helpful to reading and spelling. Learning is more meaningful when curriculum areas are interwoven, and constant reinforcement of skills is necessary for lasting learning. Keeping these two principles in mind, as well as the needs of the individual children in your class, will aid you in planning a program and selecting activities that provide real learning situations for the children.

Alphabetical Order

Children must know the alphabet thoroughly to use a telephone directory, a card catalog, a book index, an encyclopedia, or a dictionary both rapidly and efficiently. Activities for helping children learn letter names and alphabetical order are used principally in the primary grades, but the intermediate grades teacher should not ignore them, since it is possible (and in some situations even probable) that some fifth and sixth grade children will not have this skill.

In the early grades, the letters of the alphabet should be visible to the children throughout the school day. You might want to sing the ABC song as part of your opening exercises. Stress left-to-right order at the same time, using a pointer or yardstick to indicate each letter as it is sung.

Primary children can also make their own ABC books, using pictures cut from magazines or catalogs. Assigning children to locate a picture of something that begins with B or some other letter can make them feel very important. Judgment should be exercised about using a picture of bread or a block; some teachers prefer not to use these "blend" pictures.

Large sheets of paper can be used to make a class ABC book, either before the children make individual books or at the same time. Use any available wall space to post the individual pages, being sure to keep the letters in alphabetical order and to show both the capital and lowercase forms for each letter. As the children bring in pictures to paste on the pages, they will be practicing pronunciation, learning to work cooperatively, and gaining skill in finding the letters quickly. An activity such as this will add color to the room and will promote interest among parents if it is started before "Open House" time.

Many ABC books should be kept on the library table in the primary classroom. Read to the children from these, encourage them to "read" along with you, and allow pupils to look at them individually. A few are listed here; the librarian can suggest others.

Chess, Victoria. *Alfred's Alphabet*. Greenwillow Books, 1979.
Crews, Donald. *We Read: A to Z.* Harper and Row, 1967.
Elting, Mary, and Folsom, Michael. *Q is for Duck.* Clarion Books, 1980.
Federico, Helen. *ABC*. Golden Press, 1974.
Feelings, Muriel. *Jambo Means Hello: Swahili Alphabet Book.* Dial Press, 1974.
Fujikawa, Gyo. *A to Z Picture Book.* Grosset and Dunlap, 1974.
Grant, Sandy. *Hey, look at me!* Bradbury Press, 1973.
Lobel, Anita and Arnold. *On Market Street.* Greenwillow Books, 1981.
Moncure, Jane Belk. *Magic Monsters Act the Alphabet.* Children's Press, 1980.
Ruben, Patricia. *Apples to Zippers.* Doubleday, 1976.
Tobias, Hosea, and Baskin, Liza. *Hosie's Alphabet.* Viking Press, 1972.
Wall, Elizabeth. *Computer Alphabet Book.* Bayshore Books, 1979.
Wildsmith, Brian. *Brian Wildsmith's ABC.* Watts, 1963.

Select ABC books with more in mind than the purpose of teaching letter names and their sounds in words. Certainly this is their primary purpose and it should be uppermost in your mind, but there are other purposes as well. *Brian Wildsmith's ABC* could be selected for its illustrations alone; *We Read: A to Z* uses the letters of the alphabet to introduce concepts which primary children need to understand (Ii is for inside, Ll is for left); *Q is for Duck* introduces the letters through riddles (A is for zoo because animals live in the zoo; Q is for duck, of course, because they quack). The latter might prove useful in the second or third grade with children who need reinforcement or are still having trouble with letter names and sounds, as might *Jambo Means Hello*—its softly colored illustrations and words in the Swahili language add variety and introduce children to another culture. The city child will like *Hey, look at me!*, which uses actual photographs of city children performing actions which begin with the various letters: Digging, Eating, Splashing, Itching, etc. There is an alphabet book suitable to virtually any child, but of course there should be a variety available so that children may broaden their experiences.

You can help children become familiar with letter names by such a simple procedure as calling letter names when you have them line up for lunch, to make teams for a game, or for some other real purpose: "If your name begins with T, line up." Use either first or last names, or vary for different purposes. An alphabet-soup party can also add spice; some children may not know about alphabet soup and they will have a great deal of fun with it. This might be combined with a health unit in which the children plan a lunch and make their own butter and applesauce to go with the soup—another opportunity for combining areas of the curriculum.

An alphabet procession game, using old shoe boxes, can help children to associate the letter name with its written forms. For this, put a letter (both capital and lowercase forms) on each box. The children then bring from home inexpensive articles to place in the boxes. For example, the C box might have a comb, a toy car, and a candle in it. During free time children can empty two or three boxes, mix up the contents, and then place the articles in the boxes according to beginning letters. Articles placed in the boxes should not be valuable or expensive, and it is important to stress that

Urge parents to share alphabet books with their children.

Keep the "room alphabet" on display during all alphabetizing activities.

everything in a box belongs to someone and may not be taken by another person—children often have a crow-like tendency to pick up bright objects!

From the very beginning, children should be made aware of the difference between capital and small letters. At the primary level, they should begin to learn that their names, the names of the streets they live on, and the name of the school begin with capitals, while the names of most of their possessions begin with small letters. Also, as you write sentences on the board, point out that each sentence begins with a capital.

A number of activities can be devised with a pack of 5×8 cards and a magic marker to write the letters—one set of capitals and one set of lowercase letters. Begin with something simple, such as distributing the cards and then designating a pupil who stands and says, "I am capital D. Where is small d (or capital S, or any other letter)?" The child who has this letter identifies himself and asks for another, and so on. Later the children can place their cards in the chalk tray in alphabetical order as they are called. Another game with cards calls for holding up a card and asking a child to name an object that begins with that letter. For example, a small b might produce *bear, bunny,* or *box,* and a capital D could result in *Dorothy* or *Dr. Dolittle.* An activity of this type is good to use just before lunch or before children go home. Once they have the idea, they can play in small groups when they first come to school in the morning or when they have free time during the day.

Games are also useful in teaching letter sequence. Perhaps you might say "I am the letter after d (or I am the letter between k and m). Who am I?" The child who identifies the letter then gives the next clue, and so on.

This type of game is fun as a beginning activity, but it is likely to have the same disadvantage as the old-fashioned spelling bee—the children who get the most practice are those who need it least. To avoid this, turn again to the 5×8 cards mentioned earlier. Shuffle these and pass them around the room until the entire deck has been distributed. Then say, for instance, "Capital S, go to the front of the room." As soon as this child has done so, ask the children with the two letters that go before S to go to the front, then the two that come after. This could be varied by dividing the class into teams, one using the capitals and the other using the small letters. Points could be given for completing the sequence first.

The teaching of alphabetical order can be combined with practice in handwriting. On the chalkboard or a chart, place rows of letters, with one letter missing at the beginning or end of each row. The children copy these, filling in the missing letters:

abcde__   __bcdef

This can also be done with uppercase and lowercase letters:

A__B__C__D__   __a__b__c__d

After the children become proficient at this, let them work with only one letter as a cue—for example, __g and g__. Later they may move to __k__ and __ __c, __ __z. The "room alphabet" should remain visible during this activity so that children can check themselves if they are not sure of the correct order. Incorrect habits should not become established.

Exercises such as those suggested above can also be placed on ditto sheets to furnish practice for children who need recurring experiences with alphabetical order. Actually writing all the letters in order provides reinforcement for the learning and gives more handwriting practice, but it is more time consuming for both teacher and pupils. Thus it might be wise to keep a box of dittoed exercises that those children who need extra practice may use at odd moments during the day.

Alphabetical order and handwriting can both be combined with other areas of the curriculum. Perhaps in health class children might make a list of green vegetables. The next day for handwriting they could copy this list from the board, placing the words in alphabetical order. This activity is meaningful, and it will keep those who are working on it busy, freeing you to work with small groups or individuals.

Most of the activities suggested in the preceding paragraphs are principally intended for the early primary grades, though, as mentioned before, if children have not learned alphabetical order, practice is appropriate at any grade level. To supplement those suggested previously—or variations of them—a few more exercises suitable for the later primary or middle grades are listed below.

1. Have each reading group keep a dictionary to which individual children add their new words daily, placing each word neatly under the correct letter. These words will serve as a reading review and as a beginning dictionary for a child to refer to for the spelling of a word needed in writing. Or, if you prefer, each child may keep a personal dictionary.

2. When teaching about the telephone, make a class directory in connection with a handwriting lesson. Children can copy the names and numbers from the board in alphabetical order, probably doing only a few each day until the directory is completed. Addresses may or may not be included, depending on the age of the children.

3. From the picture file, select pictures showing things whose names begin with a variety of letters. Hold up a picture, and let children tell you the name of the picture, the letter the name begins with, and whether that letter is found at the beginning, the middle, or the end of the alphabet. A card with this information on it can be stapled to the back of each picture so that children can play the game when they have free time. Or cards can be separate, and children can match them with the pictures.

4. After children know letter names and sequence, begin having them alphabetize words by second letters, and later by third letters. Using reading, vocabulary, or spelling words for this exercise will make it more meaningful and help to fix words in the children's minds.

Dictionary Skills

Test yourself:

Can *you* turn quickly to the portion of a dictionary where a specific letter is located?

Although dictionary skills are usually taught in the fourth grade, children should begin in the first grade to learn the uses of this valuable tool. Every primary classroom should have at least one picture dictionary, and children should have specific instruction in its use. Begin by making certain that they understand the relationship between the illustration and the printed word, as well as the arrangement of the words in the book. As they begin to write, help them to discover how the arrangement helps them to find words quickly and how the dictionary can help them to find the correct spelling of words they want to write.

As children progress through school, their knowledge and use of the dictionary will increase. In other words, dictionary usage is a developmental activity in which skills are taught, reinforced, and added to as children move through the elementary grades. These skills and understandings fall into four general categories.

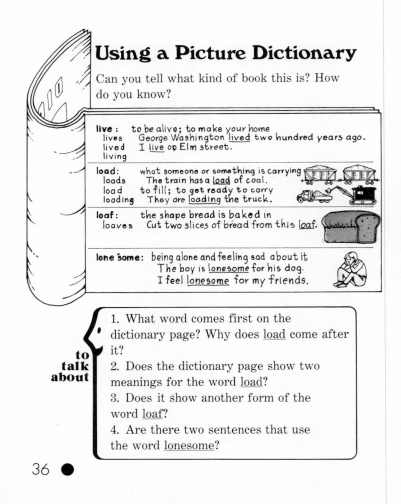

Using a Picture Dictionary

Can you tell what kind of book this is? How do you know?

live : to be alive; to make your home
lives George Washington lived two hundred years ago.
lived I live on Elm street.
living

load : what someone or something is carrying
loads The train has a load of coal.
load to fill; to get ready to carry
loading They are loading the truck.

loaf : the shape bread is baked in
loaves Cut two slices of bread from this loaf.

lonesome : being alone and feeling sad about it
The boy is lonesome for his dog.
I feel lonesome for my friends.

to talk about

1. What word comes first on the dictionary page? Why does load come after it?
2. Does the dictionary page show two meanings for the word load?
3. Does it show another form of the word loaf?
4. Are there two sentences that use the word lonesome?

36 ●

Using a dictionary may begin in the primary grades.

The first category is that discussed in the preceding section—alphabetical order. Children should recognize early that not only dictionaries but nearly all other references they will use are arranged in alphabetical order by the first, second, third, etc., letters in the words. Thus efficient use of a dictionary requires a virtually automatic familiarity with letter sequence, as well as with the relative positions of letters (the d's come in the first third of the dictionary, the y's in the final third, and so on).

The second category involves understanding the particular characteristics of the dictionary that aid one in using it efficiently. Children should learn to use guide words to locate the page on which a word may be found and that words are listed by their base forms (*have* is listed, but *having* is not).

The third group consists of pronunciation aids provided by the dictionary: accent marks, phonetic respellings, diacritical markings, and key words. In this connection, children also need to understand how syllabication is shown and how it is useful to pronunciation and to division of words in writing.

Finally, there is much information other than definitions and pronunciations that the dictionary can provide. It may give abbreviations, synonyms, antonyms, variant meanings of words; it may show related forms, irregular plurals, principal parts of irregular verbs, meanings of prefixes, etc.; and it may contain many special features, such as tables of weights and measures, a gazetteer, a list of foreign words and phrases, and so forth.

Beginning Dictionary Activities

The activities suggested here are intended for several levels of dictionary users. There is a general progression from the general and simple skills to the more specific, although many of the activities can be used in varying ways and at varying levels. Select those which appear suitable for the children in your class, and supplement them with others of your own devising as they are needed.

1. Make a large chart-size classroom picture dictionary by having the children bring in pictures, which are then pasted on the chart with the name of the picture (*cat*, *house*, etc.) written below. Both capital and lowercase letters should appear at the top of each page. Refer to this picture dictionary throughout the day when talking to the children about words.

2. Have the children make individual picture dictionaries. Since they will need help writing the words, it would be wise to limit this in some way. For example, each child might bring only one picture per day—or he or she could bring several, but select one to be used for the dictionary. An orderly way of organizing the activity is to progress through the alphabet, with each child bringing an A picture the first day, B the second, and so on. Each day the words are written on the chalkboard as the children name their pictures (undoubtedly there will be many duplications) and then copy them from the board. It is a good idea to have a supply of old magazines for those who have not been able to find a picture or have forgotten to bring one. Be prepared to improvise, too—help a child to draw a large question mark for Q, color a yellow flower for Y, or draw a picture of a zebra.

Picture Dictionaries

Charlie Brown Dictionary (Prentice-Hall, 1973)
The Macmillan Picture Dictionary (Macmillan, 1983)
My First Picture Dictionary by William A. Jenkins and Andrew Schiller (Scott, Foresman, 1982)
My Picture Dictionary (Ginn, 1977)
The New Color Picture Dictionary for Children by Archie Bennett (Children's Press, 1981)
The New Golden Dictionary by Bertha Morris Parker (Western Publishing Co., 1977)

3. Individual picture dictionaries are also helpful to older children who do not know letter names or alphabetical order or who are having difficulty with reading.

4. Word and picture associations can be strengthened by using words from reading lessons. Have the children find pictures named by the words, paste them on 5 × 8 cards, and print the words below. Children can shuffle the cards and then arrange them in alphabetical order.

5. Some picture dictionaries have category words together—*farm, city, people, animals,* etc. The children may want to bring in pictures for categories they select. Although this does not involve alphabetical order, the activity does help promote early organizational skills.

6. Select a word from a picture dictionary and ask one child to find it for you. This child then gets to select a word and ask another to find it.

7. From the picture file, select several pictures of objects whose names are in the picture dictionary. Show a picture to the class and say, "I can't spell the word for this picture. Who can find it for me in the picture dictionary?" After doing this a few times, leave the pictures out so that children can play the game in small groups.

8. Point out the glossaries in books the children are using. Help children to develop the habit of looking up the word meanings needed for comprehension in reading.

9. As children progress in their dictionary skills, they may begin using a dictionary such as those listed on this page. Such dictionaries usually have sections explaining their use, and some have teacher's guides and/or exercises to give children practice in using dictionary skills.

10. Teach new vocabulary words associated with the dictionary itself. Show and explain *entry words, guide words,* and *definitions.* It might be helpful to make a bulletin board showing a sample page from the dictionary, with the guide words, entry words, and definitions labeled.

11. Have the children write on 3 × 5 cards questions that can be answered by using a dictionary and then exchange questions. Each child finds the answer, writes it on the back of the card along with the number of the page where the answer was found, and then reads it to the class. (Encourage good sentence formation, handwriting, capitalization, and punctuation on the cards.) Make a tree of knowledge on the bulletin board with these cards. The following are a few sample questions:

Does a badger wear a badge?
Does a foothill wear a shoe?
Could a person play an oboe?

12. Select a list of words from your readers. Have the children divide the words into syllables and place the accent marks where they feel they should go. Then have them check their answers in the dictionary.

13. Randomly select a guide word from the dictionary and say the word. The first child to find that word gets to say a guide word for the others to locate.

14. Write phonetic spellings of several words on the board. Children are to determine what each word is and then write a sentence using it. Allow them to use the dictionary to check their answers.

15. Children can make their own glossaries of library, social studies, health, or science words.

Beginning Dictionaries

Ginn Beginning Dictionary (Ginn, 1973)
Macmillan Beginning Dictionary (Macmillan, 1981)
Macmillan First Dictionary (Macmillan, 1981)
My First Dictionary (Houghton Mifflin, 1981)
Scott, Foresman Beginning Dictionary (Scott, Foresman, 1979)
Webster's Elementary Dictionary (American Book, 1977)
Weekly Reader Beginning Dictionary (Grosset and Dunlap, 1973)

16. Have the children learn a word a day, with each child getting a turn to select the word. The others locate it in the dictionary, discuss it, record the meanings and part (or parts) of speech it may be, and write a sentence or two using it.

17. To develop speed in locating letters in the dictionary, give a letter name such as I. The child who opens to the letter I or closest to it gets to say the next letter.

18. Children in the upper intermediate grades should be taken to see the different dictionaries in the library. Allow them sufficient time to look through these and discover their special features.

19. Have children compare a dictionary with a thesaurus and list differences and similarities in both format and use.

Other Activities and Exercises

Children who have had a great deal of practice in using the dictionary from the time they first began to read should not need much teaching of dictionary skills in the middle and upper grades. However, some children have not learned to use this valuable tool—and all may need occasional refresher practice. Many of the activities suggested in the preceding section can be used in, or adapted for, the middle and upper grades; in addition, language texts often contain units on the use of dictionaries and other reference tools. But it may also prove helpful to keep a file of dictionary exercises to be used by one, several, or all of the children when specific skills need to be learned or reinforced. The suggestions below can be adapted to fit the needs of particular classes.

Commercially prepared masters designed to reinforce dictionary skills can be time-saving, but be sure they fit the needs of your children.

1. *Guide Words:*
   a. You might run into the words below when studying about airplanes. Find each of the words in your dictionary and write the two guide words that are on that page.

Word	*First guide word*	*Second guide word*
autopilot		
runway		
pressurized		
jet propulsion		
air drop		
beacon		
radar		
ceiling		

   b. *Nest* and *new* are the guide words on page 268 in a certain dictionary. Underline the words in the following list that would be found on this page.

lake	nerve
net	neither
neutral	nail
neglect	nettle
nestling	next

2. *Syllabication and Accent:*

a. Divide the following words into syllables and place accent marks where they belong. Use your dictionary if you are not sure. When you are finished, use the dictionary to check *each word,* even if you are sure you were right.

galaxy	lunar	geography	continent
atmosphere	astronaut	mountainous	ocean

b. Sometimes two-syllable words are accented on the first syllable when they are nouns and on the second when they are verbs. Look up the following words and write three sentences for each, using a different meaning in each sentence. In each underline the syllable which should be accented.

conduct	compress	project	contrast

3. *Diacritical Markings and Key Words:* After each of the following words, write the phonetic spelling you find for it in the dictionary. Be sure to show the accent and the diacritical marks above the vowels. In the third column write the key words that will help you to pronounce each word. Be prepared to pronounce each word correctly.

Word	*Phonetic spelling*	*Key word(s)*
menace	_____	_____
vegetation	_____	_____
mammal	_____	_____
locust	_____	_____
debris	_____	_____
swarm	_____	_____
rubbish	_____	_____
larva	_____	_____
mesquite	_____	_____
retrieve	_____	_____

4. *Selecting Appropriate Meanings:* In front of each sentence below put the number of the meaning which fits that sentence. Use the word in four other sentences, one for each of the four meanings.

sup-port (sup-port'), v. 1) To hold up; to keep from sinking or falling; as, pillars support the porch. 2) to bear; to endure; as, he could not support the pain any longer. 3) to take sides with; to back up; as, to support a candidate. 4) to provide with food, clothing, shelter, etc.; as, he supports his mother.

1. She could not support the suspense any longer.
2. Many people must support a man to get him into office.
3. She helped to support her family by working after school.
4. The shelf was supported by braces.

5. *Finding Correct Spellings:* Below you will find the phonetic spellings of a number of words. Using your knowledge of the way various sounds may be spelled, find these words in the dictionary and write their correct spellings. [For this exercise be sure to use the phonetic spellings that are found in the particular dictionary that your children use. Select words that have appeared in reading they have done or that might appeal to them. Begin with simple words that the children know and work up to those which might be spelled in a number of ways—pneumonia, physical, pylon, heather, etc.]

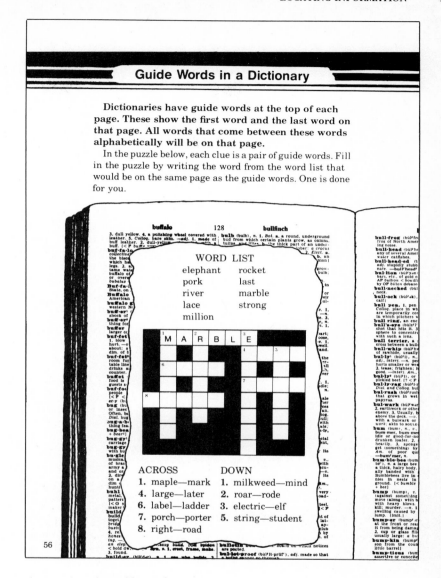

An exercise using guide words.

From *Using Our Language Workbook*, 1977 edition, Level 4; copyright © by Bowmar/Noble Publishers, a Division of The Economy Company. Used by permission of the publisher.

These exercises are intended, of course, as examples only. Wherever possible, practice in using the dictionary—or any other reference tool—should be done in connection with actual needs. For example, new words in a science unit might be used for finding diacritical markings and phonetic spellings—and meanings, too, of course.

Note Taking

The abilities required for taking effective notes are essentially those required for reading comprehension—getting the main idea, selecting supporting facts or important details, putting ideas into sequence—plus the ability to skim. These skills are discussed in later sections of this chapter. Even at the primary level, however, there are many activities that can help children to develop the habit of organized thinking which is so necessary to these skills. For example, children can compose titles for pictures. Discuss the pictures first, then let them suggest various titles and select the most appropriate one. They can also help to make charts showing what to do during a fire drill, who is responsible for various housekeeping chores during the day or week, or what activities are planned for the week. Following a trip, have the children dictate while you write an experience chart that lists what was observed and learned. After a story, ask them to recall the events; list these on the board in sequence. Or read a short description to the class and have them draw pictures, supplying as many of the details as they can. (You may need to read the description more than once.)

As children advance in reading and writing skills, group activities can be used to help them learn how to take notes. Before such an activity begins, however, the children should be helped to develop standards for note taking. At first these may be quite simple.

TIPS FOR NOTE TAKING
1. Decide exactly what you want to find out.
2. Write down only important facts on the particular information you are looking for.
3. Use your own words. *Do not copy*.

With the standards firmly in mind, try these activities:

1. From one of the class texts choose several paragraphs that are particularly easy to take notes on. (This is an opportunity to integrate; don't simply select at random, but choose material that you had planned to assign anyway and that the children will be expected to understand.) Have all the children read the material and take notes, reminding them of the standards that have been established. After all have finished, select several to go to the board and write what they have written. Compare these and compile a composite, letting the children decide which facts to include and add any important information they think has been omitted.

2. Use an opaque or overhead projector to show a brief article from a magazine or book. Again, this should be something that pertains to the curriculum. Follow the procedure suggested above, or use the projector to show individual children's notes. (Papers should be handed in without names, so no child will be embarrassed.)

3. Have children take notes as a film is shown. Before showing the film, write on the board a list of questions for which they should find answers. After the film, have each child use his or her notes to write answers to the questions. The questions should include some that call for specific information and some that require drawing inferences.

Note-taking skills facilitate independent learning.

4. Use films and recordings on tapes or cassettes frequently to give children practice in noting only important details or finding answers to specific questions. This will help them to avoid the usual tendency beginning note-takers have to write down everything they read or hear, since the time will be controlled. Do this regularly throughout the year in connection with units of study in content areas, making sure always to provide guidance by giving children specific information to look for.

5. Have children watch specific television shows or particular kinds of shows at home and take notes on advertising techniques, use of dialects, new vocabulary words, etc. Let children who have seen the same show compare information and prepare a group report for presentation to the class.

6. Let individual children who need practice work with tapes or cassettes in the listening center, making sure that they have questions to guide their listening. Allow them to stop the tape or replay portions in order to find the information they need, just as one would reread a portion of a book or article.

In the middle and upper grades, children will be preparing reports to give to the class, and for these they will need to use reference materials obtained from the library. Since the individual child will be using several sources and will be investigating different sources to discover material, standards will need to be more refined and inclusive:

1. Skim. Glance through the article to see whether it contains information that is important to the report.

2. Write down the name of the book, author's name, and page numbers on which the information is found. For encyclopedias, write the name of the encyclopedia, volume number, subject heading, and page numbers.

3. Write down only the important facts or the particular information you are looking for. Use your own words; *do not copy.*

4. If you do wish to use the author's words for some particular reason, use quotation marks and *write down the exact page number.*

Point out to children that these steps are really only an adaptation of the study steps suggested on page 355.

5. Check names, dates, and figures for accuracy.

6. Skim once more to see if you have missed anything important.

When children first start making individual reports based on notes they have taken from several sources, teacher guidance is particularly important so that they learn to locate materials quickly and to select the important information, as well as to avoid the pitfalls of unintentional plagiarism and forgetting to write down sources.

ORGANIZING AND REPORTING INFORMATION

The skills required to write the actual sentences and paragraphs of a report are essentially those required for any writing; these are discussed in Chapter 8. Of particular concern to the total report are organization, language level, and giving credit to sources of information.

Outlining

Perhaps the most difficult point in preparing a report comes when a child has collected the information needed and is ready to begin writing. Faced with what seems to be a welter of disorganized facts, the child must somehow put them in order. The solution is to use an outline.

Actually, all writing should begin with an outline. Even before beginning to collect information for a report, either oral or written, a child should make a tentative outline; it will serve as a guide in deciding what information to look for. The outline may be quite brief and certainly it may need to be revised in light of the information found, but it does provide guidance. In the same way, the child who is going to write a business letter should jot down ideas about what items to include and the order in which they are to be placed. In writing a story, there is need to plan the sequence of events and provide for the inclusion of those details that will be important to plot development and reader interest. Such outlines can be very informal, but children should learn that preplanning not only saves time but results in better organization and thus more effective writing.

Not only written activities but all the activities of the classroom at every grade level need organization. Children should learn at an early age that they cannot even have a successful class picnic without planning what they will need and who will provide it. Later, they should be shown that a written outline can help keep a speaker from omitting important points, that outlining study notes can be helpful in studying for a test, and so on.

READINESS ACTIVITIES. The following activities are suggested for helping primary grade children develop the ability to find the main idea, locate supporting details, and determine the sequence of events in what is read or heard.

Coordinate the teaching of listening skills with activities such as these.

I. Main idea
   A. Readiness books contain many pictures, most of them designed to assist children in gaining the main idea. Use these for discussions of "what the story is about."
   B. Using picture books such as *Rosie's Walk* by Pat Hutchins, have children tell what is happening in each picture, then see if they can tell what the whole story is about.
   C. Bring in pictures and ask the children to tell the main idea each one illustrates.
   D. Show a picture and have the children dictate a story about it. Write it on chart paper and evaluate it with the class as to its accuracy and completeness in telling about the picture.
   E. When you have finished reading a story to the class or when they have finished reading one, select a child to pretend he or she is sick in bed. A second child visits the sick classmate and tells the story heard in school that day.
   F. A variation of this is to have one child pretend to be a parent; the second comes home and relates the major happenings of the school day.
   G. Select an animal every week. Have the children dictate daily stories about the made-up adventures of David Donkey or Harry Hippopotamus, for example. When the daily story is completed on the experience chart, children select a title (main idea) for that story.

II. Details
   A. Take the children for a walk in the schoolyard or to another room in the school (gymnasium, principal's office, another classroom), first telling them that they will be asked to describe what they saw. On returning, list on the chalkboard all the details they can recall. Use questions to elicit specifics: What was on the principal's desk? What did the principal look like? Were there pictures on the wall?
   B. Before reading a story to the class, tell them that when the story is finished they are to draw a picture of their favorite part. Remind them to listen carefully so that they can include every detail they need.
   C. Homework for a primary grade child could be to study something in his or her home, paying particular attention to details such as size, shape, color, and texture. The next day the child may describe the object in detail, with the other children trying to guess what is being described.
   D. Ask one child to stand up, walk around the room, and then stand at the back. Have children describe his or her appearance without turning around to look. Include details such as color of eyes, type of shoes, etc.
   E. Help the children make a mural of something they are studying, such as different types of homes for humans. Details will be important in the pictures. When the mural is completed, the children may dictate experience chart stories describing the houses. Children may also draw their own pictures of the different houses and copy the experience stories. Both can be put into individual books which may be taken home.
   F. Show children a simple article such as a sweater, then put it away and ask them for words that describe it: soft, gray, old, buttons, collar, etc. (Not all need be adjectives.) Show the article again and let the children decide which words are appropriate.

III. Sequence of events
   A. After reading a story such as "The Three Billy Goats Gruff," ask children what happened first, next, and last.

B. In connection with teaching children to tell time, make up ditto sheets of clocks or have children draw clocks. Help them to place the hour and minute hands on the correct numbers to show what time they come to school, what time they have lunch, and so on throughout the day. The children can then draw pictures of themselves performing a particular activity underneath the clock that shows when that activity takes place. Start with the early morning hours and do one clock a day. It is possible that some children may come from homes where no one pays much attention to time. Be patient and consistent in your efforts to teach time sequence.

C. Questions of a cause-and-effect nature help children to understand the importance of sequence. Use such questions as listening purposes: "As I read this story, listen for the one event that caused Harry to get into trouble. Listen and remember what happened to him because of that."

D. Teaching the days of the week and months of the year helps children to become aware of sequence.

E. Tape or staple comic strips to cardboard. Cut them apart and place them in envelopes. During free time children can place the comics in correct sequence.

F. Ask children to name all the holidays that occur during the school year and then put them in the order in which they occur.

PRIMARY GRADES. Children can become familiar with outline form in the early grades. The outline below entitled "Our Trip" illustrates the type of outline that might be put on the chalkboard or on a chart for pupils to see. They should participate in preparing it, although they may need help in putting the statements into the correct form.

I. On the bus
   A. Stay in seats.
      1. Talk quietly to neighbors.
      2. Keep hands inside.
   B. Do not eat.
      1. Keep food in a bag.
      2. Don't trade food or bags.

II. At the zoo
   A. Find the animals that live in a warm climate.
   B. Find the animals that live in a cold climate.

III. Return to school
   A. Write a report about the zoo.
   B. Draw pictures.

Opportunities for using outlines in planning and reporting class activities are numerous. For instance, directions or plans for a class picnic or luncheon can be outlined on the board. Or, when children have finished reading or listening to a story, ask them to dictate the first main idea, details, and sequence, then the second main idea, and so on. Write these on the board or on chart paper; then reread the story to check the outline form. This kind of activity will help demonstrate to children how their own stories can be improved if they jot down their ideas and organize them into a meaningful sequence. As a follow-up, have them suggest several story ideas; then, with you as scribe, they can decide on a series of events and select the supporting details for each. At first, simply list the suggestions; then work with them to organize these into an outline for the story. Several of these might be written on charts to serve as models. The final step is to use one of them as the basis for a class story. You might divide the class into groups, having each group either develop one of the outlines or make their own outline and write a story from it.

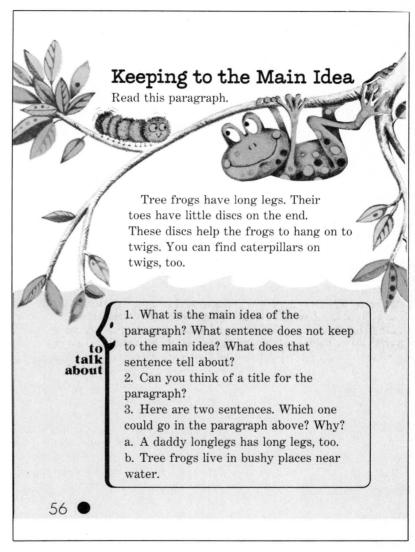

Keeping to the Main Idea

Read this paragraph.

Tree frogs have long legs. Their toes have little discs on the end. These discs help the frogs to hang on to twigs. You can find caterpillars on twigs, too.

to talk about

1. What is the main idea of the paragraph? What sentence does not keep to the main idea? What does that sentence tell about?
2. Can you think of a title for the paragraph?
3. Here are two sentences. Which one could go in the paragraph above? Why?
a. A daddy longlegs has long legs, too.
b. Tree frogs live in bushy places near water.

56 ●

Organization is important to all communication.

MIDDLE GRADES. Outlining must have a purpose to have value to children. Many children will outline simply because they are told to, but it is important to convince them that outlining has value whenever they sit down to write or whenever they plan for something they are to talk about.

Outlining form can best be taught through use of a chalkboard, chart, or overhead projector. Although the use of an outline is the most important point for a child to learn, some attention needs to be given to outline form and why such form is followed. The following should be taught:

I. Use Roman numerals for main topics—the most important points.
    A. Indent and capitalize letters for subtopics.
        1. Use Arabic numbers for the details.
        2. Because you have one, you need at least one more detail about subtopic A.
    B. This is another subtopic of Roman numeral I.
        1. Give one detail about B.
        2. One B detail needs a second.
II. List another main topic.
    A. Subtopic.   Details may or may not be needed here.
    B. Subtopic.   Again, if there are two or more parts or details, there will need to be a division of the subtopic.

A common experience such as a movie is excellent for teaching outline form. The movie should be carefully selected with a view toward its suitability for outlining, and preparation should be thorough so the children will not be frustrated in selecting important points. Before the movie begins, the class should be instructed to take notes so that they can outline the content when it is over.

Once the movie is over, ask the children to tell what they saw or learned, and write everything they say on the board. The next step is to organize the information—select the first main idea, then the details, the next main idea, details, and so on until everything has been covered. As the children select the main ideas and details, help them to make the outline, using the overhead projector or chart paper. When the lesson is completed the children can copy the outline and file it in a booklet of "Movies I Have Learned From" or with pictures, reading notes, etc., from the same unit. Naturally, the outline and movie should be an integral part of a particular unit of study—there is no point in showing a film or making an outline that does not pertain to anything the class is doing.

The discussion of content area subjects in class also provides good opportunity for teaching the value of outlining. As discussion takes place, write in outline form any information that you want the class to remember. The children can copy it in their notebooks and use it as a basis for study.

UPPER GRADES. Continue to give upper grade children practice in outlining skills if they appear to need it and to insist that outlining precede both oral and written activities. Show your own reliance on this skill by outlining important facts on the board as you discuss them, by distributing written outlines of a projected plan for a unit of work, etc.

At this level, children may need help in correlating information from several sources for an oral or written report. If they do, the following procedure should prove helpful:

1. Using an overhead projector, show three different articles about the same subject. All should contain some common information, but each should include facts not found in the others.

2. Have the children take notes on each selection. This may be a group effort, with notes being taken on the chalkboard.

3. With the children's help, outline the notes from each selection.

4. Make a composite outline, including important points from all three. You may wish to have the children place numbers (1, 2, 3) in parentheses after each point, both to illustrate how the material is correlated and to help them locate information quickly if they need to refer to the articles in writing their summaries (step 5).

5. Have each child use the outline to write an individual summary of the information obtained from all three selections.

Preparing Footnotes and Bibliographies

A first grader is often heard to say, "My teacher says . . ." or "My father told me . . ." This is the foundation for learning that we depend on sources outside ourselves for much of what we know. As the same child learns to read and write, he or she will refer to a dictionary for the meaning or spelling of a word and later will consult various references for needed information—especially if this sort of searching is encouraged. Help children to recognize that no one—not even you—knows everything, that what we know today, and what we will discover tomorrow, is built on knowledge that has been accumulated by others. As they begin to use reference materials in preparing reports, help them to understand that appending a bibliography strengthens a report in two ways: first, if a writer has authorities to back up what is said, the reader will know that the subject has been studied and that the writer knows what he or she is talking about; and second, the bibliography gives readers the opportunity to find out for themselves if they doubt the information or wish to learn more about the subject.

Children love big words, and there is no reason why they should not use the word *bibliography* to show their sources. In the beginning, form should be simple. A chart may be used to help with the punctuation and with the spelling of *bibliography*.

BIBLIOGRAPHY

Adams, Richard. *The Story of Canada*, pages 21–26.
The World Book, Vol. C, pp. 1166–1195.

By the time children reach the sixth or seventh grade, they should be ready to include slightly more information in bibliographies. For example, the items given below should probably be included. Again, charts should be used to help with punctuation and order of items; children should not be expected to remember these, especially since various authorities suggest different punctuation. We suggest that the punctuation items and order given in the language text the class uses be the guide.

Trade Books	Encyclopedias	Periodicals
author	title	author (if named)
title	most recent copyright date	title of article
publisher	volume number or letter	title of magazine
copyright date	pages	date
page numbers		pages

In the upper grades, some children may learn how to use footnotes. Generally in the elementary grades there is little need to require the use of footnotes, particularly for anything other than direct quotations. In a short paper, the source of a particular item of information can be found, if needed, by checking the bibliography or the pupil's notes. They will later learn that in longer papers it is sometimes desirable to footnote certain types of information that is not directly quoted; however, elementary school children should *never* be assigned to write long "term papers." The important learning involved is the ability to correlate information from several sources and to organize it into a well-written report; if subjects are sufficiently limited in scope, children can concentrate on organization and good form in writing rather than sloppily throwing together a great volume of information.

As mentioned earlier, standards for note taking should be established as soon as children begin to take notes from reference materials, and one of these should always be a prohibition against copying. Point out to children that borrowing words is like borrowing books: people do not write their own names in books borrowed from friends or from the library; neither should they pretend that someone else's words are their own. As they begin to write longer reports and take notes from several sources, some children may find it less time consuming to copy some information than to rephrase every item. This is the time to point out that notes can become extremely voluminous (and therefore more difficult to organize later) if too much copying is done. It is also the time to emphasize that they should *never* copy directly from a source without putting quotation marks around the words that were copied so that they will not "borrow" another's words without meaning to. Introduce the word *plagiarism*, explain its meaning, and invoke severe penalties if it should occur, however unintentionally—they will thank you for it later. Take the time to check sources if you are suspicious—the formation of bad habits negates the positive aspects of note taking and reporting.

Help children to learn that a paper should be more than simply a series of quotations strung together, however well organized, and that it is "dirty

Point out that copying dates and figures (e.g., relating to population or area) is not considered plagiarism, and credit need not be given.

pool" merely to transpose a few words or phrases and consider the writing original. The ideas and information in a report are gathered from other sources, but the organization and wording should be original. Quoting is done when it will strengthen the report in one of two ways. First, the writer may wish to use an author's own words to illustrate a point. For example, in discussing a poet, one might well quote from one or more poems; or a paper about a famous person might be enriched by the use of that person's own words. Second, it is sometimes desirable to use a quotation to show a particular person's opinion, especially if he or she is a well-known authority.

Footnotes may be in simple form. Author, title, and page number are sufficient; anyone who wishes more complete information can check the bibliography. There is no need to add the extra burden of learning about specialized forms, such as *ibid.* and *op. cit.* The important facts for children to learn are that they may not copy someone else's words without giving credit and how this credit may be given. Footnote form, like bibliography form, can be illustrated on charts to help children with punctuation and order of items. There is no need for them to memorize these, since, as mentioned earlier, forms vary. Point this out and explain that they should use whatever form is required by a particular teacher or school.

USING READING SKILLS

There are many skills needed for effective reading. The foundational ones were discussed in the preceding chapter; those discussed here are the ones particularly associated with the study skills—skimming and critical reading.

Skimming

Children should be taught how to skim in the intermediate grades, as this important skill will help them to study and to locate information more efficiently. Skimming is not a skill that is simply acquired as children grow in reading abilities; it must be specifically taught. Habits to be developed are discussed in the following sections.

READING THE FIRST AND LAST SENTENCES OF A PARAGRAPH. Both you and the children should be aware that the topic sentence of a paragraph is not always first or last, but it is frequently in one of those positions. Even when it is not, these sentences should give clues to the general content. In longer selections, the first and last paragraphs might be read quickly.

LOOKING FOR CUE WORDS. Cue words are of two types. First, if a child is looking for a specific piece of information, he or she should watch for words related to that information. For example, if a child only wants to find out where a particular tribe of Indians lived, then place names—California, northern plains, Mississippi River valley, etc.—should be looked for. Second, there are general cue words. The way they are used is illustrated in this paragraph. The heading has given the main idea. The first sentence uses the words *two types;* the words *first* and *second* lead immediately to these two types. Number words (or the numbers themselves) are perhaps the most helpful of all cue words. If these had been omitted, however, *For example* in sentence three should send your eyes back to the preceding sentence to discover one of the two types. Other cue words that can help children to locate ideas are words like *causes, reason, however, principal,* and *furthermore* and phrases such as *in addition, on the other hand,* and *in conclusion.*

USING FORMAT CLUES. As we suggested in the section concerning study steps, one of the quickest ways to discover the general content of a long selection is to glance through it and read the various types of section headings, as well as captions for pictures, graphs, maps, etc. A child who is preparing a report can be led immediately to the information needed by using this technique, particularly if it is used in conjunction with the card catalog, table of contents, index, etc. (see Chapter 14).

Materials used for teaching skimming should be selected carefully if these habits are to be established. This does not mean that they should not be related to the subject matter of content areas—only that you must select them with an eye to their suitability in developing a particular habit or skill.

Begin with short selections that clearly illustrate the habit you are developing. The first few times you may wish to underline the parts that are important—beginning and ending sentences, cue words, or topic headings. Give the children specific questions to answer and discuss what procedures might be used to find the answers. At first, simply ask them to decide what the selection is about. Later, proceed to more detailed questions, such as "What kind of homes did the Indians live in?" or "Find three reasons why the colonists came to America."

Using an overhead projector to show practice exercises makes it possible to control the time more easily. Another method is to write the selection on the chalkboard in a spot where it can be covered by a pulldown map or screen. The time allowed can be cut as the children become more skilled in using clues. Regular, brief practice will improve speed. For example, say to the class, "Turn to page 142 in your text and find the name of the Indian who guided the Smith family through the forest. As soon as you have found it, close your book and hold up your hand. Remember, find the name of the Smiths' Indian guide."

To help children who have difficulty in scanning, some teachers have tried drawing a vertical red line through the middle of a paragraph. As they look for clues, the children are to look only at the words that touch this line instead of letting their eyes go across the type line horizontally. Or you might try two vertical lines, dividing the page approximately into thirds. The idea is to help children learn to move their eyes quickly *down* the page, looking for clues, rather than looking *across* each line horizontally.

Observe children as they study and work on reports from supplementary reading. Guide individual children by reminding them of clues to look for, and provide reinforcement exercises when the need is indicated.

Try dividing the class into teams for skimming practice. Award points for finding a correct answer first, but subtract points for incorrect answers.

Critical Reading and Thinking

Children show a tendency to believe everything they read. Most people eventually learn that not everything in print is true, but often they do not learn this well enough or soon enough. Thus, thinking critically about issues, listening critically to what is heard on radio or television, and reading information critically need to be taught. Many of the ways words are used to give a false impression are well known. For example, a newspaper reports that a large number of young people attending a music festival were treated at the medical center for overdoses of drugs, upset stomachs, and cut feet. This is a fairly unadorned statement of fact, yet some readers might conclude from it that the use of drugs at the festival was widespread and that the principal cause of treatment at the center was drug overdose. This conclusion could be due (perhaps largely) to the readers' own preconceptions, but it is encouraged by the use of the term *large number*, the placement of the drug item in first position in the list, and the lack of specific numbers or percentages. Even numbers can be misleading, of course. Let us presume that 10 percent of those who came to the center were treated for drug overdose; this percentage is still not meaningful unless the reader knows the total number treated and how this number relates to the total number attending the festival.

It is important not only that we teach children to read but that we teach them to read critically. To develop into critical readers, children must learn to approach the printed words with inquiring minds, to evaluate what is read in the light of known facts or objective evidence, to examine the logic of the presentation, and to distinguish between fact and opinion. All learning, of course, is related to previous knowledge and experience, but the critical reader learns to suspend judgment and personal opinion until the total selection has been evaluated and assimilated, to seek out other knowledge and opinions, and to draw inferences from what has been read.

Reading materials designed for classroom use commonly provide children with the opportunity to make inferences or "read between the lines." This kind of reading can be encouraged by asking questions: Why do you think _____? Could this be true? What do you think really happened? It is important to stress that answers must be based on information given or knowledge gained from other sources, not simply on opinion or personal preference. One way to help children develop this kind of thinking is to begin with sentences from which inferences can be drawn.

> It is a beautiful day for a walk, but there is a sharp wind blowing. (Perhaps we will need jackets when we go out.)
> Bruce Smith has been practicing running and passing all summer. (He wants to go out for football this fall.)
> Mrs. Jones puts on her glasses the minute she gets up in the morning. (She can't see well without them.)
> Ordinarily, we have frequent showers in the summer, but this year the grass is brown and the trees look thirsty. (This has been an unusually dry summer.)

Another way to help children learn to draw inferences and base their thinking on known facts is to read or have them read part of a story and

Studying together is often helpful to children.

then ask them to write or tell a possible ending. This need not be the same as the ending used by the writer of the story, but it should be logical in terms of what is known about the characters and the events that have gone before. Begin with something short and fairly obvious, like "The Boy Who Cried Wolf," and advance to stories in which character might decide the outcome.

As in developing other language abilities, it is wise to begin teaching critical thinking with group activities so the children may learn from each other. This can be done even at the kindergarten level with activities such as the one suggested in the preceding paragraph. Be sure to ask not just "What do you think happened next?" but also "Why do you think so?" Try to get a number of responses, examine them critically (in a constructive way), and decide together which ones fit best with the known facts.

Besides supplementary reading materials, there are also filmstrips and cassettes designed to further critical thinking. These are useful because they are more readily associated with television, which influences so much of our thinking these days. They also provide variety, and they can be used with the entire class, with groups, or by individual children who need additional experience.

Closely allied to drawing inferences is distinguishing fact from opinion. Activities such as these can help children to develop this ability:

1. Have the children select famous personalities and write opinions about them: "I think Laura Ingalls Wilder must have lived in South Dakota because she wrote about life there so realistically" or "I Think Pedro Guerrero hit more home runs last year than any other player in the National League." Then have them use their library skills to show whether these are opinions only or actual facts.

2. Cut from magazines several full-page color advertisements, clipping off all printed material pertaining to the product. Show only the pictures to the children and ask them to write statements of fact and opinion about them. For example:

Fact

a. A woman is sitting on a patio with a collie.
b. The woman is smiling.
c. There are flowers and trees surrounding the patio.

Opinion

a. The woman is smiling because her new toothpaste got her teeth so white.
b. She is smiling because the flower seeds she bought made her yard so beautiful.
c. She is smiling because a particular fertilizer made her garden grow especially well.
d. She is smiling because her dog likes that new dog food.

Check to make sure the facts are really facts, and lead the children into a discussion of whether such statements as "The woman is beautiful" or "The collie is a thoroughbred" are fact or opinion. Then show the printed material that was cut from the picture so children can find out which of their opinions were correct (at least according to the advertisement!).

3. Help children evaluate newspaper accounts by looking for key words that indicate opinion rather than fact. Here are some statements of the type to look for.
   a. There is *probably* more snow here than any other place in the country.
   b. The remains just discovered *may* be the missing link.
   c. This *appears* to be the driest spot in the nation.
   d. The students *think* that this is the best school in the city.

4. A variation of the above is to have children separate fact from opinion.
   a. Yesterday's rain, which lasted for five hours, was probably the worst downpour in our history.
      Fact: It rained yesterday. The rain lasted five hours.
      Opinion: It was the worst downpour in our history.
   b. Jim Simmons, who is exactly six feet tall, must be the tallest boy in school.
      Fact: Jim Simmons is six feet tall.
      Opinion: He is the tallest boy in school.
   c. Mrs. Gotrocks, often said to be the wealthiest woman in the country, was shopping yesterday in Zayre's.
      Fact: Mrs. Gotrocks was in Zayre's yesterday.
      Opinion: Mrs. Gotrocks is the wealthiest woman in the country.

5. Have the children listen to television newscasts for several days and make a collection of phrases that are used to introduce statements that are not definitely known to be true, such as "It has been reported that," "Reliable sources inform us," "One witness said that," "Rumor has it," etc.

6. Children should also be shown how the choice of words can sway opinion. Let them try showing opposing views of the same event:
    a. Congressman Wilkins smirked sardonically, then snapped, "I have nothing to say at this time."
    b. The weary Congressman attempted a smile, then said simply, "I have nothing to say at this time."

7. As a follow-up to the above, have the class compare newspaper accounts of the same event written by different writers. A football game between teams from two cities, for example, would be written up quite differently by sports writers from each of those cities. Follow by having them attempt to sort out facts and opinions.

We are bombarded daily by propaganda of various sorts; those who have learned the skills of critical thinking are better prepared to make decisions based on reason rather than emotion. By the time children reach the middle grades, they should begin to draw conclusions from what they read or hear, distinguish between fact and opinion, and recognize that words have connotations as well as denotations. At this point they are ready for a more direct study of the ways in which people attempt to influence our thinking. Perhaps a good place to begin is with advertising techniques, since advertising is the most obvious type of propaganda. Begin with the most common categories:

- *Plain folks:* The president of the company started as a janitor. He still enjoys pitching horseshoes with the boys during the noon-hour break. (He understands ordinary people and wouldn't try to cheat them.)
- *Bandwagon:* More doctors recommend this pill than any other. (Notice that it doesn't say any other *what.*)
- *Repetition:* Sticky Goo holds your false teeth so you can munch, munch, munch for your lunch, lunch, lunch. (A more common type of repetition currently appears to be the use of frequently repeated slogans or "spot" ads which appear so often on TV that even small children can repeat them.)
- *Testimonial:* The star pitcher for the Oakland A's eats Ironies for breakfast. (If you eat Ironies, you can be a big leaguer too.)
- *Snob appeal:* Come out and see this executive house in an exclusive neighborhood. (Buy here and you can be part of an exclusive group.)
- *Emotional words:* Good mothers buy Junkie sneakers for their children. (If you don't buy your child Junkie sneakers, you aren't a good mother.)
- *Rewards:* Buy at Smith Brothers' Store and get Pink Stamps. (You can use Pink Stamps to get beautiful gifts for your family or home.)

A bulletin board might be a starting point. Ask children to bring in examples of the various advertising techniques and let them judge which ones are the most representative and therefore the best to post. They may also enjoy collecting phrases commonly found in advertising. These might include the following:

huge savings	for better mileage
this week only	discount prices
buy with confidence	money-back guarantee
service with a smile	for preferred customers

An extension of this study that will appeal to children is to have them watch television commercials and decide which groups they are directed at—small children, women, teenagers, etc.—and which techniques are used for each group. They will be fascinated to discover that variations of the same technique may be used for every age level: the four-year-old demands a certain cereal because there is a toy in the box, and the child's father buys a particular car because the company pays him a cash bonus.

As the children become expert in detecting the techniques, have them watch for overlapping ones. For example, "All responsible parents buy Dryer raincoats for their children. Your children deserve the best" includes the bandwagon, emotional, and snob appeal approaches.

As a concluding activity for the unit, divide the class into small groups and let each group select an item to shop for in the advertisements. Each group should collect all the advertisements they can locate about their item. Then they should evaluate each one, write reactions to it, and report their findings to the class, including the reasons they decided to buy a particular brand or shop at a particular store. Items might include a swimming pool, a pool table, a jar of peanut butter, a snowmobile, a video game, or a pair of jeans.

If it is valuable to recognize the advertising ploys used by those who are trying to sell their products, it is even more important to recognize that virtually the same techniques are used by those who want to sell us *ideas*. During every political campaign, for example, we are bombarded by the same spot announcements on TV and radio to keep candidates' names before us, film stars and other entertainers endorse their favorites, and so on. In fact, we are surrounded daily by propaganda of many types.

Children should learn to recognize propaganda, but they should also learn that it is not necessarily bad. Rather, it is a part of our way of life. TV stations, for instance, commonly telecast what they sometimes term "public service announcements," warning young people against the use of drugs, advertising public clinics that give immunizations against various diseases, etc.; prominent athletes plug not only shaving cream but also fund drives against multiple sclerosis or heart disease. No one is completely without bias; therefore, what a person writes or says is colored by his or her own beliefs. This "slanting" may be intentional, or the writer may make every effort to present an objective view. But the important thing is that children should learn to search for bias or motive, to distinguish fact from opinion, to examine opposing views, and to draw their own conclusions. The following are some of the types of activities that can help them to recognize and evaluate propaganda.

1. Use reading exercises that call for making inferences and for distinguishing fact from opinion, as suggested earlier.

2. Begin even in the early grades to help children find themes in stories they read, for these are a type of propaganda—they represent the writers' beliefs. Begin with simple questions: Do you think the person who wrote this story likes dogs? What makes you think so? As children mature, they can grasp more subtle and complicated themes.

3. To help children think about the purposes and qualifications of writers in evaluating what they have to say, show a variety of articles from newspapers and magazines by means of an opaque or overhead projector. Then discuss such questions as the following:

   a. Did the writer simply want to sell more newspapers or magazines? (New Clues Uncovered!)

   b. Is the writer encouraging you to vote for a candidate or an issue? (Mr. Christopher is an all-around family man who lives in a neat, modest suburban home.)

   c. Is the writer qualified and competent to write on this subject? (Has the writer studied the subject sufficiently or had enough personal experience with it to know what he or she is talking about?)

   d. Does the writer present both sides of an issue or only one? (Those who oppose this issue base their objections on emotion alone; there can be no valid objection.)

4. Have children bring in two accounts of a political speech appearing in newspapers with opposing political views, or have them listen to reports of a speech on different television channels—or both. Then compare these and note the ways in which each supports its point of view.

5. An extension of this is to videotape the speech itself and compare the various reports concerning it as to both accuracy and bias.

6. Have the children write papers either supporting or opposing a particular school or community issue on which opinions are strongly divided. Then have the class research the subject through whatever means are available— guest speakers, reading, etc.—and write new opinions based on what they have learned, telling why they have or have not changed their minds.

A BULLETIN BOARD IDEA

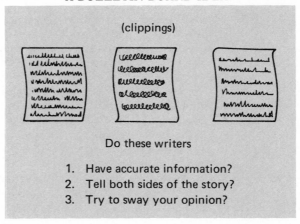

(clippings)

Do these writers

1. Have accurate information?
2. Tell both sides of the story?
3. Try to sway your opinion?

7. Bring in several articles concerning a current problem or issue. Show these on the opaque or overhead projector and have the children evaluate them in terms of propaganda techniques used, presentation of facts rather than opinions, use of "loaded" or emotional words, and use of logical reasoning.

Developing critical thinking takes time and effort. Broaden the children's horizons by providing many experiences and materials of various kinds. Make your classroom one in which a spirit of inquiry exists, where questions are freely asked and answers diligently sought. Help children to question what they read and hear and to acquire the desire and the skills to find answers.

References

Carin, Arthur A., and Sund, Robert B. *Developing Questioning Techniques.* Charles E. Merrill, 1971.

Crawford, Marion. *Teaching Study Skills.* The Instructor Publications, 1973.

Farr, Roger, and Roser, Nancy. *Teaching a Child to Read.* Harcourt Brace Jovanovich, 1979, Chap. 8

Fry, Edward B. *Skimming and Scanning.* Jamestown Publishers, 1978.

Hill, Walter R. *Secondary School Reading: Process, Program, Procedure.* Allyn and Bacon, 1979.

Mattleman, Marciene S., and Blake, Howard E. "Study Skills: Prescriptions for Survival." *Language Arts* 54 (November/December 1977), pp. 925–927.

May, Frank B. *To Help Children Communicate.* Charles E. Merrill, 1980, Module 9.

Robinson, H. Alan. *Teaching Reading and Study Strategies: The Content Areas.* 3rd ed. Allyn and Bacon, 1983.

Sanders, Norris M. *Classroom Questions: What Kinds?* Harper and Row, 1966.

Simpson, Dorothy M. *Learning to Learn.* Charles E. Merrill, 1970.

Teaching Resources

FILMSTRIPS

The Alphabet. Society for Visual Education (series of 6 strips with cassettes and duplicating masters; primary).

Bookmark Reading Filmstrips. Harcourt Brace Jovanovich (includes titles such as *Reading Between the Lines, Using a Dictionary, Drawing Conclusions, Get the Study Habit;* primary through intermediate).

The Dictionary. Thomas S. Klise Co. (filmstrip, cassette, and guide; upper grades).

Learning to Use the Dictionary. Pacific Productions (set of 8 strips).

Library Series. McGraw-Hill Films (strips on using dictionary and other books).

Using a Dictionary. Webster Publishing Co. (intermediate).

Your Dictionary and How to Use It. Society for Visual Education (set of 6 strips; intermediate).

KITS

Learning to Study Kits. EBSCO Curriculum Materials (filmstrips, cassettes, worksheets; middle and upper grades).

Let's Learn to Study. Guidance Associates (filmstrips, cassettes, teacher's guides; middle and upper grades).

Reading Minisystems. Coronet (cassettes and activity sheets; middle grades).

Report Writing Skills. Random House (8 cassettes with worksheet masters; middle and upper).

OTHER AIDS

Dictionary Skills. Scholastic Book Services (series of 3 workbooks for primary and middle grades).

Dictionary Study Skills. Macmillan (64 duplicating masters at varying levels).

Doing Research and Writing Reports. Scholastic Book Services (3 workbooks; middle grades).

Exploring Language with the Dictionary. Prentice-Hall (workbooks on four levels, including teacher's editions, plus pre- and posttests).

Strategies in Study Skills. Milton Bradley (self-instructional cassette program in dictionary, reference skills, etc.).

Random House has an extensive series of cassettes (with sets of student activity sheets) on critical reading, dictionary skills, reference skills, and study skills; middle grades.

Activities for Preservice Teachers

1. Plan the assignment for a specific lesson at a grade level of your choice. Show exactly how you would prepare the children for this assignment. Include motivation, background, and specific purposes.

2. Begin a picture file that would be useful for teaching alphabetical order (and for many other purposes as well). See if you can find a picture suitable for each letter of the alphabet.

3. Examine counting books and those which teach concepts children should know. Bring several to class and demonstrate how you would use them with children.

4. Observe in several classrooms to determine the extent to which the teachers make assignments similar to the example in this chapter. Note, too, the extent to which they integrate the teaching of language arts with the teaching of the content subjects.

5. Using a textbook for a grade level of your choice, plan a dictionary exercise to be used in connection with a particular story, lesson, or unit.

6. Select or compose three paragraphs that might be used in teaching note taking by the method suggested in this chapter. Be sure to integrate them in some way with the ongoing activities of a particular class or grade level.

7. Plan a lesson in drawing inferences for a grade level of your choice.

8. Find a selection that would be particularly useful for teaching skimming, and show how you would use it in a demonstration lesson.

9. Make a bulletin board display that could be used in connection with a lesson on advertising techniques or propaganda.

Activities for Inservice Teachers

1. Evaluate the way you assign homework. When you begin a new unit in social studies or science, experiment with the techniques suggested in this chapter for helping children learn how to study. Include in your experimenting an assessment of the effectiveness of the study procedures in terms of how well the children learned.

2. Coordinate dictionary activities with other subject areas and activities. For example, make a list of new words in a science lesson; after introducing them, have students use the dictionary and/or thesaurus to find variant meanings, synonyms, etc. This will not only help them to better understand the new words but also enrich their vocabularies.

3. Examine filmstrips, transparencies, cassettes, and other materials designed to teach skills discussed in this chapter and select those that you would like to have added to the materials center in your school. Present your list to the person who orders such materials, along with your reasons for believing they are needed.

4. Select three movies from your school media center, or send for some that fit well with your curriculum. Use these in teaching outlining. Plan carefully, making sure by previewing that the films are suitable for outlining. You may need to show the film several times when you first start this project.

5. With your class, select several topics for reports, perhaps from a social studies unit. Divide the class into groups (one for each topic), and then help the students to locate materials in the library, take notes, and correlate information from several sources. Each group will make an outline, write a rough draft, prepare a bibliography, and write a final copy. This can be done early in the year to prepare children for individual reports.

6. Collect a number of pictures from magazines. Have children write sentences identifying fact and opinion.

Have them search headlines and newspapers for further evidence of fact vs. opinion.

7. Develop critical listening and reading skills through a study of propaganda techniques used in television and magazine advertising. Begin with a class discussion of favorite commercials and magazine advertisements. Select one topic and develop a series of lessons on it. Conclude by having the children invent a product and prepare the advertising.

Independent Activities for Children

1. Put lists of words on cards—on the front in any order and on the back in alphabetical order. Vary the difficulty to provide for differences in the abilities of the children. An individual child can select a card, put the words in alphabetical order on paper, and check by looking at the back of the card.

2. A child may prepare a bulletin board display showing parts of the dictionary—guide words, entry words, pronunciation key, syllabication, etc.

3. Provide a set of miniature animals with which children may play "Noah's Ark." That is, two children take turns naming the animals and placing them in alphabetical order to go onto the Ark.

4. To aid the child who has difficulty with organizational skills, prepare several outlines with main topics listed in order on one side of the page and subtopics in jumbled order on the other side. Have the child select appropriate subtopics for each main idea and place them in logical sequence.

5. Encourage individual children to use note cards in giving oral book reports, putting one principal idea on each card and listing important details they want to include under each main point.

6. A child can preview filmstrips and recordings in order to determine their value for use in a social studies unit, taking notes and preparing a brief summary or list of material covered. He or she may then compare this list with the topics covered in the text to decide which filmstrips or recordings would add or relate to the material there.

7. Be sure that your listening center is well supplied with tapes and/or records designed to build skill in finding main ideas, putting items in sequence, using the dictionary, etc. Children who need practice with specific skills may use these during free time.

8. Let an individual child (or a group) select a brief article from a current newspaper—possibly an account of a sports event or whatever else is of special interest to the children. Then have the child list facts and opinions stated in the article.

9. Select articles such as those suggested above and place them in plastic envelopes or folders. Individual children can use these to practice many types of study skills—e.g., to make an outline, to separate fact from opinion, to find words or phrases which denote order of items or events (*then, in the final two minutes,* etc.).

10. Dictionary exercises for individual children may include the following:
a. Circle the words that come between *club* and *enough* in the dictionary.

clown	easy	draw	country
family	dust	cover	evening
oval	cloth	egg	explore
desk	close	ever	could

b. Write the entry words for each of these dictionary respellings.

bütz _____   kül _____
mün _____   tüth _____

11. Prepare specific questions related to the content being studied in social studies, science, etc. The child will utilize the study skills in locating answers to these questions.

12. A child can look in a thesaurus to find synonyms and antonyms for each word in the spelling list for the week.

13. A child who needs practice in putting items in sequence or selecting details can draw a picture sequence of everything he or she did between getting up and arriving at school. The pictures might then be put into a sort of comic strip, with dialogue added where appropriate.

14. Practice in finding the main idea can be gained by having a child read articles in a certain section of the school newspaper or one such as *My Weekly Reader* and put the main thought of each article into a single sentence.

14 | Children and the Library

Today's library is indeed a storehouse of pleasure and information, containing not only the books, magazines, and newspapers traditionally found in libraries, but also records, tapes, cassettes, filmstrips, videotapes, picture files, and displays of many kinds. In addition, many libraries have special rooms or areas for listening or viewing, computers and the cassettes or other software to accompany them, even areas (and equipment) for making videotapes, filmstrips, slides, and other visual aids. For this reason some school libraries now bear such names as *Instructional Materials Center*. This too, however, could be considered a misnomer, since it seems to emphasize the teaching/learning aspects only, ignoring the delight, inspiration, and simple contentment we would like children to find there as well.

Whatever its name, though, one of the most important—and, we feel, pleasant—tasks a teacher has is to help children develop the habit of turning to the library for both pleasure and information. To do this, they must have the ability to locate the information needed or the particular item that will provide pleasure. This chapter will discuss ways of developing the needed library skills: helping children to get familiar with the library as a whole, use the card catalog, locate books and other materials, and become acquainted with special references of many kinds.

GUIDING PRINCIPLES

The most valuable ally to enlist in teaching the library skills is the librarian, since most librarians have chosen their profession because they like books and want to share them, just as most teachers like children and want to help them grow. Naturally not all of the teaching can or should be turned over to the librarian. To a great extent, motivation for using library skills must come from the classroom activities, and children will need a great deal of individual help and reinforcement both in the library and in the classroom. But an enthusiastic librarian who believes that books and other materials should be off the shelves and in children's hands will do much toward providing a stimulating and interesting environment in which children may learn.

Library skills must be taught directly and completely if they are really to be learned and used. Like any other skills, they are best learned in a situation where they are being used for a meaningful purpose. Therefore

388

they are best introduced when children want to locate information, find a book about something of interest, listen to a cassette as they read a particular story, or perhaps simply explore what this fascinating place is all about.

A spirit of discovery must exist in a classroom for library skills to be needed. As children explore, seeking to satisfy their curiosity, motivation for learning the library skills will be created. The major task, then, is introducing children to ideas, to information that appeals to them, and to new thoughts. Reading frequently to children—and this should be a habit exercised daily—is a good way to introduce them to the world beyond their experience and at the same time show the importance of books. A multimedia and multitext approach to teaching in all areas will also help children to learn to look beyond a single source for information. This does not mean that every child must have several texts for each subject, but rather that additional resources of many kinds should be available to children and should be a part of their daily activities.

A classroom such as this will of course have an attractive and well-supplied room library which children are allowed and encouraged to use. The room library can supply the initial focus for teaching beginning library skills as you help children look up information, find books for pleasure reading, or locate a filmstrip for viewing.

Your own attitude is a vital factor. Even a simple act like looking up the correct spelling of a word in the dictionary or turning to the atlas for a specific fact will demonstrate to children the usefulness of library tools. Bringing in additional resources, showing your own interest in books, and encouraging (and helping) children to look up information will provide motivation for acquiring library skills.

A final *must* is knowing the children, their interests and abilities, and what they do outside school. A child who doesn't know how to use the card file or take notes is ill prepared to go to the library alone to find information for a report. Neither can a reluctant reader whose only interest in life is football be expected to become enthusiastic about learning library skills in order to find out about the history of ballet—but he might do surprisingly well at finding out about the career of Terry Bradshaw or how and when football was first played. Thus knowing when individual children are ready to take the next step and building upon the knowledge they already have are as vital to teaching library skills as they are to any other learning activity.

INTRODUCTORY ACTIVITIES

At the primary level, as children are first beginning to look at and read books, they can also learn how to use and handle them, how to talk about them, how to locate the ones they want, and how to check out and return them. The same applies, of course, to materials and equipment in the media center.

These learnings can begin in the room library. Some teachers like to make this a materials center (especially if the school library is set up in this

Room libraries are more fully discussed both in the following section and in Chapter 15.

Provide time—and a place—for individual reading in every school day and at every level.

fashion), housing filmstrips, cassettes, picture files, and so on, as well as books. Certainly such an arrangement fosters the understanding that libraries contain more than books, but it has the disadvantage of increased noise and traffic. If you prefer this arrangement—or if space requires it—be sure to have a "quiet spot" nearby where children can read comfortably and without distraction.

However, most libraries—including those in many schools—have separate areas, even separate rooms, for different kinds of materials or activities. Therefore it would seem that the best arrangement is to have the media center adjoin the library, possibly with a central "check-out" for both (if your school permits books and/or other materials to be taken home).

The Media Center

Most children in schools today have watched a great deal of television; many may even have played video games, or watched others play them, and possibly have had some experience with cassettes or other software. Thus they are at least partially prepared for the media center. Not all will be equally prepared, however, and all will need guidance in using and caring for materials. Even very young children can learn to use filmstrip and slide projectors, insert a cassette, or operate a computer, but they should also learn from the beginning that these are not toys and must be used and cared for properly. Work with them as they learn, and help them to set up their own list of standards for the media center. These might be something like the following:

> IN THE MEDIA CENTER
> 1. Work quietly and don't disturb others.
> 2. Don't get fingerprints on filmstrips, slides, records, lenses.
> 3. Don't tear or bend filmstrips.
> 4. Be sure you know how to work machines before using them.
> 5. Put materials away when you are finished.

Select materials for your media center as carefully as you select books for the library—there is great variation in quality. And use them to enrich the curriculum as well as to guide children to books. For example, a beginning reader may well enjoy listening to a cassette recording as he "reads" Ezra Jack Keats's *Whistle for Willie,* and children will rush for Pat Hutchins's *Rosie's Walk* after viewing the film (Weston Woods).

The supply of software is growing like Pinocchio's nose, so consult with the librarian, read current reviews in professional magazines, and check sources such as Green and Schoenfield's *Multimedia Approach to Children's Literature* (American Library Association). And by all means preview all materials before using them or placing them in the media center.

The Room Library

In this age of television, too many children come to school having had only limited experience with books or with seeing others read. It is the job of the school not only to teach children to read, but to teach them to *enjoy* reading and to turn readily to books for information. The television set can furnish both information and entertainment, but books give depth to understanding and become lifelong companions during leisure hours.

The library corner, then, should be the most inviting spot in the room and should contain as many books as possible. The teacher must know about books suitable for children and make many of these known to them. There are numerous aids available for this purpose: books on children's literature, such as those by Huck, Sutherland, Glazer and Williams, Stewig, and Cullinan; lists published by professional organizations and publishers; reviews of children's books which appear regularly in magazines such as *Language Arts, School Library Journal, The Horn Book,* and *The Reading Teacher;* and special lists, such as those of the Newbery and Caldecott Award winners. The school librarian, if there is one, or the children's librarian at the city or county library should have many of these and should also be able to make recommendations. In addition, you should be familiar with many children's books, particularly those which you select for the room library.

Books in the room library should be changed often so that no child will be unable to find one that interests him or her, although special favorites may be retained or brought back, since young children particularly love to "reread." Books should vary in level of difficulty and should be of many types. The following list may serve as a guide.

The Newbery Medal is awarded annually for the most distinguished contribution to children's literature published in the United States during the preceding year.

The Caldecott Medal, also awarded annually, is given for the most distinguished picture book for children published in the United States during the preceding year.

Picture or "Easy" Books

Crews, Donald. *Truck.* Greenwillow, 1980.
Edmondson, Madeleine. *The Witch's Egg.* Seabury, 1974.
Hutchins, Pat. *Rosie's Walk.* Macmillan, 1968.
Keats, Ezra Jack. *Pet Show.* Macmillan, 1970.
Lobel, Arnold and Anita. *On Market Street.* Greenwillow, 1981.
Matsuno, Masako. *A Pair of Red Clogs.* World, 1960.
Plume, Ilse. *The Bremen-Town Musicians.* Doubleday, 1980.
Scarry, Richard. *Best Mother Goose Ever.* Western, 1970.
Seuss, Dr. *The Cat in the Hat.* Random House, 1957.
Wildsmith, Brian. *Brian Wildsmith's Birds.* Franklin, 1957.

Idea or Theme Books

Alexander, Martha. *Nobody Asked Me If I Wanted a Baby Sister.* Dial, 1971.
de Paola, Tomie. *Watch Out for the Chicken Feet in Your Soup.* Prentice-Hall, 1974.
Gramatky, Hardie. *Little Toot Through the Golden Gate.* Putnam's, 1975.
Hutchins, Pat. *Happy Birthday, Sam.* Greenwillow, 1978.
Keller, Holly. *Cromwell's Glasses.* Greenwillow, 1982.
Lexau, Joan. *Emily and the Klunky Baby and the Next-Door Dog.* Dial, 1972.
Paris, Lena. *Mom Is Single.* Children's Press, 1980.
Steptoe, John. *Stevie.* Harper and Row, 1969.

Viorst, Judith. *Alexander and the Terrible, Horrible, No Good, Very Bad Day.* Atheneum, 1972.
Wolf, Bernard. *Anna's Silent World.* Lippincott, 1977.

Animal Stories

Barrett, Judi. *Animals Should Definitely Not Wear Clothing.* Atheneum, 1970.
Du Bois, William Pine. *Bear Circus.* Viking, 1972.
Griffith, Helen V. *Alex and the Cat.* Greenwillow, 1982.
Hogrogian, Nonny. *Carrot Cake.* Greenwillow, 1977.
Lionni, Leo. *Fish Is Fish.* Pantheon, 1975.
Lobel, Arnold. *Frog and Toad Together.* Harper and Row, 1972.
Oakley, Graham. *The Church Mice at Bay.* Atheneum, 1978.
Oxenbury, Helen. *Pig Tale.* Morrow, 1973.
Peppi, Rodney (Told by). *Three Little Pigs.* Lothrop, 1980.
Tresselt, Alvin. *The Beaver Pond.* Lothrop, 1970.

Many other types should also be included: ABC books, counting books, picture and beginning dictionaries, books which help develop concepts children should learn, stories of other lands, fables, poetry, and so on. Choose carefully, keeping in mind the interests, backgrounds, and needs of the particular children in your class. And choose books that you like so that you will be enthusiastic about sharing them. If you love books and if there are books suitable for every child in the class, motivation will be created for acquiring the beginning library skills.

Even in as small a place as the room library, books should be arranged on the shelves in some sort of logical way so children may learn that there is a pattern to the way libraries are set up and that the purpose of this pattern is to help them find books. This arrangement may be by type, by level of difficulty, or perhaps alphabetical (this would give meaningful practice with alphabetical order). Whatever the arrangement, explain it to the children, show them how to look for particular books, and teach them to return books to their proper places so that others will be able to find them.

When children first begin to handle books, they should also learn how to take care of them, and, as in other matters, they should help to formulate the standards themselves. Perhaps they will come up with something like this:

TAKING CARE OF BOOKS

1. Always have clean hands.
2. Don't write in a book that isn't yours.
3. Protect books from rain or snow.
4. Keep books away from younger brothers or sisters who don't know how to handle them.
5. Be careful not to tear pages.
6. Return books as soon as you are through with them.

As children learn to handle and care for books, they can also learn the terms used in talking about them. The most important terms (and the concepts they represent) that primary children can learn to use when talking about books are *title, author, illustrator,* and *table of contents.*

The concept of *title* is not a difficult one for children to grasp. They are already aware of their own names and those of their pets, the school, and so on. It is a simple matter, then, to explain that the name of a book is called a title and that this often helps to tell what the book is about—for example, *Curious George, My First Pictionary, Millions of Cats.*

Author and *illustrator* can also be related to the children's own names. Just as children put their names on their papers, the person who writes a book puts his or her name on it. Most children know Dr. Seuss, for example, and can understand that if they liked *Horton Hatches the Egg* they might also like other books by the same author. Several authors the children are familiar with might be used to illustrate this point, thus laying the foundation for using the card catalog and the alphabetical arrangement of books by author to find books they will enjoy.

The illustrator is of great importance to a book for young children, who usually select books by the pictures alone. Again, just as children put their names on their own drawings, a person who draws in a book has his or her name on the cover. And just as authors may write more than one book, so they may sometimes illustrate their own books. Show children books by such author-illustrators as Maurice Sendak, Arnold Lobel, Ezra Jack Keats, Nonny Hogrogian, and Leo Lionni and discuss ways in which the illustrations add to the books. Having copies of the same story—a fairy tale, for example—with pictures by different illustrators can add much to this discussion. Children will also enjoy drawing pictures about stories that are read or told; these can be posted, with captions showing the name of the story, the author, and the phrase "Illustrated by _____."

At the primary level there is little need for children to be concerned with publication information, but they should know that they can find the title of a book and the names of the author and illustrator on the title page. If they are curious about the other items found on this page, these can be explained simply, but they should not be emphasized, nor should children be required to know them.

Children ought to know that books contain more than stories and poems. The selection of books in the room library will demonstrate this, as will the regular use of resource materials. When discussing weather, for example, obtain from the library books that contain factual material at the children's level, including at least one that has a table of contents. Point out again that the title gives a general idea of what the book is about; then turn to the table of contents and show how it gives much more specific information. Understanding and competence in using this aid can be furthered by writing the name of the daily story on the chalkboard and having the children look up the page number in the table of contents.

The important concern at this level—or any other—is not the terminology of books, but the concepts related to the terminology and the understanding that books may provide not only pleasure but also knowledge of many kinds.

As soon as possible, arrange to take the class to the school and community libraries. Involving parents in the latter trip may encourage them to help their children to obtain library cards as soon as this is permitted in the particular library or to get cards for themselves and check out books for

Informational Books for Young Children

ABC's of the Ocean by Isaac Asimov (Walker, 1970)

The Amazing Dandelion by Millicent E. Selsam and Jerome Wexler (Morrow, 1977)

A Book about Pandas by Ruth Belov Gross (Dial, 1972)

Building a House by Byron Barton (Greenwillow, 1981)

How Far Is Far? by Alvin Tresselt (Parents', 1964)

How the Forest Grew by William Jaspersohn (Greenwillow, 1980)

Less Than Nothing Is Really Something by Robert Freeman (Crowell, 1973)

My Puppy Is Born by Joanna Cole (Morrow, 1973)

Squirrels by Brian Wildsmith (Watts, 1974)

their children. Many parents are probably unaware of the vast array of beautiful children's books that are now available. These visits should be prearranged so that the librarians will be available to talk to the children. It is important for children to know the librarians' names and to look on them as friends and helpers.

Before making these trips, teach library behavior and explain the reasons for library rules. If, as suggested in the preceding paragraphs, children have learned how to handle and care for books, they will not be unwelcome guests in the library. If they have learned consideration for others, they will understand the need for quiet. The librarian can explain rules about checking out books, how long they may be kept, and so forth.

In some schools, library rules forbid young children to check out books. If this is true, it is still possible to schedule regular trips to the library to let the children help select books for the classroom. The librarian can explain the fun of browsing, help in selecting books, and show them where the various kinds of books may be found and how they are arranged. And children should be allowed to explore for themselves as well.

As soon as children are old enough to check out books, they should be taught borrowing procedures. Here again it is a good idea to enlist the aid of the librarian. Actually checking out books is the best way to learn the procedures, but reinforcement and clarification of library terms may be provided by a bulletin board designed around a favorite book, showing the book card and the date due slip as they are found in your particular library. For example:

card that is in the pocket inside the cover

call number	j C	2 copy number
author title	Cleary, Beverly Ramona Quimby Age 8	
	Date Due	Borrower's Name
date due	Feb. 19	David George your name

date due is found inside the book on a slip like this

j C Cleary Ramona Quimby Age 8			
Date Due			
Jan. 14 Apr. 29			
Library Name City, State			

At this level, call number and copy number, like the publication information on the title page of the book, need not be stressed; if the children ask questions about these items, explain simply that they help to identify the book and show the librarian where it belongs on the shelves.

If your school does not allow primary children to check out books, you might prepare them for later use of the library by making sample cards for the books in the room library. (You may want to do this anyway if children need practice.) Let the children select a different librarian daily and practice checking out and returning the books. Be sure to use the same procedure as that in the school library, and show children the importance of placing their full names—in their best printing—in the correct space on the card so that there is no confusion about who has checked out a book.

Many city and county libraries are now using a photocopy system of checking out books rather than the one illustrated above. If this is the case in the library you visit with the children, ask the librarian to show them how the procedure operates—they will not only be fascinated but will also be better prepared for using large libraries.

SKILLS AND ACTIVITIES FOR THE MIDDLE GRADES

Intermediate grade children's knowledge about books and libraries will vary widely. Most children entering the fourth grade will have visited libraries, will know where to find picture and storybooks, and will have had some

Factual Books for Older Children

Being Blind by Rebecca B. Marcus (Hastings House, 1981)

The Hospital Book by James Howe (Crown, 1981)

How Did We Find Out about Germs? by Isaac Asimov (Walker, 1974)

A Natural History of Giraffes by Dorcas Mac-Clintock (Scribner's, 1973)

Seeing What Plants Do by Joan Elma Rahn (Atheneum, 1972)

A Snake-Lover's Diary by Barbara A. Brenner (Young Scott, 1970)

Thor Heyerdahl and the Reed Boat Ra by Barbara Beasley Murphy and Norman Baker (Lippincott, 1974)

experience in checking out books. By this time, too, most children will have had experience with filmstrips, cassettes, picture files, and various types of displays in the classroom and will know that libraries have these items (especially if your school library is the media center) and that they can be checked out or used in the library just as books can.

During the intermediate grades, children will be embarking on more and more independent study and preparing both oral and written reports. Therefore, no later than about the fourth grade you should have a series of lessons and activities specifically designed to help children learn about the many kinds of materials to be found in libraries and how to locate them. It goes without saying, of course, that these lessons should be planned in conjunction with actual needs for finding and using information. Most language arts textbooks for the intermediate grades contain one or more units on using the library. If these are suited to the children, their needs, and the particular library or libraries they will be using, by all means use them. Be very sure, however, that the materials you select are both adequate and suitable, for this is one of the most valuable lessons you will teach. There is little point in teaching children to read and enjoy books and the knowledge to be found in them if they are unable to find the books and other materials they want and need.

Basic Library Skills

As suggested previously, children should be exposed to books from the very beginning of the school year. Make sure that the library corner is stocked with a variety of books—stories, poems, factual books, humor, fantasy, stories about problems children face, etc. Read some of these to the children; then talk about the library, mentioning shelf arrangements (left to right), shelf labels, and different classifications (easy books, juvenile, etc.).

Ask the librarian to give the class a tour of the library, explaining where different books, magazines, and newspapers are located and why they are located in these places. Comparing a library with a supermarket may help children to understand that, just as all the fruits and vegetables are located near each other, all the books on similar subjects are located together: stories are together, biographies are together, and nonfiction books on topics such as conservation, hobbies, sports, and archaeology are grouped.

Intermediate children should have in mind the concepts related to book vocabulary, such as *title, author, illustrator, cover,* and *spine.* These may need review. To aid them in studying efficiently and in gathering and reporting information, they also need to develop an understanding of the purposes and uses of the various parts of a book. This knowledge can be developed over a period of time, as children have need to use various kinds of books and refer to various sections of them. They should become familiar with the following terms:

Publisher	The company that printed the book and put it together.
City	Place where the book was published.
Copyright date	When the book was published.
Title page	A page containing the title, author, and publisher.
Dedication	A special page in the book where the author thanks people, often special friends or members of his or her family.
Introduction, Preface, or Foreword	Any one of these names can be used for the section in the front of the book that tells briefly what the book is about or why it was written.
List of illustrations	A list usually found in a book with many pictures, maps, or charts.
Table of contents	A list of stories or chapters. [Refer to this throughout the school year in all subject areas so that children become familiar with it. If you are using a basal reader, have children use the table of contents to find their story.]
Glossary	A small dictionary that defines words used in this particular book. [In elementary grades this is often found in the back of a basal reading, social studies, or science book. Basal series frequently provide experiences in using the glossary. Capitalize on these.]
Index	A list of subjects, found in the back of most books. It is the principal means for locating information. [Several lessons will be needed so that children develop an understanding of the arrangement of indexes, their location, the symbols and pronunciation keys used, any subtopic arrangements, and the relationship to the table of contents in amount of detail.]

Ideally, before children are asked to use the library to prepare an oral or written report, they should have visited it many times and checked out books; they should have had opportunities to browse among the different kinds of materials to be found there and to know the librarian as a friend and helper. Try to see that the children in your class have as much preparation of this kind as possible. Improvise where necessary (some suggestions are included in the following sections), but try to avoid simply having available in the classroom everything that they will need to prepare a report. Children need to learn how to locate information for themselves; they cannot forever be dependent on the teacher.

However, children should not be expected to learn all at one time both the skills of organizing material from several sources and those of using the library to locate information. Using the room library, give them practice in taking notes and correlating information from two or three sources; then let them advance to using the school library for further information. Using the library to locate information involves using the card catalog, knowing the difference between fiction and nonfiction, understanding what call numbers signify, and perhaps even knowing the basic elements of classification systems. These skills are interdependent. There are many things to be learned at the same time; thus some practice exercises may need to be provided. If the need for the skills is real, however—that is, if children are preparing reports to be used in connection with a particular unit of study—practice exercises will be more meaningful.

The skills discussed in the two following sections are interrelated and must be presented at the same time. They are separated here for purposes of organization; for the same reason, practice exercises may also need to be presented separately. But library skills should never be taught in isolation from any real need for their use.

Using the Card Catalog

On their initial visit to the library, the librarian will undoubtedly show the children the card catalog and explain its use. Later, when the opportunity arises, this learning can be reinforced. A child may say, "This was a good book. I would like to read another one like it." This is the time to suggest that he or she look in the card catalog to see if there is another book by the same author or on the same subject. Another child might report, "Someone

Children should learn to use a card catalog by using one.

told me the name of a good book, but I don't know how to find it in the library." Thus the use of title cards can be introduced. Then when children are ready to prepare reports, the catalog will not be entirely unfamiliar to them. Before they can be truly independent in using it, however, they will need a lesson or series of lessons demonstrating the various kinds of cards and how they can be of help.

Begin with the physical setup of the catalog. In most libraries author, title, and subject cards are all filed together. Cards for audiovisual items may or may not be in the same catalog; alert children to this possibility. Libraries that middle grade children use, however, are likely to file all—or most—cards together. In this case they will probably use a color-coding system, which is especially useful, since it helps both you and the children to discover quickly and easily whether the library has a filmstrip, cassette, etc., that might be useful in presenting a report or teaching a particular unit. In this system, each type of material is assigned a particular color. That is, cards for filmstrips might have a strip of green tape across the top, cassettes a red one, films a blue one, and so on. These items will be filed alphabetically according to both subject and title.

A helpful technique is to go to the school or community library and sketch the outside of the card catalog, including guide letters. Display this sketch on a chart or bulletin board and use short oral drills to provide practice. Stress the alphabetical arrangement, point out that even the books listed under an author's name are in alphabetical order, and call attention to the fact that articles (*a, an,* and *the*) are not considered in alphabetizing titles.

CHART OR BULLETIN BOARD

A	E–Fi	Ji–Le	Nu–Pe	Sh–To
B–Ce	Fl–G	Li–Mc	Ph–Rh	Tr—V
Ch–Dw	Ha–Je	Me–No	Ri—Se	W–Z

Ask questions such as these:

In which drawer would you find:
Julie of the Wolves?
information about firefighting?
basketball stories?
a biography of Abraham Lincoln?
a cassette recording of *And Now Miguel?*
a Halloween poem?

Continue this type of exercise only as long as seems necessary, making sure to include a variety of topic headings, as well as many that might be found under more than one heading. And help children learn to explore all possible headings—for example, a Halloween poem might be located under "Halloween," "holidays," or even "poetry" or "poems"; and the cassette could be listed in the general file or in a special one.

Children who are ready to use the card catalog will have had much experience already in using other materials that are alphabetically arranged—dictionaries, indexes, telephone directories, etc. Therefore, they should have little difficulty in understanding the alphabetical nature of the catalog. The important part of this learning is understanding the different kinds of cards in the catalog and how to use them to find books and information. In conjunction with teaching about the physical setup of the catalog, then, explain the cards themselves. A bulletin board showing enlarged drawings of actual cards from the catalog of the school or community library is almost a must. (See pages 404–409 for types of cards that should be included.) These can be placed below the chart showing the outsides of the drawers. Both color and meaning can be added by putting explanatory notes on colored cards and attaching each to the item it refers to with a piece of colored yarn. Be sure to include all types of cards and to keep the display up until after the children have had actual experience in using the catalog to find information for a report.

Children will have many questions about the cards and the items on them: Is a book listed only once in the catalog? What does the call number mean? Answer these questions as thoroughly as possible to help children feel competent and at ease in using library aids. Some questions may not have particularly logical answers; when this is true, simply say so. For example, why are an author's first *and* last names capitalized when only the first word of a book title is? Why does one card contain more complete information than another card on the same book?

If children have had a limited amount of library experience, they may need practice exercises to ensure that they know exactly how to use the card catalog. For example, they might report on how many books the library has by Lois Lenski, Beverly Cleary, or some other author they like; they could begin with a list of book titles (both fiction and nonfiction) and find the names of the authors and where the books are located in the library; or each child could select a subject and find three books containing information about it, what subject headings they are listed under, and where they are located on the shelves. Again use only as much of this kind of drill as seems necessary; if some children are already fairly adept at using the catalog, let them work on special reports or serve as "assistant teachers" for those who need practice.

As soon as possible, each child should select a topic and go to the library to find information for a brief oral report; purposeful activities will provide greater reinforcement than any number of practice drills. Frequent opportunities to use the library in connection with units of study in all areas of the curriculum will both enrich the curriculum and help learnings to become well established.

Teaching activities related to cards should be designed to make sure the children learn the following:

1. Author, title, and subject cards are all arranged in alphabetical order.

2. Cards for media may be filed in the general catalog or in a separate one. These are filed, also in alphabetical order, under both subject and title.

3. Titles beginning with *A*, *An*, or *The* are alphabetized according to the second word.

4. A number in the title is always spelled out.

5. Abbreviated words are listed as if they were spelled out. For example, for "U.S. Government," the alphabetical arrangement would have this entry as if it were spelled out—"United States Government." The same would apply to such abbreviations as *Dr., Mrs., Mr., St.,* etc.

6. Author cards for books by the same writer are filed according to the alphabetical order of the titles of the books: "Politi, Leo, *Butterflies Come, The*" comes before "Politi, Leo, *Song of the Swallows.*"

If your school library does not have a card catalog or if your school does not have a library, make a card catalog for the books in the room library so that children will have an opportunity to learn how to use this valuable aid. Use shoe boxes or metal file boxes for the drawers, making author, title, and subject cards for each book. Set up the library corner as much like a real library as possible, and allow children to take turns being the class librarian, checking out books and seeing that they are returned to their correct places on the shelves. Even though this catalog will be small, children will have fun "playing library" while they learn that the catalog can help them:

- Find a book quickly when they know the title but not the author.
- Find out whether the library has another book by an author whose work they have enjoyed. (It could be checked out and therefore not visible on the shelf.)
- Find out whether the library has a book on a particular subject.

Another possibility is to enlist the cooperation of one or two other teachers in making a cooperative catalog. The call number for each book could show which room the book is in and where it can be found in that room, and children would be allowed to check books out from any of the several rooms. Thus many more books would be available to each child. This would entail a great deal of work initially, but it would be well worth the time spent, particularly in a small school or with children who, for one reason or another, do not have the opportunity to use a large library regularly.

Using Call Numbers

Children should learn about call numbers while they are learning to use the card catalog. They should also learn the difference between fiction and nonfiction and understand the meaning of biography. Middle grade children can understand that fiction is a story that someone made up, even though some characters may be real people and some incidents true; that nonfiction contains true information which the author has tried to verify and which may or may not be in story form; and that biography is the true story of the life of a real person.

The following understandings should be developed:

1. Books of fiction are shelved together and arranged in alphabetical order according to the author's last name. Just as children's books and adult books are in different sections, sometimes picture books and books for older children can be found in separate sections—in fact, many libraries have added a third group that includes books for children in the upper grades. A fiction book for young readers will have j on its spine, possibly followed by a capital letter indicating the first letter of the author's last name. These letters constitute the call number of the book. If the library has a special section for older children, books shelved there will be marked y (young adult) rather than j (juvenile). Cards for both groups, as well as those for picture books, will be found in the children's catalog.

2. Biographies are usually shelved together and arranged alphabetically, but in most libraries they are alphabetized by the name of the person the book is about rather than that of the author. Thus all the books about the same person can be together, so that if a child is looking for a biography of Abraham Lincoln, for example, there will be only one place to look instead of several. A biography will have on its spine the letter B, and underneath it the first letter of the subject's last name.

3. Other nonfiction books (biography is nonfiction) are arranged in numerical order according to numbers that indicate what each book is about. Thus, as with biographies, all the books about the same subject can be shelved together. Call numbers are assigned according to a classification system that has been worked out to include all subject areas. There are two of these systems; one or the other is used in almost every library of any size. General reference books such as encyclopedias and dictionaries which contain information about many subjects are another special category of nonfiction. These usually have the letter R on their spines, are kept in a special area, and can seldom be checked out of the library.

4. Media items have call numbers similar to those for books and are often grouped together for ease of care, use, and storage—that is, records are together, cassettes together, pictures in a special file, etc. In the juvenile sections of some libraries, however, a record might be found on the shelf next to the book that is recorded, a cassette could be packaged in a plastic bag with its book and kept in a special place, and so on. The librarian is the person to ask for help if these materials cannot be located.

Children who understand how to use the card catalog and what the call numbers mean are well on their way to being able to find what they are looking for, even in the large libraries they will encounter later. It is important to help them understand that this is not simply a complicated system set up by adults to try to confuse them. Rather, the card catalog is like a telephone directory; just as a child can look in the telephone directory to find out where a friend lives, so he or she can look in the card catalog to find out where a particular book—or information about a particular subject—can be located. The call number is the book's "address"; it shows where the book is shelved in the library, and it helps the librarian to put the book away quickly so another child will be able to find it.

Children should *never* be required to memorize either the Dewey Decimal or Library of Congress system of classification; there is no more point in this than in memorizing the call numbers of individual books. The important concept to learn is that the numbers will guide them in locating the books they want. If they are curious about what the numbers mean, a simple explanation can help them to understand why books about the same subject have the same or similar numbers and to recognize that there is order in the arrangement.

Although most university and other large libraries now use the Library of Congress system, many small libraries—including those in schools—find the Dewey Decimal system better suited to their needs. Begin with whichever is used in libraries available to the children, although it would be a good idea to point out that this is not the only system. If neither is used, teaching should be postponed until it can be meaningful.

DEWEY DECIMAL SYSTEM. In the Dewey Decimal System, books are arranged numerically on the shelves; thus anyone who can count and knows the call number of the book he or she wants can find it easily—the call number, of course, is found by looking in the card catalog. The numbers represent ten general subject areas, as follows:

000–099	Reference books, such as encyclopedias, and books about books (bibliographies). These books usually have R on the spine and can seldom be checked out of a library.
100–199	Philosophy, psychology, ethics (conduct).
200–299	Religion, including mythology and religions of all peoples.
300–399	Social sciences: law, government, education, vocations, civics, economics.
400–499	Language: dictionaries and books about the study of all languages.
500–599	Science: mathematics, physics, chemistry, biology, zoology, botany.
600–699	Useful arts: medicine, engineering, agriculture, aviation, manufacturing, etc.
700–799	Fine arts: painting, music, photography, recreation.
800–899	Literature: poetry, plays, novels, and criticisms of these.
900–999	History, geography, travel, biography.

Each of these general areas is divided into many subtopics, each of which has its own number. For example, the 630s are devoted to agriculture, and a book on forestry will be numbered 634, probably with a decimal to indicate a further subdivision.

LIBRARY OF CONGRESS CLASSIFICATION. The Library of Congress classification may also be explained if it is used in your library. By the time children reach the upper grades, they should at least be aware that there is more than one system of classification, since they may be using more than one library.

A	General works—polygraphy
B	Philosophy—religion
C	History—auxiliary sciences
D	History and topography (except America)

CATALOG CARDS
DEWEY DECIMAL SYSTEM

author card

book is located in nonfiction section	551.6 Davis, Hubert
	D A January fog will freeze a hog, and
	other weather folklore. Compiled and
	edited by Hubert Davis. Illus. by John
	Wallner. Crown, 1977
	unp. illus.

book is located in
nonfiction section

551.6   Davis, Hubert
D   A January fog will freeze a hog, and
other weather folklore. Compiled and
edited by Hubert Davis. Illus. by John
Wallner.   Crown, 1977
unp.   illus.
Thirty sayings used to predict the
weather are accompanied by a factual
explanation, the origin of the saying,
and its general reliability.

1. Weather lore. I. Wallner, John
II. Title

author
title

publisher

cards also under
these headings

title card

A January fog will freeze a hog, and
other weather folklore

551.6   Davis, Hubert
D   A January fog will freeze a hog, and
other weather folklore. Compiled and
edited by Hubert Davis. Illus. by John
Wallner.   Crown, 1977
unp.   illus.

1. Weather lore. I. Wallner, John
II. Davis, Hubert

remember that this
card will be found
under J, not A

pages are not
numbered

book is illustrated

subject card

note that cards are
alphabetized by first
letter at top of card,
regardless of
indentation

WEATHER LORE

551.6   Davis, Hubert
          A January fog will freeze a hog, and
other weather folklore. Compiled and
edited by Hubert Davis. Illus. by John
Wallner.   Crown, 1977
          unp.   illus.
          Thirty sayings used to predict the
weather are accompanied by a factual
explanation, the origin of the saying,
and its general reliability.

          1. Weather lore. I. Wallner, John
II. Title

there will also be a
card for this book
under the illustra-
tor's name

title card

book may be found
in juvenile fiction

          The great Gilly Hopkins

j   Paterson, Katherine
Fiction   The great Gilly Hopkins. New York:
          Crowell, 1978.

cards for fiction are
virtually the same in
Dewey Decimal and
Library of Congress
systems

author card

> j   Paterson, Katherine
> Fiction   The great Gilly Hopkins. New York:
> Crowell, 1978.
>
>   1. Title

when illustrator
is important,
there may be a
third card

see and see also cards

there is nothing cat-
alogued under this
heading; look under
woodcarving for in-
formation about
whittling

> WHITTLING   see
>
> WOODCARVING

some information
can be found under
this heading; you
may find additional
information under
the second heading

> AIRPLANES   see also
>
> AERONAUTICS

CATALOG CARDS
LIBRARY OF CONGRESS SYSTEM

author card

call number—book
is in juvenile
nonfiction

jPN	Bishop, Ann
6371.5	Noah riddle? Pictures by
B52	Jerry Warshaw. Chicago,
	J. Whitman, 1970.

40 p.   col. illus.   22 cm.

book has 40 pages
and color
illustrations

A collection of riddles about
Noah and the animals in his
ark.

1. Warshaw, Jerry
I. Riddles II. Title

title card

jPN	Noah riddle?
6371.5	
B52	Bishop, Ann
	Noah riddle? Pictures by
	Jerry Warshaw. Chicago,
	J. Whitman, 1970.

40 p.   col. illus.   22 cm.

A collection of riddles about
Noah and the animals in his
ark.

1. Bishop, Ann   2. Warshaw, Jerry
I. Riddles

subject card

RIDDLES

jPN   Bishop, Ann
6371.5   Noah riddle? Pictures by
B52   Jerry Warshaw. Chicago,
          J. Whitman, 1970.

          40 p.   col. illus.   22 cm.

          A collection of riddles about
          Noah and the animals in his
          ark.

              1. Bishop, Ann   2. Warshaw, Jerry
              I. Title

illustrator card

          Warshaw, Jerry

jPN   Bishop, Ann
6371.5   Noah riddle? Pictures by
B52   Jerry Warshaw. Chicago,
          J. Whitman, 1970.

          40 p.   col. illus.   22 cm.

          A collection of riddles about
          Noah and the animals in his
          ark.

              1. Bishop, Ann
              I. Riddles   II. Title

cassette cards

Oversize
probably means that
the cassette is
packaged with the
book by the same
name and kept in a
special place in the
library; ask the
librarian about
location

CASSETTE	McDermott, Gerald
j	Arrow to the sun. Narra-
Oversize	tor: Gerald McDermott. Sound:
PZ	H. D. Buch. Sound recording.
8.1	Weston Woods LTR 184C,
.M159	p 1975
Ar	

1 cassette 2½ × 4 in. 1⅞ ips.

1. Pueblo Indians—Legends
I. Title

publisher and
order number of
cassette

CASSETTE	Arrow to the sun
j	
Oversize	McDermott, Gerald
PZ	Arrow to the sun. Narra-
8.1	tor: Gerald McDermott. Sound:
.M159	H. D. Buch. Sound recording.
Ar	Weston Woods LTR 184C

1 cassette 2½ × 4 in. 1⅞ ips.

1. McDermott, Gerald
1. Pueblo Indians—Legends

remember these
cards will be color-
coded if in the
general file

---

cards for other
media will be similar
to these

PUEBLO INDIANS—Legends

CASSETTE	
j	McDermott, Gerald
Oversize	Arrow to the sun. Narra-
PZ	tor: Gerald McDermott. Sound:
8.1	H. D. Buch. Sound recording.
.M159	Weston Woods LTR 184C
Ar	

1 cassette 2½ × 4 in. 1⅞ ips.

1. McDermott, Gerald
I. Title

E & F	America
G	Geography—anthropology
H	Social science
J	Political sciences
K	Law
L	Education
M	Music
N	Fine arts
P	Language and literature
Q	Science
R	Medicine
S	Agriculture—plant and animal industry
T	Technology
U	Military service
V	Naval service
Z	Bibliography and library science

Using Media

As we have emphasized throughout this chapter, the elementary school library now usually contains many materials other than books. A well-stocked library may have pictures, graphics of many kinds, films and filmstrips, slides, records and cassettes, programmed materials, kits and games, models—possibly even videotapes and computers. And nearly every library will have at least some of these. Children will have had experience with these in the classroom, and they should learn to find and use them in the library, as a source of both pleasure and information. Further, they should learn to use such aids to supplement and/or add interest to reports, just as you do in preparing your lessons for the class.

As soon as children have become sufficiently familiar with the card catalog—and the library itself—to prepare simple reports using more than one source, plan for reports in several subject areas for which children may use various audiovisual aids. They should already have learned to use pictures, charts, and so on in giving oral reports (see Chapter 6), so this should not be entirely unfamiliar to them. Make sure, however, that the aids are included in the organizational plans for the reports. Point out that if a particular filmstrip, for example, cannot be included in the outline for the report, it should not be a part of that report, however interesting it may be.

Such reports, when well prepared, not only will enrich classroom activities but will help to prepare children for the kinds of presentations that many will be expected to make during later school years and in adult life.

SPECIAL REFERENCES

Chapter 13 has teaching suggestions for locating specific information and taking notes.

The use of an encyclopedia, atlas, almanac, biographical dictionary, fact book, or similar reference involves many of the same skills as those needed for effective use of a dictionary or a library card catalog. In addition, skillful use of most reference books requires the ability to locate the particular section, paragraph, or sentence within a topic or a book that gives the specific information sought, and some familiarity with each of the reference sources—familiarity gained through practice in using them.

Encyclopedias

An encyclopedia such as *Childcraft* can provide the primary grade child with good experiences in seeking and locating information in an encyclopedia. You can introduce encyclopedia use by demonstrating that you use the index to find where to look for information, and that you can then turn to the correct page and read the information you were looking for. Do this frequently as more information is needed on subjects being discussed. Tell and show the children what you are doing, and read what you find. Primary grade children should be permitted to browse in the encyclopedias available to them, and as soon as they have learned to read with sufficient skill they may be assigned simple facts to look up.

Intermediate grade children should receive more direct instruction, which should include the following skills and understandings:

- The form in which material in an encyclopedia is arranged, and differences in arrangement in the encyclopedias available for their use.
- Knowledge of the location of the index and the meanings of guide letters on the covers of volumes. Particular attention should be given to boldface type, parentheses, italics, etc.
- The use of pronunciation keys, cross reference listings, bibliographies at the close of articles.

Compton's Encyclopedia has Fact Indexes—each volume has its own—that will be most helpful when they are used correctly. If *Compton's* is available to your class, practice in using the index can be provided by having students pick a subject related to something the class is studying, decide which facts to look up, and use the index to help find these facts. For example, a subject like "waterfalls" will give the class an opportunity to explore and have experience with the arrangement of an encyclopedia, the use of an index, cross references, guide words, and the help given by pictures, charts, and their captions. The number of times instruction in using the encyclopedia is given will depend upon the particular class; they may need daily exposure in a meaningful setting for some time.

Many good encyclopedias for children are available—*The World Book, Collier's, Compton's, Americana, Britannica Junior*, and *Merit Student's Encyclopedia*, to name a few—and most school libraries have several of these. Children should have experience with all that are available to them. In connection with learning to take notes, each child might select a topic and look for information about it in all of the encyclopedias available. Comparing the information found can help children to discover the importance of looking in several sources for information. This should be done a number of times with a number of subjects; repeated lessons under guidance are essential for effective use of these materials.

Children can work both individually and in groups to gather information for oral reports. A group report can be valuable in several ways: the children can learn organization through planning what information each will look up and report, they can help each other in both finding and organizing material, and together they can present a more complete coverage of material than if each child were working individually.

Opportunities should also arise in an activity of this sort for children to discover that different sources sometimes present conflicting or different facts. Discuss how this might happen and emphasize the importance of using several sources to try to verify facts insofar as is possible. It is also helpful to point out that the copyright date of a book may have a bearing on the accuracy of certain facts—population figures and scientific data, for example. In other words, information might not have been wrong—or known to be wrong—at the time it was printed.

Children enjoy working with encyclopedias and other reference tools, and this type of experience provides opportunities for learning to locate information; to read critically; to take notes on, summarize, and outline what they have read; to prepare an oral or written report; to use handwriting, spelling, and punctuation skills; to compose with specific information and an audience in mind; and to do proofreading and editing. Thus learning to use the encyclopedia not only is valuable in itself, but also involves practice in a wealth of related language skills.

Atlases

Use of the atlas is frequently taught in connection with social studies, but, as with most social studies and other subject matter teaching, the tools and skills are those of the language arts.

Like use of the encyclopedia, use of the atlas should be taught first through demonstration. If the atlas includes a section which tells how to get the most out of it, this should be used as an aid. *The World Book Atlas*, for example, has at the beginning a section called "How to Get the Most out of *The World Book Atlas*," which explains how to find places, directions, and distances; how to understand symbols and population figures; how to pronounce names of cities; and how to understand abbreviations and foreign geographical terms. This atlas is also color keyed to help the user find quickly sections such as the United States, Asia, Africa, the index, etc. Children using this atlas to learn about the United States can find both physical and political maps of the entire country, as well as maps of regions and individual states. There are historical maps showing colonial America, the U.S. at the time of the Revolution, territories opened up by 1800, westward expansion from 1800 to 1850; maps showing positions and routes of the forces during the Vicksburg, Chattanooga, and Atlanta campaigns of the Civil War; plus two maps of the eastern theatre in 1862–1863 and 1864–1865.

Other maps show principal air routes, railroads, and highways; charts give populations and areas of states and major cities and distances between these cities. In addition, the student can learn that New York is the largest city in North America, that the highest elevation is Alaska's Mt. McKinley at 20,320 feet, and that the lowest spot is California's Death Valley, 282 feet below sea level. And this is only a part of what the atlas can reveal; there are maps and charts showing weather, population density, average income, available medical care, and so on. Children will be truly amazed at the variety of information that can be gleaned from a single book.

To give children experience with the atlas, have each child choose a city in the United States that he or she would like to visit. Help to direct selections so that each city will be large enough to be shown on maps and listed in at least some tables. Then have each child see how much information can be found about the city chosen and write this information on a small card. Perhaps the class could discuss the kinds of facts it would be desirable to know and formulate a list of questions such as the following:

> How far is the city from where we live?
> What route would I take to get there by plane? train? car?
> What kind of weather does the city have?
> What is its population?
> How many miles above sea level is the city?
> Is it located in an agricultural or industrial area?

The information gained through such an activity can be used to make a very attractive bulletin board—a map of the United States surrounded by the cards the children have made, each connected with a piece of colored yarn to a pin showing the location of the city. A map can be made very easily by taping a piece of white shelf paper or tagboard to the chalkboard, using the opaque projector to focus a picture of the map on the paper, and then drawing the outline with a felt pen. The children can color the states and locate their cities and other points of interest.

Once the children have learned to find places through the use of the index and map searching, teach them about directions and aids to pinpointing places. Parallels of latitude and meridians of longitude should be explained and discussed. Ask the children questions: Which is farther from our city—Houston, Texas or Tallahassee, Florida? If you were traveling from Louisville, Kentucky to Memphis, Tennessee, which direction would you travel?

Other atlas activities include these:

1. The reading of map symbols is necessary for understanding a map. The children can make a bulletin board showing the common map symbols and their meanings. Allow the children to copy these symbols from actual maps in an atlas. Perhaps the class could make up a game that involves identifying map symbols.

2. Determining distances on maps can and should be taught as part of the arithmetic class. It will take the pain out of arithmetic for some.

3. Abbreviations and foreign geographic terms become understandable to children once they are able to read and understand the tables where these are listed. When children are aware of the tables, they will enjoy looking for their new-found words or abbreviations on the maps.

4. An atlas also gives a great deal of information about a country—the area in square miles, the population and population density, the form of government, the capital and the largest cities, official and major languages—all on one easy-to-read table. It also gives information about the world as a whole—the

largest countries of the world in population and in area, climates, rainfall, etc. Give the children questions that require them to find such information: What is the coldest it ever got in North America and where was this? Where was it the warmest in North America and what was the temperature? In what countries—or on which continents—do most of the people in the world live?

5. Teaching about relief maps found in an atlas can be related to the making of salt-and-flour maps. Salt-and-flour maps can be made of a state, of a country, or of areas to help develop concepts such as peninsula, gulf, bay, or plateau. A child who uses an atlas as a guide in making a salt-and-flour map of a plateau will have solid knowledge of that term. Activities of this type are particularly beneficial for children who have difficulty with reading. (Make the salt-and-flour mixture with one cup each of salt, flour, and water, plus one tablespoon of powdered alum. The mixture can be stored in old coffee cans until you are ready to use it. If it dries out, add more water.)

Other References

Children will be fascinated with the many kinds of one-volume references to be found in the library. Here are a few; let them see how many others they can find.

Book of Lists
Dictionary of Art and Artists
Dictionary of Costume
Encyclopedia of Animals
Encyclopedia of Sports
The Ethnic Almanac
Geographical Dictionary
Guiness Book of World Records
Webster's Sports Dictionary

A library contains a wealth of other reference materials that children should become familiar with; the following may be of particular interest. In addition, permitting children to browse in libraries and encouraging their reporting on interesting things they discover may suggest other areas of study.

ALMANACS. The best way to teach children what an almanac contains and how to use it is to provide them with copies for exploration. Once they have done some browsing, a few specific lessons should be sufficient to acquaint them with this interesting tool. Following are a few suggestions:

1. Ask each class member to write the name of a magazine or newspaper that is in his or her home. Then let each one use the almanac to find what the circulation of that magazine is.

2. Have each child select a city and use the almanac to find out its population, the height of its tallest building, etc.

3. Let each child look for a famous person with his or her last name. The class might even like to make a *Who's Who* of these famous "relatives."

4. Have children make up questions for which answers can be found in the almanac—for example, "Who won the National League batting championship in 1971?" These can be placed on cards and exchanged, perhaps with children divided into teams and competing to see which team can find all the answers first.

FAMOUS FIRST FACTS. Intermediate grade children have been known to get into a "He did"—"He didn't" type of argument. Many times such an argument can be settled by the use of *Famous First Facts.* The index in this book is different from others children may be familiar with. Each child might use this index to make a list of all the important events that occurred on his or her birthday or on a particular holiday. These could be incorporated into a bulletin board entitled "Famous Days," which would include a picture of each child, the date of his or her birthday, and a list of the events that happened on that date written by the child concerned. A similar bulletin board might show famous events of a particular year—the year most of the children were born, the year they started attending school, etc. This type of activity can stimulate conversation and lead to other language activities.

BOOKS OF QUOTATIONS. Books of quotations may be introduced in a manner similar to that used to introduce almanacs and *Famous First Facts*. The primary objective is for children to become aware that there are books like this and to understand how they are organized and in what ways they are helpful. Again, a bulletin board can be useful. It might be entitled, "I Wish I'd Said That," with each child selecting an author—perhaps just because the name appeals—and then finding a quotation from the author selected. These may be written on cards, along with credit to the author and the source, and placed on the board. To extend this activity, children might check for facts about the person in an encyclopedia, take notes, and give orally or write a brief report.

The references mentioned above are intended as suggestions only—so many excellent books are available that it would be impossible to teach about all of them. The important thing is for children to become aware of the many resources to be found in libraries and to become familiar with ways to use them. Plan lessons around those that are of special interest to your class or that may be used in conjunction with class activities or units of study.

ACTIVITIES FOR THE UPPER GRADES

Children in the upper grades are apt to vary widely in library skills, especially considering today's mobile population. Some may still be learning to use the card catalog and the special references discussed in the previous sections. Many will still be taking notes that are either too copious or inadequate. And nearly all will need help in combining information from several sources into an organized report. These are learnings essential to a child's success in school and to his or her personal growth. Make sure, then, that upper grade children have practice in these skills as need is indicated.

Begin with simple, short reports, possibly even requiring only one source of information. Or perhaps you might assign group reports, with each child responsible for only one aspect. Go with the class to the library and observe children as they work, to discover individual and group needs. Then, if necessary, design individual or group exercises (similar to those suggested for the middle grades) to meet these needs. Continue this sort of practice, along with short reports, as long as necessary.

As children advance to longer reports using several sources of information, stress the need for beginning with an outline so they will know what they are looking for and thus not take unnecessary notes. And, of course, emphasize the importance of outlining as a means of organizing material after it is obtained. These outlines need not be formal, though children should know outline form by the time they reach the upper grades.

At *no* point should elementary school children be required to write long "term papers." Rather, emphasize the skills of locating information, organizing it, using audiovisual aids to supplement oral reports, and choosing the best way to convey ideas, either orally or in writing.

Children in the seventh or eighth grade who have become adept at locating and using materials may be ready for an introduction to *The Reader's Guide*. It should be stressed, however, that the child who has not learned to use an encyclopedia easily, who does not readily use the table of contents or index of a book to locate information, or who has not learned to organize materials from two or more sources is *not* ready for this more complicated source. If, however, you do have a few children who seem ready, select a time when the children are working on group or individual reports to introduce these few to this valuable research tool. Bring in a volume of *The Reader's Guide*—or if this is not possible, copy a few pages on one of the machines now available in most libraries. Show the children how to find out what periodicals are included and how to interpret the entries; then let them practice looking up sources of specific information. (Very little instruction or practice should be needed if they are truly familiar with other references.) Then arrange a trip to the library, either for these children or for the entire class, so they may have actual experience in using the *Guide* and finding magazine articles listed there.

Again, learning to use a public library is crucial, since it is a public library that is used or not used by adults.

Upper grade children should be aware that the city, county, or university library is a veritable treasure house of records, tapes and cassettes, picture files, films, micro-recorded materials, and equipment to use them. In addition, there are pamphlet files, newspaper files, bound volumes of innumerable periodicals, art objects, dioramas, and exhibits of many kinds. There are soundproof rooms where one may go to listen to recordings, and machines for copying pages from books. If there is such a library in your area, upper grade children should visit it. Possibly you could arrange a guided tour by the children's librarian or someone else who knows and understands children. This may help them to be less awed when they are ready to take advantage of the library's resources.

A FINAL WORD

Teaching children to know about and use the library and all its resources should be a vital part of your program in all areas. There is little doubt that the child who knows how to use library aids will, in all probability, be a better student. But the greatest reward will come when the child reaches maturity, for then he or she will be able to find information and to locate books and other materials that enrich life and aid personal fulfillment.

References

Beck, Margaret V., and Carney, Vera M. *Guidebook for Teaching Library Skills*. T. S. Denison and Co., 1981.

Bell, Irene Wood, and Weickert, Jeanne. *Basic Media Skills Through Games*. Libraries Unlimited, 1979.

California Association of School Librarians. *Library Skills*. Fearon Publishers, 1973.

Davis, Ruth Ann, ed. *The School Library Media Center: A Force for Educational Excellence*. R. R. Bowker Co., 1974.

"Getting Kids into Libraries—and Vice Versa," *Learning* 5 (April 1977): 60–63.

Glasser, J. F. *The Elementary School Learning Center for Independent Study*. Parker Publishing Co., 1971.

Holstrop, R. W. *Education Inside the Library Media Center*. Shoestring Press, 1973.

Margrabe, Mary. *The New Library: A Stations Approach*. Acropolis, 1973.

Polette, Nancy. *E Is for Everybody*. Scarecrow Press, 1976.

Richardson, Selma K. *Periodicals for School Media Programs*. American Library Association, 1978.

Start Early for an Early Start. American Library Association, 1976.

Walker, H. Thomas, and Montgomery, Paula Kay. *Teaching Media Skills*. Libraries Unlimited, 1977.

Teaching Resources

FILMS

The Library, A Place for Discovery. Encyclopaedia Britannica Educational Corp. (11 min.; color; primary).

Look in the Answer Book. Encyclopaedia Britannica Educational Corp. (17 min.; color; intermediate).

FILMSTRIPS

Hooray for the Library. Eye Gate Media (series of 4 filmstrips and cassettes; primary).

How to Use the Card Catalog. Society for Visual Education (intermediate).

Using the Elementary School Library. Society for Visual Education (6 sound color strips; intermediate).

KITS

An Introduction to the Library. Prentice-Hall Media (4 filmstrips, cassettes, and teacher's guide).

Library Services. Eye Gate Media (series of 4 filmstrips with sample catalog cards; intermediate and upper).

Using Reference Skills. Eye Gate Media (reproducible exercises; puzzles, games, cassette with lessons; intermediate and upper).

OTHER AIDS

Barnes, Donald L., and Burgdorf, Arlene B. *Study Skills for Information Retrieval*. Allyn and Bacon (series of workbooks on locational skills; middle and upper grades).

Cleary, Florence Damon. *Discovering Books and Libraries*. H. W. Wilson Co., 1977 (a handbook for middle and upper grades).

Getting to Know the Library, Books A, B, C. Scholastic Book Services (3 workbooks; grades 1–6).

How to Use the Reader's Guide to Periodical Literature. H. W. Wilson Co., 1978 (pamphlet; free in reasonable quantities).

Library Skills. T. S. Denison and Co. (workbooks and teaching guides on how to use the library; grades 4–6).

Map Skills Workbooks. Scholastic Book Services (grades 1–6).

Activities for Preservice Teachers

1. Investigate the possibility of involving parents as librarians or library helpers. Be prepared to report to the class.

2. Gather materials on book fairs. What does a school need to do to get a traveling exhibit?

3. Survey several classrooms to determine how many pupils have public library cards. Inquire how often those with cards use them.

4. Plan a lesson for a particular primary grade that would necessitate looking up information in a beginning encyclopedia. Be sure to find out whether this information can be found in an encyclopedia that would be available to a class at this grade level.

5. Visit the library to obtain lists of Newbery and Caldecott award winners. Familiarize yourself with as many of these books as possible, and begin a card file of annotations for primary, middle, or upper grades.

6. Select a fifth grade text for a subject area of your choice. Using the text as a base, make a unit lesson plan that would require children to go to the library for added information. Be sure to provide for differences in library experience and language ability.

7. Familiarize yourself with at least one set of encyclopedias, one atlas, and one of the other references listed in this chapter. Note particularly organization, teaching aids provided, types of information included, and grade levels for which each might be suitable.

8. Plan an activity designed to familiarize children with the use of a reference tool other than the encyclopedia. Demonstrate to the class exactly how you would present it.

9. Plan a unit for a subject area and grade level of your choice. Include at least three different types of media aids and tell how you would use them.

Activities for Inservice Teachers

1. Visit libraries in your area. Discuss with librarians the ages, interests, and reading abilities of your class. Find out what each library has to offer of a special nature for children. Find out what the librarian would like children of the ages of those in your class to know about the library.

2. Prepare a bulletin board designed to teach the use of the card catalog. Make large sample cards, similar to those in this chapter, with explanations (including pictures) of the various entries on the cards.

3. Plan a library skills unit for your class. Include visits to libraries in your plans.

4. Prepare activities that require children to use particular library skills—for example, finding several references about a topic, using an atlas, finding fiction books by a particular author, or locating a specific issue of a magazine.

5. Make a survey of the amount of library-use teaching done in your school. Report the results of your survey.

6. Plan a unit in some subject area for which children will prepare individual or group reports, using audio-visual aids. Report to the class on the number and types of aids used—and how successful they were.

Independent Activities for Children

1. A child might go to the library for the purpose of reporting back to the class about the different kinds of atlases (or almanacs, encyclopedias, fact books, etc.) that the library has. The report should be complete enough for the pupils to really see differences among the references in a category. Possibly permission could even be obtained to bring one or more of these references to the classroom at the time of the report for purposes of illustration.

2. Ability to read symbols—verbal and pictorial—related to air and auto travel is important. A child or group of children might prepare a chart bulletin board showing the different types of signs one might see on a visit to the grocery store, in an airport, on the highway, etc.

3. Have the child find the title and call letters for a book by each of these authors:

Lois Lenski   Robert Lawson
Eleanor Estes   Ludwig Bemelmans
Maurice Sendak   Laura Ingalls Wilder

Then reverse the process and give titles of books for which the child is to find the names of the authors.

4. Prepare sheets containing various types of information, some true and some false. Individual children who need additional practice in locating information can use library and study skills to find out whether or not the information is true. Sample statements might be as follows:

Henry and Ribsy was written by Roald Dahl.
Hailstones and Halibut Bones is a book of poems about holidays.
Chicago is approximately 850 miles from Boston by air.
The piranha is a flesh-eating fish that is found in the Amazon River.

5. At the beginning of the football (or baseball, ice hockey, etc.) season, a sports-minded pupil might prepare a bulletin board about the sport, using pictures cut from magazines and newspapers along with information gathered from almanacs and other sources to give interesting information about the game.

6. Have a child prepare a report on the library to present to another class. This should include the use of visual aids—for example, reproductions of various types of cards from the card catalog, a floor plan of the library, books with different types of call numbers, etc.

7. A child can use an atlas to plan an imaginary trip, plotting the route to be taken, places of interest to visit, time necessary for traveling, method of travel, kinds of clothing needed, etc.

8. An individual child can prepare a report for the class about the Caldecott or Newbery Award. This might include such items as when the award was first given, what factors enter into the selection, and which books and authors that the class is familiar with have won it. Several books that have received the award might be used to illustrate the report.

9. When the class is working on a project for which supplementary material is needed (this will occur often in a program that is vital and broad), a child—or several children—could go to the library to locate and examine materials that might be useful. The child could then check out these materials for class use (arrangements will need to be made with the librarian for this) or prepare a list to be placed on the bulletin board, giving title, author, a few words about content, and the call number or location for each item.

15 | *Literature for Children*

Teaching a child the basic reading skills is necessary if the child is to succeed in school, since such a large portion of the learning that takes place in school involves reading; but if that teaching also results in the child's learning to *enjoy* reading, that learning will aid the child in becoming a more complete person throughout life. The reading program, then, should be two-pronged. First, it must give each child the skills he or she needs to read well, for if these skills are not learned there will be little or no seeking of the knowledge, pleasure, and insights that reading can provide. Second, if a child is to discover these things, there must also be specific provision for the kinds of literary experiences that will encourage and develop appreciation of the written word and the desire to read.

VALUES OF LITERATURE

The principal value of literature is surely the pleasure and enrichment it brings to the individual. A child who loves to read will never be at a loss for something to do and will spend many pleasant hours with books as companions. This reading will enlarge and extend the reader's world and should result in his or her gaining greater appreciation of the beauty and power of language—the way words can stir the imagination, arouse the emotions, and develop new insights.

Books can also help children to understand both themselves and their relationships with other people, and this understanding can often help an individual child to improve his or her self-concept. This is a central theme of an increasing number of books written for primary children. For example, there is Pat Hutchins's *Titch*, which exemplifies the frustrations of innumerable small children, for Titch is the youngest and smallest member of his family. *Emily and the Klunky Baby and the Next Door Dog*, by Joan Lexau, will strike a response not only from children of divorced parents but also from those whose parents are very busy and those who must help care for younger brothers or sisters. The illustrations in this book will bring gleeful giggles as the huge, shaggy next-door dog steals rides on Emily's sled, making it heavier and heavier for her to pull until she finally decides not to run away from home after all. A fifth grade girl whose family has recently moved might find solace in *The Cat Across the Way;* one who lives in a foster home would surely respond to *The Great Gilly Hobson* and her yearning to find her "real" mother, while Lila Perl's Fat Glenda should appeal to any girl in the upper grades who is overweight and longs to be attractive to boys. Equally, the boy who is beginning to feel independent can surely empathize with Dave, in Emily Neville's *It's Like This, Cat,* who wants a cat simply because his father thinks he should have a dog. There are books about old age, death, the problems of adolescence, and so on. In short, there are innumerable opportunities for children to discover that they are not alone in their problems, to find inspiration for setting and seeking goals, and to learn how they can adjust to situations and personal problems.

Children need not only to understand their own problems, but also to recognize that other people have problems not unlike their own. This may lead to the realization that people are not so different after all. For example, the white child who reads Ezra Jack Keats's *Whistle for Willie* will not be able to help identifying with this black boy who cannot whistle for his dog; likewise, the child of divorce—or of poverty—must surely feel kinship with Rafer in Joan Lexau's *Me Day*. Progressing to such books as *Stevie* by John Steptoe, *Watch Out for the Chicken Feet in Your Soup* by Tomie de Paola, *Zia* by Scott O'Dell, and *The Turning Point* by Naomi Karp can lead children to a better understanding of other cultures and other races.

Equally important in these days of mainstreaming and the struggle for equality by the handicapped are books that help to develop an awareness of those who are physically or mentally different. There are many of these, even at the primary level—for example, Joe Lasker's *He's My Brother* (slow learner), Bernard Wolf's *Anna's Silent World* (deafness), or Ezra Jack Keats's *Apt. 3* (blindness). Thus reading can help children to gain a greater understanding of people and the world in which they live. This understanding can be further increased by reading literature of and about the past. It has long been recognized that literature is a major avenue for transmitting to the present the values, ideas, and experiences of past generations. Knowing about the past can provide a new perspective on problems of the present and increase children's appreciation of both their own heritage and that of others.

There can be little doubt that wide experience with books increases a child's vocabulary. Children whose parents have bought them books and have read to them frequently are better prepared for the language of the school. Educators who plan kindergarten and primary programs advise teachers to use many books and to read and tell many stories to help the children learn new words and acquire new meanings for words they already know. As children advance in school, reading can continue to enrich vocabulary in these ways.

Reading is also an important way to build and extend concepts. For example, a common word like *home* may have different connotations for different children. One may think of home as a two-story frame house in a typical suburban neighborhood, another may think of it as a crowded apartment in a city tenement, and possibly neither has ever heard of a home called an *igloo* or *hogan*. Books may introduce these and many other words that hold the concept of *home*, along with the emotional factors with which this word may be associated. And as they advance in reading skills and experience, children can acquire and broaden many concepts and ideas.

Bibliographies Helpful for Building Social Awareness

American Potpourri: Multi-Ethnic Books for Children and Young Adults (U.S. Office of Education, 1977)

The Black Experience in Children's Books by Augusta Baker (New York Public Library, 1971)

Multi-Ethnic Books for Young Children by Louise Griffin (National Association for the Education of Young Children, 1970)

Reading Ladders for Human Relations, edited by Eileen Tway (National Council of Teachers of English, 1981)

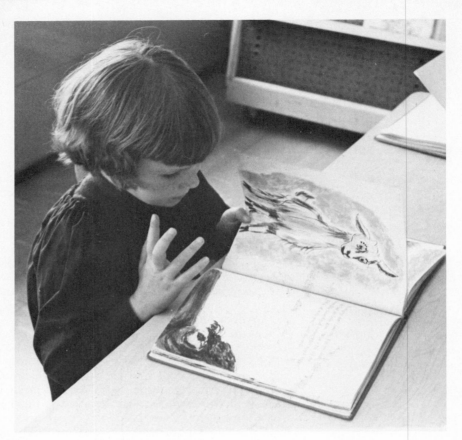

Reading is total involvement.

In addition to providing vocabulary and ideas, books can help children learn to express their own thoughts and to become familiar with the language patterns they meet in reading and in listening to others. The child who comes to school with a limited language background is especially helped by hearing many stories both read and told, but all children need to become acquainted with many types of sentence structure, the use of figurative language, the language of poetry, the formal language of research, and so forth, if they are to learn to use language effectively. And perhaps one of the most valuable corollaries of reading is that it stimulates the child's imagination and helps to stir creative talents. There is no child who cannot write something creative with the proper encouragement and a wealth of models.

Finally, any program that is tied to a single textbook is almost bound to be both narrow and uninteresting. Resource materials are invaluable, but why not add a third dimension through the use of imaginative literature?

Benjamin Franklin becomes a real person, not just a character in history, when viewed through the delightful *Ben and Me;* Patricia Clapp's *Witches' Children* helps readers experience vicariously the events which culminated in the infamous Salem witch trials; Wilder's *Little House* tales have surely made the westward expansion more real to many, while Mike Fink, Paul Bunyan, and Pecos Bill lend color and humor to that same study. Pupils with a scientific bent might enjoy reading science fiction and trying to decide whether the events depicted could really happen; a letter-writing unit can be enriched by the addition of letters written by famous people; and, of course, biography can be useful in any area. Finding just the right materials to make the best use of literature in the total program may take a little time, but the rewards are immeasurable.

CREATING THE CLIMATE

Just as you are the model for children's speaking, so will you be a model for their attitude toward books and reading. Thus a cardinal requisite for guiding children toward a love for reading is to enjoy books yourself. Even an avid reader of adult books may find it difficult to communicate this enjoyment to children; it is therefore vital that you become widely acquainted with books written expressly for children. A good first step is to take a course in children's literature, if this is possible. In addition, books written about children's literature, book reviews, and bibliographies of various types can serve as guides to specific titles. (See the list of aids to book selection at the end of this chapter.) But these are only guides. Simply knowing *about* books or knowing specific titles and authors is only the beginning; to really *know* children's books, it is necessary to read them. Spend time regularly in the children's section of the library making notes of books that would be good for reading aloud, those that would be good additions to the room library, those that would interest a particular child in your class, those that would be useful as supplementary reading for a particular unit of study, etc. This should not be an onerous task; the world of children's books is a delightful and colorful one.

For aids to teaching literature, write to The Children's Book Council, 67 Irving Place, New York, NY 10003.

Demonstrating Interest in Books

The daily activities of the classroom provide many opportunities to demonstrate to the children your own interest in and dependence on books. First, make it a point to show your own reliance on books. Let the children see you reading, use stories and poems to illustrate situations and show how ideas have been expressed by others, and use quotations when they are appropriate—perhaps putting a daily or weekly quotation on the bulletin board. This can be overdone, however; quotes should be used naturally and only when they are suitable to the occasion, or children will become bored with them.

Second, make time in the schedule to read aloud to the children at least once every day. This practice should be continued even after children have

Ideas

Children's Book Week in early November is a good time to promote children's books. Write to The Children's Book Council, 67 Irving Place, New York, NY 10003.

Also remember Library Week. Write to National Library Week, 58 W. 40th St., New York, NY 10036.

If you want to have a book fair, write to The Children's Book Council and to *Scholastic Teacher*, 50 W. 44th St., New York, NY 10036.

acquired the skills to read on their own. In fact, it is perhaps more important in the upper grades, since young children are ordinarily eager to read and to be read to, whereas the interest of older children, whose horizons are expanding, may tend to diminish unless it is carefully nurtured. The reading may be only a short poem, or it may be a story, a chapter in a book, or something interesting and informative that you wish to share with them. Learn to read well, and let the children see that you enjoy reading.

Third, discuss books with the children. Ask them questions about books they are reading or have read, let them recommend selections to be read aloud to the class, help individual children to find books that are suited to their interests and needs, and seek their opinions about books that you have especially liked—or perhaps even ask them to evaluate a book you did not like and see if they can decide why you didn't. Your attitude should show that you value their opinions and that not everyone has to like the same book, even if it is supposed to be "good."

And, finally, although reference materials are not, strictly speaking, "literature," you can foster the idea that books are friendly helpers by turning to books regularly for information and assistance. Children need to learn that not even the teacher knows everything—that it is the most natural thing in the world to turn to the dictionary to check a spelling, to seek out additional information on a subject you are studying, or to look up something you do not know.

The Room Library

The appeal of the corner of the room devoted to the room library is an important factor in creating an atmosphere that encourages reading. If the reading corner is nothing more than simply an area with some bookshelves and perhaps a table and a chair or two, it will do little to reinforce the attitude that reading is a pleasant and satisfying experience. The reading corner should be warm and bright—one of the most attractive spots in the room—and should have enough light so the children can read comfortably and can see to find books on the shelves. Chairs arranged invitingly in groups around a low table on which books are attractively displayed will provide motivation.

And now that so many filmstrips and cassettes of children's stories are available and the "hardware" for seeing and hearing them can easily be operated even by primary children, a filmstrip machine and a recorder should be nearby. Be sure to allow children free access to both materials and machines.

Some teachers like to obtain children's lounge or rocking chairs to make the reading corner inviting. Another possibility is to seek contributions from parents—an outmoded sofa, chairs, lamps, even a plant or two. A more informal atmosphere can be provided by strewing large cushions on the floor or even filling an old bathtub or rowboat with pillows. Let space, availability of "furnishings," your own imagination, and the ages and backgrounds of the children be your guides.

Provide informal places to read.

A bulletin board devoted exclusively to books is also an important part of the book corner. The children themselves can help to make displays and see that they are changed regularly. Here are a few ideas:

1. Place at the top a caption reading "Can You Match These?" On one side put pictures of well-known authors of children's books, and on the other put either actual book jackets or some that have been drawn by the children for books that were written by these authors. Provide lengths of colored yarn which the children can use to connect each writer with his or her book as they discover which ones belong together.

2. Use the same type of setup as above to match characters and the books they are in or quotations and the characters who said them (Chicken Little—"The sky is falling"; The Little Engine—"I know I can, I know I can"; etc.).

3. To create interest in a particular book, cut pictures representing characters and scenes in the book from publishers' advertisements, book jackets, or magazines, mount them attractively, and arrange them around a replica of the book.

4. Let children write captions for pictures or draw their own illustrations for stories they particularly like. These can be used to make a bulletin board about a particular book or about several books with a common theme, the same author, the same setting, etc.

5. Let the children write "advertisements" for books they particularly like and post them on the bulletin board. This would be excellent in connection with a study of advertising techniques.

6. Regularly center a display around a particular ethnic or national group. This might include authors, illustrators, or even favorite characters in books.

7. Cut a large tree from construction paper and place it in the center of the bulletin board. At the lower corners tack envelopes containing apples, oranges, or whatever, also cut from construction paper (it could even be a magic tree, bearing many different kinds of fruit). When a child finishes reading a book, the child writes his or her name and the name of the book on one of the pieces of fruit and fastens it to the tree.

8. Have the children write letters to their favorite authors, and make a display of the answers received so that all the children can enjoy them.

9. Many of the activities suggested in the later section on book reports can provide attractive and interesting bulletin boards.

Of course, there is no point in making an attractive book corner unless the children are allowed to use it. The schedule should provide daily time for children to read, listen to stories, work on book reports, and discuss the books they have enjoyed, and they should be allowed and encouraged to browse when they arrive at school early or when they have finished assigned work and the other children are still busy. There is no need for absolute quiet in the room library—if the children enjoy books, they will want to share their pleasure. The classroom atmosphere—not just during the library period, but at all times—should be one in which children feel free to ask questions, share information, and help each other. However, they should at the same time recognize that consideration for others demands that they do this without disturbing others or disrupting the activities of the class.

Naturally, the most important furnishings for the room library are the books themselves. Beginning with the very first day of school, the library should be well stocked with books, records, and tapes, including both fiction and nonfiction of many types and covering many areas. Books should have eye appeal—attractive illustrations and easy-to-read type—and there should be a few books for advanced readers that are above grade level, as well as a good number with high interest and simple vocabulary for the reluctant and poor readers, who are especially difficult to entice. Books should also be changed regularly so that no child will be unable to find something of interest that he or she has not already read.

Knowing the children, their interests, and their abilities is the best aid in selecting books and other materials that will be particularly suitable for them. Another aid is the children themselves. Allowing several (not the same ones each time) to go along on trips to the library will help them to become familiar with the library and library procedures. They can help not only in selecting books, but also in "taking orders" for particular kinds of books from the other children, thus freeing you to browse among new additions and find those suitable for children with special interests or needs. In the middle grades (if this is permitted in the school or library) two or three children might occasionally go by themselves to select books, again taking orders from the others. To avoid confusion and the "bandwagon" effect that might result from taking oral orders, these could be written on slips of paper and placed in a box kept on the table in the library corner or in a colorfully decorated envelope thumbtacked to the bulletin board. Pupil selection, however, should be an addition to, not a substitute for, teacher selection, since pupils cannot have a total picture of class needs.

Reading Aloud

As suggested earlier, providing time during each school day for reading aloud to the children will do much to stimulate interest in books. Sometimes this reading will be spontaneous (a particular situation simply demanding the reading of a certain selection), but most of the time reading should be planned. There are two reasons for this: first, it is not possible to have at hand every selection that you might want to read; second, reading aloud requires preparation.

Many selections are now available on records or cassettes; both the quality and the quantity of these are increasing almost daily. However, allowing individual children to select and listen to records or cassettes—or playing them for the entire class—should supplement, not supplant, reading aloud. This is a time for sharing an enjoyable experience with the children, for building rapport, for discovering their interests and tastes, and for broadening interests and improving tastes. Sometimes, of course, you may wish to use a recording in order to free your hands for manipulating visual aids or in order to join the children in enjoying an especially well read story or poem. But this should be the exception rather than the rule; the avenue of pleasure for children should be your own voice, not that of an unseen actor.

Becoming a good reader may require practice. Even an experienced reader should not read a selection without going over it first. It is a good idea to borrow a tape recorder from the school and listen to your own voice as you read. This will provide an opportunity for you to make sure that the

Unless you are one of the few who read dialect well, use a recording of a story which makes extensive use of dialect—but be *sure* it's a good one!

pitch is pleasant and loud enough to be heard, to check speed and enunciation, or to listen to an entire selection to see if it gives the desired impression.

In general, select for reading aloud only those stories or poems that you personally enjoy. Just as you would probably do a poor job of teaching something you don't really think the children need to learn, so you will not read well a story you do not particularly like. The pleasure the children get from listening is in direct proportion to the pleasure you have in reading.

Be constantly on the alert for selections that would be appropriate for reading aloud. Making a card file is one way to be sure you will find the right story for the right time. Cards might be organized according to the particular units or areas the class will be studying, or they might simply be under rather general headings, with the possible addition of special categories such as Christmas, Personal Problems, or Stories for a Dreary Day. Each card should contain enough information to aid you in deciding which particular story to use and to help you find it quickly. It might include the following items:

- Title and author.
- Where it may be found—Is it in a collection? In what library? Call number?
- Audiovisual possibilities—Are the illustrations suitable for showing? Are filmstrips, slides, etc., particularly good? Is there a record or cassette that might be used with visual aids?
- Time required for reading.
- Brief summary—only as much as is needed for a reminder.

With the exception of poetry, which in most cases is meant to be read aloud, there is no point in reading something the children could just as easily read for themselves. Reading time is precious; it should be reserved for those things which children might have difficulty reading for themselves or which they might not appreciate as thoroughly. For example, humor—particularly subtle humor—is sometimes not evident to children when they read silently, although they respond delightedly when it is read well to them. Dialect, too, poses a problem, as may stories containing foreign words and names, because the words do not *look* familiar. And many children's classics contain a number of words that children can understand in context but have difficulty reading for themselves. Marguerite Henry's *King of the Wind*, for instance, is neglected by many middle graders until the teacher selects it for reading aloud. Thus, reading aloud is an excellent way to improve children's tastes and increase their perception. Reasons for reading aloud, then—or for using records and cassettes—might include one or more of the following:

1. The selection is high in interest level, but vocabulary or sentence structure is difficult for the children. (This might apply to anything read to kindergarten or first grade children, but should be particularly considered at higher levels.)

2. The selection is of particular interest, but not enough copies are available for individual reading.

3. The selection is of high interest, but print in available copies is difficult to read and illustrations are poor.

4. The selection is particularly suitable for reading aloud. Sounds of the words and phraseology add markedly to enjoyment, and/or appreciation is particularly heightened by oral interpretation.

Not everything that is of value is suitable for reading aloud. Check by asking yourself these questions:

1. Is the action (of a story) fast moving and easy to follow?
2. Is the length suitable for reading at one sitting (the length of a sitting should depend on the age and maturity level of the children)? If it is long, could it be satisfactorily divided—e.g., chapters in a novel?
3. Is the vocabulary such that children will understand what is happening even if there are a few words they do not know?
4. Will it be of interest and value to all the children?
5. Is the content pertinent to something that the children are studying or that they are interested in?

The atmosphere for reading or storytelling should be pleasant and informal. If at all possible, gather the children around you in such a way that they can see illustrations easily without delaying the reading unduly. Illustrations are often important to enjoyment (it would be a shame to read *Where the Wild Things Are* without letting the children see those marvelous "wild things"), so they should be large enough to be seen by all the children. If not, consider other possibilities: larger pictures placed on a flannel board, transparencies made for the overhead projector, or perhaps a filmstrip. In such cases it might be helpful to tape the story or to use a commercially produced tape, thus freeing your hands to manipulate the aids. This is useful also when realia are being used, as, for instance, when reading is being used to develop vocabulary for primary children. It is not necessary, however, to use visual aids every time a story is read. In fact, with some children (such as educationally disadvantaged children, whose attention spans may be short), visual aids may prove to be a distraction. A child may become more interested in what makes the figures stick on the flannel board or how the projector works than in the story and interrupt the reading to investigate. Thus discretion is needed in deciding when and how to use visual aids. Certainly good illustrations should always be shared, and aids can add variety. They can also be incorporated into the discussions that precede or follow the reading of a selection when this seems appropriate.

Successful reading or storytelling is an act of sharing. Hold the book away from your face so the children can see your expression as you read, and maintain eye contact by looking up at them occasionally. The reading should move along smoothly or interest will lag, but children should be allowed to see illustrations, to laugh at a humorous line or situation, or even to ask a question that can be answered in one or two words. Other questions can be answered with a friendly smile and "Let's find out" or some similar remark. Too many interruptions may mean that you are not reading well or loudly enough or that the children find the story uninteresting. In the latter case, it may be best simply to put the book away until another time. The possible cause of the inattention should then be considered. Possibly the story was too difficult in concepts or language, there was too little action, or the characters did not seem believable. If so, look for another story that will serve the same purpose but have more appeal for the children. However, if you consider the story suitable and wish to try it again at a later time, perhaps the visual aids could be changed or omitted entirely, the story told instead of read, or some other variation applied.

In some schools teacher's aides, senior citizens, cafeteria workers, and others who have the time and interest are enlisted to read to children. This makes possible reading to small groups or even to individual children (with the child perhaps sitting on the reader's lap), as well as providing a more informal atmosphere and allowing for greater attention to the needs, interests, and abilities of each child. If you have such "helpers," work closely with them: aid them in finding suitable stories, familiarize them with the children's needs and interests, make them an integral part of your total program. But remember always to use these people to enrich the program, not as a substitute for your own reading or to free you for grading papers or going to the teachers' room.

Volunteer readers not only enrich a language arts program but can do much to foster good school-community relations.

Storytelling

A good storyteller is always in demand. None of us ever grows too old to enjoy a well-told story, but storytelling is a particularly useful tool with young children, since their attention span is short. Telling a story instead of reading it also frees your hands for illustrating it with flannel board figures or some other aid. More important, it permits you to maintain eye contact and makes you seem closer to the children—there is not even a book between you. Further, storytelling permits the insertion of synonyms or appositive phrases to explain an unfamiliar word or a definition of a foreign term (*hombre*—that means *man* in Spanish) without interruption of the story.

The criteria for selecting a story to be told are much the same as those for choosing one to read, with one important addition: it is important that the story not lose by being translated into your own words. For example, *The Elephant's Child* without Kipling's "great, gray-green, greasy Limpopo River" or *The Wonderful O* in any language but Thurber's own would surely be less effective. Of course, it is possible to memorize a story, but this is not advisable except in very special cases. Memorization takes a great deal of time, and a story can be ruined if you forget something at a crucial point. Therefore, if the author's words are vital to full enjoyment, reserve the story for reading aloud.

A good storyteller commands a great fund of words and can find exactly the right way to describe a character or an event. A good storyteller loves words, loves telling stories, and communicates this enthusiasm to the listener. There are few "born storytellers"; thorough preparation is the key to success.

Like reading aloud, storytelling is an act of sharing, but it is even more intimate. Therefore the experience should be truly enjoyable for both the teller and the listeners. Choose a physical setting that is comfortable and relaxing—possibly the library corner, where children may sit beside you,

Books with Many Helpful Ideas about Storytelling

Children's Literature through Storytelling by Joseph A. Wagner (William C. Brown, 1970)
Handbook for Storytellers by Caroline Feller Bauer (American Library Association, 1977)
Storyteller by Ramon R. Ross (Charles E. Merrill, 1972)
Storytelling by Eileen Colwell (The Bodley Head, 1981)
The Way of the Storyteller by Ruth Sawyer (Viking Press, 1970)

Check with the school librarian, language arts supervisor, or audiovisual coordinator, and watch for reviews of new aids in such sources as *Booklist* and *School Library Journal*.

on the floor, or on cushions, each one close enough to hear well and to see gestures, facial expressions, or other aids used. Select for telling only stories that you particularly enjoy, with plots which are easily followed and with characters and situations suited to the age and experiential backgrounds of the children. Study the characters thoroughly and decide what kinds of voices and mannerisms they would have. Visualize the setting and think of words that will convey this image concisely. Determine the mood of the story and what vocabulary, phrasing, and tone of voice will best express it. Examine the wording of the story to see whether retaining some of the author's words or phrases will heighten enjoyment, either because they are particularly colorful or because they form a repetitive pattern. Decide where gestures would be effective and whether visual aids are needed, such as pictures, flannel board figures, puppets, a filmstrip, or realia. Remember, however, that a well-told story often needs no embellishment. And finally, make sure that you know the exact sequence of events, including any details that are important to appreciation or to later events. The effect is lost when important information is omitted and has to be inserted at a later time.

Practice and rigid self-evaluation are essential to good storytelling. Using a tape recorder, experiment with pitch, intonation, phrasing, and use of pauses; practice telling the story before a mirror to judge the effect of gestures and facial expressions; time several tellings so you will know how much time is needed to tell the story effectively. All this will seem very time consuming at first, but it will prove to be time well spent. And a story once learned can be told again and again—possibly even to the same children. In this connection, it should be noted that even a story that has been told many times before should be mentally reviewed to make sure of details and sequence. A set of cards containing names of characters, important details, the sequence of events, and useful visual aids can help you to review. These cards can be filed with those containing information about stories for reading aloud.

Using Media

Much has already been said in this chapter about using audiovisual aids, and many of these will and should be products of your own ingenuity or that of the children. However, school libraries are increasingly becoming treasurehouses of many materials other than books. A well-stocked library may contain files of book jackets, pictures, flannel board figures, overhead transparencies, realia of many kinds, films, filmstrips, tapes, records, and cassettes, as well as the equipment for utilizing all of these. Often information about such aids is included in the library catalog on color-coded cards so that particular types of material can be identified and located quickly. That is, a card for a filmstrip might have a strip of red tape across the top edge, a cassette card might have a green tape, and so on. Use these materials wisely.

Plan carefully, so that they will enhance the literature program, *not* replace it. Plan for variety as well; use flannel board figures one day, a filmstrip and/or cassette another, and simply tell or read a story when that seems to be the best method. And by all means, try to use the method best suited to the material you are presenting. Keeping media information in your book file can be helpful here; memories are short, and this will be a valuable asset in planning. For convenience, cards may be color coded in a manner similar to that used by libraries (see above). Cards can be marked with colored tape, crayon, or felt-tipped pen.

An almost endless number and variety of commercial materials are available for use as aids in presenting literature to children. Many children's stories have been made into movies that are available to schools at low cost. Well-known actors have recorded stories and poems; authors have recorded their own works. Nearly all of the Newbery Award books are available in filmstrip/cassette or filmstrip/record form, as are interviews with many well-known authors and illustrators. In fact, most companies are now producing these combinations of filmstrips and records or cassettes, thus using both audio and visual means of telling a story. These often can be purchased—and certainly can be used—separately if desired. In addition, multimedia kits include multiple copies of a book, plus a filmstrip, a cassette, or both, as well as a teacher's guide and sometimes even duplicating masters for children's responses. Such materials can be used by the entire class, by small groups, or by individual children in the library corner or media center.

Do preview all audiovisual materials before using them. There is great variety in these; some authors do not read their own works as well as professional actors do.

HELPING CHILDREN SELECT BOOKS

Developing an understanding of each child's interests, expanding those interests, and helping the child to develop new interests is the responsibility of each teacher. In order to help a child select books, it is vital to know the child and his or her interests. This is one reason for staying with the class when they go to the library. The librarian can offer suggestions and help children find books, but the librarian cannot be expected to know individual interests and abilities as a teacher does.

Begin by reading the cumulative records for your class before school starts. These records will furnish background information on age, sex, health problems, family structure, abilities, and perhaps interests. Knowing that Lily Jones hates her name or that the biggest child in your fifth grade has first grade reading ability, for example, will be helpful when you select books for the class and for individuals.

Interests by Age and Sex

Naturally children differ in reading interests just as they do in every other respect. Children in general, however, appear to show certain preferences at certain age levels, and these are discussed below. They should not be thought of as absolutes, but only as guidelines to be used in conjunction with a knowledge of the interests of the specific children in a class.

A list of children's choices
for reading is published annually by The International
Reading Association and
The Children's Book Coun-
cil. For a free copy, write
to Children's Choices, c/o
International Reading
Association.

PRIMARY GRADES. Primary children select books principally by their pictures; therefore the illustrations are of primary importance. Bright colors
are preferred over pastels, and pictures should occupy a major portion of
the space, with only a few words on each page. Illustrations may be fanci-
ful, but objects should be readily recognizable. Young children love animal
stories, like *The Surprise Party* and *It's Not My Fault;* stories about mechanical objects, like *Little Toot Through the Golden Gate;* and some stories
about those who have problems they can identify with, like Jim in *Will I
Have a Friend?,* who wonders apprehensively if he will find a friend on his
first day at school, or the boy in Marchette Chute's poem, who says,

I told them I didn't WANT mittens
And they've given me mittens again!*

Folk and fairy tales are perennial favorites, and children love fantasy as
long as the characters have human feelings and reactions. For example,
Horton may sit on the egg without breaking it, but he must shiver when
the winter winds blow and grow lonely sitting there on the nest alone.

MIDDLE GRADES. Middle grade children continue to like fantasy and folk
tales, but as their knowledge and experiences broaden, so do their reading
interests. They are interested in the world around them, both near and far,
today and yesterday. Many books appeal to the middle grader—histories,
biographies, stories of other lands; adventure tales about pirates, cowboys,
and the frontier; books that explain the wonders of the world about them.
In the upper middle grades, boys particularly begin to be interested in
sports and science, and both sexes continue to enjoy animal stories. As a
rule, these children are interested in a wide variety of subjects and types;
their principal criterion, as far as fiction is concerned, is that the plot move
fast and have plenty of action.

UPPER GRADES. Most of the interests pupils have in the middle grades continue into the upper grades. At this level, however, the sexes begin to differentiate. The boys often prefer sports, action, adventure, and mystery,
whereas many girls begin to enjoy a bit of love interest. It might be said
that the girls' interests are broader, since they often enjoy the same books
as the boys, while boys scoff at love and tend to avoid books in which the
principal character is feminine.

At all ages, children enjoy and should be exposed to humor as well as to
stories about those who have problems to which they can relate. Humor is
a safety valve for emotions, and it is important that children learn to
laugh—at themselves as well as others. By all means encourage the enjoyment of humor: problems at which we can laugh grow small enough to at-

*"Presents" by Marchette Chute. Copyright 1932, 1960 by Marchette Chute. From the book
Around and About by Marchette Chute. Copyright © 1957 by E. P. Dutton & Co., Inc., publishers, and used with their permission.

For a free copy of *Choosing a Child's Book,* write to The Children's Book Council. This pamphlet gives suggestions for choosing books for various age levels and lists other sources of information about children's reading.

tack. Similarly, children need to be exposed to stories about both personal and social problems. The important factor here is to make sure that the problem is not too great for the children's experience and is one to which they can relate.

Another factor to be considered at all levels is the size of print and general attractiveness of the books. As mentioned earlier, young children select books primarily by their illustrations. Appearance continues to be important, even in the upper grades; children will seldom select a book that has very small print and no illustrations. Naturally, the size of print can decrease as children mature, as can the amount of space devoted to illustrations, but it is important that books be attractive and not too difficult to read. This is especially true for children who do not read well.

Reading Ability

It is relatively easy to find books for good readers, but a major problem for most teachers is helping those children who have limited reading ability select books that will interest them and that they can read. This is not an easy task; it is one that will require a great deal of patience and ingenuity. A few guidelines may prove helpful:

1. Determine the child's independent reading level. If you don't know how this is done, consult a diagnostic reading book or the reading consultant in your school or district. (A frequently used "rule of thumb" is to estimate a child's independent reading level to be one grade level below his or her instructional level.)
2. Determine the child's interests by observing and listening.
3. Use the knowledge you have gained about the child's interests and particular characteristics to guide you in selecting material for that child.
4. Branch out in the use of resources. Perhaps magazines rather than books can furnish the necessary stimulus.
5. Help the child maintain self-respect by finding easy-to-read materials that are not beneath his or her age level. Help the child gain standing in the other children's eyes. Make the most of other abilities the child has.

Magazines for Children

Artsporation, College of Fine Arts, The University of Texas, Austin, TX 78712 (grades 4–6)
Cricket, Box 2670, Boulder, CO 80302 (grades 1–4)
Children's Digest, Children's Health Publications, Box 567B, Indianapolis, IN 46206 (grades 3–6)
Highlights for Children, P.O. Box 269, Columbus, OH 43216 (grades 3–6)
National Geographic World, National Geographic Society, 17th and M Sts., N.W., Washington, DC 20036 (grades 3–6)
Odyssey, Astromedia Corp., P.O. Box 92788, 625 E. St. Paul Ave., Milwaukee, WI 53202 (grades 4–8)
Ranger Rick's Nature Magazine, National Wildlife Federation, 1412 18th St., N.W., Washington, DC 20036 (grades 2–5)
3-2-1 Contact, Children's Television Workshop, P.O. Box 2934, Boulder, CO 80321 (grades 4–8)

Children have been known to extend themselves in reading ability if they are sufficiently motivated. For example, a thirteen-year-old with third grade reading ability and an interest in fast cars might be successfully tempted by Lerner Publications' series about racing. This series includes books about the Indianapolis 500, race-car drivers, drag racing, motorcycle racing, and even snowmobile racing. Watts has a similar series, written by E. and R. S. Radlauer, which has great appeal to children in the middle and upper grades. Both have middle grade reading levels and are amply illustrated with actual photographs filled with action and excitement. Such materials might also be utilized to improve reading skills so that reluctant readers can advance to higher levels of ability and appreciation.

Children are no different from adults when it comes to reading. Age, sex, environment, interests, and ability all influence what a person selects to read. A wise teacher knows each child and guides each child in the selection of books.

More Magazines for Children

Ebony Jr., Johnson Publishing Co., 820 S. Michigan Ave., Chicago, IL 60605 (grades 4–8)

The Electric Company Magazine, P.O. Box 2924, Boulder, CO 80321 (grades 1–4)

Jack and Jill, Children's Better Health Institute, P.O. Box 567B, Indianapolis, IN 46206 (grades 1–3)

Penny Power, Consumer's Union of the United States, P.O. Box 1906, Marion, OH 43302 (grades 4–8)

Stone Soup, Children's Art Foundation, P.O. Box 83, Santa Cruz, CA 95063 (grades 4–8; articles and illustrations by children)

Again, a useful aid is a set of file cards. In this case, the cards can be used to record the children's interests so that you can help them to discover books they will enjoy and profit from. Let the children start the cards themselves; at the beginning of the year, have each child fill out a card, giving his or her name and age and the answers to a few simple questions, such as:

> Of all the books you have read (or stories you have heard), which did you like the best?
> What was one you didn't like very well?
> What is your favorite TV show?
> What do you like most to do after school or at recess?
> If you could go anywhere you wanted, where would you go? Why?

Other questions may be more suitable for a particular class or grade; the important thing is to keep to a few that can be answered briefly. Use the cards as a beginning and add to them as you talk to the children, jotting down names of books they seem to enjoy, hobbies, problems, etc. Thumb through the cards before going to the library, making notes of particular types of books, authors the children have enjoyed, special problems, etc., to guide you in the selection of books for the room library or for reading to the class. In addition, a "request box" might be kept in the library corner, where individual pupils could place requests for particular books or books about particular subjects. And, whenever possible, several children might go along to help make selections.

Book Lists

Ask the librarian to help you compile a list of suggested books for:

1. Reading aloud.
2. Helping children to find in library.
3. Suggesting to relatives as gifts.

Give the lists to parents at parent-teacher conferences, possibly making specific recommendations for individual children.

Although you and the children will make the final selection of books for the room library, the librarian can be extremely helpful in making suggestions. Most librarians will go to great pains to help find exactly what is wanted, if they are only asked. In addition, a librarian usually has a number of book lists to guide him or her in book selection. Such lists are generally annotated and arranged by subject areas, with age or grade levels indicated. The librarian will also have lists of Newbery and Caldecott Award winners; these are excellent both for the children and for reading aloud.

Naturally you will want to read or skim all the books you select for the room library, but these lists and the librarian can save you a considerable amount of time by leading you to specific titles and authors.

THE INSTRUCTIONAL PROGRAM

If children are exposed to a wide variety of good books, have a teacher who enjoys reading, and are given the time to become acquainted with literature, they may very well develop a taste for reading and some discrimination in selecting what they read. If literature is integrated with other areas of the curriculum, there is little doubt that both the curriculum and individual children will be enriched. And if the kinds of activities discussed in later sections result from reading, children's language skills will surely improve. But if careful planning of literary experiences coordinates all of these, the benefits will be even greater.

Planning, however, does not mean that children's reading should be circumscribed, nor that they should be limited to a specific reading list. Experience with this type of approach in the secondary school has shown that it does little to inspire enthusiasm for reading. Rather, the program should include both planned experiences and free choice, and it must be built around the interests, needs, and abilities of the particular children for whom it is planned. There should *not* be a specified reading list for each grade which all children are expected to follow, but there should be specific planning for the *kinds* of literary experiences that will be included in the program, not just at one grade level but at all levels. With planning, one experience builds upon and relates to another. Without it, children may have many valuable and enjoyable experiences, but they may also wind up being "introduced" to haiku (for example) in the fifth grade, again in the sixth grade, in the seventh grade—and even again in the secondary school.

Instructional Considerations

A number of factors need to be considered in planning, both for a single grade level and for the entire program. These are discussed in the following sections.

VARIETY. Selections chosen for the entire group—to be read either by or to the children—should include a variety of kinds and styles. This variety should embrace genre (stories, poems, plays, etc.), theme, tone, humorous selections as well as serious ones, and type (fantasy, folklore, adventure, history, biography, etc.). In addition, there should be some older classics and some new ones. Not all of these are suitable at every grade level, of course, but every effort should be made to see that children at all levels become acquainted with many kinds of writing and many styles.

EXPERIENCE LEVEL. Like any other area of the curriculum, the literature program must begin where the children are. If the language and sentence structure are too difficult for them, they will probably find a selection boring. Further, the concepts must be ones to which they can relate. For example, the first grader who has never seen snow is less likely to respond to *A Snowy Day* than is one accustomed to wintry weather. This is not to say that children can relate only to that which is within their immediate experience—part of the value of literature lies in the vicarious experience it provides—but there must be a basis for relating. Primary children, for instance, can enter readily into a story in which animals speak, especially since they themselves frequently carry on lengthy conversations with pets, dolls, and even imaginary playmates. This is "pretend," and they understand that, as long as there is some other basis for relating. Thus they delight as Roald Dahl's "Fantastic" Mr. Fox outwits Farmers Boggis, Bunce, and Bean, because they recognize the parent's role as provider for the fam-

Books for Special Events

Children's Books for the Holidays (National Council of Teachers of English). An annotated list of books for Christmas and Hanukkah (K–7).

The Crowell Holiday Books (Thomas Y. Crowell Co.). These include books about St. Valentine's Day, Halloween, Thanksgiving Day, Passover, and others.

Jewish Holidays by Betty Morrow and Louis Hartman (Garrard Publishing Co., 1967).

Let's Find Out About New Year's Day by Martha and Charles Shapp (Franklin Watts, Inc., 1968).

Light the Candles (The Horn Book, Inc., 585 Boylston St., Boston, MA 02116). An annotated bibliography of books for the Christmas season.

Turkeys, Pilgrims, and Indian Corn by Edna Booth (The Seabury Press, 1975).

Children's Press has a series of seven books about special days (Halloween, Easter, Valentine's Day, and others) by Jane Belk Moncure. Each contains illustrated suggestions for projects and activities.

Garrard Press has books at the third-grade reading level about special days, as well as a series about holidays in other lands.

ily and also because the three obnoxious farmers represent the adult world which so often circumvents their own desires.

INTEGRATION. If literature is to be an integral part of the curriculum, consideration must also be given to how this integration is to be accomplished. Just as overall planning requires decisions about experiments, field trips, and audiovisual aids, so it requires decisions about literary experiences that may enrich and be supplemented by other curriculum areas and that are suited to the particular children involved. Should a social studies unit include the tall tales of the expanding frontier? If so, should this be balanced by a realistic story of life in the early days? Does a group of reluctant readers need a story to "spice up" their interest in the American Revolution, such as *A Spy in Williamsburg* by Isabelle Lawrence? How can poetry be used? What kinds of literary experiences have these children had, and what kinds do they need?

FLEXIBILITY. If the literature program is truly to be adapted to the needs of the children and if it is to supplement and enrich their experiences as well as the curriculum, it must be flexible. No plan is so good that it cannot be changed. Suppose, for example, you had planned to have the children read a particular book as a group, but, as the year progresses, you discover that it is too difficult for a number of them. Possibly you might read it aloud if it is suitable for oral reading; perhaps the substitution of another book that is easier to read but has a similar theme or setting would be desirable; or the class might be divided into several groups, each reading a different book and preparing some sort of report on it for the rest of the class. The important fact to remember is that the interests, needs, and abilities of the children are at the heart of any successful program.

GROWTH. In order to provide for the needs of *all* the children, the program must include both group and individual experiences. Some selections can be read to or by the entire class, so that they develop understandings and broaden concepts through guided discussions and shared reactions. Sometimes small groups may read different selections to accommodate differing interests and abilities. Above all, the program must provide opportunity and encouragement for each child to explore in the area of his or her own interests, to discover new ones, and to grow in understanding and appreciation through individual reading. Be sure to make recreational reading a part of your daily plan. Do not allow pressures of time and subject matter to interfere with the establishment of lifetime habits.

Objectives of the Literature Program

Underlying all of the considerations discussed above is the most important element in planning—consideration of the objectives of the literature program. First, of course, are the underlying objectives, embodied in the earlier section on the values of literature as well as in the preceding paragraphs. These must be the overriding considerations in planning for both group and individual reading. Second are the immediate objectives—what are the specific outcomes desired from reading? These will be discussed in the following sections.

Since we have grouped the language arts into two categories—receptive and expressive—let us consider the specific objectives of the literature program in the same way. Those having to do with reception involve understanding and appreciating what is read; those having to do with expression involve both oral and written responses to what is read, including creative responses.

RECEPTIVE ABILITIES. In considering the objectives of the literature program, it is vital to remember that elementary school children should *not* engage in critical analysis—this should be reserved for university students and possibly some secondary students. However, some understanding of genre, theme, plot, setting, characterization, and point of view can be developed gradually during the elementary and secondary years, and these will lay the foundation for greater perception and appreciation. Children need not know the meaning of a word such as *genre,* but they will understand the concepts all these terms embody if they have been exposed throughout the elementary years to a program that has provided many experiences with them. For example, the primary child can certainly understand that Nonny Hogrogian's *One Fine Day* is a story, while the book that tells about the weather or how to feed the fish in the class aquarium is not. Perhaps factual material might even be kept on a different shelf in the room library to further this concept. This child also begins to realize that some stories are about people who could be real (*A Snowy Day,* for example), while one like *Where the Wild Things Are* is pure make-believe. Thus the child is laying the foundation for understanding the difference between fiction and nonfiction and between fantasy and realism, although none of these words are known.

The child can also begin to recognize that poetry is different from prose, particularly if rhyme and rhythm are pointed out. Much is done with both rhythm and rhyme in readiness activities, and many children's stories are written in rhyme. Primary children will enjoy clapping their hands softly to the rhythm of a poem or song, and they may even attempt to write simple poems if poetry has been made a vital part of their reading experiences.

Talking about things is an important part of language development, especially at the primary level. Suppose you interrupt the reading of a story to ask, "What do you think will happen next?" You are giving the children an opportunity not only to express themselves and to think critically, but also to understand a basic element of plot construction—the way a story turns out is built upon the events that have gone before and the kinds of characters involved. Having children recap the sequence of events in a story builds organizational skills and also helps to develop the concept of plot. "Why did Horton keep sitting on the egg when he was so cold and miserable?" "What kind of boy is Archie?" "What did you learn from this story?" Questions like these are concerned with theme and characterization and will help children learn to think about and evaluate what they read.

In the middle and upper grades these concepts can be further developed.

Children who are going to use the library independently need to know the difference between fiction and nonfiction and to understand what biography is. To write reports and stories they must understand sequence and organization. Some direct instruction will be needed, but the best teacher is example. Certainly no child should be asked to write a story without having heard or read many stories. In addition, discussions can point out sequence in plot development and the need for *cause* to be established before *effect* is reasonable.

Children of this age should also be aware of figurative language. They can talk about phrases like "the *heart* of the problem" and "matters came to a *head*." They can compose similes and metaphors (note that they should compose these, not just identify them in someone else's writing); they may even experiment with personification, describing an event from the viewpoint of an old house, a pet, or a piece of furniture. Dealing with figurative language, however, requires many examples and much familiarity with both written and spoken language.

As children discover the thought and work that go into writing well, their appreciation for good writing will grow. This appreciation and the understandings that effect it develop slowly, and only as a result of wide acquaintance with books over a long period of time. Children cannot be told to understand a concept or to appreciate a poem—the foundation for understanding and appreciation must be carefully laid through experience.

EXPRESSIONAL ABILITIES. If literature is truly made an integral part of the activities and program of the classroom, it will be inextricably interwoven with the use of language in all its aspects. Children may develop both oral and organizational skills as they plan the dramatization of a scene from a favorite story (see Chapter 6 for suggestions). Shy children who have difficulty in making oral presentations may tell a story through the use of puppets, thus taking a first step toward developing oral abilities (Chapter 6 gives directions for making several kinds of puppets). Children may read aloud stories or poems they particularly like, or they may participate in choral reading activities.

A good literature program should also stimulate creative writing of many kinds: children write stories, poems, accounts of incidents that might have occurred before or after the action of a particular story, letters from one character to another, etc. Book reports, too, can take both conventional and creative forms; this will be discussed in the next section.

In doing any kind of writing or talking about a book (other than merely recounting the plot), the child must do some evaluation. If he or she is going to write a different ending for a story, it must fit the events that have gone before and the characters who are involved. If a poem is written, it should capture the mood of the story. If an illustration is drawn, the setting must be accurate. Discussions of common reading are a good way to help children see the considerations that must enter into this kind of expression. Such evaluation, in turn, should help them to make their own writing and speaking more effective.

In planning the literature program, then, you should take into account the kinds of expressional activities the children need to engage in. Naturally, not all oral and written expression must result from literature, nor is it necessary that expressional activities result from everything read—this would be proselytizing in the worst way. However, reading *may* stimulate expression, and it certainly can and should provide models, particularly for creative writing.

Book Reports

Make book reports—like science reports or those in any other curriculum area—an integral part of your oral language program.

The book report has been used and abused for years. Too often it is dull to read or hear and consists of little more than a recounting of the plot. This type of report has some value; it gives practice in using the skills of writing or speaking as well as in selecting important details and arranging events in sequence. But a good book report can do this and much more.

To begin with, not every book read needs to be reported on. If you wish to keep a record of the children's reading—and this is a good idea for many reasons—each child might keep a card on which he or she records the names and authors of the books read, along with the date on which each was finished. As an added bonus, the children might use a numerical system to evaluate books:

1—Excellent. I recommend it highly.
2—Very good, but not everybody would like it.
3—Not bad, but I wouldn't particularly recommend it.
4—I didn't like it much.

These cards could be kept in a room file; children could glance through them for recommendations, and they could serve as an extra check before the regular trips to the library.

However, most books read should be reported on, because a pleasant experience should be shared and because books make excellent springboards to both oral and written expression. Some suggestions follow, and both you and the children can probably think of more.

ORAL ACTIVITIES. Oral activities may take a variety of forms. A few suggestions are these:

1. A child might read a particular incident from the book to the class. This requires preparation so that it will be read well; also, the incident selected should be complete in itself or listeners will lose interest.
2. Several children who have read the same book could dramatize a scene.
3. Children who have read books about the same period of history could have a panel discussion comparing the information learned—or developing different aspects of life during the period.
4. An individual child could demonstrate skills learned from a book—card tricks, a sports skill, etc.

5. A child could pretend to be one of the characters in a book giving an interview to a newspaper or TV reporter. Another pupil would act as interviewer and would be given a list of questions to ask.

6. A child could prepare a speech explaining why a particular character would or would not make a good friend.

WRITTEN ACTIVITIES. These should vary according to the age and abilities of the children; some of the following might be appropriate:

1. An imaginary letter written by one character to another at a particular point in the story.

2. An estimate of what kind of people might enjoy the book and why.

3. A review or advertisement for the class or school paper.

4. A first-person description of a particular event in the story, told as though the writer had been an onlooker. (This observer could even be a dog or some inanimate object rather than a human being.)

5. A character sketch of one of the people in the book. It should include both a physical description and a discussion of the kind of person this character was (using specific actions to prove points).

6. A description of the setting of the book, telling why it was or was not important to the story.

7. A TV script based on the book. If equipment is available, it might actually be dramatized and videotaped as a group or class activity, thus calling for both oral and written expression as well as planning and organizational skills.

8. Book reviews. As children reach the upper grades, they should learn how to write a good book review. Prepare for this by bringing in sample reviews from magazines and papers.

OTHER ACTIVITIES. Nonlanguage activities can be useful in two ways: they create an opportunity for children who are not highly verbal to make something the other children will admire, and they can add interest and color to the library corner. Such activities might include the following:

1. Making models, dioramas, or maps. For example, one child might use sand, twigs, and other items to show the setting for the battle at Little Big Horn, another might make a scale model of the Kon Tiki, a third might draw a map showing Huck Finn's trip down the Mississippi, etc.

2. Drawing illustrations for a particular story. These can make excellent bulletin boards.

3. Drawing a cartoon strip showing the action in a certain event (also good bulletin board material).

4. Dressing a doll in a costume that might have been worn by a character in a story.

5. Making a mobile depicting characters or objects in a book. It can be hung in the library corner.

Activities such as these can be used to encourage a shy child to speak before the group. For instance, the child who drew the map might be asked to explain briefly where various incidents took place, or the one who made a model could explain what it represents. These explanations can be done very informally, with the children grouped around and looking at the object being shown rather than at the one who is speaking.

POETRY IN THE CLASSROOM

Many adults think they do not like poetry, but children love rhythm, rhyme, and the sounds of words. Mother Goose has remained in good standing for years, and Dr. Seuss is an undisputed favorite with young readers. Unfortunately, teachers and textbooks must take a large share of the blame for this shift in values. Selections inappropriate to the age, experience, and interests of children have made poetry dull; teachers have read beautiful poems badly; forced memorization has placed poetry in the same category as multiplication tables; and an overemphasis on analysis has made poems seem like scientific data to be studied rather than an experience to be enjoyed.

Poetry offers a way to express ideas and feelings, it stimulates the imagination and provides an outlet for the emotions, it motivates children to express their own creativity, and it furnishes a way of showing children the beauty and expressiveness of language. What better reasons can be offered for using poetry with children?

Guidelines

Poetry had its birth in song, and, as with song, its aural qualities are among its chief assets. Thus, with a few rather obvious exceptions, poems are meant to be heard, not seen. This does not mean that the children may not have copies to follow as a poem is read—in fact, this may sometimes increase their enjoyment—but it should be read aloud, not silently, and it should be read in such a way that the greatest appreciation is obtained. This means preparation; attention must be given to the speed at which individual lines should be read, what the cadence is, which words should be emphasized, and what tone and pitch will best express the poem's meaning. Reading poetry well requires even more practice than reading stories well; again, the tape recorder can be a valuable ally.

Poetry should become a natural part of the ongoing activities of the classroom. Opportunities are endless; children love Indian chants, folk ballads, songs of the riverboatmen, etc. Many of these are available on records or in filmstrip-record packages. When possible, arrangements might be made to have someone come in to play and sing some of these for the class; older children will particularly enjoy this.

The use of poetry might be occasioned by a holiday, a change in the weather, a circus in town, or animals or insects brought in by the children. There have been poems written about every imaginable subject or situation, for poetry is truly a natural form of expression. For example, sixth graders struggling with fractions might find a moment of relaxation with Carl Sandburg's "Arithmetic"; or on a dreary day when the schoolyard is a sea of mud, you might say to the children, "Do you know what? I know a poem about mud."

MUD

Mud is very nice to feel
All squishy-squash between the toes!
I'd rather wade in wiggly mud
Than smell a yellow rose.
Nobody else but the rosebush knows
How nice mud feels
Between the toes.*

Select poems carefully and choose only those you and the children will enjoy. Too few children have regular exposure to enjoyable experiences with poetry after they have passed the nursery-rhyme stage. Therefore, at any grade level it is important to start with poems that the children will understand and like. Children will not learn to love poetry or any other type of literature by being forced to read particular poems simply because they are reputed classics or because they are in a particular textbook. There are plenty of good poems; it requires only a little time and effort to find those that appeal to the children in a particular class.

For example, if you should read the poem quoted above, you might ask, "What are a rosebush's toes? Do you suppose it can really feel the mud?" Or possibly, "I like the words 'squishy-squash,' don't you? Can you think of other words about mud?" Sandburg's fog that comes "on little cat feet" might initiate a discussion of which animals might represent other weather phenomena: could a distant thunderstorm be a growling dog threatening to attack, fleecy clouds be swans floating gracefully across the sky? Through such questions and discussion, children can develop a true understanding of such techniques as metaphor or onomatopoeia without ever hearing the words. And, with encouragement, they will experiment with their own word pictures and colorful language when they write.

Studies have shown that children prefer humorous poems to serious, meditative ones and that they like narrative poems and poems about animals or about experiences that are familiar and enjoyable to them. They respond to rhythm, rhyme, and sound in poems, but they reject those that rely heavily on imagery and figurative language, finding these difficult to understand. Select poems with concrete, well-defined images. Ask questions that bring forth individual responses and encourage appreciation for the "special" language of poetry. Help children to *discover* images; do not test for "correct" responses. Then, as children grow in experience and understanding, they will be ready for figurative language and more subtle types of imagery.

*By Polly Chase Borden. From *Child Life,* copyright © 1930.

Older children will enjoy learning the names of poetic techniques, but keep in mind that a poem should *never* be analyzed like a specimen under a microscope lens. Call attention to rhythm, a particular rhyme pattern, alliteration, metaphor, onomatopoeia, and other techniques as they aid in creating the total effect of a poem, not as items to be memorized and tested for at a later date. If children can see that the "Beat, beat, beat of the tom-tom" not only imitates the sound of the drums by its rhythm but emphasizes it through the use of hard vowels, they can begin to appreciate that the ordering and the sounds of words do much more than merely state facts. As you point out these techniques, follow with writing activities in which they are used—as a class, in groups, or individually.

Poetry may be reacted to in many ways other than writing or discussion, of course. Children may simply clap to the rhythm of a poem, dramatize all or a part of it, make a drawing or painting, or create a dance reflecting its rhythm or feeling. A poem with a repeated refrain might inspire choral reading, either spontaneous or planned. Encourage many kinds of responses; but, above all, make every effort to ensure that poetry is an avenue for the enjoyment, enrichment, and appreciation of the beauty and power of words.

Poetry File

Be selective—gather quality, not quantity. And by all means choose only poems that you like yourself.

The file in which you keep records of stories to be told or read should also contain poems. A file is probably even more important for poetry than for stories, since poems are short and it is virtually impossible to remember exactly where to find a particular one. Very short poems may simply be clipped or copied and placed in the file; other entries might show only where the particular poem is to be found. It is also a good idea to keep at least one good anthology (preferably several) in the classroom so that poems are quickly available. These should not be the only sources of poems, but they should be selected with great care.

Another possibility is to clip a card with titles and sources of poems to pictures in your picture file. These can provide a quickly assembled—and effective—bulletin board for some special occasion.

Suggested Activities

Primary children should participate in rhythmic activities to help them develop coordination and aural discrimination. Select poems with a strong, regular beat, preferably ones the children know and like, and let them clap out the rhythm as you read. They will also enjoy acting out nursery rhymes as you read them; try simple ones first, such as "Humpty, Dumpty," "One, Two, Buckle My Shoe," "Jack and Jill," and "Three Little Kittens."

Children love familiar poems just as they love to have the same story read again and again. When they ask for particular poems, you can begin to develop appreciation by asking questions such as the following: Why do you like this poem so much? Which words do you like the best? Does this line make you see a picture? When the three little kittens say "Mew, mew, mew," does it sound as though they're crying? How do they feel when they say "Purr, purr, purr"?

Such questioning should not be overdone, however. The important goal is to have the children enjoy the poem. Let the questions come as a spontaneous expression of your own appreciation; use them to increase pleasure, just as you point out illustrations in a book to make the story more enjoyable.

Young children love rhythm and rhyme. Seek out opportunities to capitalize on and develop this interest whenever you can. For example, when you talk about rhyming words in developing reading skills, let the children make couplets using the words that rhyme. You be the scribe, furnishing spelling, punctuation, and capital letters. They will enjoy this and learn to put a thought into a few words:

> The sky is black
> Because night came back.
>
> See what I found!
> A ball that's round.

Primary children can also participate in simplified choral reading—that is, you might read the verse, while they recite the refrain. Intermediate children can progress to more complex types of choral reading; in fact, students of all ages will enjoy this activity if poems are carefully selected.

Intermediate and upper grade children also enjoy reading aloud poems they particularly like. This is an excellent way to introduce a poetry unit. It is important here to accept any poem a child selects, even if it is not a very good one. The selections children make can serve as a guide to discovering other poems that they can understand and enjoy.

As middle grade children expand concepts and vocabulary and begin to feel more at ease with writing and spelling, they should also be increasing their appreciation of the ways words are used. Choosing exactly the right word to use is important to all writing, but it is especially vital to poetry. This is a time for emphasizing the fact that the sound of a word, as well as its meaning, contributes to the effect of a poem. An excellent vehicle for this is a sampling from Mary O'Neill's *What Is That Sound!* For instance:

GROWL?

> When a surly dog
> Complete with scowl
> Goes rumbly-grumbly
> That's a growl.
> Growl's sound is surly
> Snarly-gray,
> And when you hear it
> Back away. . . .*

---

*Mary O'Neill, "Growl?" in *What Is That Sound!* (Atheneum, 1966). Used by permission.

Talk about the sound of words like *rumbly-grumbly*, *surly*, and *snarly:* Do they sound unpleasant? Why do you suppose she called a snarl *gray* instead of some other color? Certainly it rhymes with *away*, but is that the only reason?

The introductory poem from the same volume is excellent for building vocabulary as well as for talking about the images words create.

SOUND OF WATER

The sound of water is:
Rain,
Lap,
Fold,
Slap,
Gurgle,
Splash,
Churn,
Crash,
Murmur,
Pour,
Ripple,
Roar,
Plunge,
Drip,
Spout,
Slip,
Sprinkle,
Flow,
Ice,
Snow.★

Experiment with reading this poem in such a way that each word sounds like its meaning, and be sure to point out the rhyme if children have missed it. Then let them try to create a similar poem about the sound of food, paper, the classroom, etc. Be sure to give several choices.

Almost every child can be inspired to be creative in some way. Perhaps this creativity will consist merely of finding and cutting out pictures from magazines that will illustrate a particular poem for a bulletin board display, but even this is a beginning and should be praised. Many children can write surprisingly good poems if they are motivated. Free verse may be good for some children because they can concentrate on choosing the best words instead of on form. However, free verse is not as easy as it seems, and many children prefer poems that rhyme. Middle and upper grade children like limericks and consider it fun to try writing them. They will also meet with success in forms such as cinquain (see Chapter 8 on creative writing).

As with any writing, children should begin with short poems so they can concentrate on excellence rather than length. Praise for their efforts and constructive criticism will encourage further efforts with other types of poetry. If sufficient interest is displayed, they might work in groups to create

---

★Mary O'Neill, "Sound of Water," in *What Is That Sound!* (Atheneum, 1966). Used by permission.

a class poetry book, with some children doing the major portion of the writing, while others draw illustrations, develop a format, plan organization, design a cover, etc. It is vital to remember, however, that, before being asked to write, children should see and hear many models and should thoroughly understand the particular characteristics of the kind of poem they are going to write; *this* is the time for talking about poetic techniques.

EVALUATION OF THE PROGRAM

Since the principal value of literature is the pleasure and enrichment it brings to an individual, some people oppose evaluating the literature program. Our viewpoint throughout this book, however, is that evaluation is an integral part of teaching. Without evaluation how does a teacher know what he or she has done well or needs to do? Also, with regard to evaluation of literature programs, there is a special need for a teacher to evaluate since literature so frequently receives only peripheral attention in the crowded school curriculum.

Because what one gains from literature is a very personal matter, we do not advocate giving tests over literature selections. Such tests usually measure reading comprehension and reflect an adult's point of view as to what should have been gained from the reading. We do believe, however, that you should ask yourself a number of questions:

1. Do the children show interest in reading beyond that which is assigned?
2. Do I read to the children and in reading introduce them to various genres and types of content?
3. Do the children share their reading with me and the other children?
4. Is the reading corner or center a busy place when children have "spare" time?
5. Do the children use the library or media center?
6. Is there evidence that children with personal problems have been affected by their reading?

These are not the only questions you might ask, and the answers to them may be more reminders to you than measures of the program in any objective sense. But consider them carefully in deciding whether your program is meeting its objectives and in making future plans. Strive for a hearty "yes" in answer to each question.

References

Boyd, Gertrude A. *Teaching Poetry in the Elementary School*. Charles E. Merrill Publishing Co., 1973.

Carlson, Ruth K. *Literature for Children: Enrichment Ideas*. William C. Brown Co., 1970.

Cullinan, Bernice. *Literature and the Child*. Harcourt Brace Jovanovich, 1981.

Glazer, Joan I., and Williams, Gurney, III. *Introduction to Children's Literature*. McGraw-Hill, 1979.

Huck, Charlotte S. *Children's Literature in the Elementary School*. Holt, Rinehart and Winston, 1976.

Lamme, Linda Leonard, *et al. Raising Readers: A Guide to Sharing Literature with Young Children*. Walker, 1980.

Lonsdale, Bernard I., and Mackintosh, Helen K. *Children Experience Literature*. Random House, 1973.

Reasoner, Charles F. *Bringing Children and Books Together: A Teacher's Guide to Early Childhood Literature*. Yearling Books, 1979.

———. *Where the Readers Are*. Dell Publishing Company, 1972.

Shapiro, Jon E., ed. *Using Literature and Poetry Affectively*. International Reading Association, 1979.

Stewig, John Warren. *Children and Literature*. Rand McNally, 1980.

Sutherland, Zena; Monson, Dianne L.; and Arbuthnot, May Hill. *Children and Books*. 6th ed. Scott, Foresman, 1981.

Tiedt, Iris. *Exploring Books with Children*. Houghton Mifflin, 1979.

Trelease, Jim. *The Read-Aloud Handbook*. Penguin Books, 1982.

Teaching Resources

GUIDES FOR SELECTING BOOKS FOR CHILDREN

Bibliography of Books for Children. Association for Childhood Education International, 1977.

Children's Books of the Year. Child Study Association of America, published annually.

Cianciolo, Patricia, ed. *Adventuring with Books*. National Council of Teachers of English, 1977.

Gillespie, John T., and Gilbert, Christine B., eds. *Best Books for Children: Preschool Through the Middle Grades*. R. R. Bowker, 1981.

Haviland, Virginia, ed. *Children's Books of International Interest*. American Library Association, 1978.

Hearne, Betty. *Choosing Books for Children: A Commonsense Guide*. Delacorte Press, 1981.

Hopkins, Lee Bennett. *The Best of Book Bonanza*. Holt, Rinehart and Winston, 1980.

Kimmel, Margaret Mary, and Segel, Elizabeth. *For Reading Out Loud: A Guide to Sharing Books with Children*. R. R. Bowker, 1983.

Lima, Carolyn W. *A to Zoo: Subject Access to Children's Picture Books*. R. R. Bowker, 1982.

Matthews, Judy, and Drag, Lillian, eds. *Guide to Children's Magazines, Newspapers, Reference Books*. Association for Childhood Education International, 1974.

Paperback Books in Print. R. R. Bowker (annual).

Rollock, Barbara, ed. *The Black Experience in Children's Books*. New York Public Library, 1974.

Selecting Materials for Children and Young Adults: A Bibliography of Bibliographies and Review Sources. American Library Association, 1977.

Smith, Dorothy B. Frissell, and Andrews, Eva L., eds. *Subject Index to Poetry for Children and Young People*. American Library Association, 1977.

Spirt, Diana L. *Introducing More Books: A Guide for the Middle Grades*. R. R. Bowker, 1978.

Subject Guide to Children's Books in Print. R. R. Bowker, 1977.

Tarbert, Gary C., ed. *Children's Book Review Index: Master Cumulation, 1969–1981*. Gale Research Company, 1982.

Tway, Eileen, ed. *Reading Ladders for Human Relations*. National Council of Teachers of English, 1981.

CHILDREN'S BOOKS REFERRED TO IN THIS CHAPTER

Brandenberg, Franz. *It's Not My Fault*. William Morrow and Company, 1980.

Clapp, Patricia. *Witches' Children*. William Morrow and Company, 1982.

Cohen, Miriam. *Will I Have a Friend?* Macmillan, 1967.

Dahl, Roald. *The Fantastic Mr. Fox*. Alfred A. Knopf, 1970.

de Paola, Tomie. *Watch Out for the Chicken Feet in Your Soup*. Prentice-Hall, 1974.

Gramatky, Hardie. *Little Toot Through the Golden Gate*. G. P. Putnam's Sons, 1975.

Henry, Marguerite. *King of the Wind*. Rand McNally, 1945.

Hogrogian, Nonny. *One Fine Day*. Macmillan, 1971.

Huston, Anne. *The Cat Across the Way*. Seabury Press, 1968.

Hutchins, Pat. *The Surprise Party*. Macmillan, 1969.

———. *Titch*. Macmillan, 1971.

Karp, Naomi. *The Turning Point*. Harcourt Brace Jovanovich, 1976.

Keats, Ezra Jack. *Apt. 3*. Macmillan, 1971.

———. *The Snowy Day*. Viking Press, 1962.

———. *Whistle for Willie*. Viking Press, 1964.

Kipling, Rudyard. *The Elephant's Child*. Follett, 1969.

Larrick, Nancy, ed. *Poetry for Holidays*. Garrard, 1966.

Lasker, Joe. *He's My Brother.* Albert Whitman, 1974.

Lawrence, Isabelle. *A Spy in Williamsburg.* Rand McNally, 1955.

Lawson, Robert. *Ben and Me.* Little, Brown, 1951.

Lexau, Joan. *Emily and the Klunky Baby and the Next-Door Dog.* Dial, 1972.

———. *Me Day.* Dial, 1971.

Neville, Emily. *It's Like This, Cat.* Harper and Row, 1964.

O'Dell, Scott. *Zia.* Houghton Mifflin, 1976.

O'Neill, Mary. *Hailstones and Halibut Bones.* Doubleday, 1961.

Paterson, Katherine. *The Great Gilly Hopkins.* Thomas Y. Crowell Company, 1978.

Perl, Lila. *Hey, Remember Fat Glenda?* Clarion Books, 1981.

Sendak, Maurice. *Where the Wild Things Are.* Harper and Row, 1963.

Seuss, Dr. *Horton Hatches the Egg.* Random House, 1940.

Southall, Ivan. *Let the Balloon Go.* St. Martin's Press, 1969.

Steptoe, John. *Stevie.* Harper and Row, 1969.

Thurber, James. *The Wonderful O.* Simon and Schuster, 1957.

Wolf, Bernard. *Anna's Silent World.* Lippincott, 1977.

BOOKS ABOUT AUTHORS AND ILLUSTRATORS OF CHILDREN'S LITERATURE

de Montreville, Doris, and Crawford, Elizabeth D. *Fourth Book of Junior Authors and Illustrators.* H. W. Wilson, 1978.

de Montreville, Doris, and Hill, Donna, eds. *Third Book of Junior Authors.* H. W. Wilson, 1972.

Fuller, Muriel, ed. *More Junior Authors.* H. W. Wilson, 1969.

Something About the Author. (A regularly updated series containing facts and pictures about contemporary authors and illustrators of books for young people.) Gale Research Company, 1971–1982.

FILMS

Millions of Cats, Whistle for Willie, The Foolish Frog, Harold's Fairy Tale, and many others are available from Weston Woods. This company also has a number of films featuring authors and illustrators such as Robert McClosky, Maurice Sendak, and Ezra Jack Keats.

Random House/Coronet, Encyclopaedia Britannica, McGraw-Hill, and others also have many literature films.

FILMSTRIPS

American Folk Heroes and Tall Tales. Troll Associates (6 color filmstrips, including tales of Paul Bunyan, Rip Van Winkle, Pecos Bill, Johnny Appleseed, John Henry, and Ichabod Crane; grades K–5).

Asian Fairy Tales. Prentice-Hall Media (5 filmstrips of fairy tales from Lebanon, Arabia, China, Japan, Turkey; grades K–3).

Beloved Fairy Tales. Troll Associates (6 strips; grades K–4).

Enrichment Filmstrips. Enrichment Teaching Materials (also records; based on Landmark Books).

Favorite Poems to Read. Troll Associates (6 strips; elementary grades).

First Stories for Little Folk. Listening Library (sound filmstrips; color; primary).

Myths and Legends of Ancient Greece. Troll Associates (5 color filmstrips including such myths as *Prometheus and the Gift of Fire* and *Theseus and the Minotaur;* upper grades).

Pick a Peck o' Poems. Miller-Brody Productions (6 color filmstrips with cassettes or records; lower elementary).

The Story Tree. Developmental Learning Materials (filmstrips, guide; primary).

Tales from Grimm and Andersen. Prentice-Hall Media (7 filmstrips; primary).

Weston Woods has sound filmstrips of a great many Caldecott Medal winners and other favorite children's stories; they are also available in multimedia kits.

What Is Poetry? Caedmon Records (includes 10 color filmstrips with accompanying records, teacher's guides, and duplicating masters; elementary).

KITS AND OTHER AIDS

Best in Children's Literature. Bowmar/Noble (4 series, 374 selections; records or cassettes; teaching guides).

Best in Children's Literature. Troll Associates (20 cassettes; grades K–3).

Caedmon Records has many recordings of both prose and poetry suitable for every grade level and read by authors or well-known actors. For example, Carl Sandburg tells the Rootabaga Stories, Carol Channing reads *Madeline,* Boris Karloff reads *The Reluctant Dragon,* and Ed Begley tells tall tales.

Literature for Children (Series 7A and 7B). Pied Piper Productions (sets of tapes and filmstrips, guide sheets, masters; titles include *Curious George, Leo the Late Bloomer, Umbrella, A Lion in the Meadow;* primary).

Miller-Brody Productions has nearly all of the New-bery Award–winning books on both records and cassettes. A great many of these are available also in sound filmstrips and in multimedia kits which include paperback or hardcover copies of the book.

My Favorite Fairy Tales. Troll Associates (8 cassettes; grades K–3).

The National Council of Teachers of English distributes many recordings.

Reading for the Fun of It: Getting Hooked on Books. Guidance Associates (filmstrips, cassettes; grades 5–9).

Scholastic Record and Book Companion Series. Scholastic Records.

Tell Me a Story. Garrard (filmstrips, cassettes, script books).

Ten Tales of Mystery and Terror. Troll Associates (includes *Dr. Jekyll and Mr. Hyde, Pit and the Pendulum,* and others; grades 5–8).

Treasury of Classroom Poetry. Troll Associates (7 6-min. cassettes; grades K–4).

Activities for Preservice Teachers

1. Read several research studies about children's interests in literature and compare the results. Report your findings to the class.

2. Check with the audiovisual or instructional materials center for children's literature films, filmstrips, and records. Preview several of these, making notes to remind you of them later.

3. Learn a story to tell to children. Review the section on storytelling and read some of the suggested references before you begin.

4. Begin a collection of pictures of authors of children's books.

5. Visit the children's section of a public library. Inquire about the most popular books, the frequency of children's visits, and the method used to select books for the collection.

6. Visit a library or bookstore and investigate collections of poetry for children. Select at least one that you would like to have as a part of your personal collection of children's literature.

7. Begin a collection of poems about holidays that occur during the normal school year. Confine your selections to those suitable for a particular age group (primary, middle, or upper grades), and try to include as many poems and as many holidays as possible.

8. Begin a file of stories for reading or telling to children. Concentrate on primary, middle, or upper grades.

9. Plan an activity designed to aid sixth grade children in understanding and using figurative language. Use a story or poem as a motivating device. Outline carefully each step you would use in teaching the concept.

10. Visit a public library during the storytelling hour. Observe and report to the class on storytelling techniques used, choice of stories, and the children's reactions.

Activities for Inservice Teachers

1. Instead of, or in addition to, providing comfortable spots for readers in the library corner, some teachers like to set up "quiet areas" where children can sit on chairs or recline on mats while they enjoy their books. Experiment with this, and, with the children, set up standards for behavior in these areas.

2. Listen to a record such as Ruth Sawyer's *Storyteller* (available from Weston Woods). Relate her comments

about storytelling to the stories she tells on the record. Play the record for your class, using this as a first step in a study of storytelling.

3. Investigate the availability of paperback books for children. Where can they be obtained? How durable are they? What do they cost?

4. Add to the independent activities for children suggested in this chapter.

5. Compile a file of poetry appropriate for particular days, such as the first day of spring, the first snow, a foggy day, Christmas, Valentine's Day, etc.

6. With your class make a bulletin board about a favorite author.

7. With the children, organize a book fair and book swap. The children can bring favorite books, books they want to trade, and books obtained from neighbors (watch these for appropriateness). Assemble the books in an attractive and organized manner in an area of the room where children can easily go to browse and to make selections. Bulletin boards, book displays, mobiles, posters, and the children's own book-sharing devices (a card file of reactions to books that have been read, dioramas, art work, objects that have been constructed or collected, etc.) may be used to enhance the appeal of the book area.

8. List the stories, poems, and books you have read to your class this year. Are you reading a variety of literature, presenting new authors, and introducing new literary forms?

9. A walk to the local library with your class can be an enjoyable learning experience. Check with your library to make arrangements for a visit. Some will plan a special story to read to your class.

Independent Activities for Children

1. Encourage children to make their own poetry anthologies and illustrate the poems with their own drawings or pictures cut from magazines. These should not be collected or graded (although they may be shared if the children wish). Poems might be written by the children themselves, might be ones they especially like, or both.

2. Have individual children select favorite poems and record them on tape. They can then use the tapes to judge their own reading for speed, expression, enunciation, etc. After a child feels that an effective reading level has been achieved, he or she may read the poem to the class.

3. Allow a child to go to the library and select books about a topic being studied by the class. This child may then be responsible for helping other children select from them either for personal enjoyment or for reporting to the class.

4. Have a child interview classmates and other children in the school about their favorite books. Urge the child to find out *why* each book is a favorite. He or she may report the results of the interviewing to the class and show copies of some of the books.

5. One or several children might stage a puppet show based on an incident in a story or book.

6. Have a child look through magazines for pictures to illustrate a favorite story for telling to the class.

7. A child can prepare a bulletin board display advertising a favorite book. A colorful jacket, sketches of characters, and a biography of the author might be included. Lists of "good" words, appealing passages, and chapter titles may also be part of the display.

8. Have the child select a character from a story that he or she knows well and finds especially appealing. The child then lists words, phrases, or sentences (either those used in the story or ones selected from his or her own impressions) that describe the character.

9. In the upper grades many children are beginning to play the guitar. Such a child may prepare for the class a program of ballads or folk songs from a particular era or locality in conjunction with a social studies or literature unit.

10. Mobiles illustrating a story or several stories may be made. These might show principal characters, location of action, or anything else the child wishes to express.

11. Many opportunities for independent activities are presented by audiovisual aids. Individual children or groups can listen to taped or recorded stories and poems, view filmstrips, prepare flannel board stories to tell, etc. Sometimes this individual activity can lead to class viewing or listening. A child may wish to write a comparison of a filmstrip and a recorded version of the same story, or children may simply view or listen for pure pleasure.

12. A child may write a letter to an author or illustrator of a book that he or she has particularly enjoyed. Make sure that the letter includes particular reasons for liking the book (or the illustrations) or points out parts that were especially enjoyed. As an alternative, some piece of creative writing or art work that resulted from the reading might be sent to the author or illustrator.

16 | Children with Special Needs

While every child is special and has special needs, for the past 150 years it has been the practice in the United States to identify some children as "special" or "exceptional." This practice began with concern for educating children with visual impairments, referred to until relatively recent times as "blind children." Later, special attention was given to children with hearing losses, speech impairments, physical handicaps, and mental retardation. Next, children of high intelligence were identified as "special," and then those with special talents, but attention to these has been somewhat sporadic. More recently the category of special children has been extended to include those with learning disabilities and emotional problems. Parents and teachers prompted much of the attention given to these children over the years, were largely responsible for the establishment of special schools and classes, and are the forces behind recent changes in policies specifying which children are "special" and how they should be educated.

In addition to those children defined as special, there are thousands of children entering classrooms each year who are unable to speak English and are unprepared by their cultural backgrounds for the environment of the school. Still other children enter school speaking a dialect different from that used by the teacher and found in textbooks. Both of these groups of children are also special and add to the range of differences among children.

It is important, though, that this increase in the extent of differences not be overemphasized. In most classrooms there is a rather wide range of differences in the intellectual abilities of children, and even where there is a narrow range, children differ in learning rates and styles. There are also children who are undernourished, fatigued, or burdened with anxiety or health problems—any or all of which may or may not be temporary. In the preceding chapters we have stressed the importance of a teacher's giving each child as much individual attention as possible and have suggested procedures and activities for accomplishing this. This chapter simply seeks to remind readers that there are children who need more individual attention than most do and that these children are found in "regular" classrooms in increasing numbers. We make suggestions regarding the special needs of these children and outline procedures that may be appropriate for dealing with those needs. Since this book is intended for teachers in regular classrooms, we do not attempt to discuss the needs and teaching of children who are so severely handicapped mentally, physically, emotionally, or by some combination of these that they will seldom if ever be assigned to regular classrooms. Too, the proliferation of categories within the rubric of "learning disabled" will receive less attention than some readers might desire.

SPECIAL CHILDREN: AN OVERVIEW

For information, write to:

Council for Exceptional
  Children
1920 Association Dr.
Reston, VA 22091

National Easter Seal
  Society
2023 W. Ogden Ave.
Chicago, IL 60612

Office of Handicapped In-
  dividuals Clearing House
Rm. 3517 Switzer Bldg.
330 C St., S.W.
Washington, DC 20201

While historically the attention given to the educational needs of special children has resulted in some improvements, authorities conceded in 1975 that many children with impairments, handicaps, and learning problems were not being adequately served by the existing programs. One reason was that the education offered these children differed from state to state, with some of the children denied schooling altogether, others placed in institutions which emphasized care rather than education, and still others labeled mentally retarded on faulty evidence. Demands by leaders of minority groups, teachers, and, particularly, parents for reform of this condition led to tne passage of the Education for All Handicapped Children Act (P.L. 94–142). Since the passage of this law, there has been a huge jump in the number of school-age handicapped children receiving special education, including education in regular classrooms; but few would maintain that the educational needs of the special children have been met.

How Many Children?

Estimates as to the number of children directly affected by P.L. 94–142 vary. One writer (Blake–see References) states that approximately 10 percent of the school-age population is handicapped, with the category breakdown ranging as follows:

speech impaired	2.5–4%
learning disabled	1–3%
mentally retarded	1.5–2.5%
emotionally disturbed	1.25–2%
orthopedically impaired	0.1–0.75%
hearing disabled	0.35–0.65%
visually handicapped	0.01–0.175%

In addition, Blake estimates that 3 to 5 percent of school children are gifted and/or talented. But these are estimates, and while the estimates regarding the numbers of those whose handicaps can be specifically identified do not vary greatly, such is not the case for all categories of "special." For example, as one publication (see Lewis) put it, "If those with different viewpoints as to what constitutes giftedness could fill a small auditorium, scholars with irreconcilable views as to what constitutes 'learning disabilities' (LD) could fill Yankee stadium."

As to the numbers or percentages of children whose cultural backgrounds make them "special," there are no satisfactory estimates. One reason is that increasing numbers of children whose native language is not English are being enrolled in the schools. At the same time, the number of children who speak English dialects that are enough different from school and textbook English to cause learning difficulties for the speakers is likely decreasing.

Mainstreaming

The term *mainstreaming* does not appear in Public Law 94–142, but the philosophy embodied in it does, since the law requires that states provide, to the maximum extent appropriate, that handicapped children be educated along with children who are not handicapped. The law implies, too, that some alternatives for educating special children are more appropriate than others. This has led to the term *least restrictive environment* and the assumption that *all* children fall along a continuum of special needs. Thus, mainstreaming should include:

1. Providing each child with the most appropriate education in the least restrictive environment.
2. Looking at the educational needs of children rather than at their clinical or diagnostic labels.
3. Seeking and creating alternatives in the educational programs of regular classrooms to serve minimally handicapped children.
4. Uniting special education programs with general education programs for the educational benefit of these children.

The law prescribes that a written educational plan must be developed and maintained for each handicapped child placed full- or part-time in a regular classroom; that this plan should be developed by a team consisting of the classroom teacher, principal, school psychologist, and support specialists; and that parents must be permitted to examine the school records, methods of instruction used, and support services available for their child.

It seems to us that the philosophy of mainstreaming is applicable to all school settings and all children. All children are entitled to an environment that maximizes their growth, and their needs should be the bases of instruction.

Labeling Children

Traditionally various labels have been attached to special children—often misleading ones. For example, individuals who have relatively minor hearing losses have been labeled "deaf." And labeling of children as "slow learners" has sometimes limited their development—the Pygmalion effect. Too often such labeling has been a diversion used by the educational system to avoid facing up to the teaching problems some children present. And while there has been a decline in such labeling, some relatively new labels—"learning disabled," "emotionally and behaviorally maladjusted"—are now being increasingly applied. Whether this labeling has resulted or will result in more effective instruction of the children so labeled, rather than extending the stigmatizing of children or providing an excuse for poor teaching or parental neglect, remains to be seen. We believe that children should be put into a category or given a label only if doing so helps in the selection of an educational program or other treatment, provides evidence of what can be expected from such a program, and achieves desirable results.

Use of labeling has diminished in some communities since the early

Yesterday.

Today.

Yesterday is gone.
Today is right now.
Tomorrow comes after
today.

Tomorrow.

25

Modern texts are cognizant of mainstreaming.

1970s, partially because of a trend toward what has come to be called "non-categorical" special education. This term is interpreted in different ways. A few educators believe that, except for the gifted, children considered "special" or "exceptional" have so much in common that in terms of educational needs they can be considered as a single group. Other educators are unwilling to go that far, but they do believe that the learning disabled, the mildly disturbed, and the mildly retarded are more alike than different (with regard to intelligence, personality and adjustment, and achievement) and thus require similar teaching methods.

Labeling has not disappeared, and it will not, since proper planning of educational programs requires its use to some degree. However, combining categories for instructional purposes and reducing the harshness of some labels by using such terms as "visual impairments," "hearing disorders," and "orthopedic impairments" helps reduce the differences in the minds of both special children and so-called normal children and will lead to better understanding and a better education for all.

Instructional Considerations

Help parents to accept their children's limitations and to recognize their potential.

While there are children who are so severely handicapped that they cannot receive any of their education in regular classrooms, for those children who can be in a regular classroom—even for part of the school day—the same teaching procedures as normally used are required, but with modifications. Special children, in general, need to learn the concepts, skills, abilities, and attitudes that other children need to learn. The mainstreaming procedure, however, forces an attention to individual needs, to learning environments, and to the effectiveness of teaching methodology that often is missing in regular classrooms. A written educational plan requires systematic attention to the following:

- Gathering objective data regarding performance.
- Establishing priorities among the skills, knowledge, etc., that need to be acquired now and in the future.
- Identifying the prerequisites necessary to develop the skills, abilities, etc., that have been prioritized.
- Using data from assessments to extend or revise teaching/learning procedures.

CHILDREN WITH SPEECH DISORDERS

Write to American Speech-Language-Hearing Association, 9030 Old Georgetown Rd., Washington, DC 20014.

Although problems of speech are the handicapping condition most frequently encountered by classroom teachers, the number of children in any classroom with problems that may be called speech disorders—disorders requiring extended training of the child by specialists—is likely to be rather small. However, it is important that teachers identify these children and provide for their instruction, as well as helping others whose speech problems are less severe or are transitory.

Normal Speech Problems

When a child first enters school, his or her speech may retain vestiges of "baby talk." Estimates indicate that over 40 percent of kindergarten children and 25 percent of those in the first grade show such retention. The speech of many of these children is characterized by one or more of the following: reversals (for example, *aminal* for *animal*), inability to articulate some blends (*st*, *th*, *str*, etc.) and individual speech sounds, mispronunciations, and divergencies in pitch and loudness.

A child with any of these speech characteristics may be referred to a speech correctionist, who will probably simply wish to observe the child's maturation but may suggest activities similar to those in this chapter.

The child of eight or nine (and often younger) certainly should be able to produce all of the speech sounds unless he or she has a genuine speech handicap. The child may, of course, have certain speech habits (saying *deese* for *these*, for example) that need attention and may continue to have problems of voice quality and control.

Speech handicaps that go beyond the speech characteristics of many young children, with the exception of those associated with a psychological disturbance, are discussed below. Most of these problems call for the services of a speech correctionist either directly or in giving the classroom teacher suggestions or assistance. However, since speech specialists are not always available, these suggestions may be useful.

Types of Abnormal Speech

Speech problems may be manifested in a variety of forms. These can be grouped, though, in four major categories: (1) articulatory, or pronunciation, disorders; (2) voice disorders—malfunctioning of the sound-producing mechanism; (3) linguistic, or language, disorders; and (4) disorders of speech rhythm.

ARTICULATION DISORDERS. Probably as many as 70 percent of all speech problems found in the normal elementary school classroom are those in which the speaker cannot make certain speech sounds either in isolation or in blends with other speech sounds. Most frequently these articulation problems consist of sound substitutions, omissions, reversals, and additions in the speech of children older than eight years. This persistence of common speech characteristics of young children is called "infantile perseveration" and may be caused by poor muscular coordination, illness, retarded physical maturation, low intelligence, short auditory memory span, poor auditory discrimination, or various environmental factors (overprotection by a parent, desire for attention, jealousy of a younger sibling, etc.). There are other articulatory disorders identified by speech specialists—the most common of which is probably lisping—but they are also manifested in problems with specific individual speech sounds.

VOICE DISORDERS. Voice disorders are those in which speech sounds are articulated acceptably but the voice has a quality that is unpleasant to the hearer. Few children have this problem beyond the primary years. The most common voice disorder is nasality, usually caused by a physical problem, the most serious of which is a cleft palate. Other voice disorders include hoarseness, an unnaturally high or low pitch, and excessive loudness or softness.

LANGUAGE DISORDERS. Language disorders are the result of physical, environmental, or psychological problems which have interfered with language learning. The language disorders most often found in the elementary school are delayed speech and childhood aphasia. Delayed speech may mean that a child does not know some sounds or has a very limited vocabulary. Victims of delayed speech range from the child who suffers a mild delay in the appearance of a few sounds to the one who reaches the primary grades with the ability to say only three or four words. When seriously delayed language development is shown, the cause is usually brain damage; the condition is known as aphasia.

RHYTHM DISORDERS. The principal speech disorder of a rhythmic nature is stuttering. Some stutterers block on producing sounds; some repeat sounds, syllables, or words; some speak very slowly or very rapidly; some prolongate sounds; and others have spasms of the speech mechanism. There may be combinations of the above in the speech of a stutterer, and there are usually times when there is no evidence of stuttering. Speech specialists generally state that there is no definite cause of stuttering, and no certain cure.

Teaching Considerations

Children suspected, as determined by a screening procedure, of having a speech disorder should be referred to a specialist for diagnosis and remediation. After seeing the child, the speech specialist will contact the parents and will involve a physician, a psychologist, and others if there is a serious speech disorder. Unless the child is totally removed from his or her regular classroom, the teacher will be brought into the planning for remediation. Important in treating any speech problem is getting the child to want to talk. This requires much encouraging. The teacher should not cut off any speaking efforts by finishing sentences or by suggesting that another start be made. Nor should classmates be permitted to make fun of the child's speech. A program which makes it possible for children to talk together in small groups will benefit a child with a speech problem. The activities suggested in Chapters 5 and 6 which avoid singling out the child's speaking will help. In addition, a teacher should give special attention to the way he or she speaks to this child. Looking directly at the child when speaking helps, as does speaking in a well-modulated voice and in an unhurried and pleasant manner.

Never display impatience with a child who has faulty speech. The child must feel accepted and secure.

Activities

Activities that may modify or remedy speech defects should be used to meet specific needs; they should not be used indiscriminately. It is much more

Working relationships between teachers and parents are important to teaching all special children.

For material on speech problems, write to Alexander Graham Bell Association for the Deaf, 3417 Volta Place, N.W., Washington, DC 20007.

important for children—including those who have speech handicaps—to engage in genuine communication situations than to practice speech exercises. Speech activities such as those suggested here are certainly important and necessary when speech correction is needed, but they are only part of a total speech improvement program.

Relaxing exercises such as falling completely relaxed into a chair, dropping the head and letting the arms dangle, shaking the hands and arms, and rotating the head on the chest and shoulders may help a child whose speech problem is related to tenseness. Breathing exercises, such as taking short quick breaths, inhaling deeply, taking in a quick breath and exhaling slowly (by counting), and doing specific acts (smelling a flower, saying "ah" for the doctor, showing surprise), may also be helpful. To correct excessive nasality, try such activities as yawning, panting, and "blowing out" vowel sounds (or blowing out a candle, blowing a pinwheel, etc.).

Ear training exercises are also important, since good speech depends on aural acuity and the ability to discriminate between correct and incorrect production of a sound. These exercises include discriminating among sounds (the ringing of a small bell, the sound of a triangle), telling when two words begin with the same sound (or end with the same sound, or have the same middle sound), and selecting objects whose names contain a particular sound.

In helping the child who retains vestiges of baby talk, the first task is to identify the particular sounds the child does not produce correctly. Then attempt to have the child distinguish between words correctly and incorrectly spoken: *fadder—father; wittle—little; thithter—sister*. It may be necessary for the child to use a mirror so that he or she can watch lip and tongue movements. Tape-recording these efforts may also help. Another useful technique is to have the child recite poems and sing songs containing the sounds that are troublesome.

Tongue exercises are helpful in remedying simple articulation problems. These should be done individually with the aid of a mirror. They include stretching the tongue out and down, up toward the nose, inside the lips, etc. There are also activities suitable for groups, such as saying the following rhymes:

> Little kitty laps her milk,
>   Lap, lap, lap!
> Her tongue goes out,
> Her tongue goes in,
>   Lap, lap lap!
>
> Little kitty likes her milk,
>   Lap, lap, lap!
> Oh, see her tongue
> Go out and in,
>   Lap, lap, lap!
> ("Make your tongue go like kitty's.")
>
> Tick! Tock! Tick! Tock!
> The clock goes ticking all the day.
> Tick! Tock! Tick! Tock!
> It has no other words to say.

Tick! Tock! Tick! Tock!
It ticks all night; it ticks all day.
And when I sleep, or when I play,
The clock goes on the same old way.
Tick! Tock! Tick! Tock!

Exercises for correcting the production of specific sounds may be used when particular faults have been identified. For example, for the sound represented by "s" the following might be done.

1. Say lists of words.

see	pencil	nice
sit	answer	dress
sun	dressing	house
soup	insect	base
salt	groceries	tennis

2. Repeat "s" sentences.

My sister is sick.
We ate soup, salad, roast, and carrots.

3. Say contrasting words.

some—thumb	sick—thick	so—though
seem—theme	thin—sin	

THE HEARING IMPAIRED

The total incidence of hearing losses among the children in schools is not known, since these losses range from very slight ones to total deafness. Hearing losses and learning difficulties are not necessarily related, but the fact that so much instruction is on an aural-oral basis means that there may be problems. Most children with hearing losses that are less than total deafness can be successful in the regular classroom if sensitivity is shown for their handicaps and instructional adjustments are made.

Screening for Hearing Losses

The best procedure for a school to use to determine whether a child has a hearing loss is to test the child with an audiometer. This test requires a competent operator for the equipment, so often every child is screened on a systemwide, regional, or statewide basis. If such a testing service is not available, a child with a suspected hearing loss should be referred to a physician.

It is possible to test children informally to determine the need for audiometric testing or referral by having them listen to a ticking watch or to whispering. The watch should have a fairly loud tick, one that would be heard at about four feet from the ear by a child with normal hearing. Each ear should be tested separately; the actual testing is done by holding the watch near the ear and moving it away until the child signals that he or she can no longer hear it. The whispering testing is done by whispering directions (e.g., "raise your left hand," "close your fist," etc.) at increasing distances from the ear being tested.

A teacher also needs to be alert to children's behavior or habits that indicate a hearing impairment or an impending difficulty with hearing properly. These conditions include recurring earaches, the tendency to favor one ear in listening, rubbing an ear, headaches, head noises, and dizziness. Excessive inattention, reflected in poor achievement and the failure to follow directions, may also signal a hearing problem. Sometimes, too, faulty pronunciation, heavy breathing through the mouth, and an unnatural pitch of voice are signs of hearing impairment.

Children with hearing losses often need professional treatment. The teacher is usually informed about the diagnosis and treatment, particularly if there is a responsibility the physician thinks the school should assume. For example, if a child is given a hearing aid, he or she has to be helped in getting accustomed to using it. If a child is receiving instruction in lip reading, the teacher should know this. Likewise, if there is medication prescribed, this should be known. Do not hesitate to inquire of parents or the school physician about these matters.

Helping the Child

Children don't like to be too different. The child with a hearing loss should be given the consideration needed to aid learning without excessive attention being called to the problem. For example, when directions are given or other talking is done with this child, he or she should be faced as directly as possible. The child will learn to watch faces (some children even learn to read lips). Do not shout or exaggerate lip and facial movements. Try looking in the mirror sometime while reciting "Mary Had a Little Lamb" with exaggerated facial expression and a shouting voice. Who would want to look at such efforts all day? Remember to hold hands and books away from the face when speaking to a child with a hearing loss. And if the child does not understand, rephrasing or restating is better than repeating what was said.

Seating arrangements should be such that a child with a hearing loss has his or her back to the light (actually a good idea for seating all children). With the light off the child's face, he or she will be better able to watch the speaker.

It is also important to keep in mind that lip reading requires constant attention and concentration (try it for half an hour; ask a friend to whisper while you watch his or her lips). Thus the child who depends heavily on lip reading will get tired and need time to rest.

Because hearing loss often affects speech and confidence in oral language situations, particular attention should be given to structuring activities that the child can engage in successfully. Others in the school—special teachers, clerks, etc.—should be aware of the child's hearing loss so that they can cooperate with you in your efforts. A child with a hearing loss often needs to develop skill in auditory discrimination. Although not every child with a hearing loss has undeveloped auditory discrimination skill, and not every child who needs auditory discrimination training is suffering from a hearing loss, being able to discriminate among speech sounds is important to success in using language. Listening and readiness activities such as those suggested in Chapters 5, 7, and 12 will help children develop this ability.

CHILDREN WITH VISUAL IMPAIRMENTS

Children who are visually impaired may, depending on the severity of the handicap, present particular teaching problems in most areas of the language arts. Children who are blind or nearly so generally will not be in a regular classroom, although with mainstreaming they may be for a portion of the school day. There are now in classrooms, however, a good many children who have visual problems of a less severely handicapping nature. These children often have difficulty seeing the board, charts, and/or the print in books. They may also reflect such handicaps in their writing.

Identifying the Children

For information, write to:

American Foundation for
the Blind
15 W. 15th St.
New York, NY 10011

Division for the Blind and
Physically Handicapped
Library of Congress
Washington, DC 20542

National Society for the
Prevention of Blindness
78 Madison Ave.
New York, NY 10016

Symptoms of possible visual problems include losing one's place while reading, avoiding close work, poor posture while reading, holding the reading material closer or farther away than normal, holding one's body rigid while looking at distant objects, rubbing the eyes, tilting the head to one side, frowning, blinking, scowling while reading or writing, excessive head movement while reading, inflamed eyelids, and frequent headaches. Children in the primary grades who have difficulty learning their colors may be suspected of having color "blindness."

Most schools make some provision for screening children's vision. Usually the screening is done with the Snellen Chart, a procedure that checks vision at 20 feet but does not check near-point vision or measure fusion ability, muscular imbalance, or other visual abnormalities. A lesser number of schools also screen with a chart held at a distance of 14 inches from the eye, which does adequately screen near-point vision.

There are other testing instruments sometimes used in schools (such as the Keystone Telebinocular or the Titmus Vision Tester), usually by a school nurse or some other specialist rather than the classroom teacher. The classroom teacher can check on symptoms by having material on the chalkboard read and by close questioning about letters and words in near-point reading. All children suspected of having problems seeing properly should be referred to specialists.

Instructional Provisions

When referred to a specialist, a child who has a vision problem usually receives attention, glasses, supervised muscle training, and so on. However, the attention needed may take most of the school year to materialize. And even if a child does receive the kind of special assistance he or she needs, there are still some ways a teacher can help. These include the following:

1. Seat the child so that he or she can see the board as well as possible.
2. Arrange the child's desk to avoid glare.
3. Prevent the child from facing sharp contrasts in the amount of direct or reflected light.
4. Use reading materials that are not "slick" or glossy.
5. Remove the glossy finish from the top of the child's desk.
6. Use a typewriter with large type to make materials for the child.

Assignments can be given orally, the child can be read to by other children, and the answers to questions can be given orally rather than in writing. Information, directions, and even literary selections can be recorded on tape for the child to listen to, particularly if other pupils are enlisted to aid in preparing the tapes. Extra attention should be given to teaching listening skills, since the child with a vision problem must depend more heavily on listening than does the child with normal vision. Recognition will need to be given to the fact that partially sighted children usually take longer to complete assignments than those with normal vision. Teachers may need to shorten written assignments for these children or allow them more time for completion.

OTHER PHYSICAL HANDICAPS

Children who are physically handicapped can usually be taught in the regular classroom if sensible adjustments are made to accommodate their handicaps so that learning problems do not develop or are not aggravated. In working with any physically handicapped child, a teacher must help the child acquire a commonsense viewpoint in regard to personal strengths and limitations and to life itself and must provide experiences that are realistic but that can be handled with the particular handicap.

Types of Handicaps

There are many types of physical handicaps other than hearing and vision losses, and some speech problems have a physical base. Many of these physical handicaps are manifested in slight impairments of movement. Children with severe handicaps, such as serious cardiac conditions, will usually not be placed in regular classrooms. But many children with serious physical problems, such as epilepsy or the loss of a limb, have learned to function in a group setting like the classroom. In general, doctors recommend that physically handicapped children associate with their peers in normal settings. There are also many borderline "special" children—children with a rather minor physical defect, a physical problem such as being grossly overweight, or a temporary crippling condition. These children are generally included in the regular classroom, and they may be especially sensitive to their physical problems, even though such problems may not be of a serious nature. Certainly any child who regards himself or herself as handicapped must be treated as a "special" child.

Instructional Provisions

Special classroom arrangements must be made for a child who is in a wheelchair or who otherwise needs help in moving about. Special tables, desks, and other work areas will need to be arranged, and usually changes will need to be made in schedules and routine activities of the classroom.

Many children with physical defects have gaps in their experiential lives. They have missed some of the so-called normal experiences that much of the school curriculum is built upon. Thus, special provision may need to be made for extra films, excursions, and demonstrations. These extra activities can be the basis for many language arts activities—and physically handicapped children can engage in most language activities.

Attention often needs to be given to the child's special social needs—relationships with parents, peers, and the personnel of the school. The child may need social contacts that have not been experienced, physical activity that has been avoided, and the general opportunity to extend himself or herself as a person. Certainly physical limitations and any special problems related to them must be known before efforts are made in these areas. This means that the teacher must have some contact with the child's physician, parents, and other specialists who are also working with him or her.

A physical handicap often brings about an emotional condition that is reflected in behavior and learning problems. Helping the child to overcome such problems and to adjust to conditions that cannot be overcome is often the teacher's most important task, and there is no easy way to do this. Certainly a teacher must extend himself or herself as a sensitive human being—this is a broad concept, one that includes the very best of teaching practices and true attention to needs, interests, and abilities. The basis for the teaching that needs to be done is often in providing a means for the child to recognize his or her own problem and to work on it.

CHILDREN WITH LEARNING PROBLEMS

This section deals with children who have more difficulties learning than most children but whose problems are not so severe that they are excluded from some participation in regular classrooms. These children may be mildly mentally retarded, learning disabled, or mildly emotionally disturbed. Their particular disabilities may differ, but they have some common characteristics, and similar instruction is needed.

Definitions and Characteristics

Like other children with learning problems, children who are mentally retarded have many of the same needs as all other children. They want and need to explore and extend their environment. They need firsthand experiences—the concrete more than the abstract. Children commonly labeled mentally retarded now in regular classrooms or likely to be in mainstreaming programs are "borderline" or mildly retarded. They are slow learners; their development is slower than average. Their short- and long-term memory deficits are greater than those of normal children, and they have more problems in focusing and maintaining attention. Yet they can learn many of the things taught to other children if the teaching respects their limitations.

A learning disability may be defined as a condition that prevents an intellectually and physically normal child from absorbing knowledge, organizing experience, and expressing the synthesis of these in ideas and actions at the level of his or her true potential. This is a broad definition—and deliberately so, since there tend to be many definitions and interpretations of definitions. The common element in the definitions—and in terminology related to them—is that learning achievement is highly unsatisfactory when compared to the apparent learning potential. As with children who are mildly retarded, attention and memory are the two characteristics showing consistent deficiencies. Most identifications of children as learning-disabled occur because of the difficulties these children have with reading comprehension.

Some educators use the term "learning disorder" rather than learning disability, since they believe that something is out of order and can be remedied. Others state that learning disabilities may be due to brain injuries, perceptual handicaps, or minimal brain dysfunctions.

As with the learning disabled, how one defines the emotionally or behaviorally disturbed child depends largely on who is doing the defining. Many teachers, at one time or another, have considered a child who misbehaves more than the other children in a class to be emotionally disturbed. The same feelings have surely also been experienced by some parents.

In considering emotional and behavior problems, one must recognize the fact that every child is growing, changing, and developing in a nonstatic world and that so-called normal behavior in that world is difficult to describe. What is acceptable behavior at one time and place may not be in another. Definitions which indicate that an emotionally disturbed child is one who cannot function emotionally, socially, and intellectually in a manner acceptable to all the individuals he or she encounters at home, at school, or in the community are less than helpful, since they bring to mind the question "Who can?"

It is true that there are children with psychoses, neuroses, and personality disorders—just as there are such people in the adult population. A physical or intellectual handicap may bring about emotional maladjustments. Similar maladjustments may arise from the child's size, appearance, or degree of social maturity. The child who is careless, lazy, spoiled, or immature has a learning maladjustment. So does the one who displays an antisocial attitude, emotional instability, or hyperactive behavior.

On the other hand, many children manifest transient and situational behaviors that do not warrant their being identified as emotionally disturbed. The increase in the number of children labeled emotionally disturbed and

Possible Symptoms of Learning Disabilities

inattentiveness
aggressiveness
impulsiveness
shyness
lack of organization
overexcitability
speech irregularities
perceptual difficulties
lethargy

Children from other cultures and those who are economically or socially handicapped may have emotional and/or motivational problems in some school settings. This does not mean that these children are disabled learners. Of course, some may be.

A teacher should know if a child is receiving medical or psychological treatment. If you do not know but suspect that this may be the case, ask the parents.

For information, write to:

Association for Children
    with Learning
    Disabilities
4156 Library Rd.
Pittsburgh, PA 15234

League for Emotionally
    Disturbed Children
171 Madison Ave.
New York, NY 10017

National Association for
    Retarded Citizens
2709 Avenue E East
P.O. Box 6109
Arlington, TX 76011

the refuge into treatment by drugs should cause all teachers to think seriously about whether the roots of many of the problems of these children may not lie in the teaching practices and the school program. Simply identifying children's particular problems is not providing the teaching they need. Of course, the determination of a child's specific problems and needs should lead to more effective instruction; the question is whether or not this is happening.

Instructional Considerations

While many teaching techniques and procedures have been suggested and tried with children who have learning problems, there is a lack of conclusive evidence to support particular procedures or techniques. However, the techniques and procedures *proven by research and practice* to be effective with so-called normal children appear to be, with some modifications, generally effective with these children. The modifications made are usually in terms of the rate of learning and the reinforcement of perception and retention, but the teacher of a child with a learning problem—whatever the categorization within this larger one—needs to try various procedures. What works for some children will not necessarily work for others. In short, attention must be given to individual differences in attitudes, interests, needs, and abilities—which of course is the essence of all good teaching.

Usually, these children need to develop patterns of behavior that they can follow without conscious thought. They need to be taken to foundational levels of visual, auditory, and motor learning skills that were not acquired in earlier learning opportunities. Attention does need to be focused on specific needs and problems, with what is to be learned presented in a graduated sequence of small steps. Teachers should stress the social value of what is to be learned and respect each child as an individual.

These children do not respond positively to prodding or coercing. Such procedures will usually reactivate or reinforce behaviors that may well be major aspects of their learning problems—withdrawal, rebelliousness, negativism, or escapism. To gain any rapport at all with many of these children requires a great deal of patience. This patience needs to be shown in understanding, sympathy, and friendliness, but it also needs to be shown in firm controls and fair limitations. The children need to feel that they are accepted, but that they are expected to learn.

In light of the lengthy discussion of these particular "special" children, some readers may question the emphasis placed here on using the same techniques as those used with normal children. Surely if these children have been in school for any length of time, such techniques have already been tried! Keep in mind, however, that emphasis has been placed on using techniques *proven by research and practice*—unfortunately not used by all teachers in all schools—and on using these *with modifications*. Authoritative reports (see articles in the 1983 edition of the *Encyclopedia of Educational Research*) would seem to confirm the value of this approach; however, they also suggest that for some children with severe learning problems, the modifications may require teaching outside the classroom.

In sum, the instructional planning described in Chapter 2 and the many activities suggested throughout the book are appropriate for children who have learning problems—particularly if the following suggestions are kept in mind:

1. Establish short-range goals, and be sure the child understands them.
2. Break up the content of the material into smaller than usual units.
3. Keep directions simple; ask that they be repeated.
4. Provide materials the child is capable of using.
5. Make instruction systematic and orderly.
6. Provide adequate time for the child to accomplish selected or assigned tasks.
7. Talk to the child directly and calmly.
8. Minimize the complexity of language used, the number of items or concepts presented at a given time, and the memory load required.
9. Minimize distractions.
10. Make sure the child attains a measure of success.
11. Make sure the child is aware of his or her accomplishments.
12. Be patient and understanding and sensitive to interests and needs.

TEACHING GIFTED AND TALENTED CHILDREN

For information, write to:

American Association for
  Gifted Children
15 Grammercy Park
New York, NY 10003

Association for Gifted
  Children
2179 Gregory Dr.
Hot Springs, AR 71901

Children with unique abilities or talents are frequently not thought of as children with special needs. A general point of view is that the extremely bright among these children will learn almost regardless of conditions; likewise, the ones with special talents are considered either to be maturing lopsidedly or to be stubborn and arrogant. As a consequence of these and other misconceptions, programs in language arts and other curriculum areas have generally not provided for gifted children in systematic and continuing ways.

Identifying the Children

Various definitions have been advanced for the gifted and talented. Possibly the most practical one is that these are children who show outstanding ability in a variety of areas—general intelligence, specific aptitudes, creativity, leadership, artistic skill, or athletic prowess. The identification of children as gifted or talented should be done by professionals—teachers, psychologists, and others. The identification should not be based solely on intelligence tests, since high intelligence as measured by these tests does not necessarily correlate highly with some of the talents, aptitudes, and other characteristics of individuals who are gifted. Giftedness is composed of above-average general ability, a high level of task commitment, and high levels of creativity. Individuals possessing some talents may not have all of

Keep in mind that an individual may be gifted and also handicapped. The best known example is Helen Keller.

these characteristics; however, most people would agree that the creative and/or talented individuals in our society are quite intelligent and are committed to their specialties, whether they are ice skating, writing fiction, designing buildings, or whatever. Thus, task commitment is a criterion that should not be overlooked when gifted and talented children are being identified.

Instructional Suggestions

Children who are gifted or talented are still children, not adults. Their interests and needs often are little different from those of other children. They may have broader interests, however, if they are academically gifted, or they may have special interests if they possess particular talents or aptitudes. A major question regarding the academically gifted is whether their movement through the normal school curriculum should be accelerated or whether the curriculum should be enriched at each level to better accommodate their needs and interests. This question is most frequently answered in favor of the latter alternative, with the child often leaving the regular classroom for part of the school day in order to engage in enrichment activities. This exiting from the classroom is not necessary, though, if *all* children in a classroom are treated as unique individuals, are permitted to pursue their interests, and have appropriate challenges presented to them.

If the classroom experiences of gifted children are to meet their needs, the extension of the curriculum should not be "more of the same." Gifted children don't need longer lists of spelling words, more questions to answer, more book reports, and the like. They do need more stimulating ideas, more opportunities to extend their interests, and most of all a teacher who is neither threatened by their intellects and talents nor prone to be too demanding of them. The teacher should share interests with these children, discuss things with them—particularly abstract ideas—introduce areas of potential interest, encourage wide exploring of topics, and pose questions which require critical thinking and problem solving.

Children who are especially creative or talented in some area may not need curriculum enrichment of the same type as that needed by the academically gifted. However, enrichment is often necessary to meet their needs. Perhaps they may be given leadership roles in small group discussions, on the class or school newspaper, in planning a dramatization, or in organizing class sporting events. Extra time might be given to them to pursue their special interests or assignments made which capitalize on their talents. Possibly they are (or could become) interested in and capable of taking photos; making films, filmstrips, slides, audio- and videocassettes; or preparing other materials for classroom use. If microcomputers are available, another avenue is open for the extension of the curriculum. Many of the activities suggested throughout this book can be made challenging to the gifted and talented; these should be reviewed and considered in planning curriculum enrichment.

OTHER SPECIAL CHILDREN

Who are the children?

black children who live in the ghettos of cities or in poor rural areas

children without English language backgrounds, especially Puerto Ricans, Cubans, and immigrants from eastern and southern Europe and Mexico

children of poor whites in the South, the Appalachian mountain regions, and the city locations to which these people have moved

American Indian children

children of migrant workers

Education has always been a major road to social advancement and economic success in society, but there have been blocks in this road, and many of them remain. In the past, the schools dealt reasonably well with some immigrant children and less well with others. However, the failures of those times received little general attention. Today, though, with the influx of immigrants from Spanish-speaking areas of the Americas and from some sections of Asia, failure to properly educate the children of these immigrants is receiving widespread attention. Possibly a reason for this is a decline in public acceptance of the "melting pot" concept—a decline evidenced in the desire of many groups to preserve aspects of their cultural heritages.

Children of racial minorities—blacks and native Americans—have also encountered road blocks, though these have been fewer in recent years. Children in or from some relatively remote areas, as well as children of the economically poor—of any race or nationality—have not always found an open road.

While all children in the above groups *should* be considered "special," those who are undereducated and many whose native language is not English or whose dialect differs markedly from "school" English *must* be so classified.

Understanding the Children

Since the use of language is fundamental to the task of the school, children who do not speak English are faced with a problem that may affect them psychologically as well as limit their learning. Children whose native language is English but whose dialect is substantially different from what they hear at school have a similar problem. Such directions as "Hang up your wraps" or "Wash after you go to the lavatory" may be confusing for them and may result in what is interpreted by the teacher as defiance or inattention. The non-English speaker will be even more confused. In either case the cause of this lack of understanding must be overcome if the development of feelings of insecurity and inferiority is to be avoided; either the teacher must change what he or she says so that it will be understood, or the child must learn the language the teacher uses.

A child with a speech or hearing impairment may also be a "quiet one."

If communication is limited because of either language or dialect difference, the children will withdraw from situations and activities in which their participation would otherwise be natural. Other possible causes of withdrawal and seeming inattention may be hunger and fatigue, for these children often come from poor homes and these are conditions usually associated with poverty.

These children need much understanding and assistance in overcoming inferiority feelings and in becoming contributing members of their group. At the same time, they need to get this help in a manner that does not single them out as being particularly different from or inferior to the other children. They and the other children need to be shown that they are all much more alike than different, but that each is different in minor ways from any of the others.

Building a Child's Identity

Build the child's self-concept:

1. By taking pictures of him and things he has done.
2. By listening to her tell about herself and sometimes writing accounts of her experiences for her.
3. By having objects or pictures related to his race or culture in the classroom.
4. By making her the leader in games and other activities she does well.
5. By respecting him as a person at all times.

In teaching a child the English of the school, it is crucial to truly believe that neither a child's thinking abilities nor any other of his or her qualities as a human being are being "improved." Yet we do believe that non-English speakers need to learn to speak and write English with some effectiveness. We also believe that it is important that native English speakers not use a dialect which will handicap them in school or when they seek employment as adults. We recognize, of course, that many who learn English as a second language need not become so proficient that they could qualify as TV commentators. Likewise, we are aware that it is impossible to define, for all possible conditions, what might be considered a "handicapping" dialect.

A teacher must remember that family and cultural ties are important to every person and must be given prime consideration in instruction. A child's earliest thoughts are of home and family, and his or her native language or dialect is a very important part of this background. Personal dignity is inseparable from early background—a fact that every teacher should remember. To abuse or dishonor a child's heritage by condemning his or her language in any way degrades the child and shows a lack of sensitivity to humankind. Beyond that, there is the very practical fact that the desire a child has to learn a new language depends heavily on an attitude about his or her own worth as an individual.

A first step in helping non-English-speaking children retain their identity while they learn the language of the school is to understand their heritage. Learn as much as possible about the children's native country, its customs and history, its values and traditions, and its language. Although it may not be possible to learn the language, some expressions—greetings, school and home words, and other words that are used often—can be learned.

Perhaps the children can be encouraged to teach the other children words and customs that have been and still are important to them. Someone from the children's native land—possibly an English-speaking parent—can be invited to the classroom for a special program or as a resource person when the children's homeland is being studied. Since all children are interested in the dress, art, music, customs, and food of a country, this is a good opportunity not only to enhance the non-English-speaking children's self-image but also to make all the children knowledgeable about and appreciative of other cultures.

In a similar manner, children who speak nonstandard English can be made to feel that their identities are important. This will not be as difficult as some might imagine, since we are a mobile people, each of us retaining at least some elements of our heritage. Exchanging information about words and expressions, customs, favorite foods, etc., can enrich all the children.

In addition to having a positive feeling about himself or herself, the child needs a similar attitude toward school and the language used in school. Thus the child needs affirmation not only of his or her identity as a person but also of the ability to achieve success in this new world. Whether in the kindergarten or a higher grade, the child needs to participate in classroom activities—games, duties, projects—that he or she is capable of handling and that are enjoyable. The child needs to gain new confidence about this strange place before undertaking difficult tasks.

Self-images are not built in a few months or even a few years; the feelings children have about themselves are the result of all their experiences, including their environment, their family, and their observations of others. But working for even a short time (e.g., the year a child is in your class) on helping a child build a more positive feeling toward himself or herself is worthwhile and is fundamental to teaching the skills and knowledge the child needs.

Dialects and Teaching

It is important for a teacher to be fully aware of the implications of the fact that we all speak in different ways as we engage in different activities. Not only do well-educated, partly educated, and uneducated people speak the dialects of their geographical regions and societal settings, but they all speak different varieties of those dialects. In addition, almost everyone has differences in levels of style or formality in speaking and writing.

Educators have increasingly come to accept the point of view that it is educationally unsound to attempt to obliterate a child's native dialect and to replace it with standard English. This has led to an emphasis on functional bidialectalism, in which the speaker uses the dialect appropriate to the situation in which he or she happens to be. Yet even this viewpoint has come under attack by those who insist that in a pluralistic society, the child's language should not be tampered with at all. However, dialect switching is essentially little different from the switching of speech styles that most of us do in moving from a formal to a casual situation.

We believe, as was discussed in Chapter 3, that children who speak dialects which differ quite noticeably from standard English should at least learn to use language that is not stigmatizing. There is a problem of motivation for this learning, though, since a speaker of a nonstandard dialect has little or no trouble understanding most speakers of standard English— or at least grasping their fundamental meaning (though the opposite is less likely to be true). But the level of understanding may suffer considerably as standard English is met in print.

Points of interference or difference between standard and nonstandard English have been identified by linguists. These features or points of interference can serve as the bases for teaching standard English using foreign language teaching procedures.

Teachers themselves can determine in a nontechnical way the features of two dialects that are different. Both phonological and grammatical differences should be noted if they appear consistently and are such that their use would sound out of place in conversation among educated Americans.

In essence, the strategy for teaching a second dialect is to identify a limited number of items—genuinely significant ones—and make every effort possible to use them consistently in the classroom. Implementing this strategy successfully requires a long-term teaching effort that helps children to

Idiomatic expressions are especially difficult for non-English-speaking children to learn.

From *Skills Book*, Level 12, of *The Laidlaw Reading Program*, Second Edition, Copyright © 1980 by Laidlaw Brothers. Used by permission of the publisher.

recognize that the dialects are different, to understand the reasons for language differences between people, and to know the social situations in which it is appropriate to use the second dialect rather than the first. Although children can be taught to hear phonological differences and to recognize grammatical ones and can be drilled so that they repeat phrases and sentences in the second dialect, the new dialect will not be used effectively if the children do not have a favorable attitude toward it.

Teaching English as a Second Language

A catalog listing materials, objects, and symbols related to learning English as a second language can be obtained from Bilingual Education Services, P.O. Box 669, 1603 Hope St., South Pasadena, CA 91030.

Various methods and programs have been used with children whose native language is not English to bring these children into the mainstream of education. One is an attempt at immersion; that is, the child is placed in a classroom in which English is the only language used. The child is thus forced to learn English. However, this may be traumatizing to the child and may not really be immersion, since the child will return to a home where English is probably not spoken. On the other hand, if there are only a few children in a classroom who do not speak English, it may be the most practical approach to use.

The teacher does not need to assume total responsibility for teaching the non-English-speaking child; the children in the class who speak English can help. Although children are naturally accepting, they can also be cruel, so they must be shown how to give this help. First, like the teacher, they must learn to respect the child's native language and culture. Imitation of teacher attitudes and general classroom atmosphere are factors here, but it is also a good idea to plan a study of the country, language, and customs of each non-native child early in the year.

Even before that, though, a child who speaks English can be asked to serve as a "special friend" to a non-English-speaking one. This special friend will be particularly helpful, since the two children will soon learn to communicate with each other. Children assigned as "special friends" can be given some quick coaching, but they will usually take their assignments seriously and may do more for the non-English-speaking child than you can.

However, even when there are only a few non-English-speaking children in a classroom, direct instruction in English is also called for, and when there are more such children in the class, the need is imperative. The following are guidelines for this teaching:

1. The focus should be on oral activity. Specific English expressions should be listened to and spoken.
2. The language forms or patterns taught should be taken from the natural English speech of children. Attention should be given to the conversational speed, intonation patterns and stress, and idiomatic uses of the native child speaker of English.
3. The tape recorder provides a good means for gaining samples of speech, for listening to the forms being taught, and for allowing the child to listen to himself or herself. Other audiovisual aids are particularly helpful in teaching meanings of words and expressions through pictures and actual objects.
4. The teacher sets a model for quality of speech, so he or she must actually be this model or provide the model by means of tapes and records.

5. The child should not be pushed into reading. Not only does the child have a language handicap, but he or she has had a different experiential background from that of native speakers of English. Attempting to teach a child to read before he or she has the language and experiential readiness for it is an inexcusable waste of both your time and the child's.

6. The basic procedure should be one of drill on language patterns selected on the basis of a contrastive analysis of English and the child's native language. The emphasis in the drill should be on the language patterns known to be the most difficult to learn.

7. Language drills should be related as closely as possible to actual classroom experiences. The emphasis in the drill is on imitation of the model, including the pronunciation the model gives to words. Some separate drill on making particular sounds will probably be needed.

8. Making the sounds of English is difficult, so a sympathetic noncritical climate in the classroom is important. Overcorrecting a child's pronunciation, accent, or speech patterns should be avoided.

9. The child's native language should not be used during the teaching or drill sessions, since translation interferes with the automatic responses that are necessary.

Suggested Items for an Object Box

knife	mirror
fork	comb
spoon	hairbrush
plate	watch
glass	button
chalk	eyeglasses
notebook	purse
scissors	string
key	hammer
soap	nail
money	shoelaces

Whenever possible, an object, a specific action, or an idea should be associated with the word or expression that names, describes, or explains it. A very useful tool to have is an "object box." Objects can be selected from the box and identified by a simple sentence—for example, "This is a spoon." At first, the teacher should select the object, but later a child can select objects, or two children can use the box for a game (one should be a native speaker of English). The child should always repeat the entire sentence, usually while handling the object.

For direct teaching of action words and expressions, objects will not be helpful (except in the teaching of words such as *cut*, in which case scissors,

Motivating language learning with games.

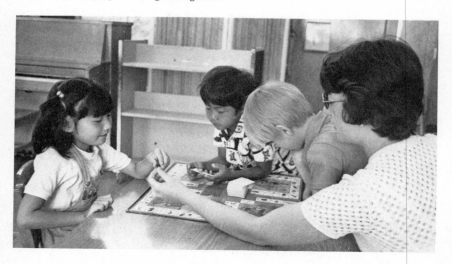

a knife, etc., would be needed). Many actions can be demonstrated by the teacher, an aide, or other children.

Ideas can be directly shown by placing something *in* a box, holding an object *above* a desk, taking a book *from* a shelf, etc. Of course, more complicated ideas are difficult to show directly because they involve several concepts. Some of these—for example, "helping one another"—can be demonstrated in the classroom if a little time and thought are devoted to the effort.

Pictures can be helpful in teaching about ideas and actions. For example, they can become the basis for stories and games in which the idea or action is pointed to and appropriate sentences are constructed for the child to repeat. Pictures can also be used as the basis for questions that require the beginning speaker of English to formulate responses. A picture file (added to regularly) is of course helpful to every teacher, whether or not he or she has non-English speakers in class. The file should be organized by major topics—communications, sports, animals, ways people live, bodies of water, foods, etc.—with subdivisions for each and perhaps some cross-referencing so that pictures can readily be found and related to the vocabulary and structures that need to be taught.

In a similar way, other materials can be used for children to talk about and as a basis for the construction of drill sentences. These include advertisements, news items, comic strips, games, and books.

Stories and poetry can also be used to present new vocabulary and structures. The selection should be read and reread—possibly only one section at a time—until the children show understanding by their ability to answer specific questions. Using several readings will also help lead children into understanding new concepts by relating them to known ones, and will aid them in memorizing many structures. If this memorization does not occur from the repetition of the reading, memorization drills may be used for teaching the most important structures.

For direct instruction to be effective a teacher must have at least a basic knowledge of the child's native language. Because many teachers are likely not to have such a knowledge of even one non-English language, many schools place non-English-speaking children in a classroom taught by a teacher who is competent in the children's native language, sometimes for only part of the school day. A variation of this, and the program probably most widely used now, calls for the non-English-speaking children to be taught subject matter in their native language for half of a school day, with the other half devoted to learning English—particularly learning to read it. Still another type of program seeks first to teach the children to more effectively use their native language, since many, particularly some Hispanic children, do not speak the standard dialect of their native language. Proponents of this program stress the need for children to be proficient in their first language in order to develop their cognitive abilities. In this program, children are mainstreamed only after several years of schooling in their first or native language.

Bilingual programs are controversial in many areas of the country, primarily because of the impression many people have that not enough stress is given to teaching English and too much attention is given to the cultures of the children's native countries. There are also disputes about the effectiveness of any second-language program—disputes both in the United States and in other countries that are bilingual or have substantial minorities who cannot speak the national language. More research is obviously needed to identify the program or programs which are genuinely effective in teaching the principal language—in this country, English—to children who are not competent in using it, in order to maximize their potential for economic and social well-being.

A FINAL WORD

Careful planning of language arts programs and sensitive and informed teaching are necessary for effective teaching in a classroom containing special children, and most classrooms include children with some of the impairments, disabilities, handicaps, or problems identified in this chapter. With the increased mainstreaming of children formerly segregated into special education classrooms, as well as the increasing elimination of racial and social/economic segregation of children, a good many schools need to look at their curriculum and teaching practices. But, as we have tried to stress throughout this book, there is no substitute for good teaching. Good teaching means acceptance of all children, diagnosis of their needs and interests, and direct and individualized attention to those needs and interests.

References

Baskin, Barbara H., and Harris, Karen H., eds. *The Special Child in the Library*. American Library Association, 1976.

Bishop, Milo E., ed. *Mainstreaming: Practical Ideas for Educating Hearing Impaired Students*. Alexander Graham Bell Association for the Deaf, 1979.

Blake, Kathryn A. *Educating Exceptional Pupils*. Addison-Wesley, 1981.

Cheney, Arnold B. *Teaching Children of Different Cultures in the Classroom*. 2nd ed. Charles E. Merrill, 1976.

Fishman, Joshua A., and Keller, Gary D., eds. *Bilingual Education for Hispanic Students in the United States*. Teachers College, 1982.

Fox, Robert P., ed. *Teaching English as a Second Language and as a Second Dialect*. National Council of Teachers of English, 1973.

Gallagher, James. *Teaching the Gifted Child*. 2nd ed. Allyn and Bacon, 1975.

Haring, Norris G. *Exceptional Children and Youth*. 3rd ed. Charles E. Merrill, 1982.

Hart, Verna. *Mainstreaming Children with Special Needs*. Longman, 1981.

Heimberger, Mary J. *Teaching the Gifted and Talented in the Elementary Classroom*. National Education Association, 1980.

Knight, Lester N. *Language Arts for the Exceptional: The Gifted and the Linguistically Different*. F. E. Peacock Publishers, 1974.

Lewis, Angelo John. *New Vistas in Special Education, Focus 8*. Educational Testing Service, 1980.

Meyen, Edward L. *Exceptional Children and Youth*. 2nd ed. Love Publishing Co., 1982.

Radabaugh, Martha, and Yukish, Joseph. *Curriculum Methods for the Mildly Handicapped*. Allyn and Bacon, 1982.

Renzulli, Joseph S. "What Makes Giftedness?" *Phi Delta Kappan* 60 (November 1978), pp. 180–184.

Safford, Philip L. *Teaching Young Children with Special Needs*. The C. V. Mosby Co., 1978.

Suran, Bernard G., and Rozzo, Joseph V. *Special Children: An Integrative Approach*. Scott, Foresman, 1979.

Teaching Resources

There are many books for children related to the content of this chapter, and new ones are coming out each year. The lists on these pages merely suggest some that you may want to examine.

BOOKS ABOUT GIFTED CHILDREN

Barne, Kitty. *Barbie*. Little, Brown, 1969.
Fitzhugh, Louise. *Harriet the Spy*. Harper and Row, 1964.

BOOKS ABOUT MENTALLY RETARDED CHILDREN

Byars, Betsy. *Summer of the Swans*. Viking Press, 1970.
Little, Jean. *Take Wing*. Little, Brown, 1968.
Wrightson, Patricia. *A Racecourse for Andy*. Harcourt Brace Jovanovich, 1968.

BOOKS ABOUT CHILDREN WITH PHYSICAL HANDICAPS

Angelo, Valenti. *Hill of Little Miracles*. Viking Press (crippled).
Beim, Jerrold. *Sunshine and Shadow*. Harcourt Brace Jovanovich (paralyzed).
Branfield, John. *Why Me?* Harper and Row (diabetic).
Burnett, Frances H. *The Secret Garden*. J. B. Lippincott (crippled).
Canty, Mary. *The Green Gate*. David McKay (blindness).
Cunningham, Julia. *Burnish Me Bright*. Pantheon (mute).
de Angeli, Marguerite. *The Door in the Wall*. Doubleday (crippled).
Frick, C. H. *Five Against the Odds*. Harcourt Brace Jovanovich (lameness).
Garfield, James. *Follow My Leader*. Viking Press (blindness).
Killilea, Marie. *Wren*. Dodd, Mead (cerebral palsy).
Little, Jean. *Mine for Keeps*. Little, Brown (cerebral palsy).
Robinson, Veronica. *David in Silence*. J. B. Lippincott (hearing).
Southall, Ivan. *Let the Balloon Go*. Martins (spastic).

BOOKS ABOUT CHILDREN WITH BEHAVIOR AND PERSONALITY PROBLEMS

Beim, Jerrold. *Just Plain Maggie*. Harcourt Brace Jovanovich (social immaturity; intermediate).
_____. *Taming of Toby*. William Morrow (self-control; primary and intermediate).
Boutwell, Edna. *Red Rooster*. E. P. Dutton (self-image; primary).
Calhoun, Mary. *The Nine Lives of Homer C. Cat*. William Morrow (show-off; primary).
Eichenberger, Rosa K. *Bronko*. William Morrow (immigrant adjustment; intermediate and upper).
Estes, Eleanor. *The Hundred Dresses*. Harcourt Brace Jovanovich (superiority; intermediate).
Fern, Eugene. *The Most Frightened Hero*. Coward-McCann (timidity; primary).
Forbes, Esther. *Johnny Tremain*. Houghton Mifflin (arrogance; upper).
Friedman, Frieda. *Janitor's Girl*. William Morrow (snobbishness; intermediate and upper).
Harrison, Crane Blossom. *The Odd One*. Little, Brown (antisocial; upper).
Henry, Marguerite. *Geraldine Belinda*. Platt and Munk (selfishness; primary).
L'Engle, Madeline. *Meet the Austins*. Vanguard Press (spoiled; upper).
Lexau, Joan. *Benjie*. Dial (shyness; primary).
Lord, Berman. *Rough Ice*. Henry C. Walck (procrastination; intermediate).
Miller, Jane. *The Ill-Tempered Tiger*. J. B. Lippincott (bad manners; primary).
Schlein, Miriam. *The Way Mothers Are*. Whitman Publishing Co. (anxieties; primary).
Tunis, John. *Highpockets*. William Morrow (conceit; upper).
Wilson, Christopher B. *Hobnob*. Viking Press (sharing; primary).

BOOKS ABOUT CHILDREN WITH APPEARANCE PROBLEMS

Barr, Catherine. *Little Ben*. Henry C. Walck (undersize; primary).
Beim, Jerrold. *Smallest Boy in the Class*. William Morrow (undersize; primary).
Felsen, Gregor. *Hepatica Hawks*. Macmillan (fat; upper).
Godden, Rumer. *The Fairy Doll*. Viking Press (short, fat and clumsy; upper).

McGinley, Phyllis. *Plain Princess*. J. B. Lippincott (plain; primary).

Meader, Stephen. *Spark Plug of the Hornets*. Harcourt Brace Jovanovich (undersize; intermediate).

Stanek, Muriel. *Tall Tina*. Albert Whitman and Company (large size; intermediate).

BOOKS ABOUT PUERTO RICAN CHILDREN

Anderson, Mary. *Just the Two of Them*. Atheneum, 1974.

Bouchard, Lois. *The Boy Who Wouldn't Talk*. Doubleday, 1969.

Buckley, Peter. *I Am from Puerto Rico*. Simon and Schuster, 1971.

Edell, Celeste. *Present from Rosita*. Julian Messner, 1967.

Keats, Ezra Jack, and Cherr, Pat. *My Dog Is Lost*. Thomas Y. Crowell Company, 1960.

Lewiton, Mina. *Candita's Choice*. Harper and Row, 1959.

Mann, Peggy. *How Juan Got Home*. Coward-McCann, 1972.

Mohr, Nicholasa. *Nilda*. Harper and Row, 1973.

Sonneborn, Ruth A. *Friday Night Is Papa Night*. Viking Press, 1970.

Weiner, Sandra. *They Call Me Jack*. Pantheon, 1973.

BOOKS ABOUT CHICANO CHILDREN

Agnew, Edith J. *Treasure for Tomas*. Friendship Press, 1964.

Buffler, Esther. *Rodrigo and Rosalita*. The Steck Company, 1949.

Bulla, Clyde Robert. *Benito*. Crowell-Collier Press, 1961.

Clark, Ann Nolan. *Paco's Miracle*. Farrar, Straus, 1962.

Ets, Marie Hall. *Gilberto and the Wind*. Viking Press, 1963.

Krumgold, Joseph. *And Now Miguel*. Crowell-Collier Press, 1953.

Lampman, Evelyn S. *Go up the Road*. Atheneum, 1976.

Lecht, Jane. *Two Surprises*. American Book Company, 1965.

Politi, Leo. *Rosa*. Charles Scribner's Sons, 1963.

Schweitzer, Byrd Baylor. *Amigo*. Macmillan, 1963.

BOOKS ABOUT NATIVE AMERICANS

Baker, Alex W. *The Picture-Skin Story*. Holiday House, 1968.

Baker, Betty. *Little Runners of the Longhouse*. Harper and Row, 1962.

Beatty, Hetty B. *Little Owl Indian*. Houghton Mifflin, 1951.

Brewster, Benjamin. *The First Book of Indians*. Franklin Watts, 1950.

Bulla, Clyde Robert. *Indian Hill*. Thomas Y. Crowell, 1963.

Clark, Ann Nolan. *Sun Journey*. U.S. Government Printing Office, 1945.

Clymer, Eleanor. *The Spider, the Cave and the Pottery Bowl*. Holt, Rinehart and Winston, 1973.

Floethe, Louise Lee. *Sea of Grass*. Charles Scribner's Sons, 1963.

Kirk, Ruth. *David, Young Chief of the Quileutes: An American Indian Today*. Harcourt Brace Jovanovich, 1967.

Lampman, Evelyn S. *The Potlatch Family*. Atheneum, 1976.

Louis, Ray Baldwin. *Child of the Hogan*. Brigham Young University Press, 1975.

Momaday, Natachee Scott. *Owl in the Cedar Tree*. Northland Press, 1975.

Showers, Paul. *Indian Festivals*. Thomas Y. Crowell, 1969.

Waltrip, Lela, and Waltrip, Rufus. *Quiet Boy*. David McKay, 1961.

Worthylake, Mary M. *Children of the Seed Gatherers*. Melmont, 1964.

Yellow Robe, Rosebud. *An Album of the American Indian*. Franklin Watts, 1969.

BOOKS ABOUT CHILDREN OF OTHER NATIONALITIES

Bulla, Clyde Robert. *Johnny Hong of Chinatown*. Crowell-Collier Press, 1952 (Chinese).

Cohen, Barbara. *Gooseberries to Oranges*. Lothrop, Lee and Shepard, 1982 (Russian).

Estes, Eleanor. *The Hundred Dresses*. Harcourt Brace Jovanovich, 1964 (Polish).

Greene, Constance. *The Unmaking of Rabbit*. Viking Press, 1972 (Polish).

Hunt, Mabel L. *Stars for Christy*. J. B. Lippincott, 1956 (Italian).

Judson, Clara I. *The Green Ginger Jar*. Houghton Mifflin, 1949 (Chinese).

Molnar, Joe. *Sherman: A Chinese-American Child Tells His Story*. Franklin Watts, 1973.

Oakes, Vanya. *Willy Wong, American*. Julian Messner, 1951 (Chinese).

BIBLIOGRAPHIES AND SOURCES OF BOOKS

Bibliography of Books for Handicapped Children Part I/ Part II. (Available on request to Division for Book

Promotion and International Exchange, Unesco, 7 place de Fontenoy, 75700 Paris, France.)

Carlson, Ruth Kearney. *Emerging Humanity: Multi-Ethnic Literature for Children and Adolescents*. Wm. C. Brown, 1972.

Dreyer, Sharon S. *The Bookfinder*. American Guidance Service, 1977 (categorizes 1,031 current children's books by psychological, behavioral, and developmental topics).

Griffin, Louise. *Multi-Ethnic Books for Young Children*. National Association for Education of Young Children, 1970.

Kircher, Clara J., comp. *Behavior Patterns in Children's Books: A Bibliography*. Catholic University Press, 1966 (organized by behavior/personality headings).

Rolleck, Barbara, selector. *The Black Experience in Children's Books*. New York Public Library, 1974 (annotation of 900 titles).

Tanyzer, Harold, and Karl, Jean, eds. *Reading, Children's Books, and Our Pluralistic Society*. International Reading Association, 1972 (ethnic-related bibliographies since 1967).

FILMS

Circle of the Sun. McGraw-Hill (29 min.; b/w; middle grades and up).

CRM McGraw-Hill Films has these film titles: *Fulfillment of Human Potential, Hidden Handicaps, First Steps, One Step at a Time, It's Cool to Be Smart*, etc.

How Come It's Thundering—You Don't See the Moon? Brandon Films (13 min.; color).

Nicky: One of My Best Friends. McGraw-Hill (15 min.; color; grades 4–12).

Whistle for Willie. Weston Woods (6 min.; primary).

FILMSTRIPS

Approaches to Mainstreaming. Teaching Resources (filmstrips and resources for teachers).

Feeling Fine. Scholastic Book Services (filmstrips and discussion guides).

Five Children. Scholastic Book Services (children visit a ranch, a Puerto Rican family, a fisherman, a southern farm, and a Chicago suburb).

Five Families. Scholastic Book Services (children visit San Francisco's Chinatown, piñata party in Phoenix, a New York apartment, a Navajo family, and a circus family).

Mainstreaming. SFA James Stanfield Film Associates (6 sound filmstrips on hearing, visual, orthopedic handicaps, development disabilities, learning disabilities, behavior disorders; for teachers).

On Our Block. McGraw-Hill Films, 1970 (color; 5-strip series for primary and above).

The Skyline Series. New York: McGraw-Hill Films (6 strips; disadvantaged children in urban areas).

Why Am I Different? Barr Films (4 sound filmstrips about blind, deaf, and physically handicapped; discussion and activity guide).

Why Billie Couldn't Learn. Association for Children with Learning Disabilities (40 min.; color; adults).

KITS

Approaches to Mainstreaming. Teaching Resources (2 units with 4 filmstrips, cassettes, etc.; for teachers).

Beginning Fluency in English as a New Language. Bowmar/Noble (5 sets of filmstrips, cassettes, records, booklets).

Children of Courage. Spoken Arts (4 color filmstrips and cassettes or records, ethnic tales).

Kids Come in Special Flavors. EBSCO Curriculum Materials (cassette, equipment for orthopedic impairments, simulating materials, guide).

OTHER AIDS

Mainstreaming Series. Teaching Resources (15 paperbound books, each on a topic relevant to mainstreaming).

Encyclopaedia Britannica has a special catalog of instructional materials for special children.

Activities for Preservice Teachers

1. Visit a school when hearing-loss screening is occurring. Report your observations to the class.

2. Examine materials used in schools for testing children's vision. Familiarize yourself with the way these are used.

3. Inquire at one or more nearby elementary schools about the special teaching considerations in effect to meet the needs of gifted and talented children. Report to the class about what you found out—and possibly observed.

4. Examine the educational literature published during the past five years for definitions of "learning disabled." What are your conclusions?

5. With others in the class, plan a panel discussion in which the issues involved in "special learning disabilities" are presented. Make certain you deal with the apparent increased incidence of learning disabilities and the influx of commercial materials presumed to attack learning disorders.

6. Visit special classrooms for mentally retarded children. Note the basic language arts emphasized in these classrooms.

7. Find out if the schools in your local community are teaching English as a second language. If they are, what procedures are being used?

8. If you have not observed in schools in ghetto or slum areas, do so in connection with reading this chapter. What differences do you note among the children? How do the classroom conditions and activities compare with those you have observed in more prosperous areas?

9. Visit an Indian reservation and/or a migrant labor camp to observe the environment of the children living there.

10. Develop a plan for learning songs, stories, customs, and the history of a particular country whose emigrants you might sometime have in class. Begin the execution of your plan.

11. Prepare a bulletin board directed at building interest in some of the children's books suggested in the references for this chapter.

Activities for Inservice Teachers

1. How do the percentages of children with various types of handicaps as given in this chapter compare with those in your school and the other institutions and agencies in your community? Does your school district compile such statistics? If not, is there a city, county, or state agency that does?

2. What problems with mainstreaming are present in your school? What do the teachers think about mainstreaming? Do you and they believe that the concept is working in practice?

3. As you look at your class, identify in your mind children who may be "special" as described in this chapter. Search through all records (test results, etc.) that you can find. Confer with parents. Then plan changes in your program to better meet the needs of these children.

4. Record sentences for a child to listen to and repeat, recording his or her effort at repeating. The child can then listen to both sentences and make his or her own comparison.

5. Let two children work together with a tape recorder—one who has always spoken only English and a second who has not. The first child makes a state-ment and the second repeats it. Then the second child says the same thing in his or her native language and the first one repeats it. After repeating this procedure a number of times, they may listen to the tape. This should help both children to understand the problems involved in learning a new language—the native-born child should be less critical, and the non-English-speaking child should feel less frustrated in his or her attempts at speaking English.

6. Current research and theory suggest that children who are mildly mentally retarded, learning disabled, or mildly mentally disturbed be considered as a single group for instructional purposes. What is your opinion? Is it the policy of your school system to take this point of view? If not, do you know why not?

7. Prepare activities "special" children can do individually to learn language skills. Those suggested in the following section will give you a start.

8. Give special attention to possible vision problems in your classroom. Begin with a visual screening as suggested in this chapter, then institute as many adjustments as appropriate.

Independent Activities for Children

Each previous chapter has activities that can be used or adapted for the children in this chapter.

THE SLOW LEARNER

1. Slow learners will profit from many kinds of readiness games, such as matching objects of the same shape, size, or color; putting pictures in sequence for a story; etc.

2. Provide many recorded or taped stories for the children to listen to; these will help build vocabulary and concepts for reading and writing.

3. Obtain an old book of flocked wallpaper samples from a wallpaper store. Let individual children use them to trace and cut out letters. They can use these letters to become more familiar with letter shapes and to put together spelling words.

4. Let the slow learner make captions for pictures or write titles for stories in the class newspaper so that he or she will feel a part of the class activities.

THE GIFTED

1. These children can make spelling and vocabulary charts, design bulletin boards, design and make games, and do many similar tasks that interest and challenge them.

2. Provide time and a place for them to write stories, scripts, reports, etc. Encourage them to write to favorite authors, TV producers, etc.

THE VISUALLY HANDICAPPED

1. Provide recorded and taped stories and poems for the visually handicapped child to listen to as a substitute for at least a part of the independent reading other children do. He can report on these as others report on their reading.

2. Let the child make a special bulletin board illustrating her view of things about her. For example, she might draw a picture of the way a familiar object or scene looks to her without her glasses, the way small print looks, the size letters that are comfortable for her, etc. This will help the other children to be more aware of her problem and therefore more understanding. It will also make her feel important if she is

helped to recognize that only she can provide this understanding for the others. (A child who is unwilling should not be forced, however.)

3. Utilize activities suggested in Chapter 7 to increase the child's listening skills.

CHILDREN WITH SPEECH HANDICAPS

1. Prepare tapes directed at the specific speech sounds the child has difficulty with so that he can listen to them and practice the sounds.

2. Provide short selections that the child can read aloud on tape. She can then listen to the recorded speech, practice needed corrections, record again, and compare the two readings.

3. Consult the speech therapist for specific activities that might help the child.

CHILDREN WITH HEARING IMPAIRMENT

1. Provide the child with reading material containing the information provided in oral reports given by other children—children speaking before a group are often difficult to hear.

2. This child will frequently not participate in discussions, since he will not hear everything that is said and thus may be hesitant to comment. In order that he does not become withdrawn from class activities, appoint him to perform special functions, let him prepare oral and written reports, and capitalize on any special talents he has to make him feel important.

CHILDREN WITH PHYSICAL HANDICAPS OR PERSONALITY MALADJUSTMENTS

1. Make it a special point to provide stories for independent reading that may help these children. Learning that others, too, have problems may help them to adjust to theirs.

2. Seek out the special talents which these children have and provide opportunities to use them. For example, the child who likes to draw might illustrate a story the class has written or design the cover for a creative writing booklet; a very shy child could tape a story for individual listening activities; a hyperactive one might be put in charge of keeping library books shelved; etc.

CHILDREN SPEAKING A DIVERGENT DIALECT OR OTHER LANGUAGE

1. Children may make alphabet books with words in their own language as well as in English for each letter.

2. Have a child make a bulletin board centered around the country of her origin. This might include a picture of the flag of that country, pictures of its people and their homes, a map, a list of principal occupations and products, etc.

3. Let a child prepare for the class a program of folk songs, stories, and/or poems from his native land or culture.

4. A child may invite a speaker to talk to the class about her native country. She will be responsible for introducing the speaker and providing any audiovisual aids or other articles that might be needed (a table for displaying handiwork, a projector and screen, etc.).

5. Children working in pairs with a simple camera can take pictures of one another. Each child can then use his pictures, examples of his classwork (stories, pictures drawn, etc.), and pictures from magazines of things he is interested in to make a booklet about himself.

6. Materials suggested above might also be used by individual children to make bulletin boards about themselves. Perhaps a bulletin board could be marked off into quarters and entitled "Our Class." When a child has gathered the particular objects she would like to display, she could arrange them in one of the sections to make a picture story about herself.

7. Provide materials for a child to read and record so that he can listen to his own speech; have short stories and poems that he can listen to for cadence and word order, record questions for him to answer, etc.

8. A child who speaks a nonstandard dialect might prepare a story for the class using particular idioms or expressions that are peculiar to that dialect. This may be used in connection with a study of dialects to help children understand the many variations that are present in speech even within the same country.

ADDRESSES OF PUBLISHERS AND ORGANIZATIONS

Acropolis Books
17th Street, NW
Washington, DC 20009

Addison-Wesley Publishing Co.
2725 Sand Hill Road
Menlo Park, CA 94025

Allyn and Bacon, Inc.
7 Wells Avenue
Newton, MA 02159

American Book Co.
135 West 50th Street
New York, NY 10020

American Guidance Service
Publishers' Building
Circle Pines, MN 55014

American Library Association
50 East Huron Street
Chicago, IL 60611

Association for Childhood
  Education International
3615 Wisconsin Avenue, NW
Washington, DC 20016

Association for Children with
  Learning Disabilities
4156 Library Road
Pittsburgh, PA 15234

Atheneum Publishers
122 East 42nd Street
New York, NY 10017

Bailey Film Associates
11559 Santa Monica Boulevard
West Los Angeles, CA 90025

Bantam Books, Inc.
666 5th Avenue
New York, NY 10019

Barnell Loft Publications
958 Church Street
Baldwin, NY 11510

Barr Films
P.O. Box 5667
Pasadena, CA 91107

Bayshore Books
Box 848
Nokomis, FL 39555

Benefic Press
10300 West Roosevelt Road
Westchester, IL 60153

BFA Educational Media
2211 Michigan Avenue
Santa Monica, CA 90404

Bobbs-Merrill Co., Inc.
4300 West 62nd Street
Indianapolis, IN 46268

The Bodley Head, Ltd.
9 Bow Street
London WC2E 7AL
England

R. R. Bowker Co.
1180 Avenue of the Americas
New York, NY 10036

Bowmar/Noble Publishing Co.,
  Inc.
P.O. Box 25308
Oklahoma City, OK 73125

Boynton/Cook Publishers, Inc.
206 Claremont Avenue
Montclair, NJ 07042

Bradbury Press
2 Overhill Road
Scarsdale, NY 10583

Brandom Films, Inc.
221 West 57th Street
New York, NY 10019

Brigham Young University Press
218 University Press Building
Provo, UT 84602

Wm. C. Brown Company
2460 Kerper Boulevard
Dubuque, IA 52001

Buffalo Public Schools
City Hall
Buffalo, NY 14202

Caedmon Records, Inc.
1995 Broadway
New York, NY 10023

Catholic University of America
  Press
620 Michigan Avenue, NE
Washington, DC 20064

Centron Educational Films
1621 West 9th Street
Lawrence, KS 66044

Children's Book Council
67 Irving Place
New York, NY 10003

Children's Press
1224 West Van Buren Street
Chicago, IL 60607

Churchill Films
662 North Robertson Boulevard
Los Angeles, CA 90069

Citation Press/Scholastic (see
  Scholastic Book Service)

Clarion Books
52 Vanderbilt Avenue
New York, NY 10017

Clearinghouse on Reading and
  Communication Skills
1111 Kenyon Road
Urbana, IL 61801

Coronet Instructional Media
65 East South Water St.
Chicago, IL 60601

Coward, McCann, and
  Geoghegan, Inc.
200 Murray Hill Parkway
Rutherford, NJ 07073

CRM McGraw-Hill Films
110 15th Street
Del Mar, CA 92014

Crowell-Collier Press
866 3rd Avenue
New York, NY 10022

Thomas Y. Crowell
10 East 53rd Street
New York, NY 10022

Crown Publishers, Inc.
1 Park Avenue
New York, NY 10016

Curriculum Associates, Inc.
5 Esquire Road
North Billerica, MA 01862

Delacorte Press
c/o Dell Publishing Co.

Dell Publishing Co.
1 Dag Hammarskjold Plaza
245 East 47th Street
New York, NY 10017

T. S. Denison and Co.
9601 Newton Avenue
Minneapolis, MN 55431

Developmental Learning
Materials
P.O. Box 4000
1 DLM Park
Allen, TX 75002

Dial Press
1 Dag Hammarskjold Plaza
New York, NY 10017

Dodd, Mead and Co.
79 Madison Avenue
New York, NY 10016

Doubleday & Co., Inc.
501 Franklin Avenue
Garden City, NY 11530

E. P. Dutton & Co., Inc.
2 Park Avenue
New York, NY 10016

EBSCO Curriculum Materials
Box 11542
Birmingham, AL 35202

The Economy Co.
1901 North Walnut
P.O. Box 25308
Oklahoma City, OK 73125

Educational Development Center,
Inc.
55 Chapel Street
Newton, MA 02160

Educational Progress
4235 South Memorial Drive
Tulsa, OK 74145

Educational Testing Service
Rosedale Road
Princeton, NJ 08541

Educators Publishing Service
75 Moulton Street
Cambridge, MA 02238

Elsevier Science Publishing Co.,
Inc.
52 Vanderbilt Avenue
New York, NY 10017

Encyclopaedia Britannica, Inc.
425 North Michigan Avenue
Chicago, IL 60611

Enrichment Teaching Materials
246 5th Avenue
New York, NY 10001

ESP, Inc.
1201 East Johnson
Jonesboro, AR 72401

Eye Gate Media
146-01 Archer Avenue
Jamaica, NY 11435

Farrar, Straus & Giroux, Inc.
19 Union Square West
New York, NY 10003

Fearon-Pittman
6 Davis Drive
Belmont, CA 94002

Field Educational Publishers
Merchandise Mart Plaza
Rm. 510
Chicago, IL 60654

Filmstrip House, Inc.
432 Park Avenue South
New York, NY 10016

Focus Publishing Co.
P.O. Box 2862
Farmington Hills, MI 48018

Folkway Records
43 West 61st Street
New York, NY 10023

Follett Education Corp.
1010 West Washington
Boulevard
Chicago, IL 60607

Four Winds Press
Box 126
Bristol, FL 32321

Franklin Book Co.
P.O. Box 208
East Millstone, NJ 08873

The Free Press
866 3rd Avenue
New York, NY 10022

Friendship Press
475 Riverside Drive
Rm. 772
New York, NY 10027

Gage Educational Publishing,
Limited
P.O. Box 5000
Agincourt, Ontario M153C7
Canada

Gale Research Company
Book Tower
Detroit, MI 48226

Garrard Publishing Co.
1607 North Market Street
P.O. Box A
Champaign, IL 61820

Ginn and Company
191 Spring Street
Lexington, MA 02173

Golden Press
850 3rd Avenue
New York, NY 10022

Good Apple
P.O. Box 299
Carthage, IL 62321

Greenwillow Books
105 Madison Avenue
New York, NY 10016

Grosset and Dunlap
51 Madison Avenue
New York, NY 10010

Guidance Associates
90 South Bedford Road
Box 3000
Mount Kisco, NY 10549

Hammond, Inc.
515 Valley Street
Maplewood, NJ 07040

Harcourt Brace Jovanovich
757 3rd Avenue
New York, NY 10017

Harper and Row
10 East 53rd Street
New York, NY 10022

Hart Publishing Co.
15 West 4th Street
New York, NY 10012

Harvard University Press
79 Garden Street
Cambridge, MA 02138

Harvey House, Publishers
20 Waterside Plaza
New York, NY 10010

Hastings House Publishers, Inc.
10 East 40th Street
New York, NY 10016

D. C. Heath
125 Spring Street
Lexington, MA 02173

Heinemann Educational Books
4 Front Street
Exeter, NH 03833

Holt, Rinehart and Winston
383 Madison Avenue
New York, NY 10017

Houghton Mifflin
1 Beacon Street
Boston, MA 02108

Human Resources Development
Press
22 Amherst Road
Amherst, MA 01002

Indiana University
School of Education
W. W. Wright Education Bldg.
3rd and Jordan
Bloomington, IN 47405

Instructor Publications, Inc.
Instructor Park
Dansville, NY 14437

International Reading Association
800 Barksdale Road
P.O. Box 8139
Newark, DE 19711

Jamestown Publishers
P.O. Box 6743
Providence, RI 02940

Kendall/Hunt Publishing Co.
2460 Kerper Boulevard
P.O. Box 539
Dubuque, IA 52001

Thomas S. Klise Co.
P.O. Box 3418
Peoria, IL 61614

Alfred A. Knopf
201 East 50th Street
New York, NY 10022

Laidlaw Brothers
Thatcher and Madison
River Forest, IL 60305

Lakeshore Curriculum Materials
Co.
2695 E. Dominguez Street
P.O. Box 6261
Carson, CA 90749

Larousse & Co., Inc.
572 5th Avenue
New York, NY 10036

The Learning Co.
4370 Alpine Road
Portola Valley, CA 94025

Lerner Publications Co.
241 1st Avenue North
Minneapolis, MN 55401

Libraries Unlimited, Inc.
P.O. Box 263
Littleton, CO 80160

Lippincott Books
10 East 53rd Street
New York, NY 10022

Listening Library, Inc.
P.O. Box L
Old Greenwich, CT 06870

Little, Brown and Co.
34 Beacon Street
Boston, MA 02106

Longman, Inc.
9 West 44th Street
New York, NY 10036

Lothrop, Lee and Shepard
105 Madison Avenue
New York, NY 10016

Love Publishing Co.
1777 South Bellaire Street
Denver, CO 80222

McGraw-Hill Book Co.
1221 Avenue of the Americas
New York, NY 10020

McGraw-Hill Films (see
McGraw-Hill Book Co.)

David McKay Co., Inc.
2 Park Avenue
New York, NY 10016

Macmillan Publishing Co.
866 3rd Avenue
New York, NY 10022

Melmont Children's Press
1224 West Van Buren Street
Chicago, IL 60612

Charles E. Merrill
1300 Alum Drive
Columbus, OH 43216

Julian Messner
1230 Avenue of the Americas
New York, NY 10020

Miller-Brody Productions
342 Madison Avenue
New York, NY 10017

Milton Bradley, Inc.
Springfield, MA 01101

William Morrow and Co., Inc.
105 Madison Avenue
New York, NY 10016

The C. V. Mosby Co.
11830 Westline Industrial Drive
St. Louis, MO 63141

Nancy Renfro Studios
1117 West 9th Street
Austin, TX 78703

National Association for the
Education of Young Children
1834 Connecticut Avenue, NW
Washington, DC 20009

National Council of Teachers of
English
1111 Kenyon Road
Urbana, IL 61801

National Education Association
1201 16th Street, NW
Washington, DC 20036

National Geographic Educational
Services
17th and M Streets, NW
Washington, DC 20036

New Plays Books
Trolley Place
Rowayton, CT 06853

New York Public Library
5th Avenue and 42nd Street
New York, NY 10018

The Northeast Regional
Exchange, Inc.
101 Mill Road
Chelmsford, MA 01824

Northland Press
P.O. Box N
Flagstaff, AZ 86002

Oddo Publishing, Inc.
Storybook Acres
Box 68
Fayetteville, GA 30214

Opportunities for Learning, Inc.
8950 Lurline Avenue
Chatsworth, CA 91311

Oxford University Press
200 Madison Avenue
New York, NY 10016

Pantheon Books
201 East 50th Street
New York, NY 10022

Parents Magazine Press
685 3rd Avenue
New York, NY 10017

Parents' Pointers Publications
Route 1
Box 238
Lawrenceburg, TN 38464

Parker Publishing Co.
Route 9W
Englewood Cliffs, NJ 07632

F. E. Peacock Publishers
115 North Prospect Avenue
Itasca, IL 60143

Penguin Books
40 West 23rd Street
New York, NY 10010

Phi Delta Kappa Educational
Foundation
P.O. Box 789
Bloomington, IN 47402

Pied Piper Productions
P.O. Box 320
Verdugo City, CA 91046

Platt and Munk Publishers
200 Madison Avenue
New York, NY 10016

Plays, Inc.
8 Arlington Street
Boston, MA 02116

Clarkson N. Potter Books
1 Park Avenue
New York, NY 10016

Prentice-Hall
Route 9W
Englewood Cliffs, NJ 07632

Prentice-Hall Media
150 White Plains Road
Tarrytown, NY 10591

Putnam Publishing Group
51 Madison Avenue
New York, NY 10010

Rand McNally & Co.
P.O. Box 7600
Chicago, IL 60680

Random House
201 East 50th Street
New York, NY 10022

Reader's Digest Service, Inc.
Pleasantville, NY 10570

St. Martin's Press, Inc.
175 5th Avenue
New York, NY 10010

Scarecrow Press, Inc.
52 Liberty Street
Box 656
Metuchen, NJ 08840

Scholastic Book Services
50 West 44th Street
New York, NY 10036

Scholastic Records (see Scholastic
Book Services)

Science Research Associates
155 North Wacker Drive
Chicago, IL 60606

Scott, Foresman and Co.
1900 East Lake Avenue
Glenview, IL 60025

The Scribner Book Co.
597 5th Avenue
New York, NY 10017

Seabury Press, Inc.
815 2nd Avenue
New York, NY 10017

The Shoestring Press, Inc.
995 Sherman Avenue
Hamden, CT 06514

Simon and Schuster
1230 Avenue of the Americas
New York, NY 10020

Slosson Educational Publications
P.O. Box 280
East Aurora, NY 14052

Society for Visual Education,
Inc.
1345 West Diversey Parkway
Chicago, IL 60614

Speech Communication
Association
5105 Baclick Road
Annandale, VA 22003

Spoken Arts
310 North Avenue
New Rochelle, NY 10801

State University of New York at
Buffalo
Amherst, NY 14260

Steck-Vaughn Company
Box 2028
Austin, TX 78768

Sterling Publishing Co., Inc.
2 Park Avenue
New York, NY 10016

Stuart Finley
3428 Mansfield Road
Falls Church, VA 22041

SubLOGIC
713 Edgebrook Drive
Champaign, IL 61820

Sunburst Communications
39 Washington Avenue
Pleasantville, NY 10570

Teachers College Press
1234 Amsterdam Avenue
New York, NY 10027

Teaching Resources Corp.
50 Pond Park Road
Hingham, MA 02043

Technomic Publishing Co.
265 Post Road West
Westport, CT 06880

Television Information Office
745 5th Avenue
New York, NY 10022

3M Co.
Visual Products Division
3M Center
St. Paul, MN 55101

Troll Associates
320 Route 17
Mahwah, NJ 07430

University of Chicago Press
5801 Ellis Avenue
Chicago, IL 60628

University of Illinois Press
54 East Gregory Drive
P.O. Box 5081, Sta. A
Champaign, IL 61820

University of Massachusetts Press
P.O. Box 429
Amherst, MA 01004

University Park Press
300 North Charles Street
Baltimore, MD 21201

Vanguard Press
424 Madison Avenue
New York, NY 10017

Viking Penguin
625 Madison Avenue
New York, NY 10022

Wadsworth Publishing Co.
10 Davis Drive
Belmont, CA 94002

Henry Z. Walck, Inc.
19 Union Square West
New York, NY 10003

Walker and Co.
720 5th Avenue
New York, NY 10019

Franklin Watts, Inc.
387 Park Avenue South
New York, NY 10016

Webster Division
McGraw-Hill Book Co.
1221 Avenue of the Americas
New York, NY 10020

Western Publishing Co., Inc.
850 3rd Avenue
New York, NY 10022

Weston Woods
389 Newtown Pike
Weston, CT 06883

Albert Whitman and Co.
5747 West Howard Street
Niles, IL 60648

John Wiley & Sons
1 Wiley Drive
Somerset, NJ 08873

H. W. Wilson Co.
950 University Avenue
Bronx, NY 10452

World Publications, Inc.
P.O. Box 366
Mountain View, CA 94043

Yearling Books
1 Dag Hammarskjold Plaza
245 East 47th Street
New York, NY 10017

Young Scott Books
Reading, MA 01867

Zaner-Bloser
2500 West 5th Avenue
P.O. Box 16764
Columbus, OH 43216

Index